# Measurement for Evaluation

*in Physical Education
and Exercise Science*

# Measurement for Evaluation

in Physical Education
and Exercise Science

*Fifth Edition*

**Ted A. Baumgartner**
**University of Georgia**

**Andrew S. Jackson**
**University of Houston**

**WCB Brown & Benchmark**
PUBLISHERS

Madison, Wisconsin • Dubuque, Iowa

## Book Team

Executive Editor  *Edward Bartell*
Editor  *Scott Spoolman*
Developmental Editor  *Suzanne Guinn*
Production Editor  *Patricia A. Schissel*
Designer  *Anna Manhart*
Art Editor  *Joyce Watters*
Photo Editor  *Laura Fuller*
Visuals/Design Developmental Consultant  *Janice Roerig-Blong*
Production Manager  *Beth Kundert*
Visuals/Design Freelance Specialist  *Mary L. Christianson*
Marketing Manager  *Pamela S. Cooper*

## WCB Brown & Benchmark

A Division of Wm. C. Brown Communications, Inc.

Executive Vice President/General Manager  *Thomas E. Doran*
Vice President/Editor in Chief  *Edgar J. Laube*
Vice President/Marketing and Sales Systems  *Eric Ziegler*
Vice President/Production  *Vickie Putman*
National Sales Manager  *Bob McLaughlin*

## Wm. C. Brown Communications, Inc.

President and Chief Executive Officer  *G. Franklin Lewis*
Senior Vice President, Operations  *James H. Higby*
Corporate Senior Vice President and President of Manufacturing  *Roger Meyer*
Corporate Senior Vice President and Chief Financial Officer  *Robert Chesterman*

Cover photo © Gray Mortimore/Tony Stone Images

**Consulting Editor**
Physical Education
Aileen Lockhart
Texas Women's University

Copyedited by Jane DeShaw

Copyright © 1975 by Houghton Mifflin Co.

Copyright © 1982, 1987, 1991, 1995 by Wm. C. Brown Communications, Inc.
All rights reserved

A Times Mirror Company

Library of Congress Catalog Card Number: 94–70432

ISBN 0–697–15218–9

No part of this publication may be reproduced, stored in a retrieval
system, or transmitted, in any form or by any means, electronic,
mechanical, photocopying, recording, or otherwise, without the
prior written permission of the publisher.

Printed in the United States of America by Wm. C. Brown Communications, Inc.,
2460 Kerper Boulevard, Dubuque, IA 52001

10  9  8  7  6  5  4  3  2  1

# Contents

## Chapter 4  Reliability and Objectivity  113

## Chapter 5  Validity  139

## Chapter 6  Evaluating Achievement  153

# Part 3 Performance Testing

# Chapter 7 The Nature of Tests and Their Administration: With Applications to Individuals with Disabilities  177

# Chapter 8 Measuring Physical Abilities  193

# Chapter 9 Evaluating Youth Fitness  245

## Chapter 14  Measuring Psychological Dimensions of Physical Education, Exercise, and Sport Psychology  417

# Preface

In previous editions we responded to changes in the field by adding information for students seeking careers in areas other than teaching, expanding the application of microcomputers, and reorganizing the text. The result was a text that contained all of the information needed by the physical education teacher or exercise specialist.

In preparing this fifth edition of the book, our first step was to seek the advice of instructors currently using the book. We combined their suggestions with input from other successful professionals and our own expertise. The resulting text is one that we feel will serve you well.

The text has 14 chapters as in the fourth edition. The order of chapters remains unchanged.

Following is a list of all the specific changes in the fifth edition of the text:

Chapter 1 has been revised to be consistent with the emerging view that sedentary lifestyle and obesity are major public health problems. The objectives of the *Healthy People 2000* public health initiative are provided and discussed.

Chapter 2 was revised to be consistent with the dramatic changes in computer technology.

Chapter 3 has been upgraded with a new example data set and expanded discussion of prediction. Numerous small changes have been made in the chapter.

Chapters 4 and 5 deal with reliability of validity and were changed slightly in response to the new issues and changes in measurement and evaluation.

Chapter 6 was shortened with less emphasis on grading.

Chapter 7 was upgraded with more information for exercise specialists and increased information on testing individuals with disabilities.

Chapter 8 contains expanded coverage on the use of physical tests for preemployment testing in physically demanding jobs.

Chapter 9 was expanded to include the three national health-related fitness programs available to evaluate youth fitness.

Chapter 10 involves expanded coverage of field tests that can be used to evaluate aerobic fitness. The chapter was revised to minimize the need for quantitative skills. Generic computer programs are provided to ease complicated calculations. These programs were designed for use with commercial database programs such as Lotus and Excel.

Chapter 11 was expanded to include the methods to evaluate the body composition of both adults and youth. Generic computer programs are provided to ease percent body fat calculations. These programs were designed for use with commercial database programs such as Lotus and Excel

Chapter 12 was revised by adding new AAHPERD sport skills tests and removing tests seldom administered. Also, many diagrams of test areas were removed.

Chapters 13 and 14 were changed slightly in response to the new issues and changes is measurement and evaluation. Generic computer programs are provided in Chapter 14 to ease the calculation of common psychological scales. These programs were designed for use with commercial database programs such as Lotus and Excel.

Along with upgrading the text, the fifth edition of *Measurement for Evaluation in Physical Education and Exercise Science* also features a comprehensive ancillary package. Elements of the package include:

1. A complete Instructor's Manual that features a course introduction, a list of changes to the new edition, a discussion of course format and approach, an overview of each chapter, and multiple-choice test questions for each chapter. An Instructor's Manual will be given to each adopter of the text.

2. Testpak 3.0, a complete computerized classroom management system that is designed to save time in test/quiz preparation and grading. Apple, Macintosh, and two IBM versions of this software are available. One copy of Testpak will be given to each adopter of the text.

3. *Statistics with Finesse.* This comprehensive statistics package can perform any of the procedures discussed in the text. Students will appreciate the easy input process as well as the speed of computation. One copy of *Statistics with Finesse* will be given to each adopter of the book. Instructors will also receive information on prices if they wish to make this software available to their students.

4. TSCORE software, which is also available in two versions, is designed especially to accompany this text. It can combine numerous scores for each person and allows for missing or weighted data. One copy will be given to each adopter of the text.

We have tried to present measurement in physical education from a sound theoretical standpoint. We feel that physical educators and exercise specialists will be better able to apply the theory of measurement and evaluation if they first understand it. We hope that this book prepares students to cope with any problems of measurement and evaluation that they may encounter once they are on the job.

We would like to express our gratitude to the many people who reviewed previous editions of this book or manuscripts and offered excellent suggestions for improvements. They include Professors Andrew Proctor, California Polytechnic State University, Stephen Langendorfer, Kent State University, Dale Mood, University of Colorado–Boulder, Antoinette Tiburzi, SUNY at Cortland, George McGlynn, University of San Francisco, Harry Duvall, University of Georgia–Athens, Ronald W. Deitrick, California State Polytechnic University–Pomona, Joy L. Hendrick, State University College at Cortland, Emma S. Gibbons, Texas A & M University, Martin W. Johnson, Mayville State University, Lloyd L. Laubach, University of Dayton, Marilyn A. Looney, Northern Illinois University, Patricia Patterson, San Diego State University, and Robert Sonstroem, University of Rhode Island.

In addition, we would like to extend a special thanks to the reviewers of this edition. Because of the extensive changes in the field of exercise science, these comments were especially useful. They are professors Alex Waigandt, University of Missouri and Charles W. Jackson, Old Dominion University.

We would also like to thank our wives for their patience and consideration during the preparation of the manuscript. Finally, we would like to express our thanks to former teachers, who contributed to our knowledge of measurement techniques, as well as our former students, who forced us to bridge the gap between theory and practice.

*T.A.B.*
*A.S.J.*

# To the Student

The major goal of this text is to help you apply the principles of measurement and evaluation to your job. Often evaluation is viewed as a necessary evil, not directly related to the real purpose of the job. This text was designed to help you learn how to use evaluation as an essential part of the total process.

We developed the text with two purposes in mind. First, we want to help you master the essential content, principles, and concepts needed to become an effective evaluator. We tried to provide the practical aspects, the "how" and the "why" of evaluation. We want this text to help you build a foundation based on theoretical concepts so that you can then apply these concepts in developing, using, and evaluating various tests.

Second, we designed the text to provide the practical skills and materials that you will need. We provide a wide assortment of tests, administrative instructions, and norms. We selected the tests, which provide the "how" of evaluation, either for their application to the job setting or for their value for teaching basic concepts discussed in the text.

A practical tool for you to use now and later is the computer. Practical computer applications are provided, by examples, with standard microcomputer(s) programs. As mentioned in the preface, some excellent microcomputer programs are available with the book. Profit from these programs and the chapter on microcomputers. Learn to use the computer as a student while help is available, and it will be easy to use whatever computer support is available once you are on the job.

The approach we use in the text follows a teaching method that has influenced recent educational thought. It is basically an outgrowth of Benjamin Bloom's ideas on "mastery learning." The method stresses letting the student know what is to be learned, providing the material to accomplish the learning, and furnishing evaluation procedures to determine whether the learning has been achieved.

This approach, formative evaluation, is an essential feature of mastery learning. Psychologists maintain that feedback is one of the most important factors in learning. Formative evaluation is designed to provide that feedback. It enables you to diagnose weaknesses. It lets you know the content you have mastered, so that you can put more effort into problem areas.

**Instructional objectives** at the beginning of each chapter enable you to focus your attention on the concepts to be learned. The **text**—supplemented with class lectures, discussions, projects, and laboratory experiments—provides the information you need to help you achieve the objectives. The **evaluation of objectives** at the end of each chapter help you determine whether you have mastered the skills set forth.

The formative evaluation in this text offers two types of questions. The first, in **question/answer format,** is most appropriate for testing yourself on the statistics content. If you cannot calculate a statistic, you have not mastered the technique. The second type of question requires you to define, summarize, analyze, apply, or synthesize content. This is typical of an **essay-type question,** and is more appropriate for testing yourself on basic content, principles, and concepts.

A common complaint of students is that they dislike learning by rote. We hope that the techniques of instructional objectives and formative evaluation will help you to avoid that approach. The objectives and evaluation questions identify the key points in a given chapter. Once you have read the chapter itself, you should be familiar with these points. Finally, we hope that by using this approach you will master important content rather than just isolated facts.

We are aware that each student studies differently. However, you may find that the following suggestions will help you achieve mastery learning.

1. Before reading a chapter, review the instructional objectives and formative evaluation questions for the chapter. This gives you an overview and directs your attention to the important content areas.

2. Read the chapter, underlining important content. Also underline material that you do not fully

understand. After reading the entire chapter, return to the underlined parts to reinforce the important content and to try to grasp the material you do not fully understand.

3. Without referring to the text, answer the formative evaluation questions. After you have written your answers, go back to the material in the text and check your answers. Spend additional time on the questions that you did not answer correctly. If you do not feel comfortable with your answers to some questions, spend more time on these as well.

4. Practical learning activities are provided at the end of each chapter. Try them. We have found that these exercises help students gain further insight into the statistical or theoretical concepts being stressed. (Many of these suggested activities are enjoyable as well as helpful.)

5. When studying for summative exams, use the formative evaluation questions and your corrected answers as the basis for final review of the instructional objectives of each chapter. Examine the list of key words at the beginning of each chapter. They are a second means for formative evaluation. If you find that you cannot think of a precise definition of a term, go back over the chapter until you find the term's definition.

We wish you good luck with your evaluating techniques.

*T.A.B.*
*A.S.J.*

# Introduction

# Measurement and Evaluation in a Changing Society

chapter

# 1

## Key Words

## Contents

## Objectives

The dynamic nature of society is altering the type of measurement and evaluation skills needed by physical education teachers and exercise specialists. This chapter will help you understand the place of measurement and evaluation in our changing world.

After reading Chapter 1 you should be able to:

1. Describe the demographic changes of the American population and understand the need to change program emphases.
2. Cite the medical and public health evidence supporting the role that physical activity and fitness have on public health.
3. List the physical activity and fitness objectives defined in *Healthy People 2000*.
4. Define and differentiate between measurement and evaluation.
5. Define and differentiate between criterion- and norm-referenced standards.
6. Define and differentiate between formative and summative methods of evaluation.

## INTRODUCTION

Society is constantly changing, and this is mirrored within the profession of physical education and exercise science. Graduates of physical education programs are not only becoming teachers and coaches, but also exercise specialists, physical and occupational therapists, sport psychologists and consultants, and some are even starting or entering private business. Many colleges and universities are expanding their degree programs to include sport management. While many factors influence kinesiology and physical education professional preparation programs, several contemporary forces are especially salient. Microcomputer technology is dramatically changing the way we work. Political activism of women is not only increasing the number of women elected to political office, but it is also increasing the opportunities for girls and women to compete in athletics. Women are now seeking employment in what were traditionally male-dominated jobs. Other major forces pressuring our educational and public health institutions are demographic changes. The American population is aging, and the ethnic mix is changing. Our occupations are becoming more sedentary. At the same time, medical and public health officials concluded that inactivity and obesity are major public health problems.

This chapter reviews these important changes and illustrates how this will affect your professional career. This information is integrated with sound principles of measurement and evaluation.

## Microcomputer Technology

The dramatic advances in the development of both microcomputer hardware and software have changed measurement and evaluation methods. This growth of microcomputer technology has been so dramatic in the 1980s that we now include an entire chapter (Chapter 2) that summarizes the application of microcomputers in physical education and exercise science. Additionally, we have integrated microcomputer applications in other chapters (e.g., Chapter 3, which is basic statistics).

## Employment Testing

There is a growing trend to use physical performance tests to make employment decisions concerning hiring, promoting, and dismissing an employee. In 1964 Congress passed the Civil Rights Act, and Title VII of this Act prohibits employment discrimination based on race, color, religion, sex, or national origin. The American with Disabilities Act extended legal protection from employment discrimination to handicapped Americans (Equal Employment Opportunity Commission 1991).

In ever increasing numbers, women are seeking employment in physically demanding jobs traditionally dominated by men. This is especially evident for public safety jobs, namely law enforcement officers and fire fighters. In the 1960s most public safety jobs had a height and weight requirement that the United States Supreme Court ruled illegal because the standards were discriminatory against minorities, namely women, Hispanics, and Asians, and because height and weight were not job related (Arvey & Faley 1988; Hogan & Quigley 1986). Employers now use professionally developed physical ability tests to legally hire workers for physically demanding jobs. A detailed discussion of this research is beyond the scope of this text. Chapter 8 has been expanded to provide examples and methods used for this important research, and the interested reader is directed to other sources (Hogan 1991; Jackson 1994) for extensive reviews of this topic.

The profile of the American population is changing. Our population is aging and the minority proportion is increasing. Physically active jobs are being replaced with less physically active jobs. These three demographic changes are increasing the need for health promotion that emphasizes physical activity, fitness, and weight control.

By the year 2000, the American population will grow to 270 million, and the population will be older. In 1975, the age of 50% of Americans was 29 years or younger. In the year 2000, this median age will increase to 36 years. By the year 2000, 35 million people will be over the age of 65, representing 13% of the total population. In 1950, only 8% of Americans were over age 65. The population of the "oldest old"—those over age 85—will have increased by 30%, totalling 4.6 million by the year 2000 (U.S. Public Health Service 1990).

Older Americans have more health problems and are more inactive. Over 40% of people over age 65 report no leisure-time physical activity. Less than one-third participate in regular moderate physical activity, such as walking and gardening, and less than 10% engage routinely in vigorous physical activity. In the National Health Interview Survey (Kovar 1986), nearly 40% of men and women over age 65 reported activity-dependent limitations. Data from the National Institute on Aging (Cornoni-Huntley, et al. 1986) found that many adults over age 65 cannot perform common physical tasks. As many as 51% could not do heavy housework and up to 33% could not walk a half-mile. Although some of this disability is due to chronic health problems such as arthritis, emphysema, and cardiovascular disease, it is also believed to be due, in part, to low levels of physical fitness.

A goal of aging is not just living longer and dying later, but also what Shephard (1986) terms a "quality-adjusted lifespan." For many elderly this is the capacity to function independently, which is partly dependent upon their aerobic capacity. A $\dot{V}O_2$ Max[1] of 15 ml·kg$^{-1}$·min$^{-1}$ is the projected minimum level required to meet the physiological demands needed for independent living (Shephard 1986).

Recent data (Jackson et al. In Press) showed that one's level of physical activity during adulthood is a major factor in maintaining this important "quality-adjusted lifespan." Figure 1.1 shows the theoretical decline in aerobic fitness from the level of an average 25-year-old man to that at age 70 for three different conditions. The average $\dot{V}O_2$ Max for a 25-year-old man is 48 ml·kg$^{-1}$·min$^{-1}$ and declines to 27 ml·kg$^{-1}$·min$^{-1}$ by age 70, a loss of 44% of aerobic fitness. But if this same man aerobically exercised three hours a week or more and remained lean (15% fat), his projected $\dot{V}O_2$ Max at age 70 would be 42 ml·kg$^{-1}$·min$^{-1}$, only 6 ml·kg$^{-1}$·min$^{-1}$ below the average 25-year-old man. If the man habitually exercised for just 30 to 60 minutes per week and slightly increased his body fat to 20%, his expected $\dot{V}O_2$ Max at age 70 would be 34 ml·kg$^{-1}$·min$^{-1}$, a 40-year decline of less than 30% in aerobic fitness. We have found similar trends with women (Wier et al. 1993). Regular aerobic exercise and weight control can dramatically reduce the loss of aerobic fitness and physical function associated with aging.

---

[1] $\dot{V}O_2$ Max is considered the best index of aerobic fitness. This is fully explained in Chapter 10.

**Figure 1.1**
Theoretical changes in aerobic fitness from age 25 to age 70. The average decline for the total sample was 0.478 ml·kg$^{-1}$·min/year, but staying active and controlling weight can dramatically alter the decline in aerobic fitness due to age. (Buskirk and Hodgson 1987; Jackson et al. Submitted for publication.)

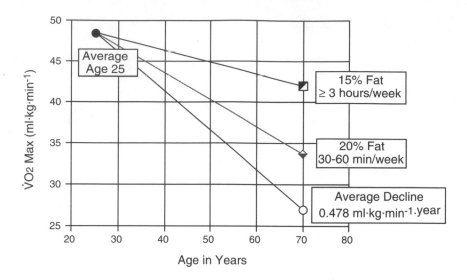

## Our Changing Ethnic Composition

The racial and ethnic composition of the American population is changing. Between the years of 1990 and 2000, the proportion of whites will decline from 76% to 72%, while the proportion of Hispanic Americans and blacks will increase from 8% to 11.3% and from 12.4% to 13.1% respectively. The remaining groups, including Native Americans, Alaska natives, Asians, and Pacific Islanders, will increase from 3.5% to 4.3% of the total American population (U.S. Public Health Service 1990).

While public health statistics document that health problems differ among minority groups, many of these differences are due more to the disparity of socio-economic status than ethnicity. Fewer whites are in the low-income group[2] than several minority groups (U.S. Public Health Service 1990). This demographic change increases the importance of youth and adult fitness programs. Low-income American adults are less physically active and have a higher overweight **prevalence.**[3]

## Changing Occupations

Between the years of 1990 and 2000, economic expansion will create up to 18 million new jobs, but the nature of the work will change. Occupations most likely to grow include service, professional, technical, sales, and executive and management jobs (U.S. Public Health Service 1990). These newly created jobs will be less physically demanding.

Occupational physical activity is related to coronary heart disease. Individuals with physically demanding jobs suffered fewer heart attacks than those with sedentary jobs. To illustrate, conductors who walked up and down the stairs of double-decker buses in London had fewer heart attacks than the more sedentary bus drivers. In the

---

[2] Low income is an annual family income <$20,000 (U.S. Public Health Service 1990).

[3] Prevalence refers to the amount of disease existing at a particular time. (U.S. Public Health Service 1990).

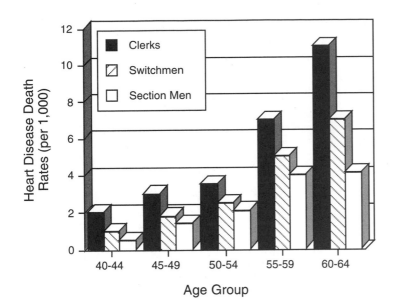

**Figure 1.2**
The relation between the specific job of railroad workers and death from heart disease. The heart disease death rate was related to the physical activity required by the occupation type. The clerks were most sedentary while the jobs of the section men were the most physically demanding. (Graph from data published by Taylor et al. 1962. Death rates among physically active and sedentary employees of the railroad industry. *American Journal of Public Health 52:* 1692–1707. From Ross, R. M. and A. S. Jackson. 1990. Chapter 2—The role of exercise on health. *Understanding exercise: Concepts, calculations, and computers,* Carmel, IN: Benchmark Press. Used with permission.)

United States, postal workers who walked and delivered the mail had a lower incidence of disease than those who stood and sorted it (Ross & Jackson 1990).

Figure 1.2 summarizes a classic occupational study (Taylor et al. 1962) that examined the role of physical activity on heart disease. Using more than 191,000 American railroad workers, the study showed that clerks had the least physically demanding job and the highest heart disease death rate. Section men had the lowest heart disease death rate. They repaired and maintained the railroad track and had the most physically demanding work. The level of physical activity required of switchmen was between that of clerks and section men, and their level of heart disease was between these two groups. These trends were consistent for all age groups.

By the year 2000, Americans will expend fewer calories during work. Paffenbarger and associates (1977) showed that longshoremen who expended the most calories during work had the fewest number of fatal heart attacks. The heart attack rate of the more sedentary workers with a history of heart disease was nearly double the rate found for the physically active workers with previous heart problems. These data showed that being physically active provided a margin of protection for those with diagnosed heart disease, supporting the value of exercise for rehabilitating the heart patient.

**Physical Activity and Fitness for Public Health**

The third trend is acceptance by public health and medical scientists that sedentary life-style and obesity are major public health problems. With increased medical evidence supporting the therapeutic value of physical activity and weight control, public health and medical organizations now endorse the value health promotion has achieved through regular physical activity and weight control. In 1992, the American

Heart Association issued a medical and scientific position statement on exercise for health promotion (Fletcher et al. 1992). In September 1990, the United States Public Health Service published *Healthy People 2000: National Health Promotion and Disease Prevention Objectives.* The next section of this chapter is devoted to this important national public health report.

## Physical Activity and Fitness—*Healthy People 2000*

*Healthy People 2000: National Health Promotion and Disease Prevention Objectives* (U.S. Public Health Service 1990) is a national strategy for significantly improving the health of Americans by the year 2000. It grew out of work initiated in 1979 with the publication of *Healthy People: The Surgeon General's Report on Health Promotion and Disease Prevention* (U.S. Public Health Service 1979) and expanded with the publication in 1980 of *Promoting Health/Preventing Disease: Objectives for the Nation* (U.S. Public Health Service 1980). This comprehensive public health study has three major goals:

- to increase the span of healthy life for Americans
- to reduce health disparities among Americans
- to achieve access to preventive services for all Americans

*Healthy People 2000* is a comprehensive national public health directive that established health promotion and disease prevention objectives. Physical activity and fitness is one of eight priority health promotion areas. An assumption of *Healthy People 2000* is that the high prevalence of sedentary life-style and overweight can be best attacked with a public health approach.

### Physical Activity, Fitness, and Public Health

There are two basic health promotion approaches: (1) Emphasize changing the behavior of the individual and (2) Emphasize changing the behavior of the target group. The public health approach is designed to change the behavior of a group. This, for example, has been used to alter tobacco use. Smoking cessation programs experience little success in changing the behavior of smokers, but public health programs have been highly successful in lowering the number of people who become smokers. A public health approach has the greatest possible impact when the prevalence is high.

Tobacco use, sedentary life-style, and obesity are health problems with a high prevalence. Tobacco use is the most important single preventable cause of death of Americans. A conclusion advanced in the *Healthy People 2000* report is that altering the American diet and increasing physical activity could have the same impact on public health as the elimination of tobacco use.

> If tobacco use in this country stopped entirely today, an estimated 390,000 fewer Americans would die before their time each year. If all Americans reduced their consumption of foods high in fat to well below current levels and engaged in physical activity no more strenuous than sustained walking for 30 minutes a day, additional results of a similar magnitude could be expected (U.S. Public Health Service 1990, p. 1).

The research published by Paffenbarger and associates (1984) illustrates the potential impact that regular, vigorous exercise can have on public health. Figure 1.3 gives the community-attributable risk estimates for the major heart disease risk factors among Harvard University alumni. Community-attributable risk estimates reflect the total reduction in heart attacks that can be expected if the risk factor was not present

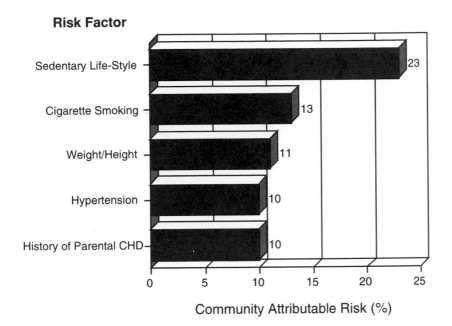

**Risk Factor**

**Community Attributable Risk (%)**

**Figure 1.3** The community-attributable risk of first heart attack of Harvard alumni. The risk estimates are the percentage reduction in heart attacks that could be expected in the total population if the adverse characteristic was not present. Becoming physically active by expending ≥2,000 kilocalories per week through vigorous exercise has the greatest potential for reducing the number of heart attacks in the group. (Graph from data published by Paffenbarger, R. S. et al., 1984. A natural history of athleticism and cardiovascular health. *Journal of American Medical Association 252:* 491–95. From Ross, R. M. and A. S. Jackson. 1990. Chapter 2—The role of exercise on health. *Understanding exercise: Concepts, calculations, and computers.* Carmel, IN: Benchmark Press. Used with permission.)

in the population. The calculation considers the prevalence of the risk factor in the population. The research showed that changing from a sedentary to active life-style had the greatest potential public health effect of all the risk factors studied. If all the college alumni were physically active,[4] the heart attack rate of this population has the potential to be reduced by nearly 25%. In contrast, if none of the alumni had high blood pressure, only a 10% reduction of heart attacks would be expected. The greater potential effect of physical activity on public health can be traced to the prevalence of each risk factor. The prevalence of hypertension among Harvard alumni was only 9%; whereas, the prevalence of sedentary lifestyle was 61%.

Physical activity is a complex behavior, and its relationship with health is multifaceted. The American Heart Association in its Position Statement on exercise concludes that regular aerobic physical activity increases exercise capacity and plays a role in both primary and secondary prevention of cardiovascular disease (Fletcher et al. 1992). Regular physical activity not only increases life expectancy (Paffenbarger et al.

**Physical Activity, Fitness, and Health**

---

[4] The definition of physically active was expending ≥2,000 kilocalories per week with moderate to vigorous exercise. This included walking, jogging, sports, play, climbing stairs, and other forms of aerobic exercise.

1986), but also helps older adults maintain functional independence and enhances quality of life at each stage of life (Katz et al. 1983). Physical activity and fitness prevents and manages coronary heart disease, hypertension, diabetes, osteoporosis, and depression (Blair et al. 1989; Harris et al. 1989; Leon 1989; Paffenbarger et al. 1984). Exercise and fitness are associated with lower rates of colon cancer (Powell et al. 1989), stroke (Solonen, Puska & Tuomelehto 1982), and back injury (Cady et al. 1979).

The reasons for the positive influence of exercise and fitness on health can be attributed to many factors. Any activity that expends energy is important for weight control. Exercise can produce changes in blood pressure, blood lipids, clotting factors, and glucose tolerance that may help prevent and control high blood pressure, heart disease, and diabetes. Activity that builds muscular strength, endurance, and flexibility may protect against injury (U.S. Public Health Service 1990).

Many public health reports have documented that sedentary life-style and obesity are major health problems for adults. Regular physical activity and exercise are critical elements of health promotion for older adults. Increased physical activity is associated with a reduced incidence of coronary heart disease, hypertension, noninsulin-dependent diabetes mellitus, colon cancer, depression, and anxiety. These are diseases prominent in older adult populations (Caspersen 1989). Much of adulthood obesity and physical inactivity has its roots in childhood. Unfortunately, the best available youth fitness data show that children are becoming less aerobically fit and fatter (Morrow et al. 1984; NCYFS 1985).

***Health Promotion Objectives*—Healthy People 2000.** The *Healthy People 2000* lists objectives for eight major health promotion efforts of which the first is Physical Activity and Fitness.[5] The strong potential public health effect of physical activity and weight control can be traced to prevalence—a large proportion of Americans are sedentary and overweight. The report lists twelve objectives for physical activity and fitness. These twelve objectives are placed into three general classes: (1) Health Status Objectives; (2) Risk Reduction Objectives; (3) Services and Protection Objectives. The three classes of objectives provide public health goals for improvement in health status, exercise goals for reaching the health goals, and methods for implementing the exercise goals. These are listed next.

***Health Status Objectives.*** These objectives focus on the medical problems that can be reduced through physical activity and physical fitness. There are two objectives.

1.1   Reduce coronary heart disease deaths to no more than 100 per 100,000 people.

1.2   Reduce overweight to a prevalence of no more than 20% among people age 20 and older and no more than 15% among adolescents age 12 through 19.

---

[5] The remaining seven health promotion priority areas include Nutrition, Tobacco, Alcohol and Other Drugs, Family Planning, Mental Health and Mental Disorders, Violent and Abusive Behavior, and Educational and Community-Based Programs.

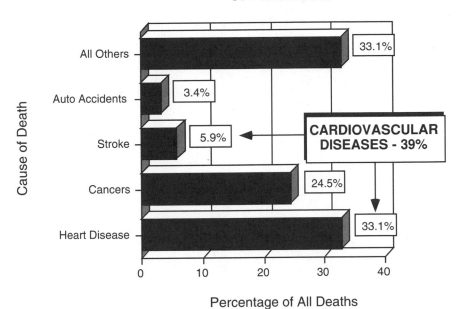

**1985 LEADING CAUSES OF DEATH OF AMERICANS**

Cause of Death

- All Others — 33.1%
- Auto Accidents — 3.4%
- Stroke — 5.9%
- Cancers — 24.5%
- Heart Disease — 33.1%

CARDIOVASCULAR DISEASES - 39%

Percentage of All Deaths

**Figure 1.4**
Leading causes of death in the United States, 1985. (Graph from data from *Health United States,* 1987. U.S. Public Health Service, Dept. of Health and Human Services, March, 1988. DHHS Pub. No. (PHS) 88–1232. From Ross, R. M. and A. S. Jackson. 1990. Chapter 2—The role of exercise on health. *Understanding exercise: Concepts, calculations, and computers.* Carmel, IN: Benchmark Press. Used with permission.)

**Coronary heart disease** (Figure 1.4) is the leading cause of death and disability in the United States. There is increasing evidence that physical activity can decrease the risk of coronary heart disease and that physically inactive people are almost twice as likely to develop coronary heart disease as those who exercise regularly (Paffenbarger et al. 1984; Powell et al. 1987).

The age-adjusted American coronary heart disease death rate in 1987 was 135 per 100,000 people. Reaching the goal of objective 1.1 by the year 2000 would amount to a 26% reduction in heart disease deaths. The heart disease death rates of black Americans is over 20% higher than the general rate. The *Healthy People 2000* report recommends that black Americans be targeted for special emphasis.

Objective 1.2 focuses on the high prevalence of overweight. The role of caloric expenditure and weight control are linked and firmly established (Ross & Jackson 1990). In 1980, the prevalence of overweight was 24% for men and 27% for women age 20 through 74 years. The height and weight ratio body mass index (BMI) was used to define overweight.[6] Chapter 11 gives the BMI standards used to define overweight.

Achieving objective 1.2 amounts to about a 25% reduction in the prevalence of overweight. The prevalence is much higher in several other groups, and a reduction to 20% would be an unrealistic goal. Table 1.1 gives the 1976–87 prevalence rates and 2000 Target for these groups.

---

[6] BMI = [Weight in Kilograms/(Height in Meters × Height in Meters)].

**Table 1.1** Target Goals for Populations with the Most Serious Levels of Overweight Prevalence

| Population | 1976–80 Baseline | 2000 Target |
|---|---|---|
| Low-Income Women (Age ≥ 20) | 37% | 25% |
| Black Women (Age ≥ 20) | 44% | 30% |
| Hispanic Women (Age ≥ 20) | | |
|   Mexican-American Women | 39% | 25% |
|   Cuban Women | 34% | 25% |
|   Puerto Rican Women | 37% | 25% |
| Native Americans/Alaska Natives | 29–75% | 30% |
| People with Disabilities | 36% | 25% |
| Women with High Blood Pressure | 50% | 41% |
| Men with High Blood Pressure | 39% | 35% |

§Estimates for different tribes

***Risk Reduction Objectives.*** The *Healthy People 2000* report lists five objectives that concentrate on increasing exercise. These objectives are as follows:

1.3 Increase to at least 30% the proportion of people age 6 and older who engage regularly, preferably daily, in light to moderate physical activity for at least 30 minutes per day.

1.4 Increase to at least 20% the proportion of people age 18 and older and at least 75% of children and adolescents age 6 through 17 who engage in vigorous physical activity that promotes the development and maintenance of cardiorespiratory fitness 3 or more days per week or more than 20 minutes per occasion.

1.5 Reduce to no more than 15% the proportion of people age 6 and older who engage in no leisure-time physical activity.

1.6 Increase to at least 40% the proportion of age 6 and older who regularly perform physical activities that enhance and maintain muscular strength, muscular endurance, and flexibility.

1.7 Increase to at least 50% the proportion of overweight people age 12 and older who have adopted sound dietary practices combined with regular physical activity to attain an appropriate body weight.

Both light to moderate and vigorous exercise have health benefits.[7] The primary benefit of light to moderate daily exercise is caloric expenditure. It is estimated that

---

[7] Light to moderate physical activity is sustained, rhythmic muscular movement that is equivalent to sustained walking, and exercise that is less than 60% of maximum heart rate. Vigorous physical activities are rhythmic, repetitive physical activities that use large muscle groups at 60% or more of maximum heart rate, over 50% of maximal aerobic capacity. Common examples of these forms of physical activity besides walking are swimming, cycling, dancing, gardening and yard work, various domestic and occupational activities, and various childhood games.

exercising at this level would involve a weekly caloric expenditure of about 1,000 kilocalories per week. Medical research (Leon 1989) suggests that caloric expenditure of this magnitude would not only help control weight, but reduce the risk of heart disease, especially for those who are sedentary.

Light to moderate daily exercise is beneficial to all, but due to the low exercise intensity, it is unlikely that this type of exercise will develop aerobic fitness. Regular vigorous exercise is needed to achieve and maintain higher levels of aerobic fitness that allow one to exercise at a high intensity for extended periods without undue stress. Sufficient aerobic fitness is needed to carry out physically demanding occupational tasks (e.g., fire fighter) and demanding leisure pursuits. Not only does vigorous physical activity enhance aerobic fitness, it also contributes substantially to caloric expenditure and provides additional protection against coronary heart disease (Blair et al. 1989; Paffenbarger et al. 1984). Baseline data shows that only 12% of adults and 66% of youth age 10 through 17 exercise to this degree. The goal is to increase this by over 60% for the population. A group with a high prevalence of inactivity is lower-income people age 18 years and older.

Objective 1.7 is directed toward the high prevalence of overweight and the failure for overweight people to lose weight by just diet restriction. The success rate for weight reduction programs that just use diet is dismal. Not only does physical activity burn calories, it alters percent body fat by increasing fat-free weight and decreasing fat weight, and it raises metabolic rate (Ross & Jackson 1990; Wood et al. 1988). Overweight occurs because too few calories are expended and too many consumed. Sound weight reduction programs focus not only on caloric restriction, but also caloric expenditure.

In 1985, only 30% of overweight women and 25% of overweight men used this combined approach. This ambitious objective deserves special importance because it targets one of our major health problems. Achieving this objective will not only help reduce one of our major nutrition problems, but also reduce the risk of degenerative diseases associated with overweight.

Both occupational and leisure-time physical activity provide health benefits. Because of the changing nature of American occupations and laborsaving devices, the amount of physical activity engaged in at work and at home has declined. For many, leisure-time activities provide the only means of being active. About 24% of men and women age 18 and older report no leisure time physical activity, and the prevalence of leisure-time sedentarism increases with age—33% for people age 45–64 years and 43% of those over age 65. Another exercise objective is to increase leisure-time activity by over 40%; this objective targets older people, people with disabilities, and lower-income people (U.S. Public Health Service 1990).

Muscular strength, muscular endurance, and flexibility are components of health-related fitness. A suitable level of this type of fitness is needed to complete daily living and occupational tasks. Cady and associates (Cady et al. 1979) reported that the incidence of back injuries for fire fighters was related to physical fitness. The reported injury rates were 7.1% for the least fit, 3.2% for the middle fit, and 0.8% for the most fit fire fighters. It is estimated that lifting causes nearly 50% of the back injuries (Ross & Jackson 1990). It appears that the workers most likely to injure themselves lifting are those without sufficient strength to meet the work demands (Chaffin 1974; Chaffin, Herrin & Keyserling 1978; Keyserling et al. 1980a; Keyserling, Herrin & Chaffin 1980b; Snook, Campanelli & Hart 1978). The logic is that if a job required lifting a

100-pound object using the back, the individual with a capacity of 100 pounds would be more prone to injury than one with a 200-pound lifting capacity (Ayoub 1982).

***Services and Protection Objectives.*** The *Healthy People 2000* services and protection objectives focus on methods for achieving the exercise and fitness objectives. These objectives are directed toward youth and adult physical education programming, expanding community exercise facilities, and increasing medical supervision and education of adult exercise programs. The five objectives are

1.8   Increase to at least 50% the proportion of children and adolescents in 1st through 12th grade who participate in daily school physical education.

1.9   Increase to at least 50% the proportion of school physical education class time that students spend being physically active, preferably engaging in lifetime physical activities.

1.10  Increase the proportion of work sites offering employer-sponsored physical activity and fitness programs as follows:

| Work site size | 1985 Baseline | 2000 Target |
|---|---|---|
| 50–99 employees | 14% | 20% |
| 100–249 employees | 23% | 35% |
| 250–749 employees | 32% | 50% |
| ≥750 employees | 54% | 80% |

1.11  Increase community availability and accessibility of physical activity and fitness facilities. The 2000 Target is based on population and recommends adding hiking, biking, and fitness trail miles; public swimming pools; and acres of park and recreation open space.

1.12  Increase to at least 50% the proportion of primary care providers who routinely assess and counsel their patients regarding the frequency, duration, type, and intensity of each patient's physical activity practices. Physicians provided exercise counseling for about 30% of sedentary patients in 1988.

School physical education is the targeted public health program for increasing physical activity and fitness of youth. In 1986, only 36% of students in 1st through 12th grade participated in daily physical education, and only 27% of class time involved some form of physical activity. These objectives call for an increase in the duration, frequency, and intensity of aerobic exercise. Lifetime activities are those activities that can be readily carried into adulthood because they generally need only one to two people. Some examples are swimming, bicycling, jogging, and racquet sports. Excluded are competitive team and group sports.

The final three services and protection objectives are designed to enhance the exercise and fitness of adults. These objectives call for an increase in adult exercise facilities and more medical supervision.

**Measurement and Evaluation**

We tend to regard test results as a valid basis for decision making. They govern matters such as student promotions, college acceptances, and designing sound exercise programs. The terms measurement and evaluation are widely used but often with little regard for their meanings. **Measurement** is the collection of information on which a decision is based; **evaluation** is the use of measurement in making decisions. This chapter should clarify these ideas with the changing context of physical education, exercise science, and health-related fitness and introduce the procedures that have evolved to meet the challenges they offer.

Measurement and evaluation are interdependent concepts. Evaluation is a process that uses measurements, and the purpose of measurement is to collect information. Tests are used for this purpose. In the evaluation process, information is interpreted according to established standards so that decisions can be made. Clearly, the success of evaluation depends on the quality of the data collected. If test results are not consistent (or reliable) and truthful (or valid), accurate evaluation is impossible. The measurement process is the first step in evaluation; improved measurement leads to accurate evaluation. People are different. They vary in body size, shape, speed, strength, and many other respects. Measurement determines the degree to which an individual possesses a defined characteristic. It involves first defining the characteristic to be measured and then selecting the instrument with which to measure it (Ebel 1973). Stopwatches, tape measures, written tests, attitude scales, skinfold calipers, treadmills, and cycle ergometers are common instruments used by physical education teachers and exercise specialists to obtain measurements.

Test scores vary between being objective or subjective. A test is **objective** when two or more people score the same test and assign similar scores. Tests that are most objective are those that have a defined scoring system and are administered by trained testers. A multiple-choice written test, stopwatch, skinfold calipers, and EKG heart rate tracing all have a defined scoring system. Testers need to be trained to secure objective measurements. For example, if percent body fat is to be measured by the skinfold method, the tester needs to be trained in the proper method of measuring a skinfold with a caliper. A **subjective** test lacks a standardized scoring system, which introduces a source of measurement error. We use objective measurements whenever possible because they are more reliable than subjective measurements.

Evaluation is a dynamic decision-making process focusing on changes that have been made. This process involves (1) collecting suitable data (measurement); (2) judging the value of these data according to some standard; and (3) making decisions based on these data. The function of evaluation is to facilitate rational decisions. For the teacher, this can be to facilitate student learning; for the exercise specialist, this could mean helping someone establish scientifically sound weight reduction goals.

Figure 1.5 is a model that can be used for evaluation. It shows the relationship of objective, instruction, testing, and evaluation. The model is equally valid for the public school physical education teacher and the adult fitness specialist.

## A Systematic Model for Evaluation

*Objective.* Preparation of the objective is the first step in the evaluation process because objectives determine what we will seek to achieve. It gives direction to the instructional or training program.

*Pretest.* With some type of pretest, one can answer three questions: (1) How much has already been learned or achieved? (2) What are the individual's current status and capabilities? (3) What type of activity should be prescribed to help achieve the objectives? Pretesting does not necessarily involve administering the same test that will be given after instruction; it can include any form of measurement that helps to answer

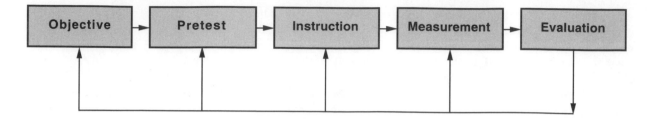

**Figure 1.5** A systematic model of evaluation.

these questions. For example, a simple health-risk appraisal might be used prior to the start of a fitness class to assess the cardiovascular risk of the participants.

*Instruction.* Sound instructional and training methods are needed to achieve the agreed-on objectives. Different instructional procedures may be needed to meet students' individual needs. A key to a successful adult fitness program is an individualized program that meets the participant's needs, interests, and capabilities.

*Measurement.* This involves the selection or development of a test to gauge the achievement of the objectives. It is crucial that the test be designed to measure the behavior specified in the objectives. Often, teachers will need to develop their own tests because standardized tests are not consistent with instructional objectives. The types of tests used in an adult fitness program may vary for several reasons. For example, if the program is medically supervised, a maximal stress test may be used to measure changes in aerobic fitness; if not medically supervised, a submaximal fitness test is the better choice.

*Evaluation.* Once the instructional or training phase has been completed and achievement has been measured, test results are judged (i.e., evaluated) to find whether the desired changes achieved the stated objective. At this stage, you may discover that the objectives are not appropriate and may need to be altered.

## Functions of Measurement and Evaluation

Too often tests are administered with no definite purpose in mind. The ultimate purpose of testing is to enhance the decision-making process so that instruction is improved. Beyond this, however, six general purposes that facilitate the instructional process are widely accepted:

*Placement.* Tests can be used to place students in classes or groups according to their abilities. Adult fitness tests are used to determine current status so an individualized program can be prescribed.

*Diagnosis.* Tests can be used to diagnose weaknesses so that individual remedial work can be given. Whereas placement usually involves the status of the individual relative to others, diagnosis is used to isolate specific deficiencies that make for low status.

*Evaluation of Achievement.* The goal of testing is to determine whether important objectives have been reached. Placement, diagnosis, and the evaluation of achievement together form the basis of individualized instruction.

*Prediction.* Test results can be used to predict one's level of achievement in future activities. Prediction is like placement in that it seeks, from a measure of present status, information on future achievement; it differs from placement in helping students to select the activities they are most likely to master. For example, a student's performance in a physical education program may suggest a high probability of success in interschool athletics. An adult found to have a high aerobic capacity may decide to engage in road racing or become a triathlete.

*Program Evaluation.* Test results of participants can be used as one bit of evidence to evaluate the program. To illustrate, fitness scores of school-aged children are falling (see Chapter 9). By plotting the results of a school district against national norms or comparing the yearly changes made within a school district, general comparisons can be made.

*Motivation.* Test scores can be motivating. Achievement of important standards can encourage one to achieve higher levels of performance.

**Formative and
Summative Evaluation**

Typically, **summative evaluation** involves the administration of tests at the conclusion of an instructional unit or training period. Motor-learning research shows that feedback is one of the most powerful variables in learning and testing during instruction, while formative evaluation enhances learning. Bloom and associates (1971) postulate that to achieve mastery, evaluation needs to be continuous.

**Formative evaluation** was developed initially for use in classroom settings. Formative evaluation begins during the early stages and continues throughout instruction. It involves dividing instruction into smaller units of learning and evaluating the student's mastery of these subunits during instruction. Its main purpose is "to determine the degree of mastery of a given learning task and to pinpoint the part of the task not mastered" (Bloom et al. 1971, p 61). The strength of formative evaluation is that it provides feedback.

In contrast, summative evaluation takes place after instruction. It is used to decide whether broad objectives have been achieved. Summative evaluation is also useful in areas of learning when goals cannot be explicitly defined. The similarities and differences between formative and summative evaluation identified by Bloom are summarized in Table 1.2.

Formative and summative evaluation and master learning were developed for use by classroom teachers (Bloom et al. 1971). However, the logic of the system can be applied to adult fitness programs. Helping adults set realistic fitness goals and using periodic testing to determine current status can be used to provide feedback facilitating achievement. A key element of a successful self-supervised fitness program for NASA executives was periodic fitness testing (Owen et al. 1980). Measuring body weight daily is a behavioral strategy used for weight-loss programs (deBakey et al. 1984). The fitness training program can become a major source of information for formative evaluation. To illustrate, increasing the intensity and/or duration of aerobic exercise is not only a sound instructional method of improving fitness, but it can provide formative evaluation. Illustrated in Chapter 2 is an example of a computer-generated exercise prescription. Over the six-step program, exercise intensity has been increased from 65% to 75% of maximal aerobic capacity and duration extended from 25 to 45 minutes. The increase in caloric expenditure can serve as a means for formative evaluation; it communicates to the participant that improvements in fitness are being achieved. A fitness test after training can serve as a summative evaluation.

You are encouraged to use the formative evaluation provided after each chapter. After you have read the chapter, attempt to answer the questions. If you cannot answer a question or if you feel unsure of your answer, this is an indication that you need additional work. The key element of formative evaluation is the feedback

**Table 1.2** Similarities and Differences between Formative and Summative Evaluation

|  | Formative | Summative |
|---|---|---|
| Purpose | Feedback to student and teacher on student progress throughout an instructional unit | Certification or grading at the end of a unit, semester, or course |
| Time | During instruction | At the end of a unit, semester, or course |
| Emphasis in Evaluation | Explicitly defined behaviors | Broader categories of behaviors or combinations of several specific behaviors |
| Standard | Criterion-referenced | Norm-referenced but can be criterion-referenced |

it provides; it communicates to the participant what yet needs to be achieved. For this course, your instructor probably will administer several major tests that will evaluate your ability to integrate and apply the readings. This would be an example of summative evaluation.

## Standards for Evaluation

Evaluation is the process of giving meaning to a measurement by judging it against some standard. The two most widely used types of standards are criterion- and norm-referenced. Glaser (1963) explains that scores on testing instruments can provide two kinds of information. **Criterion-referenced standards** are used to find if a student has attained a specified level of skill. The second is a **norm-referenced standard** that is used to judge an individual's performance in relation to the performances of other members of a well-defined group, for example, 11-year-old boys. Criterion-referenced standards are useful for setting performance standards for all students, whereas norm-referenced standards are valuable for comparisons among individuals when the situation requires a degree of selectivity.

## Nature of Norm-Referenced Standards

Norm-referenced standards are developed by testing several individuals of a defined group. Descriptive statistics are then used to develop standards. A common norming method is to use percentile ranks. This type of **norm** reflects the percentage of the group that can be expected to score below a given value. For example, a mile-run time of 11:31 for a boy 11 years of age is at the 25th percentile; only 25% ran slower, while 75% of the 11-year-old boys could be expected to exceed this time. Many fitness and motor performance tests with percentile rank norms for school-aged children are provided in this text.

Percentile rank norms are commonly used to evaluate health status. For example, percentile norms are used at the Cooper Medical Clinic, Dallas, Texas, to communicate adult fitness and health status to patients. Pollock, Wilmore, and Fox (1984) have published the Cooper percentile rank norms.

Procedures for developing percentile rank norms are fully presented in Chapter 3. Many examples of percentile rank norm-referenced standards are provided in the chapters that follow.

A major concern when using norm-referenced standards is to consider the characteristics of the group upon which the standards were developed. The norm does not always translate to desirable. This can be illustrated by examining blood cholesterol norms from the Cooper Clinic (Pollock et al. 1984). The average cholesterol of men ages 40–49 is 214 mg/dl, but this average is not considered a desirable level. A serum cholesterol of less than 200 mg/dl is considered a desirable level for health.[8] The average of the Cooper norms are typical of the general American population, and this elevated average can be traced to a diet high in calories from fats and cholesterol-rich foods. In contrast, the blood cholesterol values are much lower in vegetarians, who consume less fat and cholesterol. In this instance average is not desirable because it has been shown that there is a powerful relationship between dietary high-fat, high-cholesterol animal products and risk of coronary heart disease mortality (Stamler 1979). The heart disease rate of Americans is among the highest in the world, while the Japanese have one of the lowest.

When making norm-referenced evaluations, a useful method is to consider the norms developed on the groups being evaluated as well as other relevant groups. As an example, adult body composition standards are presented in Chapter 11. These were developed by examining normative data of adults and data published on many other groups including defined athletic groups.

A criterion-referenced standard is a predetermined standard of performance that shows the individual has achieved a desired level of performance. The performance of the individual is not compared with other individuals as is the case with norm-referenced standards, but rather just against the standard.

Many authors use the term "criterion-referenced" test, suggesting that the difference is not just with the standard, but also the method used to develop the test (Glaser & Nitko 1971; Safrit 1989). Glaser and Nitko define a criterion-referenced test as one developed to provide measurements that are directly interpretable in terms of explicit performance standards, that is, criterion-referenced. While it is true that some tests used in education were constructed to be criterion-referenced tests, the more common practice is to apply a criterion-referenced standard to a norm-referenced test. For example, the mile run is an item of Prudential FITTNESSGRAM® health-related fitness test (Glaser & Nitko 1971; Safrit 1989). The mile run previously was norm-referenced, but now, in the Prudential FITTNESSGRAM®, it is criterion-referenced. In this instance, the test itself has not changed, only the type of standard used to evaluate youth aerobic fitness. All the new health-related youth fitness tests (Chapter 9) use criterion-referenced standards.

## Limitations of Norm-Referenced Standards

## Nature of Criterion-Referenced Standards

---

[8] Standard developed from the Consensus Development Conference on lowering blood cholesterol, December 1984. These levels are also consistent with the nutrition goals set for Americans in the *Healthy People 2000* report (U.S. Public Health Service 1990).

**Figure 1.6**
A 2 × 2 table is used to determine the accuracy of a criterion-referenced test. The criterion-referenced test can be wrong in two ways—a false negative and a false positive evaluation.

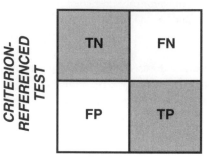

**TRUE STATE: CRITERION TEST**

**TN - True Negative**
The criterion-referenced test correctly indicates the failure to reach the criterion.

**TP - True Positive**
The criterion-referenced test correctly indicates reaching the criterion.

**FN - False Negative**
The criterion-referenced test incorrectly indicates the failure to reach the criterion.

**FP - False Positive**
The criterion-referenced test incorrectly indicates reaching the criterion.

## Limitations of Criterion-Referenced Standards

Unlike norm-referenced, which uses a continuous variable, a criterion-referenced standard is a dichotomy. Terms such as pass–fail, mastery–nonmastery, or positive-negative are used to describe the dichotomy. The validity of the criterion-referenced standard is examined by using a 2 × 2 contingency table. The accuracy of the criterion-referenced standard is analyzed by comparing the criterion-referenced standard and a criterion that represents the person's true state. This creates four possible options, which are illustrated in Figure 1.6.

The criterion-referenced approach has at least three major limitations. First, it is often not possible to define explicitly a valid criterion because a test of the true state is not available. Second, the accuracy of the criterion-referenced standard varies with the group being tested. And finally, the approach used to estimate the reliability and validity of criterion-referenced tests is different from that used for norm-referenced tests and is not familiar to most practitioners. Methods for estimating the reliability and validity of criterion-referenced tests are provided in Chapters 4 and 5 of this text. For a more complete discussion see Safrit (1989) and Looney (1989).

A common and serious limitation of the criterion-referenced approach is that it is often not possible to find a criterion that explicitly defines mastery. Assume, for example, that a physical education teacher wants a criterion for mastering volleyball skill. Tests of mastery of complex motor skills are typically not readily available and the criterion is then arbitrarily set. There are, however, situations where criterion-referenced standards can be easily set. For example, skill activities such as beginning swimming and tumbling lend themselves to the criterion-referenced approach. The successful execution of these defined skills can be clearly defined and judged.

The lack of availability of a suitable criterion is an obvious problem, but a second major problem typically not recognized by educators is that the accuracy of a criterion-referenced test will vary with the population being tested. According to Bayes' theorem, the accuracy of a criterion-referenced decision varies with the proportion of the population that exceeds the criterion (Snedecor & Cochran 1967).

The problem with varying accuracy has been studied extensively with medical tests and can be illustrated by examining the accuracy of the popular exercise stress test. A stress test is an exercise test that examines the changes in the electrical activity of the heart from rest to exercise. Explicit criteria have been established to define a

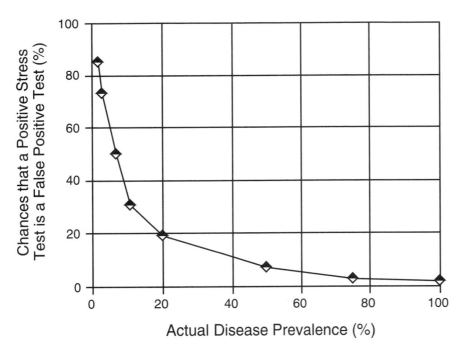

**Figure 1.7**
The accuracy of an exercise stress test increases as the disease prevalence increases in the population being tested. When the disease prevalence is very low, the chances are very high that a positive criterion-referenced test is a false positive test, but if the disease prevalence is very high, a positive criterion-referenced test is likely to be a true positive test. (Graph developed from data published by Vecchio, 1986).

positive stress test (i.e., presence of heart disease) (ACSM 1986; Ellestad 1980). The true coronary disease state is defined by the cardiac catheterization test, which involves passing a catheter into the coronary artery and then injecting dye into the artery. The flow of the dye is traced, with heart disease being defined as a coronary blood flow blockage of more than 70%. Since the catheterization test is dangerous, the exercise stress test is used first.

Researchers have discovered that the accuracy of the exercise stress test varies with disease prevalence in the group studied, that is, the percentage of patients who truly have coronary artery disease (Vecchio 1986). The problem is with **false positive tests**—the test shows that the person has reached the criterion-referenced standard when this is not so. Vecchio reported that when the disease prevalence of the population was only 1%, nearly 85% of the positive stress tests were false positive, whereas if the disease prevalence was high (75%), less than 2% of the tests were false positive tests. This change in accuracy is illustrated in Figure 1.7.

The problem in accuracy difference of criterion-referenced tests has direct application to educational settings and American society in general. If the group being tested has a low percentage of individuals who truly exceed the criterion, a high proportion of the obtained positive tests will be false positive. In an educational setting, many who have been judged to pass the criterion really did not. In other situations, the consequences of criterion-referenced decisions can be more serious. During the 1980s, some have called for mass testing for drug usage and AIDS. Public health experts have rightfully challenged this approach. Since the prevalence of AIDS and drug usage in the general population is likely to be very low, the chances that a positive test is a false positive are high. The human consequences of being labeled a drug user or having AIDS would be tragic.

**Figure 1.8.**
Curve of the relation between $\dot{V}O_2$ Max and mortality shows that low levels of aerobic fitness increase the risk of death for men and women. The curves level off at 32 ml·kg$^{-1}$·min for women and 35 ml·kg$^{-1}$·min for men and define the criterion level of aerobic fitness for health promotion.

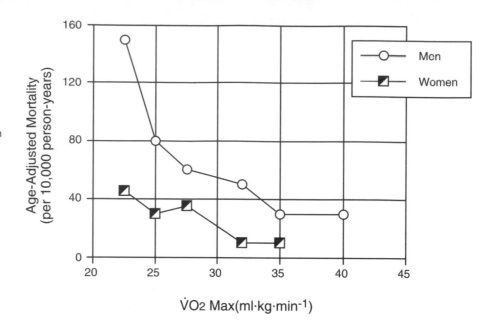

$\dot{V}O_2$ Max(ml·kg·min$^{-1}$)

## Examples in Developing Health-Related Criterion-Referenced Standards

The newly published health-related youth fitness tests (see Chapter 9) provide criterion-referenced standards, but the validity of the standards has not been determined because a criterion of true health-related fitness is presently not available. Then how were these standards developed? What may be more important in the development of criterion-referenced standards are the logic and data used to develop these standards. The Institute for Aerobics Research, which is part of the Cooper Clinic in Dallas, Texas, published and administers the FITNESSGRAM® health-related youth fitness test and includes criterion-referenced norms (Cooper Institute 1992). Provided next are the logic and data used to establish the standards for the aerobic and body composition tests.

*Aerobic Test.*  The aerobic test for FITNESSGRAM® is the 1-mile run test. Different standards (see Chapter 9) were defined for boys and girls for different ages. The factors considered to establish the criterion-referenced standards were the following:

1. Published distance run norms show performance times vary by age.

2. Gender norms are needed because of male-female differences in $\dot{V}O_2$ Max. These differences can be traced to male-female differences in blood hemoglobin, body composition, and rates of growth and development.

3. Published data (Blair et al. 1989) with adults showed that low aerobic fitness increases the risk of all-cause mortality. Figure 1.8 shows the relationship between mortality level and $\dot{V}O_2$ Max estimated from maximum treadmill performance. These data show that the criterion for maintaining health is about 35 ml·kg$^{-1}$·min$^{-1}$ and 32 ml·kg$^{-1}$·min$^{-1}$ for men and women respectively.

4. Data (Buskirk & Hodgson 1987) clearly show that aerobic fitness declines with age, but the rate of decline is related to one's life-style. Recent data (Jackson et al. Submitted for publication) show that rates of decline can be

expected for different levels of physical activity and body composition. Figure 1.1 shows the expected rate of decline in $\dot{V}O_2$ Max for three different conditions.

5. Standard equations (Ross & Jackson 1990) are available to convert running speed into level of $\dot{V}O_2$ Max. These equations were used to convert 1-mile run performance into $\dot{V}O_2$ Max estimates.

6. The FITNESSGRAM® criterion-referenced standards were derived by: (1) using the run performance $\dot{V}O_2$ Max estimates; (2) considering the expected loss in $\dot{V}O_2$ Max due to aging; and (3) considering the health promotion standards reported by Blair and associates (1989). Cureton and Warren (1990) provide a more detailed analysis of this process.

7. Chapter 9 gives FITNESSGRAM® standards. Boys and girls that meet the FITNESSGRAM® aerobic fitness standard have a good chance of maintaining a $\dot{V}O_2$ Max at a healthy level if they control their weight and remain reasonably active during adulthood.

*Body Composition.* The FITNESSGRAM® uses two methods to evaluate body composition of children or youth. The preferred method is percent body fat estimated from the sum of triceps and calf skinfolds. The second and easier method is with BMI.

1. Research has repeatedly shown that skinfolds and BMI are a valid index of body composition determined by the underwater weighing method (see Chapter 11). This is true for males and females, youths and adults.

2. The distributions of skinfolds and percent body fat of boys and girls differ.

3. Many Americans, especially young women, become overly concerned about becoming too lean. Extreme leanness can cause health problems and can even be fatal.

4. The body composition distributions of both boys and girls are positively skewed (see Chapter 3 for a discussion on skewness), which suggests that a small defined proportion are seriously overweight.

5. The mortality rates associated with body weight for a given height are U-shaped (Figure 1.9). These data show that mortality is associated with being either very thin or very overweight, but a somewhat wide range of normalcy exists between these two extremes.

The public health data, skewed skinfold fat distribution, and U-shaped weight and mortality relationship were used to define the criterion-referenced standard. The defined FITNESSGRAM® standards are consistent with public health BMI definitions of overweight (U.S. Public Health Service 1990). Lohman (1992) provides an authoritative discussion of the methods to consider when defining obesity and overweight standards for children and adolescents.

**Some Final Considerations**

Physical tests are not only useful for evaluation purposes, they also help in the educational process. Health-related fitness tests are valuable in communicating to students what it means to be fit. To illustrate, the items of the old AAHPER Youth Fitness test (AAHPER 1976) include the 50-yard dash, standing long jump, and shuttle run. This is a motor fitness

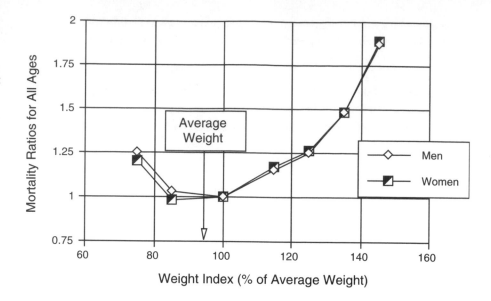

**Figure 1.9**
All-cause mortality ratio for various levels of average weight. For both men and women, when compared to average weight, the highest mortality ratios were associated with the below- and above-average groups. (Graph made from published data (Lew & Garfinkel 1979). From Ross and Jackson (1990). Used with permission.)

test that places emphasis on athletic potential. When these tests are administered to the students, they are quietly being told that fitness and athletic prowess are the same. In contrast, the health-related fitness tests communicate that physically fit individuals are aerobically fit, have a suitable body weight, and have endurance and flexibility. These are important public-health promotion goals.

A serious limitation of youth health-related fitness tests is that the criterion-referenced standards have not been validated. The criterion-referenced standards of national health-related tests are provided in Chapter 9. Of interest, the criterion-referenced standard for the mile run of the three National Youth Fitness tests are quite different. The development of health-related fitness tests is a very important step in the right direction, but more research is needed to validate health-related criterion-referenced standards. These issues are discussed in Chapter 9.

## Summary

Medical and public health scientists acknowledge that physical activity and fitness promote health. The demographic trends in America are increasing the need for exercise and weight control programs. Our population is getting older, minorities are growing, and jobs are becoming more sedentary in nature. Older Americans and those from low-income groups have a higher prevalence of inactivity and overweight than the total population. The *Healthy People 2000* public health study defines physical activity and fitness objectives to be reached by the year 2000.

Measurement uses reliable and valid tests to secure the data essential to the evaluation process. Evaluation is a decision-making process with a goal for improved instruction. Tests can be used in six ways: (1) placing students in homogeneous groups to facilitate instruction; (2) diagnosing weaknesses; (3) determining whether important objectives have been reached; (4) predicting performance levels in future activities; (5) comparing a program with others like it; and (6) motivating participants.

Evaluation is a means not only of determining whether objectives are being reached, but also for facilitating achievement. Formative evaluation clarifies what remains to be achieved; summative evaluation determines whether general objectives have been reached. Evaluation, then, is the feedback system by which the quality of the instructional or training process is monitored. Criterion-referenced standards specify the level of performance necessary to achieve specific instructional objectives; norm-referenced standards identify a level of achievement within a group of individuals.

## Formative Evaluation of Objectives

*Objective 1*  Describe the demographic changes of the American population and understand the need to change program emphases.

1. What are the demographic changes of our population?
2. How will these demographic changes affect physical educators and exercise scientists?

*Objective 2*  Cite the medical and public health evidence supporting the role that physical activity and fitness have on public health.

1. How does physical activity compare with other risk factors in reducing the risk of heart disease?
2. What is the relationship between occupational physical activity and heart disease?

*Objective 3*  List the physical activity and fitness objectives defined in *Healthy People 2000*.

1. What are the three goals of *Healthy People 2000?*
2. List the three general categories of objectives.
3. List the twelve physical activity and fitness objectives. How does this affect physical educators and exercise scientists?

*Objective 4*  Define and differentiate between measurement and evaluation.

1. The terms measurement and evaluation often are used interchangeably. Define each term.
2. What are the key differences between measurement and evaluation?
3. Although measurement and evaluation are distinct functions, explain how they are related.

*Objective 5*  Define and differentiate between criterion- and norm-referenced standards.

1. What are the key differences between criterion- and norm-referenced standards?
2. Explain how a physical education teacher or exercise specialist could use both types of standards.

*Objective 6* Define and differentiate between formative and summative methods of evaluation.

1. Many believe that greater achievement is possible if both formative and summative evaluation are used. Briefly describe formative and summative evaluation.

2. What are the key differences between formative and summative evaluation? Why could you expect to stimulate greater achievement by using both formative and summative evaluation?

## Additional Learning Activities

1. Visit physical education classes and determine if students meet the activity standards recommended in the *Healthy People 2000* report.

2. Visit a public school physical education program and discover the type of fitness test they are using. Many will not be using a health-related fitness test. Does the evidence warrant its use?

3. Visit a facility that conducts an adult fitness program. Identify the types of tests that are administered and the type of program offered.

4. Visit a public school physical education program. Analyze the program and determine the student's level of physical activity.

5. Develop a unit of instruction showing how you could use both formative and summative evaluation procedures.

6. For the same unit of instruction, develop criterion-referenced standards for the tests. Explain your logic and sources of data used to establish the standards.

7. Use an exercise physiology text to identify the caloric expenditure associated with physical activity for various work tasks.

8. Review the medical research articles cited in this chapter that relate exercise and fitness to health.

## Bibliography

AAHPER. 1976. *Youth fitness test manual.* Washington, DC: AAHPER.

AAHPERD. 1988. *Physical best.* Washington, DC: AAHPERD.

ACSM. 1986. *Guidelines for Exercise Testing and Prescription.* 3d ed. Philadelphia: Lea and Febiger.

Arvey, R. D. and R. H. Faley. 1988. *Fairness in Selecting Employees.* 2d. ed. Reading, MA: Addison-Wesley Publishing Co.

Ayoub, M. A. 1982. Control of manual lifting hazards: II. Job redesign. *Journal of Occupational Medicine 24:* 676–688.

Blair, S. N. et al. 1989. Physical fitness and all-cause mortality: A prospective study of healthy men and women. *Journal of the American Medical Association 262:* 2395–2401.

Bloom, B. S. et al. 1971. *Handbook on formative and summative evaluation of student learning.* New York: McGraw-Hill.

Buskirk, E. R. and J. L. Hodgson 1987. Age and aerobic power: The rate of change in men and women. *Federation Proceedings 46:* 1824–1829.

Cady, L. D. et al. 1979. Back injuries in firefighters. *Journal of Occupational Medicine 21:* 269–272.

Caspersen, C. J. 1989. Physical activity epidemiology: Concepts, methods, and applications to exercise science. *Exercise and Sport Sciences Reviews 17:* 423–473.

Chaffin, D. B. 1974. Human strength capability and low-back pain. *Journal of Occupational Medicine 16:* 248–254.

Chaffin, D. B., G. D. Herrin, and W. M. Keyserling. 1978. Preemployment strength testing. *Journal of Occupational Medicine 67:* 403–408.

Cooper Institute. 1992. *The Prudential Fitnessgram®: Test Administration Manual.* Dallas: Cooper Institute for Aerobics Research.

Cornoni-Huntley, J. et al. 1986. Populations for epidemiologic studies of the elderly: Resource data book. *Government Printing Office, NIH Pub. NO.86–2443.*

Cureton, K. J. and G.L. Warren 1990. Criterion-referenced standards for youth health-related fitness tests: A tutorial. *Research Quarterly for Exercise and Sport 61:* 7–19.

deBakey, M. F. et al. 1984. *The living heart diet.* New York: Simon and Schuster.

Ebel, R. L. 1973. *Measuring educational achievement.* Englewood Cliffs, NJ: Prentice-Hall.

Ellestad, M. S. 1980. *Stress testing principles and practice.* 2d ed. Philadelphia: F. A. Davis Co.

Equal Employment Opportunity Commission. 1991. Equal employment opportunity for individuals with disabilities: Final Rule. *Federal Register 56(144):* 29 CRF Parts 1602 and 1627.

Fletcher, G. F. et al. 1992. Position statement: Statement on exercise: Benefits and recommendations for physical activity programs for all Americans. *Circulation 86:* 340–344.

Glaser, R. 1963. Instructional technology and the measurement of learning outcomes: Some questions. *American Psychologist 27:* 519–521.

Glaser, R. and A. J. Nitko. 1971. Measurement in learning and instruction. In R. L. Thorndike (Ed.) *Educational Measurement.* pp. 625–670. Washington, DC: American Council on Education.

Harris, S. S. et al. 1989. Physical activity counseling for healthy adults as a primary preventive intervention in the clinical setting. *Journal of the American Medical Association 261:* 3590–3598.

Hogan, J. and A. M. Quigley. 1986. Physical standard for employment and courts. *American Psychologist 41:* 1193–1217.

Hogan, J. C. 1991. Chapter 11. Physical Abilities. In *Handbook of Industrial and Organizational Psychology.* 2d ed. Vol. 2. pp. 743–831. Dunnette, M.D. and L. M. Hough. Eds. Palo Alto: Consulting Psychologist Press, Inc.

Jackson, A. S. (1994) Pre-employment physical evaluation. *Exercise and Sport Science Review,* 22:53–90.

Jackson, A. S. et al. (In Press.) Changes in aerobic physical fitness in men ages 25–70 years. *Medicine and Science in Exercise and Sport.*

Katz, S. et al. 1983. Active life expectancy. *New England Journal of Medicine. 309:* 1218–1224.

Keyserling, W. et al. 1980a. Establishing an industrial strength testing program. *American Industrial Hygiene Association Journal 41:* 730–736.

Keyserling, W. M., G. D. Herrin, and D. B. Chaffin. 1980b. Isometric strength testing as a means of controlling medical incidents on strenuous jobs. *Journal of Occupational Medicine 22:* 332–336

Kovar, M. G. 1986. May 1 National Center for Health Statistics, Aging in the eighties, preliminary data from the supplement on aging to the national health interview survey, United States, January–June 1984. *Advanced Data From Vital and Health Statistics. No. 115. DHHS Pub. NO 86–1250.* Hyattsville, MD: Public Health Service.

Leon, A. S. 1989. Effects of physical activity and fitness on health. In *Assessing Physical Fitness and Physical Activity in Population-Based Surveys.* (N. C. F. H. Statistics Eds.), Hyattsville, MD: U.S. Department of Health and Human Services.

Lew, E. A. and L. Garfinkel. 1979. Variations in mortality by weight among 750,000 men and women. *Journal of Chronic Diseases 32:* 181–225.

Lohman, T. G. 1992. *Advances in Body Composition Assessment.* Champaign: Human Kinetics Publishers.

Looney, M. A. 1989. Chapter 7. Criterion-referenced measurement: Reliability. In *Measurement Concepts in Physical Education and Exercise Science.* (Safrit, M. J. and T. M. Wood, Eds.) Champaign, IL: Human Kinetics Books.

Morrow, J. R. et al. 1984. *Texas youth fitness study.* Austin, TX: AAHPER.

NCYFS. 1985. Summary of findings from national children and youth fitness study. *JOPERD 56:* 43–90.

Owen, C. A. et al. 1980. Longitudinal evaluation of an exercise prescription intervention program with periodic ergometric testing: A ten-year appraisal. *Journal of Occupational Medicine 22:* 235–240.

Paffenbarger, R. S. et al. 1986. Physical activity, all-cause mortality, and longevity of college alumni. *New England Journal of Medicine 314:* 605–613.

Paffenbarger, R. S. et al. 1977. Work-energy level, personal characteristics, and fatal heart attack: A birth-cohort effect. *American Journal of Epidemiology 105:* 200–213.

Paffenbarger, R. S. et al. 1984. A natural history of athleticism and cardiovascular health. *Journal of American Medical Association 252:* 491–495.

Pollock, M. L., J. H. Wilmore, and S. M. Fox, III. 1984. *Exercise in health and disease.* Philadelphia: W.B. Saunders.

Powell, K. E. et al. 1989. Physical activity and chronic disease. *American Journal of Clinical Nutrition 49:* 999–1006.

Powell, K. E. et al. 1987. Physical activity and the incidence of coronary heart disease. *Annual Review of Public Health 8:* 253–287.

Ross, R. M. and A. S. Jackson. 1990. *Exercise concepts, calculations, and computer applications.* Carmel, IN: Benchmark Press.

Safrit, M. J. 1989. Chapter 6. Criterion-referenced measurement. In *Validity in measurement concepts in physical education and exercise science.* pp. 119–136. (Safrit, M. J. and T. M. Wood Eds.) Champaign: Human Kinetics Books.

Shephard, R. J. 1986. Physical training for the elderly. *Clinical Sports Medicine 5:* 515–533.

Snedecor, G. W. and W. G. Cochran. 1967. *Statistical methods.* Ames, IA: Iowa State University Press.

Snook, S. H., R. A. Campanelli, and J. W. Hart. 1978. A study of three preventive approaches to low-back injury. *Journal of Occupational Medicine 20:* 478–481.

Solonen, J. T., P. Puska, and J. Tuomelehto. 1982. Physical activity and risk of myocardial infarction, cerebral stroke and death: A longitudinal study of Eastern Finland. *American Journal of Epidemiology 115:* 526–537.

Stamler, J. 1979. Research related to risk factors. *Circulation 68:* 1575–1587.

Taylor, H. L. et al. 1962. Death rates among physically active and sedentary employees of the railroad industry. *American Journal of Public Health 52:* 1692–1707.

U.S. Public Health Service. 1979. *Healthy People: The Surgeon General's Report on Health Promotion and Disease Prevention.* Washington, DC: U.S. Department of Health and Human Services.

U.S. Public Health Service. 1980. *Promoting Health/Preventing Disease: Objectives for the Nation.* Washington DC: U.S. Department of Health and Human Services.

U.S. Public Health Service. 1990. *Healthy People 2000: National Health Promotion and Disease Prevention Objectives.* Washington, D.C.: U.S. Department of Health and Human Services.

U.S. Public Health Service. March 1988. *Health United States 1987.* Washington, DC: Department of Health and Human Services, DHHS Pub. No. (PHS) 88–1232.

Vecchio, T. 1986. Predictive value of a single diagnostic test in unselected populations. *New England Journal of Medicine 274:* 1171–1177.

Wier, L. T., Jackson et al. 1993. The role of body composition and physical activity on the age-related decline in $V_2$ Max in women (ages 21–63). *Medicine and Science in Sport and Exercise.* 25: 5–130, Abstract.

Wood, P. D. et al. 1988. Changes in plasma lipids and lipoproteins in overweight men during weight loss through dieting as compared with exercise. *The New England Journal of Medicine 319:* 1173–1179.

# The Use of Computers in Physical Education and Exercise Science

chapter

2

## Key Words

Apple II
backup
binary digits
data
database
desktop publishing
digital
floppy disk
hard disk
hardware
K
mainframe computer
megabyte
microcomputer (PC)
microprocessor
minicomputer
MS-DOS (IBM)
Random-Access Memory (RAM)
Read-Only Memory (ROM)
software
spreadsheet
word processing

## Contents

## Objectives

Being computer literate is a desirable skill, and it is rapidly becoming a required skill of physical education teachers and exercise specialists. It is not necessary to learn computer programming; rather learn how to use computer programs that can complete desired tasks. This chapter provides an overview of computer technology and the applications (i.e., programs) that are most relevant to physical educators and exercise specialists.

After reading Chapter 2 you should be able to:

1. Differentiate between a mainframe, minicomputer, and microcomputer.
2. Be knowledgeable of the changes in computer technology and list its impact on physical education teachers and exercise specialists.
3. Be knowledgeable of the general microcomputer programs that are available.
4. Be knowledgeable of the microcomputer programs designed for the unique needs of the physical education teacher and exercise specialist.

## INTRODUCTION

This chapter is different from all others in this book because it focuses on technology that changes at an exponential rate and has applications to all segments of society. The development of electronics has produced a 20th-century quantum leap into computer technology. Evans (1980) suggested that if the automobile industry had made the same relative changes over the last 40 years, a luxury Rolls Royce automobile would now cost less than $3.00, get over 2 million miles on a single gallon of gas, and have the power to run the Queen Mary ocean liner. All of this computing power now sits on top of one's desk in the form of a microcomputer.

Our approach in this chapter[1] is to provide basic information and trends concerning computer technology and applications applicable to physical education and exercise science. We do not provide specific information on program use because when you read this chapter, it will be at least one year old, and the hardware and software will change by then.[2]

## Types of Computers

There are three general categories of computers: mainframe computers, minicomputers, and microcomputers. These computers have much in common; the differences lie in their size and computing power.

### Mainframe and Minicomputers

Most universities, governmental agencies, and major corporations have either a mainframe or minicomputer. A **mainframe computer** has enormous capacity allowing for storage of huge amounts of information and the ability to conduct complex data analyses. A **minicomputer** is smaller than a mainframe computer, but it functions in essentially the same manner. Both a mainframe and minicomputer are housed in a central location, and a user communicates with the computer through a terminal that is either directly connected (i.e., "hardwired") or uses telephone lines (e.g., personal computer with a telephone modem). To use either a mainframe or minicomputer, one not only needs to understand the computer program being used, but also the computer's operating system. Operating systems vary from center to center and are often changed, making it more difficult for the novice user.

Prior to the microcomputer era, physical educators and exercise specialists used the mainframe for data analysis. In the first three editions of this book, the mainframe statistical program SPSSx was illustrated. However, the development of microcomputer technology has been so dramatic since 1985 that all mainframe applications have been removed from the previous edition (4th) of this text. The statistical calculations that previously had to be completed on a mainframe computer can now easily be done on a microcomputer.

The computer giant IBM is the leading producer of mainframe computers. Much of their 1990s financial woes can be traced to the declining mainframe market. Mainframe computers will still have a place for large applications (e.g., Internal Revenue Service [IRS] operations), but many applications that could once only be done on a mainframe can now be done on a personal computer.

---

[1] This chapter was sent to the publisher in January 1994. It is likely that when you read this chapter it will be somewhat outdated.

[2] As an example, in the 4th edition we illustrated statistical applications with the Macintosh program Statview SE with Graphics. Macintosh stopped making the SE model and Statview's latest version (4.01) (Abacus 1993) is completely different.

A **microcomputer** is a general term referring to a complete, tiny computing system. A microcomputer, also termed a personal computer (PC), can sit easily on your desk, and now with laptops, fit into a briefcase. The trend is clear. Microcomputers are becoming more powerful, smaller, and meet general computing needs and the specific needs of teachers, coaches, sport managers, and exercise specialists. This was nicely said in 1989 by King and is even more true today.

> The rapid technological developments of the last 10 years have blurred meaningful distinctions between the capabilities of the microcomputer, the minicomputer and the mainframe computer. At the beginning of the microcomputer era, in the late 1970s, there were definite and obvious distinctions between the three types of machines: the microcomputer sat on one's desk and was operated interactively; it had limited memory capability; its speed of operation was relatively slow; its high-level languages were primitive; its graphic capability was meager; it was relatively friendly; and it often had color capability. Mainframe and minicomputer characteristics were generally opposite to these. The low cost of microcomputers, their friendliness, and their ability to play fanciful games established them as tools to be used and enjoyed by educators and the general public alike. In a mere eight years, these distinctions have become so blurred that the separate consideration of different types of computers is generally unimportant and irrelevant for the great majority of purposes (King 1989, p. 347).

The **Apple II** series were popular machines that found their way into public schools. While there still are many Apples being used, their limited power led to their death. The Apple II models are no longer being produced. Presently, there are four general categories of microcomputers that use different operating systems. The operating systems Unix and IBM OS/2 are designed for high power, network intensive work environments. These are the computer systems used by businesses and large agencies that need to link several computers together and communicate with each other. The other two major operating systems are Macintosh and **MS-DOS.** These are the machines you will likely encounter. The common MS-DOS machines include Compaq, Dell, Zenith, IBM, Packard Bell, and many other brands that are often called "IBM clones."

A microcomputer's operating system is the software that allows you to use the machine. In the initial stages of microcomputer development, operating systems tended to be somewhat difficult to use, and many people were intimidated and avoided computers. The Macintosh changed this with the development of their graphic user interface operating system. This user-friendly operating system uses icons and pull-down menus (Figure 2.1). Both Unix and IBM's OS/2 operating systems have moved to a graphic user interface. With the development of powerful MS-DOS machines, the Microsoft Software's program Windows now provides a graphic user interface for the newer, powerful MS-DOS machines.[3] It is now difficult to distinguish the difference in which Macintosh and MS-DOS with Windows operate.

**Essential Definitions**

To gain an understanding of PCs, it is important to first understand some basic terms. **Hardware** refers to the electronic and mechanical equipment used to process data. This would include the PC, printer, or other auxiliary equipment such as a scanner. **Software** refers to the programs that allow one to use a computer.

---

[3] These personal computers have the Intel's 486 and Pentium chips.

**Figure 2.1**
The standard PCs are graphic interface operating systems with pull-down menus.

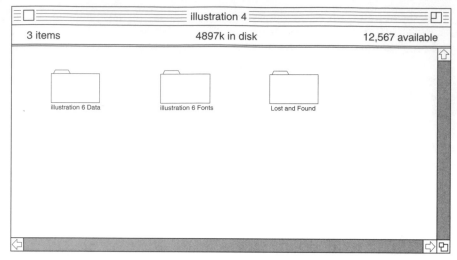

A microcomputer is designed to express its commands in a **digital** form. In a digital computer, all information is stored, transferred, or processed by a dual-state condition, a binary digit or bit (e.g., on/off or yes/no). **Binary digits** are used to quantify the capacity of a microcomputer.

The term **K** is used to express the storage capacity of a PC disk. For example, in the late 1980s the 3.5-inch disk came in two sizes, single-sided 400 K and double-sided 800 K. A **megabyte** is equal to 1,024 K. The capacity of today's 3.5-inch disk is 1.4 megabytes. These units of measurement are somewhat difficult to visualize, but the capacity can be illustrated with an example. The initial draft of this chapter was about 6,400 words in length and when stored on a 3.5-inch disk only consumed 41 K, less than 3% of the 1.4 megabyte disk's total capacity.

Each microcomputer has two types of memory, RAM and ROM. The **read-only memory (ROM)** is a semiconductor memory device where information needed to operate the system is stored permanently on the computer. ROM information stays when you turn off the machine, and you typically cannot alter ROM. It contains the programs built into the computer by the manufacturer.

**Random-access memory (RAM)** allows for information to be "written in" or "read out" very rapidly. Information stored in RAM is stored on a temporary basis and will disappear when the computer is turned off. Since RAM is used to run a program, the size of the RAM is an indication of a PC's power. Think of RAM as your "work space." You can increase the power and speed of a PC by increasing RAM, which is possible by adding RAM chips to a computer. It is likely that if you buy a PC you are likely to get the error message "there is not enough RAM to complete this operation." It is a good idea to double the RAM on any new computer.

Microcomputer programs and data are stored on a disk. A disk can be a floppy or hard disk. A **floppy disk** can transfer information with a PC through a disk drive, while a **hard disk** is either part of the PC (internal disk) or connected to it. Both the floppy and hard disk function in the same manner; they store data and computer programs (also called applications) and allow the user to communicate with the machine. The major difference between a floppy and hard disk is storage capacity. The 3.5-inch floppy disk can store 1.4 megabytes of information, whereas, hard disks well over 100 megabytes are commonplace. In our previous edition, the common size of the Macintosh SE computer was 20 megabytes. Now (November 1993), the minimum size available in current models is 80 megabytes. Many MS-DOS machines come with internal disk drives with over 300 megabytes of storage.

**Spiraling Microcomputer Power**

The history of computer technology reveals a general trend. Computer companies develop computers that exceed the capacity of the programs being written. Software developers then redesign their programs to take advantage of this additional capacity. This motivates computer companies to increase the capacity of their machines, and the process continues to spiral. The result is the constant development of more powerful hardware and software. This process marked the evolution of mainframe computers and is being repeated with PCs.

The development in microcomputer power can be documented by observing the evolution of the popular Macintosh computer. The Macintosh appeared in 1984 with only 128 K RAM, and it would only accept 400 K disks. There were few programs available (e.g., MacWrite® and MacPaint®), and the machine was slow and greatly limited by the small RAM. The Macintosh SE30 was marketed in 1989. It is over 100 times faster than the original Macintosh and comes with one megabyte (1,024 K) of RAM. The minimum RAM in the 1993 Macintosh is 4 megabytes, and this is often too small. A more realistic minimum is 8 megabytes. Now there are thousands of computer programs available that will do anything from producing high-quality color magazines to keeping your checkbook straight and computing your taxes.

The speed of a computer is determined by its **microprocessor.** The microprocessor of the first PCs was 8-bit, 4.77 MHz machines. Microcomputers are **binary** machines, using a numbering system based on the digits 0 and 1. A **bit** is a binary digit. An 8-bit machine simply means that a series of 8 binary digits is simultaneously moved with each clock click of the processor. The most common PCs are 32-bit machines, but the MS-DOS machines with the new Intel Pentium chip are 64-bit machines— the same as mainframe computers. When you read this chapter, all new PCs will likely be 64-bit machines. Quite simply, a 64-bit machine can move eight times more data than an 8-bit computer.

MHz is used to quantify the electronic speed at which a computer can operate. It is like a clock in that with each click a specified number of operations can be completed. The processors of the first PCs were 4.77 MHz, which meant that 4.77 million operations could be completed per second. A common speed for 1993 PCs is 33 MHz, or about 6.9 times faster. Thus, today's 32-bit, 33 MHz machines can move 33 million, 32-bits of information per second. In comparison to the 8-bit, 4.77 MHz machine, the

32-bit, 33 MHz PC is over 55 times faster.[4] Illustrated another way, a computer operation that took 5 minutes to complete with these early machines would be completed in about 5.5 seconds with these faster machines.

The MS-DOS machines use Intel's microprocessors chip. These machines have gotten progressively faster with each new chip, i.e., the 286, 386, and 486 microprocessors. The 286, 386, and 486 machines are 32-bit machines that run at speeds ranging from 25 to 50 MHz. The newest Intel chip for MS-DOS machines is the Pentium, and it is a 64-bit machine likely to operate at 66 MHz. The current 486 machines are extremely powerful. The new MS-DOS with the Pentium chip will be over twice as powerful.[5] The new 64-bit, 66 MHz machines that use Intel's Pentium chip are over 4 times faster than the 32-bit, 33 MHz Macintosh Power Book 230 Duo, which is being used to write this chapter. A program that takes me 20 seconds to run would only take 5 seconds with the 1993–94 MS-DOS machines with the Intel Pentium microprocessor. The speed and power will continue to spiral.

## Computer Literacy

In Texas, along with many other states, computer literacy is now a graduation requirement for education majors. What is computer literacy? This idea has evolved from a view of designing and writing computer programs to one of learning how to use PC systems and programs. Computer literacy is the ability to have a basic understanding of PCs and a working knowledge of the applications needed by someone in that profession. The type of literacy needed by a physical education teacher will not be the same as that of the exercise specialist or sport manager. Being computer literate involves having a working knowledge of both common computer programs, such as word processing, and the programs unique to one's profession. This involves learning both generic and specialized applications.

For the novice, a computer can be intimidating. This does not need to be the case. In comparison to a mainframe or minicomputer, PCs are user-friendly, which means they are easy to learn and use. Following is some advice that can enhance your computer skills and literacy.

1. *Master one of the common PC systems.* Each of the popular systems is different and has unique characteristics. The popularity of the Macintosh computer can be traced to the ease in which it can be learned. The MS-DOS machines that do not have a graphic interface are difficult for novice users to learn, but Microsoft Windows changed this. A MS-DOS machine with Microsoft Windows operates much the same way as a Macintosh.

2. *Find programs that serve your needs and master them.* It is our experience that most programs are not used to their fullest capacity. The more you use a program, the more you will find new things that it can do. All Macintosh programs are icon-oriented and menu driven. These are very easy to learn. Microsoft Windows uses the same format, but older MS-DOS models do not have the power to operate in the Window environment. This will change dramatically in the next few years.

---

[4] MHz is the abbreviation for megahertz, which is the clock frequency. A hertz is the international unit of frequency and equals one cycle per second. Megahertz is one million hertz. The change in speed is the product of the increase in bit size and MHz, i.e., $[(32/4) \times (33/4.77)] = 55.3$.

[5] In November 1993, the Dell Dimension XPS P60 used Intel's Pentium chip. The projected cost of this machine with a 450 megabyte hard drive and 8 megabytes of RAM is less than $3,000.

3. *Buy your programs rather than "pirate" them.* Not only is it illegal to copy commercial programs, using "pirated programs" can cause serious problems. When you have purchased a program, the company often provides a technical service that can help you use the program. Additionally, software manufacturers revise their programs every two years or so. The company will offer former customers the new version at a much reduced cost. The revised program will always be improved, and if you have learned one version, the new version will easily be mastered. A major problem with pirated programs is they are more likely to have a computer virus[6] that can infect your entire system, and you may lose important data.

4. *You can only become computer literate by sitting down and using the computer.* No matter how clearly a manual is written, you can only learn a program by using it.

5. *Computer users tend to be user-friendly.* We have all suffered the "agony of defeat and joy of victory"—not being able to get something to work and then finally figuring out how to get a program to run. An excellent way to solve problems is to work with other computer users who use the same computer system and program.

6. *Backup. Backup. Backup.* Something will happen that will cause you to lose important data. It happens to everyone, and it will happen to you. The way to protect yourself is to **backup,** or simply make copies of important information (files). The typical method is to copy important information on another disk or to an external hard disk. Many organizations have automatic backup systems.

## Microcomputer Programs—Software

Computer programs[7] or software are the instructions that allow a computer to perform desired functions. An operating system is the software program that operates the PC. Examples are MS-DOS with Windows and Macintosh System Software. There are many other programs or applications that allow you to do tasks like producing a graph, writing a term paper, or writing an exercise prescription. We have categorized PC programs into two categories: general programs, and those designed for specific applications used by teachers or exercise specialists.

## General Programs

General programs are those that are commercially available and designed to do a general category of tasks such as word processing. There are many different types of general programs. The general programs that are especially applicable to teachers, sport managers, and exercise specialists are word processing, graphics, desktop publishing, database and/or spreadsheets, writing aids, and statistics. Examples of some of the more popular programs are presented in Figure 2.2.

---

[6] A computer virus is a program that alters the way a PC operates without your knowledge or permission. Often the virus has been maliciously written and spreads from one computer to another in various ways (e.g., copying someone else's program). A virus can be benign—does not cause any real damage, or malignant—one that can inflict damage to your computer or alter the way one of your programs will operate.

[7] The term "applications" is often used instead of program.

**Figure 2.2**
List of some of the more
popular Macintosh and
MS-DOS general programs.
In the 1991 edition of this
text, Macintosh (Mac) and
MS-DOS had different
programs. This has
changed. Many software
companies are writing the
same program for the two
machines.

## Word Processing

Microsoft Word (Mac & MS-DOS)
WordPerfect (Mac & MS-DOS)
MacWrite (Mac)
WriteNow(Mac)

## Desktop Publishing

Pagemaker (Mac & MS-DOS)
Framemaker (Mac & MS-DOS)
QuarkXPress (Mac)

## Database/Spreadsheet

Filemaker Pro (Mac)
Foxbase (Mac & MS-DOS)
Panorama (Mac)
Lotus 123 (Mac & MS-DOS)
Microsoft Excel (Mac & MS-DOS)
DbaseIV (MS-DOS)
Quattro Pro (MS-DOS)

## Graphics

Canvas (Mac & MS-DOS)
Aldus Freehand (Mac & MS-DOS)
Adobe Illustrator (Mac & MS-DOS)
Freelance Graphics (MS-DOS)
Harvard Graphics (MS-DOS)
Corel Draw (MS-DOS)
MacPaint (Mac)
MacDraw (Mac)
CA Cricket Draw (Mac & MS-DOS)
CA Cricket Graph (Mac & MS-DOS)
Delta Graph (Mac)

## Quantitative Methods

Minitab (Mac & MS-DOS)
Mathematica (Mac & MS-DOS)
Systat (Mac & MS-DOS)
Statview (Mac)
SuperAnova (Mac)
JMP (Mac)
SAS (MS-DOS)
SPSS (MS-DOS)
BMD-P (MS-DOS)

*Word Processing.* The most popular type of general PC program is **word process-ing.** The popularity of these applications has led to the demise of typewriters. Word processing programs allow for easy typing, editing, cutting, pasting, and revising of the entered text. All good word processing programs come with spell checkers that can identify and correct misspelled words. Most have a thesaurus. Word processing programs allow you to combine graphics with text.

Word processing programs are not only useful for writing tasks, but also for learn-ing how to use a PC. By learning a word processing program, you also learn how to use the operating system, and this knowledge transfers to other programs. This is the most common way a novice starts to become computer literate. Once you learn how to use a word processing program, it will be easier to learn other programs.

*Graphic Programs.* The second type of general program provides a variety of graphic capabilities. PCs, especially the Macintosh, are much better for graphics than a mainframe or minicomputer. The availability of these programs can turn you into a graphic artist. There are at least three general types of graphic programs.

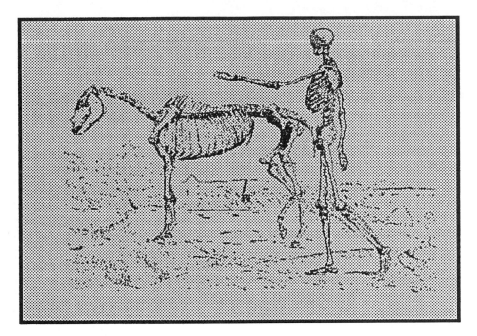

**Figure 2.3**
An example of a bitmap drawing. The drawing was made using a Macintosh computer and Apple Laser printer. The drawing was made by first scanning the figure and then using the program Cricket PAINT® (Cricket Software, Malvern, PA) to "touch up" the drawing. Looking very closely you can see that the drawing consists of a series of small dots which vary in concentration to achieve the desired effect. The grey background was added for effect. (From Ross, R. M. and A. S. Jackson. 1990. Chapter 2—The role of exercise on health. *Understanding exercise: Concepts, calculations, and computers.* Carmel, IN: Benchmark Press. Reprinted by permission.)

1. *Bitmap Programs.* A bitmap is a set of bits or pixels that, when combined in a pattern, construct a graphic image. Each bit is one dot (i.e., pixel) within the image. By altering the concentration of bits, an image can be made. The Macintosh program Macpaint® was one of the first popular bitmap programs. The bitmap process is used to make newspaper pictures. If you look at a greatly magnified newspaper photograph, you will see it is a series of dots that vary in density. An example of bitmap drawing is presented in Figure 2.3.

2. *Object-Oriented Drawing Programs.* Rather than painting an object (e.g., square, circle, line, etc.), the objects are part of the program. The advantage of this type of program is that objects can be easily recreated, drawn, altered, resized, and given special effects. The drawing can be printed on a variety of printers at its maximum resolution. The quality of this type of program was greatly enhanced with the development of the laser printer. A laser prints at a concentration from 300 to 600 dots per square inch (dpi) compared to a letter-quality dot matrix printer that prints at only 72 dpi. The dramatic effect of a laser printed object-oriented drawing is illustrated in Figure 2.4.

3. *Scientific Graphic Programs.* The graphs presented in Chapter 1 were all completed on a standard, scientific graphic program (Cricket Graph III) and made in just a few minutes. Prior to the PC era, such graphs were made by an artist using graph paper, and it was an expensive, laborious task. In addition, the better scientific graphic programs can be used with a laser printer, which results in crisp images and allows one to print mathematically defined curves. These programs are especially valuable for presenting statistical data.

**Figure 2.4**
Logo for the Udde Yacht and Rowing Club made by the author with the Macintosh program Canvas (3.5). The sailboat and sculling oars were photocopied and faxed to a Macintosh Power Book computer. The fax images were traced and embellished with the Canvas drawing tools. The fish is a clip art image, that is, images commercially produced.

*Desktop Publishing.*    Microcomputers have changed the art of printing. Individuals are now publishing materials that could previously only be done by a professional publisher. Newsletters, reports, and even books are being produced by desktop means. The advance in desktop methods can be linked to the development quality desktop publishing programs and laser printers. **Desktop publishing** programs are specially designed to allow one to integrate text and graphics. Images from graphics programs can be inserted any place on a page and resized to any degree. Laser printers produce a clear image that can be easily reproduced by modern printing methods. A book or journal, for instance, could be done by desktop method. You are directed to other sources for examples of desktop published exercise science books (Ross and Jackson 1990; Rudisill and Jackson 1992) and a diet book written by a leading psychologist (Foreyt and Goodrick 1992).

*Database and/or Spreadsheet.*    Database and spreadsheet are general programs that have been developed primarily for use in business, but they have excellent applications for teachers, exercise specialists, and especially those who must make and administer budgets (e.g., sport managers). Spreadsheets and database programs are very similar. The purposes of a **spreadsheet** program are to allow the user to work with numbers in rows and columns and to use equations to complete various calculations, but newer database programs also have this capacity.

A **database** is a structured collection of information that is arranged consistently and logically. Phone books and library card catalogs are examples of databases. We have always had databases, but they typically were in paper form (e.g., a teacher's grade book). A computer database offers several advantages over a paper database.

1. *Information in a computerized database can be located quickly.* Rather than sorting through stacks of paper or cards, one can rapidly search a computer database. It is not uncommon to search thousands of records in a single second.

2. *Computerized databases are easy to reorganize.* A major advantage of a database is that you can reorganize it in many ways. With a paper database, such as a teacher's grade book, it is typically organized one way, alphabetical, by last name. With a computer database, it can be quickly reorganized. For example, a teacher may want records sorted by test score performance, from highest to lowest. This is easily done with a database program.

3. *Computerized databases are easy to categorize and summarize.* Individuals belonging to a group of interest can be quickly located and summarized. For example, assume that part of a health promotion program includes hypertension screening. A list of those individuals with high blood pressure can be easily obtained.

4. *Computerized databases are physically compact.* A single 3.5-inch disk can hold the equivalent of an entire file cabinet of information. To illustrate, a data set of 101,052 numbers (2,406 subjects and 42 variables) used 332 K or about 24% of the capacity of a 1.4 megabyte 3.5-inch disk.

5. *Computerized databases are designed to enhance **data** entry.* A major problem when entering data into a mainframe computer is that the columns must be properly aligned. Missing by just one column would result in a serious error. Computerized databases are designed to enhance data entry. As a very useful example, the database can be designed to accept only numbers or letters for a variable. This eliminates the error of mistaking the letter O for the numeral 0, which is a common problem when entering data into a mainframe or minicomputer.

6. *A computerized database can perform complicated calculations.* Database programs have the capacity to perform both simple and complex mathematical functions that alter or form new variables. The use of standard scores is outlined in Chapter 3. A computerized database can be designed to make these calculations easily and instantly. Chapters 10 and 11 include several complicated equations used to evaluate the fitness of adults. These are easily done with database programs and are illustrated at the end of these chapters.

7. *Data from a database can be exported and then imported into other programs.* It is a simple task to move the data from a database into a statistical package for data analysis or into a word processing program to develop, for example, a list of students and their test scores.

***Telecommunications.*** With a modem and proper software, PCs can interact via telephone with a mainframe or other personal computer. It is then possible to transmit data from one computer to another. For example, a university professor can stay home and conduct complex data analyses on the university's mainframe computer with a PC. Rather than going to a library, a computer literature search can be easily conducted with a PC. It is then possible to get the abstract of each important article, which can be stored in the PC or printed. The fax is another example of a growing computer science application. With proper hardware and software, your PC becomes a fax machine.

The e-mail network is providing a way for individuals to communicate with each other on a worldwide basis. This network gives an individual with a PC and modem and an e-mail address[8] the capacity to send and receive information with others worldwide. This form of communication became a reality by linking telephone networks, mainframe computers, and communication satellites to PCs.

***Writing Aids.*** There are several programs available to enhance writing proficiency. Grammar checkers are useful for finding basic errors and recommending changes. Bibliographic database programs are especially useful for writing term papers. Libraries have computer facilities to search bibliographic databases and allow you to identify articles using key words. Presently, you can get the identified references in "hard copy" form or "down-loaded" onto a computer disk. There are programs[9] that aid writing in several ways.

1. Some programs move the identified information from the library's computer system into a bibliographical database on your PC. This not only includes the bibliographic entry, but also the provided abstract. This eliminates the need to type reference materials.

2. Bibliographic database programs function in a method similar to what is required in basic composition classes, namely, keeping the reference on one card and notes on another card. These programs have a place to type notes that later can be copied and easily inserted (i.e., pasted) into a paper.

3. The Macintosh Endnote version can be open with your word processing program. This gives you the capacity to cite a reference by simply pasting into your paper a generic reference form.

4. When the paper is done, the program has the capacity to reformat it into final form by replacing the generic reference listing with the appropriate citation; then the program builds the bibliography for all references cited in the paper. There are several different reference styles that can be used (Figure 2.5).

***Statistics Programs.*** Mainframe statistics programs are excellent and have been illustrated in previous editions. The most popular mainframe programs are SPSSx, SAS, and BMD-P. Each of these three packages provides statistical procedures ranging from simple descriptive statistics to the most complex techniques used by researchers. Each of these programs is now available for MS-DOS PCs, and there is a definite trend in colleges, universities, public school districts, hospitals, and other organizations engaged in data analysis to use the PC versions. In their initial version, the commands of the PC versions are nearly identical with the mainframe versions. For the novice, these PC programs are difficult to use. At the time this chapter was being written, these MS-DOS programs were being written for use with Microsoft Windows. This will dramatically enhance the ease in which the programs can be used.

---

[8] Dr. Maureen Weiss, editor of the Research Quarterly for Exercise and Sport has an e-mail address for manuscript inquiries. For illustration, the e-mail address to the editorial office of the journal is rqes@oregon.uoregonledu.

[9] These programs, Endlink and Endnote (Niles and Associates, Berkeley, CA), are available for Macintosh and MS-DOS machines. Endlink has the capacity to download a library search and load it into Endnote, the database program used to develop reference lists.

## GENERIC FORMAT

While it has been known for over 50 years that maximum aerobic exercise capacity declines with age [Robinson, 1938 #160], cross-sectional and longitudinal data do not agree on the rate of decline [Buskirk, 1987 #60]. Kasch and associates [Kasch, 1990 #325] compared 25-year changes of physically active and inactive men, and Rogers and associates [Rogers, 1990 #373] studied the rate of $\dot{V}O_2$ Max with 15 master athletes.

## RESEARCH QUARTERLY FOR EXERCISE AND SPORT FORMAT

While it has been known for over 50 years that maximum aerobic exercise capacity declines with age (Robinson, 1938), cross-sectional and longitudinal data do not agree on the rate of decline (Buskirk & Hodgson, 1987). Kasch and associates (Kasch, Boyer, VanCamp, Verity, & Wallace, 1990) compared 25-year changes of physically active and inactive men, and Rogers and associates (Rogers, Hagberg, Martin, Ehsani, & Holloszy, 1990) studied the rate of $\dot{V}O_2$ Max with 15 master athletes.

### REFERENCES

Buskirk, E. R., & Hodgson, J. L. (1987). Age and aerobic power: the rate of change in men and women. *Federation Proceedings, 46,* 1824–1829.

Kasch, F. W., Boyer, J. L., VanCamp, S. P., Verity, L. S., & Wallace, J. (1990). The effect of physical activity and inactivity on aerobic power in older men (a longitudinal study). *The Physician and Sportsmedicine 18,* 73–81.

Robinson, S. D. (1938). Experimental studies of physical fitness in relation to age. *Arbeitphysiologie, 10,* 251–323.

Rogers, M. A., Hagberg, J. M., Martin, W. H., Ehsani, A. A., & Holloszy, J. O. (1990). Decline in $\dot{V}O_2$ Max in master athletes and sedentary men. *Journal of Applied Physiology, 68(5),* 2195–2199.

## MEDICINE AND SCIENCE IN SPORTS AND EXERCISE FORMAT

While it has been known for over 50 years that maximum aerobic exercise capacity declines with age [3], cross-sectional and longitudinal data do not agree on the rate of decline [1]. Kasch and associates [2] compared 25-year changes of physically active and inactive men, and Rogers and associates [4] studied the rate of $\dot{V}O_2$ Max with 15 master athletes.

### REFERENCES

1. Buskirk, E. R. and J. L. Hodgson. Age and aerobic power: the rate of change in men and women. *Federation Proc* 46:1824–1829, 1987.
2. Kasch, F. W., J. L. Boyer, S. P. VanCamp, L. S. Verity, and J. Wallace. The effect of physical activity and inactivity on aerobic power in older men (a longitudinal study). *Phys. Sportsmed.,* 18:73–81, 1990.
3. Robinson, S. D. Experimental studies of physical fitness in relation to age. *Arbeitsphysiologie* 10:251–323, 1938.
4. Rogers, M. A., J. M. Hagberg, W. H. Martin, A. A. Ehsani, and J. O. Holloszy. Decline in $\dot{V}O_2$ Max in master athletes and sedentary men. *J. Appl. Phyol.* 68(5):2195–2199, 1990.

**Figure 2.5** Examples of the use of the Endnote bibliographic program. Provided first is the example of the general citation used when drafting the paper. When in final form, the program replaces the generic text citations with proper citations and develops the reference list using the selected style. Shown are the formats required for publication in the *Research Quarterly for Exercise and Sport,* and *Medicine and Science in Sports and Exercise.*

Major advantages of the present generation of PC statistical programs over mainframe and early MS-DOS versions include data entry and graphics capabilities. This is shown next.

In mainframe versions, data entry was especially difficult. The data had to be entered into a certain column in the data field. For example, assume a person's age needs to be entered into columns 3, 4, and 5. If that age is 23, and it is mistakenly entered only in columns 3 and 4, the computer would read the age as 230; if it is entered only in columns 5 and 6, the age would be read as 2. Some variables were entered names. For example, the variable gender would be male and female. If a word was misspelled (e.g., mael rather than male), the computer would not recognize the

| | AGE | $\dot{V}O_2$ MAX | GENDER | INPUT COLUMN |
|---|---|---|---|---|
| 1 | 39 | 37.3 | MALE | |
| 2 | 45 | 33.5 | FEMALE | |
| 3 | 56 | 31.6 | FEMALE | |
| 4 | 38 | 40.4 | MALE | |
| 5 | 45 | 30.8 | FEMALE | |
| 6 | 62 | 28.1 | MALE | |
| 7 | 48 | 28.0 | FEMALE | |
| 8 | 39 | 29.1 | FEMALE | |
| 9 | 48 | 30.1 | MALE | |
| 10 | 45 | 36.6 | MALE | |
| | | | | |

mistake. Microcomputer data entry methods have minimized these types of problems. Figure 2.6 shows the data entry format for the Macintosh program Statview (4.01). The variables are entered into a cell that is programmed to accept a certain format. Some common formats are integer, real number (can specify the number of decimal points), categorical (e.g., male or female), currency, and date. When integer and real are specified, only number will be accepted. The letter O would not be accepted as a zero value. The Statview program allows you to specify the names of the variables in a category. For the example shown in Figure 2.6, the names for the variable GENDER are MALE and FEMALE. To enter the name, just the first letter needs to be entered, that is, entering M results in MALE being placed in the cell. This eliminates the possibility of misspelling words.

A major development in PC statistical packages is the graphic presentation of data. The graphic output is publication quality. Figures 2.7 and 2.8 illustrate the professional quality of the graphic output of the Macintosh statistical program Statview (4.01). Graphics of this publication quality can be quickly and routinely made. Throughout the statistics and measurement theory chapters, output from PC programs is illustrated.

## Physical Education and Exercise Science Programs

A variety of computer applications is available for use in exercise science and physical education. Microcomputers have several direct applications to the area of exercise science. Much of the sophisticated scientific equipment is interfaced with a PC. With the development of the health promotion, commercial programs are available to evaluate fitness and diet, assess cardiovascular disease risk, and monitor exercise. Publishers are now using computer programs to help teach important exercise concepts. Many teachers in the public schools monitor the fitness of their students with economical programs. And finally, a variety of shareware programs is available to teachers to perform a wide range of functions.

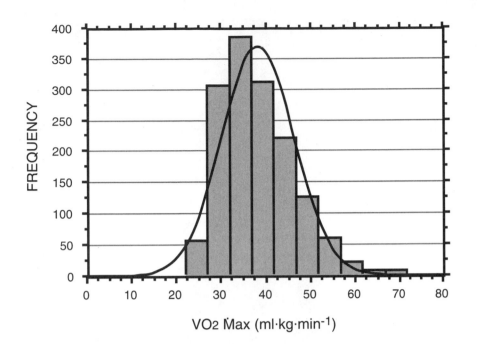

**Figure 2.7**
Histogram of the aerobic fitness of 1,604 men tested at the Cardio-pulmonary Laboratory at NASA/ Johnson Space Center, Houston, Texas. The Statview (4.01) not only has the capacity to produce the histogram, but also to superimpose a normal curve over the distribution (Abacus 1993). This provides a way to evaluate visually the shape of the distribution. These distribution characteristics are discussed in Chapter 3.

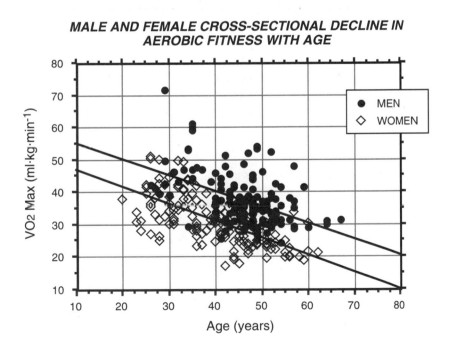

**Figure 2.8**
Scattergram and male and female linear regression lines defining the cross-sectional decline of $\dot{V}O_2$ Max with age. The Statview (4.01) program not only has the capacity to generate the bivariate plot, but also to compare group trends (Abacus 1993). These data show that the aerobic capacity of men and women declines at the same rate, but the aerobic capacity of women is lower than that of men of the same age. Graph developed from data on 300 men and women randomly selected from a large database. (Jackson et al., 1990.)

**Figure 2.9**
Maximal oxygen uptake
(VO$_2$ Max) can be easily
measured with a
computerized metabolic
system. (Courtesy of Pat
Bradley.)

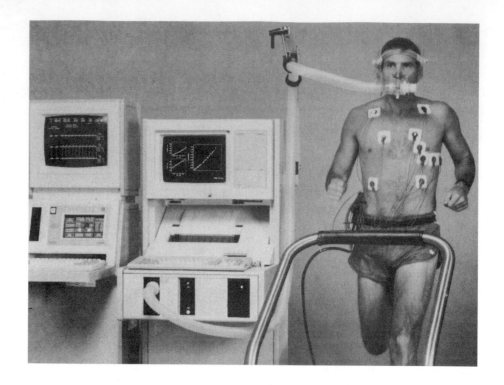

***Scientific Instrumentation.*** Computers are now being interfaced with various types of research equipment to automate data collection and complete complex calculations; for example, the calculation of VO$_2$ Max (see Chapter 10). Prior to the computer era, VO$_2$ Max was very time-consuming to measure because expired gases had to be collected in a bag for analysis. Now this analysis can be done quickly and accurately with a computer (see Figure 2.9). Another example is with isokinetic strength testing, illustrated in Chapter 8.

***Adult Fitness and Health Promotion.*** The use of PC technology in adult fitness and the health promotion industry is growing at an accelerated pace. This trend was started in the late 1960s by Dr. Kenneth Cooper when the Institute for Aerobics Research developed a computer system for the quantification of exercise with aerobics points (Cooper 1970). This computer system was designed to develop a database for studying the effects of exercise on health. When the Tenneco Corporation of Houston, Texas, developed their employee health and fitness program, a computerized system was developed to quantify exercise by caloric expenditure (Baun and Baun 1985). The Tenneco example was especially important because it signaled that the trend in the corporate fitness industry was a commitment to computerization.

Tenneco's development of its own customized computer software was a very expensive venture. Now, more affordable commercial software is available. Besides general applications such as locker assignments, the general capabilities of this commercial software include the following:

Fitness assessments (see Figure 2.10)

Exercise prescriptions (see Figure 2.11)

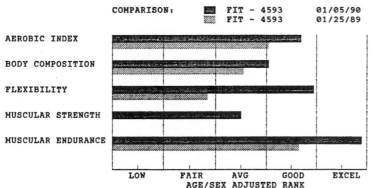

```
                FITNESS  PROFILE
        UNIVERSITY  OF  HOUSTON

Evaluation of:  JOE FIT                        Date:   01/05/90
Member Number:  4593

Age:  33        Sex:  Male        Height: 5 ' 10 "     Weight:  170.0
% Body Fat:  15.4   Ideal Weight (16 - 19 %):  171.1 - 177.5   Wt Diff:  -4.

              COMPARISON:    ████   FIT - 4593    01/05/90
                             ▓▓▓▓   FIT - 4593    01/25/89

AEROBIC INDEX

BODY COMPOSITION

FLEXIBILITY

MUSCULAR STRENGTH

MUSCULAR ENDURANCE

              LOW      FAIR     AVG     GOOD     EXCEL
                   AGE/SEX ADJUSTED RANK
```

## BODY MEASUREMENTS        ## CARDIOVASCULAR

|                    | 01/05/90 | 01/25/89 |
|--------------------|----------|----------|
| HEIGHT             | 70       | 70       |
| WEIGHT             | 170      | 185      |
| CHEST              | 42       | 42       |
| ARM                | 16       | 16       |
| WAIST              | 36       | 38       |
| HIPS               | 40       | 42       |
| THIGH              | 22       | 22       |
| CALF               | 16       | 16       |
| SUM OF SKIN FOLDS  | 50       | 70       |

|                       | 01/05/90 | 01/25/89 |
|-----------------------|----------|----------|
| RESTING BP            | 120/80   | 120/80   |
| RESTING HR            | 63       | 63       |
| VO2 MAX ml/kg/min     | 49       | 42       |

## FLEXIBILITY        ## RESPIRATORY

|               |    |    |
|---------------|----|----|
| SIT & REACH   | 21 | 12 |
| HIP ABDUCTION |    |    |
| 3rd FLEXIBILITY |  |    |

|                  |         |       |       |
|------------------|---------|-------|-------|
| VC      (6.0 l)  |         | 113.3 | 93.5  |
| FEV1    (5.0 l)  |         | 120.9 | 95.2  |
| FEV1/VC (%)      |         | 83.0  | 80.0  |

## MUSCULAR  STRENGTH        ## MUSCULAR  ENDURANCE

|                |     |
|----------------|-----|
| BENCH PRESS    | 100 |
| LEG PRESS  1RM |     |
| COMB HAND GRIP |     |

|               |    |    |
|---------------|----|----|
| SIT UPS       | 84 | 52 |
| PUSH-UPS      |    |    |
| 3rd ENDURANCE |    |    |

**Figure 2.10**
Sample computer output used for adult fitness assessment. This program has the capacity to not only evaluate initial fitness status, but also to evaluate changes in fitness. Shown is the output of the program that evaluates changes that have been made. The program allows for V̇O₂ Max to be estimated by all methods illustrated in Chapter 10. (Courtesy of CSI Software Company, 15425 North Freeway, Houston, TX 77090.)

**Figure 2.11**
Once a general fitness assessment is made (see Figure 2.10), an individualized exercise prescription can be made. The program allows the exercise specialist to alter exercise intensity and duration to personalize exercise. Exercise intensity is determined from $\dot{V}O_2$ Max measured during the fitness assessment. The caloric expenditure provides a means of relating exercise to energy expenditure, which is important for health promotion. (Courtesy of CSI Software Company, 15425 North Freeway, Houston, TX 77090.)

UNIVERSITY OF HOUSTON

JOE FIT                    Member no. 4593          Date: 01/05/90

### WARM UP

Smoothly perform 2-3 repetitions for each flexibility exercise. Attempt to hold stretch for 10-20 seconds.

```
HEAD CIRCLES
SHOULDER FLEX DRILL
TORSO TWIST
WALL BAR WAIST STRETCH
ROCKER LIFT
ALL OVER STRETCH
WALL HIP STRETCH
BALLET STRETCH
KNEELING BACKWARD BEND
LEGS FALL APART
LUNGE POSITION STRETCH
ANKLE ROTATIONS
```

### AEROBICS: (15-45 min)

This is the HEART of your conditioning program. Once you reach your Maintenance Level, perform your aerobic exercise in your training heart rate zone (THRZ).

The TRAINING LEVELS (Distance and Time) in the Maintenance Program should be used only as a guide. Modify them appropriately, according to your actual pulse rate (THRZ) or your perceived exertion level. As you improve, you will go further or perform more work at the same training heart rate.

#### WALK-JOG PROGRAM

Build up to the appropriate pace gradually over 2-3 min. Exercise at the prescribed pace at least 3 sessions/week.

Conditioning Program - Start here if out of shape.

| STEP | METS | MILES | LAPS | PACE (min/mi) | CAL/WEEK | TIME/SESSION |
|------|------|-------|------|---------------|----------|--------------|
| 1 | 9.1 | 1.37 | 5.5 | 10:59 | 553 | 15:00 |
| 2 | 9.3 | 1.63 | 6.5 | 10:43 | 662 | 17:30 |
| 3 | 9.6 | 1.91 | 7.7 | 10:27 | 775 | 20:00 |
| 4 | 9.8 | 2.21 | 8.8 | 10:12 | 893 | 22:30 |
| 5 | 10.0 | 2.51 | 10.0 | 09:58 | 1016 | 25:00 |
| 6 | 10.3 | 2.82 | 11.3 | 09:44 | 1144 | 27:30 |

Exercise logging and storage (see Figure 2.12)

Cardiovascular disease risk analysis

Health-risk appraisal

Dietary analysis (CSI 1989)

These systems are not only useful for data analysis and storage, but also for education, providing opportunities to enhance health and fitness concepts. For example, one of the most popular aspects of the highly successful Tenneco Health and Fitness

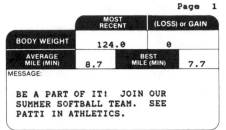

**Figure 2.12**
Sample output of the CSI EXERLOG™ program. The program allows an individual to quantify the results of his or her exercise by many different units and provides totals for different time periods.
(Courtesy of CSI Software Company, 15425 North Freeway, Houston, TX 77090.)

| | | | | |
|---|---|---|---|---|
| BODY WEIGHT | **MOST RECENT** 124.0 | **(LOSS) or GAIN** 0 | | |
| AVERAGE MILE (MIN) 8.7 | | BEST MILE (MIN) 7.7 | | |

DATE: 05/05/89   MEMBER # 2222A

FREDA A FITNESS
2345 FRED STREET
HOUSTON, TX 77001-1111

MESSAGE:
BE A PART OF IT!  JOIN OUR
SUMMER SOFTBALL TEAM.  SEE
PATTI IN ATHLETICS.

THIS MONTH'S ACTIVITIES

| DATE | ACTIVITY | UNITS | DURATION | AEROBIC POINTS | CALORIES | AEROBIC MINUTES |
|---|---|---|---|---|---|---|
| 04/05/89 | WALK/JOG/RUN | 5.8 MI | 45:00 | 33.5 | 566 | 43.0 |
| 04/06/89 | TREADMILL | | 45:00 | 32.7 | 554 | 41.0 |
| 04/06/89 | STAIRMASTER | | 55:00 | 55.2 | 560 | 50.0 |
| 04/06/89 | SWIMMING | 1.2 MI | 45:00 | 25.1 | 354 | 35.0 |
| 04/07/89 | CYCLING (ROAD) | 25.0 MI | 120:00 | 23.5 | 985 | 100.0 |
| 04/08/89 | CYCLE ERGOMETER | | 55:00 | 55.2 | 560 | 50.0 |
| 04/09/89 | AEROBIC DANCE | | 55:00 | 11.0 | 411 | 35.0 |
| 04/09/89 | PROG RESISTANCE | | 30:00 | 6.0 | 189 | 10.0 |
| 04/10/89 | SUPER CIRCUIT | | 25:00 | 6.5 | 187 | 10.0 |
| 04/10/89 | TENNIS DOUBLES | 3.0 SET | 75:00 | 1.2 | 391 | 30.0 |
| 04/11/89 | WALK/JOG/RUN | 3.0 MI | 30:00 | 14.0 | 295 | |
| 04/11/89 | SCHWINN AIRDYNE | | 45:00 | 17.5 | 458 | 30.0 |
| 04/12/89 | WALK/JOG/RUN | 6.2 MI | 48:00 | 36.2 | 610 | 48.0 |

TOTALS

| ACTIVITY | PREVIOUS TOTAL | THIS MONTH'S TOTAL | CUMULATIVE YEAR'S TOTAL |
|---|---|---|---|
| WALK/JOG/RUN (MI) | 38.30 | 15.00 | 53.30 |
| STAIRMASTER (HRS) | 4.00 | 0.92 | 4.92 |
| CYCLE ERGOMETER (HRS) | 3.82 | 0.92 | 4.74 |
| SWIMMING (MI) | 3.30 | 1.20 | 4.50 |
| CYCLING (ROAD) (MI) | 127.00 | 25.00 | 152.00 |
| TOTAL CALORIES (1.7 lbs) | 46194 | 6120 | 52314 |
| TOTAL AEROBIC MINUTES | 2993 | 482 | 3475 |
| TOTAL AEROBIC POINTS | 1507 | 317 | 1825 |

**AEROBIC POINTS:** ONE POINT EQUALS APPROXIMATELY 7.0 ML/KG/MIN OF OXYGEN UPTAKE ABOVE RESTING. TRY TO OBTAIN AT LEAST 30 POINTS PER WEEK.
**AEROBIC MINUTES:** THE NUMBER OF MINUTES YOUR HEART IS PERFORMING IN ITS TRAINING ZONE. TRY TO OBTAIN AT LEAST 60 PER WEEK.
**CALORIES:** 3500 CALORIES REPRESENTS THE ENERGY DERIVED FROM LOSING APPROXIMATELY 1 LB. OF WEIGHT.     CSI 1987

Program has been their computer logging program.[10] The computer gives the employee instant feedback on the calories expended during his or her exercise session, allowing the employee to determine in an objective way what has been accomplished and make intelligent exercise choices.

---

[10] Personal communication between A. Jackson and William Baun, Director of Health and Fitness, Tenneco Corporation, Houston, TX.

***Teaching Exercise Science Principles.*** Exercise science microcomputer programs provide a means of integrating exercise science principles with computer output. At least two texts have been published that integrate exercise science principles with commercial computer programs (Jackson and Ross 1992; Ross and Jackson 1990). This allows the computer not only to serve as a tool for data analysis and data management, but also to provide laboratory experiences that reinforce exercise science concepts presented in the text. The integration of this printed and computer medium allows for the following:

Individualized fitness assessment of each student (Figure 2.10)

Individualized exercise prescription based on their fitness assessment (Figure 2.11)

Quantification of each student's exercise program in terms of caloric expenditure (Figure 2.12)

Evaluation of fitness changes accomplished in the course (Figure 2.10)

Development of a normative database unique to University of Houston students

Computerized grading system

The educational impact of the PC explosion is just starting to be realized. Another excellent example of integrating exercise science and computer technology is illustrated in an innovative exercise physiology lab manual that includes twenty computer-simulated exercise physiology laboratories (Morrow and Pivarnik 1989). The programs are written for the MS-DOS and Apple II computers. The manual and programs are written so basic exercise physiology concepts can be learned through computer simulation.

***Evaluation of Youth Fitness.*** One of the more useful PC programs for physical education teachers is the software designed to educate students about health-related fitness. The health-related fitness tests are fully presented in the youth fitness chapter (Chapter 9). The Chrysler-AAU (1992) and Prudential FITNESSGRAM® (1992) health-related fitness programs provide a PC program. These programs are very easy to use; either the teacher or student can enter fitness test results. The programs are designed to generate a variety of reports that provide summary results for various groups such as students, parents, school boards, or evaluation teams.

The Prudential FITNESSGRAM® (1992) is a national program developed by the Institute for Aerobics Research, Dallas, TX. This is one of the most successful computer programs[11] available to evaluate youth fitness. The Institute will send you a free copy of the computer program and the only cost to the school is for the Prudential FITNESSGRAM® computer paper. The graphic output offers students a visual picture of their fitness status. An example of FITNESSGRAM® output is presented as Figure 2.13.

---

[11] The current (November 1993) programs are written for the Macintosh and MS-DOS machines with and without Microsoft Windows. To obtain information, write the Prudential FITNESSGRAM®, Cooper Institute for Aerobic Research, 12330 Preston Road, Dallas, TX 75230. (214) 701–8001.

# The Prudential FITNESSGRAM

## COMMITTED TO HEALTH RELATED FITNESS

Jane Jogger
FITNESSGRAM Jr. High
FITNESSGRAM Test District

Instructor: Bridgman
Grade: 04          Period: 09    Gregg    Age  09

| Test Date | Height | Weight |
|-----------|--------|--------|
| MO - YR | FT - IN | LBS |
| 10.92 | 5.00 | 101 |
| 05.93 | 5.01 | 106 |

### AEROBIC CAPACITY

#### HEALTHY FITNESS ZONE

One Mile Walk/Run

| Needs Improvement | Good | | Better |
|---|---|---|---|

10:00                                    07:30

|  | Current | Past |
|---|---|---|
| min:sec | 9:01 | 9:12 |
| ml/kg | 47 | 47 |

Max VO₂ Indicates ability to use oxygen. Expressed as ml of oxygen per kg body weight per minute. Healthy Fitness Zone = 35+ for girls & 42+ for boys.

### MUSCLE STRENGTH, ENDURANCE & FLEXIBILITY

#### HEALTHY FITNESS ZONE

Curl-up (Abdominal)

| Needs Improvement | Good | Better |
|---|---|---|

21                                    40

| # performed | |
|---|---|
| 12 | 05 |

Push-up (Upper Body)

| Needs Improvement | Good | Better |
|---|---|---|

12                                    25

| # performed | |
|---|---|
| 27 | 20 |

Trunk Lift (Trunk Extension)

| Needs Improvement | Good | Better |
|---|---|---|

9                                     12

| inches | |
|---|---|
| 10 | 10 |

The test of flexibility is optional. If given, it is scored pass or fail and is performed on the right and left.
Test given:  Back Saver Sit and Reach

| Right | P |
|---|---|
| Left | P |

### BODY COMPOSITION

#### HEALTHY FITNESS ZONE

Percent Body Fat

| Needs Improvement | Good | Better |
|---|---|---|

25.0                                   10.0

| % fat | |
|---|---|
| 27.0 | 31.1 |

You can improve your abdominal strength with curl-ups 2 to 4 times a week. Remember your knees are bent and no one holds your feet.

Your upper body strength was very good. Try to maintain your fitness by doing strengthening activities at least 2 or 3 times each week.

To improve your body composition, Jane, extend the length of vigorous activity each day and follow a balanced nutritional program, eating more fruits and vegetables and fewer fats and sugars. Improving body composition may also help improve your other fitness scores.

Your aerobic capacity is in the Healthy Fitness Zone. Maintain your fitness by doing 20-30 minutes of vigorous activity at least 3 or 4 times each week.

Developed by
The Cooper Institute
for Aerobics Research
Dallas, Texas

Sponsored by
The Prudential
Insurance Company
of America

**To parent or guardian**: *The Prudential FITNESSGRAM is a valuable tool in assessing a young person's fitness level. The area of the bar highlighted in yellow indicates the "healthy fitness zone." All children should strive to maintain levels of fitness within the "healthy fitness zone" or above. By maintaining a healthy fitness level for these areas of fitness your child may have a reduced risk for developing heart disease, obesity or low back pain. Some children may have personal interests that require higher levels of fitness (e.g. athletes).*

*Recommended activities for improving fitness are based on each individual's test performance. Ask your child to demonstrate each test item for you. Some teachers may stop the test when performance equals the upper limit of the "healthy fitness zone" rather than requiring a maximal effort.*

*Developing good exercise habits is important to maintaining lifelong health. You can help your son or daughter develop these habits by encouraging regular participation in physical activitiy.*

**Figure 2.13** Computer output for the Prudential FITNESSGRAM® health-related youth fitness program. The program is used by over 3 million students. (Courtesy of the Institute of Aerobics Research, Dallas, Texas.)

**SHAREWARE PROGRAM CATEGORIES**

| | | |
|---|---|---|
| Activity Aids | Fitness Testing | Instruction |
| Administration | Games | Sports Statistics |
| Appleworks | Grading Programs | Statistics |
| Computer Aids | Graphics | Teacher's Aids |
| Exercise Physiology | Health & Fitness | Utilities |
| Biomechanics | Hypercard | Writing Aids |

*Shareware Programs.* In 1985, the SOFTSHARE program started as a co-sponsored project of California State University at Fresno and the Western Society for Physical Education of College Women. The purpose of SOFTSHARE is to make available inexpensive, practical software to physical educators. In 1989, SOFT-SHARE became the sole responsibility of the University.[12]

The SOFTSHARE catalog describes over 450 programs listed under 18 different categories. Listed are programs that perform a wide range of tasks. Figure 2.14 lists these 18 categories. These programs are written for MS-DOS, Macintosh, and Apple II machines. Copies of the programs can be obtained for a small charge for the disk.

The programs distributed by SOFTSHARE are public domain and may contain "glitches," of commands that are not compatible with your computer system. Many of the programs are *shareware* software, meaning that when you first try the program, the software author requests that you send a nominal user fee. Interested programmers are encouraged to submit copies of their programs to be listed in SOFTSHARE.

## A Look at the Past and to the Future

The fourth edition of this text was written in 1990, and we raised questions and made some predictions concerning the changing computer environment. This final section is devoted to seeing how accurate we were and to make some new predictions. The first section lists the observations made in 1990 followed by what has happened at the date this chapter was sent to the publisher (November 30, 1993).

1990 Observation. "There have been many different types of microcomputers, but the three most popular categories of microcomputers are: Apple II series (i.e., II, IIe, IIc, and IIgs); MS-DOS machines; and the Apple Macintosh. A question that should be on the minds of educators is: What will happen to the Apple II series?"

11/30/93 Status. The Apple II series is dead, it is no longer being manufactured. Although there are many Apple II computers still functional in public schools, they are being replaced with MS-DOS and Macintosh machines. The Apple II machines at my (ASJ) university are "collecting dust."

1990 Observation. "You can be certain that microcomputers in the 1990s will be much different than what we presently have. You may not be able to distinguish the difference between a Macintosh and MS-DOS computer since they will both be operating under the same operating system. The rapid rise in the popularity of the Macintosh computer can be linked to its "window-and-icon format" and graphic capabilities. It is becoming apparent that this approach is likely to become the industry standard for all microcomputers."

---

[12] For a catalog of available programs contact Sally Ayer/SOFTSHARE, Physical Education and Human Performance, 5275 North Campus Drive, California State University, Fresno, CA 93740–0028. Telephone, (209) 278–2650 FAX, (209) 278–7010.

11/30/93 Status. Macintosh and MS-DOS machines still do not use the same operating system, but a graphic user interface became the PC standard. Microsoft Windows was introduced for MS-DOS machines. This MS-DOS "window-and-icon" operating system allows the machine to operate like Macintosh. Microsoft Windows was so similar to the Macintosh operating system that Apple initiated legal action.

While not using the same operating system, it is very easy to transfer files in text and numeric format between MS-DOS and Macintosh machines. Macintosh computers come with a program called "Apple File Exchange" that easily translates information in either direction. The new Mac Power PC runs both Mac and MS-DOS applications.

1990 Observation. "It is hard to predict with accuracy, but it is apparent that microcomputers of the future become more powerful and will be linked together."

11/30/93 Status. They are much more powerful as was discussed in this chapter. It is extremely easy to link computers together. For example, Apple Share is part of the operating system of Macintosh computers. This allows you, for example, to link several machines to a common printing source, to transfer data between machines, and use a program that is not on your machine but on a different machine.

And now for our predictions for the future.

Microcomputers will become smaller without losing power. It is likely students will be the next big market for the laptop models. In 1992, Macintosh produced the Newton, a hand-held computer that has FAX capabilities.

Again, we will predict that Macintosh and MS-DOS machines will move toward a common operating system. It was announced that Compaq Computer Corporation with IBM is negotiating with Apple to build a Macintosh clone or an IBM-compatible machine that can run Macintosh software.[13] The current Apple Macintosh machines use Motorola's 68000 microprocessors, but starting in spring of 1994, Apple will switch to the Power PC, a chip designed in Austin, Texas by an alliance consisting of IBM, Apple, and Motorola. The computer will still operate like a Macintosh but will run IBM-compatible software and be much faster. This new processor is a 64-bit chip with a speed of 66 MHz. The Power PC is now being sold.

Educational programs will become more multimedia because of the development of CD-ROM technology. The term CD-ROM stands for Compact Disc Read-Only Memory, which means you cannot record on them. This technology gives you the capacity to mix video and text. In 1992, there were 800 CD-ROM titles and this has grown to 3,000 in 1993. The number of PCs with CD-ROM drives is expected to grow from 5.3 million in 1993 to 17 million in 1995.

**Summary**

Computers may be classified as a mainframe computer, minicomputer, and microcomputer. The major difference in these computers is in their size and computing power. Microcomputers or personal computers are small, but powerful enough to meet the needs of teachers and exercise specialists. Computer literacy is the ability to have a basic understanding of PCs and a working knowledge of the applications needed by someone in that profession. The general programs useful to the physical education teacher and exercise specialist include word processing, graphics, databases, desktop publishing, and statistics. Several programs are available to physical education teachers for the evaluation of youth health-related fitness. Programs designed to evaluate adult fitness and prescribe and evaluate exercise are available to the exercise specialist.

---

[13] From the November 20, 1993 business section of the Houston Chronicle newspaper.

## Formative Evaluation of Objectives

*Objective 1*  Differentiate between a mainframe, minicomputer, and microcomputer.

1. What are the differences between these three types of computers?
2. Which are you most likely to use? Why?

*Objective 2*  Be knowledgeable of the changes in computer technology and list its impact on physical education teachers and exercise specialists.

1. What are the reasons that microcomputers can now replace what was previously done with a mainframe or minicomputer?
2. What does the term "computer literacy" mean?
3. How does computer literacy for physical education teachers differ from that of exercise specialists?

*Objective 3*  Be knowledgeable of the general microcomputer programs that are available.

1. List the general types of PC programs that are available to you.
2. Which of these general computer programs are most appropriate for a measurement course?

*Objective 4*  Be knowledgeable of the microcomputer programs designed for the unique needs of the physical education teacher and exercise specialist.

1. What specific types of computer programs are available for physical education teachers?
2. Describe how an exercise specialist could use computer programs to individualize an adult fitness program.

## Additional Learning Activities

1. Visit a microcomputer store and have various computers and programs demonstrated. In most stores they will encourage you to try a computer.
2. Find a MS-DOS and Macintosh microcomputer and try each. See if you can find an Apple II and compare the difference.
3. Try a MS-DOS machine that has and does not have Microsoft Windows.
4. Attend a meeting of a PC user group. Colleges and universities often have user groups where programs and equipment are demonstrated. If you are interested in computers, you will find this stimulating.
5. Visit a fitness facility or school district that uses PCs and observe how they are being used. If they are not using computers, they will be in the future.

## Bibliography

AAU. 1992. *Chrysler Fund-AAU Physical Fitness Program 1992–93 Testing Packet.* Bloomington, IN.

Abacus. 1993. *StatView (4.01).* Berkeley, CA: Abacus Concepts.

Baun, W. B. and M. Baun. 1984. A corporate health and fitness program motivation and management by computers. *JOPERD 55:* 43–45.

Cooper, K. H. 1970. *The new aerobics.* New York: Bantam Books.

CSI. 1989. *CSI Software User's Manual.* Houston, TX: Cardio Stress Software.

Evans, C. 1980. *The micro millennium.* New York: Viking Press.

Foreyt, J. P. and G. K. Goodrick. 1992. *Living without dieting.* Houston: Harrison Publishing.

Jackson, A. S. et al. 1990. Prediction of functional aerobic capacity without exercise testing. *Medicine and Science in Sports and Exercise 22:* 863–70.

Jackson, A. S. and R. M. Ross. 1992. *Understanding exercise for health and fitness.* 2d ed. Houston Cardio Stress Software Company.

King, H. A. 1989. Chapter 16. Computers in measurement and testing. In *Measurement Concepts in Physical Education and Exercise Science* (pp. 345–63) (Safrit, M. J. and T. M. Wood, Eds.) Champaign, IL: Human Kinetic Books.

Morrow, J. R., Jr. and J. M. Pivarnik. 1989. *Simulated exercise physiology laboratories.* Champaign, IL: Human Kinetic Books.

*Prudential FITNESSGRAM Test Administration Manual.* 1992. Dallas: The Cooper Institute for Aerobic Research.

Ross, R. M. and A. S. Jackson. 1990. *Exercise concepts, calculations, and computer applications.* Carmel, IN: Benchmark Press.

Rudisill, M. E. and A. S. Jackson. 1992. *Theory and application of motor learning.* Onalaska, TX: MacJR Publishing Company.

# Quantitative Aspects of Measurement

# Statistical Tools in Evaluation

## Key Words

analysis of variance
bell-shaped curve
central tendency
coefficient of determination
continuous scores
correlation
correlation coefficient
cross-validation
curvilinear relationship
dependent variable
discrete scores
frequency polygon
independent variable
interval scores
leptokurtic curves
linear relationship
mean
median
mode
multiple correlation
multiple prediction (regression)
negatively skewed curve
nominal scores
normal curve
ordinal scores
percentile
percentile rank
platykurtic curves
positively skewed curve
prediction
range
rank order correlation coefficient
ratio scores
regression line
simple frequency distribution
simple prediction (regression)
standard deviation
standard error of prediction
standard error of the mean
standard score
T-score
t-test
variability
variance
z-score

## Contents

## Objectives

This chapter presents statistical techniques that can be applied to evaluate a set of scores. Not all techniques are used on every set of scores, but you should be familiar with all of them in order to select the appropriate one for a given situation.

After reading Chapter 3 you should be able to:

1. Select the statistical technique that is correct for a given situation.
2. Calculate accurately with the formulas presented.
3. Interpret the statistical value selected or calculated.
4. Make decisions based on all available information about a given situation.
5. Utilize the microcomputer to analyze data.

# INTRODUCTION

Once test scores have been collected, they must be analyzed. You can use the techniques presented here to summarize the performance of a group and to interpret the scores of individuals within that group. Many of these techniques are used and discussed in later chapters.

You may find a good elementary statistics book such as Bloomers and Lindquist (1960), Bloomers and Forsyth (1977), Ferguson and Takane (1989), Glass and Hopkins (1984), or Roscoe (1975) helpful when studying the material in this chapter. Many other good books are also available.

## Elements of Score Analysis

There are many reasons why we analyze sets of test scores. For a large group, a simple list of scores has no meaning. Only by condensing the information and applying descriptive terms to it can we interpret the overall performance of a group, its improvement from year to year or since the beginning of a teaching or training unit, or its performance in comparison to other groups of like background.

Score analysis is also used to evaluate individual achievement. Once information on the overall performance of a group has been obtained, an individual's achievement can be evaluated in relation to it. Analysis also helps the teacher develop performance standards, either for evaluative purposes or simply to let students know how they are doing.

## Type of Scores

Scores can be classified as either continuous or discrete. **Continuous scores,** as most are in physical education and exercise science, have a potentially infinite number of values because they can be measured with varying degrees of accuracy. Between any two values of a continuous score exist countless other values that may be expressed as fractions. For example, 100-yard dash scores are usually recorded to the nearest tenth of a second, but they could be recorded in hundredths or thousandths of a second if accurate timing equipment was available. The amount of weight a person can lift might be recorded in 5-, 1-, or ½-pound scores, depending on how precise a score is desired. **Discrete scores** are limited to a specific number of values and usually are not expressed as fractions. Scores on a throw or shot at a target numbered 5-4-3-2-1-0 are discrete because one can receive a score of only 5, 4, 3, 2, 1, or 0. A score of 4.5 or 1.67 is impossible.

Most continuous scores are rounded off to the nearest unit of measurement when they are recorded. For example, the score of a student who runs the 100-yard dash in 10.57 seconds is recorded as 10.6 because 10.57 is closer to 10.6 than to 10.5. Usually when a number is rounded off to the nearest unit of measurement, it is increased only when the number being dropped is 5 or more. Thus, 11.45 is rounded off to 11.5, while 11.44 is recorded as 11.4. A less common method is to round off to the last unit of measure, awarding the next higher score only when that score is actually accomplished. For example, an individual who does 8 pull-ups but cannot complete the 9th receives a score of 8.

We can also classify scores as ratio, interval, ordinal, or nominal (Ferguson & Takane 1989). How scores are classified influences whether calculations may be done on them. **Ratio scores** have a common unit of measurement between each score and a true zero point so that statements about equality of ratios can be made. Length and weight are examples, since one measurement may be called two or three times another. **Interval scores** have a common unit of measurement between each score but

Part 2  Quantitative Aspects of Measurement

do not have a true zero point. (A score of 0 as a measure of distance is a true zero, indicating no distance. However, a score of 0 on a knowledge test is not a true zero because it does not indicate a total lack of knowledge; it simply means that the respondent answered none of the questions correctly.) In physical education, most scores are either ratio or interval. **Ordinal scores** do not have a common unit of measurement between each score, but there is an order in the scores that makes it possible to characterize one score as higher than another. Class ranks, for example, are ordinal: if 3 students receive push-up scores of 16, 10, and 8 respectively, the first is ranked 1, the next 2, and the last 3. Notice that the number of push-ups necessary to change the class ranks of the second and third students differs. Thus there is not a common unit of measurement between consecutive scores. **Nominal scores** cannot be hierarchically ordered and are mutually exclusive. For example, individuals can be classified by sport preference, but we cannot say that one sport is better than another. Gender is another example.

Many scores are recorded in feet and inches or in minutes and seconds. To analyze scores, they must be recorded in a single unit of measurement, usually the smaller one. Thus distances and heights are recorded in inches rather than feet and inches, and times are recorded in seconds rather than minutes and seconds. Recording scores in the smaller unit of measure as they are collected is less time-consuming than translating them into that form later.

**Common Unit of Measure**

Score analysis should be accurate and quick. Particularly when a set of scores is large, say 50 or more, calculators and computers should be used to ensure both accuracy and speed. Today calculators are available in desktop and pocket forms, and pocket calculators especially are inexpensive. A pocket calculator will serve you well as a student and later on the job. Your calculator should have the four basic mathematical operations, plus square root and squaring keys, a memory, and some of the basic statistical values.

**Calculators and Computers**

Calculators work well to a point, but when the number of scores is very large, the use of a calculator is time-consuming and the user tends to make more errors. Computers are very fast and accurate. As discussed in Chapter 2, computers are increasingly available in school districts and universities, agencies, and businesses. Provided with each statistical example in this chapter is an example of the microcomputer application. Sometimes the output from the microcomputer program will have more on it than has been discussed in this chapter. In these cases do not be concerned.

Throughout Chapter 3, we will reference microcomputer programs from the *Statistics with Finesse* package (Bolding 1989). These programs run on either the Apple II or IBM-PC. The programs are on several disks. One disk is a file management system for creating and modifying a data file on disk. The programs have all the nice features desired—user-friendly, menu, good prompts, and user's manual. Further, the disks of programs are very reasonably priced, and the complete set of disks should satisfy the statistical needs of any teacher, exercise specialist, or researcher. For instructors who have adopted this textbook, a copy of the *Statistics with Finesse* package is available from Wm. C. Brown Publishers at no charge. Lacking in this package of programs is the capacity to graph data. Graphic output from the Macintosh program *Statview SE + Graphics* is used to illustrate graphics examples (Feldman et al. 1987).

The *Statistics with Finesse* package of programs allows you to enter the data from the keyboard when the computer is ready for it. The problem with this is when the microcomputer is turned off the data is lost. If you should need to reanalyze the data because of a mistake in the original analysis or need to conduct a different analysis, the data must be entered again. This happens quite often, and for large amounts of data it is an inconvenience. It is possible to save the data on a floppy disk just like a microcomputer program is saved. Thus, when using *Statistics with Finesse* or some other microcomputer program, it is recommended that the data be entered and saved on disk prior to using the program. One of the questions a friendly computer program will ask you is whether your data are on disk or will be entered from the keyboard. If the data were saved on disk, it had to be saved as a file with a name, so the program will ask the name of the data file to be analyzed.

Microcomputer programs come with an instruction manual. The user must read the manual to learn how to use the program.

The following steps are used to enter and save data using the file management system of the IBM version of *Statistics with Finesse,* with the file management system on floppy disk:

1. Boot DOS.
2. Remove DOS and put the File Management disk in A drive and a formatted disk in B drive.
3. At A> type STARTSWF.
4. From the main menu of the File Management disk select "Start a New File."
5. Inform the computer that the disk for storing the data to be entered is in drive B and type a name for the data file to be created (B:filename).
6. Type a name for the data to be analyzed. If each person has multiple scores (age, height, weight, test score) a name for each variable is typed.
7. After the last variable name has been typed, type "go."
8. Enter all the data for a person before starting on another person.
9. After the last score of the last person has been typed, type "go." Then press "m" to return to the main menu of the File Management disk.
10. At the main menu, the user can either edit the data file, display the file on the screen, or print the file. Eventually, the user should either display the file on the screen or print the file to verify that the data are correct.
11. After the data have been checked, remove the File Management disk, insert and boot DOS, insert the Descriptive Statistics disk or one of the other data analysis disks, and at A> type STARTSWF.

With microcomputers having a hard disk, all of the *Statistics with Finesse* programs are stored on the hard disk in the same organization as on floppy disk. The following steps are used to enter and save data using the file management system of the IBM version of *Statistics with Finesse,* with the file management system on hard disk:

1. At C:\ > put a formatted disk in A drive and type CD SWF.
2. At C:\SWF> type STARTSWF.

3. From the menu of *Statistics with Finesse* disks select the File Management disk.

4. From the main menu of the File Management disk select "Start a New File."

5. Inform the computer that the disk for storing the data to be entered is in drive A and type a name for the data file to be created (A:filename).

6.–10. Do steps 6–10 under floppy disk.

11. After the data have been checked, from the main menu of the File Management disk press "m" to return to the menu of the *Statistics with Finesse* disks and select the Descriptive Statistics disk or one of the other data analysis disks.

## Organizing and Graphing Test Scores

### Simple Frequency Distribution

The 50 scores in Table 3.1 are not very useful in their present form. They become more meaningful if we know how many students received each score when we order the scores. To do this, we first find the lowest and highest scores in the table. Now we find the number of students who received each score between the lowest (46) and the highest (90) by making up a tally like the one in Figure 3.1.

Notice that all possible scores between 40 and 99 appear on the chart. The first score in Table 3.1 is 66, so we make a mark in row 60 under column 6 (60 + 6 = 66). This mark indicates that one score of 66 has been tabulated. We continue through the table, making a mark in the appropriate row and column for each score.

Once the scores are ordered, it is easy to make up a simple frequency distribution of the results, as shown in the first two columns of Table 3.2. We list the scores in descending order with the best score first. In most cases, the higher scores are better scores, but this is not true of running events, golf scores, numbers of errors, etc. A **simple frequency distribution** of a running event would list the lower scores first.

From a simple frequency distribution we can determine the range of scores at a glance, as well as the most frequently received score and the number of students receiving each score. For example, from Table 3.2 we can see that the scores ranged from 90 down to 46, that the most frequently received score was 68, and that with one exception all scores had a frequency of 3 or less.

With a large number of scores, forming a simple frequency distribution is time-consuming without a computer. The computer allows you to enter the scores into the computer and to analyze them using any one of a number of programs. Most packages of statistical programs for mainframe and microcomputers have a frequency count program. FREQUENCIES (Numbers Only) on the Descriptive Statistics disk in the *Statistics with Finesse* package (Bolding 1989) is one such microcomputer package.

|    | 0 | 1 | 2 | 3 | 4 | 5 | 6 | 7 | 8 | 9 |
|----|---|---|---|---|---|---|---|---|---|---|
| 40 |   |   |   |   |   |   | / | / | / | / |
| 50 |   |   |   |   | / | / | /// |  | // | / |
| 60 | / |   | // | / | / | /// | // | / | ŦĦĹ / |  |
| 70 | / | // | / | / |   | /// | /// | / | // | / |
| 80 |   |   | / | // | / |   |   |   |   |   |
| 90 | // |   |   |   |   |   |   |   |   |   |

**Figure 3.1**
Ordering a set of scores.

**Table 3.1** Standing Long Jump Scores for 50 Junior High-School Boys

| | | | | |
|---|---|---|---|---|
| 66* | 67 | 54 | 63 | 90 |
| 56 | 56 | 65 | 71 | 82 |
| 68 | 68 | 76 | 55 | 78 |
| 47 | 58 | 68 | 78 | 76 |
| 46 | 68 | 68 | 90 | 62 |
| 58 | 49 | 62 | 84 | 75 |
| 75 | 65 | 66 | 72 | 73 |
| 71 | 75 | 83 | 83 | 64 |
| 60 | 76 | 65 | 79 | 56 |
| 68 | 70 | 48 | 77 | 59 |

*66 inches

**Table 3.2** Simple Frequency Distribution of Standing Long Jump Scores of 50 Junior High-School Boys in Table 3.1

| Score | Freq. | Cum. F | Percent | Cum. % |
|---|---|---|---|---|
| 90 | 2 | 50 | 4.00 | 100.00 |
| 84 | 1 | 48 | 2.00 | 96.00 |
| 83 | 2 | 47 | 4.00 | 94.00 |
| 82 | 1 | 45 | 2.00 | 90.00 |
| 79 | 1 | 44 | 2.00 | 88.00 |
| 78 | 2 | 43 | 4.00 | 86.00 |
| 77 | 1 | 41 | 2.00 | 82.00 |
| 76 | 3 | 40 | 6.00 | 80.00 |
| 75 | 3 | 37 | 6.00 | 74.00 |
| 73 | 1 | 34 | 2.00 | 68.00 |
| 72 | 1 | 33 | 2.00 | 66.00 |
| 71 | 2 | 32 | 4.00 | 64.00 |
| 70 | 1 | 30 | 2.00 | 60.00 |
| 68 | 6 | 29 | 12.00 | 58.00 |
| 67 | 1 | 23 | 2.00 | 46.00 |
| 66 | 2 | 22 | 4.00 | 44.00 |
| 65 | 3 | 20 | 6.00 | 40.00 |
| 64 | 1 | 17 | 2.00 | 34.00 |
| 63 | 1 | 16 | 2.00 | 32.00 |
| 62 | 2 | 15 | 4.00 | 30.00 |
| 60 | 1 | 13 | 2.00 | 26.00 |
| 59 | 1 | 12 | 2.00 | 24.00 |
| 58 | 2 | 11 | 4.00 | 22.00 |
| 56 | 3 | 9 | 6.00 | 18.00 |
| 55 | 1 | 6 | 2.00 | 12.00 |
| 54 | 1 | 5 | 2.00 | 10.00 |
| 49 | 1 | 4 | 2.00 | 8.00 |
| 48 | 1 | 3 | 2.00 | 6.00 |
| 47 | 1 | 2 | 2.00 | 4.00 |
| 46 | 1 | 1 | 2.00 | 2.00 |

The output from FREQUENCIES (Numbers Only) for the data in Table 3.1 is presented in Table 3.2. From Table 3.2 it can be seen that test scores were from 46 to 90, and six people scored 68. Other useful information provided are the percent of the total group receiving each score (PERCENT column), the cumulative summing of the frequency column (CUM. F column), and the percent column (CUM. % column) starting with the worst score and working upward to the best.

We could present the information in Table 3.2 in the form of a graph. If there are many different scores, the graph is usually formed by grouping like scores together. A graph shows the general shape of a score distribution. In grouping a set of scores, we try to form about 15 groupings. To do this, divide the difference between the largest and smallest scores by 15 and round off the result to the nearest whole number if necessary (Interval size = [largest score – smallest score]/15). This number, the interval size, tells us how many scores to group together. Design the first grouping to contain the best score.

*Problem 3.1.* Group the 50 standing long jump scores listed in Table 3.2.

*Solution.* Before we can determine the actual groupings, we must determine the interval size.

### Step 1
From the table we see that the largest score is 90 and the smallest is 46, giving us an interval size of 3:

$$\text{Interval size} = \frac{90 - 46}{15} = \frac{44}{15} = 2.9 = 3.$$

### Step 2
The first grouping must contain 3 possible scores, including the score 90 (the best score). The first grouping of 89–91 was selected. Once the first grouping is established, it is easy to work up the rest as presented in Figure 3.2.

Figure 3.3 is a graph of the 50 scores. Test scores, in intervals of 3 (only midpoints are plotted), are listed along the horizontal axis with low scores on the left to high scores on the right. The frequency is listed on the vertical axis starting with 0 and increasing upward. We place a dot above each score to indicate its frequency. For example, the dot above score 66 is opposite the frequency value 6, indicating that 6 students received scores in the grouping 65–67. By connecting the dots with straight lines, we complete the graph, forming an angled figure called a **frequency polygon.**

By smoothing out the frequency polygon, we create a curve that, by its shape, tells us the nature of the distribution. In Figure 3.3 the smoothing out is indicated by the broken line. If that line resembles the curve in Figure 3.4, the graph is called a **normal** or **bell-shaped curve.** The normal curve is discussed in detail later in the chapter.

When a smoothed graph has a long, low tail on the left, indicating that few students received low scores, it is called a **negatively skewed curve.** When the tail of the curve is on the right, the curve is called **positively skewed.** A curve is called **leptokurtic** when it is more sharply peaked than a normal curve and **platykurtic** when it is less sharply peaked (see Figure 3.5). Leptokurtic curves are characteristic of extremely homogeneous groups. Platykurtic curves are characteristic of heterogeneous groups.

**Figure 3.2**
Grouping of data in Table 3.2.

| Grouping | Tally | Frequency |
|----------|-------|-----------|
| 89–91 | // | 2 |
| 86–88 | | 0 |
| 83–85 | /// | 3 |
| 80–82 | / | 1 |
| 77–79 | //// | 4 |
| 74–76 | //// / | 6 |
| 71–73 | //// | 4 |
| 68–70 | //// // | 7 |
| 65–67 | //// / | 6 |
| 62–64 | //// | 4 |
| 59–61 | // | 2 |
| 56–58 | //// | 5 |
| 53–55 | // | 2 |
| 50–52 | | 0 |
| 47–49 | /// | 3 |
| 44–46 | / | 1 |

**Figure 3.3**
A graph of standing long jump scores recorded in inches.

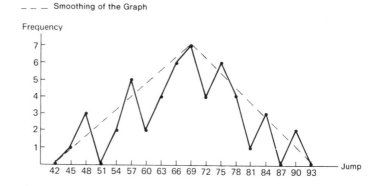

**Figure 3.4**
A normal curve.

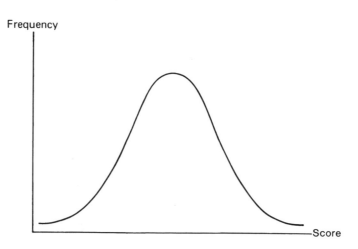

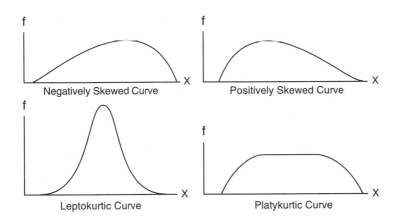

A microcomputer can be utilized to form a graph. An option of most microcomputer programs is any number of groupings and several different types of graphs. Another type of graph that is quite common is a *histogram*. Again, the frequencies for the intervals are plotted and bars are constructed at the height of the frequency running the full length of the interval. A histogram generated by a microcomputer for the data in Figure 3.2 is presented in Figure 3.6. Notice the intervals in Figure 3.6 differ from those in Figure 3.2. This is because the microcomputer picked a different number of groupings.

## Descriptive Values

Once a large set of scores has been collected, certain descriptive values can be calculated— values that summarize or condense the set of scores, giving it meaning. Descriptive values are used, not only to evaluate individual performance by the physical educator or exercise specialist who administered the test, but also to describe the group's performance or compare its performance with that of another group.

## Measures of Central Tendency

One type of descriptive value is the measure of **central tendency,** which indicates those points at which scores tend to be concentrated. There are three measures of central tendency: the mode, the median, and the mean.

*Mode.*    The **mode** is the score most frequently received. It is used with nominal data. In Table 3.2 the mode is 68: More students received a score of 68 than any other one score in the set. It is possible to have several modes if several scores tie for most frequent. The mode is not a stable measure because the addition or deletion of a single score can change its value considerably. Unless the data is nominal or the most frequent score is desired, other measures of central tendency are more appropriate.

*Median.*    The **median** is the middle score; half the scores fall above the median and half below. It cannot be calculated unless the scores are listed in order from best to worst. Where n is the number of scores in the set, we can calculate the position of the approximate median using the following formula:

$$\text{Position of approximate median} = \frac{n+1}{2}$$

**Figure 3.6**
Computer-generated histogram for the Figure 3.2 data using Statview SE with graphics.

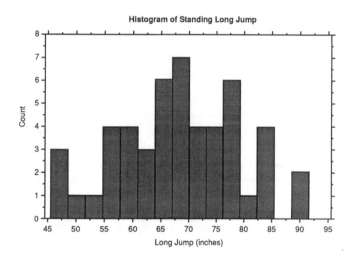

$X_1$ : S-Long Jump

| Bar: | From: (≥) | To: (<) | Count: | Percent: | |
|---|---|---|---|---|---|
| 1 | 46 | 49 | 3 | 6% | |
| 2 | 49 | 52 | 1 | 2% | |
| 3 | 52 | 55 | 1 | 2% | |
| 4 | 55 | 58 | 4 | 8% | |
| 5 | 58 | 61 | 4 | 8% | |
| 6 | 61 | 64 | 3 | 6% | |
| 7 | 64 | 67 | 6 | 12% | |
| 8 | 67 | 70 | 7 | 14% | - Mode |
| 9 | 70 | 73 | 4 | 8% | |
| 10 | 73 | 76 | 4 | 8% | |
| 11 | 76 | 79 | 6 | 12% | |
| 12 | 79 | 82 | 1 | 2% | |
| 13 | 82 | 85 | 4 | 8% | |
| 14 | 85 | 88 | 0 | 0% | |
| 15 | 88 | 91 | 2 | 4% | |

**Histogram of Standing Long Jump**

Notice that the formula calculates the median's position, or rank, in the listing—not the median itself. The approximate value, always a whole or half number, is that score in the position determined by the equation.

*Problem 3.2.* Find the approximate median score for the 9 numbers 4, 3, 1, 4, 10, 7, 7, 8, and 6.

*Solution.* First, order the listing of scores. The approximate median score is the 5th score in the ordered listing, or the score 6.

$$\text{Position of approximate median } = \frac{9+1}{2} = \frac{10}{2}$$
$$= 5, \text{ or the 5th score}$$

10, 8, 7, 7, 6, 4, 4, 3, 1

Median

*Problem 3.3.* Find the approximate median score for the 6 numbers 1, 3, 4, 5, 6, and 10.

*Solution.* First, order the listing of scores. The approximate median score is that score that falls halfway between the 3rd and 4th scores in the ordered listing, or the score 4.5.

$$\text{Position of approximate median} = \frac{6+1}{2} = \frac{7}{2}$$

$$= 3.5, \text{ or the 3.5th score}$$

10, 6, 5, 4, 3, 1

           Median

The approximate value of the median is often used by teachers, exercise specialists, and other practitioners in preference to the exact value, which is harder to obtain and unnecessarily precise. Notice that the value of the median is affected only by the position, not the value, of each score. If, in Problem 3.2, the scores were 10, 8, 7, 6, 6, 3, 2, 1, and 0, the approximate median would still be 6. This characteristic of the median is sometimes a limitation.

When scores are listed in a simple frequency distribution, we can obtain either an approximate or an exact value of the median. The approximate value of the median for the scores in Table 3.2 falls halfway between the 25th and 26th scores, at a median score of 68. Notice that we count up the frequency column from the lowest score to the 25th and 26th scores received; we do not work in the score column until we have reached the approximate median value.

Researchers are likely to need an exact value of the median. When scores in a simple frequency distribution are listed from best to worst, we can calculate the exact value of the median.

The calculation of the median is a 3-step process:

**Step 1**
Order the scores in a simple frequency distribution, listing the best score first (see columns 1 and 2 of Table 3.2).

**Step 2**
Make a cumulative frequency (cf) column by adding the frequencies, starting with the worst score and working upward to the best (see column 3 of Table 3.2).

**Step 3**
Calculate the median using the following formula:

$$\text{Median} = \text{lrl} + \left( \frac{.5n - \text{cfb}}{\text{fw}} \right)(\text{UM})$$

where X is the score that contains the median score (the score below which at least half of the frequencies lie), lrl is the lower real limit (X − .5UM), n is the number of scores (the sum of the frequency column), cfb is the cumulative frequency below (the number of scores below X), fw is the frequency within (the frequency for X), and UM is the unit of measurement in which the scores are expressed.

*Problem 3.4.* Find the exact median score for the scores listed in Table 3.2.

*Solution.* Because the scores in Table 3.2 are presented in a simple frequency distribution, **Step 1** has been done.

**Step 2**
To make the cumulative frequency column (cf), we begin adding the frequencies from the worst score (46) up to the best score (90). Thus, the starting values are 1, 2(1 + 1), and 3(2 + 1) as seen in the chart below:

| x | f | cf | x | f | cf |
|---|---|---|---|---|---|
| 90 | 2 | 50 | 60 | 1 | 13 |
| . | . | . | 59 | 1 | 12 |
| . | . | . | 58 | 2 | 11 |
| . | . | . | 56 | 3 | 9 |
| 70 | 1 | 30 | 55 | 1 | 6 |
| 68 | 6 | 29 | 54 | 1 | 5 |
| 67 | 1 | 23 | 49 | 1 | 4 |
| 66 | 2 | 22 | 48 | 1 | 3 |
| 65 | 3 | 20 | 47 | 1 | 2 |
| 64 | 1 | 17 | 46 | 1 | 1 |
| 63 | 1 | 16 | | | |
| 62 | 2 | 15 | | | |

**Step 3**
Where X is 68 (looking at the cf column in Step 2, at least half the scores are below 68), lrl is 67.5 (68 − .5), n is 50, cfb is 23, and UM is 1 (because the scores are recorded in whole numbers [inches], UM is 1), the exact median score is 67.83:

$$\text{Median} = 67.5 + \left(\frac{25 - 23}{6}\right)(1)$$

$$= 67.5 + \left(\frac{2}{6}\right)(1) = 67.5 + .33 = 67.83.$$

Notice how close this is to the approximate median score, 68.

When the scores in a simple frequency distribution are listed from lowest to highest, as they would be in a running event, we use a different formula to calculate the exact median score:

$$\text{Median} = \text{url} + \left(\frac{\text{cfb} - .5\text{n}}{\text{fw}}\right)(\text{UM})$$

where url is the upper real limit (X + .5UM).

*Problem 3.5.* Find the exact median score of the 100-yard dash times listed in the following frequency distribution.

| x | f | cf |
|------|---|----|
| 10.0 | 1 | 36 |
| 10.1 | 2 | 35 |
| 10.2 | 4 | 33 |
| 10.3 | 7 | 29 |
| 10.4 | 8 | 22 |
| 10.5 | 9 | 14 |
| 10.7 | 4 | 5 |
| 11.0 | 1 | 1 |

*Solution.* Where X is 10.4, url is 10.45 (10.4 + .05), n is 36, cfb is 14, fw is 8, and UM is .1 (because the scores are in tenths of a second, UM is .1), the exact median score is 10.4:

$$\text{Median} = 10.45 + \left( \frac{14 - 18}{8} \right)(.1)$$

$$= 10.45 + \left( \frac{-4}{8} \right)(.1) = 10.45 + (-.5)(.1)$$

$$= 10.45 + (-.05) = 10.45 - .05 = 10.4.$$

**Mean.** The mean is ordinarily the most appropriate measure of central tendency with interval or ratio data. It is affected by both the value and the position of each score. The **mean** is the sum of the scores divided by the number of scores.

$$\overline{X} = \frac{\Sigma X}{n}$$

where $\overline{X}$ is the mean, $\Sigma X$ is the sum of the score, and n is the number of scores.

*Problem 3.6.* Calculate the mean of the following scores: 2, 3, 6, 7, 1, 5, and 10.

*Solution.* Where $\Sigma X$ is 34 and n is 7, the mean is 4.86:

$$\overline{X} = \frac{34}{7} = 4.857 = 4.86.$$

Notice that the scores need not be ordered hierarchically to calculate the mean. For example, the mean for the scores in Table 3.1 is 67.78, the sum of the randomly ordered scores divided by 50.

When the graph of the scores is a normal curve, the mode, median, and mean are equal. When the graph is positively skewed, the mean is larger than the median; when it is negatively skewed, the mean is less than the median. For example, the graph for the scores 2, 3, 1, 4, 1, 8, and 10 is positively skewed with the mean 4.14 and the median 3.

The mean is the most common measure of central tendency. But when scores are quite skewed or lack a common interval between consecutive scores (as do ordinal scores), the median is the best measure of central tendency. The mode is used only when the mean and median cannot be calculated (e.g., with nominal scores) or when the only information wanted is the most frequent score (e.g., most common uniform size, most frequent error).

## Measures of Variability

A second type of descriptive value is the measure of **variability,** which describes the set of scores in terms of their spread or heterogeneity. For example, consider these pull-up scores for 2 groups:

| Group 1 | Group 2 |
|---------|---------|
| 9 | 5 |
| 1 | 6 |
| 5 | 4 |

For both groups the mean and median are 5. If you simply report that the mean and median for both groups are identical without showing the scores, another person could conclude that the two groups have equal or similar ability. This is not true: Group 2 is more homogeneous in performance than is Group 1. A measure of variability is the descriptive term that indicates this difference in the spread, or heterogeneity of a set of scores. There are two such measures: the range and the standard deviation.

*Range.* The range is the easiest measure of variability to obtain and the one that is used when the measure of central tendency is the mode or median. The **range** is the difference between the highest and lowest scores. For example, the range for the scores in Table 3.2 is 44 (90 – 46). The range is neither a precise nor stable measure because it depends on only two scores and is affected by a change in either of them. For example, the range of scores in Table 3.2 would have been 38 (84 – 46) if the students who scored 90 had been absent.

*Standard Deviation.* The **standard deviation** (symbolized s) is the measure of variability used with the mean. It indicates the amount that all the scores differ or deviate from the mean—the more the scores differ from the mean, the higher the standard deviation. The sum of the deviations of the scores from the mean is always 0. Provided are two equations: (1) the definitional formula; and (2) a calculational formula. The definitional formula illustrates what the standard deviation is, but is more difficult to use. The calculational formula is easier to use if you have only a simple calculator to use. They will both be illustrated by example.

The definitional formula for the standard deviation is:

$$s = \sqrt{\frac{\Sigma(X - \overline{X})^2}{n}} \text{ (definitional formula)} \tag{1}$$

where s is the standard deviation, X is the scores, $\overline{X}$ is the mean, and n is the number of scores.

Some books, calculators, and computer programs will use the term n –1 rather than n in the denominator of the standard deviation formula. The use of n is preferred in this chapter. Either can be used because the difference is minimal unless n is very small. If n – 1 is used, the formula for the standard deviation is:

$$s = \sqrt{\frac{\Sigma(X - \overline{X})^2}{n - 1}}. \tag{2}$$

If the group tested is viewed as the group of interest, it is considered the *population* and formula (1) is used. If the group tested is viewed as a representative part of the population, it is considered a *sample* and formula (2) is used. In other words, if the standard deviation calculated on sample data is to be used as an estimate of the population standard deviation, formula (2) is used. Many introductory statistics books have a comprehensive discussion of this point.

*Problem 3.7a.* Compute the standard deviation using the definitional formulas for the following set of scores:
7, 2, 7, 6, 5, 6, 2.

*Solution.* The process is 4 steps: calculate the mean, subtract the mean from each score, square the differences, and determine s. After calculating the mean we can combine Steps 2 and 3 by creating a table, working across the rows, and then totaling the columns. Finally s is calculated.

**Step 1**

$$\overline{X} = \frac{\Sigma X}{n} = \frac{35}{7} = 5$$

**Steps 2–3**

| $X$ | $(X - \overline{X})$ | $(X - \overline{X})^2$ |
|:---:|:---:|:---:|
| 7 | 2 (7 – 5) | 4 |
| 2 | –3 (2 – 5) | 9 |
| 7 | 2 | 4 |
| 6 | 1 | 1 |
| 5 | 0 | 0 |
| 6 | 1 | 1 |
| 2 | –3 | 9 |
| $\Sigma = 35$ | $\Sigma = 0$ | $\Sigma = 28$ |

**Step 4**

$s = \sqrt{28/7} = \sqrt{4} = 2$ (by formula [1]) or

$s = \sqrt{28/(7-1)} = \sqrt{4.67} = 2.2$ (by formula [2])

Since n is small, the difference in using n or n – 1 is somewhat large. Some calculators will calculate the standard deviation once the data is entered. These calculators provide the option of using n or n – 1. Microcomputer programs usually use n – 1.

The definitional formula is seldom used to calculate the standard deviation by hand because it is cumbersome when the mean is a fraction. Instead, the following formula is used to calculate s:

$$s = \sqrt{\frac{\Sigma X^2}{n} - \frac{(\Sigma X)^2}{n^2}} \text{ (calculational formula)} \qquad (3)$$

where $\Sigma X^2$ is the sum of the squared scores, $\Sigma X$ is the sum of the scores, and n is the number of scores. If n – 1 is used in the formula, it is

$$s = \sqrt{\frac{\Sigma X^2 - (\Sigma X)^2/n}{n-1}}. \qquad (4)$$

Formula (3) will be used most often in this chapter.

*Problem 3.7b.* Compute the standard deviation using the computational formula for the following set of scores: 7, 2, 7, 6, 5, 6, 2.

*Solution.* The process is 3 steps: calculate $\Sigma X$, calculate $\Sigma X^2$, and determine s. We can combine the first 2 steps by creating a table, working first across the rows and then totaling the columns:

| X | $X^2$ |
|---|---|
| 7 | 49 |
| 2 | 4 |
| 7 | 49 |
| 6 | 36 |
| 5 | 25 |
| 6 | 36 |
| 2 | 4 |
| $\Sigma = 35$ | $\Sigma = 203$ |

Where $\Sigma X$ is 35, $\Sigma X^2$ is 203, and n is 7, the standard deviation is 2:

$$s = \sqrt{\frac{203}{7} - \frac{35^2}{7^2}} = \sqrt{\frac{203}{7} - \frac{1225}{49}} = \sqrt{29 - 25} = \sqrt{4} = 2$$

or 2.2:

$$s = \sqrt{\frac{203 - 35^2/7}{7 - 1}} = \sqrt{\frac{203 - 1225/7}{6}} = \sqrt{\frac{203 - 175}{6}}$$

$$= \sqrt{4.67} = 2.2.$$

Notice that with this formula the scores are listed in a column and the square of each score is listed in a second column. The sums of these two columns are needed to calculate the standard deviation.

Remember that the standard deviation indicates the variability of a set of scores around the mean. The larger the standard deviation, the more heterogeneous the scores. The minimum value of s is 0.

The calculations in Problem 3.7 are easy because the number of scores is small and the number for which we needed the square root (4) is a perfect square. Unhappily, you will usually be working with between 50 and 300 scores and a number that is not a perfect square. You can speed up the calculations using a calculator. In fact, there are calculators that, by pushing the appropriate key, compute the mean and standard deviation once the data are entered. Remember, though, that if the number of scores is very large, you may find a computer more accurate and faster than a calculator.

Computer programs that calculate means and standard deviations are very common. The MEAN AND STANDARD DEVIATION program on the Descriptive Statistics disk in the *Statistics with Finesse* package can be utilized. In calculating the standard deviation it uses n – 1 in the denominator. The output from this program for the data in Table 3.1 is presented in Table 3.3.

Computer programs that calculate the median are not numerous. However, later in the Percentiles section an example is given.

**Variance.** A third measure of variability that is commonly calculated is the **variance.** It is not used as a descriptive term like the range and standard deviation but

**Table 3.3** Output from the Mean and Standard Deviation Program for the Data in Table 3.1

| Variable | N | Mean | Std Dev | Low | High |
|----------|-----|-------|---------|-----|------|
| Score | 50 | 67.78 | 10.74 | 46 | 90 |

rather as a useful statistic in certain high level statistical procedures like regression analysis or analysis of variance, which will be discussed later in this chapter. The variance is the square of the standard deviation. If, for example, the standard deviation is 5, the variance is $25(5^2)$. The calculation of the variance is the same as for the standard deviation, except the square root step is eliminated.

**Measuring Group Position**

**Percentile Ranks**

After a test session, most individuals want to know how their performance compares with those of others in the group. Ranks can be calculated by assigning the individual who earned the best score the rank of 1, the individual who earned the next best score the rank of 2, and so on. But rank has little meaning unless the number of individuals in the group is known. A rank of 35 is quite good when there are 250 individuals in the group; it is very poor when there are 37. **Percentile ranks** that indicate the relative position of an individual in a group indicate the percentage of the group that scored below a given score.

The calculation of percentile ranks is a 3-step process:

**Step 1**
Order the scores in a simple frequency distribution, listing the best score first (see Table 3.2).

**Step 2**
Make a cumulative frequency (cf) column, by adding the frequencies, starting with the worst score and working upward to the best.

**Step 3**
Calculate the percentile rank of a given score using the following formula:

$$PR_x = \left( cfb + \frac{fw}{2} \right)\left( \frac{100}{n} \right)$$

where $PR_x$ is the percentile rank of score X, cfb is the number of scores below X (the entry in the cf column one level below X), fw is the frequency of X, and n is the number of scores (the sum of the frequency column).

*Problem 3.8.* Given the following scores and frequencies, determine the percentile rank for a score of 6:

| x | f |
|-----|-----|
| 10 | 1 |
| 6 | 4 |
| 5 | 10 |
| 4 | 6 |
| 3 | 3 |
| 0 | 1 |

*Solution.* Because the scores are presented in a simple frequency distribution, **Step 1** has been done.

**Step 2**

To make the cumulative frequency column, we begin adding the frequencies from the worst score (here, 0) up to the best score (10). Thus the entry in the cf column opposite score 3 would be 4 $(1 + 3 = 4)$; and the entry opposite score 4 would be 10 $(4 + 6 = 10)$. The final chart would look like this:

| x | f | cf |
|---|---|----|
| 10 | 1 | 25 |
| 6 | 4 | 24 |
| 5 | 10 | 20 |
| 4 | 6 | 10 |
| 3 | 3 | 4 |
| 0 | 1 | 1 |

**Step 3**

The percentile rank of score 6 where cfb is 20, fw is 4, and n is 25 is 88:

$$PR_6 = \left(20 + \frac{4}{2}\right)\left(\frac{100}{25}\right)$$

$$= (20 + 2)(4) = (22)(4) = 88.$$

Of the scores received, 88% are below 6.

In the percentile rank formula, the term cfb $+ \dfrac{fw}{2}$ is the number of scores in theory below the score (x). This is based on the assumption that half the individuals who have received a given score actually scored below that score before rounding off. That is, when four people receive a score of 10, we assume that two of them originally had scores between 9.5 and 10.0.

Usually the percentile rank for each score in a set is calculated. Because the value of $\dfrac{100}{n}$ in the formula is seldom a whole number, computing PRs can be tedious without a calculator. Using a calculator, carry $\dfrac{100}{n}$ out to three digits to the right of the decimal point (thousandths), rounding off the PR to a whole number only after multiplying the cfb $+ \dfrac{fw}{2}$ value by $\dfrac{100}{n}$. For example, if n in our set of scores in Problem 3.8 had been 26 rather than 25, the value of $\dfrac{100}{n}$ would have been 3.846 $\left(\dfrac{100}{26} = 3.846\right)$ and the PR for score 6 would have been 85:

$$PR_6 = (22)(3.846) = 84.612 = 85.$$

*Disadvantages.* Percentile ranks are ordinal scores. There is no common unit of measurement between consecutive percentile rank values because they are position measures, totally depending on the scores of the group. We can see this clearly in the following PR column, the percentile ranks for the complete set of scores with which we have been working.

| x | f | cf | PR |
|---|---|----|----|
| 10 | 1 | 25 | 98 |
| 6 | 4 | 24 | 88 |
| 5 | 10 | 20 | 60 |
| 4 | 6 | 10 | 28 |
| 3 | 3 | 4 | 10 |
| 0 | 1 | 1 | 2 |

As the scores go up from 4 to 5 and from 5 to 6, notice that the percentile ranks rise at different rates: 32 and 28 respectively. For this reason Bloomers and Lindquist (1960) and Downie and Heath (1965) maintain that it is inappropriate to add, subtract, multiply, or divide percentile rank values.

Another disadvantage is that a small change in actual performance near the mean results in a disproportionate change in percentile rank; the opposite is true of changes at the extremes. We can see this in the columns above, where a change of 1 from $X = 4$ to $X = 5$ is a PR change of 32, while a score change of 4 from 6 to 10 is a PR change of only 10.

We often express test standards, or norms, in percentile ranks that are multiples of 5 (5, 10, 15, and so on). To develop these norms we must first determine the test score, or **percentile,** that corresponds to each rank. Here we have a percentile rank from which to calculate a test score (percentile). When the larger score is the better score, we use the following formula to calculate the test score that corresponds to a particular rank:

**Percentiles**

$$P = 1rl + \left[ \frac{\frac{(PR)\,(n)}{100} - cfb}{fw} \right] (UM)$$

where P is the test score (percentile) that corresponds to the percentile rank, X is the score that contains the percentile (the score below which the wanted percentage of frequencies fall), lrl is the lower real limit $(X - .5UM)$, PR is the percentile rank, n is the number of scores (sum of the frequency column), cfb is the number of scores below X, fw is the frequency for X, and UM is the unit of measurement in which the test scores are expressed.

**Note:** When the smaller score is the better score, the formula becomes

$$P = url + \left[ \frac{cfb - \frac{(PR)\,(n)}{100}}{fw} \right] (UM)$$

where url is the upper limit $(X + .5UM)$. Note that the formulas for calculating the median are a special case of these formulas.

*Problem 3.9.* Given the scores and frequency distribution in Table 3.4, determine which score has a percentile rank of 45. (What is P for a PR of 45?)

**Table 3.4** Sample Scores and Frequency Distribution

| x | f | cf |
|---|---|---|
| 21 | 2 | 52 |
| 18 | 3 | 50 |
| 15 | 3 | 47 |
| 14 | 4 | 44 |
| 13 | 4 | 40 |
| 11 | 10 | 36 |
| 10 | 7 | 26 |
| 9 | 4 | 19 |
| 8 | 6 | 15 |
| 7 | 5 | 9 |
| 6 | 2 | 4 |
| 5 | 1 | 2 |
| 1 | 1 | 1 |

*Solution.* Before we can solve the formula for P, we must determine the value of X that gives us terms lrl, cfb, and fw:

$$\frac{(PR)\,(n)}{100} = \frac{(45)\,(52)}{100} = \frac{2340}{100} = 23.4.$$

So X is the 23.4th score from the bottom. Looking at the cf column in Table 3.4, we see that score 10 contains the 23.4th score. Now we can solve for P. Where lrl is 9.5 (10 − .5), PR is 45, n is 52, cfb is 19, fw is 7, and UM is 1, P is 10:

$$P = 9.5 + \left[\frac{\dfrac{(45)\,(52)}{100} - 19}{7}\right](1)$$

$$= 9.5 + \left[\frac{\dfrac{2340}{100} - 19}{7}\right](1) = 9.5 + \frac{23.4 - 19}{7}$$

$$= 9.5 + \frac{4.4}{7} = 9.5 + .63 = 10.13 = 10.$$

The score below which 45% of the scores fall is 10; it has a percentile rank of 45.

**Using the Computer**

Percentiles and percentile ranks can be obtained from a computer. PERCENTILES on the Test and Questionnaire Analysis disk in the *Statistics with Finesse* package provide these statistics (Bolding 1989). Percentile ranks are automatically printed. After this select "Percentiles" to obtain percentiles. For the data in Table 3.1 the printout of Percentiles is presented in Table 3.5, and the printout of Percentile Ranks is presented in Table 3.6. Notice in Table 3.5 that a score (Point) is calculated for each percentile (centile), but in Table 3.6 a percentile rank is calculated for each score. Also, notice in Table 3.5, the 50th centile is the median score.

**Table 3.5** Percentiles Output for the Table 3.1 Data

| Centile | Point |
|---------|-------|
| 100 | 90.50 |
| 99 | 90.25 |
| 98 | 90.00 |
| 97 | 89.75 |
| 96 | 87.00 |
| 95 | 84.00 |
| . | . |
| . | . |
| . | . |
| 50 | 67.83 |
| . | . |
| . | . |
| . | . |
| 5 | 48.00 |
| 4 | 47.50 |
| 3 | 47.00 |
| 2 | 46.50 |
| 1 | 46.00 |
| 0 | 45.50 |

**Table 3.6** Percentile Rank Output for the Table 3.1 Data

| Score | Percentile Rank |
|-------|-----------------|
| 90 | 98.00 |
| 84 | 95.00 |
| 83 | 92.00 |
| 82 | 89.00 |
| 79 | 87.00 |
| . | . |
| . | . |
| . | . |
| 54 | 9.00 |
| 49 | 7.00 |
| 48 | 5.00 |
| 47 | 3.00 |
| 46 | 1.00 |

Computer programs usually assume that a large score is good. In situations where a small score is good (50-yard dash), subtract the percentile rank for each person from 100 to get the correct percentile rank.

## Standard Scores

**Standard scores** are used frequently to evaluate students at the end of a semester or to determine class ranks based on all the tests administered over a period of time. When each student has scores, for example, on sit-ups, a dash, and a standing long jump, how does the teacher determine which student's overall performance is best? A fitness specialist working in a health club or corporate fitness program could face the same problem. The three scores cannot be added together because the unit of measurement differs from test to test (executions, seconds, inches). We eliminate this problem by translating each test score into a standard score and summing the standard scores for each student or participant. The individual with the largest sum is the best overall.

## z-Scores

A **z-score** indicates how many standard deviations above or below the mean a test score lies. We calculate z-scores with the following formula:

$$z = \frac{X - \overline{X}}{s}.$$

A person who scores at the mean receives a z-score of 0; a person who scores $\frac{1}{2}$ standard deviation below the mean receives a z-score of –.5. Thus, the mean z-score is 0, and the standard deviation for a distribution of z-scores is 1.

## T-Scores

Because z-scores are usually fractional and can be negative, physical educators are more likely to use T-scores to combine different tests together. **T-scores** are usually rounded off to the nearest whole number and are rarely negative. The mean T-score is 50, and the standard deviation for a distribution of T-scores is 10. The formula for calculating T-scores is as follows:

$$T = \frac{10(X - \overline{X})}{s} + 50.$$

Note that the term $\frac{(X - \overline{X})}{s}$ in the T-score formula is the equation for determining the z-score. We could restate the T-score formula, then, as follows:

$$T = 10z + 50.$$

*Problem 3.10.* Given a mean of 87 and a standard deviation of 2.35, determine the T-score for a score of 90.

*Solution.* Where X is 90, $\overline{X}$ is 87, and s is 2.35, T is 63:

$$T = \frac{(10)(90 - 87)}{2.35} + 50 = \frac{(10)(3)}{2.35} + 50$$

$$= \frac{30}{2.35} + 50 = 12.76 + 50 = 62.76 = 63.$$

Notice that T-scores rise as performances rise above the mean. When smaller scores are better, T-scores must rise as performances fall below the mean. Thus, for speed events, we use the following formula to calculate T-scores:

$$T = \frac{10(\overline{X} - X)}{s} + 50.$$

The relationship among test scores, z-scores, and T-scores for a hypothetical test with mean 75 and standard deviation 8 is shown in Table 3.7. From the table we can see that a T-score of 50 is equivalent to a z-score of 0, or a test score equal to the test mean. Also a test score 2 standard deviations above the mean equals a T-score of 70.

T-scores are easy to interpret if we remember the mean T-score is 50 and the standard deviation for T-scores is 10. For example, a T-score of 65 is 1.5 standard deviations above the mean, a T-score of 40 is 1 standard deviation below the mean, and a T-score of 78 is 2.8 standard deviations above the mean.

**Table 3.7** Relationship among Test Scores (Mean 75, Standard Deviation 8), z-Scores, and T-Scores

| | Score Position | | | | | | |
| --- | --- | --- | --- | --- | --- | --- | --- |
| | $\overline{X} - 3s$ | $\overline{X} - 2s$ | $\overline{X} - s$ | $\overline{X}$ | $\overline{X} + s$ | $\overline{X} + 2s$ | $\overline{X} + 3s$ |
| Hypothetical test scores | 51 | 59 | 67 | 75 | 83 | 91 | 99 |
| z-scores | −3 | −2 | −1 | 0 | 1 | 2 | 3 |
| T-scores | 20 | 30 | 40 | 50 | 60 | 70 | 80 |

The T-scores for 20 students with 3 test scores are listed in Table 3.8. Student 6 is the best overall student because the sum of that student's scores (206) is the largest.

***Methods for Determining T-Scores.*** Obviously, translating test scores to T-scores takes time and effort. Few physical education teachers or exercise specialists, given 5 to 15 scores for each of a hundred or more individuals, have the time to calculate T-scores by hand. However, it would be unfortunate to bypass a good, easy technique for lack of time. There are two methods that allow us to obtain T-scores quickly: calculated conversion tables and computer analysis.

Calculated Conversion Tables. For most tests, each score will be obtained by several people. For example, we can see in Table 3.8 that ten students did no pull-ups, six students did 1 pull-up, and so on. Once the T-score for test score is determined, it is not necessary to recalculate the T-score every time that test score is repeated. Instead, we develop a test score–T-score conversion table. The method of development is either calculation by hand or by using the computer.

When the number of different scores is small, we can construct the test score–T-score conversion table by hand, calculating the T-score for each existing test score and expressing the T-score as a whole number. For example, from the pull-up scores in Table 3.8 we can develop this conversion table:

| X | | | 0 | 1 | 2 | 3 | 4 | 5 | 6 | 7 | 8 |
|---|---|---|---|---|---|---|---|---|---|---|---|---|
| T | | | 43 | 48 | 54 | 59 | 64 | 69 | 74 | 80 | 85 |

**Table 3.8** T-Scores Calculated by Formula and Rounded to Whole Numbers

| Student | Mile Run* | Pull-Up† | Sit-Up‡ | Mile Run T | Pull-Up T | Sit-Up T | Sum T |
|---|---|---|---|---|---|---|---|
| 1 | 407 | 0 | 43 | 64 | 43 | 52 | 159 |
| 2 | 511 | 4 | 45 | 51 | 64 | 54 | 169 |
| 3 | 478 | 2 | 50 | 55 | 54 | 60 | 169 |
| 4 | 525 | 1 | 51 | 49 | 48 | 61 | 158 |
| 5 | 480 | 4 | 53 | 55 | 64 | 64 | 183 |
| 6 | 440 | 8 | 51 | 60 | 85 | 61 | 206 |
| 7 | 519 | 1 | 39 | 50 | 48 | 47 | 145 |
| 8 | 488 | 2 | 43 | 54 | 54 | 52 | 160 |
| 9 | 510 | 0 | 30 | 51 | 43 | 37 | 131 |
| 10 | 456 | 3 | 47 | 58 | 59 | 57 | 174 |
| 11 | 603 | 1 | 38 | 40 | 48 | 46 | 134 |
| 12 | 495 | 0 | 40 | 53 | 43 | 48 | 144 |
| 13 | 435 | 1 | 45 | 60 | 48 | 54 | 162 |
| 14 | 588 | 1 | 29 | 42 | 48 | 36 | 126 |
| 15 | 630 | 0 | 29 | 37 | 43 | 36 | 116 |
| 16 | 638 | 0 | 42 | 36 | 43 | 51 | 130 |
| 17 | 511 | 0 | 40 | 51 | 43 | 48 | 142 |
| 18 | 721 | 0 | 28 | 26 | 43 | 35 | 104 |
| 19 | 482 | 0 | 52 | 55 | 43 | 62 | 160 |
| 20 | 630 | 0 | 30 | 37 | 43 | 37 | 117 |
| 21 | 360 | 1 | 54 | 69 | 48 | 65 | 182 |
| 22 | 540 | 0 | 30 | 48 | 43 | 37 | 128 |

*Mean 520.32; standard deviation 83.47.
†Mean 1.32; standard deviation 1.92.
‡Mean 41.32; standard deviation 8.59.

When the number of different test scores is large, the computer method should be utilized. From the computer output, conversion tables can be developed.

Computer Analysis. The fastest and easiest way to calculate T-scores is through computer analysis. In fact, with a large amount of data it may be the only feasible method. The "z-scores and T-scores" option in the *Statistics with Finesse* calculates z-scores and T-scores for one score per person. Since, in most cases each person will have scores on several different tests, this program is not very handy. So, a computer program (TSCORE) is discussed in this section of the chapter.

## Using the Computer

The TSCORE program is available for several types of microcomputers (Prusaczuk & Baumgartner 1986). (For instructors who have adopted this textbook, a copy of the TSCORE program is available from Wm. C. Brown Publishers at no charge.) It is entirely user-friendly, menu driven, full of prompts, able to output to screen or printer, able to handle missing data for a subject, and able to run on a desktop computer with one disk drive. When TSCORE starts up, a menu is displayed with several options:

1. create a new data file;
2. add a subject to a file;
3. edit an existing file;
4. print an existing file;
5. compute T-scores; and
6. compute percentile ranks.

The typical user will select Option 1, inputing the data to be analyzed and saving it on disk, followed by Option 5.

Table 3.9 lists the scores of 45 students on a fitness test. The scores were analyzed using the TSCORE program. The output of that program is shown in Table 3.10.

From Table 3.10 we can see each subject's (student) T-scores listed for each test and the sum of each subject's T-scores is listed as well. For example, the sum of Subject 1's T-scores is 261.47. Mean and standard deviation are provided for each test. The printout also shows that for the 44 subjects who were measured on all 5 tests (Subject 45 did not take all the tests), the mean and standard deviation for the sum of the T-scores were 249.72 and 33.78 respectively. Finally, at the bottom of Table 3.10 are percentile ranks for each test score, as well as a percentile rank for the sum of each subject's T-scores. For example, Subject 1 had a percentile rank of 48 on the sit-up test and an overall percentile rank of 60.

General database computer programs can also be used to calculate T-scores. These programs must be programmed to produce the desired results by using the T-score equation. The advantage of TSCORE is that it is designed to complete all the necessary calculations, whereas, a database program is more difficult to use. The advantage of a database program is that it can be used for many different functions other than just T-scores.

**Table 3.9** Scores of 45 Students on a Fitness Test

| Student | Skinfold | Mile Run | Sit-and-Reach | Pull-Up | Sit-Up |
|---------|----------|----------|---------------|---------|--------|
| 1 | 27.00 | 407.00 | 38.00 | 0.00 | 43.00 |
| 2 | 24.00 | 511.00 | 45.00 | 4.00 | 45.00 |
| 3 | 22.00 | 478.00 | 22.00 | 2.00 | 50.00 |
| 4 | 24.00 | 525.00 | 38.00 | 1.00 | 51.00 |
| 5 | 23.00 | 480.00 | 40.00 | 4.00 | 53.00 |
| 6 | 16.00 | 440.00 | 41.00 | 8.00 | 51.00 |
| 7 | 31.00 | 519.00 | 39.00 | 1.00 | 39.00 |
| 8 | 33.00 | 488.00 | 34.00 | 2.00 | 43.00 |
| 9 | 28.00 | 510.00 | 40.00 | 0.00 | 30.00 |
| 10 | 27.00 | 456.00 | 39.00 | 3.00 | 47.00 |
| 11 | 28.00 | 603.00 | 37.00 | 1.00 | 38.00 |
| 12 | 39.00 | 495.00 | 31.00 | 0.00 | 40.00 |
| 13 | 24.00 | 435.00 | 37.00 | 1.00 | 45.00 |
| 14 | 22.00 | 588.00 | 36.00 | 1.00 | 29.00 |
| 15 | 25.00 | 630.00 | 34.00 | 0.00 | 29.00 |
| 16 | 38.00 | 638.00 | 28.00 | 0.00 | 42.00 |
| 17 | 43.00 | 511.00 | 35.00 | 0.00 | 40.00 |
| 18 | 37.00 | 721.00 | 28.00 | 0.00 | 28.00 |
| 19 | 22.00 | 482.00 | 37.00 | 0.00 | 52.00 |
| 20 | 25.00 | 630.00 | 37.00 | 0.00 | 30.00 |
| 21 | 28.00 | 360.00 | 36.00 | 1.00 | 54.00 |
| 22 | 28.00 | 540.00 | 31.00 | 0.00 | 30.00 |
| 23 | 30.00 | 507.00 | 28.00 | 2.00 | 40.00 |
| 24 | 22.00 | 454.00 | 33.00 | 2.00 | 58.00 |
| 25 | 22.00 | 472.00 | 37.00 | 2.00 | 54.00 |
| 26 | 34.00 | 588.00 | 35.00 | 1.00 | 56.00 |
| 27 | 18.00 | 588.00 | 28.00 | 1.00 | 42.00 |
| 28 | 37.00 | 524.00 | 22.00 | 0.00 | 48.00 |
| 29 | 38.00 | 713.00 | 21.00 | 0.00 | 37.00 |
| 30 | 19.00 | 440.00 | 28.00 | 3.00 | 42.00 |
| 31 | 28.00 | 417.00 | 25.00 | 0.00 | 30.00 |
| 32 | 40.00 | 720.00 | 28.00 | 0.00 | 47.00 |
| 33 | 19.00 | 525.00 | 21.00 | 2.00 | 30.00 |
| 34 | 21.00 | 400.00 | 17.00 | 1.00 | 25.00 |
| 35 | 20.00 | 390.00 | 27.00 | 5.00 | 53.00 |
| 36 | 17.00 | 375.00 | 33.00 | 13.00 | 52.00 |
| 37 | 30.00 | 390.00 | 26.00 | 2.00 | 49.00 |
| 38 | 18.00 | 385.00 | 25.00 | 4.00 | 49.00 |
| 39 | 23.00 | 390.00 | 34.00 | 5.00 | 51.00 |
| 40 | 14.00 | 342.00 | 30.00 | 13.00 | 45.00 |
| 41 | 42.00 | 384.00 | 10.00 | 1.00 | 36.00 |
| 42 | 15.00 | 510.00 | 31.00 | 3.00 | 35.00 |
| 43 | 40.00 | 592.00 | 24.00 | 0.00 | 43.00 |
| 44 | 19.00 | 500.00 | 35.00 | 5.00 | 63.00 |
| 45 | 22.00 | | 32.00 | | 47.00 |

**Table 3.10** Sample Computer Printout of Data in Table 3.9

**T-Scores:**

| Subj # | SC 1 | SC 2 | SC 3 | SC 4 | SC 5 | Sum |
|--------|------|------|------|------|------|-----|
| 1 | 49.62 | 59.77 | 59.42 | 42.81 | 49.85 | 261.47 |
| 2 | 53.49 | 48.98 | 69.42 | 56.26 | 52.03 | 280.18 |
| 3 | 56.06 | 52.40 | 36.57 | 49.54 | 57.47 | 252.04 |
| 4 | 53.49 | 47.52 | 59.42 | 46.17 | 58.55 | 265.15 |
| 5 | 54.77 | 52.20 | 62.28 | 56.26 | 60.73 | 286.24 |
| 6 | 63.78 | 56.35 | 63.70 | 69.71 | 58.55 | 312.09 |
| 7 | 44.47 | 48.15 | 60.85 | 46.17 | 45.50 | 245.14 |
| 8 | 41.90 | 51.37 | 53.71 | 49.54 | 49.85 | 246.37 |
| 9 | 48.34 | 49.08 | 62.28 | 42.81 | 35.71 | 238.22 |
| 10 | 49.62 | 54.69 | 60.85 | 52.90 | 54.20 | 272.26 |
| 11 | 48.34 | 39.43 | 57.99 | 46.17 | 44.41 | 236.34 |
| 12 | 34.17 | 50.64 | 49.42 | 42.81 | 46.59 | 223.63 |
| 13 | 53.49 | 56.87 | 57.99 | 46.17 | 52.03 | 266.55 |
| 14 | 56.06 | 40.99 | 56.56 | 46.17 | 34.62 | 234.40 |
| 15 | 52.20 | 36.63 | 53.71 | 42.81 | 34.62 | 219.97 |
| 16 | 35.46 | 35.79 | 45.14 | 42.81 | 48.76 | 207.96 |
| 17 | 29.03 | 48.98 | 55.14 | 42.81 | 46.59 | 222.55 |
| 18 | 36.75 | 27.18 | 45.14 | 42.81 | 33.53 | 185.41 |
| 19 | 56.06 | 51.99 | 57.99 | 42.81 | 59.64 | 268.49 |
| 20 | 52.20 | 36.63 | 57.99 | 42.81 | 35.71 | 225.34 |
| 21 | 48.34 | 64.65 | 56.56 | 46.17 | 61.82 | 277.54 |
| 22 | 48.34 | 45.97 | 49.42 | 42.81 | 35.71 | 222.25 |
| 23 | 45.76 | 49.39 | 45.14 | 49.54 | 46.59 | 236.42 |
| 24 | 56.06 | 54.90 | 52.28 | 49.54 | 66.17 | 278.95 |
| 25 | 56.06 | 53.03 | 57.99 | 49.54 | 61.82 | 278.44 |
| 26 | 40.61 | 40.99 | 55.14 | 46.17 | 63.99 | 246.90 |
| 27 | 61.21 | 40.99 | 45.14 | 46.17 | 48.76 | 242.27 |
| 28 | 36.75 | 47.63 | 36.57 | 42.81 | 55.29 | 219.05 |
| 29 | 35.46 | 28.01 | 35.14 | 42.81 | 43.32 | 184.74 |
| 30 | 59.92 | 56.35 | 45.14 | 52.90 | 48.76 | 263.07 |
| 31 | 48.34 | 58.74 | 40.86 | 42.81 | 35.71 | 226.46 |
| 32 | 32.89 | 27.28 | 45.14 | 42.81 | 54.20 | 202.32 |
| 33 | 59.92 | 47.52 | 35.14 | 49.54 | 35.71 | 227.83 |
| 34 | 57.35 | 60.50 | 29.43 | 46.17 | 30.27 | 223.72 |
| 35 | 58.63 | 61.54 | 43.71 | 59.62 | 60.73 | 284.23 |
| 36 | 62.50 | 63.10 | 52.28 | 86.52 | 59.64 | 324.04 |
| 37 | 45.76 | 61.54 | 42.28 | 49.54 | 56.38 | 255.50 |
| 38 | 61.21 | 62.06 | 40.86 | 56.26 | 56.38 | 276.77 |
| 39 | 54.77 | 61.54 | 53.71 | 59.62 | 58.55 | 288.19 |
| 40 | 66.36 | 66.52 | 48.00 | 86.52 | 52.03 | 319.43 |
| 41 | 30.31 | 62.16 | 19.44 | 46.17 | 42.23 | 200.31 |
| 42 | 65.07 | 49.08 | 49.42 | 52.90 | 41.15 | 257.62 |
| 43 | 32.89 | 40.57 | 39.43 | 42.81 | 49.85 | 205.55 |
| 44 | 59.92 | 50.12 | 55.14 | 59.62 | 71.61 | 296.41 |
| 45 | 56.06 | –*– | 50.85 | –*– | 54.20 | –*– |

–*– INDICATES MISSING DATA

# Table 3.10—*Continued*

## Raw Score Summary:

| Score | Mean | Std Dev | Missing |
|---|---|---|---|
| Skin | 26.71 | 7.77 | 0 |
| Mile | 501.20 | 96.33 | 1 |
| Reach | 31.40 | 7.00 | 0 |
| Pullup | 2.14 | 2.97 | 1 |
| Situp | 43.13 | 9.19 | 0 |

## Sum of Weighted T-Scores:

| | |
|---|---|
| Mean: | 249.72 |
| Std Dev: | 33.78 |
| Missing: | 1.00 |

## Score Table:

| | |
|---|---|
| 1 | Skin |
| 2 | Mile |
| 3 | Reach |
| 4 | Pullup |
| 5 | Situp |

## Percentile Ranks:

| Subj # | SC 1 | SC 2 | SC 3 | SC 4 | SC 5 | Sum |
|---|---|---|---|---|---|---|
| 1 | 44 | 78 | 84 | 17 | 48 | 60 |
| 2 | 54 | 39 | 99 | 83 | 54 | 83 |
| 3 | 69 | 60 | 11 | 65 | 72 | 53 |
| 4 | 54 | 30 | 84 | 45 | 77 | 65 |
| 5 | 60 | 58 | 93 | 83 | 87 | 88 |
| 6 | 94 | 70 | 97 | 94 | 77 | 94 |
| 7 | 26 | 35 | 89 | 45 | 30 | 47 |
| 8 | 23 | 53 | 57 | 65 | 48 | 49 |
| 9 | 37 | 43 | 93 | 17 | 14 | 42 |
| 10 | 44 | 65 | 89 | 76 | 61 | 72 |
| 11 | 37 | 15 | 77 | 45 | 28 | 38 |
| 12 | 10 | 51 | 43 | 17 | 34 | 24 |
| 13 | 54 | 74 | 77 | 45 | 54 | 67 |
| 14 | 69 | 22 | 69 | 45 | 7 | 35 |
| 15 | 49 | 11 | 57 | 17 | 7 | 17 |
| 16 | 13 | 8 | 31 | 17 | 41 | 13 |
| 17 | 1 | 39 | 63 | 17 | 34 | 22 |
| 18 | 18 | 1 | 31 | 17 | 3 | 3 |
| 19 | 69 | 56 | 77 | 17 | 82 | 69 |
| 20 | 49 | 11 | 77 | 17 | 14 | 28 |
| 21 | 37 | 97 | 69 | 45 | 91 | 76 |
| 22 | 37 | 26 | 43 | 17 | 14 | 19 |
| 23 | 29 | 47 | 31 | 65 | 34 | 40 |
| 24 | 69 | 67 | 51 | 65 | 97 | 81 |
| 25 | 69 | 63 | 77 | 65 | 91 | 78 |
| 26 | 21 | 22 | 63 | 45 | 94 | 51 |

## Table 3.10—*Continued*

| Subj # | SC 1 | SC 2 | SC 3 | SC 4 | SC 5 | Sum |
|--------|------|------|------|------|------|-----|
| 27 | 89 | 22 | 31 | 45 | 41 | 44 |
| 28 | 18 | 33 | 11 | 17 | 66 | 15 |
| 29 | 13 | 6 | 7 | 17 | 26 | 1 |
| 30 | 83 | 70 | 31 | 76 | 41 | 63 |
| 31 | 37 | 76 | 18 | 17 | 14 | 31 |
| 32 | 7 | 3 | 31 | 17 | 61 | 8 |
| 33 | 83 | 30 | 7 | 65 | 14 | 33 |
| 34 | 77 | 81 | 3 | 45 | 1 | 26 |
| 35 | 79 | 85 | 23 | 90 | 87 | 85 |
| 36 | 92 | 94 | 51 | 98 | 82 | 99 |
| 37 | 29 | 85 | 21 | 65 | 69 | 56 |
| 38 | 89 | 90 | 18 | 83 | 69 | 74 |
| 39 | 60 | 85 | 57 | 90 | 77 | 90 |
| 40 | 99 | 99 | 39 | 98 | 54 | 97 |
| 41 | 3 | 92 | 1 | 45 | 23 | 6 |
| 42 | 97 | 43 | 43 | 76 | 21 | 58 |
| 43 | 7 | 17 | 14 | 17 | 48 | 10 |
| 44 | 83 | 49 | 63 | 90 | 99 | 92 |
| 45 | 69 | –*– | 48 | –*– | 61 | –*– |

–*– INDICATES MISSING DATA

### Score Table:

1   Skin
2   Mile
3   Reach
4   Pullup
5   Situp

**The Normal Curve**

Earlier in this chapter we discussed the normal curve as a model for the graph of a set of scores. Here we discuss the normal curve and its role in making probability statements.

**Characteristics**

The **normal curve** is a mathematically defined, smooth, bilaterally symmetrical curve, centered around a point that is simultaneously the mode, median, and mean (see Figure 3.7). Because the center point is both mode and median, it is the most frequent score and that score below which half the scores fall. The normal curve, by mathematical definition, has a mean of 0 and a standard deviation of 1. Thus, the normal curve is the graph of an infinite number of z-scores (see Figure 3.8).

**Probability**

When you flip a coin, the probability of it coming up heads is $\frac{1}{2}$: There are 2 possible outcomes, and heads represents only 1 of those outcomes—the event or outcome desired. The statement is written $P(H) = \frac{1}{2}$. In general, the probability of an event is the number of possible outcomes that satisfy the event, divided by the total number of possible outcomes.

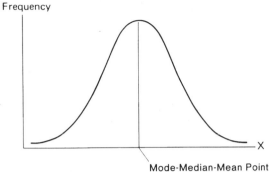

Mode-Median-Mean Point

**Figure 3.7** Normal curve for test scores.

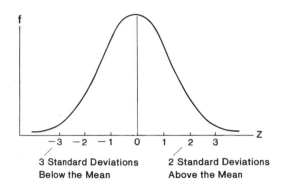

3 Standard Deviations Below the Mean

2 Standard Deviations Above the Mean

**Figure 3.8** Normal curve for Z-scores.

For example, when you flip two coins, what is the probability of their both coming up tails (TT)? You have 4 possible outcomes: both heads (HH), both tails (TT), the first coin heads and the second tails (HT), and vice versa (TH). The wanted outcome, event TT, is 1 of the 4 possible outcomes, so the probability of TT occurring is $\frac{1}{4}$:

$$P(TT) = \frac{1}{4}.$$

To use the normal curve (see Figure 3.8) to make probability statements, think of the area under the curve as 100 equal portions. If there are 100 possible outcomes under the normal curve, then 50 of these outcomes lie on each side of the mean. Because the curve is symmetrical, the number of outcomes between 0 and –1 equals the number of outcomes between 0 and 1.

*Problem 3.11.* What is the probability of a z equal to or greater than (≥) 0?

*Solution.* To begin, we must determine the percentage of the area under the curve that lies to the right of 0. From our definition we know that half of the possible outcomes lie to each side of 0 (the midpoint). Any of the 50 outcomes that lie to the right of 0 would satisfy z > 0. Thus, the probability of z ≥ 0 is $\frac{1}{2}$:

$$P(z \geq 0) = \frac{50}{100} = \frac{1}{2}.$$

This problem is simple because we have the answers to it by definition. To answer most probability statements about the normal curve, we have to use a special table, which appears here as Table 3.11. The table allows us to determine the percentage of a given area under the curve, and thus the basis for determining the probability of z falling within that area. The values along the left side and top of the table are z values, or standard deviation distances from the mean. The values in the body of the table indicate the percentage of the area under the curve between a given z-score and the mean z-score, 0.

**Table 3.11** Percentage of Total Area under the Normal Curve between the Mean and Ordinate Points at Any Given Standard Deviation Distance from the Mean

| z | .00 | .01 | .02 | .03 | .04 | .05 | .06 | .07 | .08 | .09 |
|---|-----|-----|-----|-----|-----|-----|-----|-----|-----|-----|
| 0.0 | 00.00 | 00.40 | 00.80 | 01.20 | 01.60 | 01.99 | 02.39 | 02.79 | 03.19 | 03.59 |
| 0.1 | 03.98 | 04.38 | 04.78 | 05.17 | 05.57 | 05.96 | 06.36 | 06.75 | 07.14 | 07.53 |
| 0.2 | 07.93 | 08.32 | 08.71 | 09.10 | 09.48 | 09.87 | 10.26 | 10.64 | 11.03 | 11.41 |
| 0.3 | 11.79 | 12.17 | 12.55 | 12.95 | 13.31 | 13.68 | 14.06 | 14.43 | 14.80 | 15.17 |
| 0.4 | 15.54 | 15.91 | 16.28 | 16.64 | 17.00 | 17.36 | 17.72 | 18.08 | 18.44 | 18.79 |
| 0.5 | 19.15 | 19.50 | 19.85 | 20.19 | 20.54 | 20.88 | 21.23 | 21.57 | 21.90 | 22.24 |
| 0.6 | 22.57 | 22.91 | 23.24 | 23.57 | 23.89 | 24.22 | 24.54 | 24.86 | 25.17 | 25.49 |
| 0.7 | 25.80 | 26.11 | 26.42 | 26.73 | 27.04 | 27.34 | 27.64 | 27.94 | 28.23 | 28.52 |
| 0.8 | 28.81 | 29.10 | 29.39 | 29.67 | 29.95 | 30.23 | 30.51 | 30.78 | 31.06 | 31.33 |
| 0.9 | 31.59 | 31.86 | 32.12 | 32.38 | 32.64 | 32.90 | 33.15 | 33.40 | 33.65 | 33.89 |
| 1.0 | 34.13 | 34.38 | 34.61 | 34.85 | 35.08 | 35.31 | 35.54 | 35.77 | 35.99 | 36.21 |
| 1.1 | 36.43 | 36.65 | 36.86 | 37.08 | 37.29 | 37.49 | 37.70 | 37.90 | 38.10 | 38.30 |
| 1.2 | 38.49 | 38.69 | 38.88 | 39.07 | 39.25 | 39.44 | 39.62 | 39.80 | 39.97 | 40.15 |
| 1.3 | 40.32 | 40.49 | 40.66 | 40.82 | 40.99 | 41.15 | 41.31 | 41.47 | 41.62 | 41.77 |
| 1.4 | 41.92 | 42.07 | 42.22 | 42.36 | 42.51 | 42.65 | 42.79 | 42.92 | 43.06 | 43.19 |
| 1.5 | 43.32 | 43.45 | 43.57 | 43.70 | 43.83 | 43.94 | 44.06 | 44.18 | 44.29 | 44.41 |
| 1.6 | 44.52 | 44.63 | 44.74 | 44.84 | 44.95 | 45.05 | 45.15 | 45.25 | 45.35 | 45.45 |
| 1.7 | 45.54 | 45.64 | 45.73 | 45.82 | 45.91 | 45.99 | 46.08 | 46.16 | 46.25 | 46.33 |
| 1.8 | 46.41 | 46.49 | 46.56 | 46.64 | 46.71 | 46.78 | 46.86 | 46.93 | 46.99 | 47.06 |
| 1.9 | 47.13 | 47.19 | 47.26 | 47.32 | 47.38 | 47.44 | 47.50 | 47.56 | 47.61 | 47.67 |
| 2.0 | 47.72 | 47.78 | 47.83 | 47.88 | 47.93 | 47.98 | 48.03 | 48.08 | 48.12 | 48.17 |
| 2.1 | 48.21 | 48.26 | 48.30 | 48.34 | 48.38 | 48.42 | 48.46 | 48.50 | 48.54 | 48.57 |
| 2.2 | 48.61 | 48.64 | 48.68 | 48.71 | 48.75 | 48.78 | 48.81 | 48.84 | 48.87 | 48.90 |
| 2.3 | 48.93 | 48.96 | 48.98 | 49.01 | 49.04 | 49.06 | 49.09 | 49.11 | 49.13 | 49.16 |
| 2.4 | 49.18 | 49.20 | 49.22 | 49.25 | 49.27 | 49.29 | 49.31 | 49.32 | 49.34 | 49.36 |
| 2.5 | 49.38 | 49.40 | 49.41 | 49.43 | 49.45 | 49.46 | 49.48 | 49.49 | 49.51 | 49.52 |
| 2.6 | 49.53 | 49.55 | 49.56 | 49.57 | 49.59 | 49.60 | 49.61 | 49.62 | 49.63 | 49.64 |
| 2.7 | 49.65 | 49.66 | 49.67 | 49.68 | 49.69 | 49.70 | 49.71 | 49.72 | 49.73 | 49.74 |
| 2.8 | 49.74 | 49.75 | 49.76 | 49.77 | 49.77 | 49.78 | 49.79 | 49.79 | 49.80 | 49.81 |
| 2.9 | 49.81 | 49.82 | 49.82 | 49.83 | 49.84 | 49.84 | 49.85 | 49.85 | 49.86 | 49.86 |
| 3.0 | 49.87 | | | | | | | | | |
| 3.5 | 49.98 | | | | | | | | | |
| 4.0 | 49.997 | | | | | | | | | |
| 5.0 | 49.99997 | | | | | | | | | |

From Lindquist, E. F., *A First Course in Statistics* (Boston: Houghton Mifflin, 1942), p. 242. By permission.

*Problem 3.12.* What percentage of the area under the normal curve lies between $0(z = 0)$ and $1.36(z = 1.36)$?

*Solution.* Because

$$1.36 = 1.30 + .06$$

we read down the left side of the table to 1.3 and across the row to column .06. The value listed there, 41.31, is that percentage of the area under the normal curve that lies between 0 and 1.36 (see Figure 3.9).

Part 2 Quantitative Aspects of Measurement

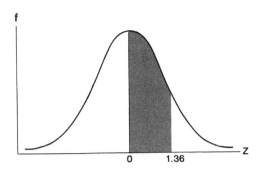

**Figure 3.9**  Normal curve graph for Problem 3.12.

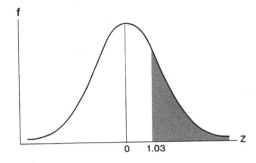

**Figure 3.10**  Normal curve graph for Problem 3.13.

Once we know the possible outcomes that satisfy an event, we can determine the probability of that event happening. The probability that z falls between 0 and 1.36 on the normal curve is the satisfactory outcomes (41.31) divided by the possible outcomes (100), or .41:

$$P(z \text{ between } 0 \text{ and } 1.36) = \frac{41.31}{100} = .4131 = .41.$$

Because the normal curve is symmetrical, the values in Table 3.11 hold true for equivalent distances from the mean to the left of it. That is, the percentage of the area under the normal curve between 0 and −1.36 is still 41.31, and the probability that z falls somewhere between 0 and −1.36 is still .41.

Although the table lists percentages only from the mean, we can extrapolate from it, remembering that 50% of all possible outcomes lie to each side of the mean.

*Problem 3.13.* What is the probability that z is equal to or greater than 1.03?

*Solution.* First we determine the overall area between 0 and 1.03. Reading down the left side of Table 3.11 to 1.0 and across to column .03, we see that 34.85% of the total area to the right of the mean lies between 0 and 1.03 (see Figure 3.10). Because we know that the possible outcomes to the right (or left for that matter) of 0 represent $\frac{50}{100}$, we can subtract the amount we know, $\frac{34.85}{100}$, from $\frac{50}{100}$. The result is our answer. The probability that z is equal to or greater than 1.03 is .15.

$$P(z \geq 1.03) \quad = \frac{50}{100} - \frac{34.85}{100}$$

$$= .50 - .3485 = .1515 = .15.$$

Often the probability statement requires a translation from test score X to the equivalent z, or vice versa, as we can see in the following problems.

*Problem 3.14.* A teacher always administers 100-point tests and always gives As to scores of 93 and above. On the last test the mean was 72 and the standard deviation was 9. Assuming test scores are normally distributed, what was the probability of receiving an A on that test?

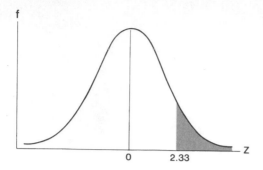

**Figure 3.11** Normal curve graph for Problem 3.14.

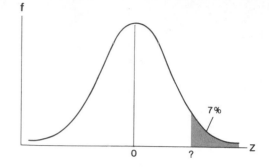

**Figure 3.12** Normal curve graph for Problem 3.15.

*Solution.* This is the same as asking what percentage of the class probably received As: What is the probability that a score X was greater than or equal to 93? Before we can solve the probability statement, then, we must change score 93 to a z-score. Where X is greater than or equal to 93, $\overline{X}$ is 72, and s is 9, the z-score must be greater than or equal to 2.33:

$$z \geq \frac{93 - 72}{9} \geq \frac{21}{9} \geq 2.33.$$

Now, using Figure 3.11 and Table 3.11, it is easy to determine the probability. At the intersection of z row 2.3 and column .03, we see that the percentage under the normal curve between 0 and 2.33 is 49.01. By subtracting that amount from the percentage of possible outcomes above 0, we see that the probability that z is greater than or equal to 2.33 is .01.

$$P(z \geq 2.33) = \frac{50}{100} - \frac{49.01}{100} = \frac{.99}{100} = .0099 = .01.$$

*Problem 3.15.* To develop some performance standards, a teacher decides to use the normal curve to determine that score above which 7% of the scores should fall. That is, what is the z-score above which 7% of the area under the normal curve falls (see Figure 3.12)?

$$P(z \geq ?) = \frac{7}{100}$$

*Solution.* We know that 43% of the area under the curve lies between 0 and the unknown z-score. If we scan Table 3.11, we see that percentage 43.06 is closest to 43%. Because 43.06 is at the intersection of z row 1.4 and column .08, the unknown z-score (the z-score above which 7% of the area falls) is 1.48. Thus, the teacher would use the following formula to calculate X:

$$X = \overline{X} + z(s)$$

$$X = \overline{X} + 1.48(s)$$

and if $\overline{X} = 31.25$, s = 5.0 then

$$X = 31.25 + 1.48(5.0) = 31.25 + 7.4 = 38.65$$

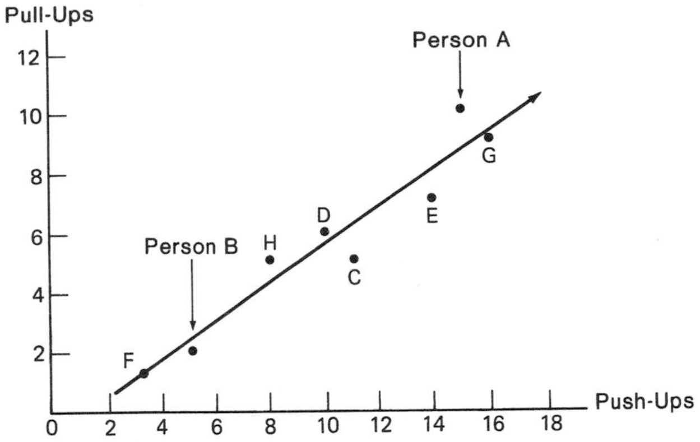

Figure 3.13
Graph of a positive
relationship.

| Person | Push-Ups | Pull-Ups |
|--------|----------|----------|
| A | 15 | 10 |
| B | 5 | 2 |
| C | 11 | 5 |
| D | 10 | 6 |
| E | 14 | 7 |
| F | 3 | 1 |
| G | 16 | 9 |
| H | 8 | 5 |

## Determining Relationships between Scores

There are many situations in which the physical education teacher and exercise specialist would like to know the relationship between scores on two different tests. For example, if speed and the performance of a sport skill were found to be related, the physical education teacher might try to improve the speed of poor performers. Or, if weight and high-jump ability were found to be related, the instructor might want to use a different evaluation standard for each weight classification. Knowing the relationship between scores can also lead to greater efficiency in a measurement program. For example, if there are seven tests in a physical fitness battery and two of them are highly related, the battery could be reduced to six tests with no loss of information. We use two different techniques to determine score relationships: a graphing technique and a mathematical technique called correlation.

## The Graphing Technique

The graphing technique is quicker than the mathematical technique but not as precise. It requires that each individual have a score on each of the two measures. To graph a relationship, we develop a coordinate system according to those values of one measure listed along the horizontal axis and those of the other measure listed along the vertical axis. We plot a point for each individual above his score on the horizontal axis and opposite his score on the vertical axis, as shown in Figure 3.13. The graph obtained is called a "scattergram."

The point plotted for Person A is at the intersection of push-up score 15 and pull-up score 10, the scores the person received on the two tests. The straight line—the **line of best fit** *or the* **regression line**—represents the trend in the data, in this case that individuals with large push-up scores have large pull-up scores, and vice versa. When large scores on one measure are associated with large scores on the other measure, the relationship is *positive*. When large scores on one measure are associated with small scores on the other measure, as shown in Figure 3.14, the relationship, is *negative*.

Chapter 3 Statistical Tools in Evaluation

Figure 3.14
Graph of a negative
relationship.

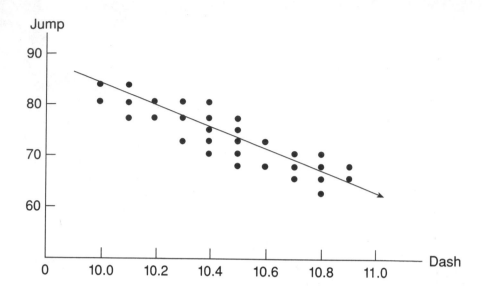

Figure 3.15
Graph of no relationship.

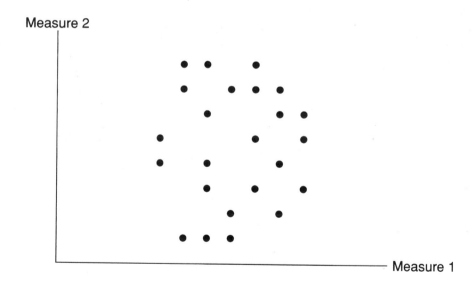

The closer all the plotted points are to the trend line, the higher or larger the relationship. The maximum relationship occurs when all plotted points are on the trend line. When the plotted points resemble a circle, making it impossible to draw a trend line, there is no linear relationship between the two measures being graphed. We can see this in the graph for Figure 3.15.

**Table 3.12** Scores for Correlation Calculation

| Individual | Pull-Up (X) | Push-Up (Y) | XY | X$^2$ | Y$^2$ |
|---|---|---|---|---|---|
| A | 10 | 15 | 150 | 100 | 225 |
| B | 2 | 5 | 10 | 4 | 25 |
| C | 5 | 11 | 55 | 25 | 121 |
| D | 6 | 10 | 60 | 36 | 100 |
| E | 7 | 14 | 98 | 49 | 196 |
| F | 1 | 3 | 3 | 1 | 9 |
| G | 9 | 16 | 144 | 81 | 256 |
| H | 5 | 8 | 40 | 25 | 64 |
| n = 8 | ΣX = 45 | ΣY = 82 | ΣXY = 560 | ΣX$^2$ = 321 | ΣY$^2$ = 996 |

Microcomputer programs have scattergram graphic programs that facilitate plotting data. Examples of computer-generated graphs are presented later in the regression analysis section of this chapter.

**The Correlation Technique**

**Correlation** is a mathematical technique for determining the relationship between two sets of scores. The formula was developed by Karl Pearson to determine the degree of relationship between two sets of measures (called X measures and Y measures):

$$r = \frac{n\Sigma XY - (\Sigma X)(\Sigma Y)}{\sqrt{[n\Sigma X^2 - (\Sigma X)^2][n\Sigma Y^2 - (\Sigma Y)^2]}}$$

where r is the Pearson product-moment correlation coefficient, n is the number of individuals, $\Sigma XY$ is the sum of each individual's X times Y value, $\Sigma X$ is the sum of the scores for one set of measures, $\Sigma Y$ is the sum of the scores for the other set of measures, $\Sigma X^2$ is the sum of the squared X scores, and $\Sigma Y^2$ is the sum of the squared Y scores.

*Problem 3.16.* Using the scores in Table 3.12, determine the correlation between the pull-up scores (X) and the push-up scores (Y).

*Solution.* Where n is 8 (the number of individuals), $\Sigma XY$ is 560 (the sum of column XY), $\Sigma X$ is 45 (the sum of column X), $\Sigma Y$ is 82 (the sum of column Y), $\Sigma X^2$ is 321 (the sum of column X$^2$), and $\Sigma Y^2$ is 996 (the sum of column Y$^2$), the correlation coefficient r is 0.96:

$$r = \frac{(8)(560) - (45)(82)}{\sqrt{[(8)(321) - 45^2][(8)(996) - 82^2]}}$$

$$= \frac{4480 - 3690}{\sqrt{(2568 - 2025)(7968 - 6724)}} = \frac{790}{\sqrt{(543)(1244)}}$$

$$= \frac{790}{\sqrt{675492}} = \frac{790}{821.88} = .96.$$

## Table 3.13 Examples of Perfect Relationships

| Individual | Height | Weight | Individual | 100-Yard Dash | Pull-Up |
|---|---|---|---|---|---|
| A | 60 | 130 | A | 10.6 | 14 |
| B | 52 | 122 | B | 10.6 | 14 |
| C | 75 | 145 | C | 11.2 | 8 |
| D | 66 | 136 | D | 11.7 | 3 |
| E | 70 | 140 | E | 10.5 | 15 |
| | r = 1 | | | r = −1 | |
| Exact formula: weight = height + 70 | | | Exact formula: dash = 12 − .1 (pull-up) | | |

## Table 3.14 Example of an Imperfect Correlation

| Individual | Height (Inches) | Weight (Pounds) |
|---|---|---|
| A | 60 | 130 |
| B | 52 | 125 |
| C | 75 | 145 |
| D | 66 | 136 |
| E | 70 | 150 |
| | r = .91 | |

**Correlation coefficients** have two characteristics, direction and strength. Direction of the relationship is indicated by whether the correlation coefficient is positive or negative, as indicated under the graphing technique. Strength of the relationship is indicated by how close the r is to 1, the maximum value possible. A correlation of 1 (r = 1) shows a perfect positive relationship, indicating that an increase in scores on one measure is accompanied by an increase in scores on the second measure. A perfect negative relationship (r = −1) indicates that an increase in scores on one measure is accompanied by a decrease in scores on the second. (Notice that a correlation of −1 is just as strong as a correlation of 1.) Perfect relationships are rare, but any such relationship that does exist is exactly described by mathematical formula. An example of a perfect positive and a perfect negative relationship is shown in Table 3.13. When the correlation coefficient is 0 (r = 0), there is no linear relationship between the two sets of scores.

Because the relationship between two sets of scores is seldom perfect, the majority of correlation coefficients are factions (.93, − .85, and the like). The closer the correlation coefficient is to 1 or −1, the stronger the relationship. When the relationship is not perfect, the scores on one measure only tend to change with the scores on the other measure. Look, for example, at Table 3.14. The correlation between height and weight is not perfect: Individual C, whose height is 75 inches, is not heavier than Individual E, whose height is only 70 inches.

When the scores for the two sets of scores are ranks, a correlation coefficient called *rho* or *Spearman's rho* or the **rank order correlation coefficient** may be calculated. The formula is just a simplification of the Pearson correlation formula. Since the same value will be obtained by applying the Pearson correlation formula to the two sets of ranks (provided no tied ranks exist) the formula is not presented, but is commonly included in microcomputer statistical programs.

*Interpreting the Correlation Coefficient.* A high correlation between two measures does not usually indicate a cause- and effect-relationship. The perfect height and weight relationship in Table 3.13, for example, does not indicate that an increase in weight causes an increase in height. Also, the degree of relationship between two sets of measures does not increase at the same rate as does the correlation coefficient. The true indicator of the degree of relationship is the **coefficient of determination**— the amount of variability in one measure that is explained by the other measure. The coefficient of determination is the square of the correlation coefficient ($r^2$). For example, the square of the correlation coefficient in Table 3.14 is .83 ($.91^2$), which means that 83% of the variability in height scores is due to the individuals having different weight scores.

Thus when one correlation coefficient is twice as large as another, the larger coefficient really explains four times the amount of variation that the smaller coefficient explains. For example, when the r between agility and balance is .80 and the r between strength and power is .40, the $r^2$ for agility and balance is $.80^2$, or 64%, and the $r^2$ for strength and power is $.40^2$, or 16%.

Remember, when you interpret a correlation coefficient, there are no absolute standards for labeling a given r "good" or "poor"; only the relationship you want or expect determines the quality of a given r. For example, if you or others had obtained a correlation coefficient of .67 between leg strength and standing long jump scores for males, you might expect a similar correlation coefficient in comparing leg strength and long jump scores for females. If the relationship between the females' scores were only .45, you might label that correlation coefficient "poor" because you expected it to be as high as that of the males.

There are two reasons why correlation coefficients can be negative: (1) opposite scoring scales and (2) true negative relationships. When a measure on which a small score is a better score is correlated with a measure on which a larger score is a better score, the correlation coefficient probably will be negative. Consider, for example, the relationship between scores on a speed event like the 50-yard dash and a nonspeed event like the standing long jump. Usually the best jumpers are the best runners, but the correlation is negative because the scoring scales are reversed. Two measures can be negatively related as well. We would expect, for example, a negative correlation between body weight and measures involving support or motion of the body (pull-ups, dips).

*The Question of Accuracy.* In calculating r we assume that the relationship between the two sets of scores is basically linear. A **linear relationship** is shown graphically by a straight line, as is the trend line in Figure 3.13. However, a relationship between two sets of scores can be represented by a curved line, a **curvilinear relationship.** A curvilinear relationship between two measures is best described by a curved line. If a relationship is truly curvilinear, the correlation coefficient will underestimate the relationship. For example, r could equal 0 even when a definite curvilinear relationship exists. More concerning curvilinear relationships is presented later in the regression section of this chapter.

Although we need not assume when calculating r that the graph of each of the two sets of scores is a normal curve, we do assume that the two graphs resemble each other. If they are dissimilar, the correlation coefficient will underestimate the relationship between the scores. Considerable differences in the two graphs are occasionally found, usually when the number of people tested is small. For this reason, the correlation coefficient ideally should be calculated with the scores of several hundred people.

Other factors also affect the correlation coefficient. One is the reliability of the scores; low reliability reduces the correlation coefficient (see Chapter 4). Another factor is the range in the scores; the correlation coefficient will be smaller for a homogeneous group than for a heterogeneous group. Ferguson and Takane (1989) suggest that generally the range in scores increases as the size of the group tested increases. Certainly small groups exhibit a greater tendency than large groups to be either more homogeneous or more heterogeneous than is typical for the group measured and the test administered. This is another reason to calculate the correlation coefficient only when the group tested is large. Ferguson and Takane (1989) and Walker and Lev (1969) cover this subject in greater detail.

The calculation of the correlation coefficient in Problem 3.16 was easy because the number of scores was small and the values of the scores were small. Usually you will be working with between 25 and 500 scores that may be three or four digit numbers. In this case the use of a calculator to speed up the calculations is essential. Many calculators have a correlation key so only the X and Y scores have to be entered into the calculator and it does the rest.

When the group tested is large or when the physical education teacher and exercise specialist want the correlation between all possible pairings of more than two tests (pull-up and sit-up, pull-up and mile run, sit-up and mile run), using a computer is the most efficient way to obtain the correlation coefficients. Computer programs that calculate correlation coefficients are commonly found in packages of statistical programs for microcomputers. In the *Statistics with Finesse* package, the PEARSON CORRELATION option on the Descriptive Statistics disk and the CORRELATION MATRIX option on the Multivariate Techniques disk will calculate the correlation between two variables or among all variables at one time. For example, the correlation between pull-up and push-up scores in Table 3.12 or among all the variables in Table 3.9 could be calculated.

Presented in Table 3.15 is the correlations obtained from the PEARSON CORRELATION option in the *Statistics with Finesse* package for the data in Table 3.12. This printout format is not economical in terms of space if many variables are correlated. A more common printout format using the CORRELATION MATRIX option is presented in Table 3.16 for the data of subjects 23–44 in Table 3.9. In Table 3.16 the correlation between any two tests is found by finding the value listed in the cell formed by the row and column of the two tests. For example, the correlation between shuttle run and 50-yard dash is .69.

**Prediction-Regression Analysis**

The terms correlation, regression, and prediction are so closely related in statistics that they are often used interchangeably. Correlation refers to the relationship between two variables. When two variables are correlated, it becomes possible to make a prediction. Regression is the statistical model used to predict performance on one variable

**Table 3.15** Output from Pearson Correlation Program for the Data in Table 3.12

**Correlations For Variable Pull-Up**

| Variable | N | Correlation | Prob. |
|---|---|---|---|
| Pull-up | 8 | 1.00 | .0001 |
| Push-up | 8 | 0.96 | .0004 |

**Correlations For Variable Push-Up**

| Variable | N | Correlation | Prob. |
|---|---|---|---|
| Pull-up | 8 | 0.96 | .0004 |
| Push-up | 8 | 1.00 | .0001 |

**Table 3.16** Correlations Among All the Variables for Subjects in Table 3.9 using the Correlation Matrix Program

| Label | Skin | Mile | Reach | Pullup | Situp |
|---|---|---|---|---|---|
| Skin | 1.00 | 0.52 | −0.44 | −0.61 | −0.09 |
| Mile | 0.52 | 1.00 | 0.01 | −0.56 | −0.04 |
| Reach | −0.44 | 0.01 | 1.00 | 0.38 | 0.70 |
| Pullup | −0.61 | −0.56 | 0.38 | 1.00 | 0.31 |
| Situp | −0.09 | −0.04 | 0.70 | 0.31 | 1.00 |

from another. An example is the prediction of percent body fat from skinfold measurements. This is illustrated in Chapter 11.

Teachers, coaches, exercise specialists, and researchers have long been interested in predicting scores that are either difficult or impossible to obtain at a given moment. **Prediction** is estimating a person's score on one measure based on the person's score on one or more other measures. Although prediction is often imprecise, it is occasionally useful to develop a prediction formula.

Simple predictions predict an unknown score Y′ for an individual by using that person's performance X on a known measure. To develop a **simple prediction,** or regression formula, a large number (at least n = 50, with n > 100 even better) of subjects must be measured and a score on the **independent** or **predictor variable** X and the **dependent** or **criterion variable** Y obtained for each.

**Simple Prediction**

$$Y' = \left[ r\left(\frac{s_y}{s_x}\right) \right](X - \overline{X}) + \overline{Y}$$

where Y′ is the predicted Y score for an individual, r is the correlation between X and Y scores, $s_y$ is the standard deviation for the Y scores, $s_x$ is the standard deviation for the X scores, X is the individual's known score on measure X, $\overline{X}$ is the mean for the X scores, and $\overline{Y}$ is the mean for the Y scores. Once the formula is developed for any given relationship, only the predictor variable X is needed to predict the performance of an individual on measure Y. One index of the accuracy of a simple prediction equation is r.

*Problem 3.17.* A coach found the correlation coefficient between physical fitness and athletic ability to be .88. The mean of the physical fitness test is 12; its standard deviation is 5.15. The mean of the athletic ability test is 9; its standard deviation is 4.30. What is the predicted athletic ability score for an athlete with a physical fitness score of 14?

*Solution.* Where r is .88, $s_y$ is 4.30, $s_x$ is 5.15, X is 14, $\overline{X}$ is 12, and $\overline{Y}$ is 9, the athlete's predicted athletic ability score, Y', is 10.46:

$$Y' = \left[ (.88) \left( \frac{4.30}{5.15} \right) \right] (14 - 12) + 9$$

$$= (.73)\,(2) + 9 = 1.46 + 9 = 10.46.$$

Prediction being a correlational technique, there is a *line of best fit* or *regression line* that can be generated (see graphing technique pp. 89–90). In case of simple prediction, this is the regression line for the graph of the X variable on the horizontal axis and the Y variable on the vertical axis.

The general form of the simple prediction equation is

$$Y' = bX + c$$

where b is a constant and termed the slope of the regression line. The slope is the rate at which Y changes with change on X. The constant, c, is called the Y-intercept and is the point at which the line crosses the vertical axis. It is the value of Y that corresponds to an X of 0. Sometimes calculators and computer programs report the simple prediction equation in terms of slope and Y-intercept. If a calculator or computer is programmed to obtain the simple prediction equation, only the X and Y scores have to be entered.

### The Standard Error of Prediction.
An individual's predicted score, Y', will not equal the actual score, Y, unless the correlation coefficient used in the formula is perfect—a rare event. Thus, for each individual there is an error of prediction. We estimate the standard deviation of this error, the **standard error of prediction,** using the following formula:

$$\text{estimated } s_{y \cdot x} = s_y \sqrt{1 - r^2}$$

where $s_{y \cdot x}$ is the standard error of score Y predicted from score X, $s_y$ is the standard deviation for the Y scores calculated with formula 4 on page 71, and $r^2$ is the square of the correlation coefficient (the coefficient of determination) for the X and Y scores. (Notice that the larger the coefficient, the smaller the standard error.) This estimate of $s_{y \cdot x}$ is sufficiently accurate if the number of individuals tested (n) is large (at least n = 50, with n > 100 even better). The exact formula for $s_{y \cdot x}$ can be found in many statistics and advanced measurement books (Kachigan 1991; Safrit & Wood 1989, p. 190). Actually multiplying the estimated $s_{y \cdot x}$ by (n − 2) / (n − 1) yields the exact value. Computer programs that provide the standard error of prediction should provide the exact value. The standard error of prediction is another index of the accuracy of a simple prediction equation.

The standard error of prediction is not a good index of the error associated with a single prediction. When a Y′ is calculated from the X-score of a certain person, the error in it will be smaller when X is near $\overline{X}$ than when X is far from $\overline{X}$. Thus, the formula for the standard error of prediction for a Y′ based on a certain X-score is

$$s'_{y \cdot x} = s_{y \cdot x} \sqrt{1 + \frac{1}{n} + \frac{(X-\overline{X})^2}{(n-1)(s_x^2)}}$$

where $(X - \overline{X})$ is the difference between the certain X-score and the mean X-score. Using this formula, confidence limits (boundaries) for the Y-score of a person can be calculated. For example, the probability is .68 that the Y-score of a person falls between $Y' \pm s'_{y \cdot x}$.

*Problem 3.18.* What is the standard error of prediction and .68 confidence limits for the Y-score predicted in Problem 3.17?

*Solution.*

Where $n = 5$, $\overline{X} = 12$, $s_x = 5.15$, $\overline{Y} = 9$, $s_y = 4.30$, $r = .88$, Y′ for X of 14 = 10.46:

A. estimated $s_{y \cdot x} = s_y \sqrt{1 - r^2} = 4.30 \sqrt{1 - (.88)^2}$

$$= 4.30 \sqrt{.23} = (4.30)(.48) = 2.06$$

B. exact $s_{y \cdot x} = \left(\frac{n-2}{n-1}\right)(\text{estimated } s_{y \cdot x}) = \left(\frac{5-2}{5-1}\right)(2.06)$

$$= (.75)(2.06) = 1.55$$

C. $s'_{y \cdot x}$ for X of 14 $= s_{y \cdot x} \sqrt{1 + \frac{1}{n} + \frac{(X-\overline{X})^2}{(n-1)(s_x^2)}} = 1.55 \sqrt{1 + \frac{1}{5} + \frac{(14-12)^2}{(5-1)(5.15)^2}}$

$$= 1.55 \sqrt{1 + \frac{1}{5} + \frac{4}{(4)(26.52)}} = 1.55 \sqrt{1 + .2 + .04} = 1.55 \sqrt{1.24}$$

$$= (1.55)(1.11) = 1.72$$

D. .68 confidence limits for the Y-score of person with X-score of 14 is

$$Y' \pm s'_{y \cdot x} = 10.46 \pm 1.72$$

The probability is .68 that the Y-score of a person with an X-score of 14 falls between 8.74 (10.46 − 1.72) and 12.18 (10.46 + 1.72).

If the prediction formula and standard error seem acceptable, the physical education teacher or exercise specialist should try to prove the prediction formula on a second group of individuals similar to the first. This process is called **cross-validation.** If the formula works satisfactorily for the second group, it can be used with confidence to predict score Y for any individual who resembles the individuals used to form and cross-validate the equation. If the formula does not work well for the second group, it is unique to the group used to form the equation and has little value in predicting performance.

| Multiple Prediction | A prediction formula using a single measure X is usually not very accurate for predicting a person's score on measure Y. *Multiple correlation-regression* techniques allow us to predict score Y using several X scores. For example, a **multiple prediction** formula has been developed to predict arm strength in pounds (Y′) using both the number of pull-ups ($X_1$) and pounds of body weight ($X_2$): |
|---|---|

$$Y' = 3.42(X_1) + 1.77(X_2) - 46.$$

A multiple regression equation will have one intercept and several bs, one for each independent variable. The general form of two and three predictor multiple regression equations are

$$Y' = b_1X_1 + b_2X_2 + c$$

$$Y' = b_1X_1 + b_2X_2 + b_3X_3 + c.$$

The *multiple correlation coefficient R* is one index of the accuracy of a multiple prediction equation. The minimum and maximum values of R are 0 and 1 respectively. The percentage of variance in the Y scores explained by the multiple prediction equation is $R^2$. A second index of the accuracy of a multiple prediction equation is the standard error of prediction. Multiple prediction formulas and **multiple correlations** are presented in later chapters of this book (see Chapter 11, Body Composition). More comprehensive coverage of multiple regression can be found in Cohen and Cohen (1975), Ferguson and Takane (1989), Kerlinger and Pedhazur (1973), the SPSS manual (Nie et al. 1975), and Safrit and Wood (1989).

***Nonlinear Regression.*** The regression models discussed to this point assume a linear relationship. With some data, this is not the case. For example, when relating age and strength, the relation is linear for the ages of 10 through 17 because the person is growing and gaining muscle mass, but for ages 18 through 65 the relationship would be nonlinear. As one starts to reach middle age, aging is associated with a loss of lean body weight, which results in a loss of strength. As explained in the correlation section, if the relationship is not linear, the linear correlation will be lower than the true correlation. Microcomputer programs have what is termed a "polynomial regression" program to compute the curvilinear correlation. Polynomial regression analysis is beyond the scope of this text.

| Using the Computer | The simple prediction and multiple prediction equations are both time-consuming and complicated, especially when the number of people being tested is large. (It is suggested that prediction equations be developed using the scores of several hundred people.) Computer programs that do either simple or multiple prediction are commonly available for both the mainframe and microcomputer. |
|---|---|

In the *Statistics with Finesse* package, a simple prediction equation can be obtained by selecting LINEAR REGRESSION option from the main menu of the Descriptive Statistics disk. In this package both a simple and a multiple prediction equation can be obtained by selecting the MULTIPLE REGRESSION FROM RAW SCORES option on the Multivariate Techniques disk. In both options the variables to be used must be identified, and then the dependent variable (Y) and the predictor (independent) variables (Xs) must be identified.

**Table 3.17** Output from Multiple Regression Using the Data of Subjects 23–44 in Table 3.9

| Dependent Variable: | Mile | |
|---|---|---|
| R = 0.5162 | R-Square = 0.2664 | |
| Predictor | Coefficient | B-Weight |
| Skin | 6.0590 | 0.5162 |
| Constant | 326.2088 | |

| Dependent Variable: | Mile | |
|---|---|---|
| R = 0.6015 | R-Square = 0.3618 | |
| Predictor | Coefficient | B-Weight |
| Skin | 3.2684 | 0.2784 |
| Pull | –11.4077 | –0.3898 |
| Constant | 431.7084 | |

Using the MULTIPLE REGRESSION FROM RAW SCORES option and the data of subjects 23–44 in Table 3.9 with Y equal to the mile run, and X equal to the skinfold, a simple prediction equation was obtained (see Table 3.17). The prediction equation is Y′ = 6.0590(Skin) + 326.2088. The R (.5162) and the R-Square (.2664) values for the prediction equation suggest that it is not very accurate. In an effort to obtain a more accurate prediction equation, a multiple prediction equation with Y equal to the mile run, $X_1$ equal to the skinfold, and $X_2$ equal to the pull-up was obtained (see Table 3.17). The prediction equation is Y′ = 3.2684(Skin) – 11.4077(Pull) + 431.7084. The R (.6015) and R-Square (.3618) values for the prediction equation suggest that it is not very accurate and not much better than the simple prediction equation. In a multiple prediction equation, a high correlation between the Y-score and each X-score but a low correlation among the X-scores is desirable. Note in Table 3.16 all three variables used in the multiple prediction equation correlated about the same amount (.52 – .61) with each other.

## Reliability of the Mean

Throughout this chapter we have placed considerable emphasis on the usefulness of the mean in describing the performance of a group. The mean is not constant: It can vary from day to day among the same individuals in a retest or from year to year if a new but similar group of individuals is tested. The performance of a group of individuals changes from day to day, even if ability has not changed, simply because people have good days and bad days. And the mean performances of different groups of individuals are seldom identical, even when the subjects are apparently equal in ability. If we can expect little variation in the mean, it is a highly reliable indicator of group ability; if we can expect considerable variation, it is not very reliable. We call the estimated variability of the mean the **standard error of the mean.** It is found using the following formula:

$$s_{\overline{x}} = \frac{s}{\sqrt{n}}$$

where $s_{\bar{x}}$ is the standard error of the mean, s is the standard deviation for the scores (s = $\sqrt{(\Sigma X^2 - (\Sigma X)^2/n)/(n-1)}$ ), and n is the number of individuals in the group.

Statistics books show that when many groups—all members of the same larger group, or population—are tested, the graph of the means is normal, centered around the population mean. The standard error is the standard deviation of the group means. The standard error can be used with the normal curve in the same manner as can the standard deviation; that is, 68% of the group means will be within one standard error of the population mean.

*Problem 3.19.* The mean for an agility test performed by 81 senior citizens is 12.5; the standard deviation is .81. Determine the standard error of the mean.

*Solution.* Where s is .81 and n is 81, the standard error of mean 12.5 is .09:

$$s_{\bar{x}} = \frac{.81}{\sqrt{81}} = \frac{.81}{9} = .09.$$

If 12.5 is the population mean, 68% of the means for groups belonging to this population (senior citizens) will fall between 12.41 (12.5 − .09) and 12.59 (12.5 + .09). Thus any senior citizens' groups with agility test means between 12.41 and 12.59 are probably similar in ability. In fact, if the group with mean 12.5 is tested on another day, the probability is 68% that its mean performance will fall between 12.41 and 12.59.

## Additional Statistical Techniques

The statistical techniques presented to this point are those commonly used in measurement situations. There are times when the goal is to determine if various groups are different, that is, males vs. females, or various groups of athletes. Researchers commonly use **t-tests** (not to be confused with T-scores) and Analysis of Variance (ANOVA) to determine if there is a large enough difference between two or more groups in mean performance to conclude that the groups are not equal in average performance. A detailed discussion of t-tests and ANOVA is beyond the scope of this book, but a brief introduction into the logic is presented. If you wish a more detailed coverage of t-tests and ANOVA, an excellent nonmathematical discussion may be found in Baumgartner and Strong (1994) and Huck, Cormier, and Bounds (1974). A more complete coverage of t-tests and ANOVA can be found in any introductory level statistics book. The presentations by Roscoe (1975) and Ferguson and Takane (1989) are easy to follow. Microcomputer packages of statistical programs include t-test and ANOVA.

## Background to Statistical Tests

Often researchers are interested in the characteristics of a large group. For example, what is the mean percent body fat for the 40,000 males who work for a particular industry or which of three fitness training techniques is best for the 40,000 workers? To answer the first question, a researcher might measure all 40,000 males for percent body fat and then calculate the mean. This would be very time-consuming and expensive, and likely impossible. Instead of testing all of the large group of interest, called the *population,* the researcher tests some part of the population, called a *sample.* The mean for the sample is calculated, and then the researcher assumes the sample and population mean are equal. In other words, if the sample mean is 17, the researcher infers that the population mean is 17. In the earlier example of which fitness training technique is best, the researchers would obtain three samples and use a different fitness training technique on each sample. After the training technique had been used for a length of time (e.g., 6 weeks or longer) the researcher would test all the subjects and determine if the mean performance of the groups was equal. Whatever the outcome, the researcher would infer the sample finding to the population.

In order to make this inference, the sample should be representative of the population and randomly selected. For a sample to be representative it must be taken from an identified population and it must be sufficiently large (i.e., 30 or more) so that all different abilities in the population are represented. Random selection of subjects guarantees that all members of the population have an equal chance of being selected. In a research setting, this is done with a special table called a table of random numbers, but in a practical setting it might be accomplished by placing each person's name on a piece of paper, putting all the pieces of paper in a container, drawing out 50 pieces of paper, and designating the people drawn as the sample.

A researcher starts out with a statement concerning what he or she thinks may be the case at the population level. This statement is called the *null hypothesis*. For example, eighteen percent is the mean percent body fat for adult males, or the three fitness training techniques are equally effective so the means of the three groups are equal. Usually the mean or means obtained from the sample(s) will not equal the values in the null hypothesis. Then the question is whether the difference between what was hypothesized at the population level and found at the sample level is large enough to suggest that the null hypothesis is false or whether the difference is due to sampling error. *Sampling error* is due to the sample not being 100% representative of the population. For example, if the mean percent body fat was hypothesized to be 18 but was 17 in the sample, is the hypothesis false or is this difference due to sampling error? If all three samples do not have the same mean after receiving their respective training technique, does this indicate that the hypothesis is false? To be able to make an objective decision, a statistical test is conducted. This statistical test is much like the probability statements earlier in this chapter. Based on the statistical test, the probability of the sample finding occurring if the null hypothesis is true can be determined. If the probability is quite small, the null hypothesis is rejected and the difference is considered to be real. Otherwise it is accepted and the difference is considered to be due to sampling error. Thus, a researcher must select some probability level that warrants rejection of the null hypothesis. This probability level is called the *alpha level,* and it is usually specified as .05 or .01. What most researchers do is look in the appropriate statistical table to find the value of the statistical test needed to reject the null hypothesis at the alpha level selected. Many microcomputer programs provide a probability level (p) for the value of the statistical test. In this case the researcher rejects the null hypothesis if the p-value is less than or equal to the alpha level. All of this will become clearer with the examples provided, each with a different research design and statistical test.

## t-Test for One Group

### Step 1
The researcher's null hypothesis was that the mean percent body fat for the population was 18, so the hypothesized population mean (u) is 18 ($H_0$:u = 18). As alternatives to this hypothesis, the researcher thought it possible that the mean could be less than 18 ($H_1$:u < 18) or greater than 18 ($H_2$:u > 18).

**Step 2**

An alpha level of .05 was selected.

**Step 3**

Knowing that a t-test would be the statistical test and the sample size would be 41, the researcher went to the t-tables and found that to reject the null hypothesis at alpha level .05 the value of the t-test would have to be at least ±2.021. This step is not needed if a microcomputer program is used because p-values are calculated.

**Step 4**

The researcher randomly selected 41 men from the population as the sample, measured their percent body fat, calculated the mean and standard deviation for the body fat measurements, and calculated the t-test.

$$\overline{X} = 16.50 \quad s^1 = 2.50 \qquad n = 41$$

$$t = \frac{\overline{X} - u}{s/\sqrt{n}} = \frac{16.50 - 18}{2.50/\sqrt{41}} = \frac{-1.50}{2.50/6.40}$$

$$= \frac{-1.50}{.39} = -3.85.$$

**Step 5**

Since the calculated value of t (−3.85) at Step 4 is less than the tabled value of t (−2.021) at Step 3, the research concludes that the difference between the null hypothesis valued (18) at Step 1 and the sample value (16.50) at Step 4 is real and not due to sample error. Thus, the researcher rejects the null hypothesis and accepts the most likely alternate hypothesis, which in this case is $H_1$, the population mean is less than 18, since the sample mean was less than 18.

Now a few points of information about what was presented in the five-step example. At Step 3 when the researcher went to the t-tables (the tables in Ferguson & Takane were used) to identify the t-value needed for rejecting the null hypothesis, he had to line up a value called *degrees of freedom* and the alpha level to find the t-value. The degrees of freedom for this t-test is (n − 1) where n is the sample size. Since there were two alternate hypotheses, the researcher used the alpha level under a *two-tailed test*. For a two-tailed test this value is always interpreted as both plus and minus. If there had been only one alternate hypothesis, the alpha level under *one-tailed test* would have been used and the value read from the table would have been interpreted as either plus or minus, depending on whether the alternate hypothesis was greater than (table value plus) or less than (table value minus). The tabled value is sometimes called the *critical value* or *critical region*. At Step 5 if the value of the statistical test at Step 4 is equal to or greater than the tabled value at Step 3, the difference and the statistical test are called *significant* (the difference is considered to be real), and the null hypothesis is rejected. If the value of the statistical test at Step 4 is not equal to or greater than the table value at Step 3, the difference and statistical test are called *nonsignificant* (the difference is considered to be due to sampling error), and the null hypothesis is accepted.

---

[1] Note: In this case $s = \sqrt{\dfrac{\Sigma X^2 - \dfrac{(\Sigma X)^2}{n}}{n - 1}}$

**Table 3.18** Scores for Three Groups on a Sit-and-Reach Test

| Group A | Group B | Group C |
|---------|---------|---------|
| 12 | 7 | 13 |
| 15 | 10 | 14 |
| 10 | 11 | 10 |
| 11 | 8 | 9 |
| 9 | 9 | 12 |
| 14 | 10 | 11 |
| 12 | 12 | 11 |
| 13 | 9 | 15 |

**Table 3.19** Output of the One-Sample t-Test of Group A in Table 3.18

| | |
|---|---|
| Sample Size | 8 |
| Sample Mean | 12.00 |
| Population Mean | 10.00 |
| Difference | 2.00 |
| Standard Deviation | 2.00 |
| t-value | 2.83 |
| Significance One-Tailed | 0.0127 |

This t-test is useful in any measurement situation where the mean performance of a group is being compared to an expected mean or a standard or norm expressed as a mean. Does the mean of the group really differ from the expected mean?

Now, this t-test we just studied is one of three t-tests available, and the other two t-tests are not as easy to calculate by hand. Fortunately most computer packages of statistical programs contain all three t-tests. In *Statistics with Finesse* the t-test for one group is called ONE-SAMPLE t-TEST. It can be selected from the main menu of the t-test and ANOVA disk. The computer will ask for the null hypothesis value.

Presented in Table 3.18 are the scores of three groups on a sit-and-reach test. The scores of Group A were analyzed using the One-Sample t-test program to test the null hypothesis that the population mean equals $10(H_0:u = 10)$. The output of this program is presented in Table 3.19. Notice in Table 3.19 that the computer provides a one-tailed significance value (.0127 in our example) so that looking up a table value is not necessary.

Doubling the one-tailed significance value provided by the computer yields the two-tailed significance value (.0254) if it is needed. In either case, if the significance value is less than or equal to the alpha level selected, the value of the statistical test is significant and the null hypothesis ($H_0$) is rejected. Otherwise the null hypothesis is accepted.

### t-Test for Two Independent Groups

In this situation either two samples are drawn from the same population and each sample is administered a different treatment or a sample is drawn from each of two populations. In the first case, two samples of size 75 each were drawn from a population of female college freshmen. Each sample received a different fitness program (treatment). Then a fitness test was administered to all the subjects in both samples.

After the treatments were administered, each sample represented a different population. In the second case, samples of size 40 were drawn from populations of last year's participants in a fitness program and this year's participants in the same fitness program. Then a fitness test was administered to all subjects in both samples. In either case, in the end the two samples represent different populations, and the question is whether there is a difference between the two samples in mean performance as an indication whether there is a difference at the population level.

This t-test is useful in any measurement situation where the mean performances of two groups are being compared. For example, is the mean for a group in a fitness program last year equal to the mean for a group in the same fitness program this year, or are two groups in different fitness programs equal in mean performance?

**Step 1**

$H_0: u_1 - u_2 = 0$ (hypothesis that population means are equal)

$H_1: u_1 - u_2 > 0$

$H_2: u_1 - u_2 < 0$

**Step 2**

Alpha = .05

**Step 3**

Find t-test table value with degrees of freedom equal $(n_1 + n_2 - 2)$ where $n_1$ is the sample size for Group 1 and $n_2$ is for Group 2.

**Step 4**

Conduct the study, collect the data, and calculate the t-test.

**Step 5**

Compare the calculated t at Step 4 to the table value t at Step 3 and draw a conclusion to accept or reject $H_0$.

The t-TEST FOR INDEPENDENT SAMPLES on the t-test and ANOVA disk in the *Statistics with Finesse* package does this t-test. The data of Groups A and B in Table 3.18 are used for an example analysis with this program. If a data file containing the data of the two groups is developed, each subject must have a variable identifying group membership and a second variable that is his score. The results of the analysis are presented in Table 3.20, where one can see that there is a significant difference between the two groups in favor of Group A. The one-tailed significance (.0077) is less than .05, indicating significance. (The computer program only provides a one-tailed p-value.) (The two-tailed p-value would be .0154, which is also significant at .05.) With 14 degrees of freedom $(8 + 8 - 2)$ and alpha .05, the two-tailed tabled t-value is 2.145, which also indicates significance. In either case, significance indicates that the null hypothesis $(H_0)$ is rejected.

## t-Test for Two Dependent Groups

One example of this t-test is a group of subjects who were measured on two different occasions, usually the beginning and end of the treatment condition. In this case there is some degree of correlation or dependency between the two columns of scores. This t-test is useful in any measurement situation where you want to determine whether the mean performance of a group changed over time or as the result of an instructional/training program.

**Table 3.20** Output of the t-Test for Independent Samples for Groups A and B in Table 3.18

| Item | Group A | Group B |
|---|---|---|
| Sample Size | 8 | 8 |
| Mean | 12.00 | 9.50 |
| Standard Deviation | 2.00 | 1.60 |
| t-value | −2.7584 | |
| One-Tailed Significance | 0.0077 | |
| Point-Biserial Correlation | −0.5934 | |

**Table 3.21** Output of the t-Test for Dependent Measures Treating the A and B Groups Data in Table 3.18 as Repeated Measures

| Item | Score 1 | Score 2 |
|---|---|---|
| *N* | *8* | *8* |
| Mean | 12.00 | 9.50 |
| Std. Dev. | 2.00 | 1.60 |
| Difference in Means | −2.50 | |
| t-value | −2.89 | |
| Significance One-Tailed | 0.0139 | |

Suppose eight subjects were selected and initially (I) measured for number of mistakes when juggling a ball. Then the subjects were taught to juggle and finally (F) retested. Let us say that in Table 3.18 the Group A scores are the initial scores and the Group B scores are the retest. To determine if the subjects improved in juggling ability as a result of the juggling instruction, a t-test for dependent groups is conducted.

**Step 1**
$H_0: u_I - u_F = 0$
$H_1: u_I - u_F < 0$

**Step 2**
Alpha = .05

**Step 3**
Find t-test table value with degrees of freedom equal n − 1, where n is the number of subjects. In this example the degrees of freedom is seven (8 − 1), and the tabled t-value is −1.895 for alpha equals .05 and a one-tailed test.

**Step 4**
Conduct the study and calculate the t-test.

The t-TEST FOR DEPENDENT MEASURE on the t-test and ANOVA disk in *Statistics with Finesse* was used to analyze the example data. The data had to be entered in pairs, so the initial and final scores for Subject 1 (12,7) were entered, followed by the initial and final scores for Subject 2 (15,10), etc. The printout of this analysis is presented in Table 3.21.

**Table 3.22** Output from One-Way ANOVA for the Data in Table 3.18

| Source | Sum of Sqr. | DF | Var. Est. | F-Ratio | Prob. F |
|--------|-------------|-----|-----------|---------|---------|
| Among | 31.75 | 2 | 15.88 | 4.45 | 0.0244 |
| Within | 74.88 | 21 | 3.57 | | |
| Total | 106.63 | 23 | | | |

| Group | N | Mean | Std. Dev. |
|-------|---|------|-----------|
| A | 8 | 12.00 | 2.00 |
| B | 8 | 9.50 | 1.60 |
| C | 8 | 11.88 | 2.03 |

**Step 5**

Since the probability in Table 3.21 is less than the .05 alpha level selected, the difference between the initial and final means is significant, and the null hypothesis is rejected. Notice that the calculated t exceeds the tabled t and the same conclusion would be drawn.

**One-Way ANOVA**

There are many research situations where there are more than two independent groups. This is just an extension of the two independent group situations already discussed. In these situations the statistical analysis is a one-way **analysis of variance** (one-way ANOVA). Actually one-way ANOVA can be used with two or more independent groups, so it could be used rather than the t-test for two independent groups. The null hypothesis being tested is that the populations represented by the groups (samples) are equal in mean performance. The one alternate hypothesis is that the population means are not equal. One-way ANOVA is presented in Chapter 4 of this book, but with an application to measurement rather than research. However, the calculations are similar or the same with both applications.

ONE-WAY ANOVA on the t-test and ANOVA disk in the *Statistics with Finesse* package will do the analysis. As in the "t-test for Independent Samples" when the data are entered, there must be a variable identifying group membership and a variable that is the score of a subject. "ONE-WAY ANOVA" was applied to the data in Table 3.18. The output from ONE-WAY ANOVA for the data in Table 3.18 is presented in Table 3.22.

The statistical test in ANOVA is a F-ratio. From Table 3.22 it can be seen that the probability of the F of 4.45 is .0244. Since this probability is less than an alpha level of .05, a researcher would conclude that there is a significant difference among the means and accept the alternate hypothesis.

**Two-Way ANOVA, Repeated Measures**

This is just an extension of the t-test for dependent groups with subjects repeatedly measured. In this case each subject is measured on two or more occasions. Thus, if there are only two measures for each subject, this ANOVA design is an alternative to the t-test for dependent groups, but if there are more than two measures for each subject, this ANOVA design must be used. The null hypothesis being tested is that at the population level the means for the repeated measures are equal. The alternate hypothesis is that the means are not equal. This ANOVA design is presented

**Table 3.23** Fitness Scores for a Two-Way Factorial ANOVA Design

| Group | B1 | B2 | B3 |
|-------|-----|-----|-----|
| A1 | 12, 10, 9, 11, 10 | 10, 11, 9, 10, 11 | 10, 9, 8, 7, 8 |
| A2 | 14, 12, 13, 15, 12 | 8, 9, 10, 9, 11 | 6, 7, 5, 6, 4 |

in Chapter 4 of this book, but with an application to measurement rather than research. However, the calculations are similar or the same with both applications.

REPEATED MEASURES ANOVA on the t-test and ANOVA disk in the *Statistics with Finesse* package will do the analysis. Since this program and its use is presented in Chapter 4, nothing further will be presented in this chapter.

It is very common in research situations to administer a different combination of two treatments to each of the several groups participating in the research study. For example, in Table 3.23 there is an A-treatment, which is how many days a week people participated in an adult fitness program (A1 = 1, A2 = 3) and a B-treatment, which is how many minutes each day people participated (B1 = 15, B2 = 30, B3 = 45). Five subjects are randomly assigned to receive each treatment combination for a six-month period. So, for example, the A1-B1 group participates 1 day a week, 15 minutes a day for the six-month period. After the six-month period, all subjects are tested and their fitness level is the data presented in Table 3.23. (The fitness test was timed; thus, a low score reflects high fitness.)

*Two-Way ANOVA, Factorial Design*

There are three null hypotheses that are usually tested in this ANOVA design. One, there is no interaction between the row and column variables. If there is no interaction effect, the difference between any two column means is the same for each row and vice versa. For example, if there is no interaction effect, the difference between the A1B1 and A1B2 means is the same as the difference between the A2B1 and A2B2 means. Two, the row means are equal. Three, the column means are equal.

A two-way factorial ANOVA was conducted on the data in Table 3.23 using the TWO WAY ANOVA option on the t-test and ANOVA disk in the *Statistics with Finesse* package. In entering the data there was a variable for the A-treatment, a variable for the B-treatment, and a variable for the score of a person.

Based on Table 3.24, there is not a significant difference between the row means (F = .42, p = .52). For the difference to be significant, the p-value would have to be .05 or smaller. However, there was a significant interaction effect (F = 15.89, p = .0001) and significant difference among the column means (F = 45.89, p = .0001). An inspection of the column means (Table 3.24) shows that the means get progressively smaller as the subjects exercise more per day. Provided in Figure 3.16 is a plot of the means that illustrates the significant interaction. As shown for those who participated only one day per week (A1), 45 minutes of exercise per day is better than 15 or 30 minutes; however, the group that exercised three days per week (A2) enhanced their fitness by exercising more minutes per day. The significant interaction can be easily seen in the graph because the lines formed by the group means are not parallel.

**Table 3.24** Output from Two-Way ANOVA for the Data in Table 3.23

| Source | Sum of Sqr. | DF | Var. Est. | F-Ratio | Prob. F |
|---|---|---|---|---|---|
| Rows | 0.53 | 1 | 0.53 | 0.42 | 0.5226 |
| Columns | 116.27 | 2 | 58.13 | 45.89 | 0.0001 |
| Interaction | 40.27 | 2 | 20.13 | 15.89 | 0.0001 |
| Error | 30.40 | 24 | 1.27 | | |
| Total | 187.47 | 29 | 6.46 | | |

| Row Var. | | N | Mean | | Std. Dev. |
|---|---|---|---|---|---|
| 1: | | 15 | 9.67 | | 1.35 |
| 2: | | 15 | 9.40 | | 3.40 |

| Column Var. | | N | Mean | | Std.Dev. |
|---|---|---|---|---|---|
| 1: | | 10 | 11.80 | | 1.87 |
| 2: | | 10 | 9.80 | | 1.03 |
| 3: | | 10 | 7.00 | | 1.83 |

| Combination | | N | Mean | | Std. Dev. |
|---|---|---|---|---|---|
| 1 & 1: | | 5 | 10.40 | | 1.14 |
| 1 & 2: | | 5 | 10.20 | | 0.84 |
| 1 & 3: | | 5 | 8.40 | | 1.14 |
| 2 & 1: | | 5 | 13.20 | | 1.30 |
| 2 & 2: | | 5 | 9.40 | | 1.14 |
| 2 & 3: | | 5 | 5.60 | | 1.14 |

**Figure 3.16**
A plot of the means for the data in Table 3.23.

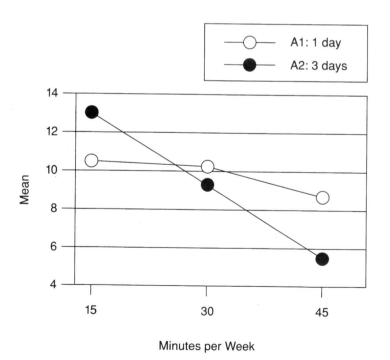

Part 2 Quantitative Aspects of Measurement

You should be sufficiently familiar with each of the techniques presented in this chapter to determine when it should be used, to calculate its value, and to interpret the results. Among the techniques discussed, means and standard deviations are most widely used. T-scores, a very useful measure, are being used more frequently every year. The concept of correlation is crucial to the determination of reliability and validity, as will be discussed in Chapters 4 and 5. Also, you will find that percentile-rank norms accompany most physical performance tests.

Some understanding of the additional statistical techniques presented will certainly be helpful in reading the research literature. Good ability to use the microcomputer is an essential outcome of this chapter.

**Summary**

*Objective 1*   Select the statistical technique that is correct for a given situation.

1. The situations listed below are common to most physical education teachers and exercise specialists. In each case, determine what statistical value(s) is(are) needed.

   a. Determining the typical group performance.
   b. Determining which of two groups is the more heterogeneous in performance.
   c. Determining whether a group has improved in performance during a 6-week training unit.
   d. Determining what percentage of the class scores fall below 70 on a 100-point knowledge test.
   e. Determining on which of four fitness tests an individual performed best in reference to the mean performance of his or her peers.
   f. Determining whether a certain test discriminates against heavy individuals.
   g. Determining whether a performance standard for a test is realistic in regard to the mean and standard deviation of the test.
   h. Determining the typical group performance if the scores are ordinal or the distribution of scores is skewed.

2. One reason for calculating various statistical values is to help in describing group performance. What statistics must be calculated to adequately describe the performance of a group?

**Formative Evaluation of Objectives**

*Objective 2*   Calculate accurately with the formulas presented.

1. The ability to calculate accurately using the formulas presented in the text is vital. To check your ability to work with the formulas, use the following scores to calculate

   a. The three measure of central tendency and the standard deviation for the 50 scores.
   b. The mean and standard deviation for each column of scores.

c. The percentile rank for scores 66 and 82.

| 84 | 82 | 95 | 92 | 83 |
|----|----|----|----|----|
| 80 | 58 | 82 | 81 | 60 |
| 79 | 87 | 71 | 90 | 69 |
| 82 | 75 | 70 | 89 | 85 |
| 69 | 79 | 80 | 74 | 69 |
| 84 | 81 | 71 | 90 | 87 |
| 66 | 79 | 52 | 92 | 72 |
| 70 | 86 | 87 | 77 | 87 |
| 90 | 89 | 69 | 68 | 83 |
| 85 | 92 | 76 | 74 | 89 |

2. There are many reasons why physical education teachers and exercise specialists use T-scores. You should not only realize when T-scores are needed, but you should also be able to calculate them.

   a. Determine the T-score when X is 60 for a 2-minute sit-up test with mean 42 and standard deviation 8.
   b. Determine the T-score when X is 11.3 for a 100-yard dash with mean 11.6 and standard deviation .55.
   c. Use the information below to determine which individual did best overall when both tests are considered.

|  | **100-yard dash** | **600-yard run** |
|----|----|----|
| Tom | 10.50 | 2 minutes |
| Bill | 11.10 | 1 minute, 35 seconds |
| Mean | 10.74 | 2 minutes |
| Standard Deviation | 1.12 | 20 seconds |

3. It is possible to solve probability statements using the normal curve, and there are several advantages to doing so. Consider the following probability statements, and solve them using the normal curve.

   a. $P(0 < z < 1.5)$     e. $P(.5 < z < 1.5)$
   b. $P(-.78 < z < 0)$     f. $P(z < .53)$
   c. $P(z < -1.34)$     g. $P(X > 15$, if $\overline{X} = 11$ and $s = 2.5)$
   d. $P(X > \overline{X} + 2s)$     h. $P(z < ?) = (10/100)$

4. The median is sometimes used instead of the mean. Use the counting method to determine the median for each set of the following scores.

   a. 1,13,12,1,8,4,5,10,2,5,6,8,9
   b. 7,13,2,1,1,9,12,5,6,11,4,10
   c. 5,1,4,8,14,7,1,2,5

5. Correlation coefficients have many uses in physical eduction as you will see in the next chapter. A correlation coefficient should be calculated using the scores of a large number of people, but to give you practice, the following are scores of a few people. Calculate the correlation coefficient for the two sets of scores.

| Person | Long Jump | Dash |
|--------|-----------|------|
| A | 67 | 5.2 |
| B | 68 | 5.4 |
| C | 57 | 6.1 |
| D | 60 | 5.5 |
| E | 71 | 5.1 |

*Objective 3*  Interpret the statistical value selected or calculated.

1. In addition to being able to calculate with the formulas presented in the chapter, you should be able to interpret the statistical values you have selected or calculated. For each situation below, indicate how you might explain or describe the statistical value to a group with which you typically work.

   a. Mean 11.67 and standard deviation 2.39 for a pull-up test
   b. Percentile rank 83 for a 100-yard dash score of 11.9
   c. T-score 61 for the test described in Part a

2. In the next chapter, correlation coefficients are used and referenced extensively. It is essential, then, that you understand both the term and its interpretation. In your own words, summarize what a correlation coefficient is and how to interpret either a positive or negative value.

*Objective 4*  Make decisions based on all available information about a given situation.

1. The text presents several methods for calculating T-scores for the entire class. Identify which formulas you would use if a calculator was to be used.

*Objective 5*  Utilize the microcomputer to analyze data.

1. Use the microcomputer to analyze several of the sets of scores in this chapter and check your answers against those in the chapter.

**Additional Learning Activities**

1. Using the techniques presented for finding T-scores for the entire class, determine the T-score for each score in a set of scores.

2. Select three units you would teach during a semester and decide which tests you would administer after each unit. Now decide which statistical techniques you would apply to the scores collected during the semester.

**Bibliography**

AAHPER. 1976. *Youth fitness test manual.* Washington, D.C.

Baumgartner, T. A. and C. H. Strong. 1994. *Conducting and reading research in health and human performance.* Dubuque, IA: Brown and Benchmark.

Bloomers, P. and E. F. Lindquist. 1960. *Elementary statistical methods.* Boston, MA: Houghton Mifflin.

Bloomers, P. J. and R. A. Forsyth. 1977. *Elementary statistical methods.* 2d ed. Boston, MA: Houghton Mifflin.

Bolding, J. 1989. *Statistics with finesse.* Fayetteville, AR: Bolding.

Cohen, J. and P. Cohen. 1975. *Applied multiple regression/correlation analysis for the behavioral sciences.* New York: Wiley.

Downie, N. M. and R. W. Heath. 1965. *Basic statistical methods.* 2d ed. New York: Harper & Row.

Feldman, D. S., Jr. et al. 1987. *Statview SE + graphics.* Berkeley: Abacus Concepts, Inc.

Ferguson, G. A. and Y. Takane. 1989. *Statistical analysis in psychology and education.* 5th ed. New York: McGraw-Hill.

Glass, G. and K. Hopkins. 1984. *Statistical methods in education and psychology.* 2d ed. Englewood Cliffs, NJ: Prentice-Hall.

Huck, S. W., W. H. Cormier, and W. G. Bounds. 1974. *Reading statistics and research.* New York: Harper & Row.

Kachigan, S. K. 1991. *Multivariate statistical analysis.* 2d ed. New York: Radius.

Kerlinger, F. N. and E. J. Pedhazur. 1973. *Multiple regression in behavioral research.* New York: Holt, Rinehart and Winston.

Nie, N. H. et al. 1975. *Statistical package for the social sciences.* 2d ed. New York: McGraw-Hill.

Prusoczuk, K. and T. Baumgartner. 1986. *TSCORE.* Dubuque, IA: Wm. C. Brown.

Roscoe, J. T. 1975. *Fundamental research statistics for the behavioral sciences.* 2d ed. New York: Holt, Rinehart and Winston.

Safrit, M. J. and T. M. Wood. 1989. *Measurement concepts in physical education and exercise science.* Champaign, IL: Human Kinetics Publishers.

Walker, H. M. and J. Lev. 1969. *Elementary statistical methods.* 3d ed. Chicago, IL: Holt, Rinehart and Winston.

# Reliability and Objectivity

## Key Words

analysis of variance
criterion score
internal-consistency reliability
  coefficient
intraclass correlation coefficient
kappa coefficient
objectivity
proportion of agreement
  coefficient
reliability
stability reliability coefficient
standard error of measurement
test-retest method
validity

## Contents

## Objectives

This chapter discusses the methods used to estimate reliability and objectivity, and the factors that influence both of these values.

Many physical performance tests can be given several times in the same day. When there are multiple trials of a test, the physical education teacher and exercise specialist must decide how many to administer and what trial(s) to use as the criterion score.

After reading Chapter 4 you should be able to:

1. Define and differentiate between reliability and objectivity for norm-referenced tests and outline the methods used to estimate these values.
2. Identify those factors that influence reliability and objectivity for norm-referenced tests.
3. Identify those factors that influence reliability for criterion-referenced tests.

## INTRODUCTION

There are certain characteristics essential to a measurement; without them, little faith can be put in the measurement and little use made of it. Measurement theory, the discussion of these characteristics, is covered in detail in this chapter and is referred to throughout the book.

One important quality of a measurement is **reliability.** A reliable test or instrument measures whatever it measures consistently. That is, if an individual whose ability has not changed is measured twice with a perfectly reliable measuring device, the two scores will be identical.

A second important characteristic is **validity.** A test or measuring instrument is valid if it measures what it is supposed to measure. Validity is discussed in greater detail in Chapter 5.

A third important characteristic of a measurement is objectivity. **Objectivity** is sometimes called rater reliability because it is defined in terms of the agreement of competent judges about the value of a measurement. Thus, if two judges scoring the same individual on the same test cannot agree on a score, the test lacks objectivity and neither score is really reliable nor valid. A lack of objectivity, then, reduces both reliability and validity.

The majority of this chapter deals with reliability and objectivity for norm-referenced tests. Since criterion-referenced tests are becoming quite common, reliability for criterion-referenced tests is presented in the last section of the chapter.

## Reliability Theory

This discussion and the reliability methods, and discussion based upon it, are for norm-referenced tests. We can better understand reliability for norm-referenced tests if we understand the mathematical theory underlying it. Reliability can be explained in terms of "observed scores," "true scores," and "error scores." Reliability theory assumes that any measurement on a continuous scale contains an inherent component of error, the measurement error. Any one or more of the following factors can be a source of measurement error:

1. lack of agreement among scorers (i.e., objectivity);
2. lack of consistent performance by the individual tested;
3. failure of an instrument to measure consistently; and
4. failure of the tester to follow standardized testing procedures.

Assume that we are about to measure the heights of five boys, all 68 inches tall. If we report any scores other than 68, an error of measurement has occurred. Thus, the variance for the reported heights is a good indicator of the amount of measurement error. The variance is the square of the standard deviation and is symbolized as $\sigma^2$ for the variance of a population or $s^2$ as the variance of a sample. A population is all the people who have a specified set of characteristics; a sample is a subgroup of a population. If all reported scores are 68, the measurement error is not serious and the variance is small. However, if the five boys are not all the same height, the variance for the reported heights may be due either to a true difference in height or to an error of measurement. In either case, the variance cannot be used as an indicator of measurement error.

In theory, the observed (recorded) score X is the sum of the true score t and an error of measurement score e:

$$X = t + e.$$

For example, if an individual who is 70.25 inches tall (t) has a recorded height of 70.5 (X), the error of measurement (e) is .25:

$$70.5 = 70.25 + .25.$$

If that individual is measured again and the recorded score is 69.5, the error of measurement equals –.75.

$$69.5 = 70.25 + -.75$$

The variance for a set of observed scores equals the variance of the true scores plus the variance of the error scores:

$$\sigma_x^2 = \sigma_t^2 + \sigma_e^2$$

where $\sigma_x^2$ is the variance of the observed scores, $\sigma_t^2$ is the variance of the true scores, and $\sigma_e^2$ is the variance of the error scores.

Reliability, then, is the ratio of the true-score variance to the observed-score variance:

$$\text{Reliability} = \frac{\sigma_t^2}{\sigma_x^2} = \frac{\sigma_x^2 - \sigma_e^2}{\sigma_x^2} = 1 - \frac{\sigma_e^2}{\sigma_x^2}.$$

We can see from this formula that, when no measurement error exists—that is, when $\sigma_e^2$ equals 0—the reliability is 1. As measurement error increases, $\sigma_e^2$ increases and reliability decreases. Thus, reliability is an indicator of the amount of measurement error in a set of scores.

Reliability depends on two basic factors:

1. reducing the variation attributable to measurement error; and
2. detecting individual differences (i.e., variation of the true scores) within the group measured.

The reliability of an instrument, then, must be viewed in terms of its measurement error (error variance) and its power to discriminate among different levels of ability within the group measured (true-score variance).

## Types of Reliability

The reliability of physical performance measures has traditionally been estimated by one of two methods. Because each yields a different reliability coefficient, it is important to use the most appropriate method for a given measuring instrument. It is also important to notice the methods others have used to calculate their reliability coefficients. Remember too that a test may be reliable for one group of individuals and not for another. For example, a test that is highly reliable for college students may be only moderately reliable for high school students or participants in a fitness program.

An issue involved in the calculation of a reliability coefficient is whether the reliability coefficient should indicate stability or internal consistency.

## Stability Reliability

When individual scores change little from one day to the next, they are stable. When scores remain stable, we consider them reliable. We use the test-retest method to obtain the **stability reliability coefficient.** Each person is measured with the same test or instrument on several (usually 2) different days (Day 1, Day 2, and so on). The correlation between the two sets of scores is the stability reliability coefficient. The closer this coefficient is to positive one (+1), the more stable and reliable the scores.

Three factors can contribute to poor score stability (a low stability reliability coefficient):

1. the people tested may perform differently;
2. the measuring instrument may operate or be applied differently; and
3. the person administering the measurement may change.

Lack of sleep, minor injuries, and anxiety all tend to lower one's level of performance. Also, if the instrument is not consistent from day to day—for example, if a stopwatch slows down or a measuring tape is bent—or if the procedures used to collect the measures change, stability reliability decreases. Finally, if the way in which the administrator scores the people tested or perceives their performances changes, reliability decreases.

As a rule of thumb, test-retest scores are collected 1 to 3 days apart. However, for a maximum-effort test, we advise retesting 7 days later because fatigue and soreness can affect test scores. If the interval between measurement is too long, scores may change because of increased maturation or practice, factors that are generally not considered sources of measurement error.

Some physical education teachers and exercise specialists object to the **test-retest method** because of the time required to administer a measuring instrument at least twice. Also, only the Day-1 scores are used as performance measures; subsequent scores are used solely to determine reliability. Yet the method is probably the most appropriate of the procedures for determining the reliability of physical performance measures. Without test-retest consistency, we lack a true indicator, not only of each person's ability, but of the faith we can place in the measure.

To save time, it is acceptable to calculate the test-retest reliability coefficient by retesting only part of the individuals tested. The typical procedure is to administer the test to all people on Day 1, and then to pick thirty to sixty people at random to be retested. (Draw names from a hat or use any procedure that gives all people an equal chance of being selected.) The test-retest reliability is then calculated using the scores of the randomly selected people.

Most physical measures are stable from day to day, exhibiting test-retest reliability coefficients between .80 and .95. There are others, however, that are not particularly stable from day to day. Baumgartner (1969b) found that scores may not be stable if subjects have not had prior experience and/or practice with the test prior to being measured. Of course, the reliability of a test or instrument depends on the type of measure, the age and gender of the subjects, the abilities of the administrator, and other factors, making it impossible to specify a universal minimum acceptable reliability. Each physical education teacher and exercise specialist must base his or her minimum acceptable reliability on the degree of reliability necessary and that which other people have obtained with similar individuals.

Many physical education teachers and exercise specialists use an internal-consistency coefficient as an estimate of the reliability of their measures. The advantage of this coefficient is that all measures are collected in a single day. Internal consistency refers to a consistent rate of scoring by the individuals being tested throughout a test or, when multiple trials are administered, from trial to trial.

Multiple trials are commonly administered by physical education teachers and exercise specialists. Examples are multiple measures of the skinfold at a site, multiple measures of the strength of a muscle or muscle group using Cybex equipment, and multiple trials of a physical performance test.

To obtain an **internal-consistency reliability coefficient,** the evaluator must give at least two trials of the test within a single day. Changes in the scores of the people being tested from trial to trial indicate a lack of test reliability. The correlation among the trial scores is the internal-consistency reliability coefficient. Obviously this technique should not be used with a maximum-performance test (e.g., the mile run) when fatigue would certainly affect the second trial scores.

The internal-consistency reliability coefficient is not comparable to the stability reliability coefficient. The former is not affected by day-to-day changes in performance, a major source of measurement error in the latter. An internal-consistency coefficient is almost always higher than its corresponding stability reliability coefficient. In fact, internal-consistency coefficients between .85 and .99 are not uncommon for motor-performance tests.

Education, psychology, and other disciplines that rely heavily on paper-and-pencil tests seldom, if ever, use the test-retest method, using instead the internal consistency method. Remember that the stability coefficient assumes that true ability has not changed from one day to the next, an assumption often unjustifiable with paper-and-pencil tests because cognitive learning usually does occur between administrations. Psychomotor learning is less apt to vary in a 1- or 2-day span, making the stability coefficient a better indicator of the reliability of data collected in physical education and exercise science.

As we have noted, theoretically an observed score X is composed of a true score t and an error score e. Furthermore, the variance of the observed scores $\sigma_x^2$ equals the variance of the true scores $\sigma_t^2$ plus the variance of the error scores $\sigma_e^2$ reliability equals the true-score variance divided by the observed-score variance. Just as observed-score variance can be divided into several parts, the total variability $s^2$ for a set of scores can be divided into several parts. To divide, or petition the variance, we use the technique of **analysis of variance** (ANOVA). We can then use these parts of the total variance to calculate an intraclass reliability coefficient.

To calculate an intraclass correlation coefficient, R, as an estimate of reliability, each subject or person tested in a physical education class, activity or fitness program, or research testing must have at least two scores. Here we replace the reliability formula

$$\text{Reliability} = \frac{\sigma_t^2}{\sigma_x^2}$$

with

$$R = \frac{MS_A - MS_W}{MS_A}$$

where R is the **intraclass correlation coefficient** (the reliability of the mean test score for each subject), $MS_A$ is the mean square among subjects, and $MS_W$ is the mean square within subjects. To obtain the two mean squares, a one-way analysis of variance was applied to the data. In other words, the term $MS_A - MS_W$ is an estimate of $\sigma_t^2$; and the term $MS_A$ is an estimate of $\sigma_x^2$. A mean square value is a variance just like the variance $s^2$ discussed in Chapter 3.

To calculate $MS_A$ and $MS_W$, we must first define six values from the sets of scores:

1. the sum of squares total, $SS_T$, and the degrees of freedom total, $df_T$, which are used to check our calculations; and

2. the sum of squares among subjects $SS_A$, the sum of squares within subjects, $SS_W$, the degrees of freedom among subjects, $df_A$, and the degrees of freedom within subjects, $df_W$, all of which are used to determine $MS_A$ and $MS_W$

$$SS_T = \Sigma X^2 - \frac{(\Sigma X)^2}{nk} \quad SS_A = \frac{\Sigma T_i^2}{k} - \frac{(\Sigma X)^2}{nk} \quad SS_W = \Sigma X^2 - \frac{\Sigma T_i^2}{k}$$

$$df_T = (n)\,(k) - 1 \qquad df_A = n - 1 \qquad df_W = n(k - 1)$$

where $\Sigma X^2$ is the sum of the squared scores, $\Sigma X$ is the sum of the scores of all subjects; n is the number of subjects; k is the number of scores for each subject, and $T_i$ is the sum of the scores for subject i. With these values in hand, it is a simple matter to calculate the mean square among subjects,

$$MS_A = \frac{SS_A}{df_A} = \frac{SS_A}{n - 1}$$

and the mean square within subjects,

$$MS_W = \frac{SS_W}{df_W} = \frac{SS_W}{n(k - 1)}.$$

*Problem 4.1.* Using one-way analysis of variance, calculate R for the data in Table 4.1.

*Solution.* To solve for R, we use a 9-step procedure:

**Step 1**
Obtain the sum of the scores, T, for each person:

| Subject | Day 1 | Day 2 | T |
|---------|-------|-------|-----|
| A | 9 | 9 | 18 |
| B | 1 | 2 | 3 |
| C | 8 | 7 | 15 |

## Table 4.1  One-Way ANOVA Data

| Student | Day 1 | Day 2 |
|---------|-------|-------|
| A | 9 | 9 |
| B | 1 | 2 |
| C | 8 | 7 |

**Step 2**

Obtain the sum of the scores, $\Sigma X$, and the sum of the squared scores, $\Sigma X^2$:

$$\Sigma X = 9 + 9 + 1 + 2 + 8 + 7^* = 36$$

$$\Sigma X^2 = 9^2 + 9^2 + 1^2 + 2^2 + 8^2 + 7^2$$

$$= 81 + 81 + 1 + 4 + 64 + 49 = 280$$

**Step 3**

Calculate the 3 sum-of-squares values:

$$SS_T = \Sigma X^2 - \frac{(\Sigma X)^2}{nk} = 280 - \frac{36^2}{(3)(2)}$$

$$= 280 - \frac{1296}{6} = 280 - 216 = 64$$

$$SS_A = \frac{\Sigma T_i^2}{k} - \frac{(\Sigma X)^2}{nk} = \frac{18^2 + 3^2 + 15^2}{2} - \frac{36^2}{(3)(2)}$$

$$= \frac{324 + 9 + 225}{2} - \frac{1296}{6} = \frac{558}{2} - 216 = 279 - 216 = 63$$

$$SS_W = \Sigma X^2 - \frac{\Sigma T_i^2}{k} = 280 - \frac{18^2 + 3^2 + 15^2}{2}$$

$$= 280 - \frac{324 + 9 + 225}{2} = 280 - \frac{558}{2} = 280 - 279 = 1$$

**Step 4**

Check your calculations. The sum of squares among subjects ($SS_A$) plus the sum of squares within subjects ($SS_W$) should equal the sum of squares total ($SS_T$):

$$63 + 1 = 64$$

(If your figures here were incorrect, you would go back and recalculate.)

---

*You could total the T column for this value as well: $(18 + 3 + 15 = 36)$.

### Step 5
Calculate the 3 degrees of freedom values:

$$df_T = (n)(k) - 1 = (3)(2) - 1 = 5$$

$$df_A = n - 1 = 3 - 1 = 2$$

$$df_W = n(k - 1) = 3(2 - 1) = 3$$

### Step 6
Check your calculations. The degrees of freedom among subjects ($df_A$) plus the degrees of freedom within subjects ($df_W$) should equal the degrees of freedom total ($df_T$):

$$2 + 3 = 5.$$

### Step 7
Calculate $MS_A$ and $MS_W$. Where $SS_A$ is 63, n is 3, $SS_W$ is 1, and k is 2, the mean square among subjects, $MS_A$, is 31.50 and the mean square within subjects, $MS_W$, is .33:

$$MS_A = \frac{63}{3 - 1} = \frac{63}{2} = 31.50$$

$$MS_W = \frac{1}{(3)(2 - 1)} = \frac{1}{3} = .33.$$

### Step 8
Place all your values in an ANOVA summary table to make sure nothing has been left out and everything is correct.

| Source | df | SS | MS |
|---|---|---|---|
| Among subjects | $df_A$ | $SS_A$ | $MS_A$ |
| Within subjects | $df_W$ | $SS_W$ | $MS_W$ |
| Total | $df_T$ | | |

| Source | df | SS | MS |
|---|---|---|---|
| Among subjects | 2 | 63 | 31.50 |
| Within subjects | 3 | 1 | .33 |
| Total | 5 | 64 | |

### Step 9
Now we can calculate R. Where $MS_A$ is 31.50 and $MS_W$ is .33, the intraclass reliability coefficient R is .99:

$$R = \frac{31.50 - .33}{31.50} = \frac{31.17}{31.50} = .99.$$

**Table 4.2** Sample ANOVA Summary Table for n Subjects and k Trials

| Source | DF | SS | MS |
|---|---|---|---|
| Among subjects | $n-1$ | $SS_S$ | $MS_S$ |
| Among trials | $k-1$ | $SS_t$ | $MS_t$ |
| Interaction | $(n-1)(k-1)$ | $SS_I$ | $MS_I$ |
| Total | $nk-1$ | $SS_T$ | |

R indicates the reliability of the mean test score for each person. When R equals 0 there is no reliability; when R equals 1 there is maximum reliability. Whenever multiple trials are administered on one day or a test is administered on at least two days, we can use R to estimate the reliability of the mean score. If the person's scores change from trial to trial or from day to day, R will be lower.

With the availability of calculators and computers, the calculation of R is quite easy. A simple or one-way analysis-of-variance computer program provides the mean squares needed to calculate R. These computer programs are easily found for any mainframe or microcomputer. In the *Statistics with Finesse* package of statistical programs, the ONE-WAY ANOVA program will do a one-way analysis of variance (see Additional Statistical Techniques in Chapter 3). If a computer program is used, notice that each subject is treated as a group. This may be a problem since the number of subjects often exceeds the maximum number of groups allowed by a computer program. Further, the data input organization for a one-way ANOVA is not compatible with the data input organization required by other statistical techniques if additional statistical analyses are applied to the data. To avoid these two problems use a repeated measures ANOVA program for the data analysis (see Computer Use section later in this chapter).

This reliability coefficient using a one-way ANOVA is only one of many intraclass reliability coefficients. It is the simplest to determine because it requires the least calculation and decision making. Slightly more advanced procedures may yield a more precise criterion score. Baumgartner (1969a) describes a selection procedure that yields a criterion score minimally influenced by learning or fatigue and the intraclass reliability for that score. Feldt and McKee (1958) present a way to estimate reliability using the intraclass method when multiple trials are administered on each of several days. Safrit (1981, 1986) discusses intraclass reliability and related topics in detail. Safrit and Wood (1989) have several strong chapters on reliability.

## Intraclass R from Two-Way Analysis of Variance

Suppose that k scores were collected for each of n subjects. These scores could have been collected over k trials or k days. For discussion purposes, we will refer to the k scores as trials. If a two-way analysis of variance were applied to the k scores of these n subjects, a summary table could be developed as shown in Table 4.2.

**Table 4.3** Two-Way ANOVA Data for 3-Trial Test Administered on 1 Day

| Subject | Trial 1 | Trial 2 | Trial 3 |
|---------|---------|---------|---------|
| A | 5 | 6 | 7 |
| B | 3 | 3 | 4 |
| C | 4 | 4 | 5 |
| D | 7 | 6 | 6 |
| E | 6 | 7 | 5 |

For two-way ANOVA, the following formulas are used to calculate the various sums of squares:

Sum of squares total $(SS_T) = \Sigma X^2 - \dfrac{(\Sigma X)^2}{nk}$

Sum of squares among subjects $(SS_S) = \dfrac{\Sigma(T_i)^2}{k} - \dfrac{(\Sigma X)^2}{nk}$

Sum of squares among trials $(SS_t) = \dfrac{\Sigma(T_j)^2}{n} - \dfrac{(\Sigma X)^2}{nk}$

Sum of squares interaction $(SS_I) = \Sigma X^2 + \dfrac{(\Sigma X)^2}{nk} - \dfrac{\Sigma(T_i)^2}{k} - \dfrac{\Sigma(T_j)^2}{n}$

where $\Sigma X^2$ is the sum of the squared scores, $\Sigma X$ is the sum of the scores of all subjects, n is the number of subjects, k is the number of scores for each subject, $T_i$ is the sum of the scores for Subject i, and $T_j$ is the sum of the scores for Trial j.

*Problem 4.2.* Using the two-way analysis of variance formulas, develop a summary table of the data in Table 4.3.

*Solution.* These first 4 steps in the procedure are similar to those used in one-way ANOVA.

**Step 1**
Set up a table to calculate the sum of scores for each subject $(T_i)$ and for each trial $(T_j)$:

| Subject | Trial 1 | Trial 2 | Trial 3 | $T_i$ |
|---------|---------|---------|---------|-------|
| A | 5 | 6 | 7 | 18 |
| B | 3 | 3 | 4 | 10 |
| C | 4 | 4 | 5 | 13 |
| D | 7 | 6 | 6 | 19 |
| E | 6 | 7 | 5 | 18 |
| $T_j$ | 25 | 26 | 27 | 78 |

**Step 2**

Calculate the values needed to determine the sums of squares:

$$\Sigma X^2, \Sigma X, \frac{\Sigma(T_i)^2}{k}, \text{ and } \frac{\Sigma(T_j)^2}{n}.$$

$$\Sigma X^2 = 5^2 + 6^2 + 7^2 + \cdots + 6^2 + 7^2 + 5^2$$

$$= 25 + 36 + 49 + \cdots + 36 + 49 + 25 = 432$$

$$\Sigma X = 5 + 6 + 7 + \cdots + 6 + 7 + 5^* = 78$$

$$\frac{\Sigma(T_i)^2}{k} = \frac{18^2 + 10^2 + 13^2 + 19^2 + 18^2}{3}$$

$$= \frac{324 + 100 + 169 + 361 + 324}{3}$$

$$= \frac{1278}{3} = 426$$

$$\frac{\Sigma(T_j)^2}{n} = \frac{25^2 + 26^2 + 27^2}{5} = \frac{625 + 676 + 729}{5} = \frac{2030}{5} = 406.$$

**Step 3**

Where $\Sigma X^2$ is 432, $\Sigma X$ is 78, n is 5, k is 3, $\frac{\Sigma(T_i)^2}{k}$ is 426,

and $\frac{\Sigma(T_j)^2}{n}$ is 406, $SS_T$, $SS_S$, $SS_t$, and $SS_I$ are as follows:

$$SS_T = 432 - \frac{78^2}{(5)(3)} = 432 - \frac{6084}{15} = 432 - 405.6 = 26.4$$

$$SS_S = 426 - 405.6 = 20.4$$

$$SS_t = 406 - 405.6 = .4$$

$$SS_I = 432 + 405.6 - 426 - 406 = 837.6 - 832 = 5.6.$$

**Step 4**

Check your calculations. The sum of the sum of squares among subjects, the sum of squares among trials, and the sum of squares interaction should equal the sum of squares total:

$$20.4 + .4 + 5.6 = 26.4$$

---

*Here too the sum of the $T_j$ column could be used.

**Step 5**

Following the procedure in Table 4.2, the summary table for the data in Table 4.3 would look like this:

| Source | DF | SS | MS |
|--------|----|----|----|
| Among subjects | 4 | 20.4 | 5.10 |
| Among trials | 2 | .4 | .20 |
| Interaction | 8 | 5.6 | .70 |
| Total | 14 | 26.4 | |

*The F-Test.* Once the summary table has been developed, we can determine whether the trial means differ significantly using the F-test formula $F = MS_t/MS_I$. For example, the F from the summary table in Problem 4.2 is .29 ($F = .20/.70 = .29$).

If the F is significant, there is real, or true, difference among the trial means. If the F is nonsignificant, the difference between trial means is not considered a true difference, but rather a chance one. (To review significance versus nonsignificance, see Additional Statistical Techniques in Chapter 3.)

For example, using the summary table in Problem 4.2, the F-table value for 2 and 8 degrees of freedom is 4.46 at the 0.5 level and 8.65 at the .01 level. Because the calculated F for the data in the problem is .29, the difference among trial means is nonsignificant.

After the F-test, there are three potential ways the analysis can progress, as shown in Figure 4.1.

*Nonsignificant F.* If there is a nonsignificant F, indicating no difference among the trial means, the reliability of the criterion score, which is the sum or mean of a subject's trial scores, is as follows:

$$R = \frac{MS_S - MS_W}{MS_S} \qquad (1)$$

where

$$MS_W = \frac{SS_t + SS_I}{df_t + df_I}.$$

Using the data in Problem 4.2, where $MS_W$ is $.6 \left( \dfrac{.4 + 5.6}{2 + 8} \right)$, R is .88:

$$R = \frac{5.10 - .6}{5.10} = \frac{4.50}{5.10} = .882 = .88.$$

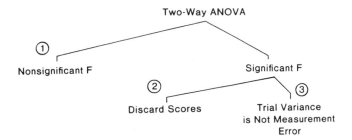

**Figure 4.1**
Two-way ANOVA decision
process.

Notice that Formula 1 is the same as the Formula for R presented with a one-way ANOVA since $SS_S$ in a two-way ANOVA is the same as $SS_A$ in a one-way ANOVA. Applying the one-way ANOVA formulas to the data in Table 4.3 we obtain the following:

$$MS_A = \frac{20.4}{5-1} = 5.1 \qquad MS_W = \frac{6}{(5)(3-1)} = .6$$

$$R = \frac{5.1 - .6}{5.1} = .88$$

*Significant F.* The other alternative ways for the analysis to go are possible when the F is significant, indicating a difference among the trial means. With the first technique (number 2 in Figure 4.1), which can be used when each subject is tested several times in 1 day or on several days, the scores from trials whose means are lower than or not approximately equal to the means of the other trials are discarded (Baumgartner 1969a). A second two-way analysis of variance is then conducted on the retained scores, and another F-test is calculated. If the recalculated F is nonsignificant, Formula 1 is used to estimate the reliability of the **criterion score,** representing the sum or mean of all the subjects' retained trial scores. For example, suppose the data for a 6-trial test were as presented in Figure 4.2. Trials 1, 2, and 6 would be discarded, and another two-way ANOVA would be conducted using the scores from Trials 3, 4, and 5.

The purpose of this technique (number 2 in Figure 4.1) is to find a measurement schedule free of trial differences and yielding the largest possible criterion score for most subjects. This criterion score is usually very reliable. Baumgartner and Jackson (1970) used this technique. Trial-to-trial variance is random after finding a nonsignificant F, so trial-to-trial variance is considered a measurement error in Formula 1. Interaction is also considered a measurement error.

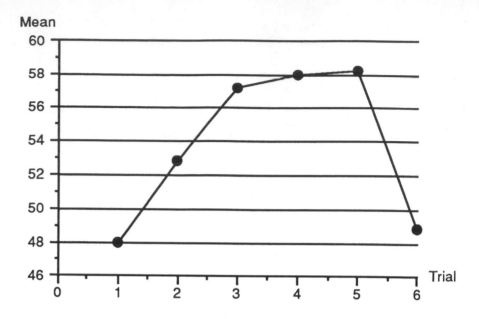

**Figure 4.2**
Graph of the means for a six-trial test.

The last alternative (number 3 in Figure 4.1) does not consider a trial-to-trial variance as measurement error. This technique is often used when it is known that subjects will improve from trial to trial. Also, this technique is often used when estimating objectivity (judges replace trials) and all judges are not expected to use the same standards. The formula for estimating the reliability of the criterion score (the sum or mean of all trials) is as follows:

$$R = \frac{MS_S - MS_I}{MS_S}.$$

(2)

For the data in Problem 4.2, using Formula 2, R is .86:

$$R = \frac{5.10 - .70}{5.10} = \frac{4.40}{5.10} = .86.$$

Measurement error is supposed to be random. Significant difference among the trial means indicates a lack of randomness. Thus, when significant difference is found, one could argue that the variance for trials should not be combined with the sum of squares interaction to form the mean square within of Formula 1. Statistically this position is defensible. However, one could counter that every source of variance not attributable to students is error-score variance. In keeping with this philosophy, you can either conduct a one-way analysis of variance with the test scores or, as Baumgartner (1969a) advocates, discard scores until no significant difference among trial means is found in the data and then use Formula 1.

Of the three potential data analyses shown in Figure 4.1, it seems that most people are using alternatives 2 and 3. Only when people must do the data analysis by hand is a one-way ANOVA initially applied to the data.

**Table 4.4** Two-Way ANOVA for the Data in Table 4.3 Using the *Statistics with Finesse* Microcomputer Program

| Source | Sum of Sqr. | DF | Var. Est. | F-Ratio | Prob. F |
|---|---|---|---|---|---|
| Between Subject | 20.40 | 4 | 5.10 | 8.50 | 0.0029 |
| Within Subject | 6.00 | 10 | 0.60 | | |
|    Treatments | 0.40 | 2 | 0.20 | .29 | 0.7588 |
|    Error | 5.60 | 8 | 0.70 | | |
| Total | 26.40 | 14 | 1.89 | | |

| Treatment | Mean | Std. Dev. |
|---|---|---|
| One | 5.00 | 1.58 |
| Two | 5.20 | 1.64 |
| Three | 5.40 | 1.14 |

*Computer Use.* Most researchers are using the computer to apply a two-way ANOVA to their data. Two-way ANOVA computer programs that will handle repeated measures on each subject are very common on microcomputers. Unless the amount of data is small, all physical educators and exercise specialists should use the computer to do a two-way ANOVA on their data. The advantage of a two-way ANOVA over a one-way ANOVA is that the computer will give you the mean for each trial, a significance test for difference among trial means is possible, and the R can still be calculated as if a one-way ANOVA was used (Formula 1) or by Formula 2 that requires a two-way ANOVA.

In the *Statistics with Finesse* package of microcomputer programs, the program REPEATED MEASURES ANOVA will analyze repeated measures on each subject (Bolding 1989). This program is referenced from the main menu of the T-Test and ANOVA disk. When entering the data in Table 4.3 there must be four variables (Subject, Trial 1, Trial 2, Trial 3). When analyzing the data, Trials 1, 2, and 3 must be identified as the treatment variables. The output from the analysis of the data in Table 4.3 is presented in Table 4.4.

In Table 4.4 the between and within subjects are the sources if a one-way ANOVA was applied to the data. The between subjects, treatments, and error are the sources if a two-way ANOVA was applied to the data. Note that within subjects from the one-way ANOVA is composed of treatment and error from the two-way ANOVA. In terms of the terminology used up to this point and in Table 4.2, treatments and error in Table 4.4 are among trials and interaction respectively. Variance estimates in Table 4.4 were previously called mean square values. Since the Prob. F for treatments (.7588) is larger than .05, there is not a significant difference among the trial means (see The F-Test p. 124), which has implications as to how R is calculated. There is sufficient information in Table 4.4 to calculate R no matter the formula that is selected.

Finally, as noted in Chapter 3 under Additional Statistical Techniques, a researcher might use the *Statistics with Finesse* program REPEATED MEASURES ANOVA to analyze data where each column of scores was a response to a different treatment. In this case the whole intent of the research is to determine whether there is a difference among the treatment means. Thus, the F-ratio for treatment is the statistical test of interest.

## Coefficient Alpha

Coefficient alpha is often used to determine the reliability of dichotomous data (see chapter 13). When the data are ordinal, we may use the coefficient alpha to determine reliability (Ferguson & Takane 1989; Nunnally 1967). In fact, with ordinal or interval data the coefficient alpha is the same as the intraclass $R \left[ R = \dfrac{(MS_S - MS_I)}{MS_S} \right]$ just discussed. Coefficient alpha is an estimate of the reliability of a criterion score that is the sum of the trial scores in 1 day. There is no reason why the coefficient could not be applied to multiple-day or multiple-judge data to estimate stability reliability or objectivity. We determine coefficient alpha using the following formula:

$$r_\alpha = \left( \frac{k}{k-1} \right) \left( \frac{s_x^2 - s_j^2}{s_x^2} \right) \tag{3}$$

where $r_\alpha$ is coefficient alpha, k is the number of trials, $s_x^2$ is the variance for the criterion scores, and $s_j^2$ is the sum of the variances for the trials.

*Problem 4.3.* Calculate coefficient alpha for the data in Table 4.3.

*Solution.* Here too the procedure is a multistep one.

### Step 1
The simplest way to do this is to set up a table like the one below:

| Subject | TRIAL 1 $X_1$ | TRIAL 2 $X_2$ | TRIAL 3 $X_3$ | TOTAL X |
|---------|------|------|------|------|
| A | 5 | 6 | 7 | 18 |
| B | 3 | 3 | 4 | 10 |
| C | 4 | 4 | 5 | 13 |
| D | 7 | 6 | 6 | 19 |
| E | 6 | 7 | 5 | 18 |
|   | 25 | 26 | 27 | 78 |

### Step 2
Have the computer calculate the variance for $X_1$, $X_2$, $X_3$, and X. Using the formula

$$s^2 = \frac{\Sigma X^2}{n} - \frac{(\Sigma X)^2}{n^2}$$

the variances are

$$s_1^2 = 2;$$

$$s_2^2 = 2.16;$$

$$s_3^2 = 1.04;$$

$$s_x^2 = 12.24.$$

If the computer calculates with the formula $s^2 = \dfrac{(\Sigma X^2 - (\Sigma X)^2/n)}{(n-1)}$, the variances above will be different. With a larger number of subjects the difference in the variances for the two formulas is slight.

**Step 3**
Now we can calculate $r_\alpha$. Where k is 3, $s_x^2$ is 12.24, and $s_j^2$ is 5.2 (the sum of $s_1^2$, $s_2^2$, and $s_3^2$: 2 + 2.16 + 1.04), the coefficient alpha r is .86:

$$r_\alpha = \left(\frac{3}{3-1}\right)\left(\frac{12.24 - 5.2}{12.24}\right) = \left(\frac{3}{2}\right)\left(\frac{7.04}{12.24}\right) = \frac{21.12}{24.48} = .86.$$

Notice R = .86 with Formula 2.

Besides providing the needed variances, the computer can also provide the correlations for the trial scores with the sum of the trial scores, which could be useful in deciding which trials to sum as the criterion score. Only trials that correlate positively at a reasonably high value with the sum of the trial scores should be retained. Normally, with motor performance tests, each trial is correlated with the sum of all trials.

**Single Score**

All the formulas for calculating the intraclass reliability coefficient thus far have been for the average or sum of all trials or days. Sometimes it is necessary to estimate the reliability of a single trial or day. Two formulas are used to calculate the reliability of a single score when there are k trials or days; the decision of which to use rests on the analysis procedure. If the procedures leading to Formula 1 were used, we calculate R with the following equation:

$$R = \frac{MS_S - MS_W}{MS_S + (k/k' - 1)(MS_W)}. \tag{4}$$

If the procedures leading to Formula 2 were used, we use this formula instead:

$$R = \frac{MS_S - MS_I}{(MS_S + (k/k' - 1)(MS_I))} \tag{5}$$

where k is the number of trials administered and k' is the number of trials for which R is estimated.

Several authors, including Safrit (1981), present these formulas for estimating or predicting what R would be if the number of trials was increased or decreased.

We can see this easily in a test-retest situation; for example, if people were tested on each of 2 days and the physical education teacher or exercise specialist wants to estimate the reliability of a score collected on one of those days. In this case, using Formula 4 the R is:

$$R = \frac{MS_S - MS_W}{MS_S + (2/1 - 1)(MS_W)} = \frac{MS_S - MS_W}{MS_S + MS_W}.$$

*Problem 4.4.* Calculating R for a single score, using the data in Table 4.1.

**Step 1**
From Step 7 in Problem 4.1, the $MS_A = 31.5$ and $MS_W = .33$.

**Step 2**
Calculate R

$$R = \frac{31.5 - .33}{31.5 + .33} = \frac{31.37}{31.83} = .98.$$

R indicates the reliability of a test score collected on 1 day.

Intraclass R in Summary

Occasionally, an intraclass correlation coefficient will be lower than wanted even though the test seemed reliable (individual scores changed little from trial to trial or day to day). This happens when the sum of squares among subjects is small, indicating a group homogeneous in ability. In a situation like this, one thing to do is to realize why the coefficient is low. The better thing to do is to try to increase test sensitivity or ability to discriminate among individuals in terms of ability. Remember though that you cannot accept something as reliable if the reliability coefficient is low.

Interval data are assumed in calculating an intraclass R. When the data are ranks, consider instead the Rho, Tau, or Concordance coefficients (Stamm 1976; Stamm & Safrit 1977) that are presented in many statistics books like Ferguson and Takane (1989).

Occasionally people want to test intraclass correlation coefficients as to value at the population level, whether two coefficients are equal, or develop confidence limits for a coefficient. Feldt (1990) and Alsawalmeh and Feldt (1992) address these needs.

**Spearman-Brown Prophecy Formula**

This equation is used to estimate the reliability of a test when its length is increased. It assumes that the additional length (or new trial), although as difficult as the original, is neither mentally nor physically tiring.

$$r_{k,k} = \frac{k(r_{1,1})}{1 + (k - 1)(r_{1,1})}$$

where $r_{k,k}$ is the estimated reliability of a test increased in length k times, k is the number of times the test is increased in length, and $r_{1,1}$ is the reliability of the present test.

*Problem 4.5.* The reliability of a 6-trial test was found to be .94. Determine the reliability if 18 trials were administered.

*Solution.* Where k is 3 and $r_{1,1}$ is .94, the estimated reliability of a criterion score based on 18 trials is .98:

$$r_{k,k} = \frac{(3)(.94)}{1 + (3 - 1)(.94)} = \frac{2.82}{1 + (2)(.94)}$$

$$= \frac{2.82}{1 + 1.88} = \frac{2.82}{2.88} = .979 = .98.$$

Baumgartner (1968) investigated the accuracy with which the Spearman-Brown prophecy formula predicts reliability. He compared the predicted reliability coefficients to the reliability coefficients actually obtained when the number of trials of a test was increased. He found that the formula's accuracy increased as the value of k in the formula decreased, concluding, then, that the reliability coefficient predicted by the Spearman-Brown formula is the maximum reliability that can be expected.

It is sometimes useful to be able to estimate the measurement error in each test score. The average amount of measurement error in test scores is estimated by calculating the standard error of measurement by the following formula:

**Standard Error of Measurement**

$$s_e = s_x \sqrt{1 - r_{x,x}}$$

where $s_e$ is the standard error of measurement, $s_x$ is the standard deviation for the test scores, and $r_{x,x}$ is the reliability coefficient for the test scores.

Since the variance of all measurements contains some measurement error, the **standard error of measurement** of a test score reflects the degree one may expect a test score to vary due to measurement error.

*Problem 4.6.* A written test has a standard deviation of 5 and a reliability coefficient of .91. Determine the standard error of measurement for the test.

*Solution.* Where $s_x$ is 5 and $r_{x,x}$ is .91, the standard error of measurement $s_e$ is 1.5:

$$s_e = 5 \sqrt{1 - .91} = 5 \sqrt{.09} = (5)(.3) = 1.5.$$

The standard error acts like a test score's standard deviation and can be interpreted in much the same way using the normal curve. From the normal curve table (Table 3.11, page 86), we know that approximately 68% of the scores lie within 1 standard deviation of the mean, which in this case is the test score. If a person who scored 73 on the test in Problem 4.6 were to take the test 100 times and his or her ability did not change, we would expect the person's scores to fall between 71.5 (73 – 1.5) and 74.5 (73 + 1.5) 68 times out of 100. The standard error, then, specifies the limits within which we can expect scores to vary due to measurement error. In fact, there is a growing tendency to report a confidence band—the score, plus and minus the standard error—with test scores. For more lengthy discussion, see Ferguson and Takane (1989) or any other statistics text that includes a chapter on measurement theory.

Many factors can affect test reliability. Among them are scoring accuracy, the number of test trials, test difficulty, instructions, and the testing environment, as well as the subject's familiarity with the test and present performance level. The range of talent and the use of a reliability coefficient also can affect reliability (Remmers et al. 1969). Ebel (1979) notes that the reliability coefficient is larger for scores from a long test than those from a short one, and for a group with a broad range of abilities than for one with a narrow range of abilities.

**Factors Affecting Reliability**

**Table 4.5** Factors Influencing Test Reliability

| Category of Factors | Illustrative Sources of Imperfect Reliability |
|---|---|
| Characteristics of the performers | Range of talent; motivation; good day vs. bad day; learning; forgetting; fatigue |
| Characteristics of the test | Length; difficulty; discriminative power; trial homogeneity; number of performers |
| Characteristics of the testing situation | Instructions; environment; class organization; class management; warm-up opportunity |
| Characteristics of the measurement process | Nature of measurement instrument; selection of scoring unit; precision; errors in measurement; number of trials; recording errors |
| Characteristics of the evaluator(s) | Competences; confidence in test; concentration on task; familiarity with instrument; motivation; number of evaluators |
| Characteristics of the mode of statistical estimation | Breakdown of observed score variance into true score and error score variance, with retest design: error source is variation within individuals between days. Does not include within-day variance. With split-trial design: variation within individuals between trials. Does not include between-day variance or variance between grouped trials. |

Table 4.5 shows a categorization proposed by Zuidema (1969) of the factors that influence test reliability. We can expect an acceptable degree of reliability when

1. the subjects are heterogeneous in ability, motivated to do well, ready to be tested, and informed about the nature of the test;
2. the test discriminates among ability groups, and is long enough or repeated sufficiently for each subject to show his or her best performance;
3. the testing environment and organization are favorable to good performance; and
4. the person administering the test is competent.

The reliability coefficient should be calculated using the scores of a large group (at least 100 people), since it is relatively easy to obtain extremely high or low correlation coefficients with a small group.

## Objectivity

Objectivity, or rater reliability, is an important characteristic of a test or measuring instrument. We can define objectivity as the close agreement between the scores assigned to each subject by two or more judges. Judges in this case could be judges in gymnastics or timers in a 100-yard dash.

### Factors Affecting Objectivity

Objectivity depends on two related factors: (1) the clarity of the scoring system and (2) the degree to which the judge can assign scores accurately. Certain tests have clearly defined methods of scoring: a 50-yard dash is scored with a stopwatch; and a long jump with a tape measure. In this type of test the rater can easily determine the subject's scores. In contrast, an essay test or a dance performance does not offer a well-defined scoring system, relying on the rater's judgment in the assignment of points.

The second factor is more obvious. If a judge does not know how to assign a score, he or she cannot do it accurately. For example, a scorer who is unfamiliar with stopwatches will probably not assign an accurate score on a timed speed event. Of course, it is a simple matter to train a scorer in the use of scoring equipment and scoring procedures.

A high degree of objectivity is essential when two or more people are administering a test. For example, say that a group of fifty people is divided into two groups and each group is tested by a different person. If a high degree of objectivity is lacking because the two scorers of the test use different administrative procedures and/or scoring standards, a subject's score is dependent on the identity of the scorer. If one scorer is more lenient than the other, the subjects tested by that scorer have an advantage.

A high degree of objectivity is also needed when one person scores on several occasions. For example, a scorer may measure one-third of a group on each of 3 days, or the entire group at the beginning and end of a teaching or training unit. Certainly, in the first case, it is essential that the same administrative procedures and scoring standards be used each day. This is true in the second case as well, where any variation in a subject's scores should represent changed performance, not changed procedures or standards.

## Estimation

To determine the degree of objectivity in a physical performance test, two or more judges score each subject as he or she is tested. Then we calculate an intraclass correlation coefficient on the basis of judges' scores of each person.

To calculate the objectivity coefficient, we think of the judges as trials, inserting their individual scores into the trial terms of our reliability formulas. If all judges are supposed to be using the same standards, we could consider a difference among judges to be measurement error and would calculate objectivity using the one-way ANOVA formula

$$R = \frac{MS_A - MS_W}{MS_A},$$

If all judges are not expected to use the same standards, we would calculate objectivity using either the alpha coefficient or the appropriate intraclass R formula (see Formula 2). Very seldom, if ever, would we discard the data of judges as was suggested by Baumgartner (1969a) with multiple trials.

## Reliability of Criterion-Referenced Tests

Criterion-referenced standards and the setting of criterion-referenced standards were discussed in Chapter 1. Based on a criterion-referenced standard a person is classified as either proficient or nonproficient, either pass or fail. For example, in a Red Cross certification course a person either meets the minimum requirements and is certified or does not meet the minimum requirements and is not certified. As mentioned in Chapter 1, the criterion-referenced standard for an adult fitness course could be the ability to jog continuously for 30 minutes. Based on this standard a

**Table 4.6** Table for Estimating Reliability of a Criterion-Referenced Test

|  |  | Day 2 | |
|  |  | Pass | Fail |
|---|---|---|---|
| Day 1 | Pass | A | B |
|  | Fail | C | D |

person is classified as either proficient or nonproficient. A very nice characteristic of a criterion-referenced standard is that there is no predetermined quota as to how many people are classified proficient.

Criterion-referenced reliability is defined differently than norm-referenced reliability. In the criterion-referenced case, reliability is defined as consistency of classification. Thus, if a criterion-referenced test is reliable, a person will be classified the same on each of two occasions. This could be trial-to-trial within a day or day-to-day.

To estimate the reliability of a criterion-referenced test form a double classification table as presented in Table 4.6. In the A-box is the number of people who passed on both days and in the D-box is the number of people who failed on both days. Notice the B-box and C-box are the numbers of people who were not classified the same on both occasions. Obviously larger numbers in the A-box and D-box and smaller numbers in the B-box and C-box are desirable because reliability is consistency of classification on both occasions.

The most popular way to estimate reliability from this double classification table (Safrit 1986) is to calculate the **proportion of agreement coefficient** (P) where

$$P = \frac{A + D}{A + B + C + D}.$$

*Problem 4.7.* Determine the proportion of agreement (P) for a criterion-referenced test using the data in Table 4.7.

*Solution.* Where the sum of the A-box and D-box is 124 and the sum of the four boxes is 150, P = .83:

$$P = \frac{84 + 40}{84 + 21 + 5 + 40} = \frac{124}{150} = .827 = .83.$$

The proportion of agreement (P) does not allow for the fact that some same classifications on both occasions may have happened totally by chance. The **kappa coefficient** (k) corrects for chance agreements. The formula for kappa is

**Table 4.7** Data for Determining the Reliability of a Criterion-Referenced Test

|  |  | **TRIAL 2** | |
|---|---|---|---|
|  |  | *Pass* | *Fail* |
|  | *Pass* | 84 | 21 |
| **TRIAL 1** |  |  |  |
|  | *Fail* | 5 | 40 |

$$k = \frac{Pa - Pc}{1 - Pc},$$

where Pa = proportion of agreement

Pc = proportion of agreement expected by chance

$$= [(A + B)(A + C) + (C + D)(B + D)]/$$

$$(A + B + C + D)^2 \text{ in a } 2 \times 2 \text{ double classification table.}$$

*Problem 4.8.* Determine the kappa coefficient (k) for a criterion-referenced test using the data in Table 4.7.

*Solution.* To solve for k, we use a 3-step procedure:

**Step 1**
Calculate Pa

$$Pa = \frac{A + D}{A + B + C + D} = \frac{84 + 40}{84 + 21 + 5 + 40} = \frac{124}{150} = .827 = .83$$

**Step 2**
Calculate Pc

$$Pc = \frac{(A + B)(A + C) + (C + D)(B + D)}{(A + B + C + D)^2}$$

$$= \frac{(105)(89) + (45)(61)}{(84 + 21 + 5 + 40)^2} = \frac{9345 + 2745}{150^2}$$

$$= \frac{12090}{22500} = .537 = .54$$

**Step 3**
Calculate kappa

$$k = \frac{Pa - Pc}{1 - Pc} = \frac{.83 - .54}{1 - .54} = \frac{.29}{.46} = .63$$

Notice that for the data in Table 4.7 there is a definite difference between the proportion of agreement (P) and coefficient kappa (k). A more extensive discussion of both coefficients is presented by Looney (Safrit & Wood 1989).

Since P can be affected by classifications by chance, values of P less than .50 are interpreted as unacceptable. Thus, values of P need to be closer to 1.0 than .50 to be quite acceptable. Values of k also should be closer to 1.0 than 0.00 to be quite acceptable.

## Summary

There are three characteristics essential to a sound measuring instrument: reliability, objectivity, and validity. Reliability and objectivity were discussed in this chapter. A test has reliability when it consistently measures what it is supposed to measure. There are two types of reliability for mean-referenced tests: stability and internal consistency.

Objectivity, the second vital characteristic of a sound instrument, is the degree to which different judges agree in their scoring of each individual in a group. A fair test is one in which qualified judges rate individuals similarly and/or offer the same conditions of testing to all individuals equally.

Reliability of criterion-referenced tests was also discussed. The definition of reliability and techniques for estimating reliability differ from those for norm-referenced tests.

## Formative Evaluation of Objectives

*Objective 1* Define and differentiate between reliability and objectivity for norm-referenced tests and outline the methods used to estimate these values.

1. Two important characteristics of all measurements are that they be reliable and objective. Describe the basic nature of each of these characteristics.

2. In theory, reliability is the ratio of the true-story variance to the observed-score variance. Observed-score variance consists of both error-score variance and true-score variance. Describe these basic sources of variance and the combination that yields the highest estimate of reliability.

3. Two basic methods are used to estimate the reliability of a measuring instrument: stability, reliability and internal-consistency reliability. Briefly describe each method and the procedure it uses to estimate reliability.

4. The standard error of measurement is an estimate of the amount of measurement error in the test score. List the formula for the standard error of measurement and describe the characteristics of the statistic.

5. Objectivity, or rater reliability, is achieved when the scores of two or more different judges closely agree. The correlation between the scores is an objectivity coefficient. Summarize the procedures that yield high objectivity.

*Objective 2*   Identify those factors that influence reliability and objectivity for norm-referenced tests.

1. Acceptable reliability is essential for all measurements. Many factors affect the reliability of a measurement, and some of these are listed below. Identify the conditions under which the highest reliability can be expected for the following factors:

   a. Subjects tested
   b. Test length
   c. Testing environment
   d. Test administrator

2. According to measurement theory, if a test is lengthened, its reliability is increased. If the reliability of a standing long-jump test composed of 2 jumps is found to be .83, how reliable might the test be if 6 jumps were scored?

3. A physical education teacher or exercise specialist can improve test objectivity in several ways. Summarize them.

*Objective 3*   Identify those factors that influence reliability for criterion-referenced tests.

1. Acceptable reliability is essential for all measurements. Many factors affect the reliability of a measurement, and some of these are listed below. Identify how each of these factors affect the estimated reliability coefficient obtained:

   a. Reliability coefficient calculated
   b. Chance
   c. Composition of the group

**Additional Learning Activities**

1. Many tests suggest 2 or 3 trials within a day. The number may have been arbitrarily selected so that the tests can be given quickly. Administer a multiple-trial test with more trials than recommended. By looking at the trial means, determine when the performance of the group reaches its maximum and becomes consistent.

2. There are many tests commonly used in testing programs (runs, jumps, maximum effort). Administer one of these tests and determine the reliability of it.

3. Construct a new physical performance test. Administer the test and decide how to calculate its reliability and objectivity.

# Bibliography

Alsawalmeh, Y. M. and L. S. Feldt. 1992. Test of the hypothesis that the intraclass reliability coefficient is the same for two measurement procedures. *Applied Psychological Measurement 16(2):*195–205.

Baumgartner, T. A. 1968. The application of the Spearman-Brown prophecy formula when applied to physical performance tests. *Research Quarterly 39:*847–56.

———. 1969a. Estimating reliability when all test trials are administered on the same day. *Research Quarterly, 40:*222–25.

———. 1969b. Stability of physical performance test scores. *Research Quarterly 40:*257–61.

———. 1974. Criterion score for multiple trial measures. *Research Quarterly 45:*193–98.

Baumgartner, T. A. and A. S. Jackson. 1970. Measurement schedules for tests of motor performance. *Research Quarterly 41:*10–17.

Bolding, J. 1989. *Statistics with finesse.* Fayetteville, AR: Publisher.

Ebel, R. L. 1979. *Essentials of educational measurement.* 3d ed. Englewood Cliffs, NJ: Prentice-Hall.

Feldt, L. S. 1990. The sampling theory for the intraclass reliability coefficient. *Applied Measurement in Education 3:*361–67.

Feldt, L. S. and M. E. McKee. 1958. Estimating the reliability of skill tests. *Research Quarterly 29:*279–93.

Ferguson G. A. and Y. Takane. 1989. *Statistical analysis in psychology and education.* 6th ed. New York: McGraw-Hill.

Nunnally, J. C. 1978. *Psychometric theory.* 2d ed. New York: McGraw-Hill.

Remmers, H. H., N. L. Gage, and J. F. Rummel. 1969. *A practical introduction to measurement and evaluation.* New York: Harper & Row.

Safrit, M. J. 1981. *Evaluation in physical education.* 2d ed. Englewood Cliffs, NJ: Prentice-Hall.

———. 1986. *Introduction to measurement in physical education and exercise science.* St. Louis: Time Mirror/Mosby.

———. et al. 1974. *Reliability theory appropriate for motor performance measures.* New York: AAHPER.

Safrit, M. J. and T. M. Wood. 1989. *Measurement concepts in physical education and exercise science.* Champaign, IL: Human Kinetics.

Stamm, C. L. 1976. An alternative method for estimating reliability. *JOPERD 47:*66–67.

Stamm, C. L. and M. J. Safrit. 1977. Comparisons of two nonparametric methods for estimating the reliability of motor performance tests. *Research Quarterly 48:*169–76.

Zuidema, M. A. 1969. A brief on reliability theory: Theoretical concepts, influencing factors, and empirical estimates of the reliability of measurements especially applied to physical performance tests. Mimeographed. Bloomington, IN: University of Indiana.

# Validity

## Key Words

concurrent validity
construct validity
criterion score
decision validity
domain-referenced validity
logical validity
predictive validity
validity

## Contents

## Objectives

This chapter discusses the methods used to estimate validity for norm-referenced tests, the relationship between reliability and validity, and the factors that influence validity.

Many physical performance tests can be given several times in the same day. When there are multiple trials of a test, the teacher and exercise scientist must decide how many to administer and what trial(s) to use as the criterion score.

Finally, the methods used to estimate validity for criterion-referenced tests are discussed.

After reading Chapter 5 you should be able to:

1. Define validity, and outline the methods used to estimate it.
2. Describe the influence of test reliability on test validity.
3. Identify those factors that influence validity.
4. Select a reliable, valid criterion score based on measurement theory.

# INTRODUCTION

There are certain characteristics essential to a measurement; without them, little faith can be put in the measurement and little use made of it. Two of these characteristics, reliability and objectivity, were discussed in Chapter 4. A third important characteristic of a measurement is validity. The American Psychological Association (1985) indicates that validity is the most important.

A test or measuring instrument is valid if it measures what it is supposed to measure. For example, pull-ups are a valid measure of arm and shoulder girdle strength and endurance because strength and endurance of the arm and shoulder girdle muscles are necessary to do a pull-up; pull-ups are not a valid measure of arm speed because the number of pull-ups one can execute is not influenced by arm speed. For a measure to be valid it must be reliable, but a reliable test may not be valid. Obviously for a test or instrument to measure what it is supposed to measure, it must first measure consistently. For example, the 50-yard dash test is reliable and is a valid measure of running speed; however, it is not a valid measure of flexibility. Thus, for a test, reliability is first determined, and then validity is determined.

Recognize that validity of a test or measuring instrument is in terms of the intended use of the data. The pull-up mentioned in the previous paragraph is an example. If the data from a test or measuring instrument are invalid in terms of their intended use, the data are useless. Any decisions made about subjects based on the invalid data probably will be in error.

# Validity for Norm-Referenced Tests

Validity may be discussed in terms of norm-referenced or criterion-referenced tests. A review of these two types of tests (see Chapter 1) might be helpful. Traditionally validity has been discussed in terms of norm-referenced tests, so first we will discuss validity from this standpoint.

When a test measures what it purports to measure, it is a valid test. To have **validity,** then, a test must be both relevant and reliable—relevant to the trait being tested and reliable as a measurement of that trait. Figure 5.1 shows the interrelationship between validity, relevance, and reliability.

In Figure 5.1 it can be seen that validity has two major components, relevance and reliability, with objectivity (sometimes called rater reliability) a component of reliability. As we demonstrated in Chapter 4, there are two general types of reliability, stability estimated by the test-retest method and internal consistency estimated by the multiple-trials-within-a-day method. As we will find in this chapter, there are three basic types of relevance with definite estimation methods leading to what is called logical validity, concurrent validity, predictive validity, and construct validity.

## Types and Estimation

A test's degree of validity should indicate to the user the degree to which that test is capable of achieving certain aims (APA 1985). These aims, and the four types of validity that parallel these aims, are logical, concurrent, predictive, and construct validity.

Validity can be estimated either logically or statistically. Recently the trend in education and psychology has been away from the statistical approach, while exercise science depends more on the statistical approach. This does not necessarily mean that physical education and exercise science should follow suit. Education and psychology work predominantly with paper-and-pencil tests, while physical education and exercise science work predominantly with physical performance tests. The test method for estimating validity must be chosen in terms of the situation, not the trend.

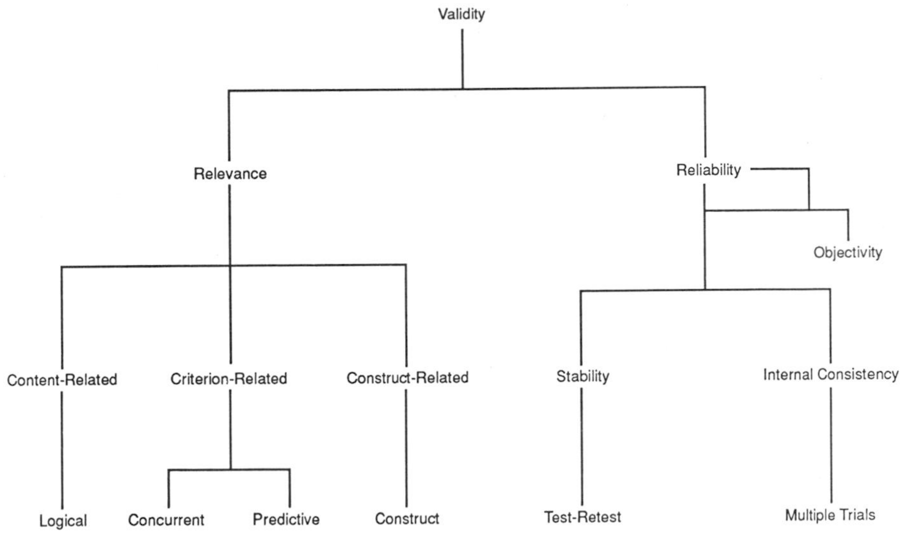

**Figure 5.1**
Relationship of relevance and reliability to validity.

An overview of the commonly used validity approaches and basic issues involved in establishing validity are presented. A more comprehensive coverage of validity is presented in Safrit and Wood (1989).

*Logical Validity.*   A measuring instrument has **logical validity** to the extent that it measures the capacities about which conclusions are to be drawn. Logical validity is established by examining the capacities to be measured and determining whether the instrument is, in fact, measuring them. For example, the 50-yard dash and 100-yard dash are obviously valid tests of running speed because they measure the speed a person can run. A written test has logical validity (often called content validity) when its questions are reliable, based on the material taught, and sample the stated educational objectives of the unit. For a complicated, multicomponent skill such as team sports, clearly defined objectives provide the only means of determining the degree of logical validity.

It is certainly true that logical validity has been both successfully used and badly misused at times. The American Psychological Association (1985) suggests that, ideally, several different types of validity evidence (content-related, criterion-related, construct-related) be provided with a test, but one solid piece of evidence is better than several weak pieces of evidence. Perhaps, if possible, logical validity should be used in conjunction with other validity evidence.

Logical validity seems to have been used quite successfully with physical fitness tests and fitness test batteries. For example, sit-ups are a measure of abdominal strength and endurance because it is required to do a sit-up. A second example, the items in the health-related physical fitness tests were logically selected based on what the biggest health problems in the United States are today. However, Jackson and Baker (1986) did not find the sit-and-reach test a valid measure of hamstring and lower back flexibility.

Logical validity seems to have been less successfully used with complex sports skills tests. Claims of logical validity for certain sports skill tests and sports skill test batteries have been occasionally questioned. The wall volley in volleyball is one example. The basic components of softball, basketball, and volleyball ability so a comprehensive skills test battery can be constructed is another.

Logical validity, then, rests solely on subjective decision making, which has led to criticism of this type of validity. However, this validity is not the only one to rest on subjective decision: Concurrent validity is often determined by using the subjective decisions of an expert judge or judges.

### Concurrent Validity.
**Concurrent validity** is a measure of a test's correlation to some specified criterion. This is a traditional procedure for establishing the validity of a test. It involves calculating the Pearson product-moment correlation coefficient or some other similar type of correlation between scores on the test and those achieved on a criterion measure. The resulting correlation coefficient—the validity coefficient—is an estimate of the validity of the test. When the validity coefficient is close to 1, the instrument is measuring similarly to the criterion measure and is valid; when the coefficient is close to 0, the instrument has little validity.

A crucial step in establishing the concurrent validity of a test is the choice of a suitable criterion measure. Expert ratings and tournament standings are commonly used for sports skills tests. Predetermined criteria such as $VO_2$ Max and body composition are commonly used criteria in exercise science.

*Expert Ratings.* One criterion measure is the subjective rating of one or more experts. Because one judge may overlook certain factors in a person's performance or may have certain biases that affect his or her ratings, the sum of several qualified judges' ratings is a more reliable criterion measure. Obviously, high objectivity among judges is vital.

Subjective ratings usually take the form of either class ranks or a point scale. Using class ranks, the subjects are ordered from best to worst on the basis of performance. Using a point scale, the subjects are scored individually on a numbered point scale, as they would be in a gymnastics meet. Class ranks become unworkable as the size of the group increases. Further, a point scale system is preferable, since it does not require that one person be ranked best and another worst. One usually obtains higher validity with a scoring system than with class ranks, provided the scoring system is well defined so that high objectivity is possible.

Expert ratings have been commonly used to estimate the validity of skill tests. A skill test has certain advantages over tests that must be judged by experts. Providing the judges are qualified, they furnish a valid index of skill performance. However, in practice it is hard to find even one expert, let alone several, who have the time to subjectively evaluate a class of students. Then, too, skill tests are usually easier to administer and less time-consuming than are subjective evaluations.

*Tournament Standings.* A second method of estimating the validity of an instrument is to correlate the scores from the instrument (using the Pearson product-moment correlation coefficient or some other appropriate correlation coefficient) with the tournament standings of the students being measured. The method assumes that tournament standing is a good indicator of overall ability in the tested skill, usually an individual or dual activity like tennis or badminton. Many teachers are eager to find an instrument that is a valid indicator of skill. Such an instrument makes it unnecessary to conduct round-robin tournaments to evaluate the skill level of the students.

*Predetermined Criteria.* The final method uses a known valid, accepted instrument, which yields a quantitative score as the criterion measure. The validity of a test is then estimated by determining the Pearson product-moment correlation coefficient between scores from the test and scores from the accepted instrument. The method is usually used in developing a test that is quicker and/or easier to administer than is the accepted instrument. For example, this procedure has been used to validate the use of skinfolds to measure body composition. A valid, accepted measure of percentage body fat can be obtained by weighing a subject under water; a person with a high percentage of body fat weighs less under water because fat tissue is less dense than muscle and bone. Skinfold measurements are easy to obtain and correlate highly (r at least .80) with the percentage of fat determined by the more complicated underwater weighing method. Further, they can be used on people fearful of being weighed under water. By obtaining selected skinfold measurements, we can estimate the subject's percent body fat using a regression equation. In fact, multiple correlation and regression equations (see Chapter 3) are often used to establish concurrent validity. In these situations, Y is the criterion score (dependent variable), and the several scores used to estimate Y are the X-scores (independent variables). In the earlier example, Y would be the underwater weight, and the X-scores would be the skinfold measures.

**Predictive Validity.** Predictive validity, like concurrent validity, is determined by using a criterion measure. **Predictive validity** represents the value of a measure for predicting performance on another measure (criterion). This may be either predicting a criterion with a regression equation (see Chapter 3) or predicting a criterion that will not be immediately available. An example of the first situation is predicting percent body fat by using skinfold measures. An example of the second situation follows.

Consider, for example, the question of predicting success in college. A student's performance on one measure such as a high school grade point average, obtained before entering college, is correlated with a criterion measure of success in college, usually the student's college grade point average. The correlation between the two measures indicates the predictive validity of the measure obtained before entering college.

For example, to determine the validity of high school grade point average for predicting college grade point average the following steps would be used:

1. for college graduates, obtain from their records the college and high school grade point average; and

2. calculate the correlation between the two measures—the predictive validity coefficient.

If the predictive validity coefficient is sufficiently high and the standard error of prediction (see Chapter 3) sufficiently low, high school grade point average is a valid predictor of college grade point average. In this case the college admissions officer would develop a simple prediction equation (see Chapter 3) to predict college grade point averages for students applying for admission to the college.

Again, multiple correlation and regression equations could be used to establish predictive validity. You could determine how valid a combination of high school grade point average ($X_1$) and a standardized test score (like ACT or SAT) ($X_2$) are in predicting college grade point average (Y). As a second example, you could determine how valid a combination of present fitness level ($X_1$), health history ($X_2$), and previous activity level ($X_3$) is in predicting how long a person would continue in an adult fitness program (Y).

*Construct Validity.* Logical validity, concurrent validity, and predictive validity are established methods for examining test validity; construct validity is a comparatively new and more complex validation procedure. It was first introduced in 1954 by the American Psychological Association and has been used extensively in psychological testing since then. Today the method is being used more and more in physical education testing as well (Safrit 1975).

Construct validity is used with abstract rather than concrete tests (Nunnally 1967). An abstract test measures something that is not directly observable. Attitudes toward physical activity are abstract human traits that are neither readily apparent nor easily understood by an untrained professional. The number of basketball free throws made out of 100 tries, on the other hand, is a concrete measure of skill.

**Construct validity** is based on the scientific method. First, there is a hunch that a test or tests measure some abstract trait. Second, a theory is developed to explain both the construct and the tests that measure it. Finally, various statistical procedures are applied to confirm or reject the theory. An excellent example of this process is shown in the work of Kenyon (1968a, b), who developed valid scales (see Chapter 14) for the measurement of attitude toward physical activity and the construct validation of distance run tests by Disch, Frankiewicz, and Jackson (1975), Safrit (1977) provides a fine overview of the construct validation process.

Construct validity is determined by judging the extent to which theoretical and statistical information supports assumed constructs. The procedure gives physical education teachers and exercise specialists a way to evaluate their tests. For example, consider a swimming test administered to intermediate and varsity swimmers. Because the varsity swimmers are known to be better swimmers, we can demonstrate construct validity whenever the mean score of the varsity swimmers is superior to that of the intermediate swimmers. Probably a statistical test of the significance of the difference between the two means at alpha equal .01 should be conducted (see Additional Statistical Techniques in Chapter 3) to make sure the two swimming groups really do differ.

A second example of this approach is the comparing of the performance of a group before and after instruction or training. This involves testing a group for initial ability, applying some instructional or training technique for multiple weeks, and then retesting the group for final ability. Since the group should have improved in ability as a result of the instruction or training, we can demonstrate construct validity if the final test mean is significantly better than the initial test mean (see the repeated measures t-test in Chapter 3).

Scientists may not consider this a scientifically "true" example of the construct validation process; however, it does demonstrate that the process can be applied in physical education and exercise science. Whenever a superior performer does not achieve a score comparable to those of previously administered tests, the teacher must be alert to the possibility that the test lacks either reliability or validity.

**Table 5.1** Rotated Factor Loadings of Running Tests

| | Factors | |
|---|---|---|
| **Distance of Run** | **I** | **II** |
| 1. 50 yards | .18 | .86 |
| 2. 100 yards | .17 | .88 |
| 3. ½ mile | .76 | .46 |
| 4. ¾ mile | .74 | .53 |
| 5. 1 mile | .84 | .38 |
| 6. 1¼ miles | .88 | .33 |
| 7. 1½ miles | .73 | .27 |
| 8. 1¾ miles | .94 | .23 |
| 9. 2 miles | .87 | .10 |
| 10. 12-minute run | −.91 | −.01 |

Factor analysis is a statistical procedure that can be used to identify constructs and the valid tests of isolated constructs. In this context the isolated factor of the analysis is an abstract construct (Safrit 1975; Yates 1977). Factor analysis has often been used to identify the basic components of fitness or a sport skill (see Chapters 8 and 12).

Factor analysis assumes that tests that correlate with each other measure the same basic factor, and that tests that do not correlate measure different factors. A factor, then, is simply a group of intercorrelations among tests that cluster together. The nature of factor analysis can best be demonstrated with data from an actual study (Disch et al. 1975) that was designed to identify the factors common to running tests. It was believed that endurance and speed were constructs common to these tests, and that the importance of endurance increased as distance increased. To prove this theory, ten tests were administered to college men. Among them were sprints of 50 and 100 yards, seven runs varying in distance from ½ mile to 2 miles, and the 12-minute run for distance.

Factor analysis determines the number of basic factors, or clusters, in a group of tests, and the degree to which each test measures each basic factor. Table 5.1 shows the final stage of the factor analysis of the intercorrelations of the ten tests, which indicates that two basic factors (I: endurance; II: speed) are represented in this group of tests. The values, called *factor loadings,* listed under columns I and II can be interpreted as the correlation between the test and the basic factors. The 50- and 100-yard dashes are highly correlated with Factor II, speed; the distance runs are highly correlated with Factor I, endurance, and there is a tendency for a higher correlation as the distance increases. The negative correlations for the 12-minute run are due to the method of scoring: a high score is a good score on the 12-minute run, whereas a low score is better on the other tests. As can be seen in Table 5.1, the 50- and 100-yard dashes measure running speed. As the runs become longer, speed becomes less important and endurance more important.

Factor analysis is useful, not only for isolating the abstract being measured, but also for selecting valid tests of the construct. By examining the factor loadings of all tests, a pattern that identifies the construct should become apparent. Once the pattern is apparent, the best test or combination of tests can be selected to measure the construct. In the running tests example, the 50-yard dash and the 12-minute run could be used to measure the endurance and speed factors. Because of the nature of endurance tests, only one test would be selected: however, a more reliable measurement of a construct would be obtained by selecting several measures of the same construct.

***Selected Criterion Measure.***   The magnitude of a validity coefficient can be affected by several factors, among them the criterion measure selected. We have suggested several possible criterion measures (expert ratings, tournament standards, predetermined criteria) to use in estimating the validity of a test. It is reasonable to expect that each measure, when correlated with the same set of test scores, would yield a different validity coefficient. This is particularly true for a test of multicomponent skills.

***Characteristics of the Individuals Tested.***   Characteristics of the individuals tested also play a part in determining validity. A test that is valid for 6-year-old children may not be valid for 15-year-old students; a test valid for males may not be valid for females; a test that is valid for beginners may not be valid for advanced students. We can assume that a test is valid only for individuals similar in age, gender, and experience to those on whom the test was validated. In fact, it is a good idea to determine validity for yourself the first time you use a test, even for like groups, because the individuals you are measuring cannot be exactly like those originally used to validate the test.

***Reliability.***   As we have said, a test must be reliable to be valid. The validity coefficient is directly related to the reliability of both the test and the criterion measure. The maximum validity coefficient possible between two tests can be estimated by:

$$r_{x,y} = \sqrt{(r_{x,x})\,(r_{y,y})}$$

where $r_{x,y}$ is the correlation between Tests X and Y, $r_{x,x}$ is the reliability coefficient for Test X, and $r_{y,y}$ is the reliability coefficient for Test Y (Ferguson & Takane 1989). For example, if the reliability of both Tests X and Y is .90, the maximum validity coefficient possible would be .90:

$$r_{x,y} = \sqrt{(.90)\,(.90)} = \sqrt{.81} = .90.$$

If the reliability of Test X is .90 and that of Test Y is only .40, the maximum validity coefficient is much lower, only .60:

$$r_{x,y} = \sqrt{(.90)\,(.40)} = \sqrt{.36} = .60.$$

***Objectivity.***   Objectivity was defined as the agreement of two or more competent judges or scorers about the value of a measurement. Note that some people call objectivity "rater reliability." If two judges or raters scoring the same individual on the same test cannot agree on a score, the test lacks objectivity and the score of neither judge is valid. Thus, a lack of objectivity reduces the validity of a test much the way a lack of reliability does.

***Lengthened Tests.***   We know that the validity of a test is influenced by its reliability. We know, from the Spearman-Brown formula, that reliability increases as the number of test trials or the length of the test increases. Further, the more measures you obtain for each individual, the more valid an indication you have of his or her true ability. For example, a dribbling test and a shooting test are better indications of basketball-playing ability than just a shooting test, but four measures of basketball-playing ability are preferable to just two. The same thing could be said for skinfold measures in terms of the number of measures taken at each site and the number of sites. Since reliability and validity are related, increasing the length of a test not only increases reliability, but also test validity.

*Size of the Validity Coefficient.*    What is an acceptable validity coefficient when determining concurrent or predictive validity? The American Psychological Association (1985) does not address the issue. Safrit (1986) suggests that if a test is being used as a substitute for a more sophisticated test, coefficients of .90 and larger are desirable, but values exceeding .80 are acceptable. This recommendation seems to be for concurrent validity with a Pearson correlation coefficient. For predictive validity she suggests that in some situations tests with values of .50 or .60 may be acceptable. When a predictive test is needed and/or high predictive validity is not required in a situation, a test with predictive validity of .50 or .60 is better than nothing and, thus, acceptable.

It seems the acceptable value of the validity coefficient must be dependent on many things, such as whether it is concurrent or predictive validity, whether it is a Pearson correlation coefficient or a multiple correlation coefficient, how good the criterion is, how high a validity coefficient is needed or expected based on what others have obtained in similar situations, how small a standard error (see Chapter 3) is needed, and how much variance must be explained. The fact that the square of the correlation coefficient indicates the amount of variance common to both tests and, thus, the degree to which the two tests measure the same thing should not be overlooked. A review of interpreting correlation coefficients in Chapter 3 might be worthwhile. It is interesting to note the variety of concurrent validity values for distance run tests reported in Chapter 12, since many of the values failed the .80 criteria suggested earlier.

## Selecting a Valid Criterion Score

### Mean Score versus Best Score

A **criterion score** is the measure used to indicate a subject's ability. Unless a test has perfect reliability it is a better indicator when it is developed from more than one trial. Multiple-trial tests are common in physical education with jumping, throwing, and short running—tests whose performance is not adversely affected by fatigue. Multiple trials with skinfold and Cybex strength tests are common in exercise science. For a multiple-trial test, the criterion score can be either the person's best score or mean score. The best score is the optimal score a person receives on any one trial; the mean score is the mean of all the person's trial scores.

Much research has been done on the selection of a criterion score (Baumgartner 1974; Berger & Sweney 1965; Disch 1975; Henry 1967; Hetherington 1973; Johnson & Meeter 1977; Whitley & Smith 1963). The choice of best or mean score should be based on the amount of time available to obtain the criterion score and the use to be made of it. It is a much slower process to calculate a mean score than to list a best score for each subject. This is probably why standardized instructions for most multiple-trial tests suggest using the best score. Certainly when the criterion score is to be used as an indicator of maximum possible performance, the best score should be used. However, the best score from several trials may not be typical, in that it is unlikely to be achieved again for a long time and may be inflated by measurement error. The most reliable criterion score and the best indicator of true ability (typical performance), then, is the mean score. In theory, the sum of the errors of measurement is 0 when all of an individual's trial scores are added together. Because in most situations one wants an indication of status or typical performance, the mean score is the preferred criterion score for a multiple-trial test. When scores are not stable, as may be true for individuals with disabilities, the mean of the scores collected on several days may well be the only indicator of true ability.

## The Role of Preparation

Preparation is an important determinant of the validity of a criterion score. A criterion score is a better indicator of true ability if individuals are measured only after they fully understand how to undertake a test. For example, suppose your instructor announces one day that he or she is going to measure your cardiorespiratory endurance by having you run a mile for time. If you have never done any distance running, you would not know how to pace yourself, how to run in a relaxed manner, how to avoid being boxed in by other runners, or how to run near the inside curve. Your score that day will not be a true indication of your cardiorespiratory endurance. If you were tested again the next day, your score would improve, not because your endurance had improved, but because you would have learned how to approach the test. And on a third day you might do better still.

Research indicates that people often need a day of practice before testing to familiarize themselves with a test, even if they have had experience with it (Baumgartner 1969; Erickson et al. 1946). This practice allows a period of relearning and reinforcement necessary because skill retention is never perfect. Studies also show that a mean trial score for a multiple-trial test will be higher if several practice trials (called practice warm-up trials) are administered just before the test (Baumgartner & Jackson 1970).

## Validity for Criterion-Referenced Tests

Generally, the definition of validity for a norm-referenced test applies to a criterion-referenced test. The techniques for validating a criterion-referenced test are different than the techniques for validating a norm-referenced test. Remember, a criterion-referenced test is used to classify people as either proficient or nonproficient, either pass or fail.

One technique for validating a criterion-referenced test is called **domain-referenced validity.** The term *domain* refers to the criterion ability or behavior the test is supposed to measure. Thus, the criterion-referenced test is logically validated by showing that the test measures the criterion ability or behavior. This technique is basically the same as the logical validity technique discussed earlier in the chapter.

Another technique for validating a criterion-referenced test is called **decision validity.** This deals with accuracy of the test in classifying people as either proficient or nonproficient. Essential to this technique is the ability to classify people as either proficient or nonproficient, independent of the test. This is often very difficult to do, but for the moment let us say that we had the ability to do it. So, independent of the test and also as a result of the test, we have classified people as either proficient or nonproficient. These classifications enable us to generate a double entry classification table as shown in Table 5.2.

From this double entry classification table the classification of outcome probabilities (C) can be calculated as an estimate of test validity.

$$C = \frac{A + D}{A + B + C + D}$$

**Table 5.2** Table for Determining the Validity of a
Criterion-Referenced Test

|  |  | **Actual Classification** | |
|  |  | Proficient | Nonproficient |
| **Test Classification** | Proficient | A | B |
|  | Nonproficient | C | D |

**Table 5.3** Data for Determining the Validity of a
Criterion-Referenced Test

|  |  | **Actual Classification** | |
|  |  | Proficient | Nonproficient |
| **Test Classification** | Proficient | 40 | 5 |
|  | Nonproficient | 10 | 20 |

*Problem 5.1.* Calculate C for the data in Table 5.3.

*Solution.* Where the sum of the A-Box and D-Box is 60 and the sum of the four boxes is 75, C = .80.

$$C = \frac{40 + 20}{40 + 5 + 10 + 20} = \frac{60}{75} = .80$$

If $C$ equals 0.50 it indicates that the classification by the test was no better than chance. For this reason a value of $C$ closer to 1.0 than 0.50 is most desirable.

Another estimate of test validity that can be calculated from a double entry classification table is phi ($\phi$).

$$\phi = \frac{(AD) - (BC)}{\sqrt{(A+B)\,(C+D)\,(A+C)\,(B+D)}}$$

*Problem 5.2.* Calculate $\phi$ for the data in Table 5.3.

*Solution.*

$$\phi = \frac{(40)(20) - (5)(10)}{\sqrt{(40 + 5)(10 + 20)(40 + 10)(5 + 20)}}$$

$$= \frac{800 - 50}{\sqrt{1687500}}$$

$$= \frac{750}{1299.04}$$

$$= .58$$

Phi values can range from –1.0 to 1.0, so phi coefficients can be interpreted like any other correlation coefficient. However, because phi is the correlation between two dicothomous variables, high values of phi should not be expected (see Chapter 3 on correlation coefficients).

Let us come back to the problem of classifying people as either proficient or nonproficient, independent of the test (the actual classification in the double entry table). In some instructional situations the proficient classification could be people who had received instruction, and the nonproficient classification could be people who had not received instruction. Also, in an instructional situation the nonproficient could be the classification of people before they received instruction, and the proficient could be the classification of the same people after receiving instruction. In some exercise science situations, an accepted standard or laboratory measure may exist that can be used for classifying people in terms of actual group membership.

Ideally the validity of criterion-referenced standards for youth health-related fitness tests would be determined by the test classification in the double entry table being the subject's classification as a youth (fit or unfit) and the actual classification in the double entry table being the subject's classification (fit or unfit) as an adult. Unfortunately, little if any data like this exists.

An excellent discussion of validity of criterion-referenced tests can be found in Safrit (1981) and Safrit and Wood (1989). Both sources contain other information related to the validity issue such as setting the cutoff score for proficiency on the criterion-referenced test. An excellent tutorial on standards setting is presented by Cureton and Warren (1990). Safrit and Looney (1992) should be read for their comments on the standards setting procedures of Cureton and Warren.

A discussion of many validity, reliability, and performance standards issues in reference to fitness tests for children is presented by Safrit (1990). She concludes that much has been done but much more remains to be done in terms of the goodness of fitness tests for children.

## Summary

There are three characteristics essential to a sound measuring instrument: reliability, objectivity, and validity. Validity for norm-referenced tests may be of four different types: content, concurrent, predictive, and construct. Content validity is a logically determined measure—the test must measure the stated instructional objectives. Both concurrent and predictive validity gauge a person's test scores against an established criterion to determine that the test does correlate to the established criterion (concurrent validity) or does predict performance (predictive validity). Construct validity, which may be established through factor analysis, is the measure used with abstract rather than concrete tests.

Another major issue in testing is the selection of a criterion score, which can be either the person's best or mean score. A knowledge of how the criterion score is used is essential to intelligent selection and ultimately to the validity of the instrument itself.

Finally, when using criterion-referenced tests, the validity of these tests must be estimated. Two methods for estimating validity were presented.

## Formative Evaluation of Objectives

*Objective 1*  Define validity, and outline the methods used to estimate it.

1. Important characteristics of all measurements are that they be reliable, objective, and valid. Describe the basic nature of validity.

2. Four types of norm-referenced test validity indicate the degree to which a test is capable of achieving certain aims: content validity, concurrent validity, predictive validity, and construct validity. Briefly describe these aims of testing and the four types of validity that parallel them.

3. Some authors refer to concurrent and predictive validity as criterion-related validity because validity is determined by the correlation between a test and criterion measure. Summarize the criterion measures especially suitable for physical education.

4. Briefly describe the two methods of estimating the validity of criterion-referenced tests.

*Objective 2*  Describe the influence of test reliability on test validity.

1. A basic principle of measurement theory is that a test must first be reliable to be valid. Why is this so?

2. What effect does objectivity have on test validity?

*Objective 3*  Identify those factors that influence validity.

1. It is well established that test reliability is an essential factor of test validity. What other factors affect test validity?

*Objective 4*  Select a reliable, valid criterion score based on measurement theory.

1. Many psychomotor tests involve several trials. In multiple-trial tests either the best score or the mean score is used as the criterion score. What can a teacher do to make sure that the criterion score is as reliable and valid as possible?

2. Why is the criterion score in athletic events the best score, while in a physical education class it is generally the mean score?

## Additional Learning Activities

1. There are many tests commonly used in testing programs (runs, jumps, throws). Administer one of these tests and determine the validity of it.

2. Construct a new sport-skill test. Administer the test and decide how to calculate its validity.

# Bibliography

American Psychological Association. 1985. *Standards for educational and psychological tests.* Washington, DC: APA.

Baumgartner, T. A. 1969. Stability of physical performance test scores. *Research Quarterly 40:*257–61.

———. 1974. Criterion score for multiple trial measures. *Research Quarterly 45:*193–98.

Baumgartner, T. A. and A. S. Jackson. 1970. Measurement schedules for tests of motor performance. *Research Quarterly 41:*10–17.

Berger, R. A. and A. B. Sweney. 1965. Variance and correlation coefficients. *Research Quarterly 36:*368–70.

Cattell, R. B. and G. F. Stice. 1957. *Handbook for the sixteen personality factor questionnaire.* Champaign, IL: Institute for Personality and Ability Testing.

Cureton, K. J. and G. L. Warren. 1990. Criterion-referenced standards for youth health-related fitness tests: A tutorial. *Research Quarterly for Exercise and Sport 61:*7–19.

Disch, J. 1975. Considerations for establishing a reliable and valid criterion measure for a multiple trial motor performance test. In *Proceedings of the C.I.C. Symposium on Measurement and Evaluation in Physical Education.* T. A. Baumgartner, (Ed.), Indiana University.

Disch, J. R., R. J. Frankiewicz, and A. Jackson. 1975. Construct validation of distance run tests. *Research Quarterly 46:*169–76.

Erickson, L. et al. 1946. The energy cost of horizontal and grade walking on the motor drive treadmill. *American Journal of Physiology 145:*391–401.

Ferguson, G. A. and Y. Takane. 1989. *Statistical analysis in psychology and education.* 5th ed. New York: McGraw-Hill.

Henry, F. M. 1967. Best versus average individual score. *Research Quarterly 38:*317–20.

Hetherington, R. 1973. Within subject variation, measurement error, and selection of a criterion score. *Research Quarterly 44:*113–17.

Jackson, A. W. and A. B. Baker. 1986. The relationship of the sit-and-reach test to criterion measures of hamstring and back flexibility in young females. *Research Quarterly for Exercise and Sport 57:*183–86.

Johnson, R. and D. Meeter. 1977. Estimation of maximum physical performance. *Research Quarterly 48:*74–84.

Kenyon, G. A. 1968a. A conceptual model for characterized physical activity. *Research Quarterly 39:*96–105.

———. 1968b. Six scales for assessing attitude toward physical activity. *Research Quarterly 39:*566–74.

Nunnally, J. C. 1967. *Psychometric theory.* New York: McGraw-Hill.

Safrit, M. J. 1975. Construct validity: Applications in physical education. In *Proceedings of the C.I.C. Symposium on Measurement and Evaluation in Physical Education.* T. A. Baumgartner, (Ed.), Indiana University.

———. 1977. Construct validity. In *Proceedings of the Colorado Measurement Symposium.* D. Mood, (Ed.), University of Colorado.

———. 1986. *Introduction to measurement in physical education and exercise science.* St. Louis: Times Mirror/Mosby.

———. 1990. The validity and reliability of fitness tests for children: A review. *Pediatric Exercise Science 2:*9–28.

Safrit, M. J. and M. L. Looney. 1992. Should the punishment fit the crime? A measurement dilemma. *Research Quarterly for Exercise and Sport 63:*124–27.

Safrit, M. J. and T. M. Wood. 1989. *Measurement concepts in physical education and exercise science.* Champaign, IL: Human Kinetics.

———. 1981. *Evaluation in physical education.* 2nd ed. Englewood Cliffs, NJ: Prentice-Hall.

Whitley, J. D. and L. E. Smith. 1963. Larger correlations obtained by using average rather than best strength scores. *Research Quarterly 34:*248–49.

Yates, M. E. 1977. Construct validity—Points to consider. *JOPER 48:*2, 64–65.

# Evaluating Achievement

## Key Words

final grades
natural breaks
program evaluation
rank order
teacher's standards

## Contents

## Objectives

In this chapter we discuss the differences between formative and summative evaluation and the standards used with each method. The attributes, issues, and techniques of grading show that the process is a complicated and often emotional one. There is no universal agreement among physical education teachers and exercise specialists as to which attributes are important or which grading system works best. Each issue, each technique, has its supporters; and each has its advantages and disadvantages as well. Finally, we arrive at program evaluation—which should also be part of every teacher's and exercise specialist's measurement program.

After reading Chapter 6 you should be able to:

1. Define and compare the terms evaluation, measurement, and grading.
2. Select the components for inclusion in a grading program and calculate grades using several methods.
3. Identify ways to make an evaluation system as quick and efficient as possible.
4. Outline the procedures used for evaluating programs.

# INTRODUCTION

Much of what is presented in this chapter is from the standpoint of grading, which is certainly the responsibility of a teacher, but seldom the responsibility of an exercise specialist. However, grading is actually just evaluating the participants in a program that happens to be an educational one. Exercise specialists must evaluate the participants in their programs. Thus, think of grading as individual evaluations, and it applies to teachers and exercise specialists. Adults, just like children, want to know how they compare to each other or a standard even though grades are not assigned. Much of the process and philosophical issues discussed in terms of grading have implications for exercise specialists in their evaluation program.

A teacher's primary function is to promote desirable changes in students. The same thing can be said of any exercise specialist in regard to the program participants. The type of change deemed important by the teacher and school system depends on two factors: the stated instructional objectives and the procedures used to evaluate their achievement. If the instructional process is to be meaningful, it is essential that (1) the instructional objectives be relevant, (2) the instruction be designed to achieve the objectives efficiently, and (3) the evaluation procedures reliably and validly assess student achievement.

We administer tests primarily to facilitate the achievement of instructional objectives. As noted in Chapter 1, tests can be used for placement, diagnosis, evaluation of learning, prediction, program evaluation, and motivation. Every teacher must formally or informally evaluate every student. The assignment of students to appropriate groups, the diagnosis of factors that inhibit learning, and the prediction of future success are all essential to individualized instruction. The evaluation of student achievement is tantamount to the evaluation of the instructional process, and so it is a vital part of that process. A student's failure to achieve important instructional objectives can indicate that the instructional program itself has failed and needs revision.

Student evaluation is not a popular issue with some teachers and prospective teachers, primarily because they think of it synonymously with grading. But, evaluation is more than grading. In fact, it need not result in the assignment of grades. This does not mean that grading itself is not necessary. Grading continues to be an integral part of the educational system and thus one of the teacher's responsibilities. A teacher who passes all students without regard to their level of achievement is ignoring a professional responsibility. Grading is too often a system of rewards and punishments, reflecting the teacher's frustrations and biases rather than a reliable, valid measure of student achievement.

## Evaluation

Evaluation often follows measurement, taking the form of a judgment about the quality of a performance. Suppose, for example, that each participant in a class or exercise program ran a mile, and their scores were recorded by the teacher or exercise specialist. When the person classified these measurements "excellent," "good," "poor," and so on, he or she was making an evaluation.

Evaluation can be subjective: The judge uses no set standards for each classification and/or evaluates during the performance without recording any measurements. The objectivity of evaluation increases when it is based on defined standards. Three common standards are (1) required levels of performance based on the exercise specialist's or teacher's experience and/or convictions; (2) the ranked performances of the rest of the group; and (3) existing standards, called norms.

Formative evaluation, as noted in Chapter 1, goes on during instruction or the exercise program to inform the participant and the teacher or exercise specialist of the participant's status. This information allows the teacher or exercise specialist to judge the effectiveness of the unit in progress and to make future plans. Participants are motivated by knowing the extent to which they are meeting the stated objectives. Thus, formative evaluation is both continuous throughout the teaching unit or program and related to the program's objectives.

Summative evaluation is the final measurement of participant performance at the end of the teaching unit or exercise program. In teaching it is often used to assign grades. This type of evaluation is likely to involve comparisons among students rather than comparisons with a single level of achievement. In an exercise program the summative evaluation is more likely to be a comparison of the participant's score to a performance goal set earlier or to an ideal standard.

*Criterion-Referenced Standards.*   Criterion-referenced standards represent the level of achievement that nearly all participants should be able to reach given proper instruction and ample practice. These standards are valuable to the participant because they specify the expected level of performance and to the teacher or exercise specialist because they clearly define participant status in relation to the standard.

Criterion-referenced standards must be used with explicit instructional objectives—objectives that ordinarily must be accomplished before broader objectives can be achieved. Thus, criterion-referenced standards can be used in formative evaluation to diagnose weaknesses and to determine when participants are ready to progress.

For example, the American Red Cross has developed a hierarchy of swimming skills that reflect criterion-referenced standards:

**Beginner Skills**
1. Breath holding—10 seconds
2. Rhythmic breathing—10 seconds
3. Prone glide
4. Back glide and recovery
5. Prone glide with kick
6. Back glide with kick
7. Beginner stroke or crawl stroke—15 yards
8. Combined stroke on back—15 yards

**Swimming Skills**
1. Sidestroke
2. Back crawl
3. Breaststroke
4. Crawl stroke
5. Surface dives—pike, tuck
6. Feet-first surface dive

Obviously these standards must be met if the participant is to achieve a wanted level of competence in swimming. The inability to meet a specified standard indicates that additional instruction or learning activities are needed. On both levels, summative evaluation would focus on combinations of these skills: at the upper level, for example, the distance a person can swim in 10 minutes using the breaststroke, sidestroke, crawl, and backstroke.

For an instructional unit on physical fitness, the criterion-referenced standards for ninth-grade boys might be a run of 1½ miles in 12 minutes, 35 bent-knee sit-ups in 2 minutes, and 3 pull-ups. Thus, criterion-referenced standards tend to be pass-fail. In this case, performance on all 3 tests (the sum of the T-scores) could be used to summatively evaluate the broader objective of total fitness.

In some educational systems there is a move to mastery of course content as the desired outcome. Thus, the evaluation of a student is in terms of the number of desired outcomes achieved and not in comparison to his/her peers. This is basically a competency based criterion-referenced standard situation. In the earlier swimming skills example, each student could be evaluated on how many of the standards were achieved. Passing the course is dependent on reaching a certain outcome if the outcomes are hierarchically ordered or mastering a certain number of outcomes if there is no ordering of outcomes.

Many different procedures are used to develop criterion-referenced standards. One method involves the following steps:

**Step 1**

Identify the specific behaviors that must be achieved to accomplish a broad instructional objective.

**Step 2**

Develop clearly defined instructional objectives that correspond to the specific behaviors.

**Step 3**

Develop standards that give evidence of successful achievement of the objective. These standards may be based on logic, expert opinion, research literature, and/or an analysis of test scores.

**Step 4**

Try the system and evaluate the standards. Determine whether the standards must be altered and do so if necessary.

Bloom and his associates (1971) have experimented extensively with criterion-referenced standards in the formative evaluation of knowledge tests. They specified, as indications of mastery criterion, levels of 80%–90%—high required levels of performance. But they also stated:

. . . This is arbitrary, however, and individual teachers may want to set the score for mastery higher or lower. If the accuracy level is too high (95 to 100 percent), it is likely to be obtained by only a few students; and there will be little positive reinforcement for mastery for very many students. On the other hand, if the mastery level is too low (50 to 60 percent), then a large number of students may have the illusion that they have mastered the unit of learning when in fact they have made many errors.

Because physical education teachers and exercise specialists use a variety of testing instruments that apply different units of measurement, the importance to them of evaluating and readjusting criterion-referenced standards is evident.

***Norm-Referenced Standards.*** Norm-referenced standards, those that compare the performances of peers, are useful for determining the degree to which students have achieved a broad instructional objective. In developing norm-referenced standards, levels of performance that discriminate among ability groups are specified; that is, the standards are set so that some students are classified "high ability" and some "low ability."

The traditional grading system (A,B,C,D,F) is based on norm-referenced standards. Grading and the development of norm-referenced standards are so important that much of this chapter is devoted to these two topics.

The improvement of grading practices has been an educational issue for the last fifty years. Although many suggestions for improvement have been made, changes have been few. Gronlund (1974) cites two reasons for this: (1) A single grading system that would satisfy students, parents, teachers, and school administrators may be impossible to find. (2) Efforts to improve grading have been directed more toward alternative symbols (satisfactory-unsatisfactory) for the traditional A-B-C-D-F system than toward basic issues. Also, considerable thought has been given to the value of a plus-minus system (A+, A, A–, etc.) over the traditional A to F system.

**Grading**

The grading process is twofold: (1) the selection of the measurements—either subjective or objective—that form the basis of the grade and (2) the actual calculation. Both steps can be undertaken in many different ways.

As described in the systematic model of evaluation (see Chapter 1), the instructional process begins with the instructional objectives and culminates with evaluation. The instructional objectives, then, are the basis on which the factors used to grade students are selected. These objectives may be cognitive, affective, or psychomotor, but, whatever, the test must be suited to their nature and content. Clearly, using only a written test to grade students in a unit on physical fitness would be illogical and unfair.

Not only must grades be based on important instructional objectives, but also the testing instruments must be both reliable and valid. If a test has no reliability, the scores by definition are due entirely to measurement error. Using such a test to calculate a student's grade is much like flipping a coin. Validity is a function of the instructional objectives: A test can be very reliable but unrelated to the objectives of the unit. Thus, when selecting testing instruments for grading, the teacher must ask: (1) What are the instructional objectives? (2) Were the students taught in accordance with these objectives? (3) Does the test reliably and validly measure the achievement of these objectives?

Whether they approve of them or not, most teachers are required by their school system to assign grades. Most people can remember taking courses that were excellent in terms of content and presentation, but the system for assigning grades was so bad that overall the course was not rated highly. Therefore, it is essential for the teacher not only to develop a good grading system, but to assign grades with skill, accuracy, and fairness.

The relative merits of various bases for grading have received much attention in professional books and journals. Such attributes as improvement, knowledge, sportsmanship, attitude, leadership, squad ranking in competition, and the like have all been mentioned. Each of these suggested attributes should be judged by three criteria:

**Attributes**

1. Is it a major objective of the physical education program?
2. Do all students have identical opportunities to demonstrate their ability relative to the attribute?
3. Can the attribute be reliably and validly measured?

Although evaluation is common before a unit is taught, grading of initial fitness or skill is not recommended because the teacher has yet to contribute to student ability.

Determination of improvement, then—the change in student performance from the beginning to the end of a course or unit—would seem valuable, but the process has three limitations:

1. Improvement scores tend to be unreliable.
2. Students who perform well at the beginning of a unit have less opportunity for improvement than students who start the unit poorly.
3. Students may purposely perform poorly on an initial test in order to attain impressive improvement scores.

Although sportsmanship, attitude, and leadership are wanted outcomes of physical education programs, their measurement is often difficult. Observation is the only means of determining whether a student has exhibited these three characteristics in desired amounts. Furthermore, opportunities for leadership must be extended to all students if they are to be graded on this attribute. Temper control in competition is impossible to judge if a student has never been observed in a trying situation.

Grades are sometimes based on squad rank in competition, with members of winning squads receiving higher grades than members of losing squads. This procedure operates to the advantage of those low-ability students who are on a squad with a number of high-ability students. However, the reverse is true for a high-ability student on a low-ability squad. It is unwise to allow a student's grade to be influenced by the performance of others.

## Issues

A teacher's philosophy on certain issues directly influences the grading system. There is no one correct approach to most of these issues, but you should consider them before developing a grading system. Remember that teachers communicate their values in their grading procedures.

If grades are assigned, it is only fair to explain to the students at the start of the course how grades will be determined. Thus, the teacher should plan the grading system before the course begins. Planning usually works, not only to lessen student complaints about assigned grades, but also to make it easier and faster to assign grades.

Grades should be based on a sufficient amount of evidence to be valid and reliable. One trial where multiple trials of a test were possible or one comprehensive exam at the end of the course is not likely to be sufficient evidence. The worst objective testing situation we can envision for a tests and measurement course is one test at the end of the course composed of one true-false question. If the student answers the question correctly, the student receives a high grade; otherwise???

The distribution of grades in summative evaluation is a controversial issue. Should physical educators, like teachers of classroom subjects, use A-B-C-D-F grades? Note that a teacher grading A through F is equivalent to an exercise specialist evaluating participants in a fitness program as excellent, above average, average, below average, or poor. Low grades tend to discourage students from continuing with a given subject once basic requirements are fulfilled. In science programs, for example, the grades D and F are assigned to discourage low-ability students from continuing to take science courses. This means that by the senior year in high school only a select group of students is still in the program. (Of course, because only the better students continue to take courses, a smaller percentage of low grades should be given in advanced courses. For example, more As and Bs should be assigned in a senior-level course than in a junior-level course.) Physical education programs are not developed along these discriminatory lines. In an effort to encourage all students—despite their ability—to continue in the program, many physical educators assign only grades A, B, and C. The equivalence to an A-B-C grading system for an exercise specialist might be classifying participants in a fitness program as above average, average, or below average but better still would be classifying participants as excellent, above average, or average.

Another consideration that relates to the distribution of grades is whether the general quality of the class, or differences among classes, should affect the assignment or distribution of grades. With ability-grouped classes, it seems unfair to assign grades A through F in each class because every student in a high-ability class would probably have received a C or better if ability grouping were not used. On the other hand, grading A through C in a high-ability class, B through D in a middle-ability class, and C through F in a low-ability class is unfair because it makes no allowance for the misclassification of students. A high-ability student could loaf and still receive a C, while a middle-ability overachiever could never earn an A.

A philosophy endorsed by many experienced teachers and most measurement specialists is that the grade a student receives should not depend on (1) the semester or year in which the class is taken; (2) the instructor (if several instructors teach the course); or (3) the other students in the course. Thus, standards should not change from semester to semester or year to year unless the course itself has been changed or upgraded. For example, if 65 sit-ups represent an A for seventh graders this semester, the same should apply next semester. Likewise, if 65 sit-ups represents an A from one instructor, the same should be true for all instructors. Inherent in this philosophy is the principle that all students should be evaluated by the same standards. Two examples may clarify this point:

1. An instructor teaches five ungrouped eleventh-grade classes, which are combined for grading purposes. The top 20% of the combined group receive As, the next 30% receive Bs, and the remaining students receive Cs. If grades had been allotted in the same percentages but assigned by classes, a student's grade would depend on those of the other students in the class. Thus, it would be possible for two students with identical scores to receive different grades if one were in a class with many good performers and the other in a class with many poor performers.

2. An instructor teaches three ability-grouped classes of eighth graders and two ability-grouped classes of ninth graders. The eighth-grade classes are composed of high, middle, and low achievers; the ninth-grade class, of low and middle achievers. Because of the age difference, higher grading standards are applied to the ninth graders than to the eighth graders, but the grading standards for each grade are applied consistently to all classes in that grade.

The teacher must decide whether a grade represents only achievement or student effort as well. The teacher must also decide what type of student achievement (fitness, skill, knowledge) should be considered and how each should be weighted in the grade.

Usually school policy governs certain issues, among them the type of grade assigned (A-B-C-D-F or pass-fail), although the teacher may have a choice. Letter grades are by far the most prevalent, but pass-fail grading is gaining popularity. This system reduces the competitive pressure of letter grading and encourages students to explore new subject areas. However, the system also provides less information about student ability.

If pass-fail grades are assigned, the teacher must decide whether, in reality, anyone will fail. It seems that in many classes, if students attend class regularly, they will not receive a failing grade. Also, the teacher must decide how much information is needed on each student to assign a grade of pass or fail. Possibly less information on each student is needed with a pass-fail system than with a letter-grade system. Finally, the teacher must decide on the standard for a passing grade. Is passing equivalent to a C or a D in a letter grade system?

## Methods

Of the four methods to be discussed, no single method of assigning grades is best for all situations or all teachers. Ordinarily, each method yields a unique distribution of grades. For example, a student who is on the borderline between an A and a B may receive an A with one grading method and a B with another. Thus, it is vital that the teacher understand the advantages and disadvantages of each grading method in order to select the one best suited to the situation. Also, these methods are not restricted to assigning grades. The exercise specialist can use these methods for classifying participants in a program. As suggested earlier in this chapter, a grade of A and a classification of excellent are equivalent.

*Natural Breaks.* When scores are ordered by rank, gaps usually occur in their distribution. The teacher may make each such break a cut-off point between letter grades as shown in Table 6.1. This is a norm-referenced standard.

The other methods to be discussed require that the teacher decide what letter grades are possible (e.g., A to F, or A to C) and usually what percentage of the students should receive each letter grade. This is not required with the **natural breaks** method. In theory, if there were no breaks in the distribution of scores, all students would receive the same grade. For the teacher who does not believe in specifying the possible grades and percentages for these grades, this is a useful method. Thus, the method has some characteristics of a criterion-referenced standard.

Although used by some teachers, this method is the poorest of the four listed here. It provides no semester-to-semester consistency and makes each student's grade dependent on the performance of other students in the class. If, in another year, the breaks in the distribution occur in different places, the cut-off points between letter grades change, as is evident in the table.

*Teacher's Standard.* Some teachers base grades on their own perceptions of what is fair and appropriate, without analyzing any data. For example, a teacher's standard for a 100-point knowledge test might be A, 93–100; B, 88–92; C, 79–87; D, 70–78; F, 0–69. If the teacher uses the same standard year after year, the grades will be consistent. Furthermore, a student's grade does not depend on the performance of other students in the class: Each student who scores 93 points or more receives an A. This is a fine method if the teacher's standards are realistic in terms of the students' abilities and if measurements are quite reliable and valid. First-year teachers, and teachers working with students younger than they are familiar with, tend to misuse this method by setting their standards too high.

**Table 6.1** Two Sets of Grades Assigned by Natural Breaks

| First Semester | | | Second Semester | | |
|---|---|---|---|---|---|
| x | f | | x | f | |
| 98 | 1 | | 92 | 1 | |
| 95 | 1 | A | 91 | 2 | |
| 93 | 2 | | 90 | 1 | A |
| 92 | 3 | | 89 | 2 | |
| | | | 88 | 2 | |
| 88 | 4 | | 87 | 3 | |
| 87 | 5 | | | | |
| 85 | 7 | B | 82 | 6 | |
| 84 | 7 | | 80 | 8 | |
| 83 | 6 | | 79 | 7 | B |
| | | | 78 | 11 | |
| 77 | 8 | | | | |
| 76 | 14 | | 73 | 12 | |
| 75 | 10 | C | 72 | 11 | |
| 72 | 5 | | 71 | 14 | C |
| | | | 70 | 6 | |
| 65 | 2 | | 68 | 1 | |
| 60 | 1 | D | | | |

The **teacher's standards** are norm-referenced, but the procedure used to develop them is very similar to that of criterion-referenced standards, in that standards are set by the teacher with no thought as to what percentage of the class receives a given grade. In theory, the entire class could receive As or Fs.

If the teacher's standards were used in a pass-fail or competent-incompetent system, the standards would be criterion-referenced. Again, in theory the entire class could be judged competent. Many teachers have difficulty selecting the standard for competence; there are no guidelines. The teacher must choose a standard that he or she believes is fair. This standard often becomes one of minimum competence. For example, the teacher might decide that hitting one out of five shots from the free-throw line in basketball is minimum competence.

One way minimum competence might be determined is by deciding what grade in a letter system corresponds to competent or pass. The letter grade D is defined as a low pass or minimum competence by some educators; it is defined as a "charity grade" by others who would assign a competent grade with a C or higher. In most colleges, the instructor does not know which students are taking a graded class on a pass-fail basis. He or she assigns a letter grade to each student, which is converted to a pass in the records office for letter grades of D or better.

*Rank Order.* **Rank order** is a straightforward, norm-referenced method of grading. The teacher decides what letter grades will be assigned and what percentage of the class should receive each letter grade; the scores are then ordered, and grades are assigned.

**Table 6.2** Rank-Ordered Scores

| x | f | | x | f | | x | f | | x | f | |
|---|---|---|---|---|---|---|---|---|---|---|---|
| 78 | 1 | | 64 | 4 | | 60 | 8 | | 51 | 2 | |
| 70 | 2 | A | 62 | 5 | B | 59 | 6 | C | 48 | 1 | D |
| 66 | 4 | | 61 | 5 | | 58 | 5 | | 41 | 1 | |
| 65 | 4 | | | | | 57 | 2 | | | | |

For example, assume there are 50 students in a class, and the teacher decides to assign grades as follows: As to 20% of the class, or 10 students [(.20)(50)]; Bs to 30% of the class, or 15 students [(.30)(50)]; Cs to 40% of the class, or 20 students [(.40)(50)]; and Ds to 10% of the class, or 5 students [(.10)(50)]. Now look at the scores and frequency distribution in Table 6.2. In the table, the first 10 scores were supposed to be As, but a choice had to be made between 7 or 11 As. It was decided to use 11 because that number was closer to the wanted number of As. To make up for the extra A, only 14 Bs were given. Then a choice had to be made between 19 or 21 Cs. The reasons for giving 21 rather than 19 Cs are twofold: (1) it is preferable to give the higher grade in borderline cases, and (2) a distinct natural break occurs below score 57.

Among the advantages of the rank-order method are that it is quick and easy to use and that it makes a student's grade dependent on his or her rank-order position rather than the instructor's feelings about the student. The system also allows grades to be distributed as wanted.

A disadvantage of the method is that a student's grade depends on the performance of other students in the class. A student with average ability will receive a higher grade in a class with low-ability students than in a class with high-ability students. Another disadvantage is that no allowance is made for the quality of the class: A certain proportion of students must get high grades and a certain proportion must get low grades. For large heterogeneous classes, in which all levels of ability are represented, this is probably not a bad method; however, it is not recommended for small or ability-grouped classes unless the teacher adjusts the percentages in light of the quality of each class. Teachers who use the rank-order method obtain grade standards that vary from semester to semester and year to year, depending on the quality of their class.

***Norms.*** Norms are performance standards based on the analysis of data, not on a subjective standard chosen by a teacher. If norm-referenced standards are being used, norms are the best type of standard. Norms are developed by gathering scores for a large number of individuals of similar age, gender, ability, and other characteristics to the subjects with whom the norms will be used. These data are statistically analyzed, and performance standards are then constructed on the basis of the analysis. Norms have many advantages over other types of standards. First, they are unaffected by the performance of the group or the class being evaluated. For example, if it is considered excellent to run the mile in 10 minutes, all the students in the class can excel if they can run the mile within that time. Another advantage is that new performance standards need not be developed each year; once norms are developed, they usually can be used for 2 to 5 years. Also, because the same standards are used to evaluate several different groups or classes of students, the grades have a high degree of consistency—a given grade indicates the same degree of ability for each group.

There are many sources for norms. (Examples are given in Chapters 8 through 11.) Statewide tests often provide norms for that state; local norms for an entire school system are not uncommon; and teachers can develop norms using the scores of former students. Although norms should be developed using the scores of students similar to those on whom the norms will be used, this is unlikely to be true of national and state norms. Teacher-developed norms are probably fairest to the students.

Norms are often used by exercise specialists to interpret the performance of adults in their fitness and rehabilitation programs. The performance score of a subject must be evaluated by comparing it to the performance of a reference group before the score has any meaning. The norms based on this reference group reflect the expected performance for each participant. This is not to suggest that the same norms are used on all participants. Norms are usually gender and age specific and often health-status specific.

The first step in developing norms is the administration of the same test each year under the same conditions as much as is possible for 2 to 5 years, until several hundred scores have been collected. These scores are then analyzed and used to develop norms that can be employed for the next 2 to 5 years. At the end of this time, several hundred more test scores have been collected, and the test is renormed. The advantages of this procedure are numerous. Because the norms are based on recent student performances, they are applicable to students currently in the class. When combined, scores collected in different years tend to cancel out any differences among years in terms of the quality of the students, and thus represent typical performance. (Norms developed on the scores of students from a single year are not representative if the students are not typical.) Because students and conditions change, norms should be revised every few years. And if major changes are made in the curriculum, norms may need to be revised.

Depending on the needs of the teacher, percentile-rank norms, T-score norms (see Chapter 3), or letter-grade norms may be constructed. Probably because they are easier to explain to students and parents, percentile-rank norms are used more often than T-score norms. In deciding on a type of norm, determine how the norms will be used and then choose the type that best meets your needs. Percentile-rank norms are easily understood and indicate how a student's performance ranks relative to his or her peers. However, they should not be added together to obtain a composite score based on several measures. If you will eventually need a composite score, choose T-score norms. If students understand T-scores, they can determine their approximate class ranks for a single test. Furthermore, if several tests have been administered, they can easily determine from their T-score norms the test on which they performed best. For example, if on 3 different tests a student had T-scores of 55, 62, and 48 respectively, he or she could identify the second test as the best performance. Examples of percentile-rank and T-score norms are shown in Tables 6.3 and 6.4.

For grading purposes, letter-grade norms must be developed. The teacher's task is to determine the test scores that constitute each letter grade to be assigned. For example, the letter-grade norms for a one-minute sit-up test for boys might be A, 59–70; B, 47–58; C, 35–46; D, 20–34; F, 0–19 using the percentile-rank norms in Table 6.3. These letter-grade norms are developed based on the decision to, over multiple years, assign basically 10% As, 30% Bs, 45% Cs, 15% Ds, and 0% Fs to students evaluated with these standards. The A-grade standard is obtained by observing in Table 6.3 that a score of 59 for boys corresponds to the 90th percentile, so 10% of the scores are 59 or larger. The minimum score to obtain a grade of B is determined by

**Table 6.3**  Sample Percentile-Rank Norms for a One-Minute Sit-Up Test

| Percentile | Boys | Girls | Percentile | Boys | Girls |
|---|---|---|---|---|---|
| 100th | 70 | 60 | 45th | 44 | 33 |
| 95th | 61 | 54 | 40th | 43 | 32 |
| 90th | 59 | 52 | 35th | 41 | 31 |
| 85th | 56 | 49 | 30th | 40 | 30 |
| 80th | 54 | 45 | 25th | 38 | 29 |
| 75th | 51 | 42 | 20th | 36 | 28 |
| 70th | 50 | 40 | 15th | 35 | 27 |
| 65th | 48 | 39 | 10th | 30 | 23 |
| 60th | 47 | 36 | 5th | 28 | 20 |
| 55th | 46 | 35 | 0 | 20 | 15 |
| 50th | 45 | 33 | | | |

**Table 6.4**  Sample T-Score Norms for a Distance Run

| T-Score | 6-Lap Run | T-Score | 6-Lap Run |
|---|---|---|---|
| 80 | 287 | 48 | 458 |
| 78 | 297 | 46 | 468 |
| 76 | 308 | 44 | 479 |
| 74 | 319 | 42 | 490 |
| 72 | 330 | 40 | 500 |
| 70 | 340 | 38 | 511 |
| 68 | 351 | 36 | 522 |
| 66 | 362 | 34 | 532 |
| 64 | 372 | 32 | 543 |
| 62 | 383 | 30 | 554 |
| 60 | 394 | 28 | 564 |
| 58 | 404 | 26 | 575 |
| 56 | 415 | 24 | 586 |
| 54 | 426 | 22 | 597 |
| 52 | 436 | 20 | 607 |
| 50 | 447 | | |

going to the 60th percentile in Table 6.3. This method of developing letter-grade norms is similar to the rank order method discussed earlier. However, these letter-grade norms could have been developed using any of the other methods previously discussed. No matter what method is used, this grading standard is used each time the one-minute sit-up test is administered. Ideally these letter-grade norms are developed on the basis of an analysis of the one-minute sit-up scores of students who have taken the test in the past.

A second example of the use of norms involves a physical fitness test with seven items. For each of the seven items, local T-score norms have been developed. When the test is administered, T-scores do not have to be calculated but can be assigned by using the norms. The sum of the T-scores for the seven items in the test is the student's fitness score. Letter-grade norms corresponding to these fitness scores have been developed:

A, 420→; B, 385–419; C, 315–384; D, 245–314; F, ← 244.

Notice that any of the grading methods discussed here can be used to develop letter-grade norms. The teacher's standard is sometimes used, but the rank-order method is more common.

At the end of a grading period a final grade must be assigned on the basis of all the information available on each student. There are many approaches to the assignment of this grade, some very simple, others more complex. The information available, the manner in which it is recorded, and the commitment of the teacher to fairly assign grades influence both the approach chosen and the time required for the procedure.

**Final Grades**

It is definitely to the teacher's advantage to adopt a simple, quick method of assigning final grades. Some teachers spend countless hours determining grades at the end of each grading period. To be fair to the students and to have a workable system, the teacher should choose a grading system before the course begins. Preplanning allows the teacher to announce the system at the beginning of the course, telling the students on what they will be measured and what standards they must meet. Preplanning is also to the teacher's advantage, allowing many time-consuming problems to be eliminated in advance.

The three common methods of assigning **final grades** are (1) the sum of the letter grades, (2) a point system, and (3) the sum of the T-scores.

***Sum of the Letter Grades.*** This method is used when test scores reflect different units of measure that cannot be summed. The scores on each test are translated into letter grades, and the letter grades, in turn, are translated into points. The sum of these points is used to assign each student a final grade.

Many teachers believe this method is quicker than translating test scores into T scores, but it is probably at best only slightly faster than calculating T-scores by hand as described in Chapter 3.

If this method is selected, a plus-and-minus system should be used when assigning letter grades to each measure. If an A-B-C-D-F system is used for a given test, only 5 scores are possible (A is 4, B is 3, C is 2, D is 1, F is 0); a plus-and-minus system allows 15 possible scores (A+ is 14, A is 13, A– is 12, and so on, including F+ and F– values). (The final grades do not have to include pluses and minuses, which are seldom recorded on transcripts.)

To compute the final grade using the plus-and-minus system, we convert the student's letter grade on each test to points, add the points, and divide the sum by the total number of tests. This point value, the mean of the student's scores, is then converted back to a letter grade. For example, in Table 6.5, the student's scores on five tests are changed from letter grades to points and then added. The total, 45, is then divided by the number of tests. The student's mean grade in points, 9, is then converted back into a letter grade, B–.

**Table 6.5** Sample Grades and Points for Calculating a Final Grade

| Test | Grade | Points |
|------|-------|--------|
| Sit-ups | B+ | 11 |
| Pull-ups | B | 10 |
| Distance run | C+ | 8 |
| Volleyball | C– | 6 |
| Tumbling | B | 10 |
| | | 45 |

**Table 6.6** Sample Grades and Points for the Best Student in the Class

| Test | Grade | Points |
|------|-------|--------|
| Sit-ups | A | 13 |
| Pull-ups | A– | 12 |
| Distance run | A– | 12 |
| Volleyball | B+ | 11 |
| Tumbling | B+ | 11 |
| | | Sum = 59 |

This process has several drawbacks. In the first place, it is a waste of time to calculate the mean. By multiplying each of the plus-and-minus values by the number of grades per student, we can express the final grade standards in terms of total points—A+ is 70 [(5)(14)], A is 65 [(5)(13)], and so on. In the second place, no allowance is made in the final grade for the regression effect—the tendency for individuals who score exceptionally high or low on one measure to score closer to the mean performance of the group on a second. Thus, a student who earns an A or an F on one test is likelier on the next to earn a grade closer to C than to repeat the first performance. The regression effect phenomenon always exists and must be allowed for in assigning final grades. Thus, it would be unusual for a student to receive an A on each of five tests, although a superior student sometimes does. It is much more common to find the best student in the class receiving grades like those in Table 6.6.

Now, according to our standards, a student needs 60 points [(12)(5)] to receive an A– in the course. If the teacher makes no allowance for the regression effect, the best student in the class (grades shown in Table 6.6) will receive a B+, and no one in the class will get an A. In fact, if no allowance is made for the regression effect, very few final grades will be high or low; most students will receive grades in the middle of the possible range.

To allow for the regression effect, the teacher might decide to give the student with 59 points an A– because the student's total is closer to an A– than a B+. Another procedure is to lower the standards when assigning final grades. For example, the teacher might decide that any student who earns at least 3 As and 2 Bs will receive an A in the course. This means that 58 points are needed to earn an A when the final grade is based on five tests and an A+ is 14 points.

If such an arbitrary adjustment is made, it must be done for each letter grade. In the bottom half of the grading system, the adjustment must be up rather than down to allow for individuals below the mean regressing up toward the mean. But you must be careful in making arbitrary adjustments. If upward adjustments are made in the bottom half of the grading system, it is possible for a student to receive a final grade lower than any grade received on a test.

Rather than make arbitrary adjustments in the total number of points needed for each final grade, it might be better to calculate the total points earned by each student and use the rank-order, or norms method to assign final grades.

All tests need not be given equal weight in calculating a student's total points. If, using the grades in Table 6.6, the instructor wants 30% of a student's final grade to represent fitness (scores on sit-ups, pull-ups, and the distance run) and the other two grades to represent 35% each, the following procedure can be used:

$$\text{Final grade} = .10 \,(\text{sit-ups} + \text{pull-ups} + \text{distance run})$$
$$+ .35 \,(\text{volleyball} + \text{tumbling})$$

$$= (.10)(13 + 12 + 12) + (.35)(11 + 11)$$

$$= (.10)(37) + (.35)(22)$$

$$= 3.7 + 7.7$$

$$= 11.4 \,(\text{B+ or A--})$$

The calculation of final grades with unequally weighted tests is very common, but it can also be time-consuming when there are a large number of tests and/or students to grade. To save time, the teacher can use a calculator or microcomputer.

*Problem 6.2.* At the end of a tennis unit you have assigned the following weights to the 6 grades that will make up the final grade: rally test, 20%; serve test, 20%; improvement, 5%; daily work, 10%; game observation, 5%; final exam, 40%. A student's scores on the items were C, B, A+, C+, C+, and C respectively.

*Solution.* When using a calculator the points from each multiplication can be summed in memory as the multiplications take place. Using 14 is an A+, 13 is A, etc., the calculation is as follows:

**Step 1**
Rally test, 20% of C is .20 times 7 is 1.4.

**Step 2**
Put 1.4 in the calculator memory.

**Step 3**

Serve test, 20% of B is .20 times 10 is 2.

**Step 4**

Add 2 to the calculator memory. (There is now 3.4 [1.4 + 2] in memory.)

The process would continue for each grade and its weight, with the final 3 steps as follows:

**Step 11**

Final exam, 40% of C is .40 times 7 is 2.8.

**Step 12**

Add 2.8 to the calculator memory.

**Step 13**

Display the sum in memory, which is 8.10 and a C+.

The calculation of final grades with unequally weighted tests using the microcomputer would involve having a program with the letter grade point values and test weightings already entered into the program so all that would have to be entered for each student would be the letter grades. Then the computer would do the calculations much like in *Problem 6.2* and provide an answer. Grading programs like this are presently available commercially or can be easily written or developed on a spreadsheet program.

*Point Systems.*   Point systems are often used by classroom teachers so that all test scores are in the same unit of measure and can be easily combined. In physical education activity classes, point systems require a great deal of planning and the development of norms. A sample point system is shown in Table 6.7. To construct this system, the total number of points was chosen, points were allotted to the various activities, and standards were developed for each activity—that is, how many sit-ups earn 8 points, 7 points, and so on.

**Table 6.7**  Sample Point System for an Activity Course

| | | | |
|---|---|---|---|
| I.  Physical ability | | | 70 points |
|    A.  Fitness | | 24 points | |
|        1.  sit-ups | 8 points | | |
|        2.  pull-ups | 8 points | | |
|        3.  distance run | 8 points | | |
|    B.  Volleyball | | 24 points | |
|        1.  serving test | 8 points | | |
|        2.  set or spike test | 8 points | | |
|        3.  game play | 8 points | | |
|    C.  Tumbling | | 22 points | |
|        1.  11 stunts | 2 points each | | |
| II.  Knowledge | | | 20 points |
|    40 questions | ½ point each | | |
| III.  Subjective | | | 10 points |
|    Instructor's assessment of effort, improvement, attitude, attendance, and the like. | | | |

An instructor using the point system in Table 6.7 would have 3 fitness scores, 3 volleyball scores, a tumbling score, a knowledge score, and a subjective score in the record book. Thus, 9 scores must be summed before assigning a final grade, a procedure made easier if certain scores are combined before the calculation of final grades. For example, at the end of the fitness unit, the 3 fitness scores could be combined to form a single score. If the same thing is done at the end of the volleyball unit, only 5 scores have to be summed to calculate the final grade.

*Sum of the T-Scores.*   When the units of measurement on a series of tests differ, some teachers translate the test scores into letter grades and the letter grades into points, and then sum the points. Another alternative is to change the test scores to T-scores and sum the T-scores, as discussed in Chapter 3. Obviously it is possible to weight each test differently in summing the T-scores by using the procedures outlined for weighting letter-grade points.

## Program Evaluation

The **program evaluation** of instructional physical education has focused on their physical characteristics. Score cards (Bookwalter 1962; LaPorte 1955a, b) have been used to determine whether the learning environment—the facilities, professional staff, curriculum, equipment, and supplies—meets specified criteria. Evaluation specialists (Wittrock & Wiley 1970), however, view the learning environment as one of the least important factors in evaluating an instructional program: A school system may have excellent facilities and equipment, trained faculty, and a published curriculum guide, and still produce little teaching or learning.

The success of an instructional program depends less on its physical characteristics than on the manner in which they are used in the instructional process. Thus, student performance offers the most valid index of the success of a program. The most crucial question is: Are students achieving important instructional objectives? If they are not, there is a need for change.

Similar statements can be made about an adult fitness program. The best facilities, staff, and program on paper cannot guarantee a successful program. Obviously a serious lack of these three essential attributes will be detrimental to a program. However, the most important indication of the success of an adult fitness program is whether participants are benefiting from the program and program objectives are being met. Both formative and summative procedures can be used to judge program effectiveness.

## Data Collection for Program Evaluation

Some data must be available in order to do program evaluation. This data may be the result of testing or good daily record keeping. For the teacher it is primarily a result of testing. Much of the data for the exercise specialist may be the result of good record keeping. In both cases some forethought and planning must occur so that data is collected and available to do the program evaluation. The teacher commonly tests students at the beginning and end of a teaching unit or school year. The exercise specialist should be doing some fitness testing, but, in addition, the exercise specialist should be keeping daily records in terms of important outcomes on each participant such as attendance, amount of exercise, intensity of exercise, estimated calories burned, weight, resting and exercise heart rate, etc. Without periodic testing and good record keeping it is impossible to document improvement in program participants. With

**Figure 6.1**
Output of a computer
program to evaluate the
use of a fitness facility.

**MEMBER MANAGEMENT SYSTEM GENERAL STATISTICS**
**Report for Director**
**Dates: 06/01/86 thru 06/01/88**

|  | Male | Female | Composite |
|---|---|---|---|
| Number of Active Members | 227 | 292 | 519 |
| Number of New Members | 87 | 117 | 204 |
| Number of Memberships Expired | 8 | 7 | 15 |
| Number of Members Who Quit | 26 | 63 | 89 |
| Number of Members Who Checked In | 174 | 218 | 392 |
| Number of Members Who Logged | 157 | 199 | 356 |
| Number of Fitness Profiles | 118 | 144 | 262 |
| Number of Health-Life Assessments | 1 | 0 | 1 |
| Number of Sessions at the Facility | 4542 | 4756 | 9298 |
| Number of Activities Logged | 12965 | 10896 | 23861 |
| Total Calories Burned ($\times$ 1000) | 3672.4 | 1820.7 | 5493.1 |
| Average Calories Burned/Session | 619 | 302 | 459 |
| Average Calories Burned/Activity | 283 | 167 | 230 |
| Average Aerobic Minutes/Session | 18 | 16 | 17 |
| Average Aerobic Minutes/Activity | 8 | 8 | 8 |
| Average Aerobic Points/Session | 9 | 4 | 6 |
| Average Aerobic Points/Activity | 4 | 2 | 3 |

many participants in a program and considerable information collected daily, record keeping is a big problem. Before starting an exercise program considerable thought needs to be done as to how to store and retrieve this data with a computer. It is not uncommon for a staff person to enter the data daily or the participant to enter the data at the end of a session. Computer programs are available to provide a detailed evaluation of the use of a fitness facility (see Figure 6.1).

Barrow, McGee, and Tritschler (1989) have a chapter on program evaluation. They present an excellent discussion of program evaluation issues and several instruments for evaluating physical education, intramural, and athletic programs.

## Formative Evaluation

Evaluation is the process of judging performance with reference to an established standard. The qualities and levels of performance that an adult fitness program is designed to produce are reflected in its stated instructional objectives and criterion-referenced standards. Let us assume that one of a program's instructional objectives is the development of (1) muscular strength and endurance of the arms, (2) muscular strength and endurance of the abdominal muscles, and (3) cardiorespiratory endurance. The tests and criterion-referenced standards are 3 two-arm barbell curls with 25 pounds, 25 bent-knee sit-ups, and a run of 1 mile in 10 minutes.

The formative evaluation of a program is the determination of the extent to which the stated standards are being achieved. The program developers may establish as a criterion that 80% of all participants should achieve these goals. Progress toward the goal is easily determined by calculating the percentage of participants who achieved the criterion-referenced standard for each fitness test. For example, assume that the percentage of participants who achieved these criterion-referenced standards is as listed in Table 6.8.

**Table 6.8** Percentage of Adult Fitness Program Participants Who Achieved the Criterion-Referenced Standards for Three Fitness Tests

| Test | 1989 | 1990 | 1991 |
|------|------|------|------|
| Two-arm curl | 80 | 79 | 83 |
| Bent-knee sit-up | 90 | 93 | 91 |
| 1-Mile run | 40 | 75 | 84 |

The program goal of 80% achievement was not reached in 1989 with the 1-mile run, which indicates that the instructional program failed in this aspect. The exercise specialist must analyze this failure and make an instructional decision. Several interpretations are possible. First, more aerobic conditioning activities may be needed. Second, it may be that the 10-minute criterion is an unrealistic standard for participants; perhaps it should be lowered to 12 minutes. Third, the value of the instructional objective may be questioned, and the objective retained or dropped.

The success of formative program evaluation depends directly on the selection of important, well-defined instructional objectives and the establishment of realistic standards. The failure to achieve a stated standard is thus a reliable indication that something is wrong. The value of formative program evaluation is that it signals that something is wrong while action can still be taken. In this sense, evaluation is a continuous process.

## Summative Evaluation in Schools

The success of an instructional program is reflected in the degree of achievement of its broad objectives. Such success can usually be judged by comparing student performance to some norm. For this type of evaluation, published national, statewide, or local norms can serve as the basis for comparison.

It is common to compare a school's performance with national or statewide norms. For example, the mean performance of students from a given school or district might be compared to the national norms that accompany the AAHPER Physical Best Test (1988) to determine whether the mean is above or below the 50th percentile ($P_{50}$ = Median = Mean in normal curve) (see Chapter 3). Although this procedure does stimulate interest, it also has several disadvantages. First, tests with national or statewide norms may not reflect the true objectives of the school district. For example, if the general objectives of a school were directed primarily toward motor-skill development, the national norms for a fitness test would not validly apply. A second disadvantage arises from the geographic and environmental factors that affect performance. Often, the testing conditions used by a school district are not similar to those used to develop national norms.

We agree with Safrit (1981) that local norms offer the most realistic basis for summative program evaluation. Although it is quite likely that all schools in a given system will be above the national norms, several of them may score considerably lower than others, indicating a need for program improvement.

**Table 6.9** Summative Evaluation of Weight Training

| Test | Norm Sample | | Fall 1994 Sample | |
|------|------|------|------|------|
| | Mean | Standard Deviation | Mean | Standard Deviation |
| 1. Dips | 17.30 | 6.65 | 19.40 | 6.91 |
| 2. Sit-ups | 24.71 | 8.17 | 25.09 | 7.70 |
| 3. Lat pull | 27.33 | 9.47 | 34.09 | 12.70 |
| 4. Arm curl | 23.45 | 9.89 | 28.02 | 9.77 |
| 5. Bench press | 17.85 | 8.34 | 23.39 | 8.69 |

Table 6.9 presents the means and standard deviations for an instructional unit on weight training. The local norm sample represents the performance of over 500 students; the Fall 1994 sample represents the performance of a group of students being compared to the established norms. As you can see, the average performance of the Fall 1994 group exceeded that of the norm group, indicating that the program is functioning properly in light of these objectives. If a school's means are considerably lower than the local norms, action can be taken to identify and correct the difficulty. If the means become progressively larger over succeeding years, this may be objective evidence that the program is improving.

## Summative Evaluation in Adult Fitness

The success of an adult fitness program can usually be judged by comparing participant performance to some norm. For this type of evaluation, published national standards or local standards can serve as the basis for comparison. Standards have been developed for body composition (see Chapter 10) and aerobic fitness (see Chapter 9).

A useful way to judge the quality of an adult fitness program is to evaluate the number who continue to exercise on a regular basis. The drop-out rate of many poor programs is extremely high. Another method that is being used is the use of caloric expenditure (see Figure 6.1). At many computerized fitness centers, participants log their exercise into a computer, and these data can be used for program evaluation. As shown in Chapter 1, caloric expenditure is related to health.

## Program Improvement

Evaluation is a decision-making process that works toward program improvement. The adoption of appropriate standards is essential for program evaluation and improvement. Bloom and his associates (1971) report that formative evaluation leads to higher-level achievement of objectives, evaluated summatively. Furthermore, the use of criterion- and norm-referenced standards helps the students or fitness program participants to determine expected levels of performance. People tend to strive to exceed standards. The use of explicit, realistic, and improvement standards, then, is necessary, not only for program evaluation, but also for motivation. A primary objective of program developers should be improved participant performance over time.

**Summary**

The method and rationale for student or fitness program participant evaluation should be determined by the instructional objectives and content of the course. It is crucial that evaluation be based on reliable, valid information and that the process be carefully planned and explained to the people in the program.

Before evaluating a class, the teacher must decide whether formative or summative evaluation is wanted. For summative evaluation, one of the grading methods described in the chapter—or a combination of several—can be used. We cannot stress enough the importance of deciding in advance how final grades will be determined.

Regular measurement and analysis of scores are essential to the ongoing process of evaluating the physical education and adult fitness program.

**Formative Evaluation of Objectives**

*Objective 1* Define and compare the terms evaluation, measurement, and grading.

1. In discussing the broad topic of evaluation the terms measurement, grading, and summative and formative evaluation often are mentioned. In your own words, discuss how these terms are related to the broad topic of evaluation.

2. Many people feel strongly that grades should be eliminated. Is it possible that they are frustrated with the faculty techniques used to assign grades rather than the idea of grades? Explain your answer.

*Objective 2* Select the components for inclusion in a grading program and calculate grades using several methods.

1. There are certain attributes commonly used for determining grades in physical education. Also, as suggested in the text, grading programs themselves have desired characteristics. There are several different methods that can be used to assign grades. Considering these three points, outline the grading procedure you would like to use as a teacher.

2. Whatever method you select for assigning grades, it is important that you apply it accurately. Below are three situations to give you practice in using the various grading methods discussed in the text.

   a. Using the rank-order method, assign letter grades for the first-semester scores in Table 6.1, assuming As, 20%; Bs, 30%; Cs, 45%; and Ds, 5%.
   b. Using the percentages in part (a) and the norms in Table 6.3, what are the scores for an A, B, C, and D for girls on the one-minute sit-up test?
   c. Using a plus-and-minus grading system with A+ = 14, A = 13, etc., what final grade would you assign a student based on the tests and percentages below?

| Test | Percentage of Final Grade | Student's Grade |
|------|---------------------------|-----------------|
| 1    | 15%                       | C–              |
| 2    | 25                        | B–              |
| 3    | 35                        | B               |
| 4    | 25                        | B+              |

*Objective 3*  Identify ways to make an evaluation system as quick and efficient as possible.

1. A common reason for not using an extensive evaluation system in physical education is lack of time. It is true that physical educators have large classes and that it does take time to combine scores from different tests and to grade knowledge tests, but with good planning, the time involved in administering an evaluation system could be minimized. List at least 5 ways to make an evaluation system as quick and efficient to administer as possible.

2. A common reason for not using an extensive evaluation/record keeping system in adult fitness is lack of time. It is true that fitness specialists often have a large number of participants and testing/record keeping is time-consuming, but with good planning more could be done. List at least 5 ways to make an evaluation/record keeping system efficient.

3. Which 3 procedures in question 1 do you think would be easiest to implement? Defend your choices.

4. Which 3 procedures in question 2 do you think would be easiest to implement? Defend your choices.

*Objective 4*  Outline the procedures used for evaluating programs.

1. Evaluation of the instructional program is an important part of the total measurement. In your own words, indicate the importance of both formative and summative evaluation.

## Additional Learning Activities

1. Interview faculty members at your school and in the local school system. Determine what attributes they consider in their grading systems, what methods they use for assigning grades, and what grading system (A-B-C-D-F, pass-fail) they use.

2. Interview fitness specialists about their evaluation/record-keeping system or survey the literature as to what is being done in some big adult fitness programs.

## Bibliography

Barrow, H. M., R. McGee, and K. A. Tritschler. 1989. *Practical measurement in physical education and sport.* 4th ed. Philadelphia: Lee and Febiger.

Bloom, B. S. et al. 1971. *Handbook on formative and summative evaluation of student learning.* New York: McGraw-Hill, 129.

Bookwalter, K. W. 1962. *A score card for evaluating undergraduate professional programs in physical education.* (C. Bookwalter and R. Dollgener, Eds.), Bloomington, IN: Indiana University.

Gronlund, N. E. 1974. *Improving marking and reporting in classroom instruction.* New York: Macmillan.

LaPorte, W. D. 1955a. *Health and physical education score card No. 1 for elementary schools.* Los Angeles, CA: University of Southern California.

————. 1955b. *Health and physical education score card No. 11 for junior and senior high schools and for four year high schools.* Los Angeles, CA: University of Southern California.

Safrit, M. J. 1981. *Evaluation in physical education.* 2d ed. Englewood Cliffs, NJ: Prentice-Hall.

Wittrock, M. C. and D. E. Wiley, (Eds.) 1970. *The evaluation of instruction: Issues and problems.* New York: Holt, Rinehart and Winston.

# Performance Testing

# The Nature of Tests and Their Administration: With Applications to Individuals with Disabilities

## Key Words

individuals with disabilities
mass testability
posttest procedures
pretest planning
useful scores

## Contents

## Objectives

In the first part of this chapter we will discuss those attributes that make up a sound measuring instrument. These include not only reliability, objectivity, and validity, but also other content-related, subject-related, and administration-related characteristics.

Pretest procedures, giving the test, and posttest procedures are also important aspects of testing. Pretest planning, in particular, is the key to a successful measurement procedure, providing the basis for all testing decisions and processes.

Finally, issues and problems associated with testing individuals with disabilities will be discussed. Realizing the problems in testing individuals with disabilities is vital.

After reading Chapter 7 you should be able to:

1. Identify the important characteristics of a test.
2. Plan the administration of a test.
3. Identify problems in measuring individuals with disabilities.

# INTRODUCTION

Many existing measurement programs are neither effective nor efficient while others produce invalid scores because the teacher, researcher, or exercise specialist has been careless in selecting tests or in planning testing procedures. The first level of planning in a good measurement program focuses on the selection or construction of a test. The second level involves the administration of the test.

Teachers almost always test a group of students at the same time with all students going through the test at the same time (the entire group running the mile for time), half the group going through the test while the other half of the group watch or assist in administering the test (half the group do the sit-up test and the other half hold the feet of those being tested and count the number of sit-ups executed), or one student going through the test while the rest of the group watch (the instructor takes skinfold measures). Sometimes researchers and exercise specialists test people in a group, but they are just as likely to test one person at a time with one person coming to be tested every 30 to 60 minutes. Testing one person at a time is a clinical model common to adult fitness, athletic training, physical therapy, and cardiac rehabilitation programs. Some of the topics discussed in this chapter may not apply to situations where one person is tested at a time. However, there are many topics that apply to all measurement situations.

## Test Characteristics

Knowing the important characteristics of a test allows the teacher, researcher, or exercise specialist to construct effective, efficient instruments, and to recognize essential features in tests constructed by others. The characteristics themselves concern the test content, the individuals tested, and the administrative procedures, and, above all, reliability, objectivity, and validity.

### Reliability, Objectivity, and Validity

The three most important characteristics of a test are reliability, objectivity, and validity (see Chapters 4 and 5). If a test does not fulfill these requirements, you need not consider it further. Yet there are no rigid standards for acceptable levels of these characteristics. Acceptability is determined by both the testing situation itself and the values others have obtained in their measurement programs. This is not to say that no standards exist. In general, the test-retest reliability of most physical measures is between .85 and .93. Objectivity coefficients of between .85 and .93 are also usually reported. Published validity coefficients vary from .80 or higher for a well-constructed, properly administered physical fitness test to between .70 and .85 for a sport-skill test. Remember, though, that a validity coefficient depends greatly on the criterion and population used and that when construct validity is used there may be no coefficient at all.

### Content-Related Attributes

These characteristics relate to the nature of the test content—what it measures and how it does so.

***Important Attributes.*** Typically, no more than 10% of the class time or adult fitness program should involve testing. To meet this goal, only the most important skills and abilities should be measured. These skills and abilities are those listed in the educational objectives for the unit, or are the important components of an adult fitness program.

***Discrimination.*** A test should discriminate among different ability groups throughout the total range of ability. Ideally, there should be many different scores and the distribution of the scores basically normal or at least not markedly skewed. Also, it is important to select a test difficult enough so that nobody receives a perfect score, but easy enough so that nobody receives a zero. Consider the problem of two individuals receiving the minimum or maximum score. Although two individuals who receive a zero on a pull-up test are both weak, they are probably not equal in strength per pound of body weight. Remember, however, that the fact that nobody receives a perfect score or a zero is no guarantee that a test discriminates satisfactorily; conversely, the fact that someone does receive a perfect score or a zero is no guarantee that the test is a poor one.

***Resemblance to the Activity.*** A test, particularly a sport-skill test, must require the subject to use good form, follow the rules of the activity, and perform acts characteristic of the activity. For example, a badminton short-serve test that does not require the serve to be low over the net is not requiring good form. And a basketball test that asks a student to run with the ball rather than dribble it, or to dribble backward the length of the course rather than forward, is neither following the rules of the game nor demanding a performance characteristic of it. The validity of a test is questionable if the test does not resemble the activity.

***Specificity.*** When a test measures a single attribute, it is possible to determine from it why a person is performing poorly; when a test measures a skill that has several components, it is more difficult to determine why a person is performing at a given level. For example, consider a basketball test of 10 shots at the basket. If the test asks the student to stand 3 feet away from the basket to shoot and the student misses all 10 shots, it is easy to determine that the student is a poor shot. If, however, the student were standing 40 feet away from the basket and missed the 10 shots, it would be difficult to determine whether the student simply shoots poorly or lacks strength.

Sometimes it is not possible to measure a single attribute; at other times your reason for testing is to measure how well a person combines several attributes. In either case, the test should be as specific as possible for whatever is being measured.

***Unrelated Measures.*** Often a single measure is inadequate to evaluate fitness or a sport skill, so you will use a battery composed of several tests. The measures in a battery should be unrelated—that is, the correlation between the tests should be low—both to save testing time and to be fair to the individuals being tested. Of course, all tests in a battery should correlate highly with the criterion used to determine validity.

When two tests are highly correlated, they are probably measuring the same ability. This wastes time and also gives the measured ability double weight in the battery, a practice unfair to individuals weak in the ability. If two tests in a battery are highly correlated, keep the better of the two and drop the other.

***Appropriateness to Students and Participants.*** Performance is influenced by the person's maturity, gender, and experience. For example, older students and boys generally score better on strength tests (push-ups, distance jumps) than do younger students and girls. The strength tests are usually valid and reliable for a variety of ages

**Student and Participant Concerns**

and both genders, but performance standards should be based on age and gender. Skill tests, on the other hand, are not universally applicable: They must apply to the age, gender, skill level, strength, and other capacities of the students. Again, skill tests that are valid and reliable with junior high students may not be valid and reliable with elementary or high school students; and tests that are valid and reliable with females may not be valid and reliable with males.

Performance is also influenced by the age and disabilities of the person. Physical performance tests (fitness tests in particular) for high school and college students are often not appropriate for adults over 30 years old and seldom appropriate for adults older than age 60 or preschool children. Individuals with disabilities often do not score as well as individuals without disabilities on most physical performance tests. Strength and skill tests for individuals without disabilities are usually not acceptable for individuals with disabilities.

***Individual Scores.*** A person's test scores should not be affected by another person's performance. That is, a test should not require several individuals to interact and then score individuals on the basis of that interaction. For example, consider a basketball lay-up shot test in which Student 1 runs toward the basket and Student 2 throws the ball to him to make the shot. If Student 2 makes a poor or late throw, even the best student is going to look bad.

***Enjoyable.*** When individuals enjoy taking a test and understand why they are being tested, they are motivated to do well, and their scores ordinarily represent their maximum capacity. To be enjoyable, a test should be interesting and challenging, within reason. People are more likely to enjoy a test when they have a reasonable chance to achieve an acceptable score. Testing comfort is also an aspect of enjoyment. Although certain cardiorespiratory endurance tests and other maximum-effort tests can be uncomfortable, avoid any test so painful that few people can do it well.

***Safety.*** Obviously, you should not use tests that endanger the people being tested. Examine each test's procedures to see whether individuals might overextend themselves or make mistakes that could cause injury. The use of spotters in gymnastic tests, soft nonbreakable marking devices for obstacle runs or marking testing areas, and nonslip surfaces and large areas for running and throwing events is always necessary. The ACSM (1986) offers guidelines for administering maximal stress tests. This is summarized in Chapter 9.

***Confidentiality and Privacy of Testing.*** Many students and participants in fitness or rehabilitation programs would prefer that others did not know how good or poor they score on a test. Often students are embarrassed when they receive a test score that is considerably better or worse than their peers. Participants in fitness and rehabilitation programs have similar feelings or just do not think that their score should be known by others. All people conducting measurement programs need to be sensitive to this issue. Testing one person at a time rather than in a group may be the only way to satisfy this concern.

***Motivation to Score at Maximum Potential.*** Students tend to try hard on tests because their grade is affected. Generally, people who are in certification programs or whose job, salary, insurance premium, and so on are affected by their score try hard on tests. But, what motivates people not in these situations to try hard on tests? Poor effort by the person being tested makes scores not valid and not reliable. The tester must motivate participants to do well and constantly watch for lack of effort by participants. Exercise specialists doing testing in therapy programs need to be particularly aware of participant effort.

***Mass Testability.*** When there is a large number of people to test in a short period of time, **mass testability** can be a vital test characteristic. The longer it takes to administer each test, the fewer tests are likely to be administered. With large groups it is essential that people be measured quickly, either successively or simultaneously. For example, a standing long jump test can be mass testable when students jump successively every 10 to 15 seconds. A sit-up test can be mass testable when half the group is tested while the other half helps with the administration. Remember too that short tests or tests that keep most of the subjects active at once help prevent the discipline problems that often result from student inactivity and reduce dissatisfaction of participants in research or fitness programs.

The teacher, researcher, or exercise specialist can become so concerned about mass testing that validity and reliability of the data suffers. With careful thought and planning this need not be true.

***Minimal Practice.*** People must be familiar with a test and be allowed to practice before testing. Familiarity, either through previous testing, the exercise program, regular class instruction, or practice sessions prior to the testing day, lessens both explanation and practice time. Even when a test is unfamiliar, if it is easy to understand little time need be spent to explain it. Avoid tests that require elaborate directions or considerable practice.

In research or rehabilitation fitness testing and strength testing situations where participants are tested on treadmill and Cybex equipment with no previous experience on the equipment and with minimum explanation and practice trials of the test, are valid and reliable scores obtained? The equipment may have the potential to provide very valid and precise scores, but if poor administrative techniques are used when testing with the equipment, the scores obtained will not be valid.

***Minimal Equipment and Personnel.*** For teachers, tests that require a lot of equipment and/or administrative personnel are often impractical. Equipment is usually expensive to purchase and maintain and can be time-consuming to assemble. In the same way, when several people are needed to administer a test, time must be spent finding and training them. Even when you plan to use members of the class or exercise group, you must expect to spend time training them.

Insufficient training of all test administrators contributes to lack of test objectivity (see Chapter 4). In some labs and rehabilitation programs where participants will be tested at regular intervals over a period of time to determine if they are improving, the same person, rather than different people, tests a participant each time to maximize the chances that improvement in the scores of the participant is really an improvement and not due to lack of objectivity.

***Ease of Preparation.*** Select tests that are easy to set up over ones that take more time, provided the first does the job well. Tests that use complex equipment or several pieces of equipment placed at specific spots or that require a large number of boundary or dimension marks on floors and walls are usually neither easily nor quickly set up.

***Adequate Directions.*** When you construct a test, you must develop a set of directions for it. When you use a test constructed by others, you must make sure that complete directions accompany it. Directions should specify how the test is set up, subject preparation, and administration and scoring procedures.

***Norms.*** When the norms provided with a test are both recent and appropriate, they can save the time necessary to develop local norms or at least offer temporary standards until local norms can be developed. Unhappily, those norms may be so old that they are no longer suitable or are based on a group of different gender, age, or experience that they are not appropriate to the individuals being tested.

***Useful Scores.*** A test should yield **useful scores.** These are scores that can be used at once or inserted into a formula with little effort. Most physical measures—push-up, pull-up, sit-up, and dash scores, for instance—can be used immediately after a measurement session. If scores must be placed in a formula before they can be used, the formula should be sufficiently simple so that calculations can be done quickly. For example,

$$Y = 2X + 5,$$

where $Y$ is the calculated score and $X$ is the score collected, is a simple enough formula that a test requiring it could be considered. However, a test that requires the calculation:

$$Y = .6754 \sqrt{X} + .2156X^2 - 3.14 \text{ or}$$

$$Y = .4521X_1 + .3334X_2 + 1.2$$

would be very time-consuming if a Y score had to be calculated by hand for each of several hundred people. With computer support, the computer program would have the formula for Y in it, and only the X score(s) for each person would have to be input to the computer. Computer support like this is quite common in adult fitness programs and should be used more in the public school setting.

## Administration

The key to good testing is the planning before the test is given and then the follow-up to that planning during and after the administration.

We plan before giving a test to be sure that our preparation is adequate and that the actual administration will proceed smoothly. **Pretest planning** is all of the preparation that occurs before test administration. It involves a number of tasks: knowing the test, developing test procedures, developing directions, preparing the subjects, planning warm-up and test trials, securing equipment and preparing the test facility, making scoring sheets, estimating time needed, and giving the test.

*Knowing the Test.*   Whenever you plan to administer a test for the first time, read the directions or test manual several times, thinking about the test as you read. This is the only way to avoid overlooking small details about procedures, dimensions, and the like.

*Developing Test Procedures.*   Once you are familiar with the test, start to develop procedures for administering it. These include selecting the most efficient testing procedure, deciding whether to test all the subjects together or in groups, and determining whether one person will do all the testing or pairs of subjects will test each other.

If you plan to administer several tests on the same day, order them so that fatigue is minimized. Do not give consecutive tests that tire the same muscle groups. Also, plan to administer very fatiguing events, such as distance runs, last.

The next step is the identification of exact scoring requirements and units of measurement. For example, in a sit-up test, you would require the subject to start in a supine position with both shoulder blades on the floor, then to sit up with hands interlaced behind the head, to lean forward until both elbows touch the thighs, and to return to the starting position, all to score one sit-up. Here too, when necessary, the unit of measurement with which you will score must be selected. For example, do you want to express distance in feet or inches or both; time in minutes or seconds or both? To obtain a score that can immediately be analyzed mathematically, only one unit of measurement—usually the smaller one—is used.

At this point you should also decide what to do if a subject makes a mistake during the test. By anticipating possible situations and rulings, you will be able to deal fairly with all subjects. For example, what do you do if a subject fails to go all the way down on a sit-up? Whether you disregard the mistake, warn the subject and count the sit-up, or discount it, you must follow the same policy for all subjects.

Finally, safety procedures are essential. Always plan to use spotters in tumbling and gymnastics tests or when testing the elderly. Consider your marking devices as well. In obstacle runs they should be soft, unbreakable, and tall enough so that subjects cannot step over them. Use marking cones instead of chairs or soda bottles when marking testing areas or obstacle courses. Think too about the testing area. Hold dashes, agility runs, and similar running events in a large enough area that subjects do not run into obstacles. Plan for organization of subjects waiting to be tested so that participants do not run into them.

If you have never administered a specific test before, try one or two practice administrations before the actual test. This is a good way, not only to see what changes and additions to the procedures must be made, but also to train administrative personnel.

***Developing Directions.*** After you have determined procedures, it is necessary to develop exact directions. It is perfectly acceptable to read these directions to a group before administering the test to them. The directions should be easy to understand and should specify the following:

1. Administration procedures
2. Instructions on performance
3. Scoring procedure and the policy on incorrect performance
4. Hints on techniques to improve scores

***Preparing the Students or Fitness Program Participants.*** Announce the test well in advance so that people can practice if they think it will improve their scores. When the class or exercise group is unfamiliar with a test, spend some time before the day of the test explaining it and the techniques that will improve test scores, and supervising pretest practice.

Even when people have had exposure to a test, they may need some time to re-learn the necessary techniques. Girardi (1971) familiarized a group of high school boys with a jump-and-reach test and a 12-minute-run test, and then tested them. Eight weeks later, he retested the students without review, and found that a number of them, particularly the poorly skilled, had forgotten the necessary techniques.

With the exception of a few research situations (e.g., learning research), people should know well in advance that they are going to be tested, what the test is, and what it involves. This allows the person to be psychologically and physiologically ready to be tested and score up to his or her potential. This is vital when important things like grades, admission to or release from programs, or health-fitness ratings are involved.

***Planning Warm-Up and Test Trials.*** We saw in Chapter 4 that reliability improves with pretest warm-up. The amount and nature of this warm-up must be planned. Ideally, warm-up should be specific to the skill being tested (that is, practice rather than calisthenics). It has been shown too that supervised warm-up, in which the tester tells the subjects what to do and ensures that all subjects receive the same amount of practice, is better than unsupervised warm-up. In some situations it is acceptable to administer multiple trials of a test and to consider the first few trials as warm-up, making each subject's score the sum or mean of the latter test trials.

***Securing Equipment and Preparing the Testing Facility.*** You should have all equipment on hand and the facility prepared before the day of the test. Having all equipment available and all boundary lines and other markings positioned correctly when the subjects arrive to be tested saves time and avoids the problems that inevitably arise when subjects are kept waiting while the test is set up.

***Making Scoring Sheets.*** At some point before the test, locate or prepare either a master scoring sheet for the entire group or individual scorecards. Enter the subjects' names on the sheets or cards before they arrive to be tested.

There are many advantages to using individual scorecards over a master score sheet. Scorecards allow subjects to rotate among testing stations and to quickly record scores when they have tested one another. Even when one person is testing and recording the scores of the entire group, time can be saved by gathering the score-cards in order after the subjects are in line to be tested rather than having the subjects get in line in the same order they are listed on the scoring sheet.

***Estimating the Time Needed.*** When a test will not take an entire class period, or when half the class will be tested on each day, you must plan some activity to fill the extra time or to occupy the rest of the class. If testing will occur during an agency or corporate fitness program, similar planning is necessary. Estimating the time needed to administer a test both minimizes confusion and maximizes the use of available time.

If you have planned properly, the testing should go smoothly. Although your primary concern on the day of the test is the administration of the test itself, you should also be concerned with subject preparation, motivation, and safety. If, after you have administered the test, you can say, "The subjects were prepared and the test was administered in a way that I would have liked if I were being tested," the testing session was undoubtedly a success.

***Giving the Test***

***Preparation.*** The subjects should already know what the test is and why it is being given, so your first concern is the warm-up or practice. Next, explain the test instructions and procedures, even demonstrating the test for them if possible. Ask for questions both before and after the demonstration. When the skill or procedures are particularly complicated, let the subjects run through a practice trial of the test.

***Motivation.*** Give all subjects the same degree of motivation and encouragement. Although we all tend to encourage poor performers and compliment superior ones, in fairness all or none of the subjects should receive a comment. Whenever possible, indicate his or her score to a subject immediately after the test trial. This can motivate subjects to perform better on a second or third trial. However, the reporting of the score should not embarrass the subject.

***Safety.*** During a testing session, watch for safety problems. Subjects often perform unsafely when they are not following instructions. Try to anticipate these or other unsafe situations.

***Posttest Procedures***

The rationale for testing is to collect information about the subjects and in education, the instructional program. Only after the test is given can the information be used. Surprisingly, many teachers and exercise specialists fail to do enough, or even any, posttest analysis. The sooner the results of tests are returned to the students, the more meaningful they will be in the educational process. **Posttest procedures** include the analyzing, reporting, and recording of test scores.

***Analyzing Test Scores.*** Shortly after a test, the scores must be analyzed using the appropriate techniques from Chapter 3. This often requires entering the data into the computer, so analysis, record keeping, and/or data retrieval is possible. Analysis serves to reveal characteristics that could influence the teaching procedures or program conduct and to provide information for the group tested and prepare the data for grading or other evaluation purposes. People are usually interested in their scores, their relative standings in the group or class, and their degree of improvement or decline since the last test. Reporting test results to subjects is an effective motivational device.

***Recording Test Results.*** The recording of test results is usually nothing more than placing the scoring sheets and your analysis of them in an appropriate file. The information makes possible comparisons between classes or groups within and between years, program evaluation over years, as well as the development of norms. Notice that these are group or class standards rather than individual standards, based solely on the scores and your analysis. Often it is not even necessary to identify the scores, particularly in situations where a permanent record card for each student or program participant is kept. It is from this card, that follows the student from grade to grade or the program participant from year to year, that you can trace individual improvement over time.

## Measuring Individuals with Disabilities*

Administering tests to individuals with disabilities can be especially difficult and requires special attention. An individual may be considered an **individual with disabilities** when special program or testing considerations must be extended to this individual due to limited ability to perform certain activities. Impairment and handicap are terms often used in place of disability, but individuals with disabilities is the accepted term at this time.

Most of the issues and problems associated with testing individuals with disabilities are beyond the scope of this text. However, some of them are discussed here. For more extensive coverage see Baumgartner and Horvat (1988). "Testing the Handicapped—A Challenge by Law" was the feature section of the January 1988 *Journal of Physical Education, Recreation, and Dance.* It is a highly recommended reading. Two other excellent sources are Seaman and DePauw (1989) and Werder and Kalakian (1985). *Physical Best and Individuals with Disabilities* (AAHPERD in progress) will be completed in 1994 and is a source to consult when it is available.

## Background

At one time individuals with disabilities tended to be sent to special schools and/or placed in special classes. This may have had some advantages. The teachers who taught these classes were trained to work with individuals with disabilities. All members of the class were approximately similar in terms of their disability and performance level. The classes were small so that individual testing was feasible even if it was time consuming and often required special teacher expertise and equipment. However, there were also many disadvantages to special schools and/or special classes.

Public Law 94–142 (U.S. Congress 1975) and its revision, Public Law 101–476 (U.S. Congress 1990), mandated that individuals with disabilities should be placed in an environment that affords the individual maximum opportunity for development and function but at the same time accommodates the individual's disabilities. This meant regular education where possible. Greater discussion of Public Law 101–476 can be found in adapted physical education books such as Eichstaedt and Lavay (1992) and Auxter, Pyfer, and Huettig (1993). One of the outcomes of the Law is that

---

*Appreciation is extended to Dr. Janet A. Seaman, California State University, Los Angeles, for suggesting many improvements to this section.

many individuals with disabilities are no longer attending special schools or classes. Rather, they are included in regular physical education classes. "Inclusion: Physical Education for All" was the feature section of the January 1994 *Journal of Physical Education, Recreation, and Dance*. Presently, approximately 93% of all students with disabilities are being served in regular classes. By law these students must be receiving appropriate activities, be tested with appropriate tests, and be evaluated with appropriate standards. Specifically, the Law states that "tests must be validated for the purpose for which they are intended." This means a test must measure motor performance and not the student's intelligence, language comprehension, etc. as is often the case if the student doesn't understand the test directions or grasp the meaning of words or concepts used during administration of the test.

There have been many positive outcomes of Public Law 101–476, but inclusion of individuals with disabilities in regular physical education classes has caused teachers some testing problems. Many physical education teachers are not properly trained to work with individuals with disabilities nor recognize their unique problems. Measurement problems arise because tests and standards traditionally used in physical education programs are not appropriate for some individuals with disabilities. One would not expect a student with one arm to do pull-ups. With large classes, limited equipment, and limited expertise on the part of the teacher, individual testing with special equipment becomes difficult if not impossible.

There may be differences among individuals with disabilities in terms of their ability to do some physical tasks. The differences can be as great as the differences among preschool, college, and retirement-aged individuals in the ability to do some physical tasks. Individuals with disabilities may have single or multiple disabilities and therefore present multiple challenges in the testing situation.

There are some problems to recognize when measuring individuals with disabilities. When testing individuals with disabilities, recognize that these problems exist and plan how to cope with them so that valid and reliable data are obtained.

**Problems in Measuring Individuals with Disabilities**

*Attributes of Individuals with Disabilities.* Individuals with disabilities may be classified by a variety of methods. Seaman and DePauw (1989) use the classifications which are presented with a brief description in Table 7.1. Each of these disabilities has degrees of severity and functional ability. Thus, two individuals with the same disability may not be the same. People with sight and/or hearing problems tend to have problems in performing motor tasks, but there is a difference between having some sight or hearing and none.

One problem in developing tests for individuals with disabilities or testing them is the need for a test battery for each possible combination of disabling conditions. This is similar to the problem of accounting for age and gender when testing individuals without disabilities.

Another problem in testing individuals with disabilities is finding norm-referenced standards. For many disabilities, adequate age and gender norms do not exist. Norms for individuals without disabilities and individuals with disabilities on the same test are not usually available but are needed to determine if individuals with disabilities should be placed in regular or special programs. For example, an individual with disabilities could be at the 99th percentile in terms of his or her peers with disabilities, which might suggest

**Table 7.1** Classifications of Individuals with Disabilities

| Classification | Description |
|---|---|
| Mentally retarded | Low IQ; mildly retarded 55–69; moderately retarded 40–54; etc. |
| Orthopedically impaired | Neurologically impaired; musculoskeletal conditions; postural deviations; trauma-caused physical impairments |
| Seriously emotionally disturbed and behaviorally disordered | Autism; depression; mental illness; schizophrenia |
| Multihandicapped and severely handicapped | Two or more handicapping conditions varying in severity; severely handicapped are in special programs |
| Speech- and/or language-disabled | Difficulty in communicating thoughts or forming or sequencing sounds |
| Other health-impaired | Examples are asthma, cardiovascular disorders, diabetes, epilepsy, obesity |
| Deaf/hard of hearing | Little or no hearing |
| Blind/visually handicapped | Little or no sight |
| Deaf-blind | Combination of both hearing and sight impairments |
| Specific learning-disabled | Learning problems not due to mental retardation or emotional disturbance |

that he or she could be moved into a regular physical education program, but only at the 1st percentile when compared to peers without disabilities.

Individuals with disabilities may be similar to individuals without disabilities who are chronologically younger. Many individuals with disabilities have a short attention span and problems with complicated directions. Often they cannot reliably test each other, even if the test lends itself to it, because they don't count accurately or are not good judges of properly executed performances.

These problems are compounded by the fact that individuals with disabilities may have physical performance needs and levels not similar to each other. Neither are they similar to individuals without disabilities, making the reliability and validity of many tests commonly used with individuals without disabilities low when used with individuals with disabilities. Many individuals with disabilities do not have as much prior experience with certain tests as individuals without disabilities, which contributes further to low reliability and validity of data collected on individuals with disabilities.

Oververbalizing or not clearly verbalizing what is expected from an individual with disabilities can lead to testing problems and lack of valid and reliable data. For example, tell a child with a language disability to "run as fast as you can" and you probably will not get a valid response. The child is language disabled, not deaf, so you will get a response. However, because the child can not relate to the meaning of "as fast as you can," the response may not be a true indication of how fast the child can really run. This disability requires that there be a beginning and an end to a task and that the child not be required to draw relationships like "as fast as you can."

***Limitations of Tests.*** Often individuals with disabilities do not stay on task and are not likely to give maximum exertion (as are young individuals without disabilities) because they may not understand why or how to give it, or do not understand the test protocol. For these reasons many field-based physical fitness batteries for individuals with disabilities do not have a valid item for cardiorespiratory endurance. The cardiorespiratory endurance tests commonly used with individuals with disabilities are distance run, step test, arm cranking, and wheelchair push. Each test has varying degrees of validity and applicability for an individual with disabilities. Certainly no single test could be used on all individuals with disabilities.

The most common cardiorespiratory endurance test is a distance run for time (6, 9, or 12 minutes) or distance (300, 600, 880, or 1,760 yards). Pizarro (1982) reported that 14- to 18-year-old individuals with mild and moderate mental retardation did not identify well with abstract concepts like run for time. Fifty percent of his subjects with mental retardation failed to complete the 9-minute run, and 70% of his subjects either quit running, walked, or completed less than 1,000 yards. So, he substituted the 880-yard run, with subjects running from the starting line 440 yards out to a marker and then back to the starting line. He used this very goal-oriented task because the subjects had trouble staying on task when running around a track or for longer distances. He still found the 880-yard run questionable for subjects with mild mental retardation and not appropriate for subjects with moderate mental retardation because they walked too much.

Exercise physiologists probably would say the 880-yard run is too short a distance to measure cardiorespiratory endurance and would recommend a run of at least a mile. The distance used should be dependent on the characteristics and abilities of the individual with disabilities being tested. The distance must be long enough to tax the cardiorespiratory system but not so long that extraneous factors like attention span and motivation influence the individual's performance and reduce test validity. One of the issues here, as it effects the valid measurement of nearly any attribute, is practice and cognition. Unless the individual knows how to do the task and understands what is asked of him or her, it will be very difficult to get a valid measure. Sometimes this takes months of training, not just 3 trials. Just as with any short-term task, you need to be sure you are measuring cardiorespiratory endurance and not learning, cognition, or language acquisition.

The 1971 California Physical Performance Test (Clarke 1976) has used the 6-minute run for some time with individuals with disabilities. Further, Disch, Frankiewicz, and Jackson (1975) found the 6-minute run to be a cardiorespiratory test rather than a speed test. The National Children and Youth Fitness Study Phase II used the one-half mile run if a child was under 8 years of age.

Some fitness test batteries for individuals with disabilities have used a 300-yard run as a measure of cardiorespiratory endurance. This is a very short distance, which may have been arbitrarily selected. Just because it is part of a test battery does not indicate that it is valid.

Finding tests appropriate for individuals with disabilities is not easy. Many tests presented in adapted physical education books are designed to test one individual at a time and often require special equipment and teacher expertise. These tests seldom will be appropriate for mass testing. Other tests are nothing more than tests for individuals without disabilities with norms for individuals with disabilities. The validity and reliability of these tests for individuals with disabilities must be determined and then maybe norms for the individuals developed. If these tests prove to be valid and reliable, then they can be used to measure an individual's progress or improvement even if norms are not developed.

Forbus (1990) investigated the suitability and reliability of the Physical Best fitness test items with individuals with learning disabilities (LD), individuals with mild mental retardation (MiMR), individuals with moderate mental retardation (MoMR), and individuals without disabilities (ND). Subjects were 11 to 15 years old. There were 25 males and 25 females from each of the four groups. Significant differences in mean score were found among all groups on each item of the Physical Best test. All of the reliability coefficients were at least .80 except for the pull-up and sit-and-reach tests for females in the MoMR and MiMR groups and the sit-up test for the LD group. Forbus concluded that the sit-and-reach test and the skinfolds test are suitable for all four groups. The sit-up test is not suitable for children with MoMR. The pull-up test is not suitable for children with MoMR, MiMR, and LD. The one-mile run/walk test is not suitable for children with MoMR and MiMR. Overall, he concluded that the Physical Best test should not be used with individuals with mental retardation. Alternative tests or modifications should be used when assessing the health-related physical fitness of individuals with mental retardation.

The health and physical fitness test in the Kansas Adapted/Special Physical Education Test Manual (Johnson & Lavay 1988) is one example of what seems to be a good test for many individuals with disabilities. Means and reliability coefficients for individuals 5–21 years of age can be found in Appendix D of Eichstaedt and Lavay (1992). In developing the manual, Johnson and Lavay used the concept of the non-classification approach to testing students. The test manual may be used with the majority of individuals with disabilities in school systems, regardless of their disability. Validity and reliability of test items were addressed.

The health and physical fitness items in the Kansas test are sit-ups as an indication of abdominal strength and endurance, sit-and-reach as an indication of lower back and hamstring flexibility, isometric push-ups (children under 13 years of age) or bench pressing a 35-pound barbell (children 13 years of age or older) as an indication of upper body strength and endurance, and aerobic movement as an indication of cardiovascular endurance. In the last test item the students may jog, march, walk with vigorous arm movement, propel themselves in a wheelchair or other appliance, ride an exercise bike, or move in any way to elevate the heart rate to 140–180 beats per minute for 12 minutes. The score of a student is the number of minutes this rate can be maintained (not to exceed 12 minutes) after 6 minutes of warm-up.

Several nationally distributed fitness tests for youth discussed in chapter 9 (Prudential FITNESSGRAM®, Chrysler Fund-AAU) have addressed testing individuals with disabilities. Modifications of these tests may be appropriate for many individuals with disabilities.

## Summary

Whether you develop your own test or select a preconstructed test, which is certainly easier, you will require certain attributes in the instrument. It is these characteristics that make the measurement procedure both efficient and meaningful.

Although the successful administration of a test depends on many factors, the key to success is good planning in the pretest stage and attention to the details of that planning during and after the testing procedure.

Both physical educators and exercise scientists will be responsible for testing individuals with disabilities. In order to obtain reliable and valid scores, the tests and test procedures must be carefully selected.

*Objective 1* Identify the important characteristics of a test.

1. The text discusses many important attributes of a test. In addition to reliability, objectivity, and validity, what are several of these attributes?

2. Certain characteristics listed in the text relate to the individuals taking the tests, while others act simply to make the procedure more efficient. What are the subject-related attributes?

*Objective 2* Plan the administration of a test.

1. The success of a testing program depends on how well the pretest planning is carried out. What type of planning and procedures would you use to administer the following tests?
   a. A timed bent-knee sit-up test
   b. A pull-up test
   c. A mile-run test or some other cardiovascular test

*Objective 3* Identify problems in measuring individuals with disabilities.

1. What are five problems in measuring individuals with disabilities no matter what the disability?

1. From the material in this book and other physical education measurement texts, develop a summary of test characteristics and a checklist of pretest planning procedures.

2. Select a test with which you are unfamiliar and administer it to individuals with and without disabilities following the pretest, administrative, and posttest procedures outlined in the text.

**Bibliography**

ACSM. 1986. *Guidelines for exercise testing and prescription.* 3rd ed. Philadelphia, PA: Lea & Febiger.

Auxter, D., J. Pyfer, and C. Huettig. 1993. *Principles and methods of adapted physical education and recreation.* St. Louis, MO: Mosby-Year Book.

Baumgartner, T. A. and M. A. Horvat. January 1988. Problems in measuring the physical and motor performance of the handicapped. *Journal of Physical Education, Recreation, & Dance 59:*48–52.

Clarke, H. H. 1976. *Application of measurement to health and physical education.* 5th ed. (p. 178). Englewood Cliffs, NJ: Prentice-Hall.

Disch, J., R. Frankiewicz, and A. Jackson. 1975. Construct validation of distance run tests. *Research Quarterly 46:*169–76.

Eichstaedt, C. B. and B. W. Lavay. 1992. *Physical activity for individuals with mental retardation.* Champaign, IL: Human Kinetics.

Forbus, W. R. III. 1990. The suitability and reliability of the Physical Best fitness test with selected special populations. Ed. D. dissertation, University of Georgia, Athens, GA.

Girardi, G. 1971. A comparison of isokinetic exercises with isometric and isotonic exercises in the development of strength and endurance. P.E.D. dissertation, Indiana University.

Johnson, R. E. & B. Lavay. 1988. *Kansas adapted/special physical education test manual: Health related fitness and psychomotor testing.* Topeka, Kansas: Kansas State Department of Education.

Pizarro, D. C. 1982. Health-related fitness of mainstreamed emr/tmr children. Ed. D. dissertation, University of Georgia, Athens, GA.

Seaman, J. A. and K. D. DePauw. 1989. *The new adapted physical education: A developmental approach.* 2d ed. Palo Alto, CA: Mayfield.

U.S. 94th Congress. 1975. Public Law 94–142. Washington, DC: Authors.

U.S. 101st Congress. 1990. Public Law 101–476. Washington, DC: Authors.

Werder, J. K. and L. H. Kalakian. 1985. *Assessment in adapted physical education.* Minneapolis: Burgess.

# Measuring Physical Abilities

## Key Words

absolute endurance
agility
balance
basic physical ability
classification index
flexibility
general motor ability
isokinetic strength
isometric strength
isotonic strength
kinesthesis
motor educability
motor skill
muscular endurance
muscular power
muscular strength
power
speed
work

## Contents

## Objectives

Physical educators have long accepted the idea of generality. General motor ability and motor educability tests were used to measure generality, but they have not proven to be valid. The theory of basic physical abilities does provide a sound measurement model. This chapter provides a discussion of the theory and practical procedures for measuring basic physical abilities in athletic and employment settings.

After reading Chapter 8 you should be able to:

1. Describe the tests historically used to measure generality.
2. Define and differentiate between basic physical abilities and a motor skill.
3. Apply the theory of basic physical abilities to the evaluation of athletes.
4. Identify the methods to develop preemployment tests for physically demanding jobs and the types of tests that comprise preemployment batteries.
5. Identify basic physical abilities and tests that validly measure each ability.

# INTRODUCTION

The assumption of the concept of generality is that the performance of many different motor tasks can be predicted from a single or limited number of test items. The principle of generality can be traced to the work of Sargent (1921), who first reported a test of generality. The Sargent Physical Test of Man simply measures the height of a vertical jump, on the assumption that a single test is sufficient to measure motor ability. This assumption paralleled the concept of generality once accepted by psychologists, who felt a g-factor, or general factor of intelligence, is adequate to represent human intellectual ability.

The interest in developing physical tests of generality peaked between 1930 and 1960. During this period, several batteries of general motor ability and motor educability were published. Research published from the discipline of motor learning cast doubt on the principle of general motor ability and the validity of these tests. This research suggested that learning motor skills was very task-specific and interest in using the general tests lessened.

More recently, psychologists interested in measuring intelligence recognized that a single g-factor of intellectual ability was not adequate; rather several abilities are needed to represent this domain. For example, both verbal and quantitative sections are used to measure intellectual aptitudes on college entrance examinations. Each is important for predicting different types of intellectual performance. Edwin Fleishman (1964), an industrial psychologist, has extended this multi-ability theory to the physical domain. His research showed that several different basic physical abilities exist and various abilities are important for predicting motor-skill performance.

Common physical abilities include strength, endurance, power, agility, balance, flexibility, and basic movement patterns that involve sprinting, jumping, and throwing. Two important uses of basic physical ability tests are for evaluating athletes and testing applicants for physically demanding jobs. This chapter examines the historical development of generality testing and provides methods for measuring important physical abilities.

## History of Generality Testing

The purpose of generality tests was to provide a method by which it would be possible to predict an individual's performance on a wide range of motor activities from a simple test battery. Several types of tests have been used by physical educators to measure generality, but their validity has not been established. A brief summary of methods used to test generality follow.

## Age-Height-Weight Classification Index

Generally, students who differ in age, height, and weight will differ in their ability to perform motor tasks. McCloy (1932) was the first to propose a system for classifying students on these age and size dimensions into homogeneous groups for instruction. The Neilson-Cozens **classification index** (CI) was used as a basis for developing norms on the AAHPERD Youth Fitness Test prior to the 1976 revision. The equation was

$$CI = 20(age) + 5.5(height) + 1.1(weight).$$

The CI score would be higher for the older and larger child, and these children were supposedly more physically capable than children with a lower CI. Age, height, and weight are correlated. As children become older, they become taller, heavier, and stronger. So, age alone has been shown (Espenschade 1963; Gross & Casciani 1962)

**Table 8.1** Test Items of General Motor Ability Batteries

**Scott Motor Ability Test**

1. Basketball throw for distance
2. Standing long jump
3. Wall pass
4. Dash (4 seconds)

**Barrow Motor Ability Test**

1. Standing long jump
2. Zigzag run
3. Softball distance throw
4. Wall pass
5. Medicine ball put
6. 60-yard dash

as useful for classifying students as the entire CI. Today, age and gender are the variables used most when making norms for evaluating motor performance.

**General Motor Ability**

According to Larson and Yocom (1951), **general motor ability** is the "present acquired and innate ability to perform motor skills of a general or fundamental nature, exclusive of highly specialized sports or gymnastic techniques." Numerous general motor ability batteries have been published, and examples of two popular tests (Barrow 1954; Scott 1939) are shown in Table 8.1. The batteries typically consist of sprinting, jumping, throwing, and agility tests.

General motor batteries are highly reliable because the individual test items that comprise the battery are very reliable. But the purpose of general motor ability tests is to measure a wide range of motor skills with a few easily administered tests, and in this sense the tests are not valid. Cumbee and Harris (1953) showed that the batteries were measuring a single factor rather than the seven or eight proposed by the test makers. A student's test score on a general motor ability test is not predictive of performance on a wide range of motor skills. Rather it represents a student's speed, jumping, and throwing abilities.

**Motor Educability**

**Motor educability** is "the ability to learn motor skills easily and well" (McCloy & Young 1954). Motor educability tests were gymnastic "stunt-like" tasks. The successful completion of these unfamiliar motor tasks was supposedly an indication of how rapidly one could learn a motor skill. Several different batteries were published (Brace 1927; Carpenter 1942; Johnson 1932; McCloy & Young 1954; Metheny 1938).

The validity of motor educability tests—their ability to predict motor-skill learning aptitude—has not been established. The reported correlations between motor-skill acquisition and motor educability are low (Gire & Espenschade 1942; Gross et al. 1956). Additionally, the correlation between different types of motor educability tests is low (.20 or less), which suggests they are not measuring the same thing (Gire & Espenschade 1942).

## Specificity of Motor Skill

In the late 1950s, Franklin Henry advanced the memory-drum theory of neuromotor reaction, claiming that motor ability is specific to a task rather than general to many tasks. In other words, a student's performance on one **motor skill** is of little or no value in predicting performance on a different task. By his theory, Henry claims that there is no such thing as general motor ability; rather each individual possesses many specific motor abilities. A student who scores well on a general motor test is gifted with several specific abilities, whereas a student who scores poorly has only a few neural patterns stored on his or her memory drum (Henry 1956; Henry 1958). The theory of specificity casts doubt on the validity of general motor ability and motor educability tests and is largely responsible for the demise of these tests.

Certainly, physical education teachers and exercise specialists must acknowledge the theory of specificity; however, complete acceptance of the theory would signal the need to measure all the specifics that enter the complex domain of motor skills. Obviously this is not feasible given the limited testing time available to most teachers. In fact, the practice of using physical abilities tests is on the rise. Testing programs for athletes are becoming common practice at public school, college, and professional levels. Physical abilities tests are now used to screen applicants for physically demanding jobs such as a fire fighter or coal miner.

## Theory of Basic Physical Abilities

The theory of **basic physical abilities** was developed by Edwin Fleishman (1964) and is especially useful for generality testing because individual performance of a specific motor skill is explained in terms of a relatively small number of psychomotor abilities. His theory is based on research conducted for the U.S. Air Force, in which tests of psychomotor abilities were found valid for predicting the subsequent performance of various air crew members (Fleishman 1956).

Fleishman distinguishes between **psychomotor skills** and **psychomotor abilities,** but considers both essential and complementary. A psychomotor skill is one's level of proficiency on a specific task or limited group of tasks. Dribbling a basketball, catching a softball, swimming the sidestroke, and playing the piano are examples of very different psychomotor skills. Learning a psychomotor skill involves acquiring the sequence of responses that results in a coordinated performance of the task. A psychomotor ability is a more general trait that may be common to many psychomotor tasks. For example, running speed is important to several different specific motor skills, such as football and the running long jump.

Fleishman describes the relationship between basic physical abilities and motor skills as follows:

> The assumption is that the skills involved in complex activities can be described in terms of the more basic physical abilities. For example, the level of performance a man can attain on a turret lathe may depend on his basic physical abilities of manual dexterity and motor coordination. However, these same basic physical abilities may be important to proficiency in other skills as well. Thus, manual dexterity is needed in assembling electrical components, and motor coordination is needed to fly an airplane. Implicit in the previous analysis is the relation between abilities and learning. Thus, individuals with high manual dexterity may more readily learn the specific skill of lathe operation (1964).

Basic physical abilities are measured with many types of tests, and individuals differ in the extent to which they possess an ability (e.g., some people run faster than others). An individual with many highly developed basic physical abilities can become proficient at a wide variety of specific motor skills. For example, the "all-around" athlete is a person who has many highly developed basic physical abilities important to many different sports. Then, too, certain basic physical abilities are more generalized than others. For example, in our culture, verbal abilities are important in a greater variety of tasks than are many other abilities. Certainly speed, jumping ability, and muscular strength are important basic physical abilities related to athletic success.

According to Fleishman (1964), both the rate of learning and the final level of skill achieved depend on an individual's level of achievement in the more basic physical abilities. In this sense a test that measures basic physical abilities (construct validity) also may demonstrate concurrent and/or predictive validity. Remember, however, that the importance of a basic physical ability varies from skill to skill, which is the crucial difference between the theory of generality and that of basic physical abilities. General motor ability combines all test scores into a single score that supposedly is highly related to many different motor skills. In contrast, basic physical ability tests are themselves combined for each skill, and their relative importance varies for each skill. For example, the basic physical abilities for learning how to swim are different from those for learning how to pass a football; but the same basic physical abilities can be important to the performance of several different gross motor skills. Muscular strength is an important ability of many sport skills.

The development of basic physical abilities is a product of both genetic and environmental influences, with the genetic factor the limiting condition. Consider, for example, muscular strength. By participating in weight training programs, we can greatly influence the development of muscular strength; but the limit of that development (the maximum strength) depends on our genetics. Basic physical abilities develop during childhood and adolescence, reaching a fairly stable level in adulthood.

Fleishman reports that both the rate of learning and the final level achieved by an individual on specific motor skills are limited by basic physical abilities. Because an ability is a lasting, stable pattern of behavior, individual differences in basic physical abilities make it possible to predict the subsequent performance of specific skills. For example, the SAT measures verbal and quantitative abilities. Using a student's score on the quantitative ability section would be predictive of success in programs such as engineering, where math skills are very important, but not predictive of success in nonmathematical majors such as English. In this same way, running speed is an important factor in the running long jump; on the basis of a student's speed, we could judge better how well he or she will do on the long jump. Coaches maintain that the major reason that the world's premier long jumper Carl Lewis is in a class of his own can be traced to his world-class sprinting speed.

Basic physical abilities tests have at least two important applications. First, for evaluating athletes, and second, for use as preemployment tests in physically demanding jobs. These applications are illustrated next.

## Application 1: Evaluating Athletes

The testing of athletes has become accepted procedure. Before the 1976 Olympics, sport scientists studied the psychological, physiological, biomechanical, and medical characteristics of twenty world-class distance runners (Pollock et al. 1978). Prior to the unification of Germany, the East German Olympic team, which has been very successful in Olympic competition, conducted an extensive testing program for its athletes. Several years before its 1978 Super Bowl victory, the Dallas Cowboys team

**Table 8.2** Types of Tests Commonly Used to Evaluate Athletes

1. Maximal oxygen uptake ($\dot{V}O_2$ Max)
2. Percent body fat
3. Muscular strength
4. 40- or 50-yard sprint
5. Vertical or standing long jump
6. Agility run test

had developed a scientific program for evaluating and training its football players. Today, most university and professional teams hire a full-time strength coach who is responsible for testing and training athletes. The United States Olympic Committee developed a central facility for testing athletes in Colorado Springs, Colorado. This facility is fully staffed with exercise scientists who provide comprehensive testing of athletes. These data are given to the athlete and coach and used to improve training and performance.

The important concern is to find the physical abilities that are most relevant to the demands placed on an athlete. The more specific the test, the more valid it will be. At the U.S. Olympic testing site, for example, different exercise modes are used to measure $\dot{V}O_2$ Max. For distance runners, a treadmill-running protocol is followed; in contrast, specially devised cycle ergometer protocols are used to evaluate cyclists.

Table 8.2 lists the physical ability tests that are most appropriate for evaluating athletes. We would suggest following six steps when developing a battery for evaluating athletes.

1. Consider the sport and the basic qualities it demands of the athlete. For example, jumping ability would be especially important for volleyball and basketball players, and $\dot{V}O_2$ Max for distance runners.

2. Select tests that measure these defined traits. The tests may be found in Chapters 8 through 11.

3. Administer the tests to as many athletes as possible.

4. From their scores, develop percentile-rank norms using the procedures furnished in Chapter 3.

5. Use these norms to evaluate your athletes. The criterion for comparison here also can be earlier data on outstanding athletes, allowing you to evaluate your athletes with both the norm and outstanding players.

6. Reevaluate your selection of tests to be sure you are measuring the abilities most relevant to the sport. You should see a tendency for the best athletes to achieve the highest scores.

Provided in Tables 8.3 and 8.4 are sample test batteries used for college football players and female volleyball players. A profile for an athlete can be obtained by simply plotting his or her score on the table. In this way an athlete's strengths and weaknesses become apparent. The performance expectations of defined groups of football players are different, so profiles for defined subgroups of players are also provided on the team norms. The subgroup profile is the mean of all players in that

**Table 8.3** Percentile-Rank Norms for High School and College Female Volleyball Players

| | High School Players | | | | College Players | | | | |
| Percentile | Height | Vertical Jump | 20-Yard Dash | Basketball Throw | Height | Vertical Jump | 20-Yard Dash | Basketball Throw | Percentage Fat* |
|---|---|---|---|---|---|---|---|---|---|
| 99 | 74.0 | 22.0 | 2.87 | 70.8 | 77.0 | 24.0 | 2.83 | 82.3 | 11.2 |
| 95 | 71.0 | 18.5 | 3.04 | 64.5 | 72.0 | 20.5 | 3.00 | 68.5 | 12.3 |
| 90 | 70.0 | 17.8 | 3.12 | 60.0 | 71.0 | 19.8 | 3.07 | 66.8 | 12.6 |
| 85 | 69.0 | 16.5 | 3.17 | 57.0 | 70.0 | 19.0 | 3.12 | 64.0 | 13.2 |
| 80 | 68.0 | 16.0 | 3.20 | 55.0 | 69.5 | 18.5 | 3.16 | 61.2 | 13.5 |
| 75 | 67.5 | 15.7 | 3.23 | 52.8 | 69.0 | 18.0 | 3.17 | 59.4 | 14.0 |
| 70 | 67.0 | 15.3 | 3.26 | 51.5 | 68.5 | 17.5 | 3.20 | 58.3 | 14.4 |
| 65 | 66.5 | 15.0 | 3.28 | 50.5 | 68.5 | 17.0 | 3.27 | 57.6 | 14.6 |
| 60 | 66.0 | 14.5 | 3.32 | 49.0 | 68.0 | 16.8 | 3.30 | 56.6 | 15.1 |
| 55 | 65.5 | 14.2 | 3.34 | 48.4 | 67.5 | 16.5 | 3.33 | 56.1 | 15.5 |
| 50 | 65.5 | 14.0 | 3.37 | 47.2 | 67.5 | 16.0 | 3.37 | 55.0 | 16.0 |
| 45 | 65.5 | 13.7 | 3.42 | 46.0 | 67.0 | 15.8 | 3.40 | 53.9 | 16.5 |
| 40 | 65.0 | 13.5 | 3.46 | 44.5 | 67.0 | 15.5 | 3.42 | 52.3 | 17.5 |
| 35 | 65.0 | 13.3 | 3.47 | 43.5 | 66.0 | 15.0 | 3.44 | 51.1 | 18.2 |
| 30 | 64.0 | 13.0 | 3.50 | 42.0 | 66.0 | 14.7 | 3.50 | 51.0 | 18.8 |
| 25 | 64.0 | 12.5 | 3.53 | 40.8 | 65.5 | 14.0 | 3.53 | 50.1 | 20.5 |
| 20 | 63.0 | 12.3 | 3.57 | 39.2 | 65.0 | 13.5 | 3.60 | 48.7 | 21.5 |
| 15 | 62.5 | 12.0 | 3.60 | 37.8 | 64.0 | 12.7 | 3.67 | 46.6 | 22.9 |
| 10 | 62.0 | 11.5 | 3.67 | 36.4 | 63.5 | 11.5 | 3.73 | 45.8 | 26.0 |
| 5 | 61.5 | 11.0 | 3.80 | 33.5 | 62.5 | 10.5 | 3.83 | 41.2 | 31.3 |

Source: Data used with the permission of Dr. James G. Disch, Associate Professor of Physical Education, Rice University, Houston, TX.
*Percentage fat was not determined for high school players. See Chapter 11 for methods and norms appropriate for high school girls.

subgroup. Thus, an athlete's profile can be compared to the entire team and any subgroup. The University of Houston players who have gone on to play professional football have all been faster, stronger, and leaner than the average for their respective subgroup. This lends credence to the system.

Percentile-rank norms allow us to plot the athletes' test scores individually in a profile that we can then examine to determine whether an athlete shows a performance level compatible to that needed for a given sport. The profile is more than an evaluative technique; identifying a variation from the general profile, it provides data for designing a training program as well. For example, assume that a profile shows an athlete with a higher level of body fat than average. With this information, the coach can initiate an individualized diet and exercise program for the athlete. The profile provides both the coach and the athlete with an objective means of designing an individualized training program and motivating the athlete. Plotting retests can be used to gauge progress. And finally, the profile may give a coach insight into an athlete's potential.

Employers have always used some method to select an employee among potential job applicants. Much of the early preemployment testing focused on cognitive abilities, but with the rise in women seeking jobs that were once male dominated, the need for preemployment physical abilities tests increased. Most major fire and police departments

**Application 2: Preemployment Testing**

**Table 8.4** Percentile-Rank Norms for University
Football Players

| Percentile | 0–5 Yards | 20–40 Yards | 0–40 Yards | Percentage Fat | Bench Press |
|---|---|---|---|---|---|
| 99 | 0.985 | 1.933 | 4.412 | 4.1 | 422 |
| 95 | 1.029 | 1.995 | 4.626 | 6.5 | 389 |
| 90 | 1.052 | 2.028 | 4.737 | 7.7 | 376 |
| 85 | 1.067 | 2.049 | 4.812 | 8.7 | 360 |
| 80 | 1.080 | 2.067 | 4.903 | 9.2 | 350 |
| 75 | 1.091 | 2.083 | 4.926 | 9.8 | 342 |
| 70 | 1.101 | 2.096 | 4.973 | 10.3 | 335 |
| 65 | 1.109 | 2.108 | 5.013 | 10.7 | 329 |
| 60 | 1.118 | 2.121 | 5.057 | 11.3 | 322 |
| 55 | 1.126 | 2.131 | 5.094 | 11.6 | 316 |
| 50 | 1.134 | 2.143 | 5.134 | 12.0 | 310 |
| 45 | 1.142 | 2.155 | 5.174 | 12.3 | 304 |
| 40 | 1.150 | 2.166 | 5.212 | 12.7 | 298 |
| 35 | 1.159 | 2.178 | 5.255 | 13.2 | 291 |
| 30 | 1.167 | 2.190 | 5.295 | 13.6 | 285 |
| 25 | 1.177 | 2.203 | 5.342 | 14.1 | 278 |
| 20 | 1.188 | 2.219 | 5.394 | 14.6 | 270 |
| 15 | 1.201 | 2.237 | 5.456 | 15.1 | 260 |
| 10 | 1.216 | 2.258 | 5.531 | 15.9 | 244 |
| 5 | 1.239 | 2.291 | 5.642 | 16.9 | 231 |
| 1 | 1.283 | 2.353 | 5.856 | 18.8 | 198 |
| Mean | 1.134 | 2.143 | 5.134 | 12.0 | 310 |
| S.D. | 0.064 | 0.090 | 0.310 | 3.1 | |

Source: Data used with the permission of William F. Yeoman, Head Football Coach, University of Houston, Houston, TX.

require applicants to pass a physical ability test. Other occupations that use preemployment tests are telephone craft workers who climb poles, steel workers, coal miners, chemical plant workers, electrical transmission lineworkers, military personnel, and freight handlers. You are directed to other sources for a more complete discussion (Hogan 1991; Jackson 1994).

There are at least three reasons physical ability tests are used as a condition for employment. First, equal employment opportunity legislation resulted in greater numbers of females and handicapped individuals seeking employment in occupations requiring high levels of physical ability. Second, there was evidence suggesting that physically unfit workers had higher incidences of lower back injuries. Third, preemployment medical evaluations used alone are inadequate for personnel selection for a physically demanding job (Campion 1983). With the passage of the American with Disabilities Act (July 26, 1992), medical examinations cannot be given until an offer of employment is made. Any medically disqualifying condition must be shown to be job-related. One possible consequence of ADA is that validated physical ability tests will play a greater role in employee selection.

***Legal Issues.*** Preemployment tests face potential legal review because physical ability[1] tests are likely to have adverse impact against females and ethnic groups such as Asians and Hispanics (Hogan 1991). Public safety jobs (fire fighters, police officers, and correctional officers) have been the target of several sex discrimination litigation, and they have not fared well. You are directed to other sources for a review of legal issues (Arvey & Faley 1988; Arvey et al. 1992; Hogan & Quigley 1986).

In the 1960s and 1970s, height and weight standards were a condition of employment of most public safety workers. Since women and some ethnic groups (Asians and Hispanics) are shorter and lighter, a lower proportion of them met the standard. Arvey and Faley (1988) reported that in 1973, nearly all the nation's large police departments had a minimum height requirement. The average requirement was 68 inches. More than 90% of the women and only 45% of the males failed the 68-inch height requirement. The rational used to defend the standard was that size was related to physical strength, and the effectiveness of an officer's job performance depended upon strength. The United States Supreme Court ruled that if strength is a real job requirement, then a direct measure of strength should have been adopted. The height and weight standards of public safety jobs are being replaced with physical ability tests.

***Preemployment Test Methodology.*** If hiring practices produce adverse impact such as was the case with a height requirement, federal law requires that a validation study must support the selection method. The steps involved in a validation study are (1) complete a task analysis; (2) validate the selected tests; and (3) establish cut scores. Each is briefly reviewed next.

Broadly defined, a job analysis is the collection and analysis of any type of job-related information by any method for any purpose (Gael 1988). The objective of a job analysis is to find measures of work behavior(s) or performance that are used for the job and find the extent that they represent critical or important job duties, work behaviors, or work outcomes (EEOC 1978). Task analyses of physically demanding jobs often follow one or more of the following approaches.

*Psychophysical methods.* This method involves developing a scale that can be used to rate the frequency and intensity or physical demands required by various work tasks. The scale is administered to several employees who are engaged in these work tasks. This provides data by which work tasks can be compared. In a recent study, employees rated the task of lifting boxes that weigh over 60 pounds to shoulder height more demanding then lifting them to waist height.

*Biomechanical methods.* The types of data collected include heights, weights of the objects lifted or transported, and forces needed to complete work tasks such as opening and closing valves, or pushing and pulling objects. Biomechanical models provide a means of evaluating the stresses that the tasks of materials handling and lifting place on the spine (NIOSH 1981).

*Physiological methods.* Work tasks such as climbing stairs and fighting fires have a significant aerobic endurance component. Physiological methods document the cardiovascular response of these work tasks. For example, heart rate response when working provides an index of a work task's level of physical demands.

---

[1]Some governmental literature uses the term physical agility. The term physical ability will be used in this document.

**Figure 8.1**
Common work sample tests
included in police officer
and fire fighter
preemployment tests
(Arvey and Faley 1988). The
content validity of the test
is judged to the extent that
the test can be shown it is
job-related.

**POLICE OFFICERS**
Scaling a wall, usually 6 feet in height
Long (broad) jumping a set distance
Crawling through openings at ground level
Running a set distance, usually a quarter mile
Dragging a heavy object a set distance
Running a course consisting of various obstacles

**FIRE FIGHTERS**
Climbing a ladder
Pushing and pulling a ceiling hook
Dragging a dummy a set time period
Running up stairs carrying hose bundles

The failure to conduct a valid task analysis is a major reason preemployment physical ability tests have been ruled by the courts to be illegal (Arvey & Faley 1988; Hogan & Quigley 1986). The task analysis becomes the framework for developing and validating a preemployment test. Validating a preemployment test involves determining the accuracy with which a test or other selection device measures the important work behaviors identified with the job analysis. There are three validation strategies that can be followed.

1. Criterion-related validity. Criterion-related validity study has data showing that the preemployment test is predictive of, or significantly correlated with, important elements of job performance. The concurrent approach uses current employees and relates tests to current job performance. In the predictive approach, test data are obtained on people prior to hire and compared with performance data obtained at a later date (EEOC 1978).

2. Content validity. This is a rational process that involves gathering evidence that shows a logical relationship between the preemployment test and important duties or job behaviors. A content validity study needs to present data showing that the content of the selection procedure represents important aspects of performance on the job for which the candidates are to be evaluated (EEOC 1978). To illustrate, a typing test is a content valid test to hire a person for jobs involving typing, but not content valid for something like shoveling coal.

3. Construct validity. This approach is more theoretical than content validity because it is necessary to establish that a construct is required for job success and that the selection device measures the same construct. The data from a construct validation study should show that the preemployment test measures the degree to which candidates have identifiable characteristics that are important for successful job performance (EEOC 1978).

There are two general types of preemployment tests: (1) work sample tests; and (2) physical ability tests. The advantage of work sample tests is that they simulate the actual working conditions and are more likely to have content validity. Lifting and carrying boxes a specified distance is an example of a materials handling work sample test. Arvey (1992) reported that many police and fire fighter physical ability tests consist of some combination of job sample tests. Figure 8.1 lists work sample tests commonly included in these public safety preemployment tests.

**Table 8.5** Correlations between the Sum of Isometric Strength and Simulated Work Sample Test

| Reference | Work Sample Test | Correlation |
|---|---|---|
| Jackson et al. 1991 | Shoveling Coal | 0.71* |
| Jackson et al. 1991 | 50-pound Bag Carry | 0.63* |
| Jackson & Osburn 1983 | 70-pound Block Carry | 0.87* |
| Jackson & Osburn 1983 | One-arm Push Force | 0.91* |
| Jackson 1986 | Push Force | 0.86* |
| Jackson et al. 1993 | Push Force | 0.78** |
| Jackson 1986 | Pull Force | 0.78* |
| Jackson et al. 1993 | Pull Force | 0.67** |
| Laughery & Jackson 1984 | Lifting Force | 0.93* |
| Jackson et al. 1992 | Valve-Turning Endurance | 0.83* |
| Jackson et al. 1993 | Box Transport Endurance | 0.76** |
| Jackson et al. 1993 | Moving Document Bags | 0.70** |

*Sum of grip, arm lift, and torso lift isometric strength.
** Sum of arm lift, shoulder lift, torso lift, and leg lift isometric strength.

While work sample tests have the advantage of appearing to be valid, Ayoub (1982) maintains that they have at least two limitations. The first is safety. Applicants seeking employment are likely to be highly motivated to pass the work sample test. A highly motivated applicant that lacks the physical capacity to perform the task is likely to increase the risk of injury (Chaffin 1974; Chaffin et al. 1978; Keyserling et al. 1980a; Keyserling et al. 1980b; Snook et al. 1978). Outdoor telephone craft jobs require employees to climb telephone poles, and accident data showed that this was a dangerous task (Reilly et al. 1979). Using a pole climbing test to screen applicants would have content validity but likely would be too dangerous for untrained or physically unfit employees.

A second limitation of job simulation tests is they do not give any information about the applicant's maximum work capacity (Ayoub 1982). A work sample test is often scored by pass or fail (e.g., lifted a 95-pound jackhammer and carried it a specified distance). Some can easily complete the test, while others may just pass and be working at their maximum. If it can be assumed that there is a linear relationship between job performance and the preemployment test performance, applicants with the highest test scores can be expected to be the more productive workers. Testing for maximum capacity not only identifies the most potentially productive workers, but also defines a level of reserve that may reduce the risk of musculoskeletal injury.

Physical ability tests are the second type of items used for preemployment tests. The most common tests used include strength, body composition, and aerobic fitness. Strength tests are the most common item used. A common strategy has been to relate strength performance to criteria of job success (Reilly et al. 1979) or work sample tests (Jackson et al. 1984; Jackson et al. 1991; Jackson et al. 1990; Jackson et al. 1992; Jackson et al. 1993; Jackson et al. 1991; Reilly et al. 1979). Table 8.5 lists the correlations we have found between isometric strength tests and work sample test performance. There is a growing trend to use an index of aerobic fitness for selecting fire fighters (Sothmann et al. 1992; Sothmann et al. 1990). A "blue-ribbon" panel suggested the fat-free weight be used to select military personnel for heavy lifting tasks (Marriott 1992). Skinfold fat was used to disqualify applicants for jobs involving climbing poles (Reilly et al. 1979).

After completing the validation study, the next, difficult step is to set a cut score. The cut score is the test score that an applicant must obtain to be considered for the job. The Uniform Guidelines merely specify that cut scores should be reasonable and consistent with normal expectations of acceptable proficiency within the work force (EEOC 1978). The cut score should be based on a rational process and valid selection system that is flexible and meets the needs of the organization. Based on legal, historical, and professional guidelines, Cascio and associates (1988) offer several recommendations.

- The cut score should be based upon the results of the job analysis. The validity and job-relatedness of the testing procedure are crucial.

- The cut score should be sufficiently high to ensure minimally accepted job performance.

- The performance level associated with a cut score should be consistent with the normal expectations of acceptable proficiency within the work force.

The strategies used to set cut scores evolved largely from preemployment studies using psychological paper and pencil tests. However, in physical testing, the discipline of work physiology is also used. This involves matching the worker to the physiological demands of the task. Maximum oxygen uptake and strength are the physiological variables used to evaluate a worker's capacity to meet the demands of the job.

A current, important research focus is to define the energy cost needed to fight fires. This research effort can be attributed to litigation leveled at the validity of fire fighter preemployment tests and the use of age to terminate employment. Several investigators (Barnard & Duncan 1975; Davis & Dotson 1978; Lemon & Hermiston 1977; Manning & Griggs 1983; O'Connell et al. 1986; Sothmann et al. 1992) published data showing that fire suppression work tasks have a substantial aerobic component. In an excellent study, Sothmand and associates (1990) showed that the minimum $\dot{V}O_2$ Max required to meet the demands of fire fighting is 33.5 ml/kg/min. Fire fighters below this level were not able to meet basic fire suppression work demands

The work of Chaffin and his associates (Chaffin 1974; Chaffin et al. 1983; Chaffin et al. 1978; Chaffin & Park 1973; Herrin et al. 1974; Keyserling et al. 1980a; Keyserling et al. 1980b) showed the importance of matching the strength of workers with the job demands. If a 75-pound load must be lifted and transported, a worker must have sufficient strength to complete the task (see Figure 8.2). The results of the studies summarized in Table 8.5 show that strength is highly correlated with many industrial work sample tasks. Figure 8.3 is a bivariate plot between the sum of isometric strength and the capacity to generate push force (Jackson et al. 1993). Regression equations define the level of strength needed to generate sufficient force to complete the work task. In this example, the work task was to push a large container full of freight.

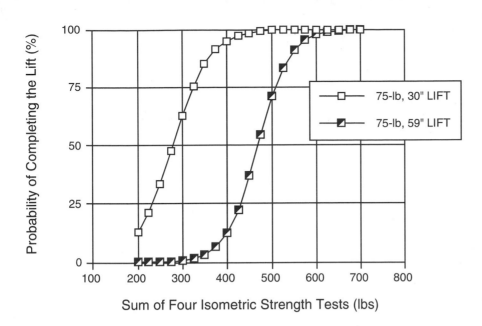

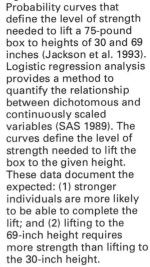

**Figure 8.2**
Probability curves that define the level of strength needed to lift a 75-pound box to heights of 30 and 69 inches (Jackson et al. 1993). Logistic regression analysis provides a method to quantify the relationship between dichotomous and continuously scaled variables (SAS 1989). The curves define the level of strength needed to lift the box to the given height. These data document the expected: (1) stronger individuals are more likely to be able to complete the lift; and (2) lifting to the 69-inch height requires more strength than lifting to the 30-inch height.

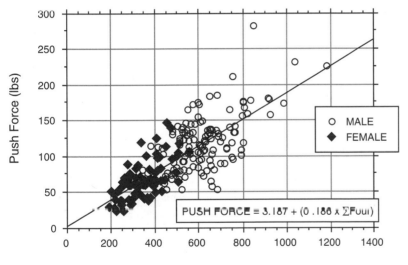

PUSH FORCE = 3.187 + (0.188 x $\Sigma$Four)

**Figure 8.3**
Scattergram and simple linear regression equation that defines the relationship between isometric strength and the capacity to generate the push force required to move freight containers. The force required to move the container was measured by pulling and recording the force with a load cell.

**Table 8.6** Basic Abilities of the Motor Performance Domain

**Muscular Strength**
1. Upper-body strength
2. Leg strength

**Muscular Power**
1. Arm power
2. Leg power

**Endurance**
1. Arm and shoulder girdle muscle endurance
2. Abdominal muscle endurance
3. Aerobic endurance ($VO_2$ Max)

**Basic Movement Patterns**
1. Running speed
2. Running agility
3. Jumping ability
4. Throwing ability

**Flexibility**

**Balance**

**Kinesthesis**

**Fine Psychomotor Abilities**

## Measurement of Basic Physical Abilities

Provided in this section are basic physical abilities and tests that can be used to measure each ability. The system for classifying basic physical abilities shown in Table 8.6 is empirical, or measurement-oriented. It rests on the findings of several factor analysis studies (Baumgartner & Zuidema 1972; Bernauer & Bonanno 1975; Considine et al. 1976; Cousins 1955; Cumbee 1954; Disch et al. 1975; Fleishman 1964; Harris 1969; Ismail et al. 1965; Jackson 1971; Jackson & Frankiewicz 1975; Jackson & Pollock 1976; Larson 1941; Liba 1967; McCloy 1956; Meyers et al. 1984; Safrit 1966; Zuidema & Baumgartner 1974). The tests listed as measures of the same ability are highly correlated with that ability; the correlations between tests of different basic physical abilities tend to be lower, closer to zero. This system allows you to develop test batteries that reliably measure different abilities. For each ability we have included at least one test.

## Muscular Strength

**Muscular strength** is the maximum force that a muscle group can exert over a brief period. Muscular strength can be measured with a maximum static contraction, isometric strength, or maximal dynamic contractions that include isotonic and isokinetic strength. Additionally, it has been shown that absolute endurance is highly correlated with strength (deVries 1980). A brief discussion of each measurement method follows.

### Isometric Strength

This method of strength testing has historically been popular. The equipment is readily available and inexpensive. A principle advantage of isometric tests is in their flexibility—if a position can be standardized, it is possible to measure isometric

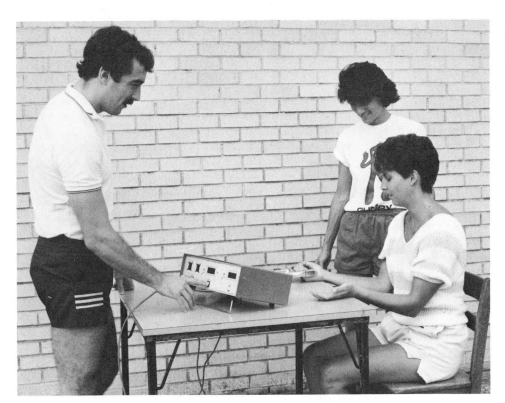

**Figure 8.4**
Isometric testing
equipment for the test
grip strength.

strength. Isometric tests have been developed to measure single muscle groups (e.g., elbow flexion or elbow extension) or a combination of muscle groups.

**Tensiometers** and **dynamometers** have been traditionally used for recording force, but electronic load cells are now replacing these mechanical devices. The National Institute for Occupational Safety and Health (NIOSH 1977) has studied the issues of isometric strength testing as it related to preemployment testing for physically demanding jobs. The recommendation of NIOSH is to replace these mechanical devices with electronic load cells. Mechanical equipment is subject to error and difficult to calibrate. An example of a load cell unit is shown in Figure 8.4.

### Isotonic Strength

A popular strength test is to measure the maximal force one can lift with one repetition (1-RM test). The most difficult part of the test is to find the subject's maximal load. Several different weights will need to be tried to find the proper 1-RM weight. This test can be administered with standard barbells, but we recommend strength development machines common to most facilities (e.g., Universal gymnasium). Because equipment varies in design, 1-RM tests need to be specific to the muscle group tested. The maximal weight lifted will be higher for progressive resistance equipment (e.g., Nautilus) because the resistance changes during the exercise.

### Isokinetic Strength

A sound way to measure strength is with isokinetic equipment. This is the method used at the U.S. Olympic Training Center to measure the strength of our Olympic athletes and by NASA scientists to measure astronauts' loss of strength during extended space missions. The speed of resistance is set at a constant rate while the subject exerts maximal force through the entire range of motion. The exerted force is recorded on graph paper, allowing the test to be scored by measuring (1) the force output achieved at a specified joint angle; (2) the peak force output; and (3) the total work applied through the range of motion, which is the area under the curve. A test position is shown in Figure 8.5. The major disadvantage of the isokinetic method is cost. The equipment is expensive and so is usually used only at well-equipped testing centers such as NASA, the U.S. Olympic Center, and modern sports medicine and physical therapy facilities.

### Absolute Endurance

Muscular strength and absolute endurance are highly correlated. In an **absolute endurance test,** a weight load is repeatedly lifted until exhaustion is reached, and the same weight is used for all subjects tested. Examples of absolute endurance tests are the strength tests recommended by the YMCA. These are provided in this chapter.

DeVries (1980) has reported that the correlations between strength and absolute endurance tests are high (at least .90). The reason for the high relation between strength and absolute endurance is that subjects are lifting at different percentages of maximal strength. For example, assume the maximal bench press strengths of two people are 120 and 125 pounds. If the weight load for the test is 110 pounds, the weaker person would be lifting at 92% of maximal while the stronger person would be lifting at 73% of maximal strength. The stronger person would complete more repetitions before becoming exhausted.

*Measuring Upper-Body Strength.* Tests of upper-body strength measure the maximum force that can be generated with the arms and back and can be static or dynamic contractions. Because muscular strength is related to the cross-sectional size of a muscle group, there is a positive correlation between strength body weight, more specifically fat-free weight. All other factors being equal, individuals with more fat-free weight can generate higher force outputs. Provided next are sample isotonic and isometric strength tests.

### Isometric Strength Test Battery[1]

Many different types of isometric strength tests have been used. Isometric strength tests have been used extensively for preemployment testing (Hogan 1991; Jackson et al. 1990; NIOSH 1977; NIOSH 1981).

*Objective:* To measure the maximal force for selected muscle groups.

*Validity:* Isometric tests have been recognized as a valid method for measuring strength. The isometric strength tests are highly correlated with simulated work tasks of physically demanding occupations.

---

[1]For a comprehensive manual for isometric strength testing contact Lafayette Instrument Company, P.O. Box 5729, Lafayette, Indiana 47903. Phone (800) 428–7545.

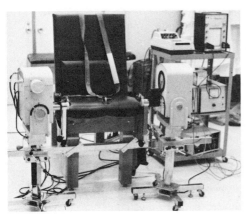

(a)

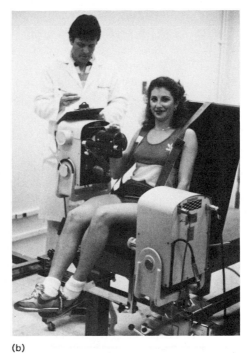

(b)

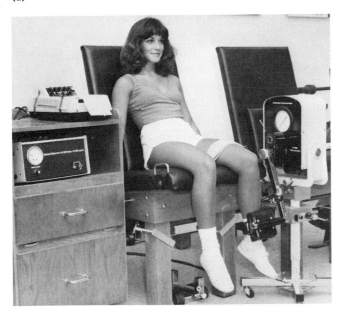

(c)

**Figure 8.5**
Cybex equipment for testing isokinetic strength. This equipment is used by NASA to evaluate the expected loss of strength as a result of extended space flight; (a) testing equipment, (b) device for testing arm strength, and (c) device for testing leg strength. (Photos courtesy of Cybex.)

*Reliability:* The reliability estimates exceed 0.90 for each test.

*Equipment:* The tests are administered on equipment manufactured by Lafayette Instrument Company, Lafayette, IN (Model 32528) and consist of a grip strength apparatus, a platform with a chain apparatus, and a load cell and digital recorder. The equipment was developed for preemployment testing for physically demanding jobs for the Shell Oil Company, Houston, TX. The equipment is now widely used in medical and rehabilitative settings.

*Procedures:* Once the subject is in the test position, the tester pushes the "start" button. A "beep" will sound and 3 seconds later a second "beep" will be heard. The subject is instructed to exert force on this first "beep" and stop on the second "beep." The equipment allows you to set the length of the trial. A 3-second trial is used during which force is recorded only for the last 2 seconds. Typically, subjects will jerk at the start of the trial. By not measuring this first second, the jerk is not reflected in the strength score, which is the average force exerted during the final two seconds. A warm-up trial at 50% effort is administered first, followed by two trials for score. External forms of motivation are to be strictly avoided. Do not encourage the subject when he/she is exerting force. Do not give the subject his/her score after completing a trial.

1. **Grip.** The grip strength is tested with the load cell attached to the grip apparatus. The subject is seated at a table with the free hand on the table. The apparatus is gripped with the palm up. Maximal force is exerted in this position (see Figure 8.4).

2. **Arm Lift.** The arm-lift apparatus is used to measure lifting strength. The load cell is attached and equipment is adjusted so the elbows are at 90° flexion. The legs should be straight and the subject is not allowed to lean back. Maximal lifting force is exerted in this position (see Figure 8.6).

3. **Shoulder lift.** The bar setting used for the arm-lift test is used for the shoulder lift. To assume the correct position, the subject moves forward until the bar touches her/his body. The cable should be at a right angle to the base. With the palms facing the rear, the subject grabs the bar so that the inside of the hands are on the inside of the black handle. In this position the elbows are pointing out, away from the body. This test measures the lifting strength of the shoulders. The subject is not allowed to lean back or use his/her legs (e.g., bending the knees and generating force with the legs). The force is correctly exerted by lifting up with the shoulders while the elbows point outward (see Figure 8.7).

4. **Torso Strength.** The Torso lift test is recommended for preemployment testing (NIOSH, 1977). Figure 8.8 illustrates the NIOSH test position. It has been our experience that many are hesitant to be tested in this position. Our research led us to the development of the Torso Pull test also shown in Figure 8.8. With a sample of 246 industrial workers and 204 students, we found a high correlation (r = 0.91) between the two tests shown in Figure 8.8. We recommend that the Torso Pull test be used. The test procedure is described next.

   The platform-chain apparatus is placed against the wall with the chain at its lowest point. The bar is set 17 inches from the base of the platform.

**Figure 8.6**
Arm-lift test.

**Figure 8.7**
Shoulder-lift test.

**NIOSH
TORSO LIFT**

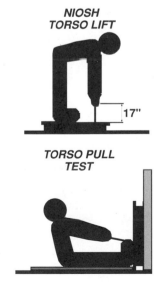

17"

**TORSO PULL
TEST**

**Figure 8.8**
The torso
strength tests.

**Table 8.7** Means, Standard Deviations, and Sample Sizes for Isometric Strength Tests Administered to College Students and Different Groups of Workers

| Sample | Grip Strength MEAN | SD | N | Arm Lift MEAN | SD | N | NIOSH Torso Lift MEAN | SD | N | Shoulder Lift MEAN | SD | N |
|---|---|---|---|---|---|---|---|---|---|---|---|---|
| **Fit College Students** | | | | | | | | | | | | |
| Females | 64.1 | 15.5 | 207 | 44.5 | 13.0 | 226 | 114.0 | 34.1 | 226 | 67.3 | 14.8 | 19 |
| Males | 99.4 | 27.0 | 193 | 85.3 | 19.4 | 224 | 195.6 | 60.5 | 224 | 108.0 | 22.7 | 31 |
| **Gas Company    Construction Workers** | | | | | | | | | | | | |
| Females | 80.2 | 23.3 | 18 | 58.4 | 16.3 | 18 | 145.2 | 60.1 | 18 | * | | |
| Males | 111.1 | 23.3 | 234 | 88.8 | 19.8 | 234 | 213.7 | 65.3 | 234 | * | | |
| **Gas Company    Service Workers** | | | | | | | | | | | | |
| Females | 70.8 | 19.0 | 34 | 49.5 | 13.3 | 34 | 128.4 | 38.0 | 34 | * | | |
| Males | 108.8 | 23.3 | 212 | 77.9 | 18.9 | 212 | 182.0 | 59.0 | 212 | * | | |
| **Public Safety    Highway Patrol Cadets** | | | | | | | | | | | | |
| Females | 71.5 | 16.2 | 17 | 53.4 | 10.3 | 17 | 150.3 | 26.4 | 17 | * | | |
| Males | 113.8 | 25.2 | 161 | 97.9 | 18.2 | 161 | 247.6 | 55.3 | 161 | * | | |
| **Coal Miners** | | | | | | | | | | | | |
| Males | 124.8 | 17.5 | 98 | 96.1 | 12.7 | 98 | 255.3 | 55.9 | 98 | * | | |
| **Express Freight Workers** | | | | | | | | | | | | |
| Females | * | | | 48.3 | 11.0 | 56 | 114.1 | 34.2 | 56 | 65.1 | 16.7 | 56 |
| Males | * | | | 88.1 | 18.2 | 101 | 203.2 | 55.2 | 101 | 120.8 | 22.8 | 101 |
| **Refinery Workers** | | | | | | | | | | | | |
| Females | 76.8 | 12.8 | 14 | 53.6 | 12.4 | 14 | 133.9 | 54.2 | 14 | * | | |
| Males | 118.1 | 23.3 | 75 | 91.1 | 16.3 | 75 | 204.3 | 56.4 | 75 | * | | |

*Test not administered to this group.

The subject sits on a mat and places his or her feet against platform. The subject uses a reverse grip (palms facing the floor) and keeps the legs straight. The force is correctly exerted by leaning and pulling back. Provided next is a regression equation that can be used to estimate the NIOSH Torso Life strength from Torso Pull.

NIOSH Torso Lift = (0.973 × Torso Pull) − 18.188

*Scoring:* The average of two trials are used for score. Table 8.7 gives the means, standard deviations, and sample sizes for physically fit college students and occupational groups contrasted by gender.

### Bench Press, Curls, and Lat. Pull Tests (Jackson & Smith 1974)

These isotonic tests are especially applicable in facilities that have strength development machines. Provided next are test items used with college students.

*Objective:* To measure 1-RM strength or absolute endurance.

*Validity:* Construct validity of muscular strength of the arms.

**Figure 8.9**
Bench press with free weights.

*Equipment:* A Universal gym or similar weight-training machine. Besides serving as a teaching station for weight-training instruction, this type of equipment is excellent for measuring arm strength. Free weights also can be used with proper spotting. In fact, the YMCA (Golding et al. 1989) recommends the bench press with free weights to measure arm strength. The bench press test is shown in Figure 8.9.

*Procedures:* If the 1-RM test is to be used, students will need to practice to find their 1-RM. This should be completed prior to the test day. If absolute endurance is to be the test, select a weight load appropriate for the group being tested. For a group of male college freshmen, the following weight loads were used: bench press, 110 pounds; curls, 50 pounds; lat. pull, 100 pounds. For different groups, other weights would be appropriate. You need to select a weight load that every student can execute with at least one repetition. For the YMCA two-arm curl test, the weights are 25 pounds for women and 40 pounds for men. For the bench press, 80- and 35-pound barbells are used for men and women, respectively.

Each repetition is done on the regulated cadence of a 3-second count. Each repetition must be completed in the 3-second limit, and each new repetition cannot begin until a new 3-second interval begins. Each effort must begin from the original starting position. The students should not drop or slam the weights.

1. **Bench press.** The student can assume any width grasp outside the shoulders. Feet must be on the floor, the back straight. After each repetition the weights must be brought back to touch the weights beneath them.

**Table 8.8** The 25th, 50th, and 75th Percentiles for Absolute Arm Endurance of Men (Adjusted for Body Weight)

| Body Weight | Bench Press | | | Curls | | | Lat. Pull | | |
|---|---|---|---|---|---|---|---|---|---|
| | $P_{25}$ | $P_{50}$ | $P_{75}$ | $P_{25}$ | $P_{50}$ | $P_{75}$ | $P_{25}$ | $P_{50}$ | $P_{75}$ |
| 100–109 | 6 | 11 | 16 | 10 | 17 | 23 | 12 | 18 | 24 |
| 110–119 | 7 | 12 | 17 | 11 | 18 | 24 | 13 | 19 | 24 |
| 120–129 | 8 | 13 | 18 | 13 | 19 | 25 | 14 | 20 | 25 |
| 130–139 | 9 | 14 | 20 | 14 | 20 | 26 | 15 | 20 | 26 |
| 140–149 | 10 | 16 | 21 | 15 | 21 | 28 | 16 | 21 | 27 |
| 150–159 | 12 | 17 | 22 | 16 | 22 | 29 | 16 | 22 | 28 |
| 160–169 | 13 | 18 | 23 | 17 | 24 | 30 | 17 | 23 | 28 |
| 170–179 | 14 | 19 | 24 | 19 | 25 | 31 | 18 | 24 | 29 |
| 180–189 | 15 | 20 | 26 | 20 | 26 | 32 | 19 | 24 | 30 |
| 190–199 | 16 | 22 | 27 | 21 | 27 | 33 | 20 | 25 | 31 |
| 200–209 | 18 | 23 | 28 | 22 | 28 | 35 | 20 | 26 | 32 |
| 210–219 | 19 | 24 | 29 | 23 | 29 | 36 | 21 | 27 | 32 |
| 220–229 | 20 | 25 | 30 | 24 | 31 | 37 | 22 | 28 | 33 |
| 230–239 | 21 | 26 | 31 | 26 | 32 | 38 | 23 | 28 | 34 |
| 240–249 | 23 | 28 | 33 | 27 | 33 | 39 | 24 | 29 | 35 |

Source: Department of HHP, University of Houston, Houston, TX.

2. **Curls.** The student stands with head, shoulders, and buttocks against a wall, feet bracing his or her back, and the feet some 12 to 15 inches away from the wall. Place a sheet of paper behind the buttocks. The student must keep the paper pinned against the wall during the exercise, which both forces the student to use the elbow flexors and prevents a rocking motion. Stop the count when the paper falls. Position the machine so that when the student holds the weight with arms fully extended, the exercise weight is suspended slightly above the remaining weight. A complete repetition occurs when the arms are fully flexed and the bar touches the chin. Be sure the student remains against the wall and fully extends the arms after each repetition.

3. **Lat. pull.** The student grasps the bar on the handle grips and kneels on the floor. The bar is pulled down behind the head to touch at the juncture of the neck and shoulders, just below the hairline. The weight should be brought back to the starting position without jerking or lifting the student off the floor.

*Scoring:* For the 1-RM test a student's score is the maximal weight lifted, and for absolute endurance it is the number of repetitions completed. Stop the count whenever a student fails to complete a repetition correctly or to maintain the 3-second cadence.

*Norms:* Percentile-rank norms developed on college men and women who have completed a 16-week weight-training program are listed in Tables 8.8 and 8.9. The norms have been adjusted for body weight.

**Table 8.9** Percentile Norms for College Women for 1-RM Bench Press Strength for Selected Body Weights

| Body Weight | Percentile* | | | | |
| --- | --- | --- | --- | --- | --- |
| | **95** | **75** | **50** | **25** | **5** |
| 90 | 93 | 73 | 65 | 55 | 43 |
| 100 | 97 | 77 | 69 | 59 | 47 |
| 110 | 101 | 81 | 73 | 63 | 51 |
| 120 | 105 | 85 | 77 | 67 | 55 |
| 130 | 109 | 89 | 81 | 71 | 59 |
| 140 | 113 | 93 | 85 | 75 | 63 |
| 150 | 117 | 97 | 89 | 79 | 67 |
| 160 | 121 | 101 | 93 | 83 | 71 |
| 170 | 126 | 106 | 98 | 88 | 76 |
| 180 | 130 | 110 | 102 | 92 | 80 |
| 190 | 134 | 114 | 106 | 96 | 84 |
| 200 | 138 | 118 | 110 | 100 | 88 |

*Data from 202 college women using the Universal Gym Spartacus (Jackson & Gibson 1984).

### YMCA Bench Press Test

The Y's Way to Physical Fitness program (Golding et al. 1989) includes a bench test to measure strength of adults. The general procedures for the YMCA test are

1. A 35-pound barbell is used for women and an 80-pound weight for men.

2. The test is to bench press the barbell at a rate of 30 repetitions per minute. A metronome is used to regulate the rate.

3. The test is terminated when

   a. a participant is unable to reach full extension of the elbows.

   b. a participant breaks cadence and cannot keep up with the rhythm of the metronome.

4. The score is the number of repetitions. Norms for men and women of selected age groups are provided in Table 8.10.

*Measuring Leg Strength.* Research shows that the muscular strength is comprised of more than a single component. Three studies (Jackson 1971; Jackson & Frankiewicz 1975; Start et al. 1966) have identified separate abilities in the arms and legs. Isometric and isokinetic strength testing equipment can be used to measure leg strength, but the availability of weight-training equipment makes 1-RM leg strength tests a realistic option. Isometric leg strength is a recommended preemployment test (NIOSH 1977).

**Table 8.10** Adult Norms for the YMCA Bench Press Test

| Percentile | Age Group 18–25 | 26–35 | 36–45 | 46–55 | 56–65 | >65 |
|---|---|---|---|---|---|---|
| *Adult Men* | | | | | | |
| 95 | 42 | 40 | 34 | 28 | 24 | 20 |
| 75 | 30 | 26 | 24 | 20 | 14 | 10 |
| 50 | 22 | 20 | 17 | 12 | 8 | 6 |
| 25 | 13 | 12 | 10 | 6 | 4 | 2 |
| 5 | 2 | 2 | 2 | 1 | 0 | 0 |
| *Adult Women* | | | | | | |
| 95 | 42 | 40 | 32 | 30 | 30 | 22 |
| 75 | 28 | 25 | 21 | 20 | 16 | 12 |
| 50 | 20 | 17 | 13 | 11 | 9 | 6 |
| 25 | 12 | 9 | 8 | 5 | 3 | 2 |
| 5 | 2 | 1 | 1 | 0 | 0 | 0 |

Source: Norms from the *Y's Way to Physical Fitness,* 1989, 3rd edition.

### 1-RM Leg Strength Test

*Objective:* To determine the greatest weight one can lift with the legs during one repetition.

*Validity:* Construct validity of leg strength.

*Equipment:* A Universal gym or similar weight-training machine. Free weights are not recommended because the need for heavy weight increases the chance of injury.

*Procedures:* Start with a weight that can be lifted comfortably, continuing to add weight until the individual's maximum value is found. The appropriate weight is easy to identify with experienced weight lifters; trial and error methods have to be used with inexperienced lifters. The Universal gym allows you to measure leg press and leg extension strength.

1. **Leg press.** The subject sits in the provided chair, fully extends the legs, and executes a maximal repetition. The starting position is shown in Figure 8.10. The seat should be adjusted to standardize the knee angle at approximately 120°.

2. **Leg extension.** The subject is in a sitting position, and the test is to extend the knee from 90° to 180°. The test position is shown in Figure 8.11.

*Scoring:* The subject's score is the maximum weight lifted during one repetition. The procedure of using the number of repetitions with a constant weight load is not recommended: Some subjects are so strong they will achieve an excessive number of repetitions, creating positively skewed distributions.

*Norms:* Wilmore (1976) provides optimal leg press strength values for males and females in Table 8.11. Furnished in Table 8.12 are leg extension norms for college women adjusted for body weight.

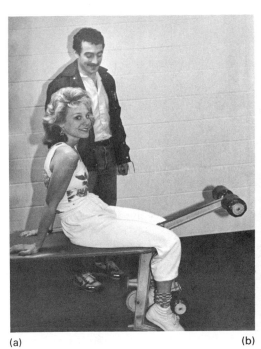

**Figure 8.10**
Using the Universal Gym to
test leg strength.

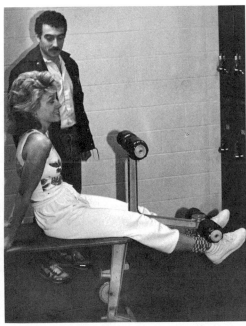

**Figure 8.11**
Leg extensions.
An individual with
knee extended
(a) 90°, and
(b) 180°.

(a)                                        (b)

Chapter 8  Measuring Physical Abilities                217

**Table 8.11** Optimal 1-RM Leg Press Standards

| Body Weight | Males | Females |
|---|---|---|
| 80 | 160 | 112 |
| 100 | 200 | 140 |
| 120 | 240 | 168 |
| 140 | 280 | 296 |
| 160 | 320 | 224 |
| 180 | 360 | 252 |
| 200 | 400 | 280 |
| 220 | 440 | 308 |
| 240 | 480 | 336 |

Data from Dr. Jack H. Wilmore, Department of Physical Education, University of Texas, Austin, TX.

**Table 8.12** Percentile Norms for College Women for 1-RM Leg Extension Strength for Selected Body Weights

| Body Weight | Percentile 95 | 75 | 50 | 25 | 5 |
|---|---|---|---|---|---|
| 90 | 104 | 84 | 65 | 45 | 23 |
| 100 | 112 | 92 | 73 | 53 | 31 |
| 110 | 120 | 100 | 81 | 61 | 39 |
| 120 | 128 | 108 | 89 | 69 | 47 |
| 130 | 136 | 116 | 97 | 77 | 55 |
| 140 | 144 | 124 | 105 | 85 | 63 |
| 150 | 152 | 132 | 113 | 93 | 71 |
| 160 | 160 | 140 | 121 | 101 | 79 |
| 170 | 168 | 148 | 129 | 109 | 87 |
| 180 | 176 | 156 | 137 | 117 | 95 |
| 190 | 184 | 164 | 145 | 125 | 103 |
| 200 | 192 | 172 | 153 | 133 | 111 |

Data from 202 college women using the Universal Gym Spartacus (Jackson & Gibson, 1984).

## Muscular Power

**Muscular power** has traditionally been defined as maximum force released in the shortest possible time. Power is the movement of one's body mass in the shortest possible time. The vertical jump, standing long jump, and shot put have been the recommended measures of power (McCloy 1932), but jumping tests are not highly correlated with mechanically measured power (Barlow 1970; Considine 1970; Glencross 1966; Gray 1962).

Muscle strength and **work** are essential in demonstrating power, as is clear from the following formula:

$$W = F \times D$$

where W is work, F is force, and D is the distance the force moves.

**Power** is the rate that work is performed and is calculated with the following formula:

P = W/T

where P is power, W is work, and T is the time required to perform the work.

Two studies have reported that arm and leg power have different components, which means that motor tasks requiring leg power differ from those that require arm power (Glencross 1966; Jackson & Frankiewicz 1975). Leg power tests generally measure the work required to move a weight load equal to one's body weight. Tests of arm power, on the other hand, involve moving a weight load that remains constant for different individuals. Examples are putting a shot and throwing a ball.

We can use these work and power formulas to illustrate the characteristics of human arm and leg power outputs. For example, if, using the bench press, a boy moves a 70-pound weight load a vertical height of 1.5 feet, the work is 105 foot-pounds:

W = (70 × 1.5) = 105 foot-pounds.

Assuming the weight was moving as fast as possible and that the boy took 0.15 seconds to move the weight load 1.5 feet, his power output is 700 foot-pounds per second:

$$P = \frac{(70 \times 1.5)}{0.15} = 700 \text{ foot-pounds per second.}$$

Let us look at another example. Assume that the same boy, who weighs 180 pounds, sprints up a 15-foot hill. The work performed equals 2700 foot-pounds:

W = (180 × 15) = 2700 foot-pounds.

If the sprint took 2 seconds, the boy's power output is 1350 foot-pounds per second:

$$P = \frac{(180 \times 15)}{2} = 1350 \text{ foot-pounds per second.}$$

*Measuring Arm Power.*   Arm power is characterized by an explosive contraction of the muscle groups of the arms and shoulder girdle. As we have said, arm power is measured by applying force to a weight load that is relatively heavy and constant for all subjects.

Researchers have measured arm power with specially developed power levers and electronic timing devices, neither of which is feasible for mass testing. Although not verified by research, putting the shot and medicine ball for distance are traditionally accepted tests of arm power (McCloy & Young 1954). Body weight is moderately correlated with arm power.

### Shot Put or Medicine Ball Put Test

*Objective:* To put a weighted object for distance with a maximal effort of the arms.

*Validity:* Construct validity of muscular strength of the arms.

*Equipment:* A 100-foot tape measure to measure the puts. A shot put that weighs from 4 to 12 pounds, or a 6- or 9-pound medicine ball may be used. The size of the weighted object depends on the age, gender, and strength of the participants. With an indoor shot put or medicine ball, the test can be administered in a gymnasium.

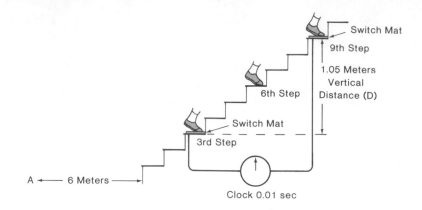

**Figure 8.12**
Margaria-Kalamen leg power test. (From Matthews, D. K. and E. L. Fox. 1976. *The Physiological Basis of Physical Education and Athletics,* 2nd ed. Philadelphia, PA: W. B. Saunders. (p. 501). Reprinted by permission of Holt, Rinehart and Winston.)

*Procedure:* The student assumes a position behind a restraining line with the shoulders in line with the test course; the side opposite the throwing arm should be facing the direction of the throw. The shot put or medicine ball should be tucked under the chin. From a standing position the student dips back, without moving the feet, to gather momentum and puts the object down the test course. In track and field terminology this is called putting from the reverse position. A run is not recommended.

*Alternative Procedures:* The test can be administered with the student sitting in a chair or on the ground.

*Scoring:* The student's score is the distance of the put measured to the last half-foot. Concentric circles drawn 1 foot apart are recommended for scoring the test, eliminating the need to measure each throw. In most situations measurements accurate to the last foot are precise enough to produce reliable data.

*Other Considerations:* The shot put is recommended over the medicine ball because many students have difficulty controlling the medicine ball. It is important that the students be allowed to practice this test before taking it. This test can be very time-consuming to administer to a large class. By taking the necessary precautions of setting up the test course so that each throw does not need to be measured, one person can easily administer three or four trials to a class in 45 minutes. By measuring to the last foot rather than the last half-foot, some precision is lost, but efficiency is gained.

### Measuring Leg Power.

Leg power is characterized by the explosive movement of the entire body. Leg power, or anaerobic power, is the power generated by the legs when moving the body. Because body weight is the mass moved, the mass varies among subjects.

Margaria and his associates (1966) were the first to publish a leg power test, which has been revised as shown in Figure 8.12 (Mathews & Fox 1971). The subject begins 6 meters from the bottom stair and runs up the stairs as fast as possible, taking three steps at a time. Switch mats are placed on the third and ninth steps. By stepping on the third stair, the subject starts a clock accurate to one-hundredth of a second;

when the subject steps on the ninth stair, the clock is stopped. The time recorded by the clock represents the time required to move the body a height of 1.05 meters. Power is calculated using the following formula:

$$\text{Power} = \frac{(W \times 1.05)}{T}$$

where W is the subject's weight in kilograms, 1.05 is the height in meters, and T is elapsed time.

Chaloupha revised this test for boys, grades 2 through 6, placing the switch mats on the second and sixth steps (Mathews 1978). It was reported that this variation represents a more valid procedure for classifying boys for age-group football teams. Margaria and his associates (1966) report that athletes have higher levels of leg power than nonathletes. Leg power is useful for predicting athletic success in a power-related sport such as football.

**Muscular endurance** is the ability to persist in physical activity or to resist muscular fatigue (deVries 1980). Endurance tests can measure absolute endurance where the weight load moved to exhaustion is the same for all subjects tested or relative endurance where the weight moved varies among the subjects tested. The muscular endurance abilities described here involve moving or maintaining one's own body weight to exhaustion. Since body weights among subjects will vary, these are tests of relative endurance. Three basic endurance abilities have been identified: (1) muscular endurance of the arms and shoulder girdle, (2) muscular endurance of the abdominal muscles, and (3) cardiorespiratory endurance. Tests used to measure these endurance abilities are included in motor fitness and health-related fitness tests (see Chapters 9 and 10).

Endurance

*Measuring Arm and Shoulder Girdle Endurance.*  Tests of this ability require the subject to move or support the body weight against the pull of gravity and may involve either isometric or isotonic contractions of the muscles executed to exhaustion. It has been claimed that tests of this ability measure both strength and endurance. Dynamic strength, arm and shoulder girdle strength, and muscular endurance are the terms used by physical educators to describe this ability. There is a negative correlation between body weight and this basic physical ability, and the correlation is even higher between percent of body fat and this basic ability.

The tests most often recommended for motor fitness or physical fitness batteries are pull-ups or chin-ups, and the flexed-arm hang. The AAHPERD Youth Fitness Test (1976) includes pull-ups for boys and the flexed-arm hang for girls. On both tests, the student is required to use the forward grip, palms facing away from the body. These tests can also be administered with the reverse grip, palms facing the body. Wells (1971) maintains that the reverse grip is the most favorable position for the biceps. With the forward grip, the function of the biceps is greatly diminished because the tendon is wrapped around the radius and the effective lever arm is reduced. Testing procedures for the AAHPERD pull-up and flexed-arm hang tests are provided in Chapter 9. Provided with the test instructions are norms.

**Table 8.13** Optimal Criterion-Referenced Standards for the Modified Pull-Up and Curl-Up Tests for Boys and Girls, Ages 5 to 17+

| Age | Boys Curl-Ups | Boys Modified Pull-Ups | Girls Curl-Ups | Girls Modified Pull-Ups |
|-----|---------|---------------|---------|---------------|
| 5 | 7 | 10 | 7 | 10 |
| 6 | 7 | 10 | 7 | 10 |
| 7 | 9 | 14 | 9 | 14 |
| 8 | 11 | 20 | 11 | 20 |
| 9 | 11 | 24 | 11 | 22 |
| 10 | 15 | 24 | 13 | 26 |
| 11 | 17 | 28 | 13 | 29 |
| 12 | 20 | 36 | 13 | 32 |
| 13 | 22 | 40 | 13 | 32 |
| 14 | 25 | 45 | 13 | 32 |
| 15 | 27 | 47 | 13 | 35 |
| 16 | 30 | 47 | 13 | 35 |
| 17 | 30 | 47 | 13 | 35 |
| 17+ | 30 | 47 | 13 | 35 |

Standards from the Prudential FITNESSGRAM® test (1992).

When preparing to measure this ability, it is important to select a test of appropriate difficulty for the group being tested. There is a tendency for these test distributions to be positively skewed. Many students (e.g., junior high girls) have difficulty maintaining or moving their body weight against gravity. A high proportion of students, especially girls, cannot complete a single pull-up. This has led to the development of modified pull-up tests. Described next are two modified pull-up tests.

**Youth Fitness Modified Pull-Up Test.** The Prudential FITNESSGRAM® (1992) and AAHPERD Physical Best Tests (1989) youth fitness tests provide an optional test. For this test, the student lies down on his/her back with the shoulders directly under a bar[2] that has been set 1 to 2 inches above the child's reach. The student grasps the bar with an overhand grip (palms away from the body). From this "down" position with the arms and legs straight, buttocks off the floor, and only the heels touching the floor, the student pulls until the chin reaches an elastic band placed on the pull-up equipment. The band is set 7 inches below the pull-up bar. Table 8.13 gives the optimal criterion-referenced standards for school-aged males and females.

**Baumgartner Modified Pull-Up Test.** The Baumgartner modified pull-up test can also be used for training (Baumgartner & Wood 1984). The student grasps the pull-up bar at the top end of the pull-up board with an overhanded grip, hands about shoulder-width apart (Figure 8.13). The student then assumes a straight-arm hanging position, pulls up the inclined board until the chin is over the bar, and returns to a

---

[2]A specially designed pull-up bar needs to be constructed to regulate differences in reach height. Plans for this are available in other sources (Prudential FITNESSGRAM® 1992) and AAHPERD Physical Best Tests (1989).

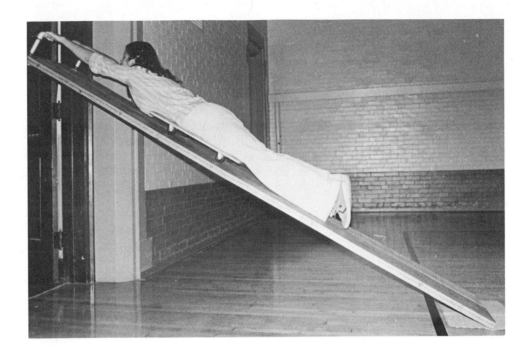

**Figure 8.13**
Baumgartner
modified pull-up test.

straight-arm hanging position. This action is repeated as often as possible. The test is scored by the number of completed repetitions. Norms for most ages 6 through college and both genders are reported by Baumgartner et al. (1984) and Jackson et al. (1982). Almost without exception scores range from 3 to 50.

***Measuring Abdominal Muscle Endurance.*** Tests of this ability require the subject to use the abdominal muscles to move or maintain the body's upper extremity to exhaustion; they may require either isometric or isotonic contractions of these muscles. Tests that measure this ability have been called measures of abdominal muscle strength or endurance.

Sit-ups are generally recommended on physical or motor fitness batteries. Prior to the 1976 revision of the AAHPERD Youth Fitness Test, the straight-leg sit-up was used. When executing a straight-leg sit-up, the hip flexors are in position for their most forceful contraction. This is due to the strong hip flexor, the iliopsoas group, shown in Figure 8.14. With a straight-leg sit-up there is a tendency to arch or hyperextend the lumbar spine during its execution. When this occurs, it indicates that the abdominal muscles do not have enough strength to prevent the hip flexors from increasing the pelvic tilt. Kendall (1965) reports that the hyperextension of the lumbar spine may result in injury to the lower back. Hyperextension of the lower back can result in ligamentous strains, muscle or tendon ruptures, and even intervertebral disc ruptures.

The hyperextended lower back may be reduced by substituting the hook-lying (i.e., flexed knee and hip joints) or bent-knee sit-up for the straight-leg sit-up. In these positions, the hip flexors are not stretched, and the abdominal muscles (flexors of the lumbar spine) assume the major responsibility for movement. It is for this reason that the flexed-leg sit-up is the recommended test.

**Figure 8.14**
Anterior view of the
iliopsoas group. (From Wells,
K. F. and K. Luttgens. 1976.
*Kinesiology: Scientific basis of
human emotion* (p. 151).
Philadelphia, PA: W. B.
Saunders. Reprinted by
permission of Holt, Rinehart
and Winston.)

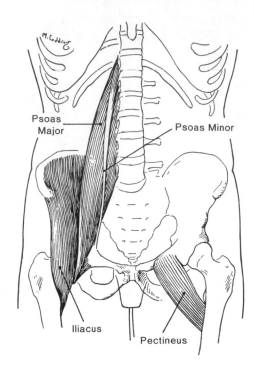

The 1-minute, flexed-leg sit-up is an item of three national health-related youth fitness tests (see Chapter 9). Testing procedures and norms for both tests are provided in Chapter 9. The Y's Way to Physical Fitness program (Golding et al. 1989) includes a timed sit-up test for evaluating abdominal endurance of adults. This is a 1-minute test with the hands held behind the head, the knees bent, and the feet held. The elbows should alternately touch the opposite knee as the participant comes into the up position. The subject's score is the number of sit-ups completed in 60 seconds. Norms for men and women of selected age groups are provided in Table 8.14.

The curl-up test was added to the National Prudential FITNESSGRAM test (1992) to minimize compression in the spine. It is likely that this will be the test of the future. This test is described next.

**Curl-Up.** This test starts with the subject in a supine position on a mat with the knees bent at an angle of about 140°, and the feet are flat on the floor. The arms are straight, parallel to the trunk with palms of the hands resting on the mat. A 3-inch-wide measuring strip is used to regulate the curl-up. Keeping their heels in contact with the mat, the student curls up slowly sliding their fingers across the measuring strip until the fingertips reach the other side (movement distance of 3 inches), and then curls back down to the starting position. The test rate is controlled at a rate of 20 curl-ups per minute—one curl-up every 3 seconds. The test ends when 1) the subject cannot maintain the pace; or 2) when a total of 75 curl-ups are completed. Norms have not been published for this test, but Table 8.13 gives the age-related optimal criterion-referenced standards.

**Table 8.14** Adult Norms for the YMCA 1-Minute Sit-up Test

| Percentile | 18–25 | 26–35 | Age Group<br>36–45 | 46–55 | 56–65 | >65 |
|---|---|---|---|---|---|---|
| *Adult Men* | | | | | | |
| 95 | 54 | 50 | 46 | 41 | 32 | 33 |
| 75 | 45 | 41 | 36 | 29 | 26 | 22 |
| 50 | 37 | 33 | 29 | 22 | 18 | 17 |
| 25 | 30 | 28 | 22 | 17 | 12 | 10 |
| 5 | 17 | 12 | 9 | 8 | 4 | 4 |
| *Adult Women* | | | | | | |
| 95 | 48 | 42 | 38 | 30 | 29 | 26 |
| 75 | 37 | 33 | 27 | 22 | 18 | 18 |
| 50 | 30 | 26 | 21 | 16 | 11 | 12 |
| 25 | 24 | 20 | 14 | 9 | 6 | 4 |
| 5 | 10 | 2 | 2 | 1 | 1 | 0 |

Source: Norms from the *Y's Way to Physical Fitness*, 1989, 3rd edition.

***Measuring Cardiorespiratory Endurance.*** Maximal oxygen uptake ($\dot{V}O_2$ Max) is considered by exercise scientists to be the best index of cardiorespiratory endurance. The most valid method of measuring $\dot{V}O_2$ Max is in the laboratory using sophisticated gas analysis equipment and motor driven treadmills. A less accurate but easier method is to measure submaximal heart rate response to exercise. A remarkably simple and easy method is the University of Houston nonexercise test (Jackson et al. 1990). The test uses age, gender, body composition, and self-report level of physical activity to estimate $\dot{V}O_2$ Max. Body composition can be measured by skinfold fat percent body fat estimates or body mass index. The body mass index is especially feasible for testing large groups of people because all data can be obtained through self-report.

The method most appropriate for use in the public schools is with distance runs either at least one mile in length or at least nine minutes in duration. The laboratory methods are fully discussed in Chapter 10 and the distance runs tests and norms for the AAHPERD Health Related (1980) and Texas Tests (1986) are furnished in Chapter 9.

The importance of basic movement patterns—running, jumping, and throwing—is recognized by physical educators, and tests of these abilities are included in published general motor ability and motor fitness batteries. These abilities are especially important for evaluating athletes.

**Basic Movement Patterns**

***Measuring Running Speed.*** Tests of running **speed** require the subject to run at maximum speed in a straight path. The basic physical ability is measured by the elapsed time required to run a specified distance (usually 10 to 60 yards) or the distance the student can run during a specified time period (usually 4 to 8 seconds). This basic physical ability is normally represented on motor ability and motor fitness test batteries by a sprinting test ranging from 40 to 60 yards in length. Several investigators (Fleishman 1964; Jackson 1971) report that sprints as short as 20 yards reliably measure this basic physical ability; however, longer sprints, 40 or 50 yards, are more reliable (Jackson & Baumgartner 1969). Most motor ability or motor fitness batteries recommend 50-yard sprints, while 40-yard sprints are universally accepted by football coaches. Testing procedures and norms for the 50-yard dash (AAHPERD 1976) are provided next.

### 50-Yard Dash (AAHPER 1976)

*Equipment:* A stopwatch accurate to one-tenth second per runner, or a stopwatch accurate to one-tenth second with a split timer, and a test course of suitable length to ensure safe stopping after the sprint.

*Procedure:* Have two students run at the same time for competition. The students assume a starting position behind the starting line. The starter uses the commands "Are you ready?" and "Go!" On "Go," the starter makes a downward sweep of the arm, giving a visual signal to the timer to start the watch. The timer, standing at the finish line, stops the watch when the runner crosses the line.

*Scoring:* The student's score is the elapsed time between the starter's signal and the instant the pupil crosses the finish line. Scores are recorded to the nearest tenth of a second. Selected AAHPERD norms for girls and boys are listed in Table 8.15.

*Other considerations:* Allow students to take one or two warm-up trials before they are timed for score.

***Measuring Running Agility.***   **Agility** is the ability to change the direction of the body or body parts rapidly. This ability is measured with running tests that require the subject to turn or start and stop. Such tests appear in most published general motor ability and motor fitness batteries. Running speed tends to be related to agility.

Research indicates that the tests used to measure running agility present a common measurement problem: Students learn to perform these tests with practice (Baumgartner & Jackson 1970). It was found that when five trials were administered, the best scores for the group were achieved on Trials 4 and 5. These tests are time-consuming, so it would not normally be feasible to allow five trials, but you should give students an opportunity to practice before the test or while other students are being tested. Proper traction is another problem posed by these tests. It is essential that students wear proper shoes and that the test be administered on a suitable surface; a tile floor or a dirty floor may be too slippery.

Many tests of running agility have been published. The shuttle run requires the subject to run back and forth between two parallel lines. A second type of running agility test requires the student to run a test course that calls for constant turning. The zigzag run is an example.

### Shuttle Run (AAHPER 1976)

*Equipment:* Floor space sufficiently large to allow acceptable traction, stopwatches accurate to a tenth of a second, and two wooden blocks ($2'' \times 2'' \times 4''$) per test station.

**Table 8.15** Percentile Rank Norms for Girls and Boys on the 50-Yard Dash (in Seconds and Tenths of Seconds)

| | Girls Age | | | | | | | |
|---|---|---|---|---|---|---|---|---|
| **Percentile** | **9–10** | **11** | **12** | **13** | **14** | **15** | **16** | **17+** |
| 95 | 7.4 | 7.3 | 7.0 | 6.9 | 6.8 | 6.9 | 7.0 | 6.8 |
| 75 | 8.0 | 7.9 | 7.6 | 7.4 | 7.3 | 7.4 | 7.5 | 7.4 |
| 50 | 8.6 | 8.3 | 8.1 | 8.0 | 7.8 | 7.8 | 7.9 | 7.9 |
| 25 | 9.1 | 9.0 | 8.7 | 8.5 | 8.3 | 8.2 | 8.3 | 8.4 |
| 5 | 10.3 | 10.0 | 10.0 | 10.0 | 9.6 | 9.2 | 9.3 | 9.5 |
| | **Boys** | | | | | | | |
| 95 | 7.3 | 7.1 | 6.8 | 6.5 | 6.2 | 6.0 | 6.0 | 5.9 |
| 75 | 7.8 | 7.6 | 7.4 | 7.0 | 6.8 | 6.5 | 6.5 | 6.3 |
| 50 | 8.2 | 8.0 | 7.8 | 7.5 | 7.2 | 6.9 | 6.7 | 6.6 |
| 25 | 8.9 | 8.6 | 8.3 | 8.0 | 7.7 | 7.3 | 7.0 | 7.0 |
| 5 | 9.9 | 9.5 | 9.5 | 9.0 | 8.8 | 8.0 | 7.7 | 7.9 |

Source: Adapted from *Youth Fitness Test Manual* (Washington, D.C.: AAHPER, 1976), pp. 42 and 50. Used by permission.

*Procedure:* The test course is comprised of two parallel lines placed on the floor 30 feet apart. The student starts from behind the first line and, after the starting command, runs to the second line, picks up one wooden block, runs back to the first line, and places the wooden block behind the line. The student then runs back and picks up the second block, carrying it back across the first line.

*Scoring:* The score is the elapsed time accurate to the nearest tenth of a second. Each student is allowed two trials and the best score is selected. The watch is started on the signal "Go," and stopped when the second block is carried across the line. Students who fall or slip significantly should be given another trial. Norms for boys and girls are listed in Table 8.16.

*Other considerations:* This test is time-consuming because the trials must be administered individually. You can save time by setting up several test courses and having enough scorers. Efficiency can also be improved when two students run the course at the same time, in which case the tester needs two stopwatches or one with a split-second timer.

**Zigzag Run Test (Texas Fitness Test 1973)**

*Objective:* To run a test course that requires turning as fast and efficiently as possible.

*Validity:* Construct validity of running agility.

**Table 8.16** Percentile Rank Norms for Boys and Girls on the Shuttle Run (in Seconds and Tenths)

| Percentile | Boys Age | | | | | | | |
| | 9–10 | 11 | 12 | 13 | 14 | 15 | 16 | 17+ |
|---|---|---|---|---|---|---|---|---|
| 95 | 10.0 | 9.7 | 9.6 | 9.3 | 8.9 | 8.9 | 8.6 | 8.6 |
| 75 | 10.6 | 10.4 | 10.2 | 10.0 | 9.6 | 9.4 | 9.3 | 9.2 |
| 50 | 11.2 | 10.9 | 10.7 | 10.4 | 10.1 | 9.9 | 9.9 | 9.8 |
| 25 | 12.0 | 11.5 | 11.4 | 11.0 | 10.7 | 10.4 | 10.5 | 10.4 |
| 5 | 13.1 | 12.9 | 12.4 | 12.4 | 11.9 | 11.7 | 11.9 | 11.7 |
| | Girls | | | | | | | |
| 95 | 10.2 | 10.0 | 9.9 | 9.9 | 9.7 | 9.9 | 10.0 | 9.6 |
| 75 | 11.1 | 10.8 | 10.8 | 10.5 | 10.3 | 10.4 | 10.6 | 10.4 |
| 50 | 11.8 | 11.5 | 11.4 | 11.2 | 11.0 | 11.0 | 11.2 | 11.1 |
| 25 | 12.5 | 12.1 | 12.0 | 12.0 | 12.0 | 11.8 | 12.0 | 12.0 |
| 5 | 14.3 | 14.0 | 13.3 | 13.2 | 13.1 | 13.3 | 13.7 | 14.0 |

Source: Adapted from *Youth Fitness Test Manual* (Washington, D.C.: AAHPER, 1976), Used by permission.

**Figure 8.15**
Test course for zigzag run.

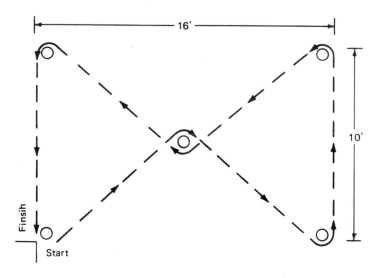

*Equipment:* A test course of appropriate size, a stopwatch accurate to a tenth of a second, and five markers to outline the test course (see Figure 8.15). Although the instructions for several agility tests recommend the use of chairs, volleyball standards, or wooden clubs for outlining the test course, we strongly recommend that you not use these objects because of possible injury to students. Rubber pylons are ideal for safely outlining the course.

**Table 8.17** Percentile-Rank Norms for Boys and Girls on the Zigzag Run

| | Boys—Age to the Last Year | | | | | | | |
|---|---|---|---|---|---|---|---|---|
| Percentile | 10 | 11 | 12 | 13 | 14 | 15 | 16 | 17 |
| 95 | 7.5 | 7.4 | 7.2 | 7.0 | 6.8 | 6.7 | 6.5 | 6.3 |
| 75 | 8.3 | 8.2 | 8.0 | 7.8 | 7.6 | 7.5 | 7.3 | 7.1 |
| 50 | 8.9 | 8.8 | 8.6 | 8.4 | 8.2 | 8.1 | 7.9 | 7.7 |
| 25 | 9.5 | 9.4 | 9.2 | 9.0 | 8.8 | 8.7 | 8.5 | 8.3 |
| 5 | 10.3 | 10.2 | 10.0 | 9.8 | 9.6 | 9.5 | 9.3 | 8.7 |

| | Girls—Age to the Last Year | | | | | | | |
|---|---|---|---|---|---|---|---|---|
| Percentile | 10 | 11 | 12 | 13 | 14 | 15 | 16 | 17 |
| 95 | 7.2 | 7.0 | 6.8 | 6.7 | 6.5 | 6.3 | 6.3 | 6.3 |
| 75 | 8.4 | 8.2 | 8.0 | 7.9 | 7.7 | 7.5 | 7.5 | 7.5 |
| 50 | 9.2 | 9.0 | 8.8 | 8.7 | 8.5 | 8.3 | 8.3 | 8.3 |
| 25 | 9.6 | 9.4 | 9.2 | 9.1 | 8.9 | 8.7 | 8.7 | 8.7 |
| 5 | 11.2 | 11.0 | 10.8 | 10.7 | 10.5 | 10.3 | 10.3 | 10.3 |

Source: (Texas Test 1973).

*Procedure:* At the signal the student begins from behind the starting line and runs the outlined course one time as fast as possible.

*Scoring:* The student's score is the elapsed time accurate to the nearest tenth of a second. Give three trials. The first should be at three-quarter speed to familiarize the student with the procedure and to serve as a specific warm-up. The score is the mean of the last two trials.

*Norms:* Norms for boys and girls ages 10 through 17 are provided in Table 8.17.

*Other Considerations:* Although some authorities recommend that the test consist of three circuits through the course, it has been found that high reliability can be achieved by using several trials of just one circuit. With ample rest between each trial, fatigue is not a factor. The test is time-consuming because each trial must be administered individually, but several test courses can be used to administer the test to a large group.

***Measuring Jumping Ability.*** Tests of this factor measure the ability to expend maximum energy in one explosive act, projecting the body through space. The vertical jump, chalk jump, Sargent jump, and standing long jump (the easiest to administer) are the most frequently used tests of the ability.

Jumping tests have been described as tests of power (McCloy & Young 1954) and of explosive strength (Fleishman 1964). Although physical educators generally refer to these tests as measures of power, research has reported low correlations between jumping tests and mechanical measures of power (Barlow 1970; Considine 1970).

The need for leg strength in jumping is self-evident; body weight, however, is negatively correlated with jumping ability. The negative relation can be largely traced

**Table 8.18** Percentile Rank Norms for Boys and Girls on the Standing Long Jump (in Feet and Inches)

| | Boys Age | | | | | | | |
|---|---|---|---|---|---|---|---|---|
| Percentile | 9–10 | 11 | 12 | 13 | 14 | 15 | 16 | 17+ |
| 95 | 6'0" | 6'2" | 6'6" | 7'1" | 7'6" | 8'0" | 8'2" | 8'5" |
| 75 | 5'4" | 5'7" | 5'11" | 6'3" | 6'8" | 7'2" | 7'6" | 7'9" |
| 50 | 4'11" | 5'2" | 5'5" | 5'9" | 6'2" | 6'8" | 7'0" | 7'2" |
| 25 | 4'6" | 4'8" | 5'0" | 5'2" | 5'6" | 6'1" | 6'6" | 6'6" |
| 5 | 3'10" | 4'0" | 4'2" | 4'4" | 4'8" | 5'2" | 5'5" | 5'3" |
| | Girls | | | | | | | |
| 95 | 5'10" | 6'0" | 6'2" | 6'5" | 6'8" | 6'7" | 6'6" | 6'9" |
| 75 | 5'2" | 5'4" | 5'6" | 5'9" | 5'11" | 5'10" | 5'9" | 6'0" |
| 50 | 4'8" | 4'11" | 5'0" | 5'3" | 5'4" | 5'5" | 5'3" | 5'5" |
| 25 | 4'1" | 4'4" | 4'6" | 4'9" | 4'10" | 4'11" | 4'9" | 4'11" |
| 5 | 3'5" | 3'8" | 3'10" | 4'0" | 4'0" | 4'2" | 4'0" | 4'1" |

Source: Adapted from *Youth Fitness Test Manual* (Washington, D.C.: AAHPER, 1976). Used by permission.

to body fatness. More force or greater muscular strength is needed to propel a heavier individual through space. Jumping ability, then, depends on individual differences in leg strength and body composition. If two individuals can generate the same amount of force, all other things being equal, the leanest person would jump highest.

The standing long jump is very easy to administer and is a common test of motor fitness batteries. The vertical jump is used by many coaches to test athletes.

### Standing Long Jump (AAHPER 1976)

*Equipment:* A tape measure at least 10 feet long and masking tape. You can construct the test station by attaching the tape measure to the floor with the starting line at 0 inches. We have found the gym floor to be a suitable surface, although mats can also be used.

*Procedure:* The student should straddle the tape measure, with feet parallel, about a shoulder-width apart, and toes behind the starting line. From this position, the student should squat and then jump horizontally as far as possible. The student should land straddling the tape measure.

*Scoring:* The recommended procedure is to administer three trials and award the student the best of the three trials. The test is scored in feet and inches to the nearest inch. Norms for boys and girls are listed in Table 8.18.

*Other considerations:* Because the test must be administered individually, it is suggested that several test stations be used. It is important that students be allowed to practice the specific test because a learning effect has been shown to exist.

**Table 8.19** Percentile-Rank Norms for Boys and Girls on the Vertical Jump

| | Boys—Age to the Last Year | | | | | | | |
|---|---|---|---|---|---|---|---|---|
| Percentile | 10 | 11 | 12 | 13 | 14 | 15 | 16 | 17 |
| 95 | 15.5 | 16.5 | 17.5 | 19.0 | 20.5 | 21.5 | 22.5 | 24.0 |
| 75 | 12.5 | 13.5 | 14.5 | 16.0 | 17.5 | 18.5 | 19.5 | 21.0 |
| 50 | 11.0 | 12.0 | 13.0 | 14.5 | 16.0 | 17.0 | 18.0 | 19.5 |
| 25 | 9.0 | 10.0 | 11.0 | 12.5 | 14.0 | 15.0 | 16.0 | 17.5 |
| 5 | 6.0 | 7.0 | 7.0 | 8.5 | 10.0 | 11.0 | 12.0 | 13.5 |

| | Girls—Age to the Last Year | | | | | | | |
|---|---|---|---|---|---|---|---|---|
| Percentile | 10 | 11 | 12 | 13 | 14 | 15 | 16 | 17 |
| 95 | 14.0 | 14.5 | 15.0 | 15.5 | 16.0 | 17.0 | 17.0 | 17.0 |
| 75 | 11.5 | 12.0 | 12.5 | 13.0 | 13.5 | 14.5 | 14.5 | 14.5 |
| 50 | 10.0 | 10.5 | 11.0 | 11.5 | 12.0 | 13.0 | 13.0 | 13.0 |
| 25 | 8.5 | 9.0 | 9.5 | 10.0 | 10.5 | 11.5 | 11.5 | 11.5 |
| 5 | 6.0 | 6.5 | 7.0 | 7.5 | 8.0 | 9.0 | 9.0 | 9.0 |

Source: (Texas Test 1973).

**Vertical Jump Test (Texas Test 1973)**

*Objective:* Using a double-foot take off, to jump vertically as high as possible with maximum effort.

*Validity:* Construct validity of jumping ability.

*Equipment:* A smooth wall of sufficient height, a yardstick, and chalk.

*Procedure:* Secure the student's standing height by having him or her stand with heels together on the floor and the side of his or her dominant hand holding a piece of chalk, next to the wall. From this position the student reaches upward as high as possible and marks on the wall. To execute the jump, the student squats next to the wall, jumps as high as possible, and marks the wall. Once in the starting position the student should not walk in or step into the jump.

*Scoring:* The height of the jump is the measured distance between the standing and jumping heights. Measurements accurate to the last inch are precise enough for reliable results. Give three trials, the first at three-quarter speed to familiarize the student with the procedure and to serve as a specific warm-up. The score is the mean of the last two trials to the nearest half inch.

*Norms:* Norms for boys and girls ages 10 through 17 are listed in Table 8.19.

***Measuring Throwing Ability.*** Test of this ability requires the subject to throw a relatively light ball (baseball, softball, or basketball) overarm for distance. These tests have been reported to measure arm and shoulder girdle strength and/or coordination. Eckert (1965) reports a high correlation between muscular strength and speed of movement when the mass of the ball is high relative to the strength of the muscle groups involved. Obviously strength is necessary to throw a ball for distance; however, the weight of the ball relative to the strength of the thrower must be considered. For example, if young and relatively weak children are required to throw a basketball, muscular arm strength or power may be the dominant factor measured; if a Little League baseball is used, throwing ability is more likely to be measured. Given adequate strength, the basic physical ability measured is the execution of a coordinated overarm pattern with maximal speed.

Orthopedic surgeons have questioned the advisability of having children throw with maximal effort. "Little League elbow" is a common injury among preteen athletes. The softball throw for distance, once an item in the AAHPERD Youth Fitness battery, was dropped with the 1975 revision. For any throw for distance, it is recommended that the students be conditioned and warmed up before testing. Do not allow the students who complain of sore arms to take the test.

### Basketball Throw for Distance Test (Disch et al. 1977)

*Objective:* To throw a basketball as far as possible.

*Validity and Reliability:* The test has been shown to discriminate among levels of performance of female volleyball players. The intraclass reliability estimates with samples of females have ranged from .85 to .97.

*Equipment:* Two basketballs and a 100-foot tape measure.

*Procedure:* The throws are made with both feet parallel to the restraining line. The subject may not take a step to throw, but may follow through by stepping over the line after the throw, minimizing the action of the lower body. In this way the throw more closely represents the overarm pattern used when spiking or serving a volleyball. Each subject is awarded five throws.

*Scoring:* The student's score is the distance thrown to the nearest half foot. This test was shown to have a warm-up effect, thus, the best score achieved is the recommended score.

*Norms:* Norms for female volleyball players are listed in Table 8.3.

## Flexibility

**Flexibility** is the range of movement about a joint. Individual differences in flexibility depend on physiological characteristics that influence the extensibility of the muscles and ligaments surrounding a joint. Physical educators agree that certain levels and types of flexibility are wanted, but the degree of flexibility desired is yet to be determined.

Leighton (1955) has published the most comprehensive battery of flexibility tests using a specially developed instrument, the Leighton Flexometer, to measure the flexibility of a joint. Physical therapists use a protractor-like instrument called a goniometer to measure joint flexibility; in research laboratories, electronic and slow-motion photographic methods are used to measure flexibility. Although these are reliable methods for measuring flexibility, the investment of time and money prohibit their use out of the laboratory setting.

Flexibility is often regarded as a single general factor or ability. Clarke (1967) represents flexibility as a component of general motor ability. Harris (1969) conducted a factor analysis study to determine whether flexibility is a single general factor. Two types of flexibility tests were used in her study: (1) tests that measure the movement of a limb involving only one joint action; and (2) composite measures of movements that require more than one joint or more than one type of action within a single joint. The analysis revealed many intercorrelations to be near zero, which implies specificity rather than generality. A factor analysis of these data revealed thirteen different factors of flexibility. Harris concluded, then, that there is no evidence that flexibility is a single general factor.

Harris' finding indicates that we must think in terms of several types of flexibilities. We can easily recognize the importance of different types of flexibility in different motor skills. Figure 8.16 shows the types of flexibility needed by the modern dancer and the football punter. These specific types of flexibility are developed over time with special stretching exercises and practice in the given skill. The specificity of flexibility, then, means that we cannot use a single test to measure the various types of flexibility necessary to the execution of different motor skills.

Fleishman (1964) has identified a factor, called dynamic flexibility, involving the ability to change direction with the body parts rapidly and efficiently. Physical educators (McCloy & Young 1954) call this factor "agility that does not involve running." The squat thrust test is reported to measure the factor and is included in some motor fitness batteries as a measure of agility. Harris (1969) identified the same factor. The tests used to measure the factor are difficult to standardize and thus tend to lack reliability and are of questionable value. Fleishman (1964) offers a full description and norms for this test.

Kraus and Raab (1961) maintain that a degree of flexibility in the back and hamstring muscle groups is essential for the prevention of lower back disorders. Kraus and Hirschland (1954) have published a battery of minimum muscular fitness tests, the Kraus-Weber Tests, developed in a posture clinic for the diagnosis and treatment of patients with low-back pain. When these ten tests were administered to several thousand European and American school children, the American failure rate was considerably higher than the European rate. The test, scored on a pass-fail basis, is described below:

> The subject stands erect in stockings or bare feet, hands at the sides, feet together. The test is for the subject to lean down slowly and touch the floor with the fingertips and hold the position for three seconds. The knees should be held straight and bouncing is not permitted.

The value of flexibility for a healthy lower back is recognized by physicians, physical therapists, and physical educators. It is for this reason that the sit-and-reach test is a recommended test of health related youth-fitness tests reviewed in the next chapter. Test procedures and norms for these tests are provided in Chapter 9.

**Figure 8.16** Different types of flexibility.

**Table 8.20** Adult Norms for the YMCA Trunk Flexion Test

| | | | Age Group | | | |
|---|---|---|---|---|---|---|
| **Percentile** | **18–25** | **26–35** | **36–45** | **46–55** | **56–65** | **>65** |
| *Adult Men* | | | | | | |
| 95 | 22 | 22 | 21 | 20 | 19 | 18 |
| 75 | 18 | 18 | 17 | 16 | 15 | 13 |
| 50 | 16 | 15 | 14 | 12 | 11 | 10 |
| 25 | 12 | 12 | 11 | 9 | 7 | 7 |
| 5 | 7 | 7 | 5 | 4 | 3 | 3 |
| *Adult Women* | | | | | | |
| 95 | 25 | 24 | 23 | 22 | 21 | 21 |
| 75 | 21 | 20 | 19 | 18 | 18 | 18 |
| 50 | 19 | 18 | 16 | 16 | 15 | 15 |
| 25 | 16 | 15 | 13 | 13 | 12 | 11 |
| 5 | 12 | 11 | 9 | 8 | 7 | 6 |

Source: Norms from the *Y's Way to Physical Fitness*, 1989, 3rd edition.

The Y's Way to Physical Fitness program (Golding et al. 1989) includes a lower back flexibility test for adults. The test is somewhat different than what is used for health-related youth fitness tests. The 15-inch mark of the yardstick is at foot placement. The test is to reach the most distant point on the yardstick. The best of three trials measured to the nearest 0.25 of an inch is the subject's score. Norms for men and women of selected age groups are provided in Table 8.20.

**Balance** is the ability to maintain body position, which is obviously essential to the successful execution of motor skills. Two general types of balance are commonly recognized: Static balance is the ability to maintain total body equilibrium while standing in one spot; and dynamic balance is the ability to maintain equilibrium while moving from one point to another. These two types of balance were first reported by Bass (1939), who stated that static balance depends on the ability to coordinate stimuli from the three semicircular canals; proprioceptive receptors located in the muscles, tendons, and joints; and visual perception. Dynamic balance depends on similar but more complex stimuli.

Singer (1968) argued against the assumption that there are only two general types of balance, claiming instead that different motor skills require different types of balance. The balance needed by the tennis player differs from that needed by the swimmer. Furthermore, he points out that different tests of balance do not correlate highly with each other. Fleishman (1964) suggests the existence of several factors in balance. He reported two factors in static balance, one measured with the eyes closed and the other with the eyes open. Because dynamic balance is more complex, it is likely to be composed of several more factors.

Due to the specificity of balance, the value of balance tests in the instructional process is yet to be determined. Balance tasks are often used by motor learning researchers because significant improvements can be noted in a relatively short time. This learning effect, inherent in balance tests, indicates that they are not reliable in

**Balance**

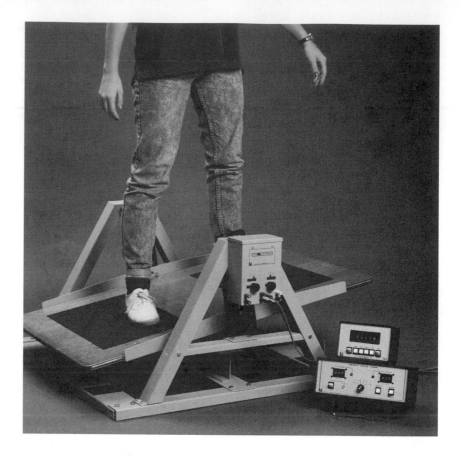

**Figure 8.17**
The stability platform is a laboratory task designed to measure dynamic balance. The apparatus uses electronic equipment to measure the time the subject can maintain balance. (Photo courtesy of Lafayette Instrument Company, Lafayette, IN.)

terms of stability. Thus, the tests do not offer stable measurements for purposes of placement, diagnosis, or prediction. By contrast, many gymnastic and tumbling stunts—among them, the headstand—involve learning a specific type of balance. Because the performance of balance stunts is an instructional objective of a tumbling or gymnastics unit, the value of measuring these specific types of balance is easily defended. Described next are common static balance tests (eyes open or shut) and a dynamic balance test commonly used to study skill acquisition.

**Static balance.** The static balance was first recommended by Bass (1939), and the test was revised by Fleishman (1964). Wooden sticks ($1'' \times 1'' \times 12''$) are taped to the floor. At the word "Ready," the subject places the supporting foot lengthwise on the stick. At the command "Go," the subject raises the free foot and holds this position as long as possible for a maximum of 60 seconds. The test is terminated if (1) either foot touches the floor; or (2) balance is maintained for 60 seconds. The subject is given three practice trials, and the subject's score is the sum of six trials of the test. Fleishman (1964) administered the test with the eyes open and closed and found they measured different factors.

**Dynamic balance.** Dynamic balance can be measured with a stability platform (Figure 8.17). The objective is to keep the balancing platform as level as possible during a regulated time period. Electronic clocks and interval timers are used to measure the subject's capacity to maintain balance for a given time period, often 30 seconds in duration. You are directed to another source (Rudisill & Jackson 1992) for a description of the equipment and task.[3]

**Kinesthesis,** or kinesthetic perception, is the ability to perceive the body's position in space and the relationship of its parts (Singer 1968). The proprioceptors, highly developed sense organs located in the muscles, tendons, and joints, compose a highly sensitive system of kinesthetic perception. They provide the brain with information about what the parts of the body are doing when executing a skill.

## Kinesthetic Perception

The need for and importance of kinesthesis for skill learning is universally acknowledged, and several physical educators (Roloff 1953; Scott 1955; Wiebe 1954; Young 1954) have tried to develop kinesthesis tests. These tests tend to have very low reliabilities, and their value for general testing is questionable. Kinesthesis is an ability that is central to the execution of motor skill, but one cannot be measured with accuracy.

Fine motor abilities are those that do not involve total body movement. Some more common abilities are simple and complex forms of hand-eye coordination, reaction time, and movement time. Common methods of measuring these psychomotor abilities in the laboratory are described in another source (Rudisill & Jackson 1992). Fine psychomotor abilities are often used to study psychomotor skill acquisition.

## Fine Psychomotor Abilities

Physical educators have traditionally accepted the notion of generality and believe that a test or group of tests are predictive of a wide range of motor skills. The theory of specificity of motor-skill acquisition was largely responsible for showing that motor ability and motor educability tests lacked validity. The age-height-weight classification indexes were found to have limited value because the addition of height and weight to age fails to improve prediction power. The theory of basic physical abilities does provide a theoretically sound base for generality testing. This theory is especially useful for use with athletes and pre-employment testing for physically demanding jobs and estimating a worker's capacity to be able to complete physically demanding work tasks.

## Summary

Researchers have identified three basic motor performance abilities—muscular strength, muscular power, and endurance—and three basic movement patterns—running, jumping, and throwing. Several different tests are available to measure each ability. Although tests can be used for general evaluation, they are especially useful for identifying students with athletic potential.

The assessment of flexibility, balance, and kinesthesis is a difficult problem. Flexibility is not a general factor; rather it is task-specific, and different types are needed to perform different motor tasks. Balance has been thought to consist of two basic types: dynamic and static. However, research suggests that several additional types of balance also exist. Kinesthesis is the ability to perceive the body's position

---

[3]Lafayette Instrument Company manufactures the electronic equipment and stability platform and distributes the lab manual (Rudisill & Jackson 1992) that describes this dynamic balance test. For information, call (800) 428–7545.

in space and the relationship of its parts. The reliability of kinesthetic tests tends to be low, making this trait difficult to measure.

## Formative Evaluation of Objectives

*Objective 1*   Describe the tests historically used to measure generality.

1. Summarize the traditional procedures used to measure the generality of motor performance.
2. Describe the differences between motor educability and general motor ability.
3. What effect did Henry's memory-drum theory have on the generality concept?

*Objective 2*   Define and differentiate between basic physical abilities and a motor skill.

1. Using their definition, distinguish between a basic ability and a motor skill.
2. The terms ability and skill are often used interchangeably. Describe the essential difference between the two.
3. Could a basic ability be considered a measure of generality?

*Objective 3*   Apply the theory of basic physical abilities to the evaluation of athletes.

1. In evaluating different groups of athletes (for example, gymnasts and basketball players), would you use the same basic abilities?
2. Outline the steps a teacher or coach could follow to develop a test for athletes.

*Objective 4*   Identify the methods to develop preemployment tests for physically demanding jobs and the types of tests that comprise preemployment batteries.

1. What are the steps used to develop a preemployment physical test?
2. What kinds of tests are used for a preemployment test?
3. What types of physical ability tests are most often used for preemployment testing?

*Objective 5*   Identify basic physical abilities and tests that validly measure each ability.

1. The text provides a system for classifying basic abilities and tests that measure each ability. Summarize the general characteristics of each basic ability and list one test that measures each.
2. Develop a five-item motor performance battery that includes tests of different basic abilities. Use tests that are feasible for mass testing.

## Additional Learning Activities

1. Summarize the research supporting the specificity of motor-skill learning. Pay close attention to the procedures used by the researcher to conclude specificity or generality.
2. Select a sport and identify the basic abilities demanded by it. Using Fleishman's theory of basic abilities, develop a test battery that could be used to evaluate athletes.

3. A test can be made more reliable, valid, and feasible for mass use by improving the procedures used to administer it. For example, some have constructed inexpensive devices to measure balance, vertical jumping, and push-ups. Try to develop equipment that would improve the testing of some basic ability.

4. Are absolute endurance and 1-RM really highly correlated? If you have access to weight-lifting equipment, devise tests that measure both. Administer the tests to a group of students and determine if the 1-RM score is correlated with the absolute endurance score.

5. Gain testing experience by using some of the tests listed in this chapter and administer the tests to a group of students. Determine how reliable your testing methods are.

**Bibliography**

AAHPER. 1976. *Youth fitness test manual.* Washington, DC: AAHPER.

AAHPERD. 1980. *Health related physical fitness manual.* Washington, DC: AAHPERD.

AAHPERD. 1989. *Physical best: instructor's guide.* Reston, VA: AAHPERD.

American Health and Fitness Foundation. 1986. FYT Program Manual. Austin, TX.

Arvey, R. D. and R. H. Faley. 1988. *Fairness in selecting employees.* 2d ed. Reading, MA: Addison-Wesley.

Arvey, R. D., S. M. Nutting, and T. E. Landon. 1992. Validation strategies for physical ability testing in police and fire settings. *Public Personnel Management 21:* 301–312.

Ayoub, M. A. 1982. Control of manual lifting hazards: II. job redesign. *Journal of Occupational Medicine 24:* 676–688.

Barlow, D. A. 1970. Relation between power and selected variables in the vertical jump. In J. M. Cooper (Ed.). *Selected topics on biomechanics* (pg. nos. 233–41). Chicago, IL: Athletic Institute.

Barnard, R. and H. W. Duncan. 1975. Heart rate and ECG responses of firefighters. *Journal of Occupational Medicine 17:* 247–250.

Barrow, H. M. 1954. Test of motor ability for college men. *Research Quarterly 25:* 253–260.

Bass, R. I. 1939. An analysis of the components of tests of semicircular canal function and static and dynamic balance. *Research Quarterly 2:* 33–52.

Baumgartner, T. A. et al. 1984. Equipment improvements and additional norms for the modified pull-up test. *Research Quarterly for Exercise and Sport 55:* 64–68.

Baumgartner, T. A. and A. S. Jackson. 1970. Measurement schedules for tests of motor performance. *Research Quarterly 41:* 10–14.

Baumgartner, T. A. and S. Wood. 1984. Development of shoulder-girdle strength-endurance in elementary children. *Research Quarterly for Exercise and Sport 55:* 169–171.

Baumgartner, T. A. and M. A. Zuidema. 1972. Factor analysis of physical fitness tests. *Research Quarterly 43:* 443–450.

Bernauer, E. M. and J. Bonanno. 1975. Development of physical profiles for specific jobs. *Journal of Occupational Medicine 17:* 22–33.

Brace, D. K. 1927. *Measuring motor ability.* New York: Barnes.

Campion, M. A. 1983. Personnel selection for physically demanding jobs: Review and recommendations. *Personnel Psychology 36:* 527–550.

Carpenter, A. 1942. The measurements of general motor capacity and general motor ability in the first three grades. *Research Quarterly 13:* 444–446.

Cascio, W. F., R. A. Alexander, and G. V. Barrett. 1988. Setting cutoff scores: Legal, psychometric, and professional issues and guidelines. *Personnel Psychology 41:* 1–24.

Chaffin, D. B. 1974. Human strength capability and low-back pain. *Journal of Occupational Medicine 16:* 248–254.

Chaffin, D. B., R. O. Andres, and A. Garg. 1983. Volitional postures during maximal push/pull exertions in the sagittal plane. *Human Factors 25:* 541–550.

Chaffin, D. B., G. D. Herrin, and W. M. Keyserling. 1978. Preemployment strength testing. *Journal of Occupational Medicine 67:* 403–408.

Chaffin, D. B. and K. S. Park. 1973. A longitudinal study of low-back pain as associated with occupational weight lifting factors. *American Industrial Hygiene Association Journal 34:* 513–525.

Clarke, H. H. 1967. *Application of measurement to health and physical education.* 4th ed. Englewood Cliffs, NJ: Prentice-Hall.

Considine, W. et al. 1976. Developing a physical performance test battery for screening Chicago fire fighting applicants. *Public Personnel Management 5:* 7–14.

Considine, W. J. 1970. A validity analysis of selected leg power tests utilizing a force platform. In J. M. Cooper (Ed.). *Selected topics on biomechanics* (pg. nos. 243–50). Chicago, IL: Athletic Institute.

Cousins, G. F. 1955. A factor analysis of selected wartime fitness tests. *Research Quarterly 26:* 277–288.

Cumbee, F. 1954. A factorial analysis of motor coordination. *Research Quarterly 25:* 412–420.

Cumbee, F. Z. and C. W. Harris. 1953. The composite criterion and its relation to factor analysis. *Research Quarterly 24:* 127–134.

Davis, P. and C. Dotson. 1978. Heart rate responses to fire fighting activities. *Ambulatory Electrocardiology 1:* 15–18.

deVries, H. A. 1980. *Physiology of exercise for physical education and athletics.* Dubuque, IA: Wm. C. Brown.

Disch, J., R. Frankiewicz, and A. S. Jackson. 1975. Construct validation of distance run tests. *Research Quarterly 46:* 169–176.

Disch, J. G. et al. 1977. The construction and analysis of a test related to volleyball playing capacity in females. Mimeographed. Houston, TX: Rice University.

Eckert, H. M. 1965. A concept of force-energy in human movement. *Journal of American Physical Therapy Association 45:* 13–18.

EEOC. 1978. Uniform Guidelines on employment selection procedures. *Federal Register 43* (38289–28309).

Espenschade, A. S. 1963. Restudy of relationships between physical performances of school children and age, height, and weight. *Research Quarterly 34:* 144–153.

Fleishman, E. A. 1956. Psychomotor selection tests: Research and application in the U.S. Air Force. *Personnel Psychology 9:* 449–467.

Fleishman, E. A. 1964. *The Structure and Measurement of Physical Fitness.* Englewood Cliffs, NJ: Prentice-Hall.

Gael, S. 1988. *The job analysis handbook for business, industry, and government.* Vol. I. New York: John Wiley & Sons.

Gire, E. and A. Espenschade. 1942. The relationship between measure of motor educability and learning of specific motor skills. *Research Quarterly 13:* 43–56.

Glencross, D. J. 1966. The nature of the vertical jump test and the standing broad jump test. *Research Quarterly 37:* 353–359.

Golding, L. A., C. R. Meyers, and W. E. Sinning. 1989. *The Y's way to physical fitness.* 3d ed. Chicago, IL: National Board of YMCA.

Gray, R. K. 1962. Relationship between leg speed and leg power. *Research Quarterly 33:* 395–400.

Gross, E. et al. 1956. Relationship between two motor educability tests, a strength test, and wrestling ability after eight weeks' instruction. *Research Quarterly 27:* 395–402.

Gross, E. and J. A. Casciani. 1962. Value of age, height, and weight as a classification device for secondary school students in the seven AAHPER youth fitness tests. *Research Quarterly 33:* 51–58.

Harris, M. 1969. A factor analytic study of flexibility. *Research Quarterly 40:* 62–70.

Henry, F. M. 1956. Coordination and motor learning. In 59th Annual *Proceedings* College Physical Education Association, 68–75.

Henry, F. M. 1958. Specificity vs. generality in learning motor skills. In 61st Annual *Proceedings* College Physical Education Association, 126–28.

Herrin, G. D., D. B. Chaffin, and R. S. Mach. 1974. *Criteria for research on the hazards of manual materials handling.* U.S. Government Printing Office. Washington, DC: NIOSH.

Hogan, J. and A. M. Quigley. 1986. Physical standard for employment and courts. *American Psychologist 41:* 1193–1217.

Hogan, J. C. 1991. Chapter 11. Physical abilities. In *Handbook of industrial and organizational psychology.* 2d ed. Vol. 2. pp. 743–831. (Dunnette, M. D. and L. M. Hough, Eds.) Palo Alto: Consulting Psychologist Press, Inc.

Ismail, A., H. Falls, and D. MacLeod. 1965. Development of a criterion for physical fitness tests from factor analysis results. *Journal of Applied Physiology 20:* 991–999.

Jackson, A. S. 1971. Factor analysis of selected muscular strength and motor performance test. *Research Quarterly 42:* 164–172.

Jackson, A. S. 1994. Chapter 3. Preemployment physical evaluation. *Exercise and Sport Science Review.* 22: 53–90.

Jackson, A. S. et al. 1990. Prediction of functional aerobic capacity without exercise testing. *Med. Sci. Sports Exerc. 22:* 863–870.

Jackson, A. S. et al. 1990. Validation of physical strength tests for the texas city plant—Union Carbide Corporation. Center for Psychological Services, Houston, TX.

Jackson, A. S. et al. 1991. Strength demands of chemical plant work tasks. *Proceedings of the Human Factors Society 35th Annual Meeting 1:* 758–762.

Jackson, A. S. et al. 1992. Validity of isometric strength tests for predicting the capacity to crack, open and close industrial valves. *Proceedings of the Human Factors Society 36th Annual Meeting 1:* 688–691.

Jackson, A. S. et al. 1993. Validation of physical strength tests for the Federal Express Corporation. Center of Applied Psychological Services, Rice University, Houston, TX.

Jackson, A. S. and T. A. Baumgartner. 1969. Measurement schedules of sprint running. *Research Quarterly 40:* 708–711.

Jackson, A. S. and R. J. Frankiewicz. 1975. Factorial expressions of muscular strength. *Research Quarterly 46:* 206–217.

Jackson, A. S. and M. L. Pollock. 1976. Factor analysis and multivariate scaling of anthropometric variables for the assessment of body composition. *Medicine and Science in Sports 8:* 196–203.

Jackson, A. S. and L. Smith. 1974. The validation of an evaluation system for weight training. Paper presented at AAHPER Convention, Anaheim, CA.

Jackson, A. S., H. G. Osburn, and K. R. Laughery. 1984. Validity of isometric strength tests for predicting performance in physically demanding jobs. *Proceedings of the Human Factors Society 28th Annual Meeting 28:* 452–454.

Jackson, A. S., H. G. Osburn, and K. R. Laughery. 1991. Validity of isometric strength tests for predicting endurance work tasks of coal miners. *Proceedings of the Human Factors Society 35th Annual Meeting 1:* 763–767.

Jackson, Allen et al. 1982. Baumgartner's modified pull-up test for male and female elementary school-aged children. *Research Quarterly for Exercise and Sport 53:* 163–164.

Jackson, Andrew S. et al. Submitted for Publication. Changes in aerobic power in men ages 25–70 years.

Johnson, G. B. 1932. Physical skill tests for sectioning classes into homogeneous units. *Research Quarterly 3:* 128–134.

Kendall, F. P. 1965. A criticism of current tests and exercises for physical fitness. *Journal of American Physical Therapy Association 45:* 187–197.

Keyserling, W. et al. 1980a. Establishing an industrial strength testing program. *American Industrial Hygiene Association Journal 41:* 730–736.

Keyserling, W. M. et al. 1980b. Isometric strength testing as a means of controlling medical incidents on strenuous jobs. *Journal of Occupational Medicine 22:* 332–336.

Kraus, H. and R. P. Hirschland. 1954. Minimum muscular fitness test in school children. *Research Quarterly 25:* 177–188.

Kraus, H. and W. Raab. 1961. *Hypokinetic disease.* Springfield, IL: Thomas.

Larson, L. A. 1941. A factor analysis of motor ability variables and tests for college men. *Research Quarterly 12:* 499–517.

Larson, L. A. and R. D. Yocom. 1951. *Measurement and evaluation in physical, health, and recreation education.* St. Louis, MO: Mosby.

Leighton, J. 1955. An instrument and technique for the measurement of range of joint motion. *Archives of Physical Medicine 36:* 571–578.

Lemon, P. W. R. and R. T. Hermiston. 1977. The human energy cost of firefighting. *Journal of Occupational Medicine 19:* 558–562.

Liba, M. R. 1967. Factor analysis of strength variables. *Research Quarterly 38:* 649–662.

Manning, J. and T. Griggs. 1983. Heart rates in fire fighters using light and heavy breathing equipment: similar near-maximal exertion in response to multiple work load conditions. *Journal of Occupational Medicine 25:* 215–218.

Margaria, R. et al. 1966. Measurement of muscular power (anaerobic) in man. *Journal of Applied Physiology 21:* 1662–1664.

Marriott, B. M. and J. Grumstrup-Scott. Editors. 1992. *Body Composition and Physical Performance: Application for the Military Services.* Washington, DC: National Academy Press.

Mathews, D. K. 1978. *Measurement in physical education.* 3d ed. Philadelphia, PA: Saunders.

Mathews, D. K. and E. L. Fox. 1971. *The physiological basis of physical education and athletics.* Philadelphia, PA: Saunders.

McCloy, C. H. 1932. *The measurement of athletic power.* New York: Barnes.

McCloy, C. H. 1956. A factor analysis of tests of endurance. *Research Quarterly 27:* 213–216.

McCloy, C. H. and N. D. Young. 1954. *Test and measurements in health and physical education.* New York: Appleton-Century-Crofts.

Metheny, E. 1938. Studies of the Johnson test as a test of motor educability. *Research Quarterly 9:* 105–114.

Meyers, D. C. et al. 1984. *Factor analysis of strength, cardiovascular endurance, flexibility, and body composition measures (Tech. Rep. R83-9).* Bethesda, MD: Advanced Research Resources Organization.

NIOSH. 1977. *Preemployment strength testing.* Washington, DC: U.S. Department of Health and Human Services.

NIOSH. 1981. *Work practices guide for manual lifting.* Washington, DC: U.S. Department of Health and Human Services.

O'Connell, E. et al. 1986. Energy costs of simulated stair climbing as a job-related task in fire fighting. *Journal of Occupational Medicine 28:* 282–284.

Pollock, M. L. et al. 1978. Characteristics of elite class distance runners. *Annals of New York Academy of Sciences 301:* 278–410.

Prudential FITNESSGRAM® Test Administration Manual. 1992. Dallas: The Cooper Institute for Aerobic Research.

Reilly, R. R., S. Zedeck, and M. L. Tenopyr. 1979. Validity and fairness of physical ability tests for predicting craft jobs. *Journal of Applied Psychology 64:* 267–274.

Roloff, L. L. 1953. Kinesthesis in relation to the learning of selected motor skills. *Research Quarterly 24:* 210–217.

Rudisill, M. E. and A. S. Jackson. 1992. *Theory and application of motor learning.* Onalaska, TX: MacJR Publishing Company.

Safrit, M. J. 1966. *The structure of gross motor skill patterns.* Washington, DC: U.S. Department of Health, Education, and Welfare. Office of Education Cooperative Research Project No. S–397.

Sargent, D. A. 1921. The physical test of man. *American Physical Education Review 26:* 188–194.

SAS. 1989. *JMP User's Guide: Version 2 of JMP.* Cary, NC: SAS Institute, Inc.

Scott, M. G. 1939. The assessment of motor abilities of college women, through objective test. *Research Quarterly 10:* 63–89.

Scott, M. G. 1955. Test of kinesthesis. *Research Quarterly 26:* 324–341.

Singer, R. N. 1968. *Motor learning and human performance.* New York: Macmillan.

Snook, S. H., R. A. Campanelli, and J. W. Hart. 1978. A study of three preventive approaches to low-back injury. *Journal of Occupational Medicine 20:* 478–481.

Sothmann, M. S. et al. 1990. Advancing age and the cardiorespiratory stress of fire suppression: Determining a minimum standard for aerobic fitness. *Human Performance 3:* 217–236.

Sothmann, M. S. et al. 1992. Heart rate response of firefighters to actual emergencies. *Journal of Occupational Medicine 34:* 797–800.

Start, K. B. et al. 1966. A factorial investigation of power, speed, isometric strength, and anthropometric measures in the lower limb. *Research Quarterly 37:* 553–558.

Texas Governor's Commission on Physical Fitness. 1973. *Physical Fitness-Motor Ability Test.* Austin, TX.

Wells, K. F. 1971. *Kinesiology.* 5th ed. Philadelphia, PA: Saunders.

Wiebe, V. R. 1954. A study of test of kinesthesis. *Research Quarterly 25:* 222–227.

Wilmore, J. H. 1976. *Athletic training and physical fitness.* Boston, MA: Allyn and Bacon.

Young, O. G. 1954. A study of kinesthesis in relation to selected movements. *Research Quarterly 16:* 277–287.

Zuidema, M. A. and T. A. Baumgartner. 1974. Second factor analysis of physical fitness tests. *Research Quarterly 45:* 247–256.

# Evaluating Youth Fitness

## Key Words

ACSM
AAHPERD YFT
AAHPERD HRFT
aerobic fitness
    (circulatory-
    respiratory endurance)
agility
body composition
cardiorespiratory function
cardiovascular disease
Chrysler-AAU test
distance run tests
exercise epidemiology
flexibility
health-related physical fitness
motor fitness
muscular endurance
muscular power
muscular strength
President's challenge
Prudential FITNESSGRAM®
skinfold fat
speed
Texas Youth Fitness Test

## Contents

## Objectives

One important goal of school physical education programs is to develop physical fitness. The two methods used to evaluate youth fitness are motor fitness and health-related fitness tests. Here we describe the AAHPERD Youth Fitness Test (YFT), the first national test available to evaluate youth fitness (AAHPER 1976). This is a motor fitness test. In 1973, the Texas test (Fitness 1973) was published and made a distinction between motor fitness and health-related fitness. After the publication of the Texas Test, several health-related youth fitness tests were published. Presently, there are three national youth fitness tests: 1) The Prudential FITNESSGRAM®; 2) Chrysler Fund-AAU; and 3) The President's Challenge. These three programs[1] are described, compared, and evaluated.

After reading Chapter 9, you should be able to:

1. Identify the general tests that comprise a motor fitness battery.
2. Identify the general tests that comprise a health-related battery.
3. Differentiate between motor fitness and health-related fitness batteries.
4. Identify and evaluate the national health-related fitness batteries.

[1]In January 1994, AAHPERD adopted the Prudential FITNESSGRAM® as its fitness test and dropped its youth fitness test, and AAHPERD Physical Best Test.

# INTRODUCTION

Since the concern for positive health extends to all ages, it is recommended that all persons be tested periodically on health-related fitness components. Periodic testing places emphases on the importance of an active life-style to achieve and maintain low amounts of fat, high levels of aerobic fitness, and sufficient muscular strength, muscular endurance, and flexibility in the lower trunk and posterior thigh areas for healthy low-back function (AAHPERD 1980; AAHPERD 1984).

In the past, physical fitness has been defined in broad terms, and tests have measured either an aspect of physiological function or selected aspects of motor performance. This type of test has been termed motor fitness and includes not only strength and endurance components, but also factors of speed, power, and agility (Clarke 1971). Motor fitness tests represent more potential for athletic excellence than fitness for health promotion. As the concept of physical fitness moved away from athletic participation toward health, the components changed to include cardiorespiratory function, body composition (leanness/fatness), strength, endurance, and low-back flexibility, traits shown by medical and exercise scientists to promote health and reduce the risk of disease.

In the text we discuss both motor fitness and health-related batteries. A review of these tests and health-related fitness programs provides you with an understanding of the essential difference between motor fitness and health-related fitness and programs available for use in the public schools.

## Motor Fitness

The terms physical fitness and **motor fitness** are often used interchangeably, but motor fitness is broader and less definitive in scope. It includes both physical fitness and motor ability factors. The seven components that define motor fitness (Clarke 1971) and tests often used to measure a component are given next.

### Components of Motor Fitness

1. **Muscular strength** is characterized by the contraction power of the muscles. This capacity involves the amount of force a muscle can exert (see Chapter 8). Pull-ups, flexed-arm hangs, or push-ups are normally included in motor fitness batteries and said to measure strength, but one can question if these items are measuring strength or endurance.

2. **Muscular endurance** is characterized by the ability to perform work. The capacity involves performing a task to exhaustion. The bent-knee sit-up is commonly used to measure this trait.

3. **Circulatory-respiratory endurance**[2] is characterized by moderate contractions of large muscle groups over long periods of time. Distance run tests measure this youth fitness component.

4. **Muscular power** is the ability to release maximum muscular force in the shortest possible time, as in executing a standing long jump.

5. **Agility** is the ability to change body position or direction rapidly and is often tested with a shuttle run test.

---

[2]Many different terms have been used to define this component. We use aerobic fitness in this text and the best test is $\dot{V}O_2$ Max (see Chapter 10).

6. **Speed** is the rapidity of movement and can be tested with the 50-yard dash.

7. **Flexibility** is the range of movement in a joint or joints, and tests are usually not included in motor fitness batteries.

Many different motor fitness tests have been published and are reported in older editions of measurement texts. The **AAHPERD YFT** was the first national youth fitness test and was used extensively in the public schools. The original AAHPERD YFT was published in 1958 and revised in 1975 and 1976. The test was developed in response to a study that reported that European children scored higher on the Kraus-Weber tests of minimum muscular fitness than did American children (Kraus & Hirschland 1954). The Kraus-Weber tests were designed to identify adults who were likely to have low-back problems.

The AAHPERD YFT was developed by a group of physical educators who met and selected tests based on logic. The YFT was not developed through test validation research. In 1975, major changes were made. The straight-leg sit-up was replaced with the bent-leg sit-up from the Texas Test (1973), and the softball throw was dropped. It was thought that the straight-leg sit-up and throw-for-distance might cause musculoskeletal injuries. In addition, the longer distance runs of the Texas Test (1973) were offered as options.

In 1976, a national normative survey was completed and national norms for the YFT were revised (AAHPERD 1976). The only distance run included in the normative survey was the 600-yard run. The six tests with national normative data are 1) Pull-up (boys) or flexed-arm hang (girls); 2) Sit-up (flexed leg, 60-second time limit); 3) Shuttle run; 4) Standing long jump; 5) 50-yard dash; and 6) 600-yard run. Test procedures and normative standards for these traditional tests are provided in Chapter 8 and in a later section of this chapter.

## Health-Related Physical Fitness

The development of **health-related physical fitness** tests represents a major innovation in youth fitness testing. These tests were developed in response to both the growing dissatisfaction with traditional motor fitness batteries and the growing body of evidence supporting the value of regular, vigorous exercise for health promotion. The goals of the Healthy People 2000 public health project (1990) support the shift from a motor to health related fitness emphasis. Provided next is a discussion of the batteries that led to the development of the health-related fitness movement. These tests are no longer used. Following this overview the current three national tests are reviewed.

### Texas Test

The Texas Governor's Commission on Physical Fitness published a test in 1973 because many felt the AAHPERD YFT was too time-consuming to administer and did not measure true components of physical fitness. The **Texas Youth Fitness Test** was a motor fitness test, but the battery was split into physical fitness components and motor ability components. Both types of abilities were measured, but the award for achievement applies only to the fitness tests. The major contribution of the Texas Test in advancing the health-related concept was the publication of true aerobic distance run tests.

A feature of the Texas battery is that different tests were provided for each component. Many of these tests and test instructions are provided in Chapter 8. The components and items of the Texas Test are as follows:

1. Physical fitness components
   a. Muscular strength and endurance of the arms and shoulder girdle: pull-ups, dips, flexed-arm hand (90 seconds).
   b. Muscular strength and endurance of the abdominal region: bent-leg sit-ups (2 minutes).
   c. Cardiorespiratory endurance in distance running: 1.5 mile- and 12-minute walk/run for distance (grades 7 to 12); 9-minute walk/run for time, 1-mile walk/run for time (grades 4 to 6).

2. Motor ability components
   a. Running speed: 50-yard timed sprint, 8-second run for distance.
   b. Running agility: shuttle run for distance (15 seconds), zig-zag run.
   c. Explosive movement: vertical jump, standing long jump.

## South Carolina Test

Using the AAHPERD position paper on physical fitness (Jackson 1976) as a guide, South Carolina published a health-related fitness test and statewide norms (Pate 1978). One unique feature of the test is its inclusion of both criterion- and norm-referenced standards. The battery includes the following components and recommended tests:

1. **Cardiorespiratory function:** 1-mile run or 9-minute run for distance.
2. Body composition: the sum of triceps and abdominal skinfolds.
3. Abdominal and low-back musculoskeletal function: bent-knee sit-ups in 1 minute, and sit-and-reach.

The test provides norms for boys and girls ages 9 to 16. Criterion-referenced standards are also included to evaluate the physical fitness status of teachers, encouraging teachers to demonstrate the importance of fitness through participation.

## Manitoba Physical Fitness Performance Test

The Manitoba Department of Education (1977) in Canada offers a health-related fitness test designed for boys and girls ages 5 to 19. The test includes fitness standards for teachers as well. The components of the test are as follows:

1. Cardiovascular endurance: 800-meter run (ages 5 to 9); 1600-meter run (ages 10 to 12); 2400-meter run (ages 13 to 60).
2. Flexibility: sit-and-reach.
3. Muscular endurance: 1-minute speed bent-knee sit-ups and flexed-arm hang.
4. Body composition: percentage fat estimated from biceps, triceps, subscapular, and suprailium skinfolds.

The test also includes an agility run, which is a motor ability rather than a health-related fitness test. The prediction of body composition with the Manitoba equation is not recommended. Chapter 11 provides valid methods for estimating percent body fat of children and youth with the sum of calf and triceps skinfolds.

After five years of development, the AAHPERD (1980; 1984) published a health-related physical fitness battery. This was the first national health-related fitness test. The components and test items include the following:

1. Cardiorespiratory function: 1-mile run or 9-minute run for all students. The Texas 1.5-mile or 12-minute run/walk tests are optional for students 13 years or older.

2. Body composition (leanness/fatness): sum of triceps and subscapular skinfolds or triceps skinfold if only one site is used.

3. Abdominal and low-back hamstring musculoskeletal function. Modified, timed (60 seconds), bent-knee sit-ups and sit-and-reach tests.

The **AAHPERD HRFT** was developed by a joint committee representing the Measurement and Evaluation, Physical Fitness, and Research Councils of AAHPERD. The manual (AAHPERD 1980) includes the test items and norms and a chapter on the general principles of exercise prescription. This allows the teacher to diagnose student weaknesses and to provide a sound, individualized physical fitness program.

The AAHPERD HRFT has not proven to be popular. Most school districts continued to use the AAHPERD YFT, which is a motor fitness test. It is likely that this first national health-related fitness test was ahead of its time. This test is important in that it established that health-related fitness was the trend in fitness testing and fitness was more than just exercise—it also included a knowledge component.

The FYT (Fit Youth Today) program is important because it set the standard for the new health-related fitness programs (1986). It was the first to be published since the development of the AAHPERD HRFT. It includes a complete program of health-related fitness for all school-age youth and was reviewed and endorsed by the **American College of Sports Medicine.** The FYT program was developed by leaders in measurement, exercise physiology, and medicine and was more than just a test; it was an educational program.

The FYT curriculum emphasized student understanding of key health-related fitness concepts. A health promotion educational component was included. It was broken down by grade level and provided questions and answers by grade level for both the instructor and the student on exercise, cardiovascular disease risk factors, diet and nutrition, tobacco use, stress, cancer, allergy and asthma, and the family role in health and fitness. The FYT conditioning protocol provides a detailed eight-week progressive aerobic conditioning program. Included are warm-up, flexibility exercises, and training ranges for the frequency, intensity, and duration of aerobic fitness.

The FYT tests are (1) 20-minute steady state run; (2) bent-knee curl-up; (3) sit-and-reach; and (4) body composition—percent body fat estimated from the sum of triceps and medial calf skinfolds. The bent-knee curl-up and sit-and-reach tests are similar to the sit-up and sit-and-reach tests previously presented in this chapter. The percent body fat methods follow standard procedures that are shown in Chapter 11.

The unique test of this battery is the 20-minute steady state run. This test is to be administered after an 8-week training program. The test is to jog continuously for 20 minutes. Rather than using age levels, the FYT program established criterion-reference

**Table 9.1** Criterion-Referenced Standards in Miles Traveled for Males and Females for the Texas FYT 20-Minute Steady State Run

| Grade Level | Males | Females |
|---|---|---|
| 4 | 1.8 | 1.6 |
| 5 | 2.0 | 1.8 |
| 6 | 2.2 | 2.0 |
| 7–12 | 2.4 | 2.2 |

norms for grades. Table 9.1 presents the criterion-referenced 20-minute steady state norms for males and females in grades 4 to 12.

## National Health-Related Youth Fitness Tests

In the early stages of development, youth fitness programs were just a test battery. The public school fitness programs consisted of just testing students. The Texas FYT and AAHPERD HRFT programs changed this by developing educational programs that integrated a health and fitness curriculum with testing. In 1993, there were four national youth fitness tests for use in the public schools. The test items of AAHPERD's Physical Best and the Prudential FITNESSGRAM® were nearly identical. In January 1994, AAHPERD adopted the popular Prudential FITNESSGRAM® in an effort to help create a single youth fitness program for all of the nation's schools. Table 9.2 lists the fitness components and the tests of the three national tests. The broad scope of these programs prohibits their duplication in this text. Provided next is a description of the test items and award programs. You are encouraged to write to each organization to obtain the entire program materials.

## Prudential FITNESSGRAM®

The most comprehensive and academically sound health-related fitness program is the **Prudential FITNESSGRAM®.** This program was developed by a team of professionals working with personnel from the Institute for Aerobics Research of the Cooper Clinic (1992).[3] The program is sponsored by the Prudential Insurance Company of America and has been consistently revised in light of new scientific evidence.

This popular test is a comprehensive youth fitness program that not only includes an excellent health-related fitness test with sound criterion-referenced standards and well-developed educational materials, but also has the best computerized reporting system (see Chapter 2). The program is not only designed to enhance physical fitness, but also to develop affective, cognitive, and behavioral components that enhance participation in regular physical activity.

***Test Items.*** *Aerobic Capacity.* The 1-mile walk/run test can be used for all students, but performance standards have purposefully not been established for students in grades K–3. The goal for these young children is to complete the 1-mile distance at a

---

[3]The Prudential FITNESSGRAM®, Cooper Institute for Aerobic Research, 12330 Preston Road, Dallas, TX 75230. (214) 701–8001.

**Table 9.2** A Comparison and National Youth Fitness Test Batteries Contrasted by Fitness Component and Test Item

| Fitness Component | President's Challenge | Chrysler Fund-AAU | Prudential FITNESSGRAM® |
|---|---|---|---|
| **Aerobic Fitness** | 1-Mile Run | 1-Mile Run<br>Endurance Shuttle Run | 1-Mile Run<br>The PACER |
| **Body Composition** | None | None | Skinfolds or<br>Body Mass Index |
| **Strength and Endurance Components** | | | |
| Abdominal | Sit-ups | Sit-ups | Curl-up |
| Upper Body | Pull-ups<br>Flexed-Arm Hang | Pull-ups<br>Flexed-Arm Hang<br>Isometric Push-up | Pull-ups<br>Flexed-Arm Hang<br>Modified Pull-up |
| Trunk & Lower Body | None | Isometric Leg Squat | Trunk Lift |
| **Flexibility** | Sit-and-Reach<br>V-Sit | V-Sit | Back Saver Sit-and-Reach<br>Shoulder Stretch |
| **Motor Fitness Components** | Shuttle Run | Shuttle Run<br>50–100 Yard Run<br>Standing Long Jump | None |

comfortable pace. The PACER is an optional test that is strongly recommended for participants in grades K–3. This progressive aerobic cardiovascular endurance run (PACER) is a 10-meter shuttle run that becomes progressively more demanding. The pace is regulated with a tape recording. A time of 9 seconds is allowed to run the 20 meters during the first minute, and each minute the pace increases by reducing the 20-meter run time requirement by about a half second. This requires the student to increase exercise intensity at a systematic rate and is the same physiological principle used to regulate the power output of treadmill and cycle ergometer tests (see Chapter 10).

*Body Composition.* **Body composition** can be measured by percent body fat estimated from the sum of triceps and calf skinfolds and body mass index. The equations developed by Lohman (1992) are used to estimate percent body fat. Chapter 11 gives the equations, test methods, and criterion-referenced standards.

*Curl-Up Test.* This test replaces the sit-up test common to most motor and health-related test batteries.[4] The objective of the curl-up test is to complete as many curl-ups as possible at a defined rate. Special equipment is used to measure the distance the student curls up. A completed curl is the initial phase of the sit-up and involves raising

---

[4]A limitation of the bent-leg sit-up test is the use of the hip flexor muscles besides the abdominal muscles. Excessive use of the hip flexor muscles increases low-back compression forces. Excessive low-back compressive forces are associated with low-back problems (NIOSH 1977; NIOSH 1981; Ross & Jackson 1990).

the head and shoulders off the exercise mat. Music is provided to control the rate of exercise at 20 curl-ups per minute. The test is to maintain the exercise rate as long as possible or complete a maximum of 75 curl-ups.

*Trunk Lift.* The trunk-lift test measures the student's trunk extensor strength and flexibility. The test requires the student to lift the upper body to a maximum of 12 inches off the floor using the back muscles. The score is the height the student can hold his/her chin off the floor. Students are encouraged not to exceed 12 inches because excessive arching can cause compression of the discs.

*Upper Body Strength.* The Prudential FITNESSGRAM® provides four standard tests to choose from. These include 1) push-up; 2) modified pull-up; 3) pull-up; and 4) flexed-arm hang. The general types of tests are discussed in Chapter 8, and the instructions for the pull-up and flexed-arm hang tests are furnished in a later section of this chapter.

*Flexibility.* Two flexibility tests are provided. The back-saver sit-and-reach test is similar to the traditional sit-and-reach test except that it is performed on one side at a time. One leg is fully extended while other knee is bent. Testing one side at a time discourages students from hyperextending. In this position, the student reaches forward as far as possible. After measuring one side, the student switches the position of the legs and reaches again. The student's score is the average of the two stretches. The second test, shoulder stretch, measures upper body flexibility. The goal is to touch the fingertips together behind the back by reaching over the shoulder and under the elbow.

***Award Program.*** The Prudential FITNESSGRAM® award program is designed not only for recognition, but also for motivation. The philosophy of the program comes from three important concepts: (1) fitness is for a lifetime; (2) fitness is for everyone; and (3) fitness is fun and enjoyable. The program refers to its system as a "recognition" program rather than an "award" program because "awards often are perceived to be something that is 'given' rather than 'earned' and because awards may be perceived as something only a select few can receive" (1992, p. 55).

The Prudential FITNESSGRAM® recognition system is based on four sources of research evidence. First, to be effective, recognition must be based on achievement of goals that are challenging yet attainable. Second, if a recognition system is not based on goals that seem attainable, children and youth will not be motivated to try. Third, intrinsic motivation for any behavior, including exercise and physical fitness behaviors, must be based on continuous feedback of progress. Awards that are perceived as controlling rather than informative do not build intrinsic motivation. Finally, awards that are given to those with exceptionally high scores on fitness tests will often go to those who have the gift of exceptional heredity, early maturity, and to those already receiving many awards for their physical accomplishments.

The Prudential FITNESSGRAM® recognition system has several levels.

1. "It's Your Move." This is for students in grades K–6. To get this recognition award, students must perform the Prudential FITNESSGRAM® assessment and complete physical activities at home, at school, and with the community.

2. Behavior Recognition, "Get Fit" and "Fit for Life." These incentive programs are designed to recognize participants for any of the following activities: (1) completion of exercise log; (2) achievement of specific goals; and (3) fulfillment of contractual agreement.

3. Performance Recognition, "I'm Fit." The Prudential FITNESSGRAM® uses criterion-referenced standards that represent a level of fitness that offers a degree of protection against disease that results from sedentary living. Performance is judged by two general categories: needs improvement and healthy fitness zone that ranges from "good" to "better." The FITNESSGRAM® computer printout given in Chapter 2 shows this system. This incentive program recognizes participants in two ways: (1) achievement of healthy fitness zone on five of six test items or on four of five test items; and (2) improvement in their performance on at least two test items.

*Educational Program.* The Prudential FITNESSGRAM® offers a sound educational program that integrates testing and a computer-generated student evaluation system with cognitive teaching materials. The Prudential FITNESSGRAM® computer output is illustrated in Chapter 2. The Prudential FITNESSGRAM® program adopted the educational materials developed for the AAHPERD Physical Best Program. These teaching materials provide teachers with sound information designed to integrate exercise with important exercise physiology and **exercise epidemiology** concepts. The Prudential FITNESSGRAM® provides teachers with the capacity to teach American youth the value of exercise for health promotion. These materials and approach are consistent with the goals of Healthy People 2000 provided in Chapter 1. Many medical scientists now view physical education as an important public health program.

The **Chrysler AAU Physical Fitness Program** is funded by the Chrysler Corporation Fund (Fund-AAU 1992).[5] This new test includes both motor fitness and health-related fitness tests.

**Chrysler Fund-AAU Physical Fitness Program**

*Test Items.* The test battery has required tests and optional tests. The required tests are summarized next.

*Endurance Run.* The distance becomes progressively longer with age. The distances for age groups are 6 and 7 years, 0.25 miles; 8 and 9 years, 0.50 miles; 10 and 11 years, 0.75 miles; and ages 12 years and above, 1 mile.

*Bent-Knee Sit-Ups.* The sit-up test is the total number of sit-ups completed in one minute. The test position is described in a later section of this chapter.

*Sit-and-Reach Test.* The test objective is to reach as far as possible on the floor with heels 12 inches apart.

*Pull-Ups and Flexed-Arm Hang.* The pull-up test is the total number completed with the palms facing either toward or away from the body. Many students cannot complete a pull-up. For these students, the flexed-arm hang can be used. These tests are described in a later section of this chapter.

The battery includes optional tests that include health-related and motor fitness items. These are summarized next.

---

[5]The Chrysler Fund-Amateur Athletic Union Physical Fitness Program, 400 E. 7th Street, Poplars Room 711, Bloomington, IN 47405. Phone 1–800–258–5497.

*Hoosier Endurance Shuttle Run.* This is an aerobic endurance test. This test involves running a 20-yard shuttle course as often as possible within a 6-minute time period for students ages 6 to 11 and 9 minutes for students age 12 or older.

*Standing Long Jump, Shuttle Run, Sprint Tests (50 yards ages 6 to 12 and 100 yards ages 13 years and older).* These are common items of motor fitness batteries. Chapter 8 gives a description of these tests.

*Isometric Push-Up and Isometric Leg Squat.* These are unique tests that require the student to hold a position as long as possible. The tests are scored by the elapsed time the student can maintain the test position. The push-up position is with elbows bent at a 90 degree angle. The leg squat position is with the back against the wall and the knees at a 90 degree angle.

***Award Program.*** The AAU test based its Award Program on data from the 1985 School Population Fitness Survey conducted by the University of Michigan Institute for Social Research. The AAU Outstanding Achievement Standard is rigorous and nearly identical with the Presidential Physical Fitness Award. The Attainment Standard is similar to the 50th percentile standard of the Presidential test. The final award is for participation. The three awards are

1. Certificate of Outstanding Achievement. The student is required to meet the outstanding standard on all four required tests and one optional event of the student's choice. The student must attain the pull-up standard to achieve this award.

2. Certificate of Attainment. The student who does not meet the outstanding achievement level, but reaches the attainment or outstanding levels on the four required tests and one optional event of the student's choice receive this certificate. The flexed-arm hand test can be substituted for the pull-up test to qualify for this award.

3. Certificate of Participation. This is awarded to students who do not reach the levels required by the two more demanding events.

## President's Challenge

The least comprehensive program is the **President's Challenge** program.[6] Prior to 1987, the AAHPERD YFT was used by the President's Council on Physical Fitness and Sports to provide the Presidential Award, but in 1987 the President's Council on Physical Fitness and Sports published The Presidential Physical Fitness Award Program. The test battery is a slight modification of the AAHPERD YFT and has five tests.

***Test Items.*** *Curl-Up.* The test is called curl-up, but it is the bent-leg, 60-second sit-up test described in a later section of this chapter.

*Pull-Ups.* This is the pull-up test completed with the overhand grip (i.e., palms facing forward). Flexed-arm hang is provided as an optional test for those who cannot do pull-ups. These test instructions and normative standards are given in a later section of this chapter.

---

[6]For information on this test write to President's Challenge, Poplars Research Center, 400 East 7th Street, Bloomington, IN 47405.

*Sit-and-Reach or V-Sit Reach.* These are two common flexibility tests. The sit-and-reach test is discussed in a later section of this chapter. The goal of the V-sit is to reach as far as possible on the floor while the legs are straight and the heels are 12 inches apart.

*One-mile Run/Walk.* This distance run test is described at the end of this chapter.

*Shuttle Run.* This is the FYT shuttle run test. This is a motor fitness, not health-related fitness, item. Test instructions and normative standards of the shuttle run are presented in Chapter 8.

***Award Program.*** Over 19,000 American boys and girls were tested in 1985, and these data were used to develop the new standards for the Presidential Physical Fitness Award. There are three awards given.

1. Presidential Physical Fitness Award. The 85th percentile was used to establish this award standard. To qualify for the Presidential Award, a student would need to reach the 85th percentile on each of the five tests. Both male and female students must reach the pull-up standard to win this award.

2. National Physical Fitness Award. The 50th percentile was used to establish this award standard. To qualify for the National Physical Fitness Award, a student would need to reach the 50th percentile on each of the five tests.

3. Participant Physical Fitness Award. Students who attempted all five test items but did not reach the 50th percentile or above on all tests receive the Participant Award. This award recognizes those students who completed all tests.

## Common Fitness Test Items

The national health-related youth fitness tests include several common test items. They include distance runs, pull-ups, flexed-arm hangs, sit-ups, and low-back flexibility. Included in this section are the test procedures for these common fitness tests and published norms. Chapter 11 gives the methods used to measure body composition with children and youth, but the special considerations applied to children are restated in this section.

## Distance Run Tests

All health-related youth fitness test batteries include **distance run tests** to measure aerobic endurance. The AAHPERD YFT (1976) included the 600-yard run as a test of endurance. But, exercise physiologists maintain that 600 yards is more anaerobic than aerobic (Balke 1963). Provided next is the evidence supporting the validity of distance run tests, test methods, and normative data.

***Validity of Distance Run Tests.*** Cooper (1968), whose study intensified efforts to establish the concurrent validity of distance runs, reported a correlation of 0.90 between $\dot{V}O_2$ Max and the distance covered during a 12-minute run/walk. Factor analysis studies have shown that distance runs normally measure two factors: (1) speed, represented in distances less than 440 yards; and (2) endurance, represented in longer distances (one mile in length or longer) or 9 minutes or longer in duration (Burke 1976; Disch et al. 1975; Jackson & Coleman 1976). Intermediate distances and duration (from 600 to 800 yards and 3 to 6 minutes) have been found to measure both speed and endurance. These studies have also shown that runs of 1 mile and 9 minutes in duration or longer measure the same basic component.

**Table 9.3** Means and Standard Deviations of $\dot{V}O_2$ Max and Concurrent Validity of Distance Run Tests with Children and Youth

| Source | Sample | Run | $\dot{V}O_2$ Max (Ml/Kg/Min) | | |
| --- | --- | --- | --- | --- | --- |
| | | | **Mean** | **SD** | $r_{xy}$ |
| Cureton et al. (1977) | 140 boys, age 10 | 1 mile | 48.0 | 6.7 | −.66 |
| | 56 girls, age 10 | 1 mile | 45.4 | 5.9 | −.66 |
| Doolittle and Bigbee (1968) | 9 boys, grade 9 | 12 minutes | * | * | .90 |
| Gutin et al. (1976) | 15 boys and girls, age 11 | 1800 yards | 47.5 | 5.8 | −.76 |
| | | 1200 yards | | | −.81 |
| Gutin et al. (1976) | 33 girls, age 11–12 | 1120 yards | 37.0 | 5.9 | −.70 |
| Jackson and Coleman (1976) | 22 boys, grades 1–6 | 9 minutes | 44.5 | 4.6 | .82 |
| | | 12 minutes | | | .82 |
| | 25 girls, grades 1–6 12 minutes | 9 minutes | 40.6 | 4.1 | .71 |
| | | | | | .71 |
| Krahenbuhl et al. (1977) | 20 boys, age 8 | .75 miles | 47.6 | 7.1 | −.64 |
| | | 1 mile | | | −.71 |
| | 18 girls, age 8 | .75 miles | 42.9 | 5.7 | −.22 |
| | | 1 mile | | | −.26 |
| Maksud and Coutts (1971) | 17 boys, age 11–14 | 12 minutes | 47.4 | 4.0 | .65 |
| Vodak and Wilmore (1975) | 69 boys, age 9–12 | 6 minutes | 53.6 | 5.6 | .50 |

*Value not published.

Distance run tests have been shown to have moderate to high correlations with $\dot{V}O_2$ Max when the runs are 1 mile or longer and 9 minutes or more in duration. The concurrent validity coefficients for running tests involving youth are listed in Table 9.3. Prior to 1973, the longer distance runs were not considered acceptable tests for public school children, but now they are. As an additional guide for evaluating distance run tests, the sample characteristics, distance run test means, and standard deviations of samples of school-age children are listed in Table 9.4.

***Distance Run Test Methods.*** Distance run tests can be scored in two ways: the elapsed time to cover a distance (e.g., one mile); and the distance traveled in a specified time, usually 9 or 12 minutes. The one-mile run has become the most popular distance run test.

*Objective:* To measure maximal aerobic fitness or $\dot{V}O_2$ Max (see Chapter 10).

*Validity and reliability:* The 1-mile and 9-minute runs are valid field tests of cardiorespiratory function and performance because they are related to $\dot{V}O_2$ Max, along with other physiological parameters of cardiorespiratory function, and provide an index of the participant's ability to run distances. Also, the proposed runs give essentially the same information as those of longer distance. The 1.5-mile and 12-minute run alternatives are offered mainly because of their current widespread use. Distance runs have acceptable reliability when administered carefully to properly prepared students. The test user should note that other factors (body fatness, running efficiency, maturity, motivation) also affect distance run time.

**Table 9.4** Descriptive Statistics for Distance Run Tests

| Source | Sample | Run | MEAN | SD |
|---|---|---|---|---|
| Cooper et al. (1975) | 778 boys and girls, grades 9–12 | 12-minute run/walk | 2235* 2640** | 475 563 |
| | 437 boys and girls, grades 9–12 | 12-minute run/walk | 2358* 2340** | 510 545 |
| Doolittle et al. (1969) | 100 girls, grades 9–10 | 12-minute run/walk | 2202 | ε |
| | 45 girls, grade 9 | 12-minute run/walk | 2296 | ε |
| Gutin et al. (1976) | 15 boys and girls, ages 10–12 | 12-minute run/walk | 2320 | 400 |
| Jackson and Coleman (1976) | 25 boys, grades 1–6 | 12-minute run/walk | 2560 | 314 |
| | 25 girls, grades 1–6 | 12-minute run/walk | 2255 | 284 |
| Maksud and Coutts (1971) | 44 boys, ages 13–14 | 12-minute run/walk | 2381 | 270 |
| Texas Test (1973) | 662 girls, grades 4–6 | 9-minute run/walk | 1536 | 277 |
| | 556 boys, grades 4–6 | 9-minute run/walk | 1778 | 355 |
| | 375 girls, grades 4–6 | 1-mile run/walk | 10:09 | 1:54 |
| | 312 boys, grades 4–6 | 1-mile run/walk | 8:54 | 1:59 |
| | 1397 girls, grades 7–12 | 12-minute run/walk | 1862 | 357 |
| | 1234 boys, grades 7–12 | 12-minute run/walk | 2543 | 428 |
| | 471 girls, grades 4–6 | 1.5-mile run/walk | 16:11 | 2:36 |
| | 745 boys, grades 4–6 | 1.5-mile run/walk | 11:29 | 1:44 |

*Pretest.
**Posttest. ε Value not given.

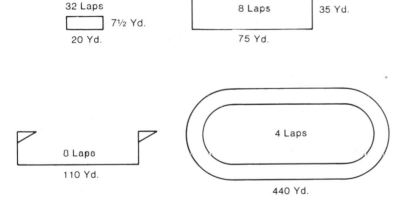

**Figure 9.1**
Test courses for administering the distance run tests of the AAHPERD Health-Related Physical Fitness Test.

*Equipment:* Either of the two distance-run tests can be administered on a 440-yard or 400-meter track, or on any other flat measured area (the 110-yard or 100-meter straight-away, other outside fields, an indoor-court area). Sample test courses are shown in Figure 9.1.

*Procedures:* Instruct students to run 1 mile in the fastest possible time. This should begin on the signal "Ready, Start!" As they cross the finish line, call out elapsed time to the participants (or their partners). Walking is allowed, but the objective is to cover the distance in the shortest possible time.

**Table 9.5** Percentile Norms for Boys for the 1-Mile Run (in Minutes and Seconds)*

| Percentile | Age | | | | | | |
| | 5 | 6 | 7 | 8 | 9 | 10 | 11 |
|---|---|---|---|---|---|---|---|
| 95 | 9:02 | 9:06 | 8:06 | 7:58 | 7:17 | 6:56 | 6:50 |
| 75 | 11:32 | 10:55 | 9:37 | 9:14 | 8:36 | 8:10 | 8:00 |
| 50 | 13:46 | 12:29 | 11:25 | 11:00 | 9:56 | 9:19 | 9:06 |
| 25 | 16:05 | 15:10 | 14:02 | 13:29 | 12:00 | 11:05 | 11:31 |
| 5 | 18:25 | 17:38 | 17:17 | 16:19 | 15:44 | 14:28 | 15:25 |

| Percentile | Age | | | | | |
| | 12 | 13 | 14 | 15 | 16 | 17+ |
|---|---|---|---|---|---|---|
| 95 | 6:27 | 6:11 | 5:51 | 6:01 | 5:48 | 6:01 |
| 75 | 7:24 | 6:52 | 6:36 | 6:35 | 6:28 | 6:36 |
| 50 | 8:20 | 7:27 | 7:10 | 7:14 | 7:11 | 7:25 |
| 25 | 10:00 | 8:35 | 8:02 | 8:04 | 8:07 | 8:26 |
| 5 | 13:41 | 10:23 | 10:32 | 10:37 | 10:40 | 10:56 |

*The complete table is available in *AAHPERD Manual* (AAHPERD 1980).

**Table 9.6** Percentile Norms for Girls for the 1-Mile Run (in Minutes and Seconds)*

| Percentile | Age | | | | | | |
| | 5 | 6 | 7 | 8 | 9 | 10 | 11 |
|---|---|---|---|---|---|---|---|
| 95 | 9:45 | 9:18 | 8:48 | 8:45 | 8:24 | 7:59 | 7:46 |
| 75 | 13:09 | 11:24 | 10:55 | 10:35 | 9:58 | 9:30 | 9:12 |
| 50 | 15:08 | 13:48 | 12:30 | 12:00 | 11:12 | 11:06 | 10:27 |
| 25 | 17:59 | 15:27 | 14:30 | 14:16 | 13:18 | 12:54 | 12:10 |
| 5 | 19:00 | 18:50 | 17:44 | 16:58 | 16:42 | 17:00 | 16:56 |

| Percentile | Age | | | | | |
| | 12 | 13 | 14 | 15 | 16 | 17+ |
|---|---|---|---|---|---|---|
| 95 | 7:26 | 7:10 | 7:18 | 7:39 | 7:07 | 7:26 |
| 75 | 8:36 | 8:18 | 8:13 | 8:42 | 9:00 | 9:03 |
| 50 | 9:47 | 9:27 | 9:35 | 10:05 | 10:45 | 9:47 |
| 25 | 11:34 | 10:56 | 11:43 | 12:21 | 13:00 | 11:28 |
| 5 | 14:46 | 14:55 | 16:59 | 16:22 | 15:30 | 15:24 |

*The complete table is available in *AAHPERD Manual* (AAHPERD, 1980).

*Scoring:* The elapsed time tests are scored to the nearest second and the distance covered tests in yards.

*Norms:* Norms were established from data collected on over 10,000 students throughout the United States and appear in Tables 9.5 through 9.9. Additional norms for boys and girls ages 6 to 9 years may be found in another source (Ross et al. 1987).

Part 3 Performance Testing

**Table 9.7** Percentile Norms for Boys for the 9-Minute Run (in Yards)*

| Percentile | Age | | | | | | |
| | 5 | 6 | 7 | 8 | 9 | 10 | 11 |
|---|---|---|---|---|---|---|---|
| 95 | 1760 | 1750 | 2020 | 2200 | 2175 | 2250 | 2250 |
| 75 | 1320 | 1469 | 1683 | 1810 | 1835 | 1910 | 1925 |
| 50 | 1170 | 1280 | 1440 | 1595 | 1660 | 1690 | 1725 |
| 25 | 990 | 1090 | 1243 | 1380 | 1440 | 1487 | 1540 |
| 5 | 600 | 816 | 990 | 1053 | 1104 | 1110 | 1170 |

| Percentile | Age | | | | | |
| | 12 | 13 | 14 | 15 | 16 | 17+ |
|---|---|---|---|---|---|---|
| 95 | 2400 | 2402 | 2473 | 2544 | 2615 | 2615 |
| 75 | 1975 | 2096 | 2167 | 2238 | 2309 | 2380 |
| 50 | 1760 | 1885 | 1956 | 2027 | 2098 | 2169 |
| 25 | 1500 | 1674 | 1745 | 1816 | 1887 | 1958 |
| 5 | 1000 | 1368 | 1439 | 1510 | 1581 | 1652 |

*The complete table is available in *AAHPERD Manual* (AAHPERD, 1980).

**Table 9.8** Percentile Norms for Girls for the 9-Minute Run (in Yards)*

| Percentile | Age | | | | | | |
| | 5 | 6 | 7 | 8 | 9 | 10 | 11 |
|---|---|---|---|---|---|---|---|
| 95 | 1540 | 1700 | 1900 | 1860 | 2050 | 2067 | 2000 |
| 75 | 1300 | 1440 | 1540 | 1540 | 1650 | 1650 | 1723 |
| 50 | 1140 | 1208 | 1344 | 1358 | 1425 | 1460 | 1480 |
| 25 | 950 | 1017 | 1150 | 1225 | 1243 | 1250 | 1345 |
| 5 | 700 | 750 | 860 | 970 | 960 | 940 | 904 |

| Percentile | Age | | | | | |
| | 12 | 13 | 14 | 15 | 16 | 17+ |
|---|---|---|---|---|---|---|
| 95 | 2175 | 2085 | 2123 | 2161 | 2199 | 2237 |
| 75 | 1760 | 1785 | 1823 | 1861 | 1899 | 1937 |
| 50 | 1590 | 1577 | 1615 | 1653 | 1691 | 1729 |
| 25 | 1356 | 1369 | 1407 | 1445 | 1483 | 1521 |
| 5 | 1000 | 1069 | 1107 | 1145 | 1183 | 1221 |

*The complete table is available in *AAHPERD Manual* (AAHPERD, 1980).

**Table 9.9** Optional Distance Run Tests for Boys
and Girls, Age 13 and Older*

| Percentile | 12-Minute Run (Yards) | | 1.5 Mile Run (Min: Sec) | |
|:---:|:---:|:---:|:---:|:---:|
| | *Boys* | *Girls* | *Boys* | *Girls* |
| 95 | 3297 | 2448 | 8:37 | 12:17 |
| 75 | 2879 | 2100 | 10:19 | 15:03 |
| 50 | 2592 | 1861 | 11:29 | 16:57 |
| 25 | 2305 | 1622 | 12:39 | 18:50 |
| 5 | 1888 | 1274 | 14:20 | 21:36 |

*Normative data from Texas Test (1973).

**Table 9.10** Percentile Rank Norms for Boys
on the AAHPER Test for Pull-Ups*

| Percentile | Age | | | | | | | |
| | 10 | 11 | 12 | 13 | 14 | 15 | 16 | 17+ |
|:---:|:---:|:---:|:---:|:---:|:---:|:---:|:---:|:---:|
| 95 | 9 | 8 | 9 | 10 | 12 | 15 | 14 | 15 |
| 75 | 3 | 4 | 4 | 5 | 7 | 9 | 10 | 10 |
| 50 | 1 | 2 | 2 | 3 | 4 | 6 | 7 | 7 |
| 25 | 0 | 0 | 0 | 1 | 2 | 3 | 4 | 4 |
| 5 | 0 | 0 | 0 | 0 | 0 | 0 | 1 | 0 |

*Source: Adapted from *Youth Fitness Test Manual* (Washington, DC: AAHPER, 1976), p. 38. Used by permission.

**Common Endurance and Flexibility Test Items**

Sit-up, pull-up, flexed-arm hang, and sit-and-reach test are items common to health-related fitness and motor fitness batteries. Provided next are test procedures and normative standards for these tests.

*Pull-Up Test.*

　*Equipment:* A horizontal bar positioned at a height that allows the student to hang without touching the ground.

　*Procedure:* The bar should be adjusted to a height that allows the student to hang free from the floor. From the hanging position with an overhand grip (palms forward), the body is pulled upward until the chin rests over the bar and then lowered until the arms are straight. This movement should be repeated to exhaustion. The student is not allowed to kick, jerk, or use a "kip" movement. The Chrysler-AAU test allows the student to use either handhold, palms forward or backward.

　*Scoring:* The student's score is the number of correctly executed chins. Selected norms are provided in Table 9.10.

**Table 9.11** Percentile Rank Norms for Girls on the AAHPER Flexed-Arm Hang Test (in Seconds)*

| Percentile | 9–10 | 11 | 12 | Age 13 | 14 | 15 | 16 | 17+ |
|---|---|---|---|---|---|---|---|---|
| 95 | 42 | 39 | 33 | 34 | 35 | 36 | 31 | 34 |
| 75 | 18 | 20 | 18 | 16 | 21 | 18 | 15 | 17 |
| 50 | 9 | 10 | 9 | 8 | 9 | 9 | 7 | 8 |
| 25 | 3 | 3 | 3 | 3 | 3 | 4 | 3 | 3 |
| 5 | 0 | 0 | 0 | 0 | 0 | 0 | 0 | 0 |

*Source: Adapted from *Youth Fitness Test Manual* (Washington, DC: AAHPER, 1976), p. 38. Used by permission.

### Flexed-Arm Hang Test

*Equipment:* A horizontal bar positioned at a height that allows the student to hang without touching the ground, and a stopwatch.

*Procedure:* The student uses the overhand grasp (palms forward). With the assistance of two spotters, one in front and one behind, the pupil raises the body off the floor to a position where the chin is above the bar, the elbows are flexed, and the chest is close to the bar. Start the stopwatch when the student reaches the hanging position. Stop the watch when (1) the student's chin touches the bar; (2) the student's head tilts backward to keep the chin above the bar; or (3) the student's chin falls below the level of the bar. The Chrysler-AAU test allows the student to use either handhold, palms forward or backward.

*Scoring:* The score is the number of seconds measured to the nearest second that the student maintained the hanging position. Selected AAHPERD norms are listed in Table 9.11.

### Bent-Knee Sit-Ups

*Objective:* To evaluate abdominal muscular strength and endurance.

*Validity and Reliability:* You can improve the validity and reliability of the test by giving students sufficient instruction and practice in the correct sit-up procedure before testing. The validity of the sit-up test has been determined logically. Studies show that abdominal muscles are being used in the performance of a sit-up. The reliability of the test has been satisfactory with test-retest reliability coefficients ranging from 0.68 to 0.94.

*Equipment:* Use mats or other comfortable surfaces for the students. A stopwatch, or watch or clock with a sweep-second hand, can be used for timing.

*Procedure:* To start, the student lies on the back with knees flexed and feet on the floor, heels 12 to 18 inches from the buttocks. Arms are crossed on the chest, with hands on opposite shoulders. The feet should be held down by a partner to keep them on the testing surface. The student, by tightening his or her abdominal muscles, curls to the sitting position, touching elbows to

**Figure 9.2**
Positions for the modified sit-up test of the AAHPERD Health-Related Physical Fitness Test; (a) on the back and (b) in the up position.

(a)

(b)

thighs. Arms must remain on the chest, as should the chin (Figure 9.2). To complete the sit-up, the student returns to the down position until the mid-back touches the testing surface.

The timer gives the signal "Ready, Go." The student starts on the word "Go" and must stop on the word "Stop." The student should know before the test begins that resting between sit-ups is allowed but that the objective is to perform as many correctly executed sit-ups as possible in a 60-second period.

*Scoring:* Record the number of correctly executed sit-ups completed in 60 seconds.

*Norms:* Tables 9.12 and 9.13 list norms for the test. These are based on data secured from over 10,000 school-aged children throughout the United States in 1979.

**Table 9.12** Percentile Norms for Boys for Sit-Ups*

| Percentile | 5 | 6 | 7 | 8 | 9 | 10 | Age 11 | 12 | 13 | 14 | 15 | 16 | 17+ |
|---|---|---|---|---|---|---|---|---|---|---|---|---|---|
| 95 | 30 | 36 | 42 | 48 | 47 | 50 | 51 | 56 | 58 | 59 | 59 | 61 | 62 |
| 75 | 23 | 26 | 33 | 37 | 38 | 40 | 41 | 46 | 48 | 49 | 49 | 51 | 52 |
| 50 | 18 | 20 | 26 | 30 | 32 | 34 | 37 | 39 | 41 | 42 | 44 | 45 | 46 |
| 25 | 11 | 15 | 19 | 25 | 25 | 27 | 30 | 31 | 35 | 36 | 38 | 38 | 38 |
| 5 | 2 | 6 | 10 | 15 | 15 | 15 | 17 | 19 | 25 | 27 | 28 | 28 | 25 |

*The complete table is available in *AAHPERD Manual* (AAHPERD, 1980).

**Table 9.13** Percentile Norms for Girls for Sit-Ups*

| Percentile | 5 | 6 | 7 | 8 | 9 | 10 | Age 11 | 12 | 13 | 14 | 15 | 16 | 17+ |
|---|---|---|---|---|---|---|---|---|---|---|---|---|---|
| 95 | 28 | 35 | 40 | 44 | 44 | 47 | 50 | 52 | 51 | 51 | 56 | 54 | 54 |
| 75 | 24 | 28 | 31 | 35 | 35 | 39 | 40 | 41 | 41 | 42 | 43 | 42 | 44 |
| 50 | 19 | 22 | 25 | 29 | 29 | 32 | 34 | 36 | 35 | 35 | 37 | 33 | 37 |
| 25 | 12 | 14 | 20 | 22 | 23 | 25 | 28 | 30 | 29 | 30 | 30 | 29 | 31 |
| 5 | 2 | 6 | 10 | 12 | 14 | 15 | 19 | 19 | 18 | 20 | 20 | 20 | 19 |

*The complete table is available in *AAHPERD Manual* (AAHPERD, 1980).

### Sit-and-Reach

*Objective:* To evaluate the flexibility of the lower back and posterior thighs.

*Validity and Reliability:* You can improve the validity and reliability of the test by giving students sufficient instruction and warm-up. Warm-up should include slow, sustained, static stretching of the lower back and posterior thighs. The test has been validated against several other flexibility tests. The validity coefficients have ranged between 0.80 and 0.90. The test also has logical validity in that a student must have good flexibility in the lower back, hips, and posterior thighs to score well. Reliability coefficients for this test have been high, ranging above 0.70.

*Equipment:* The test apparatus has a specially constructed box (12″ × 12″ × 21″) with a measuring scale where 23 centimeters is at the level of the feet. The box is shown in Figure 9.3. Plans for building it can be found in the test manual (AAHPERD 1980; 1989).

*Procedure:* To start, have the student remove his or her shoes and sit at the test apparatus with knees fully extended and feet shoulder-width apart. The feet should be flat against the end board. To perform the test, the student extends the arms forward, with hands placed on top of each other as shown in Figure 9.3. The pupil reaches directly forward, palms down, along the measuring scale four times, and holds the position of maximum reach on the fourth trial. This position must be held for one second.

**Figure 9.3**
Testing position for the sit-and-reach test from the AAHPERD Health-Related Physical Fitness Test. (Note the specially constructed box used to standardize the testing procedure.)

**Table 9.14** Percentile Norms for Boys for Sit and Reach (in Centimeters)*

| Percentile | Age | | | | | | | | | | | | |
|---|---|---|---|---|---|---|---|---|---|---|---|---|---|
| | **5** | **6** | **7** | **8** | **9** | **10** | **11** | **12** | **13** | **14** | **15** | **16** | **17+** |
| 95 | 32 | 34 | 33 | 34 | 34 | 33 | 34 | 35 | 36 | 39 | 41 | 42 | 45 |
| 75 | 29 | 29 | 28 | 29 | 29 | 28 | 29 | 29 | 30 | 33 | 34 | 36 | 40 |
| 50 | 25 | 26 | 25 | 25 | 25 | 25 | 25 | 26 | 26 | 28 | 30 | 30 | 34 |
| 25 | 22 | 22 | 22 | 22 | 22 | 20 | 21 | 21 | 20 | 23 | 24 | 25 | 28 |
| 5 | 17 | 16 | 16 | 16 | 16 | 12 | 12 | 13 | 12 | 15 | 13 | 11 | 15 |

*The complete table is available in *AAHPERD Manual* (AAHPERD, 1980).

*Scoring:* The score is the farthest point reached, measured to the nearest centimeter, on the fourth trial. The administrator should remain close to the scale and note the most distant line touched by the fingertips of both hands. If the hands reach unevenly, administer the test again.

*Norms:* Tables 9.14 and 9.15 list the norms for the sit-and-reach test. These are based on data secured from over 10,000 school-aged children throughout the United States.

*Other considerations:* Repeat the test trial if (1) the student's hands reach out unevenly or (2) the knees are flexed during the trial. You can prevent the knees from flexing by keeping your hand, or a monitor's hand, lightly on the knees. To prevent the apparatus from sliding away from the student, place it against a wall or a similar immovable object.

**Table 9.15** Percentile Norms for Girls for Sit and Reach (in Centimeters)*

| Percentile | Age | | | | | | | | | | | | |
| --- | --- | --- | --- | --- | --- | --- | --- | --- | --- | --- | --- | --- | --- |
| | 5 | 6 | 7 | 8 | 9 | 10 | 11 | 12 | 13 | 14 | 15 | 16 | 17+ |
| 95 | 34 | 34 | 34 | 36 | 35 | 35 | 37 | 40 | 43 | 44 | 46 | 46 | 44 |
| 75 | 30 | 30 | 31 | 31 | 31 | 31 | 32 | 34 | 36 | 38 | 41 | 39 | 40 |
| 50 | 27 | 27 | 27 | 28 | 28 | 28 | 29 | 30 | 31 | 33 | 36 | 34 | 35 |
| 25 | 23 | 23 | 24 | 23 | 23 | 24 | 24 | 25 | 24 | 28 | 31 | 30 | 31 |
| 5 | 18 | 18 | 16 | 17 | 17 | 16 | 16 | 15 | 17 | 18 | 19 | 14 | 22 |

*The complete table is available in *AAHPERD Manual* (AAHPERD, 1980).

## Measuring Skinfold Fat of Youth

The Prudential FITNESSGRAM® program includes skinfold tests for measuring body composition. Statistics show that the prevalence of overweight of youth is a major public health problem. The inclusion of the skinfold test in youth fitness batteries has been controversial. Many parents and physical education teachers do not feel that skinfolds should be used to test youth. Extreme care and sensitivity needs to be practiced when measuring skinfold fat of school-aged children. While the testing procedures are fully outlined in Chapter 11, we would like to emphasize the following issues when testing children.

1. The triceps, subscapula, and calf are the recommended sites for children. We recommend the use of triceps and calf skinfold because clothing does not need to be removed. Measuring the subscapular skinfold of a female requires raising the shirt in back for access to the skinfold site. This can be embarrassing for some students.
2. It is best to have a female teacher test female students.
3. Skinfold measurements should always be measured in a private setting.
4. If the student or parent objects to the skinfold test, the BMI may be used.

## Comparison of National Youth Fitness Tests

Youth fitness programs are similar to some degree. These national programs reflect a trend of providing educational materials that extends youth fitness from just testing to a program that integrates education with testing. The noted exception is the program of the President's Council on Physical Fitness and Sports; testing is still the focus of the President's Challenge. All have expanded the award programs, placing more emphasis on student motivation. Even with these similarities, the programs are different in terms of test items and defining criterion-referenced standards of health-related fitness.

## Test Items

All three programs use the 1-mile run to evaluate aerobic fitness. The pull-up and flexed-arm hang are common to all batteries. Two of the programs include the same bent-knee sit-up test to evaluate abdominal strength and endurance while the Prudential FITNESSGRAM® changed to the curl-up test that places less strain on the back.

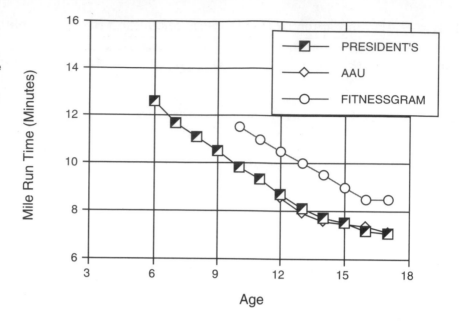

**Figure 9.4**
Mile run criterion-referenced standards needed for a boy to qualify for a performance award on each national youth fitness test. The Prudential FITNESSGRAM® standard differs from the other two and more truly represents the level of aerobic fitness needed for health promotion.

A major difference among the programs concerns the inclusion of body composition and use of motor fitness items. The President's Challenge and Chrysler Fund-AAU batteries do not include body composition items and do include one motor fitness test item. The Prudential FITNESSGRAM® program does not require a motor fitness item, but includes body composition items.

## Criterion-Referenced Standards

All programs provide criterion standards for evaluating health-related fitness levels. Because of differences in tests, it is not possible to compare performance standards across the four batteries because each includes different test items. The 1-mile run and chin-up tests are items of all four tests. Figure 9.4 graphically compares the criterion-referenced standard of each test for the 1-mile run for boys. The Prudential FITNESS-GRAM® 1-mile run standards differ substantially from the other batteries. The Prudential FITNESSGRAM® criterion-referenced standard most closely represents a health-related criterion-referenced standard. Cureton and Warren (1990) give a detailed discussion of the process followed to develop the Prudential FITNESSGRAM® standard. They make convincing arguments based on scientific evidence that the standards used with the other three tests exceed the aerobic fitness level needed for health promotion. Blair and associates (1989) showed that once a moderate level of aerobic fitness was reached, becoming more aerobically fit did not enhance health. The major reason the Chrysler Fund-AAU and President's criterion standards are more demanding is they were derived largely from normative data rather than health-promotion standards.

Figure 9.5 graphically shows the criterion-referenced standards for the pull-up test. The standards of the Prudential FITNESSGRAM® are much less demanding than the other two. These data show that both the President's Challenge and Chrysler Fund-AAU programs place emphasis on rewarding the physically elite. To qualify for the

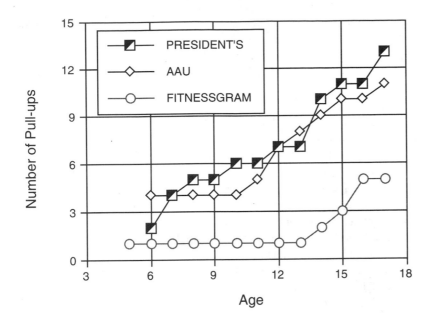

**Figure 9.5**
A graphic comparison of the criterion-referenced standards of the pull-up test for boys. The standards for the President's and Chrysler-AAU are much more physically demanding than the Prudential FITNESSGRAM®.

highest performance award a student must reach the 85th percentile on all required tests, including the pull-up test. One should expect that 15% of those tested will reach the standard on each test, but the correlations among tests are low. Therefore, performance on one test is not highly predictive of performance on the other tests—it is unlikely that if a student scores at the 85th percentile on one test, he or she will score at the same level on other tests. In practice, you would expect less than 1% of students tested to reach the 85th percentile on all five tests. These high standards endorse athletic superiority, rather than encouraging the majority of students to become physically active.

Each of the three programs expanded their award programs so all students can be involved. The combined AAHPER and Prudential FITNESSGRAM® award programs now include awards that recognize important behavioral traits. The evidence cited in Chapter 1 documents that regular participation in vigorous aerobic exercise not only enhances body composition, but also reduces the risk of major degenerative diseases such as heart disease, hypertension, and diabetes. The study by Blair and associates (1989) showed that high levels of aerobic fitness do not enhance health, but low levels place one at a health risk.

## Future Trends

The philosophy and performance standards of the Prudential FITNESSGRAM® are most consistent with the public health view articulated in the Healthy People 2000 goals (1990). These are outlined in Chapter 1. The leadership in youth fitness testing reflected in the Prudential FITNESSGRAM® program is due to their advisory board and the capacity to initiate needed changes. The Prudential FITNESS-GRAM® includes leading exercise epidemiologists, exercise physiologists, measurement specialists, psychologists, educators, and computer technologists. Not only does this group provide an important scientific thrust, but also the program is located at a leading exercise research organization, the Cooper Institute for Aerobics Research. This close relationship gives the Prudential FITNESSGRAM® the capacity to put current scientific research into practice. Since AAHPERD dropped its Physical Best test, the Prudential FITNESSGRAM® will likely become the Nation's youth fitness program.

## Summary

The evaluation of youth fitness has evolved from an emphasis on motor fitness to health-related fitness. Motor fitness tests not only include tests of strength and endurance, but also speed, power, and agility. Motor fitness tests reflect an athletic orientation and endorse the philosophy of awarding the athletically gifted. With the growing body of medical evidence supporting the role of exercise, weight control, and aerobic fitness on health, the trend in youth fitness testing has shifted away from this athletic orientation to one of health promotion. The components of health-related batteries are aerobic fitness, body composition, muscular strength and endurance, and flexibility. There are three national health-related fitness batteries available. Compared to motor fitness tests, these national health-related tests have been expanded to not only include testing, but also educational materials that integrate the cognitive and affective components with the physiological aspects of health-related fitness. The Prudential FITNESSGRAM® is a true health-related program, while the Presidential and AAU tests include motor fitness test items. The philosophy of fitness test award programs is moving from one that only rewards a high level of performance to one that encourages regular exercise designed to achieve fitness levels suitable for health promotion. Criterion-referenced standards are being refined to define the level of fitness needed for health.

## Formative Evaluation of Objectives

*Objective 1*   Identify the general tests that comprise a motor fitness battery.

1. The most popular motor fitness test is the AAHPERD YFT. List the tests that comprise this battery.
2. What is the general nature of motor fitness test items?

*Objective 2*   Identify the general tests that comprise a health-related battery.

1. What is the general nature of health-related fitness test items?
2. What are the test items of the four national health-related fitness test batteries?

*Objective 3*   Differentiate between motor fitness and health-related fitness batteries.

1. Motor fitness and health-related fitness batteries each evolved from different philosophies of fitness. Explain these philosophies.
2. Health-related fitness tests can be used to teach students the value of exercise for health promotion. For what can motor fitness tests be used?
3. What is the major difference between the test items included on motor fitness and health-related fitness batteries?

*Objective 4* Identify and evaluate the national health-related fitness batteries.

1. List and describe the four national health-related youth fitness test batteries.

2. What is the difference in philosophy concerning performance standards and awards?

1. Gain experience in youth fitness testing. Go to the public schools and help a teacher administer fitness tests.

2. Learn how to take skinfold measurements accurately. With one or more of your classmates, take triceps, subscapular, and calf skinfolds on a group of students. Compare your results with your classmates. If your scores do not agree, figure out what you are doing differently. The intraclass reliability method can be used to analyze tester differences. Check the procedures and pictures in this chapter to standardize your testing methods.

3. Order a health-related youth fitness test package. You will be surprised—they are very comprehensive.

**Bibliography**

AAHPER. 1976. *Youth Fitness Test Manual.* Washington, DC.

AAHPERD. 1980. *Health Related Physical Fitness Manual.* Washington, DC.

AAHPERD. 1989. *Physical Best: Instructor's Guide.* Reston, VA.

AAHPERD. 1984. *Technical Manual: Health Related Physical Fitness.* Washington, DC.

AAU. 1992. *Chrysler Fund-AAU Physical Fitness Program 1992–93 Testing Packet.* Bloomington, IN.

American Health and Fitness Foundation. 1986. *FYT Program Manual.* Austin, TX.

Balke, B. 1963. A simple field test for assessment of physical fitness. *Civil Aeromedical Research Institute Report:* 63–66.

Blair, S. N. et al. 1989. Physical fitness and all-cause mortality: A prospective study of healthy men and women. *Journal of the American Medical Association 262:* 2395–2401.

Burke, E. 1976. Validity of selected laboratory and field tests of physical working capacity. *Research Quarterly 47:* 95–104.

Clarke, H. H. (Ed.) 1971. *Basic understanding of physical fitness.* In physical fitness research digest. Washington, DC: President's Council on Physical Fitness and Sport.

Cooper, K. H. 1968. A means of assessing maximal oxygen intake. *Journal of the American Medical Association 203:* 201–204.

Cureton, K. J. 1977. Determinants of distance running performance in children: Analysis of a path model. *Research Quarterly 48:* 270–279.

Cureton, K. J. and G. L. Warren. 1990. Criterion-referenced standards for youth health-related fitness tests: A tutorial. *Research Quarterly for Exercise and Sport 61:* 7–19.

Disch, J., R. Frankiewicz, and A. S. Jackson. 1975. Construct validation of distance run tests. *Research Quarterly 46:* 169–176.

Doolittle, R. L. and R. Bigbee. 1968. The twelve-minute run-walk: A test of cardiorespiratory fitness of adolescent boys. *Research Quarterly 39:* 491–495.

Gutin, B. et al. 1976. Relationship among submaximal heart rate, aerobic power, and running performance in children. *Research Quarterly 47:* 536–539.

Jackson, A. S. et al. 1976. *A position paper on physical fitness. Position paper of a joint committee representing the Measurement and Evaluation, Physical Fitness, and Research councils of the AAHPER.* Washington, DC: AAHPER.

Jackson, A. S. and A. E. Coleman. 1976. Validation of distance run tests for elementary school children. *Research Quarterly 47:* 86–94.

Krahenbuhl, G. et al. 1977. Field estimation of $\dot{V}O_2$ Max in children eight years of age. *Medicine and Science in Sports 9:* 37–40.

Kraus, H. and R. P. Hirschland. 1954. Minimum muscular fitness test in school children. *Research Quarterly 25:* 177–188.

Lohman, T. G. 1992. *Advances in Body Composition Assessment.* Champaign, IL: Human Kinetics Publishers.

Maksud, M. G. and K. Coutts. 1971. Application of the Cooper twelve-minute run-walk test to young males. *Research Quarterly 42:* 54–59.

Manitoba Department of Education. 1977. *Manitoba Physical Fitness Performance Test Manual and Fitness Objectives.* Manitoba, Canada.

NIOSH. 1977. *Preemployment Strength Testing.* Washington, DC: U.S. Department of Health and Human Services.

NIOSH. 1981. *Work Practices Guide for Manual Lifting.* Washington, DC: U.S. Department of Health and Human Services.

Pate, R. R. (Ed.) 1978. *South Carolina Physical Fitness Test Manual.* Columbia, SC: Governor's Council on Physical Fitness.

*Prudential FITNESSGRAM® Test Administration Manual.* 1992. Dallas: The Cooper Institute for Aerobic Research.

Ross, J. G. et al. 1987. New health-related fitness norms. *JOPERD 66:* 18–22.

Ross, R. M. and A. S. Jackson. 1990. *Exercise Concepts, Calculations, and Computer Applications.* Carmel, IN: Benchmark Press.

Texas Governor's Commission on Physical Fitness. 1973. *Physical Fitness-Motor Ability Test.* Austin, TX.

U.S. Public Health Service. 1990. *Healthy People 2000: National Health Promotion and Disease Prevention Objectives.* Washington, DC: U.S. Department of Health and Human Services.

Vodak, P. and J. H. Wilmore. 1975. Validity of the 6-minute jog-walk and 600-yard run-walk in estimating endurance capacity in boys, 9–12 Years of Age. *Research Quarterly 46:* 230–234.

# Evaluating Aerobic Fitness ($\dot{V}O_2$ Max) of Adults

## Key Words

aerobic fitness
cycle ergometer
maximal exercise test
METs
Multi-Stage Exercise Test
oxygen uptake
power output
rating of perceived exertion
Single-Stage Exercise Test
submaximal exercise test
$\dot{V}O_2$ Max

## Contents

## Objectives

The methods used to evaluate health-related fitness of adults and youth differ. Chapter 9 covers the methods for measuring health-related fitness of school children. Distance-run tests are used to evaluate the aerobic fitness of school children while the evaluation of aerobic fitness of adults is likely to take place in a variety of places, including medical or university laboratories, YMCAs, and private or corporate fitness centers. Maximum oxygen uptake, $\dot{V}O_2$ Max, is the scientifically accepted measure of aerobic fitness, and it is used to prescribe scientifically sound individualized exercise programs, to gauge progress, and to adjust an exercise program. This testing is most likely to be done by an exercise specialist.

The purpose of this chapter is to outline the tests used to measure $\dot{V}O_2$ Max, requiring an integration of measurement theory with exercise physiology.

After reading Chapter 10, you should be able to:

1. Define the methods used to measure $\dot{V}O_2$ Max from (a) maximal tests; (b) submaximal tests; (c) walking and running field tests; and (d) nonexercise models.
2. Define the levels of aerobic fitness needed for health promotion and physically demanding exercise.
3. Identify maximal and submaximal treadmill protocols.
4. Identify cycle ergometer submaximal protocols.
5. Differentiate between a stress test and fitness evaluation.

# INTRODUCTION

Aerobic fitness is, to a large extent, dependent on and limited by the body's ability to deliver oxygen to the working muscles. The lungs, heart, blood, circulatory system, and working muscles are all factors in determining one's aerobic fitness. The public health report *Healthy People 2000* (U.S. Public Health Service 1990), reviewed in Chapter 1, places special importance on aerobic exercise and fitness for health promotion. Aerobic exercise is the most efficient form of exercise for developing aerobic fitness and expending sufficient amounts of energy (i.e., calories). Caloric expenditure is not only important for weight control and reducing the prevalence of overweight, it also provides a margin of protection from heart disease. In this chapter we discuss the methods available to the exercise specialist to evaluate aerobic fitness. A final section reviews the difference between a fitness evaluation and the medical stress test and reviews medical criteria exercise specialists need to consider when testing adults.

# Aerobic Fitness

**Aerobic fitness,** or $\dot{V}O_2$ **Max,** depends on several factors: efficient lungs, heart, and blood vessels; the quality and quantity of blood (red blood count, volume); and the cellular components that help the body use oxygen during exercise. Because an individual's ability to use oxygen during exhaustive work depends on these factors, maximal oxygen uptake $\dot{V}O_2$ Max, the maximal rate at which oxygen can be used, is an accepted test of aerobic fitness and an indicator of subsequent exercise capacity (ACSM 1990; ACSM 1991). Åstrand and Rodahl (1970) consider it to be the best index of physical fitness:

> During prolonged heavy physical work, the individual's performance capacity depends largely upon his ability to take up, transport, and deliver oxygen to working muscle. Subsequently, the maximal oxygen uptake is probably the best laboratory measure of a person's physical fitness, providing the definition of physical fitness is restricted to the capacity of the individual for prolonged heavy work (Åstrand & Rodahl 1970, p. 314).

$\dot{V}O_2$ Max can be determined from either maximal or submaximal exercise. At maximal exercise level, $\dot{V}O_2$ Max is measured directly from expired gases or estimated from exercise intensity. $\dot{V}O_2$ Max can be estimated from submaximal treadmill and cycle ergometer performance and heart rate response to the exercise. Because of the need for special equipment, treadmill and cycle ergometer tests are typically completed in a laboratory. This has led to development of submaximal walking and jogging tests that can be administered in the field. Lastly, a new method does not require exercise testing.

This chapter outlines and compares the methods used to evaluate aerobic fitness of adults. All the methods involve mathematical computations. Our approach is to minimize the mathematics and emphasize the method's physiological foundation and illustrate its applications. Chapter 2 gives an example of a commercial program (CSI Software) designed to complete all calculations described in this text. The Computer Calculations section at the end of the chapter gives all equations in a microcomputer "user friendly" way. This gives you the opportunity to develop computer applications for your purposes. With the provided equations and using commercial database and spreadsheet programs, you can develop programs to speed these computations.

The maximal volume of oxygen one can consume during exhausting exercise ($\dot{V}O_2$ Max) is considered the best index of aerobic fitness (ACSM 1990; ACSM 1991). It is best measured by slowly and systematically increasing the intensity of exercise until exhaustion is reached. Computer-controlled metabolic carts shown in Chapter 2 have the capacity to measure the volume of oxygen used during the entire test. Provided next are definitions of terms used in this chapter.

**Oxygen uptake** ($\dot{V}O_2$) is the volume of oxygen used under given conditions. This may be at rest, during submaximal exercise, or during maximal exercise (i.e., $\dot{V}O_2$ Max). Oxygen uptake is expressed in two general ways. First, by the total volume used for a standard length of time. This is expressed in milliliters (ml) or liters (l) of oxygen per minute ($min^{-1}$).[1] The total volume of oxygen used is a function of one's muscle mass—the more muscle mass, the greater volume of oxygen consumed. To control for size difference, $\dot{V}O_2$ expressed in milliliters is divided by body weight and expressed by milliliters of oxygen used per kilogram of body weight per minute. The Computer Calculations section of this chapter shows these computations. The scientific notation of these terms is $\dot{V}O_2$ $l \cdot min^{-1}$; $\dot{V}O_2$ $ml \cdot min^{-1}$; and $\dot{V}O_2$ $ml \cdot kg \cdot min^{-1}$.

Oxygen consumption is also expressed in METs. A **MET** is a $\dot{V}O_2$ of 3.5 $ml \cdot kg \cdot min^{-1}$, the amount of oxygen used at rest. The unit of METs quantifies oxygen uptake in multiples above resting. For example, the $\dot{V}O_2$ used to jog 6 miles-per-hour is 35 $ml \cdot kg \cdot min^{-1}$ or 10 METs (35/3.5 = 10), a level of exercise 10 times above the resting state.

Åstrand and Rodahl (1986) report a linear increase in oxygen uptake with a linear increase in **power output.** As the power output increases, the exercising muscle requires more oxygen. You can easily see this when you walk up a hill; as the hill gets steeper (increased power output), your **heart rate** and breathing rates increase (increased oxygen uptake), your body needs and uses more oxygen. Cycle ergometers, treadmills, and bench stepping are common methods used to regulate power output. Changing steady state jogging and walking speed is another method of changing power output. These are summarized next.

*Cycle Ergometer.* Power output is changed by increasing the resistance placed on the flywheel, altering the pedaling rate, or a combination of both. Power output of a cycle ergometer is expressed in **kilopond** meters of work per minute (**kmp**$\cdot min^{-1}$), watts, and $\dot{V}O_2$ ($ml \cdot min^{-1}$). A later section of this chapter gives common cycle ergometer power output levels.

*Treadmill.* The power output of a treadmill is regulated by changing treadmill speed, elevation, or a combination of both. Standard equations (ACSM 1991; Ross & Jackson 1990) convert treadmill speed and elevation to $\dot{V}O_2$ ($ml \cdot kg \cdot min^{-1}$).

---

[1]A liter equals 1000 milliliters.

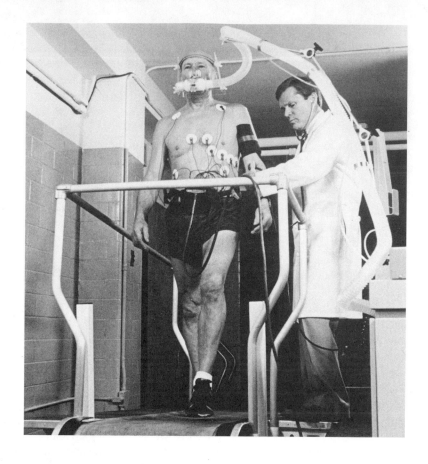

**Figure 10.1**
Dr. Michael Pollock monitoring an exercise test designed to measure VO₂ Max by analyzing expired gases. Electrodes placed on the chest provide a means of monitoring the heart's rhythm and produce an electrocardiogram (EKG). V̇O₂ Max is a fitness evaluation, while the EKG is a medical test to help diagnose heart disease. (© Patti Bose.)

***Bench Stepping.*** Bench height and stepping rate regulates the power output of bench stepping. This can be converted to $\dot{V}O_2$ (ml·kg·min$^{-1}$) or METs by a standard equation (ACSM 1991; Nagel et al. 1965).

***Walking and Jogging on Level.*** Walking and jogging movement rate defines the power output of these two exercise modes. Power output for walking and jogging is expressed by speed of movement (miles per hour and meters per minute) and $\dot{V}O_2$ (ml·kg·min$^{-1}$) (ACSM 1991; Ross & Jackson 1990).

## Maximal Oxygen Uptake (V̇O₂ Max)

**Maximal Oxygen Uptake ($\dot{V}O_2$ Max)** is the maximum volume of oxygen a subject uses during exhausting exercise (Mitchell & Blomqvist 1971; Mitchell et al. 1958; Rowell et al. 1964). In the laboratory, the test involves gradually increasing power output and measuring expired gases (Figure 10.1). $\dot{V}O_2$ Max is that point at which the increased power output does not produce an increase in oxygen uptake (Noakes 1988). Figure 10.2 shows computer-generated graphs of two $\dot{V}O_2$ Max tests. The graphs show that as power output increased (increased speed and elevation), $\dot{V}O_2$ steadily increased and then flattened out during the last two minutes of the test when each person reached his $\dot{V}O_2$ Max. The more fit man reached a higher power output than the less fit man.

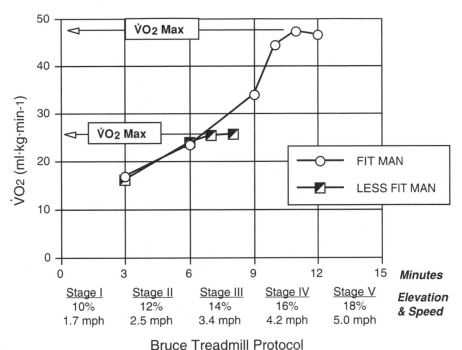

**Figure 10.2**
Oxygen uptake tests of an active and sedentary man. The fit man has the following characteristics: engages in aerobic exercise five days per week, age 46, 13.5% fat, and $\dot{V}O_2$ Max 47.2. The less fit man is sedentary, younger (age 38), has a higher percent body fat (31%), and lower $\dot{V}O_2$ Max (25.5 ml·kg·min$^{-1}$). (Data from Cardio-pulmonary Laboratory, Kelsey-Seybold Clinic, NASA/Johnson Space Center, Houston, TX)

## Evaluating Aerobic Fitness

$\dot{V}O_2$ Max assesses the physical working capacity of athletes and individuals engaged in fitness programs. There is a growing trend to include aerobic fitness as part of a medical examination.[2] The standards used for athletes would not be suitable for evaluating the fitness level of nonathletic adults. Provided in Figure 10.3 are average oxygen uptake values for elite runners and average men and women. High-level endurance athletes (e.g., cross-country skiers and long distance runners) have the highest $\dot{V}O_2$ Max, nearly double the typical person. As a group, women have a $\dot{V}O_2$ Max about 20% lower than a man of a similar age. This is primarily due to hormonal differences that cause women to have a lower concentration of hemoglobin in their blood and a higher percentage of body fat.

Most of us have neither the ability nor the motivation to become world-class endurance athletes, but a suitable level of cardiorespiratory endurance is needed for health and fitness. $\dot{V}O_2$ Max is age-dependent, steadily increasing during childhood and reaching a peak at about age 25, after which it slowly declines (Buskirk & Hodgson 1987). Table 10.1 lists low (16th percentile), average (50th percentile), and high aerobic fitness values (84th percentile) for men and women for various ages. These normative data (Jackson et al. 1990) are consistent with norms published by others (Franks & Howley 1989).

---

[2]Direct measurement of $\dot{V}O_2$ Max during a stress test is part of a NASA/Johnson Space Center employee's medical examination.

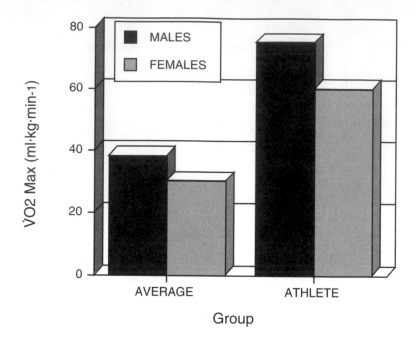

**Figure 10.3**
Average aerobic fitness of elite endurance athletes and normal adults. The VO₂ Max of the average man and women is about 50% of highly trained endurance athletes, and a women's VO₂ Max is about 80% of a man's.
(Ross & Jackson 1990.)

**Table 10.1** Normative Age-Adjusted $\dot{V}O_2$ Max $(ml \cdot kg^{-1} \cdot min^{-1})$ Standards* for Men and Women.

| | Men | | | Women | | |
|---|---|---|---|---|---|---|
| Age | Low P16 | Average P50 | High P84 | Low P16 | Average P50 | High P84 |
| 25 | 41 | 49 | 56 | 33 | 39 | 45 |
| 30 | 39 | 46 | 53 | 30 | 36 | 42 |
| 35 | 36 | 44 | 51 | 26 | 33 | 39 |
| 40 | 34 | 41 | 49 | 24 | 30 | 36 |
| 45 | 32 | 39 | 46 | 21 | 28 | 34 |
| 50 | 29 | 37 | 44 | 20 | 26 | 32 |
| 55 | 27 | 34 | 42 | 18 | 24 | 30 |
| 60 | 24 | 32 | 39 | 17 | 23 | 29 |
| 65 | 22 | 29 | 37 | 16 | 22 | 28 |

*Data source: (Jackson et al. 1990).

While the norms given in Table 10.1 describe the aerobic fitness of adults, the levels are not suitable for health promotion. Blair and associates (1989) provided the first scientific data defining the level of aerobic fitness for heath promotion. They showed that the health promotion threshold was 35 ml·kg·min⁻¹ for men and 32 ml·kg·min⁻¹ for women (see Chapter 1). The mortality rates of men and women with the lowest level of aerobic fitness was four times higher than those who exceeded these levels, but exceeding

**Table 10.2** Age-Adjusted Adult Aerobic Fitness Standards for Health Promotion*

| Age Group | $\dot{V}O_2$ Max (ml·kg$^{-1}$·min$^{-1}$) Men | Women |
|---|---|---|
| 45 and Under | 35 | 32 |
| 50 | 34 | 31 |
| 55 | 32 | 29 |
| 60 | 31 | 28 |
| 65 and Over | 30 | 27 |

*Standards developed from data (Jackson In Press; Jackson et al. Submitted for publication) and personal communication with S. Blair, September 30, 1993.

these did not provide an added margin of protection. $\dot{V}O_2$ Max declines with age (Buskirk & Hodgson 1987), but researchers showed this rate of decline can be slowed by maintaining a physically active life-style and suitable level of body composition (Buskirk & Hodgson 1987; Hagberg et al. 1985; Holloszy 1983; Jackson In Press; Pollock et al. 1987; Rogers et al. 1990; Wier, et al. 1993). The health promotion levels defined by Blair and associates were age adjusted. Table 10.2 lists aerobic fitness suitable for health promotion, accounting for the age-related loss in aerobic fitness.

## Laboratory Methods of Measuring $\dot{V}O_2$ Max

$\dot{V}O_2$ Max can be determined from either maximal or submaximal tests. At maximal exercise, it can be either measured directly from expired gases or estimated from power output. For submaximal tests, the heart rate response to the given level of treadmill and cycle ergometer power output is used to estimate $\dot{V}O_2$ Max (Figure 10.4). Single- and multi-stage models can be used to estimate $\dot{V}O_2$ Max from submaximal power output.

## Maximal Exercise Tests

The objective of a **maximal test** is to increase systematically exercise intensity until the subject reaches exhaustion. The most accurate method is to measure oxygen uptake by indirect calorimetry, that is, to measure expired gases during the exercise test (Figure 10.1). The second method is to estimate $\dot{V}O_2$ Max from maximum power output.

*Indirect Calorimetry.* Maximal oxygen uptake is most accurately determined by measuring expired gases during maximal exercise. This method is conceptually simple but most difficult to use and requires trained technicians with expensive equipment. Chapter 2 gives an example of the computerized equipment. The objective is to increase power output at linear rate (e.g., increase treadmill elevation 4% or increase cycle ergometer resistance by 150 kmp·min$^{-1}$ every three minutes) until the individual reaches exhaustion. Expired gases are collected during all stages of exercise. The volume of oxygen used at this exhausting level is $\dot{V}O_2$ Max (see Figure 10.2). The parameters needed to compute $\dot{V}O_2$ Max are oxygen and carbon dioxide concentrations of room and expired air and volume of air expired per minute. Standard methods are available for calculating $O_2$ consumption (Consolazio et al. 1963; Jones & Campbell 1982).

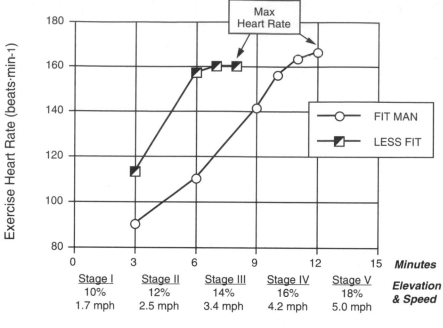

**Figure 10.4**
Heart rate increases with power output. Shown are the changes in exercise heart rate with increases in power output. These heart rates are the values of the fit and less fit man shown in Figure 10.2. (Data from Cardio-pulmonary Laboratory, Kelsey-Seybold Clinic, NASA/Johnson Space Center, Houston, TX)

The direct measurement of $\dot{V}O_2$ Max is expensive in terms of needed equipment and personnel and for these reasons, typically done in a research setting. Yet, with the advancement in microcomputer technology, several commercial systems are now available to speed these measurements. For example, at NASA/Johnson Space Center in Houston, astronauts' $\dot{V}O_2$ Max is measured yearly. Many colleges and universities now have the capacity to evaluate $\dot{V}O_2$ Max by indirect calorimetry.

***Maximum Power Output Estimates.*** $\dot{V}O_2$ Max can be measured from maximal treadmill or cycle ergometer exercise. Many people are not accustomed to riding a cycle ergometer and find it difficult to reach their maximum; their legs fatigue prior to reaching maximal exercise. So, maximum tests are more often administered on a treadmill. Power output systematically increases by time in a treadmill protocol. The elapsed time to reach exhaustion is an index of maximum work capacity (Figure 10.2). Provided in Figure 10.5 is a graphic representation of the speed and elevation for the two most common treadmill protocols. About 71% of all tests given in the United States follow the Bruce protocol and about 10% use the Balke (Pollock et al. 1984).

Several valid regression equations have been published that estimate $\dot{V}O_2$ Max ($ml \cdot kg \cdot min^{-1}$) from maximal treadmill time (Bruce et al. 1973; Foster et al. 1984; Pollock et al. 1976). Since each treadmill protocol increases power output at different rates, unique equations are needed for each protocol. The reported correlations between $\dot{V}O_2$ Max measure directly, and maximal treadmill exercise is high, ranging from 0.88 to 0.97. The standard error of prediction is about 3 $ml \cdot kg \cdot min^{-1}$.

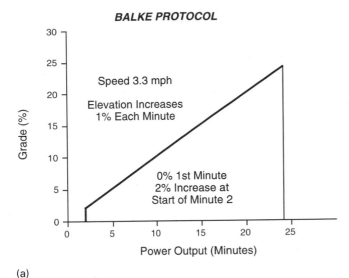

**BALKE PROTOCOL**

Speed 3.3 mph

Elevation Increases
1% Each Minute

0% 1st Minute
2% Increase at
Start of Minute 2

(a)

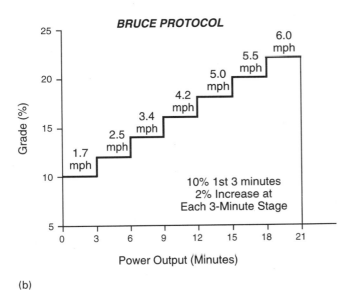

**BRUCE PROTOCOL**

6.0 mph
5.5 mph
5.0 mph
4.2 mph
3.4 mph
2.5 mph
1.7 mph

10% 1st 3 minutes
2% Increase at
Each 3-Minute Stage

(b)

**Figure 10.5**
The (a) Balke and (b) Bruce Treadmill protocols are most often used to measure $\dot{V}O_2$ Max. (Figure adopted from Pollock et al. 1980.)

Table 10.3 lists $\dot{V}O_2$ Max from treadmill time for the Balke and Bruce protocols. It takes longer to reach $\dot{V}O_2$ Max with the Balke protocol than with the Bruce. The $\dot{V}O_2$ Max of cardiac patients is slightly lower than healthy adults for the same maximum Bruce treadmill time (Foster et al. 1984); therefore, different $\dot{V}O_2$ Max estimates are needed for these groups. The Computer Calculations section at the end of this chapter illustrates the use of the maximal treadmill time equations.

The Balke protocol (Balke 1963) is at a constant speed of 3.4 mph and power output is increased by raising the grade 1% every minute. A major disadvantage of this protocol is that one minute is not long enough for the subject to reach a submaximal steady state. Typically, one must exercise at a constant submaximal intensity for

**Table 10.3** Estimated $\dot{V}O_2$ Max ($ml \cdot kg^{-1} \cdot min^{-1}$) from Treadmill Time for the Balke and Bruce Maximum Protocols

| Time (Minutes) | Balke Protocol | Bruce Protocol Cardiac | Normal |
|:---:|:---:|:---:|:---:|
| 2 | 17.9 | 14.4 | 18.6 |
| 3 | 19.3 | 15.7 | 19.9 |
| 4 | 20.8 | 17.4 | 21.6 |
| 5 | 22.2 | 19.6 | 23.8 |
| 6 | 23.7 | 22.1 | 26.3 |
| 7 | 25.1 | 25.0 | 29.2 |
| 8 | 26.5 | 28.1 | 32.3 |
| 9 | 28.0 | 31.5 | 35.7 |
| 10 | 29.4 | 35.0 | 39.2 |
| 11 | 30.9 | 38.7 | 42.9 |
| 12 | 32.3 | 42.4 | 46.6 |
| 13 | 33.8 | 46.2 | 50.4 |
| 14 | 35.2 | 50.0 | 54.2 |
| 15 | 36.6 | 53.7 | 57.9 |
| 16 | 38.1 | 57.3 | 61.5 |
| 17 | 39.5 | 60.8 | 65.0 |
| 18 | 41.0 | 64.1 | 68.3 |
| 19 | 42.4 | | 71.3 |
| 20 | 43.9 | | 74.1 |
| 21 | 45.3 | | 76.5 |
| 22 | 46.6 | | |
| 23 | 48.2 | | |
| 24 | 49.6 | | |
| 25 | 51.1 | | |
| 26 | 52.5 | | |
| 27 | 54.0 | | |
| 28 | 55.4 | | |
| 29 | 56.9 | | |
| 30 | 58.3 | | |

about three minutes to reach a steady state. This is a major requirement for estimating $\dot{V}O_2$ Max from submaximal exercise, which is illustrated later in this chapter.

***Maximal Test Procedures.*** A maximal treadmill test is performed to voluntary exhaustion. The potential for a cardiac problem during a maximal test is low, about 1 per 10,000 tests. Even with this low risk, caution needs to be exercised when testing adults, especially those at risk of cardiovascular disease. Typically, exercise heart rate and blood pressure are monitored during a maximal effort.

When true maximum heart rate is not known, exercise heart rate may not give a true reading of the individual's level of exertion. Borg's **rating of perceived exertion scale (RPE)** is often used when administering exercise tests to gain additional insight into the level of exertion (Borg 1977; Pollock et al. 1986). During the test, the subject is asked to rate exercise intensity during the last 15 seconds of each minute of the test.

**Table 10.4** Cycle Ergometer Power Output Estimates for Common Kilopond (kp) Resistance Settings Pedaling at a Rate of 50 Revolutions Per Minute.

| Scale Setting kp | kpm (min⁻¹) | $\dot{V}O_2$ (min⁻¹) | $\dot{V}O_2$ (ml·kg⁻¹·min⁻¹) For Body Selected Weights | | | |
|---|---|---|---|---|---|---|
| | | | 50 kg | 60 kg | 70 kg | 80 kg |
| .5 | 150 | 600 | 12.0 | 10.0 | 8.6 | 7.5 |
| 1.0 | 300 | 900 | 18.0 | 15.0 | 12.9 | 11.2 |
| 1.5 | 450 | 1200 | 24.0 | 20.0 | 17.1 | 15.0 |
| 2.0 | 600 | 1500 | 30.0 | 25.0 | 21.4 | 18.8 |
| 2.5 | 750 | 1800 | 36.0 | 30.0 | 25.7 | 22.5 |
| 3.0 | 900 | 2100 | 42.0 | 35.0 | 30.0 | 26.2 |
| 3.5 | 1050 | 2400 | 48.0 | 40.0 | 34.3 | 30.0 |
| 4.0 | 1200 | 2700 | 54.0 | 45.0 | 38.6 | 33.8 |
| 4.5 | 1350 | 3000 | 60.0 | 50.0 | 42.9 | 37.5 |
| 5.0 | 1500 | 3300 | 66.0 | 55.0 | 47.1 | 41.2 |
| 5.5 | 1650 | 3600 | 72.0 | 60.0 | 51.4 | 45.0 |
| 6.0 | 1800 | 3900 | 78.0 | 65.0 | 55.7 | 48.8 |
| 6.5 | 1950 | 4200 | 84.0 | 70.0 | 60.0 | 52.5 |
| 7.0 | 2100 | 4500 | 90.0 | 75.0 | 64.3 | 56.2 |

These psychophysical ratings are useful for determining when the subject is reaching his/her maximum level. Chapter 14 gives the RPE scales and test directions.

## Submaximal Exercise Tests

Exercising to $\dot{V}O_2$ Max is physical exhausting, time-consuming, and requires medical supervision when testing high-risk subjects. **Submaximal tests** provide a less accurate, but safer method of estimating $\dot{V}O_2$ Max. The measurement objective of submaximal tests is to define the slope of the individual's heart rate response to exercise and use the slope to estimate $\dot{V}O_2$ Max from submaximal parameters. $\dot{V}O_2$ Max may be estimated from a single reading (single-stage model) or several submaximal heart rates (multi-stage model).

## Regulating Power Uutput

A submaximal test estimates $\dot{V}O_2$ Max from submaximal exercise heart rate and power output. Power output can be regulated with treadmill, cycle ergometer, and bench stepping. Listed next are common submaximal protocols.

***Submaximal Cycle Ergometer Protocols.*** Mechanical and electronically braked **cycle ergometers** are used to measure $\dot{V}O_2$ Max. Exercise intensity on a mechanically braked bike is increased by (1) placing more resistance on the flywheel; (2) increasing pedaling speed; or (3) both. The most common method is to have the subject pedal at a constant rate, usually 50 revolutions per minute, and power output is increased by placing more resistance on the flywheel.

The power output for common cycle ergometer pedaling rates is provided in Table 10.4. A standard method of increasing exercise intensity is not appropriate for general cycle ergometer testing because people vary in leg strength and fitness level. A starting level for one person may be too demanding for another. So, different initial loads are recommended for men and women, and power output is increased at different

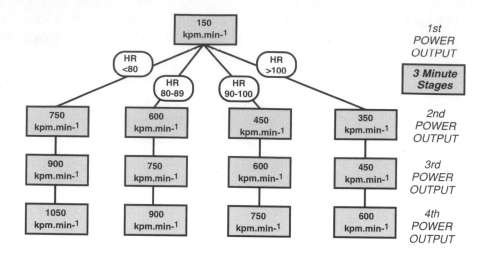

**Figure 10.6**
Cycle ergometer protocol used for the YMCA adult fitness test (Golding et al. 1989). The test starts at a low power output, and the heart rate response to the first stage determines the next power output. Each stage is three minutes in length.

rates based on the person's heart rate response. Figure 10.6 gives the YMCA test procedures (Golding et al. 1989). The suggested starting intensity is 150 kmp·min⁻¹ for women and 300 kmp·min⁻¹ for men. Åstrand and Rodahl (1986) suggest starting intensities of 450 to 600 kmp·min⁻¹ for women and 600 to 900 kmp·min⁻¹ for men; however, the level may need to be altered depending on the fitness level and leg strength of the subject being tested.

The pedaling position should be comfortable for the subject. When administering cycle ergometer tests, first adjust the seat height on the ergometer so that the knee is almost straight on the downward stroke. A suitable pedaling rate is 50 revolutions per minute. Use a metronome to standardize this pedaling rate (Golding et al. 1989).

***Submaximal Treadmill Protocols.*** Some believe that submaximal tests are administered just on a cycle ergometer. This is not so; we find that it is easier to use a treadmill. A cycle ergometer is often used because it is more portable and less expensive. Table 10.5 gives submaximal treadmill protocols suitable for submaximal testing. Although it takes longer to complete, the authors of this text prefer the Ross protocol.

The first three stages of the Bruce protocol can be used for submaximal testing. The fourth stage of the protocol is not recommended because the speed is 4.2 mph, which requires some to jog and others to walk. The Bruce protocol is better for the single-stage model than it is for the double-stage model (Mahar et al. 1985). Ross modified the Balke treadmill protocol for submaximal treadmill testing. The speed is constant, a comfortable walk at 3.4 mph. Every 3 minutes the elevation of the treadmill is increased. For men, the change is 4% per stage; the change is slightly lower for women, 3% per stage.[3]

Submaximal heart rate is measured during the last 15 seconds of every minute. Electronic equipment needs to be used to measure exercise heart rate for treadmill

---

[3]Other speeds and elevations can be used. The equations for completing the power output estimates can be found in another source (Ross & Jackson 1990) and in the Computer Calculation section of this chapter.

**Table 10.5** Submaximal Treadmill Test Protocols and the Estimated Power Output for the Last Minute of Each Stage

| Stage | Minutes | mph | % Grade | Power Output $\dot{V}O_2$ (ml·kg$^{-1}$·min$^{-1}$) | METs |
|-------|---------|-----|---------|-------------------------------------------|------|
| **Bruce Protocol** | | | | | |
| I | 1–3 | 1.7 | 10 | 13.4 | 3.82 |
| II | 4–6 | 2.5 | 12 | 21.4 | 6.12 |
| III | 7–9 | 3.4 | 14 | 31.5 | 9.01 |
| **Ross Submaximal Protocol—Women** | | | | | |
| I | 1–3 | 3.4 | 0 | 14.9 | 4.25 |
| II | 4–6 | 3.4 | 3 | 18.4 | 5.27 |
| III | 7–9 | 3.4 | 6 | 22.0 | 6.29 |
| IV | 10–12 | 3.4 | 9 | 25.6 | 7.31 |
| V | 13–15 | 3.4 | 12 | 29.2 | 8.33 |
| **Ross Submaximal Protocol—Men** | | | | | |
| I | 1–3 | 3.4 | 0 | 14.9 | 4.25 |
| II | 4–6 | 3.4 | 4 | 19.6 | 5.61 |
| III | 7–9 | 3.4 | 8 | 24.4 | 6.97 |
| IV | 10–12 | 3.4 | 12 | 29.2 | 8.33 |
| V | 13–15 | 3.4 | 16 | 33.9 | 9.09 |

tests. The movement produced by walking on a treadmill makes it very difficult to measure heart rate by palpitation. Because of differences in fitness, individuals will vary in their heart rate response to the power output. The submaximal heart rate at any stage should not exceed 150 to 155 b·min$^{-1}$. The following guidelines are offered to ensure that submaximal exercise is achieved.

*Bruce Protocol.* Do not go to the next stage if the subject's heart rate exceeds 135 b·min$^{-1}$. For most healthy adults, a heart rate between 135 and 150 will be reached in the first 6 minutes at the treadmill test.

*Ross Submaximal Protocol.* Do not go to Stage II if the heart rate exceeds 140 at Stage I; this person would be very unfit. Sages IV and V should only be used for individuals under age 50. Never go to the next stage if the heart rate exceeds 145 b·min$^{-1}$.

The Ross modification of the Balke protocol is better than the modified Bruce for the multi-stage model because power output is increased at a slower rate. Table 10.5 lists the submaximal $\dot{V}O_2$ Max power output levels for each stage. The submaximal power output levels and their associated heart rates can be used with either the single- or multi-stage models to estimate $\dot{V}O_2$ Max.

***Bench Stepping.*** Prior to the widespread use of cycle ergometers and treadmills, bench stepping was the method used to regulate power output. The Harvard step test (Brouha 1943; Sloan 1959) involved having the individual bench step at a set power output for five minutes after which recovery heart rate was measured. The test did not

**Figure 10.7**
Illustration of estimating
V̇O₂ Max with the
multi-stage model
following the methods
used for the YMCA test.
(Golding et al. 1989.)

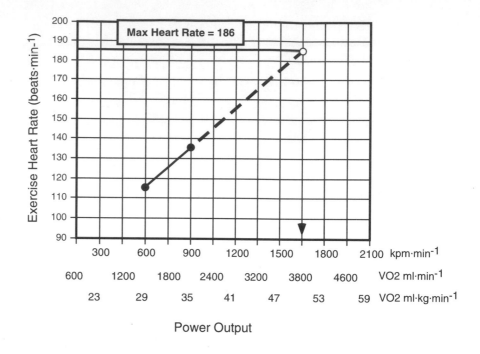

estimate V̇O₂ Max. Lower recovery heart rates were associated with high levels of fitness. As an alternate to the cycle ergometer, the YMCA test includes a 3-minute bench stepping test (Golding et al. 1989). The test uses a 12-inch bench and 24-step per minute stepping rate. The test is scored by the individual's 1-minute recovery heart rate. Age- and gender-adjusted norms are used to evaluate aerobic fitness.

## Multi-Stage Model

The **multi-stage exercise test** model requires that heart rate and power output be measured at two or more submaximal levels (Golding et al. 1989). These data points are then used to project to maximal heart rate, which is used to estimate V̇O₂ Max. The multi-stage model is the procedure used for the YMCA Adult Fitness test (Golding et al. 1989). The YMCA test uses a cycle ergometer following the protocol shown in Figure 10.6 to regulate power output for each 3-minute stage. The goal of the test is to obtain at least two submaximal heart rates between 115 and 150 b·min⁻¹. V̇O₂ Max is estimated by plotting the linear increase in exercise heart rate associated with increases in power output (Figure 10.7). Connecting the two points defines the linear power output–heart rate slope. Using the defined slope, the line is extended to maximum heart rate.[4] V̇O₂ Max is estimated by dropping the line down to the power output scale.

The YMCA test manual gives graphs for making these determinations with just a cycle ergometer where power output is expressed in kmp·min⁻¹. We have added a power output scale expressed as V̇O₂ (ml·kg·min⁻¹) to Figure 10.7, allowing the use of graphic method with treadmill testing. The Computer Calculations section gives the equations that can be used to compute V̇O₂ Max from the power output and heart rate values.

---

[4]Since maximal heart rate is typically not known, it is estimated by 220 – Age.

The **single-stage exercise test** model is both simpler to use and slightly more accurate than the multi-stage model (Mahar et al. 1985). It was initially popularized by the Åstrand- Ryhming nomogram (Åstrand & Rodahl 1970; Åstrand & Rodahl 1986; Åstrand & Ryhming 1954). The model assumes that $\dot{V}O_2$ Max can be estimated by knowing the submaximal power output and the percentage of the subject's maximum aerobic capacity. This can be easily illustrated.

Assume a person's true $\dot{V}O_2$ Max is 45 ml·kg·min$^{-1}$ and the submaximal power output ($\dot{V}O_2$ SM) is 31 ml·kg·min$^{-1}$. This submaximal power output expressed as a percentage of $\dot{V}O_2$ Max would be

$$\% \ \dot{V}O_2 \ \text{Max} = [(\dot{V}O_2 \ \text{SM}/\dot{V}O_2 \ \text{Max}) \times 100]$$

$$\% \ \dot{V}O_2 \ \text{Max} = [(31/50 \times 100] = 62\%.$$

By simply rearranging the equation, $\dot{V}O_2$ Max is the product of submaximal $\dot{V}O_2$ and the inverse of % $\dot{V}O_2$ Max.

$$\dot{V}O_2 \ \text{Max} = \dot{V}O_2 \ \text{SM} \times [1/(\% \ \dot{V}O_2 \ \text{Max} \times 100)]$$

$$\dot{V}O_2 \ \text{Max} = 25 \times [1/(62)/100] = 31 \times 1.613 = 50 \ \text{ml·kg}^{-1}\text{·min}^{-1}.$$

Obviously, if true $\dot{V}O_2$ Max is known, it would not need to be estimated. The above calculations are presented just to illustrate the physiological validity of the single-stage model. Since $\dot{V}O_2$ Max is not known, true % $\dot{V}O_2$ Max cannot be determined. But it can be estimated from exercise heart rate and maximal heart rate.[5]

Table 10.6 gives inverse of percentage of $\dot{V}O_2$ Max estimated for exercise heart rate and maximum heart rate estimated by 220 – Age. The factors represent exercise heart rates between 45% and 70% of $\dot{V}O_2$ Max. To estimate $\dot{V}O_2$ Max, the only other factor needed is submaximal power output. The ease of this calculation is shown next by example.

Assume a man's exercise heart rate is 135 b·min$^{-1}$ at stage III of the Ross submaximal treadmill protocol. The power output for stage III is 24.4 ml·kg·min$^{-1}$. If the man's age is 35, his estimated maximum heart rate is 185 b·min$^{-1}$, and the heart rate factor would be 1.69 (Table 10.6). The single-stage estimated $\dot{V}O_2$ Max would be

$$\dot{V}O_2 \ \text{Max} = \dot{V}O_2 \ \text{SM} \times \text{Heart Rate Factor}$$

$$\dot{V}O_2 \ \text{Max} = 24.4 \times 1.69 = 41.2 \ \text{ml·kg·min}^{-1}$$

The Computer Calculations section illustrates the use of the single-stage equation.

A limitation of the maximal and submaximal tests is the need for a cycle ergometer or treadmill to regulate power output. Walking and jogging on level ground is another method of regulating power output. The walking and jogging tests described next allow the person to travel at a self-determined pace. $\dot{V}O_2$ Max is estimated from movement time, and heart rate response to the exercise.

---

[5]The equation for heart rate estimate of $\dot{V}O_2$ Max is % $\dot{V}O_2$ Max = [(Sub Max HR – b)/(Max HR – b)], where b is 63 for a man and 73 for a woman (Ross & Jackson 1990).

**Table 10.6** Heart Rate Factors for Estimating $\dot{V}O_2$ Max for Men and Women from the Single-Stage Model

| Exercise Heart Rate | Maximum Heart Rate Beats per Minute (220 – Age) | | | | | | |
|---|---|---|---|---|---|---|---|
| | 200 | 195 | 190 | 185 | 180 | 175 | 170 |
| **Men[a]** | | | | | | | |
| 110 | • | • | • | • | • | • | 2.28 |
| 115 | • | • | • | • | 2.25 | 2.15 | 2.06 |
| 120 | • | • | 2.23 | 2.14 | 2.05 | 1.96 | 1.88 |
| 125 | 2.21 | 2.13 | 2.05 | 1.97 | 1.89 | 1.81 | 1.73 |
| 130 | 2.04 | 1.97 | 1.90 | 1.82 | 1.75 | 1.67 | 1.60 |
| 135 | 1.90 | 1.83 | 1.76 | 1.69 | 1.62 | 1.56 | 1.49 |
| 140 | 1.78 | 1.71 | 1.65 | 1.58 | 1.52 | 1.45 | • |
| 145 | 1.67 | 1.61 | 1.55 | 1.49 | 1.43 | • | • |
| 150 | 1.57 | 1.52 | 1.46 | • | • | • | • |
| 155 | 1.49 | 1.43 | • | • | • | • | • |
| **Women[b]** | | | | | | | |
| 120 | • | • | • | • | • | 2.17 | 2.06 |
| 125 | • | • | • | 2.15 | 2.06 | 1.96 | 1.87 |
| 130 | 2.23 | 2.14 | 2.05 | 1.96 | 1.88 | 1.79 | 1.70 |
| 135 | 2.05 | 1.97 | 1.89 | 1.81 | 1.73 | 1.65 | 1.56 |
| 140 | 1.90 | 1.82 | 1.75 | 1.67 | 1.60 | 1.52 | 1.45 |
| 145 | 1.76 | 1.69 | 1.62 | 1.56 | 1.49 | • | • |
| 150 | 1.65 | 1.58 | 1.52 | 1.45 | • | • | • |
| 155 | 1.55 | 1.49 | 1.43 | • | • | • | • |
| 160 | 1.46 | • | • | • | • | • | • |

•Below 45% $\dot{V}O_2$ Max or exceeds 7% of $\dot{V}O_2$ Max for age and gender. Heart Rate Factors (Ross & Jackson 1990)

[a]Men = [(220 – Age – 63)/(Exercise Heart Rate – 63)]

[b]Women = [(220 – Age – 73)/(Exercise Heart Rate – 73)]

*The Rockport Walk Test.* The Rockport Walk Test (Kline et al. 1987) provides a means of estimating $\dot{V}O_2$ Max from heart response to walking speed. A track and heart rate monitoring equipment are all that are needed to administer the test. The Rockport test involves walking as fast as possible for 1 mile and then measuring the exercise heart rate immediately after the walk. In the original study, heart rate was monitored electronically. Several inexpensive electronic heart rate monitors are now commercially available and recommended. The test is suitable for men and women. Table 10.7 gives the Rockport multiple regression equations to estimate $\dot{V}O_2$ Max. The data needed to estimate $\dot{V}O_2$ Max include the following:

- Weight measured in pounds.
- Mile walk time measured to 1/100th of a second. Note, a walk time of 15 minutes and 30 seconds would be 15.50.
- Exercise heart rate (beats·min$^{-1}$) measured immediately at the conclusion of the walk.
- Age measured to the last year.

**Table 10.7** Regression Equations* for the Rockport Walk Test

| Variable | Regression Equation | |
|---|---|---|
| | **Men** | **Women** |
| Age (yrs) | –0.388 | –0.388 |
| Weight (lbs) | –0.077 | –0.077 |
| Mile Walk Time (min) | –3.265 | –3.265 |
| Exercise Heart Rate (b/min) | –0.156 | –0.156 |
| Constant | 139.168 | 132.85 |

*R = 0.88; SE = 5.0 ml·kg·min$^{-1}$

**Table 10.8** Regression Equations* for the BYU Jog Test

| Variable | Regression Equation | |
|---|---|---|
| | **Men** | **Women** |
| Weight (kg) | –0.164 | –0.164 |
| Mile Walk Time (min) | –1.438 | –1.438 |
| Exercise Heart Rate (b/min) | –0.193 | –0.193 |
| Constant | 108.844 | 100.500 |

*R = 0.87; SE = 3.0 ml·kg·min$^{-1}$

All regression coefficients have a negative sign, showing that the individuals with the highest $\dot{V}O_2$ Max would be those who are younger, have less body weight, and combine a low mile walk time with a low heart rate. The Computer Calculations section of this chapter illustrates the application of the Rockport equations.

***BYU Jog Test.*** A major limitation of the Rockport Walk Test is highly fit individuals cannot walk fast enough to elevate their heart rate above 45% of $\dot{V}O_2$ Max. Researchers at Brigham Young University (BYU) developed a similar test that replaces walking with jogging (George et al. 1993). The test protocol requires the subject to jog at a steady pace for 1 mile. Exercise heart rate is measured immediately after the run.

The recommended test procedures include the following:

1. The subject first takes a 2- to 3-minute warm-up jog.

2. The goal is to jog the 1 mile at a steady and suitable pace. Many subjects tend to run at an "all-out" rate. This is a submaximal test. To ensure that it is a submaximal effort, run time and exercise heart limits are set. These limits are jogging pace, ≥ 8 minutes for males and ≥ 9 minutes for females; and exercise heart rate, ≤ 180 b·min$^{-1}$.

Table 10.8 gives the male and female regression equations. Like the Rockport Walk Test, all regression weights were negative, indicating that the individuals with the highest $\dot{V}O_2$ Max were those who could jog a fast pace with a low heart rate.

**Table 10.9** Regression Coefficients for Calculating $\dot{V}O_2$ Max ($ml \cdot kg^{-1} \cdot min^{-1}$) by the University of Houston

| Variable | % Fat Equation* | | | BMI Equation** | |
| | Men | Women | | Men | Women |
|---|---|---|---|---|---|
| Constant | 56.370 | 50.513 | Constant | 67.350 | 56.363 |
| Age | −0.289 | −0.289 | Age | −0.381 | −0.381 |
| Activity Code | 1.589 | 1.589 | Activity Code | 1.951 | 1.951 |
| %Fat | −0.552 | −0.552 | BMI | −0.754 | −0.754 |

*R = 0.81, SEE = 5.3 $ml \cdot kg \cdot min^{-1}$
**R = 0.78, SEE = 5.7 $ml \cdot kg \cdot min^{-1}$

The BYU Jog Test was developed on a homogeneous sample of young, fit college students. The test will not likely be acceptable for less fit subjects. For those subjects, the Rockport test would likely be more appropriate. The Computer Calculations section of this chapter illustrates the application of the BYU Jog Test Equations.

## Estimating $\dot{V}O_2$ Max without Exercise Testing

$\dot{V}O_2$ Max can be estimated without testing individuals (Jackson et al. 1990). It can be estimated with reasonable accuracy from the individual's gender, body composition, and self-report level of aerobic exercise over the previous 30 days. Metabolically determined $\dot{V}O_2$ Max is the test used to evaluate NASA/Johnson Space Center (Houston, TX) employees and astronauts. This has provided a very large database (N = 2,249) of men and women with a measured $\dot{V}O_2$ Max. Prior to being tested, each employee rated their physical activity (see Figure 10.8) during the previous month. Multiple regression was used to estimate $\dot{V}O_2$ Max from exercise rating in combination with age, gender, and a body composition parameter consisting of either percent body fat or body mass index (BMI). Chapter 11 gives the methods used to measure and compute percent body fat and BMI.

Table 10.9 gives the raw score regression equations for these models. The percent body fat is slightly more accurate than the model that used body mass index as an index of body composition. The regression coefficients show that those with the highest aerobic capacity are those who are younger, more aerobically active, and leaner. Tables 10.10 and 10.11 give $\dot{V}O_2$ Max estimates for men and women for selected age, levels of physical activity, and percent body fat. The Computer Calculations section provides examples of these calculations.

## Which Method Should Be Used?

$\dot{V}O_2$ Max can be used for designing individualized exercise programs and documenting fitness changes produced through exercise. Several methods are available to measure $\dot{V}O_2$ Max. The method selected depends on the degree of accuracy desired as contrasted with ease in testing. Table 10.12 summarizes the issues of strengths, limitations, and concerns to consider when comparing methods.

The direct measurement of expired gases is the most accurate but least practical method for measuring $\dot{V}O_2$ Max. This method requires expensive equipment and highly trained technicians. For this reason, the direct measurement of $\dot{V}O_2$ from expired gases is usually reserved for research.

# CODE FOR PHYSICAL ACTIVITY

Use the appropriate number (0 to 7) which best describes your general ACTIVITY LEVEL for the PREVIOUS MONTH.

DO NOT PARTICIPATE REGULARLY IN PROGRAMMED RECREATION SPORT OR HEAVY PHYSICAL ACTIVITY.

**0 - Avoid walking or exertion, e.g., always use elevator, drive whenever possible instead of walking.**

**1 - Walk for pleasure, routinely use stairs, occasionally exercise sufficiently to cause heavy breathing or perspiration.**

PARTICIPATED REGULARLY IN RECREATION OR WORK REQUIRING MODEST PHYSICAL ACTIVITY, SUCH AS GOLF, HORSEBACK RIDING, CALISTHENICS, GYMNASTICS, TABLE TENNIS, BOWLING, WEIGHT LIFTING, YARD WORK.

**2 - 10 to 60 minutes per week.**
**3 - Over one hour per week.**

PARTICIPATE REGULARLY IN HEAVY PHYSICAL EXERCISE SUCH AS RUNNING OR JOGGING, SWIMMING, CYCLING, ROWING, SKIPPING ROPE, RUNNING IN PLACE OR ENGAGING IN VIGOROUS AEROBIC ACTIVITY TYPE EXERCISE SUCH AS TENNIS, BASKETBALL OR HANDBALL.

**4 - Run less than one mile per week or spend less than 30 minutes per week in comparable physical activity.**

**5 - Run 1 to 5 miles per week or spend 30 to 60 minutes per week in comparable physical activity.**

**6 - Run 5 to 10 miles per week or spend 1 to 3 hours per week in comparable physical activity**

**7 - Run over 10 miles per week or spend over 3 hours per week in comparable physical activity.**

**Figure 10.8** Scale for rating level of physical activity. The directions are to select one value that best represents the level of physical activity for the previous month. (The scale developed for use in the Cardio-pulmonary Laboratory, NASA/Johnson Space Center, Houston, Texas.)

Estimating $\dot{V}O_2$ Max from maximal treadmill time is the next most accurate method. A major disadvantage is that the subject must reach exhaustion, and many do not enjoy the experience. When maximal tests are used, medical supervision needs to be considered for high-risk subjects. The next section of this chapter offers some guidelines to consider.

Submaximal tests are less accurate but easier to administer. The correlations between $\dot{V}O_2$ Max measured and estimated from submaximal levels range between 0.70 and 0.80 (Pollock et al. 1984). The Rockport Walk and BYU Jog Tests are promising submaximal methods that are especially feasible for field testing. The limited data on these tests suggest that they may be slightly more accurate than single- and multi-stage tests.

The nonexercise tests are especially feasible for mass testing. With the ease of test administration, one may question the accuracy of them. Figures 10.9 through 10.12 present scattergrams between measured $\dot{V}O_2$ Max and estimated from the maximal treadmill time (Foster et al. 1984), Åstrand single-stage submaximal model (Ross & Jackson 1990), and the two nonexercise models (Jackson et al. 1990). Maximum treadmill time provided the most accurate estimate of $\dot{V}O_2$ Max while the two nonexercise models were slightly more accurate than the Åstrand single-stage model.

**Table 10.10** $\dot{V}O_2$ Max (ml·kg$^{-1}$·min$^{-1}$) from the Nonexercise Model for Levels of Fatness, Age, and Self-Report Level of Physical Activity for Men

| Activity Level | Percent Body Fat Level | | | | | | | |
|---|---|---|---|---|---|---|---|---|
| | 12% | 15% | 18% | 21% | 24% | 27% | 30% | 33% |
| **Age 25 Years** | | | | | | | | |
| 7 | 53.6 | 52.0 | 50.3 | 48.7 | 47.0 | 45.4 | 43.7 | 42.1 |
| 6 | 52.1 | 50.4 | 48.7 | 47.1 | 45.4 | 43.8 | 42.1 | 40.5 |
| 5 | 50.5 | 48.8 | 47.2 | 45.5 | 43.8 | 42.2 | 40.5 | 38.9 |
| 4 | 48.9 | 47.2 | 45.6 | 43.9 | 42.3 | 40.6 | 38.9 | 37.3 |
| 3 | 47.3 | 45.6 | 44.0 | 42.3 | 40.7 | 39.0 | 37.4 | 35.7 |
| 2 | 45.7 | 44.0 | 42.4 | 40.7 | 39.1 | 37.4 | 35.8 | 34.1 |
| 1 | 44.1 | 42.5 | 40.8 | 39.1 | 37.5 | 35.8 | 34.2 | 32.5 |
| 0 | 42.5 | 40.9 | 39.2 | 37.6 | 35.9 | 34.2 | 32.6 | 30.9 |
| **Age 35 Years** | | | | | | | | |
| 7 | 50.8 | 49.1 | 47.4 | 45.8 | 44.1 | 42.5 | 40.8 | 39.2 |
| 6 | 49.2 | 47.5 | 45.9 | 44.2 | 42.5 | 40.9 | 39.2 | 37.6 |
| 5 | 47.6 | 45.9 | 44.3 | 42.6 | 41.0 | 39.3 | 37.6 | 36.0 |
| 4 | 46.0 | 44.3 | 42.7 | 41.0 | 39.4 | 37.7 | 36.1 | 34.4 |
| 3 | 44.4 | 42.7 | 41.1 | 39.4 | 37.8 | 36.1 | 34.5 | 32.8 |
| 2 | 42.8 | 41.2 | 39.5 | 37.8 | 36.2 | 34.5 | 32.9 | 31.2 |
| 1 | 41.2 | 39.6 | 37.9 | 36.3 | 34.6 | 32.9 | 31.3 | 29.6 |
| 0 | 39.6 | 38.0 | 36.3 | 34.7 | 33.0 | 31.4 | 29.7 | 28.0 |
| **Age 45 Years** | | | | | | | | |
| 7 | 47.9 | 46.2 | 44.6 | 42.9 | 41.2 | 39.6 | 37.9 | 36.3 |
| 6 | 46.3 | 44.6 | 43.0 | 41.3 | 39.7 | 38.0 | 36.3 | 34.7 |
| 5 | 44.7 | 43.0 | 41.4 | 39.7 | 38.1 | 36.4 | 34.8 | 33.1 |
| 4 | 43.1 | 41.4 | 39.8 | 38.1 | 36.5 | 34.8 | 33.2 | 31.5 |
| 3 | 41.5 | 39.9 | 38.2 | 36.5 | 34.9 | 33.2 | 31.6 | 29.9 |
| 2 | 39.9 | 38.3 | 36.6 | 35.0 | 33.3 | 31.6 | 30.0 | 28.3 |
| 1 | 38.3 | 36.7 | 35.0 | 33.4 | 31.7 | 30.0 | 28.4 | 26.7 |
| 0 | 36.7 | 35.1 | 33.4 | 31.8 | 30.1 | 28.5 | 26.8 | 25.1 |
| **Age 55 Years** | | | | | | | | |
| 7 | 45.0 | 43.3 | 41.7 | 40.0 | 38.3 | 36.7 | 35.0 | 33.4 |
| 6 | 43.4 | 41.7 | 40.1 | 38.4 | 36.8 | 35.1 | 33.4 | 31.8 |
| 5 | 41.8 | 40.1 | 38.5 | 36.8 | 35.2 | 33.5 | 31.9 | 30.2 |
| 4 | 40.2 | 38.6 | 36.9 | 35.2 | 33.6 | 31.9 | 30.3 | 28.6 |
| 3 | 38.6 | 37.0 | 35.3 | 33.7 | 32.0 | 30.3 | 28.7 | 27.0 |
| 2 | 37.0 | 35.4 | 33.7 | 32.1 | 30.4 | 28.7 | 27.1 | 25.4 |
| 1 | 35.4 | 33.8 | 32.1 | 30.5 | 28.8 | 27.2 | 25.5 | 23.8 |
| 0 | 33.9 | 32.2 | 30.5 | 28.9 | 27.2 | 25.6 | 23.9 | 22.3 |
| **Age 65 Years** | | | | | | | | |
| 7 | 42.1 | 40.4 | 38.8 | 37.1 | 35.5 | 33.8 | 32.1 | 30.5 |
| 6 | 40.5 | 38.8 | 37.2 | 35.5 | 33.9 | 32.2 | 30.6 | 28.9 |
| 5 | 38.9 | 37.2 | 35.6 | 33.9 | 32.3 | 30.6 | 29.0 | 27.3 |
| 4 | 37.3 | 35.7 | 34.0 | 32.3 | 30.7 | 29.0 | 27.4 | 25.7 |
| 3 | 35.7 | 34.1 | 32.4 | 30.8 | 29.1 | 27.4 | 25.8 | 24.1 |
| 2 | 34.1 | 32.5 | 30.8 | 29.2 | 27.5 | 25.9 | 24.2 | 22.5 |
| 1 | 32.5 | 30.9 | 29.2 | 27.6 | 25.9 | 24.3 | 22.6 | 21.0 |
| 0 | 31.0 | 29.3 | 27.6 | 26.0 | 24.3 | 22.7 | 21.0 | 19.4 |

**Table 10.11** $\dot{V}O_2$ Max (ml·kg$^{-1}$·min$^{-1}$) from the Nonexercise Model for Levels of Fatness, Age, and Self-Report Level of Physical Activity for Women

| Activity Level | Percent Body Fat Level | | | | | | | |
|---|---|---|---|---|---|---|---|---|
| | 18% | 21% | 24% | 27% | 30% | 33% | 36% | 39% |
| **Age 25 Years** | | | | | | | | |
| 7 | 44.5 | 42.8 | 41.2 | 39.5 | 37.9 | 36.2 | 34.5 | 32.9 |
| 6 | 42.9 | 41.2 | 39.6 | 37.9 | 36.3 | 34.6 | 33.0 | 31.3 |
| 5 | 41.3 | 39.6 | 38.0 | 36.3 | 34.7 | 33.0 | 31.4 | 29.7 |
| 4 | 39.7 | 38.1 | 36.4 | 34.7 | 33.1 | 31.4 | 29.8 | 28.1 |
| 3 | 38.1 | 36.5 | 34.8 | 33.2 | 31.5 | 29.8 | 28.2 | 26.5 |
| 2 | 36.5 | 34.9 | 33.2 | 31.6 | 29.9 | 28.3 | 26.6 | 24.9 |
| 1 | 34.9 | 33.3 | 31.6 | 30.0 | 28.3 | 26.7 | 25.0 | 23.3 |
| 0 | 33.4 | 31.7 | 30.0 | 28.4 | 26.7 | 25.1 | 23.4 | 21.8 |
| **Age 35 Years** | | | | | | | | |
| 7 | 41.6 | 39.9 | 38.3 | 36.6 | 35.0 | 33.3 | 31.6 | 30.0 |
| 6 | 40.0 | 38.3 | 36.7 | 35.0 | 33.4 | 31.7 | 30.1 | 28.4 |
| 5 | 38.4 | 36.8 | 35.1 | 33.4 | 31.8 | 30.1 | 28.5 | 26.8 |
| 4 | 36.8 | 35.2 | 33.5 | 31.9 | 30.2 | 28.5 | 26.9 | 25.2 |
| 3 | 35.2 | 33.6 | 31.9 | 30.3 | 28.6 | 26.9 | 25.3 | 23.6 |
| 2 | 33.6 | 32.0 | 30.3 | 28.7 | 27.0 | 25.4 | 23.7 | 22.0 |
| 1 | 32.1 | 30.4 | 28.7 | 27.1 | 25.4 | 23.8 | 22.1 | 20.5 |
| 0 | 30.5 | 28.8 | 27.2 | 25.5 | 23.8 | 22.2 | 20.5 | 18.9 |
| **Age 45 Years** | | | | | | | | |
| 7 | 38.7 | 37.0 | 35.4 | 33.7 | 32.1 | 30.4 | 28.8 | 27.1 |
| 6 | 37.1 | 35.5 | 33.8 | 32.1 | 30.5 | 28.8 | 27.2 | 25.5 |
| 5 | 35.5 | 33.9 | 32.2 | 30.5 | 28.9 | 27.2 | 25.6 | 23.9 |
| 4 | 33.9 | 32.3 | 30.6 | 29.0 | 27.3 | 25.6 | 24.0 | 22.3 |
| 3 | 32.3 | 30.7 | 29.0 | 27.4 | 25.7 | 24.1 | 22.4 | 20.7 |
| 2 | 30.8 | 29.1 | 27.4 | 25.8 | 24.1 | 22.5 | 20.8 | 19.2 |
| 1 | 29.2 | 27.5 | 25.8 | 24.2 | 22.5 | 20.9 | 19.2 | 17.6 |
| 0 | 27.6 | 25.9 | 24.3 | 22.6 | 20.9 | 19.3 | 17.6 | 16.0 |
| **Age 55 Years** | | | | | | | | |
| 7 | 35.8 | 34.1 | 32.5 | 30.8 | 29.2 | 27.5 | 25.9 | 24.2 |
| 6 | 34.2 | 32.6 | 30.9 | 29.2 | 27.6 | 25.9 | 24.3 | 22.6 |
| 5 | 32.6 | 31.0 | 29.3 | 27.7 | 26.0 | 24.3 | 22.7 | 21.0 |
| 4 | 31.0 | 29.4 | 27.7 | 26.1 | 24.4 | 22.8 | 21.1 | 19.4 |
| 3 | 29.4 | 27.8 | 26.1 | 24.5 | 22.8 | 21.2 | 19.5 | 17.9 |
| 2 | 27.9 | 26.2 | 24.5 | 22.9 | 21.2 | 19.6 | 17.9 | 16.3 |
| 1 | 26.3 | 24.6 | 23.0 | 21.3 | 19.6 | 18.0 | 16.3 | 14.7 |
| 0 | 24.7 | 23.0 | 21.4 | 19.7 | 18.1 | 16.4 | 14.7 | 13.1 |
| **Age 65 Years** | | | | | | | | |
| 7 | 32.9 | 31.3 | 29.6 | 27.9 | 26.3 | 24.6 | 23.0 | 21.3 |
| 6 | 31.3 | 29.7 | 28.0 | 26.4 | 24.7 | 23.0 | 21.4 | 19.7 |
| 5 | 29.7 | 28.1 | 26.4 | 24.8 | 23.1 | 21.5 | 19.8 | 18.1 |
| 4 | 28.1 | 26.5 | 24.8 | 23.2 | 21.5 | 19.9 | 18.2 | 16.6 |
| 3 | 26.6 | 24.9 | 23.2 | 21.6 | 19.9 | 18.3 | 16.6 | 15.0 |
| 2 | 25.0 | 23.3 | 21.7 | 20.0 | 18.3 | 16.7 | 15.0 | 13.4 |
| 1 | 23.4 | 21.7 | 20.1 | 18.4 | 16.8 | 15.1 | 13.4 | 11.8 |
| 0 | 21.8 | 20.1 | 18.5 | 16.8 | 15.2 | 13.5 | 11.9 | 10.2 |

**Table 10.12** A Comparison of the Methods Used to Estimate $\dot{V}O_2$ Max

| Method | Advantage | Limitation | Comments and Cautions |
|---|---|---|---|
| **Maximal Tests** *Indirect Calorimetry* | Most Accurate | Maximal Test; Expensive Equipment & Trained Personnel Needed | High-Risk Subjects Need Medical Monitoring |
| *Maximal Treadmill Time* | Highly Accurate | Maximal Test; Expensive Equipment & Trained Personnel Needed | High-Risk Subjects Need Medical Monitoring |
| **Submaximal Tests** | | | |
| *Single-Stage* | Submaximal Effort | Expensive Equipment; Heart Rate Variability; Estimate Max Heart Rate | Not Suitable for Individuals on Drugs that Alter Heart Rate |
| *Multi-Stage* | Submaximal Effort | Expensive Equipment; Heart Rate Variability; Estimate Max Heart Rate; Difficult to Measure Multiple Stages | Not Suitable for Individuals on Drugs that Alter Heart Rate |
| **Walk or Jog Tests** | | | |
| **Rockport Walk Test** | Submaximal Effort; Just Need a Heart Rate Monitor | Too Easy for Highly Fit | Not Suitable for Individuals on Drugs that Alter Heart Rate |
| **BYU Jog Test** | Submaximal Effort; Just Need a Heart Rate Monitor | Too Difficult for Low Fit | Not Suitable for Individuals on Drugs that Alter Heart Rate; Developed on Young, Fit Adults |
| **Nonexercise Methods** | | | |
| *Percent Fat Model* | Just Need to Test % Fat; Not Affected by Drugs | Subjective Rating of Activity; No Cardiac Function | Not Appropriate for Individuals with $\dot{V}O_2$ Max $\geq 50 \cdot ml \cdot kg$ $min^{-1}$ |
| *BMI Model* | Just Need Height/Weight; Not Affected by Drugs; Can Be All Self-Report | Subjective Rating of Activity; No Cardiac Function | Not Appropriate for Individuals with $\dot{V}O_2$ Max $\geq 50 \cdot ml \cdot kg$ $min^{-1}$ |

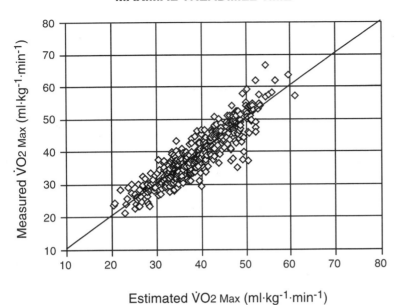

**MAXIMAL TREADMILL TIME**

**Figure 10.9**
Scattergram between
measured VO₂ Max and
estimated from maximum
treadmill time (Foster and
others 1984). (Data from
Jackson et al. 1990.)

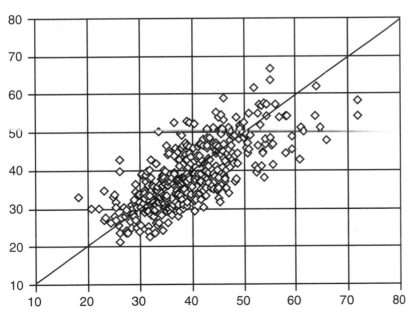

**SINGLE STAGE MODEL**

**Figure 10.10**
Scattergram between
measured VO₂ Max and
estimated from Åstrand's
single stage model
(Åstrand and Ryhming
1954; Ross & Jackson
1990). (Data from Jackson
et al. 1990.)

**Figure 10.11**
Scattergram between
measured V̇O₂ Max and
estimated from
nonexercise percent body
fat model. (Jackson et al.
1990.)

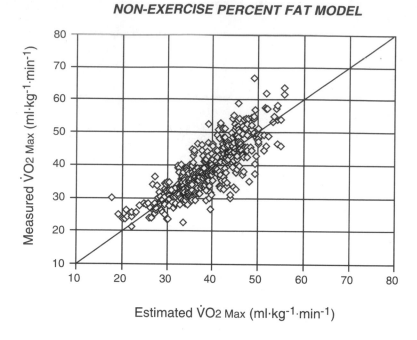

**NON-EXERCISE PERCENT FAT MODEL**

**Figure 10.12**
Scattergram between
measured V̇O₂ Max and
estimated from
nonexercise body mass
index model. (Jackson et al.
1990.)

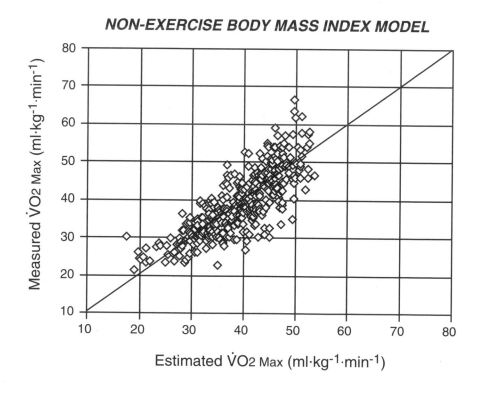

**NON-EXERCISE BODY MASS INDEX MODEL**

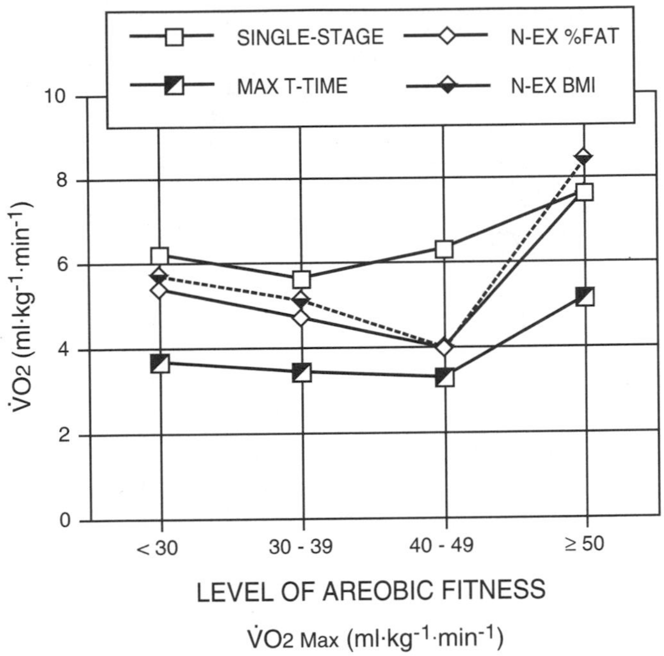

**Figure 10.13**
Comparison of standard
errors of VO₂ Max
prediction models over
levels of aerobic fitness.
(Data from Jackson et al. 1990.)

An examination of the scattergrams for the two nonexercise models shows that the models are least accurate for highly fit subjects. Figure 10.13 plots the standard error of prediction for these methods contrasted over levels of aerobic fitness. As expected, the maximum treadmill time prediction errors were the lowest over all levels of aerobic fitness. The two nonexercise models were most accurate for $\dot{V}O_2$ Max levels between 30 and 49 ml·kg·min$^{-1}$ but had poor accuracy for highly fit subjects ($\dot{V}O_2$ Max $\geq$ 50 ml·kg·min$^{-1}$). An examination of the two nonexercise scattergrams shows that at this high level, the nonexercise models underestimate true $\dot{V}O_2$ Max. Figure 10.13 shows that all four prediction models were least accurate with highly fit subjects.

The standard error of measurement for the direct measurement of $\dot{V}O_2$ Max is about 1 ml·kg·min$^{-1}$. The reported standard error for estimating $\dot{V}O_2$ Max from maximal treadmill time is about 3 ml·kg·min$^{-1}$, while the standard error for estimating $\dot{V}O_2$ Max from the other prediction models range between 5 and 6 ml·kg·min$^{-1}$. These data are clear. If accuracy is of concern, a max test must be used. Submaximal and nonexercise tests are more practical, but there is a cost—they are less accurate; this is especially true for highly fit subjects.

## Fitness Evaluation or Stress Test?

It is important to make a distinction between a fitness evaluation and a stress test. A fitness evaluation evaluates just aerobic fitness. A stress test provides both medical and fitness data. A stress test is a medical procedure administered under the supervision of a physician. The primary objective of a stress test is to "stress the heart," to see if there is any evidence of myocardial ischemia or restricted blood flow to the myocardium or heart muscle. Electrocardiographic (EKG), cardiovascular (e.g.,

**Figure 10.14**
Sample of a computerized twelve-lead exercise EKG during peak exercise. These 12-leads give the cardiologist a view of the heart's electrical activity from twelve different "windows." The figure shows the computer-smoothed twelve EKG tracings and the rhythm strip (bottom continuous tracing) in which the electrical artifacts are still present. A physician uses these data to decide if a patient may have coronary heart disease. Figure 10.1 shows the twelve-lead EKG electrode placement.

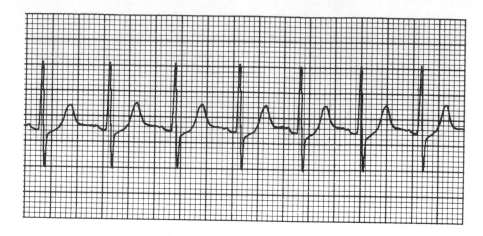

blood pressure and heart rate), and physical symptoms (e.g., shortness of breath or chest pain) are monitored during the test. The objective of a stress test is to identify patients who may have **cardiovascular disease,** particularly coronary heart disease. Healthy individuals do not get myocardial ischemia when exercising at a maximal level. The pattern of the exercise EKG (Figure 10.14) provides this important information. A stress test and fitness evaluation are both typically administered on a motor driven treadmill or cycle ergometer.

Who should have a stress test? Useful criteria have been developed to decide if an individual should have a medically supervised stress test prior to starting an exercise program. The best advice can be obtained from your physician, but the following are general guidelines.

1. Sedentary men over the age of 35 years and postmenopausal sedentary women should have a stress test prior to starting an exercise program.

2. Any individual who has chest pains or a history of heart disease.

3. Any individual of any age who has significant cardiovascular disease risk factors should consider having a stress test and a medical evaluation prior to beginning an exercise program. These risk factors include

   • A strong family history of cardiovascular disease, particularly occurring at an early age.

   • A history of high blood pressure.

   • A history of elevated cholesterol, particularly with a relatively low HDL fraction.

   • A history of diabetes.

   • A smoker, particularly if sedentary or with other cardiovascular risk factors.

   • An abnormal resting EKG.

**Figure 10.15**
The Physical Activity Readiness Questionnaire (PAR-Q) (ACSM 1991). If a person answers "yes" to any of the following questions, vigorous exercise or exercise testing should be postponed and medical clearance sought.

---

## PHYSICAL ACTIVITY READINESS QUESTIONAIRE (PAR-Q)

- Has your doctor ever said you have heart trouble?
- Do you frequently suffer from pains in your chest?
- Do you often feel faint or have spells of severe dizziness?
- Has a doctor ever told you that you have a bone or joint problem, such as arthritis, that has been aggravated by exercise or might be made worse with exercise?
- Is there a good physical reason not mentioned here why you should not follow an activity program even if you wanted to?
- Are you over age 65 and unaccustomed to vigorous exercise?

---

The Physical Activity Readiness Questionnaire (PAR-Q) is a screening method that has been used extensively in Canada to determine if individuals should not exercise or take an exercise test (ACSM 1991). Almost all individuals for whom it might be dangerous to start a moderate exercise program or take an exercise test can be identified with the PAR-Q. Answering "Yes" to any of the six questions would disqualify a person from taking any form of an exercise test without medical supervision. Figure 10.15 gives the PAR-Q.

## Computer Calculations

This section provides all equations used in this chapter. These equations are written to be compatible for use with database and spreadsheet microcomputer programs. They were used and checked for accuracy on a microcomputer database program. You will need to examine your program documentation to make the equations compatible with the program you have. The microcomputer mathematical operands are addition +; subtraction −; multiplication *; and division /.

## Some Common Conversions

Weight in pounds (WTLB) and kilograms (WTKG). Height in inches (HTIN), centimeters (HTCM), and height in meters (HTM). Body Mass Index (BMI).

```
WTKG = WTLB/2.2
WTLB = WTKG * 2.2
HTCM - HTIN * 2.54
HTIN = HTCM/2.54
HTM  = HTCM/100
BMI  = (WTKG/(HTM * HTM))
```

### CALCULATION EXAMPLES

| SUBJECT | WTLB | WTKG | HTIN | HTCM | HTM | BMI |
|---|---|---|---|---|---|---|
| JIM | 208 | 94.54 | 70 | 177.8 | 1.778 | 29.91 |
| JANE | 164 | 74.54 | 64 | 162.6 | 1.625 | 28.21 |
| BOB | 168 | 76.36 | 72 | 182.9 | 1.828 | 22.83 |
| MARY | 124 | 56.36 | 66 | 167.6 | 1.676 | 20.05 |

Chapter 10  Evaluating Aerobic Fitness ($\dot{V}O_2$ Max) of Adults

$\dot{V}O_2$ calculations when expressed as ml·kg·min$^{-1}$, $\dot{V}O_2$ KG; ml·min$^{-1}$, $\dot{V}O_2$ ML; l·min$^{-1}$, $\dot{V}O_2$ L; and METs

```
VO2KG = VO2ML/WTKG
VO2KG = (VO2L/WTKG) * 1000
METS = VO2KG/3.5
```

### CALCULATION EXAMPLES

| SUBJECT | VO2ML | VO2KG | METS |
|---------|-------|--------|-------|
| JIM | 2400 | 25.384 | 7.25 |
| JANE | 2354 | 31.578 | 9.02 |
| BOB | 3679 | 48.177 | 13.76 |
| MARY | 3258 | 57.803 | 16.51 |

Power Output (PO) Calculations (ACSM 1991; Ross & Jackson 1990)
Cycle Ergometer from kilopond meters per minute (kpm) to $\dot{V}O_2$ (ml·min$^{-1}$).

```
PO = (2 * KPM) + 300
```

Treadmill from walking speed in miles per hour (MPH) and treadmill elevation (%) to $\dot{V}O_2$ (ml·kg·min$^{-1}$)

***Total Work Method (Ross & Jackson 1986; Ross & Jackson 1990)***

```
POTW = ((262.5 + (21 * GRADE)) * (MPH/60))
```

***ACSM Method (ACSM 1991)***

```
POACSM = (((0.1 * 26.8 * MPH) + 3.5) +
((26.8 * MPH * 1.8) * (GRADE/100)))
```

### CALCULATION EXAMPLES

| SUBJECT | KPM | PO | GRADE | MPH | POACSM | POTW |
|---------|------|------|-------|-----|--------|------|
| JIM | 300 | 900 | 3 | 3.4 | 17.5 | 18.4 |
| JANE | 450 | 1200 | 4 | 3.5 | 19.6 | 20.2 |
| BOB | 1200 | 2700 | 10 | 3.8 | 32.0 | 29.9 |
| MARY | 900 | 2100 | 12 | 3.7 | 34.8 | 31.7 |

**Maximal Treadmill Time**

$\dot{V}O_2$ Max (ml·kg·min$^{-1}$) from maximal treadmill time in minutes (BKT or BRT) and cardiac health status (CHS) where 0 represents individuals with angina pectoris, previous heart attack, or heart bypass surgery, and 1 represents healthy individuals.

***Balke Protocol (Pollock et al. 1976)***

```
BKVO2 = 14.99 + (1.444 * BKT)
```

### Bruce Protocol (Foster et al. 1984)

```
BRVO2 = 13.30 - (0.03 * BRT) + (0.297* (BRT*BRT)) -
(0.0077* (BRT*BRT*BRT)) + (4.2 * CHS)
```

### CALCULATION EXAMPLES

| SUBJECT | BKT | BRT | CHS | BKVO2 | BRVO2 |
|---------|-----|-----|-----|-------|-------|
| JIM     | 7   | 6   | 0   | 25.1  | 22.1  |
| JANE    | 12  | 9   | 0   | 32.3  | 31.5  |
| BOB     | 23  | 12  | 1   | 48.2  | 46.6  |
| MARY    | 28  | 16  | 1   | 55.4  | 61.5  |

### Single-Stage Model.

Single-Stage Model (Åstrand & Ryhming 1954; Ross & Jackson 1990) uses age, one submaximal power output (POTW), and exercise heart rate (HR). The term SEX represents a 0 for women and 1 for men.

```
VO2KG = (POTW * ((220 - AGE - 73 - (SEX * 10))/
(HR - 73 - (SEX * 10))))
```

### CALCULATION EXAMPLES

| SUBJECT | POTW  | AGE | SEX | HR  | VO2KG |
|---------|-------|-----|-----|-----|-------|
| JIM     | 18.44 | 52  | 0   | 145 | 24.3  |
| JANE    | 20.21 | 55  | 1   | 148 | 25.5  |
| BOB     | 29.92 | 43  | 1   | 135 | 54.1  |
| MARY    | 31.73 | 32  | 0   | 130 | 64.0  |

### Multi-Stage Model.

Multi-Stage Model (Golding et al. 1989; Ross & Jackson 1990) uses age, two submaximal power output values (low level = PO1, high level = PO2), and two exercise heart rates (low level = HR1, high level = HR2). We have split the equation into two parts. The first step is to compute the power output–exercise heart rate slope (i.e., the unit increase in power output per beat increase in heart rate). The second equation estimates $\dot{V}O_2$ Max by using the slope to estimate. The $\dot{V}O_2$ unit of measurement is dependent upon the method used to compute power output.

```
SLOPE = ((PO2 - PO1) / (HR2 - HR1))
VO2KG = PO2 + (SLOPE * (220 - AGE - HR2))
```

### CALCULATION EXAMPLES

| SUBJECT | AGE | PO2  | PO1  | HR2 | HR1 | SLOPE  | VO2KG |
|---------|-----|------|------|-----|-----|--------|-------|
| JIM     | 52  | 18.4 | 14.9 | 142 | 125 | 0.2058 | 23.8  |
| JANE    | 55  | 22.0 | 18.4 | 149 | 130 | 0.1894 | 25.0  |
| BOB     | 43  | 29.2 | 22.0 | 138 | 122 | 0.4500 | 46.7  |
| MARY    | 32  | 29.2 | 22.0 | 135 | 118 | 0.4235 | 51.6  |

**Rockport Walk Test.** The variables needed are age, weight in pounds, mile walk time in minutes, and exercise heart rate measured after walk. The term SEX represents a 0 for women and 1 for men.

$$VO2KG = 139.168 - (0.388 * AGE) - (0.077* WTLB) - (3.265 * WMILE) - (0.156 * HR) + (SEX * 6.318)$$

### CALCULATION EXAMPLES

| SUBJECT | WTLB | SEX | WMILE | HR | VO2KG |
|---------|------|-----|-------|-----|-------|
| JIM | 208 | 1 | 18.20 | 162 | 18.3 |
| JANE | 164 | 0 | 17.60 | 174 | 26.9 |
| BOB | 168 | 1 | 12.10 | 122 | 57.3 |
| MARY | 124 | 0 | 12.30 | 118 | 58.6 |

**BYU Jog Test.** The variables needed are weight in kilograms, mile jog time in minutes, and exercise heart rate measured after the jog. The term SEX represents a 0 for women and 1 for men.

$$VO2KG = 100.5 - (0.164*WTKG) - (1.438 * JMILE) - (0.193 * HR) + (SEX * 8.344)$$

### CALCULATION EXAMPLES

| SUBJECT | WTKG | SEX | JMILE | HR | VO2KG |
|---------|-------|-----|-------|-----|-------|
| JIM | 94.54 | 1 | 14.20 | 162 | 33.3 |
| JANE | 74.54 | 0 | 15.80 | 174 | 40.3 |
| BOB | 76.36 | 1 | 8.65 | 122 | 60.3 |
| MARY | 56.36 | 0 | 9.20 | 118 | 55.3 |

## Nonexercise Models

The variables used for the nonexercise models include age, self-report exercise level (EX, score from Figure 10.8), percent body fat (%FAT) or BMI. The term SEX represents a 0 for women and 1 for men.

### Percent Body Fat Model

$$\%FATVO2 = 50.513 - (0.289 * AGE) + (1.589 * EX) - (0.552 * \%FAT) + (SEX * 5.851)$$

### Body Mass Index Model

$$BMIVO2 = 56.363 - (0.381 * AGE) + (1.951 * EX) - (0.754 * BMI) + (SEX * 10.987)$$

## CALCULATION EXAMPLES

| SUBJECT | BMI | %FAT | EX | %FATVO2 | BMIVO2 |
|---------|-------|------|----|---------|--------|
| JIM     | 29.91 | 38.2 | 0  | 14.4    | 14.0   |
| JANE    | 28.21 | 35.1 | 1  | 22.7    | 27.1   |
| BOB     | 22.83 | 18.3 | 6  | 43.4    | 45.5   |
| MARY    | 20.05 | 16.2 | 7  | 43.4    | 42.7   |

**Summary**

Aerobic fitness or $\dot{V}O_2$ Max is a major component of adult fitness tests and important for health promotion. $\dot{V}O_2$ Max may be measured by either maximal or submaximal tests. The most valid method is a maximal test where $\dot{V}O_2$ Max is measured directly from expired gases. Typically, this method is reserved for research purposes. A second maximal method is to estimate $\dot{V}O_2$ Max from treadmill time with regression equations. Submaximal tests are more realistic for mass use. $\dot{V}O_2$ Max is estimated from submaximal power output and exercise heart rate response to the exercise level. Single- and multi-stage models are available for estimating $\dot{V}O_2$ Max. A second type of submaximal test that is more practical for field testing involves measuring exercise heart rate immediately after a 1-mile walk or jog. The final method does not require exercise testing. The nonexercise $\dot{V}O_2$ Max method involves estimating aerobic fitness from age, self-report physical activity, and body composition measured by percent body fat or BMI. The maximal treadmill test is the most accurate with a standard error of about 3 ml·kg·min$^{-1}$ while the standard error of the submaximal and nonexercise models range between 5 and 6 ml·kg·min$^{-1}$.

Many universities, YMCAs, private corporations, and commercial organizations provide adult health-related fitness programs. Individuals with significant cardiovascular risk factors need a stress test prior to starting an exercise program. A stress test is a medical test designed to diagnose heart disease from the exercise EKG and cardiovascular responses to exercise. In contrast, a fitness evaluation evaluates aerobic fitness.

**Formative Evaluation of Objectives**

*Objective 1*  Define the methods used to measure $\dot{V}O_2$ Max from (a) maximal tests; (b) submaximal tests; (c) walking and running field tests; and (d) nonexercise models.

1. What is $\dot{V}O_2$ Max for the following treadmill time and protocols:

    a. 10 minutes for (1) Bruce; (2) Balke?

    b. 18 minutes for (1) Bruce; (2) Balke?

    c. Would you expect someone to last 25 minutes on the Bruce or Balke? Why or why not?

2. Calculate $\dot{V}O_2$ Max from the following:

    a. Female with a maximal heart rate of 187, and submaximal values of 6 METs and heart rate 145 b·min$^{-1}$.

    b. Male, age 37 years. Submaximal power output on a bike 900 kmp·min$^{-1}$ and heart rate 140 b·min$^{-1}$.

    c. A 28-year-old person had the following submaximal treadmill data; max heart rate, 175 b·min$^{-1}$; 3.4 mph and 9% grade after 3 minutes of exercise; and exercise heart rate of 146 b·min$^{-1}$.

3. What are the procedures you would need to follow to estimate $\dot{V}O_2$ Max with the multi-stage model?

4. What is the similarity between submaximal test methods and the Rockport Walk Test and BYU Jog Test?

5. What are the variables that comprise the nonexercise models? Explain why these variables can be expected to be related to $\dot{V}O_2$ Max.

*Objective 2* Define the levels of aerobic fitness needed for heath promotion and physically demanding exercise.

1. What are the variables used to establish normative $\dot{V}O_2$ Max standards, and what is the reason these variables are used?

2. What is the basis for health-related aerobic fitness standards?

*Objective 3* Identify maximal and submaximal treadmill protocols.

1. Define the speeds and elevations for the Balke and Bruce treadmill protocols.

2. Define the speeds and elevations for the Ross and Bruce submaximal treadmill protocols.

*Objective 4* Identify cycle ergometer submaximal protocols.

1. List the power output loads you would follow to test a typical woman.

2. List the power output loads you would follow to test a typical man.

3. What would be the power output differences for (a) single-stage model and (b) multi-stage model?

*Objective 5* Differentiate between a stress test and fitness evaluation.

1. What is the major difference between a stress test and fitness evaluation?

2. What types of individuals should have a stress test prior to starting an exercise program?

## Additional Learning Activities

A true understanding of $\dot{V}O_2$ Max is best obtained by measuring it.

1. Find a partner and measure your $\dot{V}O_2$ Max by (1) multi-stage model; (2) single-stage model; (3) the Rockport Walk Test; (4) BYU Jog Test. If your college or university has metabolic equipment, try this method and compare the results you get by maximal treadmill time and the submaximal models.

2. It may be difficult to complete some $\dot{V}O_2$ Max tests that involve testing, but this is not true for the nonexercise method. Evaluate your aerobic fitness with the nonexercise models.

3. Maximum distance run tests can be used to evaluate aerobic fitness. Conduct a validation study with the nonexercise models. Have a group of students complete the 1.5 mile walk-run test and estimate their $\dot{V}O_2$ Max with a nonexercise model. What is the correlation between the two aerobic fitness measures?

4. Develop a computer program to complete the calculations presented in this chapter. Provided at the end of the chapter are equations that can be used to make these calculations on spreadsheet or database programs.

**Bibliography**

ACSM. 1991. *Guidelines for Exercise Testing and Prescription.* 3d ed., Vol. 4. Philadelphia: Lea and Febiger.

Åstrand, P. and K. Rodahl. 1970. *Textbook of work physiology.* New York: McGraw-Hill.

Åstrand, P. O. and K. Rodahl. 1986. *Textbook of work physiology.* 3d ed. New York: McGraw-Hill.

Åstrand, P. O. and I. Ryhming. 1954. A nomogram for calculation of aerobic capacity (physical fitness) from pulse rate during submaximal work. *Journal of Applied Physiology 7:*218–221.

Balke, B. 1963. A simple field test for assessment of physical fitness. *Civil Aeromedical Research Institute Report* 63–66.

Blair, S. N. et al. 1989. Physical fitness and all-cause mortality: A prospective study of healthy men and women. *Journal of the American Medical Association 262:*2395–2401.

Borg, G. 1977. *Physical work and effort.* Proceedings of the First International Symposium, Wenner-Gren Center, Stockholm, Sweden. Oxford, England: Pergamon Press.

Brouha, L. 1943. The step tests: A simple method of measuring physical fitness for muscular work in young men. *Research Quarterly 14:*31–36.

Bruce, R. A., F. Kusumi, and D. Hosmer. 1973. Maximal oxygen intake and nomographic assessment of functional aerobic impairment in cardiovascular disease. *American Heart Journal 85:*546–562.

Buskirk, E. R. and J. L. Hodgson. 1987. Age and aerobic power: The rate of change in men and women. *Federation Proceedings 46:*1824–1829.

Consolazio, L. J., R. F. Johnson, and L. J. Pecora. 1963. *Physiological Measurements of Metabolic Functions in Man.* New York: McGraw-Hill.

Foster, C., A. S. Jackson, M. L. Pollock, et al. 1984. Generalized equations for predicting functional capacity from treadmill performance. *American Heart Journal 107:*1229–1234.

Franks, B. D. and E. T. Howley. 1989. *Fitness Facts: The Healthy Living Handbook.* Champaign, IL: Human Kinetics Books.

George, J. D. et al. 1993. $\dot{V}O_2$ Max estimation from a submaximal 1-mile track jog for fit college-age individuals. *Medicine and Science in Sports and Exercise 25:*401–406.

Golding, L. A., C. R. Meyers, and W. E. Sinning. 1989. *The Y's Way to Physical Fitness.* 3d ed. Chicago: National Board of YMCA.

Hagberg, J. M. et al. 1985. A hemodynamic comparison of young and older endurance athletes during exercise. *Journal of Applied Physiology 58:*2041–2046.

Holloszy, J. O. 1983. Exercise, health, and aging: a need for more information. *Medicine and Science in Sports and Exercise 15:*1–5.

Jackson, A. S. et al. 1990. Prediction of functional aerobic capacity without exercise testing. *Medicine and Science in Sports and Exercise 22:*863–870.

Jackson, A. S. et al. In press. Changes in aerobic physical power in men ages 25–70 years. *Medicine and Science in Sports and Exercise.*

Jones, N. L. and E. J. M. Campbell. 1982. *Clinical Exercise Testing.* Philadelphia: W. B. Saunders.

Kline, G. M., J. P. Porcari, R. Hintermeister, et al. 1987. Estimation of $\dot{V}O_2$ Max from a one-mile track walk gender age and body weight. *Medicine and Science in Sports and Exercise 19:*253–259.

Mahar, M., A. Jackson, and R. L. Ross. 1985. Predictive accuracy of single and double stage sub max treadmill work for estimating aerobic capacity. *Medicine and Science in Sports and Exercise 17:*206–207.

Mitchell, J. H. and G. Blomqvist. 1971. Maximal oxygen uptake. *The New England Journal of Medicine 284:*1018–1022.

Mitchell, J. H., B. J. Sproule, and C. B. Chapman. 1958. The physiological meaning of the maximal oxygen intake test. *Journal of Clinical Investigation 37:*538–547.

Nagel, F. J., B. Balke, and J. P. Naughton. 1965. Gradational step tests for assessing work capacity. *Journal of Applied Physiology 20:*745–748.

Noakes, T. D. 1988. Implications of exercise testing for prediction of athletic performance: a contemporary perspective. *Medicine and Science in Sports and Exercise 20:*319–330.

Pollock, M. L. et al. 1976. A comparative analysis of four protocols for maximal treadmill stress testing. *American Heart Journal 92:*39–42.

Pollock, M. L. et al. 1987. Effect of age and training on aerobic capacity and body composition of master athletes. *Journal of Applied Physiology 62:*725–731.

Pollock, M. L., A. S. Jackson, and C. Foster. 1986. The use of the perception scale for exercise prescription. In *The perception of exertion in physical work. Proceedings of an International Symposium.* G. Borg and D. Ottoson, eds. Stockholm: Wiener-Glenn.

Pollock, M. L., D. H. Schmidt, and A. S. Jackson. 1980. Measurement of cardiorespiratory fitness and body composition in the clinical setting. *Comprehensive Therapy 6:*12–27.

Pollock, M. L., J. H. Wilmore, and S. M. Fox, III. 1984. *Exercise in health and disease.* Philadelphia: W. B. Saunders.

Rogers, M. A. et al. 1990. Decline in $\dot{V}O_2$ Max in master athletes and sedentary men. *Journal of Applied Physiology 68:*2195–2199.

Ross, R. M. and A. S. Jackson. 1986. Development and validation of total work equations for estimating the energy cost of walking. *Journal of Cardiopulmonary Rehabilitation 6:*182–192.

Ross, R. M. and A. S. Jackson. 1990. *Exercise concepts, calculations, and computer applications.* Carmel, IN: Benchmark Press.

Rowell, L. B., H. L. Taylor, and Y. Wang. 1964. Limitations to prediction of maximal oxygen intake. *Journal of Applied Physiology 19:*919–927.

Sloan, A. W. 1959. A modified Harvard step test for women. *Journal of Applied Physiology 14:*235–241.

U.S. Public Health Service. 1990. *Healthy People 2000: National Health Promotion and Disease Prevention Objectives.* Washington, DC: U.S. Department of Health and Human Services.

Wier, L. T. et al. 1993. The role of body composition and physical activity on the age-related decline in $\dot{V}O_2$ Max of women (ages 21–63). *Medicine and Science in Sports and Exercise 25:5130.*

# Evaluating Body Composition

## Key Words

anorexia nervosa
Bioelectrical Impedance Analysis
    (BIA)
body composition
body density
Body Mass Index (BMI)
circumferences
desired weight
fat weight
fat-free weight
generalized equations
hydrostatic weighing
multicomponent model
obesity
overweight
percent body fat
residual lung volume
two-component model

## Contents

## Objectives

With the growing body of literature supporting the value of regular physical activity for health and fitness, the evaluation of body composition has become an important aspect of both youth and adult fitness. The purpose of this chapter is to outline the methods used to evaluate body composition and to evaluate the validity of common field methods.

After reading Chapter 11, you should be able to:

1. Identify the methods used to measure body composition of youth and adults.
2. Identify the limitations of the two-component percent body fat model when applied to children and elderly.
3. Calculate percent body fat of youth and adults from skinfold equations.
4. Be able to evaluate body composition of youths and adults.
5. Calculate weight goals for selected levels of desired percent body fat.
6. Evaluate the accuracy of the various methods used to measure body composition.

## INTRODUCTION

Health-related fitness and athletic training programs are designed to control body weight and body composition. This is accomplished through regular exercise and proper nutrition. Being overweight is associated with many medical problems such as hypertension, diabetes, and heart disease. These illnesses lead to increased morbidity and reduced longevity. It is important to realize that adulthood obesity is a complex problem with physical inactivity being just one cause among many. A detailed discussion of the causal factors and health consequences are beyond the scope of this text. The interested reader is directed to the recent Surgeon General's Report on Nutrition and Health (U.S. Department of Health and Human Services 1988) and Ross and Jackson (1986) for a more comprehensive discussion.

Suitable levels of **body composition** are also important for athletic competition. Excess body fat lowers aerobic fitness and reduces the ability to perform many activities requiring jumping and moving quickly. However, being too thin is not desirable either. Suitable body composition is important for general health and appearance and for maximizing athletic performance. For these reasons, accurate measurements of body composition are needed to develop sound preventive health and athletic programs.

## Body Density and Percent Body Fat

In simple terms, body weight consists of fat weight and fat-free weight.[1] **Percent body fat** is simply the proportion of total weight that is fat weight. Percent body fat is measured from body density. It is possible for two individuals of the same height and body weight to differ substantially in percent body fat, which is why we use it as the standard for evaluating body composition. If percent body fat (%fat) and body weight are known, it becomes possible to calculate fat weight and fat-free weight. The equations for making these calculations are

Fat Weight = [Weight × (%fat/100)]

Fat-Free Weight = Weight – Fat Weight.

Although the terms overweight and obesity are often used interchangeably, there are important differences between them. **Overweight** is weight that exceeds the "normal" weight defined for an individual on the basis of gender, height, and frame size. It is based on norms compiled by insurance companies. **Obesity** is the excessive accumulation of fat weight and is expressed as percent body fat.

The **hydrostatic** (or **underwater**) **weighing** (see Figure 11.1) method is the most common laboratory method used to measure body composition. Numerous laboratories located at universities and medical centers have the equipment for underwater weighing determinations. The measurement objective of the hydrostatic weighing is to find body volume, which is then used with body weight to calculate body density. Percent fat is calculated from body density.

---

[1]Many use the term lean body mass or **lean body weight** rather than fat-free weight. Lean body weight has a density less than 1.100 g/cc because it contains from 2 to 3% essential lipid. Lohman (1992) maintains that fat-free weight is the appropriate term.

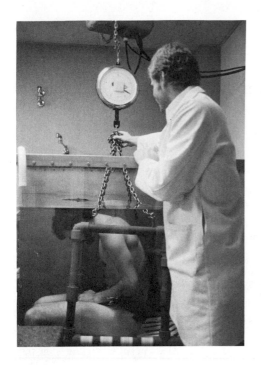 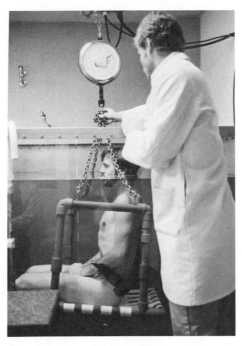

Figure 11.1
Method of
determining body
density by
underwater
weighing. (Photos
courtesy of Dr. M. L.
Pollock, University of
Florida.)

## Measuring Body Density

Variation in body density can be due to air, fat weight, and fat-free weight. The density of air is zero, and the density of **fat weight** (tissue) is about 0.90 g/cc. The density of **fat-free weight** varies from about 1.0 g/cc to as high as 3.0 g/cc with an average assumed to be 1.10 g/cc. Fat-free weight consists of muscle, blood, bone, and organs.

The underwater weighing method is based on the Archimedes Principle for measuring the density of an object. When an object, in this case a person, is submerged under water, the difference between the weight in air and under water equals the weight of water displaced. The weight of water displaced divided by the density of water is the volume of water displaced or the volume of the object (i.e., the person). The objective of underwater weighing is to measure body volume. **Body density** is the ratio of weight in air and body volume. Dry land weight, underwater weight, residual lung volume, and water density are needed to calculate body density. The basic steps needed to measure hydrostatically determined body density are summarized next.

***Determining Underwater Weight.*** Body density is typically measured in the laboratory in a specially constructed tank (see Figure 11.1), but it can be measured in a swimming pool if there is no turbulence. The subject sits on a specially devised chair that is attached to a scale, leans forward, and submerges the head while performing a maximal expiration. Since many subjects are too buoyant, it may be difficult to submerge them. In these instances, a scuba weight belt is placed on the subject's lap. Figure 11.1 shows that the subject is typically sitting on a chair. Both the weight of the chair and scuba weight belt must be subtracted from the obtained weight to calculate true underwater weight.

Underwater weight is measured to the nearest 0.01 kilogram with a calibrated scale. The Chatillon 15 kilogram scale shown is commonly used; however, electronic scales that use load cells are also commercially available. A minimum of seven to ten trials should be administered. The average of the three trials with the highest weights, and within 0.025 kilograms, are used. It has been shown that underwater weight will systematically increase. The person must practice to reach true underwater weight, which is typically reached after three to five trials. The underwater weight is greatly dependent on the amount of air in the lungs when submerged. The subject must be weighed while breath holding after a complete expiration.

***Determining Land Weight.*** Body weight can be easily and accurately determined by weighing. However, it is important to be weighed under standard conditions because total body water, which is a major determinant of body weight, can vary considerably from day to day. The body is composed of approximately 60% water. That is, a 70-kilogram individual has over 40 kilograms of body water. Heavy exercise may result in a water loss as high as 2 to 3 kilograms per hour.

***Determining Residual Volume.*** The volume of the body that is air can introduce the largest source of error in the underwater weighing method. This is primarily because the density of air and other gases in the body are so close to zero that even a small error in volume measurement makes a significant change in total body density. The major potential sources of measurement error are (1) the volume of air left in the lungs after expiration (**residual volume**) and (2) air elsewhere, particularly in the gastrointestinal tract. However, air bubbles in the hair, bathing caps, bathing suits, and on the body also can introduce errors.

The most accurate way of measuring the volume of air in the body is by use of a "body box" or body plethysmograph. This technique uses the principle of compressibility of gases. While in a box, the individual breathes in and out against a closed diaphragm. The movement causes compression of the gas in his body, leading to small changes in volume and pressure in the box. These are then measured and used to calculate the volume of air in the individual's lungs. Body boxes are expensive and not widely available. Other methods of calculating residual volume are based on dilution or wash-out techniques. Wilmore (1969) describes the methods most commonly used in body composition studies.

***Determining the Density of Water.*** The density of water is a function of its temperature and can be calculated by

$$Dw = 1.005932 - (0.0003394 \times TW)$$

where Dw is water density and TW is the temperature of water measured in centigrade.

***Computing Body Density.*** The values needed to calculate body density are body weight on land, body weight in water, and residual lung volume. Body density is calculated by

$$BD = (Wa/[(Wa - Ww)/Dw] - (RV + 100\ ml)$$

where Wa is the individual's weight in air, Ww is the individual's weight in water, Dw is the density of the water, and RV is residual lung volume. The 100-ml value is added to residual lung volume to adjust for gas bubbles in the gastrointestinal tract (Behnke & Wilmore 1974).

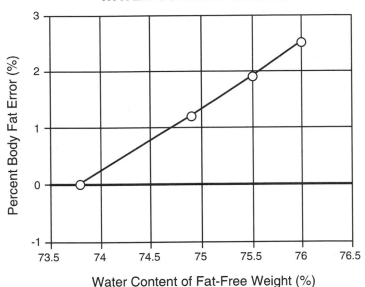

**WATER CONTENT ERRORS**

*X-axis:* Water Content of Fat-Free Weight (%)
*Y-axis:* Percent Body Fat Error (%)

**Figure 11.2**
Increases in body water content lead to overestimates of true percent body fat. Graphs made from published data (Lohman 1992). The reference body weight is 65.3 kg with a 73.8% water content of fat-free weight.

## Converting Body Density to Percent Body Fat

Researchers have developed equations for converting body density to percent body fat. These two equations, Siri (1961) and Brŏzek et al. (1963), yield nearly identical percent fat values throughout the human range of body fatness. The equations are

Siri: %fat = (495/BD) – 450

Brozek: %fat = (457/BD) – 414.

## Limitations of the Siri and Brozek Methods

The Siri and Brŏzek methods of estimating percent body fat from body density are considered by many to be the "gold standard" for assessing body composition. Each is based on the **two-component model** that assumes that the density of fat tissue is 0.9 g/cc and the density of fat-free weight is 1.10 g/cc. This is likely true for adults between the ages of 20 and 50 years. Lohman (1992) argues convincingly that the two-component model has serious limitations when measuring the body composition of elderly and children because total body water and mineral content of these extreme groups vary from the values of the 20–50-year-old subjects.

During childhood and elderly years, the body is changing more dramatically. Changes in body water and bone mineral content alter the density of the fat-free component. Figure 11.2 shows the relationship between changes in body water content on the error of percent body fat. As these values increase over reference values, there is a linear increase in percent body fat errors obtained with the two-component method.

Lohman (1992) provides an excellent discussion on the effect of bone mineral differences on the accuracy of percent body fat determinations. Changes in the body's mineral content alters the density of fat-free weight. The two major sources of differences among individuals in bone mineral content can be traced to genetics and environmental conditions. Some inherit a higher bone mineral content than others. Due to life-style, some will develop a higher mineral content. For example, it has been shown the bone diameter of the playing arm of tennis players is larger than their other arm.

Osteoporosis is a major source of bone loss in elderly, especially for women. This disease is characterized by a decrease in bone density that results in an increase in bone porosity and leads to weak, fragile bones that break easily. The reasons for osteoporosis are not known, but the lack of sufficient calcium in the diet and lack of physical activity are believed to be important determinants leading many scientists to believe that diet and strenuous exercise can help maintain skeletal integrity and reduce the risk of osteoporosis (Ross & Jackson 1990). The extent that bone mineral loss in the elderly limits the accuracy of the two-component model is a topic of current study.

Since differences in water and bone mineral content affect body density, the equations for converting body density of adults to percent body fat cannot be validly used with children. Lohman (1982; 1992) has discussed this problem and developed a multi-component equation that is an extension of the Siri equation. These methods are described in a series of reports published by Lohman and his associates (Boileau et al. 1985; Lohman 1986; Lohman et al. 1984) and summarized in Lohman's text (Lohman 1992). The **multicomponent model** not only includes body density (BD), but also water (w) and mineral (m) content. The multicomponent equation that can be used for children or adults of any age is

$$\%Fat = [(2.749/BD) - 0.727(w) + 1.146 (m) - 2.053].$$

With the development of dual energy radiography, technology is becoming available to estimate bone mineral content (g/cm) and bone density (g/cm$^2$). This presents the possibility of developing a multicomponent model that adjusts for water and mineral content variance in fat-free weight. A detailed discussion of this topic is beyond the scope of this text, and the interested reader is directed to the work of Lohman and colleagues (1992).

## Anthropometric Assessment of Body Composition

Due to the need for highly trained technicians and expensive laboratory equipment, hydrostatically determined body composition is rarely used in field settings. The most common alternative is to use some form of anthropometric method. This includes weight-height ratios, body circumferences, and skinfold measurements.

### Body Mass Index

**Body mass index (BMI)** is the weight-height ratio often used in field settings. It is the measure of body composition typically used in large-scale public health studies, but it also is an alternative item on the FITNESSGRAM® Youth Fitness battery (Chapter 9). BMI is computed by

$$BMI = [Weight/(Height \times Height)]$$

where weight is in kilograms and height is in meters.

While BMI is correlated with hydrostatically determined percent body fat, the correlations are lower than found with skinfold measurements and waist circumference (Table 11.1). The limitation of the BMI can be traced to the numerator of the equation—body weight. Body weight is not only affected by fat mass, but also fat-free mass, consisting of muscle, organs, and skeletal mass. BMI is not used to determine degree of obesity, rather it defines overweight. Table 11.2 gives the BMI criterion used

**Table 11.1.** Linear Correlations between Body Density and Anthropometric Variables for Adults (Jackson & Pollock 1978; Jackson, Pollock, & Ward 1980)

| Variables | Men (N=402) | Women (N=283) |
|---|---|---|
| **General Characteristics** | | |
| Height | −0.03 | −0.06 |
| Weight | −0.63 | −0.63 |
| Body Mass Index* | −0.69 | −0.70 |
| **Skinfolds** | | |
| Chest | −0.85 | −0.64 |
| Axilla | −0.82 | −0.73 |
| Triceps | −0.79 | −0.77 |
| Subscapula | −0.77 | −0.67 |
| Abdomen | −0.83 | −0.75 |
| Suprailium | −0.76 | −0.76 |
| Thigh | −0.78 | −0.74 |
| Sum of Seven | −0.88 | −0.83 |
| **Circumferences** | | |
| Waist | −0.80 | −0.71 |
| Gluteal | −0.69 | −0.74 |
| Thigh | −0.64 | −0.68 |
| Biceps | −0.51 | −0.63 |
| Forearm | −0.35 | −0.41 |

*$Wt/Ht^2$, where weight is in kg and height is in meters.

**Table 11.2.** BMI Criterion Used to Define Overweight for the *Healthy People 2000* Public Health Program

| Age Group | Body Mass Index Level | |
|---|---|---|
| | Males | Females |
| 12–14 | ≥24.3 | ≥24.8 |
| 15–17 | ≥25.8 | ≥25.7 |
| 18–19 | ≥23.4 | ≥25.7 |
| ≥ 20 | ≥27.8 | ≥27.3 |

BMI = [weight/(height × height)], where weight is in kilograms and height is in meters.

to define overweight for the *Healthy People 2000* project (U.S. Public Health Service 1990) outlined in Chapter 1. The criterion for overweight varies for males and females of different ages.

**Table 11.3** Generalized Regression Equations for Predicting Body Density of Men and Women from Body Circumference Measurements (Tran & Weltman 1988 and 1989)

| Regression Equation | R | g/cc |
|---|---|---|
| **Males** | | |
| $BD = 1.21142 + .00085(X_1) - .00050(X_2) - .00061(X_3) - .00138(X_4)$ | .84 | .009 |
| **Females** | | |
| $BD = 1.168297 - .002824(X_4) = .000012(X_1)^2 - .000733(X_3) = .000510(X_5) - .000216(X_6)$ | .89 | .009 |

KEY: $X_1$ = weight (kg); $X_2$ = iliac circumference (cm); $X_3$ = hip circumference (cm); $X_4$ = abdominal circumference (cm); $X_5$ = height (cm); $X_6$ = age (years).

## Body Circumferences

Table 11.1 shows that body **circumferences** are correlated with hydrostatically determined body density. The circumferences that tend to be most highly correlated are in the abdominal and hip regions. In 1981, the United States Navy changed from using height and weight standards to percent body fat estimated from body circumferences (Hodgdon & Beckett 1984a; Hodgdon & Beckett 1984b). The variables used for the navy equations are height, abdomen circumference, hip circumference, and neck circumference (Hodgdon & Beckett 1984c). Tran and associates (1989; 1988) published generalized equations for estimating hydrostatically determined body density from various combinations of circumference measurements. The subjects used varied considerably in age and body composition. Table 11.3 gives the generalized equations developed on the general population. The procedures for measuring body circumferences are given in other sources (Behnke & Wilmore 1974; Hodgdon & Beckett 1984c).

## Skinfolds

Skinfold measurements are highly correlated with underwater-determined body density. Skinfold measurements involve measuring a double thickness of subcutaneous fat with a specially designed caliper (Figure 11.3). Several acceptable calipers are available for measuring skinfold fat. A **skinfold caliper** that conforms to specifications established by the committee of Food and Nutrition Board of the National Research Council of the United States should be used. The Lange, Harpenden, and Lafayette calipers meet these criteria.[2] The Harpenden caliper gives measurements about 1 or 4 mm lower than the Lange and Lafayette calipers (Lohman 1982).

*Skinfold Sites.* A concern many express with skinfolds is accuracy. This is insured by using a suitable caliper and having a trained technician measure skinfold fat at the proper locations. Improper site selection is probably the most common reason for error in measuring skinfold fat. The skinfold sites and methods are listed here. All measurements are taken on the right side of the body. Figures 11.4 through 11.11 illustrate the measurement methods and site location.

---

[2]The Lange caliper is manufactured by Cambridge Scientific Industries, Cambridge, MD. The Harpenden caliper is manufactured by British Indicators LTD., St. Albans, Herts, England and distributed in the Untied States by Quinton Equipment, Seattle, WA. Lafayette Instrument Company, Lafayette, IN, manufactures the Lafayette caliper.

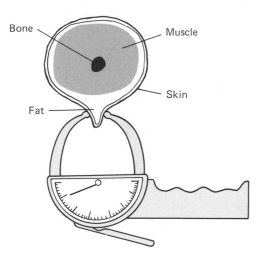

**Figure 11.3**
Measurement of skinfold fat.

Bone

Muscle

Skin

Fat

1. *Chest:* a diagonal fold taken half the distance between the anterior axillary line and nipple for men and one third of the distance from the anterior axillary line to the nipple for women (Figure 11.4).

2. *Axilla:* a vertical fold on the midaxillary line at the level of the xiphoid process of the sternum (Figure 11.5).

3. *Triceps:* a vertical fold on the posterior midline of the upper arm (over the triceps muscle), halfway between the acromion and olecranon processes; the elbow should be extended and relaxed (Figure 11.6).

4. *Subscapula:* a fold taken on a diagonal line coming from the vertebral border to 1–2 cm from the inferior angle of the scapula (Figure 11.7).

5. *Abdomen:* a vertical fold taken at a lateral distance of approximately 2 cm from the umbilicus (Figure 11.8).

6. *Suprailium:* a diagonal fold above the crest of the ilium at the spot where an imaginary line would come down from the anterior axillary line (Figure 11.9).

7. *Thigh:* a vertical fold on the anterior aspect of the thigh midway between hip and knee joints (Figure 11.10).

8. *Medial Calf:* The right leg is placed on a bench with the knee flexed at 90°. The level of the greatest calf girth is marked on the medial border. A vertical skinfold is raised on the medial side of the right calf one centimeter above the mark, and the fold is measured at the maximal girth (see Figure 11.11).

***Skinfold Test Methods.*** When taking a skinfold measurement, the left hand pinches and pulls the skin, and the caliper is held in the right hand. Grasp the skinfold firmly by the thumb and index finger. The caliper is perpendicular to the fold at approximately 1 cm (0.25 in) from the thumb and forefinger. Then release the caliper grip so that full tension is exerted on the skinfold. Use the pads at the tip of thumb and finger to grasp the skinfold. (Testers may need to trim their nails.) Read the dial to the nearest 0.5 mm approximately one to two seconds after the grip has been released. A minimum of two measurements should be taken. If they vary by more than 1 mm, a third should be taken.

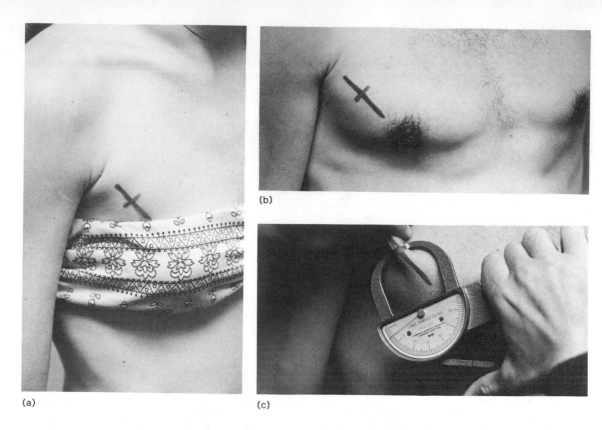

(a)                                        (b)

                                           (c)

**Figure 11.4**
(a) and (b) Skinfold test sites for men and women; (c) placement of calipers for chest skinfold test. (Photos courtesy of Pollock, M. L., D. H. Schmidt, & A. S. Jackson, *Measurement of Cardiorespiratory Fitness and Body Composition in the Clinical Setting, Comprehensive Therapy,* Vol. 6(9), pgs. 12–27, 1980. Published with permission of the Laux Company, Inc., Harvard, MA)

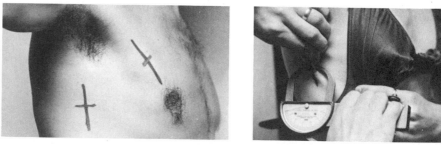

**Figure 11.5** Test site and placement of calipers for axilla skinfold. The axilla skinfold site is shown in relation to the man's chest site. (Photos courtesy of Pollock, M. L., D. H. Schmidt, & A. S. Jackson, *Measurement of Cardiorespiratory Fitness and Body Composition in the Clinical Setting, Comprehensive Therapy,* Vol. 6(9), pgs. 12–27, 1980. Published with permission of the Laux Company, Inc., Harvard, MA)

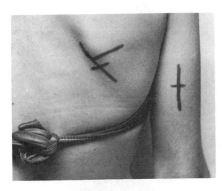
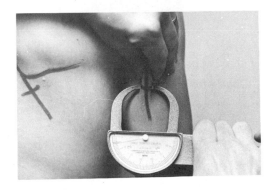

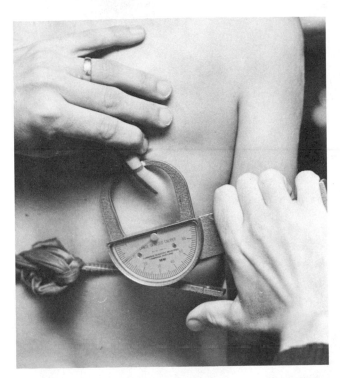

**Figure 11.6 (above)**
Test site and placement of calipers for triceps skinfold. The triceps skinfold site is shown in relation to the subscapular skinfold site. (Photos courtesy of Pollock, M. L., D. H. Schmidt, & A. S. Jackson, *Measurement of Cardiorespiratory Fitness and Body Composition in the Clinical Setting, Comprehensive Therapy*, Vol. 6(9), pgs. 12–27, 1980. Published with permission of the Laux Company, Inc., Harvard, MA)

**Figure 11.7 (left)**
Placement of calipers for subscapular skinfold. The proper site location is shown in Figure 11.6. (Photos courtesy of Pollock, M. L., D. H. Schmidt & A. S. Jackson, *Measurement of Cardiorespiratory Fitness and Body Composition in the Clinical Setting, Comprehensive Therapy*, Vol. 6(9), pgs. 12–27, 1980. Published with permission of the Laux Company, Inc., Harvard, MA)

**Figure 11.8 (below)**
Test site and placement of calipers for abdominal skinfold. The abdominal site is shown in relation to the suprailium site. (Photos courtesy of Pollock, M. L., D. H. Schmidt, & A. S. Jackson, *Measurement of Cardiorespiratory Fitness and Body Composition in the Clinical Setting, Comprehensive Therapy*, Vol. 6(9), pgs. 12–27, 1980. Published with permission of the Laux Company, Inc., Harvard, MA)

**Figure 11.9**
Caliper placement for
suprailium skinfold. The
proper site location is shown
in Figure 11.8. (Photos
courtesy of Pollock, M. L.,
D. H. Schmidt, & A. S. Jackson,
*Measurement of
Cardiorespiratory Fitness and
Body Composition in the Clinical
Setting, Comprehensive
Therapy,* Vol. 6(9), pgs. 12–27,
1980. Published with permission
of the Laux Company, Inc.,
Harvard, MA)

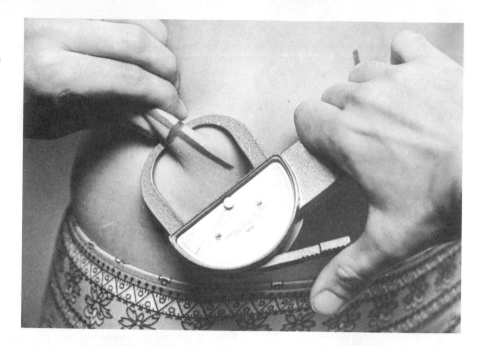

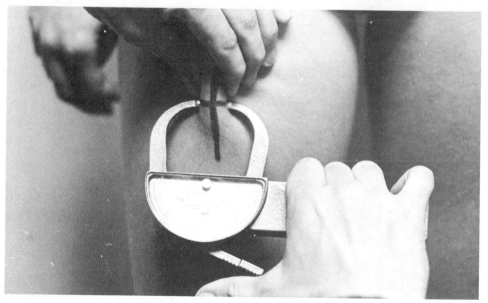

**Figure 11.10** Caliper placement for thigh skinfold. (Photos courtesy of Pollock, M. L., D. H. Schmidt,
& A. S. Jackson, *Measurement of Cardiorespiratory Fitness and Body Composition in the Clinical Setting,
Comprehensive Therapy,* Vol. 6(9), pgs. 12–27, 1980. Published with permission of the Laux Company, Inc.,
Harvard, MA)

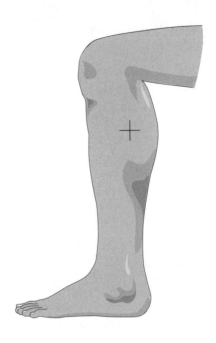

**Figure 11.11**
Test site and placement of
calipers for medial calf.

If consecutive fat measurements become smaller and smaller, the fat is being compressed; this occurs mainly with "fleshy" people. The tester should go on to the next site and return to the trouble spot after finishing the other measurements; the final value will be the average of the two that seem to best represent the skinfold fat site. Typically, the tester should complete a measurement at one site before moving to another. It is better to make measurements when the skin is dry, because when the skin is moist or wet the tester may grasp extra skin (fat) and get larger values. Measurements should not be taken immediately after exercise or when a subject is overheated because the shift of body fluid to the skin will increase skinfold size. Practice is necessary to grasp the same size of skinfold consistently at the same location every time. Consistency can be ensured by having several technicians take the same measurements and comparing results. Proficiency in measuring skinfolds may take practice sessions with up to 50 to 100 subjects.

Many people have published regression equations with functions to predict hydrostatically measured body density from various combinations of anthropometric variables. More than 100 equations appear in the literature. The results of these studies are provided in Table 11.4.

## Skinfold Assessment of Percent Fat of Adults

**Table 11.4** Means and Standard Deviations of Hydrostatically Determined Body Density and Concurrent Validity of Regression Equations for Males and Females

| Source | Age | Sample n | Body Density Mean | SD | Regression Analysis R | SE |
|---|---|---|---|---|---|---|
| **Males** | | | | | | |
| Brŏzek and Keys (1951) | 20.3 | 133 | 1.077 | .014 | .88 | .007 |
| | 45–55 | 122 | 1.055 | .012 | .74 | .009 |
| Durnin and Wormsley (1974) | 17–19 | 24 | 1.066 | .016 | † | .007 |
| | 20–29 | 92 | 1.064 | .016 | † | .008 |
| | 30–39 | 34 | 1.046 | .012 | † | .009 |
| | 40–49 | 35 | 1.043 | .015 | † | .008 |
| | 50–68 | 24 | 1.036 | .018 | † | .009 |
| Forsyth and Sinning (1973) | 19–29 | 50 | 1.072 | .010 | .84 | .006 |
| Haisman (1970) | 22–26 | 55 | 1.070 | .010 | .78 | .006 |
| Jackson and Pollock (1978) | 18–61 | 308 | 1.059 | .018 | .92 | .007 |
| Katch and McArdle (1973) | 19.3 | 53 | 1.065 | .014 | .89 | .007 |
| Katch and Michael (1973) | 17.0 | 40 | 1.076 | .013 | .89 | .006 |
| Pascale et al. (1956) | 22.1 | 88 | 1.068 | .012 | .86 | .006 |
| Pollock et al. (1976) | 18–22 | 95 | 1.068 | .014 | .87 | .007 |
| | 40–55 | 84 | 1.043 | .013 | .84 | .007 |
| Sloan (1967) | 18–26 | 50 | 1.075 | .015 | .85 | .008 |
| Wilmore and Behnke (1969) | 16–36 | 133 | 1.066 | .013 | .87 | .006 |
| Wright and Wilmore (1974) | 27.8 | 297 | 1.061 | .014 | .86 | .007 |
| **Females** | | | | | | |
| Durnin and Rahaman (1967) | 18–29 | 45 | 1.044 | .014 | .78 | .010 |
| Durnin and Wormsley (1974) | 16–19 | 29 | 1.040 | .017 | † | .009 |
| | 20–29 | 100 | 1.034 | .021 | † | .011 |
| | 30–39 | 58 | 1.025 | .020 | † | .013 |
| | 40–49 | 48 | 1.020 | .016 | † | .011 |
| | 50–68 | 37 | 1.013 | .016 | † | .008 |
| Jackson et al. (1980) | 18–55 | 249 | 1.044 | .016 | .87 | .008 |
| Katch and McArdle (1973) | 20.3 | 69 | 1.039 | .015 | .84 | .009 |
| Katch and Michael (1968) | 19–23 | 64 | 1.049 | .011 | .70 | .008 |
| Pollock et al. (1975) | 18–22 | 83 | 1.043 | .014 | .84 | .008 |
| | 33–50 | 60 | 1.032 | .015 | .89 | .007 |
| Sinning (1978) | 17–23 | 44 | 1.064 | .010 | .81 | .006 |
| Sloan et al. (1962) | 20.2 | 50 | 1.047 | .012 | .74 | .008 |
| Wilmore and Behnke (1970) | 21.4 | 128 | 1.041 | .010 | .76 | .007 |
| Young (1964) | 53.0 | 62 | 1.020 | .014 | .84 | .008 |
| Young et al. (1962) | 17–27 | 94 | 1.034 | .009 | .69 | .007 |

†Correlation not reported.

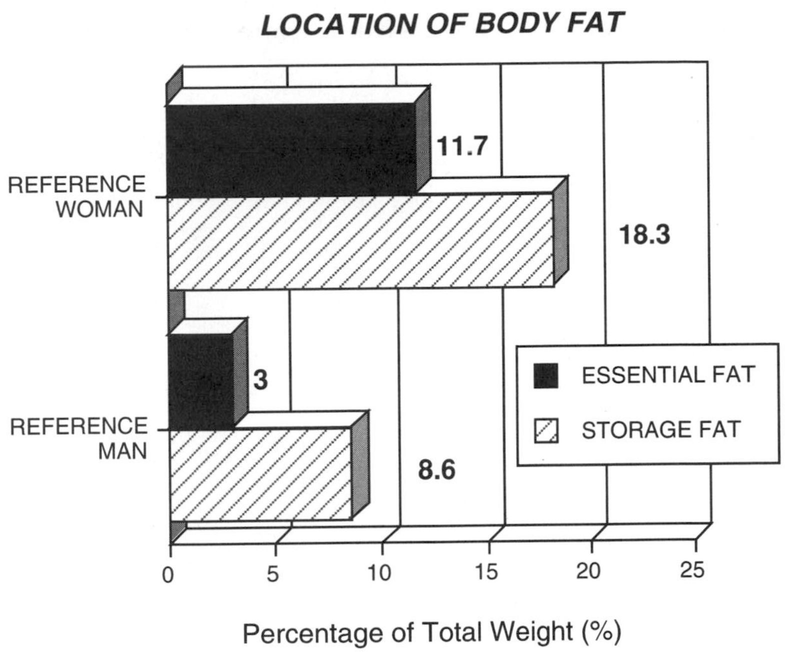

## LOCATION OF BODY FAT

**Figure 11.12**
Not only do women have a higher percentage of their weight in storage fat, but also in essential fat consisting of lipids of the bone marrow, central nervous system, mammary glands, and other organs. Graph made from published data (Lohman 1992) of the fat distribution in reference to a man and woman with the following characteristics: man, body weight 70 kilograms, 14.7% body fat; woman, body weight 56.8 kilograms, 26.9% body fat.

Early researchers developed equations for relatively homogeneous populations termed *population-specific equations.* The more recent trend is to use what is termed **generalized equations,** equations that can be validly used with heterogeneous samples. Population-specific equations were developed on relatively small, homogeneous samples, and their application is limited to that sample. The generalized equations were developed on large heterogeneous samples using models that accounted for the nonlinear relationship between skinfold fat and body density. Age was found to be an important variable for generalized equations (Durnin & Wormsley 1974; Jackson & Pollock 1978; Jackson et al. 1980). The main advantage of the generalized approach is that one equation replaces several without a loss in prediction accuracy. A detailed discussion of population-specific and generalized equations can be found in other sources (Cureton 1984; Jackson 1984; Lohman 1982).

Separate skinfold equations are needed for men and women. Men and women differ in both storage and essential fat content (Figure 11.12). Table 11.5 gives the descriptive statistics for the variables used to develop generalized equations for men and women. When all seven skinfolds[3] were summed, the mean of the men's and women's distributions were nearly the same, but men and women differed considerably at the various sites. The women's means for the limb skinfold, triceps, and thigh were substantially higher then the men's values while the men's means on the remaining five sites, mainly in the region of the trunk, tended to be higher.

**Generalized Skinfold Equations**

---

[3]The calf skinfold was not used with this adult sample.

**Table 11.5** Descriptive Statistics of Samples Used to Develop Generalized Body Density Equations for Men and Women

| Variables | Men (N = 402) | | Women (N = 283) | |
|---|---|---|---|---|
| | Mean | Sd | Mean | Sd |
| **General Characteristics** | | | | |
| Age (yr) | 32.8 | 11.0 | 31.8 | 11.5 |
| Height (cm) | 179.0 | 6.4 | 168.6 | 5.8 |
| Weight (kg) | 78.2 | 11.7 | 57.5 | 7.4 |
| Body Mass Index* | 24.4 | 3.2 | 20.2 | 2.2 |
| **Laboratory Determined** | | | | |
| Body Density (g/cc) | 1.058 | 0.018 | 1.044 | 0.016 |
| Percent Fat (%) | 17.9 | 8.0 | 24.4 | 7.2 |
| Lean Weight (kg) | 63.5 | 7.3 | 43.1 | 4.2 |
| Fat Weight (kg) | 14.6 | 7.9 | 14.3 | 5.7 |
| **Skinfolds (mm)** | | | | |
| Chest | 15.2 | 8.0 | 12.6 | 4.8 |
| Axilla | 17.3 | 8.7 | 13.0 | 6.1 |
| Triceps | 14.2 | 6.1 | 18.2 | 5.9 |
| Subscapula | 16.0 | 7.0 | 14.2 | 6.4 |
| Abdomen | 25.1 | 10.8 | 24.2 | 9.6 |
| Suprailium | 16.2 | 8.9 | 14.0 | 7.1 |
| Thigh | 18.9 | 7.7 | 29.5 | 8.0 |
| **Sum Of Skinfolds (mm)** | | | | |
| All seven | 122.9 | 52.0 | 125.6 | 42.0 |
| Chest, Abdomen, Thigh | 59.2 | 24.5 | | |
| Triceps, Suprailium, Thigh | | | 61.6 | 19.0 |

*Body mass index is weight (kg) divided by height in meters squared $(kg/m^2)$.

Multiple regression models were used to develop generalized skinfold equations for men (Jackson & Pollock 1978) and women (Jackson et al. 1980). Figure 11.13 gives the scattergram between the sum of seven skinfolds and hydrostatically measured percent body fat. The male and female bivariate distribution is similar except the distribution of women is "shifted" upward. For the same sum of seven skinfold value, women tend to have a higher percent body fat. This systematic difference is due largely to the women's higher level of essential fat.

Table 11.6 gives generalized skinfold equations for men and women. A quadratic component is used to adjust for the nonlinearity, and age is an independent variable to account for aging. The sum of three and seven skinfolds is highly correlated ($r = 0.97$), which shows that different combinations of the sum of skinfolds can be used with minimal loss of accuracy. The use of the sum of three instead of seven enhances feasibility. The logic used to develop the generalized equations is fully presented in another source (Jackson 1984).

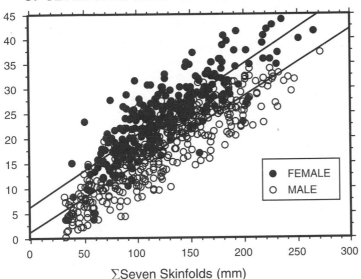

SCATTERGRAM PERCENT BODY FAT AND THE SUM
OF SEVEN SKINFOLDS FOR MALES AND FEMALES

ΣSeven Skinfolds (mm)

**Figure 11.13**
Scattergram of the sum of
seven skinfolds and
hydrostatically determined
percent body fat of men
(Jackson & Pollock 1978)
and women (Jackson et al.
1980). The regression line
shows that for a given
skinfold thickness, the
percent body fat of women
is higher than for men. This
is largely due to essential
fat differences.

## Table 11.6 Generalized Regression Equations for Predicting Body Density of Men and Women from the Sum of Skinfold Fat and Age

| Regression Equation | R | g/cc | %Fat |
|---|---|---|---|
| **Males** | | | |
| $BD(M\text{-}1) = 1.11200000 - 0.00043499(X_1) + 0.00000055(X_1)^2 - 0.00028826(X_4)$ | .90 | .008 | 3.4 |
| $BD(M\text{-}2) = 1.10938000 - 0.0008267(X_2) + 0.00000016(X_2)^2 - 0.0002574(X_4)$ | .91 | .008 | 3.4 |
| **Females** | | | |
| $BD(F\text{-}1) = 1.0970 - 0.0004697(X_1) + 0.00000056(X_1)^2 - 0.00012828(X_4)$ | .85 | .008 | 3.8 |
| $BD(F\text{-}2) = 1.099421 - 0.0009929(X_3) + 0.00000023(X_3)^2 - 0.0001392(X_4)$ | .84 | .009 | 4.0 |

Key: $X_1$ = sum of seven skinfolds; $X_2$ = sum of chest, abdomen, and thigh skinfolds; $X_3$ = sum of triceps, suprailium, and thigh skinfolds; $X_4$ = age in years.

The generalized equations can be difficult to use without computational help. The Computer Calculations section at the end of this chapter provides microcomputer equations to speed the computations. Tables 11.7 and 11.8 provide percent body fat estimates from the quadratic sum of three skinfolds and age. In the tables we have used the sum of the chest, abdomen, and thigh skinfolds for men, and the sum of the triceps, suprailium, and thigh skinfolds for women, each sum having proved the most valid for each gender. The YMCA adult fitness test (Golding et al. 1989) includes a similar table for a different combination of skinfolds.

## Table 11.7 Estimates of Percentage of Fat for Men; Sum of Chest, Abdomen, and Thigh Skinfolds

| Sum of Skinfolds (MM) | Under 22 | 23 to 27 | 28 to 32 | 33 to 37 | 38 to 42 | 43 to 47 | 48 to 52 | 53 to 57 | Over 58 |
|---|---|---|---|---|---|---|---|---|---|
| 8–10 | 1.3 | 1.8 | 2.3 | 2.9 | 3.4 | 3.9 | 4.5 | 5.0 | 5.5 |
| 11–13 | 2.2 | 2.8 | 3.3 | 3.9 | 4.4 | 4.9 | 5.5 | 6.0 | 6.5 |
| 14–16 | 3.2 | 3.8 | 4.3 | 4.8 | 5.4 | 5.9 | 6.4 | 7.0 | 7.5 |
| 17–19 | 4.2 | 4.7 | 5.3 | 5.8 | 6.3 | 6.9 | 7.4 | 8.0 | 8.5 |
| 20–22 | 5.1 | 5.7 | 6.2 | 6.8 | 7.3 | 7.9 | 8.4 | 8.9 | 9.5 |
| 23–25 | 6.1 | 6.6 | 7.2 | 7.7 | 8.3 | 8.8 | 9.4 | 9.9 | 10.5 |
| 26–28 | 7.0 | 7.6 | 8.1 | 8.7 | 9.2 | 9.8 | 10.3 | 10.9 | 11.4 |
| 29–31 | 8.0 | 8.5 | 9.1 | 9.6 | 10.2 | 10.7 | 11.3 | 11.8 | 12.4 |
| 32–34 | 8.9 | 9.4 | 10.0 | 10.5 | 11.1 | 11.6 | 12.2 | 12.8 | 13.3 |
| 35–37 | 9.8 | 10.4 | 10.9 | 11.5 | 12.0 | 12.6 | 13.1 | 13.7 | 14.3 |
| 38–40 | 10.7 | 11.3 | 11.8 | 12.4 | 12.9 | 13.5 | 14.1 | 14.6 | 15.2 |
| 41–43 | 11.6 | 12.2 | 12.7 | 13.3 | 13.8 | 14.4 | 15.0 | 15.5 | 16.1 |
| 44–46 | 12.5 | 13.1 | 13.6 | 14.2 | 14.7 | 15.3 | 15.9 | 16.4 | 17.0 |
| 47–49 | 13.4 | 13.9 | 14.5 | 15.1 | 15.6 | 16.2 | 16.8 | 17.3 | 17.9 |
| 50–52 | 14.3 | 14.8 | 15.4 | 15.9 | 16.5 | 17.1 | 17.6 | 18.2 | 18.8 |
| 53–55 | 15.1 | 15.7 | 16.2 | 16.8 | 17.4 | 17.9 | 18.5 | 19.1 | 19.7 |
| 56–58 | 16.0 | 16.5 | 17.1 | 17.7 | 18.2 | 18.8 | 19.4 | 20.0 | 20.5 |
| 59–61 | 16.9 | 17.4 | 17.9 | 18.5 | 19.1 | 19.7 | 20.2 | 20.8 | 21.4 |
| 62–64 | 17.6 | 18.2 | 18.8 | 19.4 | 19.9 | 20.5 | 21.1 | 21.7 | 22.2 |
| 65–67 | 18.5 | 19.0 | 19.6 | 20.2 | 20.8 | 21.3 | 21.9 | 22.5 | 23.1 |
| 68–70 | 19.3 | 19.9 | 20.4 | 21.0 | 21.6 | 22.2 | 22.7 | 23.3 | 23.9 |
| 71–73 | 20.1 | 20.7 | 21.2 | 21.8 | 22.4 | 23.0 | 23.6 | 24.1 | 24.7 |
| 74–76 | 20.9 | 21.5 | 22.0 | 22.6 | 23.2 | 23.8 | 24.4 | 25.0 | 25.5 |
| 77–79 | 21.7 | 22.2 | 22.8 | 23.4 | 24.0 | 24.6 | 25.2 | 25.8 | 26.3 |
| 80–82 | 22.4 | 23.0 | 23.6 | 24.2 | 24.8 | 25.4 | 25.9 | 26.5 | 27.1 |
| 83–85 | 23.2 | 23.8 | 24.4 | 25.0 | 25.5 | 26.1 | 26.7 | 27.3 | 27.9 |
| 86–88 | 24.0 | 24.5 | 25.1 | 25.7 | 26.3 | 26.9 | 27.5 | 28.1 | 28.7 |
| 89–91 | 24.7 | 25.3 | 25.9 | 25.5 | 27.1 | 27.6 | 28.2 | 28.8 | 29.4 |
| 92–94 | 25.4 | 26.0 | 26.6 | 27.2 | 27.8 | 28.4 | 29.0 | 29.6 | 30.2 |
| 95–97 | 26.1 | 26.7 | 27.3 | 27.9 | 28.5 | 29.1 | 29.7 | 30.3 | 30.9 |
| 98–100 | 26.9 | 27.4 | 28.0 | 28.6 | 29.2 | 29.8 | 30.4 | 31.0 | 31.6 |
| 101–103 | 27.5 | 28.1 | 28.7 | 29.3 | 29.9 | 30.5 | 31.1 | 31.7 | 32.3 |
| 104–106 | 28.2 | 28.8 | 29.4 | 30.0 | 30.6 | 31.2 | 31.8 | 32.4 | 33.0 |
| 107–109 | 28.9 | 29.5 | 30.1 | 30.7 | 31.3 | 31.9 | 32.5 | 33.1 | 33.7 |
| 110–112 | 29.6 | 30.2 | 30.8 | 31.4 | 32.0 | 32.6 | 33.2 | 33.8 | 34.4 |
| 113–115 | 30.2 | 30.8 | 31.4 | 32.0 | 32.6 | 33.2 | 33.8 | 34.5 | 35.1 |
| 116–118 | 30.9 | 31.5 | 32.1 | 32.7 | 33.3 | 33.9 | 34.5 | 35.1 | 35.7 |
| 119–121 | 31.5 | 32.1 | 32.7 | 33.3 | 33.9 | 34.5 | 35.1 | 35.7 | 36.4 |
| 122–124 | 32.1 | 32.7 | 33.3 | 33.9 | 34.5 | 35.1 | 35.8 | 36.4 | 37.0 |
| 125–127 | 32.7 | 33.3 | 33.9 | 34.5 | 35.1 | 35.8 | 36.4 | 37.0 | 37.6 |

**Table 11.8** Estimates of Percentage of Fat for Women; Sum of Triceps, Suprailium, and Thigh Skinfolds

| Sum of Skinfolds (MM) | Age to the Last Year | | | | | | | | |
|---|---|---|---|---|---|---|---|---|---|
| | Under 22 | 23 to 27 | 28 to 32 | 33 to 37 | 38 to 42 | 43 to 47 | 48 to 52 | 53 to 57 | Over 58 |
| 23–25 | 9.7 | 9.9 | 10.2 | 10.4 | 10.7 | 10.9 | 11.2 | 11.4 | 11.7 |
| 26–28 | 11.0 | 11.2 | 11.5 | 11.7 | 12.0 | 12.3 | 12.5 | 12.7 | 13.0 |
| 29–31 | 12.3 | 12.5 | 12.8 | 13.0 | 13.3 | 13.5 | 13.8 | 14.0 | 14.3 |
| 32–34 | 13.6 | 13.8 | 14.0 | 14.3 | 14.5 | 14.8 | 15.0 | 15.3 | 15.5 |
| 35–37 | 14.8 | 15.0 | 15.3 | 15.5 | 15.8 | 16.0 | 16.3 | 16.5 | 16.8 |
| 38–40 | 16.0 | 16.3 | 16.5 | 16.7 | 17.0 | 17.2 | 17.5 | 17.7 | 18.0 |
| 41–43 | 17.2 | 17.4 | 17.7 | 17.9 | 18.2 | 18.4 | 18.7 | 18.9 | 19.2 |
| 44–46 | 18.3 | 18.6 | 18.8 | 19.1 | 19.3 | 19.6 | 19.8 | 20.1 | 20.3 |
| 47–49 | 19.5 | 19.7 | 20.0 | 20.2 | 20.5 | 20.7 | 21.0 | 21.2 | 21.5 |
| 50–52 | 20.6 | 20.8 | 21.2 | 21.3 | 21.6 | 21.8 | 22.1 | 22.3 | 22.6 |
| 53–55 | 21.7 | 21.9 | 22.1 | 22.4 | 22.6 | 22.9 | 23.1 | 23.4 | 23.6 |
| 56–58 | 22.7 | 23.0 | 23.2 | 23.4 | 23.7 | 23.9 | 24.2 | 24.4 | 24.7 |
| 59–61 | 23.7 | 24.0 | 24.2 | 24.5 | 24.7 | 25.0 | 25.2 | 25.5 | 25.7 |
| 62–64 | 24.7 | 25.0 | 25.2 | 25.5 | 25.7 | 26.0 | 26.7 | 26.4 | 26.7 |
| 65–67 | 25.7 | 25.9 | 26.2 | 26.4 | 26.7 | 26.9 | 27.2 | 27.4 | 27.7 |
| 68–70 | 26.6 | 26.9 | 27.1 | 27.4 | 27.6 | 27.9 | 28.1 | 28.4 | 28.6 |
| 71–73 | 27.5 | 27.8 | 28.0 | 28.3 | 28.5 | 28.8 | 28.0 | 29.3 | 29.5 |
| 74–76 | 28.4 | 28.7 | 28.9 | 29.2 | 29.4 | 29.7 | 29.9 | 30.2 | 30.4 |
| 77–79 | 29.3 | 29.5 | 29.8 | 30.0 | 30.3 | 30.5 | 30.8 | 31.0 | 31.3 |
| 80–82 | 30.1 | 30.4 | 30.6 | 30.9 | 31.1 | 31.4 | 31.6 | 31.9 | 32.1 |
| 83–85 | 30.9 | 31.2 | 31.4 | 31.7 | 31.9 | 32.2 | 32.4 | 32.7 | 32.9 |
| 86–88 | 31.7 | 32.0 | 32.2 | 32.5 | 32.7 | 32.9 | 33.2 | 33.4 | 33.7 |
| 89–91 | 32.5 | 32.7 | 33.0 | 33.2 | 33.5 | 33.7 | 33.9 | 34.2 | 34.4 |
| 92–94 | 33.2 | 33.4 | 33.7 | 33.9 | 34.2 | 34.4 | 34.7 | 34.9 | 35.2 |
| 95–97 | 33.9 | 34.1 | 34.4 | 34.6 | 34.9 | 35.1 | 35.4 | 35.6 | 35.0 |
| 98–100 | 34.6 | 34.8 | 35.1 | 35.3 | 35.5 | 35.8 | 36.0 | 36.3 | 36.5 |
| 101–103 | 35.3 | 35.4 | 35.7 | 35.9 | 36.2 | 36.4 | 36.7 | 36.9 | 37.2 |
| 104–106 | 35.8 | 36.1 | 36.3 | 36.6 | 36.8 | 37.1 | 37.3 | 37.5 | 37.8 |
| 107–109 | 36.4 | 36.7 | 36.9 | 37.1 | 37.4 | 37.6 | 37.9 | 38.1 | 38.4 |
| 110–112 | 37.0 | 37.2 | 37.5 | 37.7 | 38.0 | 38.2 | 38.5 | 38.7 | 38.9 |
| 113–115 | 37.5 | 37.8 | 38.0 | 38.2 | 38.5 | 38.7 | 39.0 | 39.2 | 39.5 |
| 116–118 | 38.0 | 38.3 | 38.5 | 38.8 | 39.0 | 39.3 | 39.5 | 39.7 | 40.0 |
| 119–121 | 38.5 | 38.7 | 39.0 | 39.2 | 39.5 | 39.7 | 40.0 | 40.2 | 40.5 |
| 122–124 | 39.0 | 39.2 | 39.4 | 39.7 | 39.9 | 40.2 | 40.4 | 40.7 | 40.9 |
| 125–127 | 39.4 | 39.6 | 39.9 | 40.1 | 40.4 | 40.6 | 40.9 | 41.1 | 41.4 |
| 128–130 | 39.8 | 40.0 | 40.3 | 40.5 | 40.8 | 41.0 | 41.3 | 41.5 | 41.8 |

To use Tables 11.7 and 11.8, first select the appropriate skinfold sites and measure them following the recommended measurement procedures. Using the sum of three skinfolds and age, find the percentage fat value from the appropriate table. For example, if the sum of the triceps, suprailium, and thigh skinfolds for a 21-year-old woman was 82 millimeters, her estimated percent fat would be 30.1.

The multiple correlations and standard errors of measurement for the generalized equations are well within the range reported for population-specific equations. These findings show that a generalized equation can be used to replace several different population-specific equations and are valid for adults varying greatly in age and body fatness. Still, an important caution should be raised when using the generalized equations. They were developed on men and women ranging from 18 to 61 years of age using the two-component model that does not consider body water and mineral content. These equations should not be applied to children and may lose accuracy with the elderly (Lohman 1992). Another concern should be raised with extremely obese individuals.

## Evaluating Body Composition of Adults

It is important to assess both body weight and percent body fat because they provide two related pieces of information about a person's body composition. Body weight is easy to measure, and once someone has an understanding of a desirable body weight for his or her frame, weight can be used to monitor changes in body composition. The shortcoming of using only body weight is that the fat-free weight component, frame size, and muscle development are not accurately considered. Two individuals of the same height, gender, and age may weigh the same but have different levels of fat-free mass and body fat.

***Percent Body Fat Standards.*** What is a desirable percent fat standard for adults? Being seriously overweight clearly increases one's risk of heart disease, hypertension, and diabetes, and results in a lower life expectancy. Still, too many Americans, especially young women, are overly concerned about being thin. Being underweight also can result in serious health problems. Athletes generally have a lower percent body fat than the total population. The percent body fat level depends on the athlete's gender and event performed. Highly trained endurance athletes (e.g., distance runners) will normally have very low levels of body fat. The average percent body fat of world-class distance runners is very low, averaging about 5% for men and ranging from 12% to 15% for women. This is an unrealistically low level for most who are not exercising to the level of these athletes. Most world-class runners run from 10 to 15 miles each day of the week. At this mileage, they consume over 1,000 kilocalories a day just from exercise.

Because of the errors associated with measuring body composition, it is not possible to define exact percent body fat standards. Lohman (1992) summarizes the problems of evaluating body composition of adults.

> In adults, with aging, the fat distribution may change. Now, we cannot easily sort out the influences of changes in fat distribution with changes in density of fat-free body associated with bone mineral loss on body fatness prediction with age. For example, using the Jackson-Pollock equations on 30- and 50-year-old females with the sum of three skinfolds (triceps, abdomen, suprailiac) equal to 60 mm, we obtain a percent fat of 25.7% for the 18- to 22-year-old and 27% for the 55-year old with the same skinfold. Is this change associated primarily with a change in fat distribution or with a change in

the density of the fat-free body? All the Durnin and Womersley (1974) equations, as well as the Jackson and Pollock equations (1978; 1980), are based on the two-component model and assume constant density of the fat-free body with aging. p. 45.

Table 11.9 gives standards for evaluating body composition of adults considering these limitations. These standards were developed from major published normative databases that consider both gender and age characteristics. The interpretation of the standards is furnished in Table 11.10. These standards not only consider the problems associated with obesity, but also the problem of being underweight. The relation between weight and all-cause mortality is "J"-shaped—the highest and lowest death rates are associated with not only being too heavy, but also being too light (Lew & Garfinkel 1979). This was shown in Chapter 1. It has also been shown that failing to gain weight is associated with a shorter life expectancy compared to individuals who are at the optimal weight range for their age, sex, and height (Paffenbarger et al. 1986).

It is likely that the "J"-shaped weight and mortality rates found in epidemiological studies can be traced to some extent to wasting diseases such as cancer, but there is morbidity associated with the diet restrictions and/or high levels of exercise. For example, **anorexia nervosa** is characterized by excessive diet and exercise resulting in extreme weight loss. This often is a problem of some young women and, for too many, it is a fatal disease.

***Defining Weight Reduction Goals.***   For many adults, their goal is weight reduction. If percent fat is known, an estimate of a realistic goal can be easily obtained. The weight loss goal is the estimated body weight for a desired percent body fat level. It is estimated from fat-free weight and desired percent fat level. The equation is

Weight Goal = Fat-Free Weight/[1 − (Desired %fat/100)].

The equation can be easily illustrated. Assume the body composition characteristics of a man were weight, 187 pounds and percent body fat, 26.3%. We must first calculate fat weight and fat-free weight.

Fat Weight = [187 × (26.3 × 100)] = 49.2 pounds.

Fat-Free Weight = 187 − 49.2 = 137.8 pounds.

The weight goals for 15% and 20% fat would be

Weight Goal (15%) = 137.8/[1 − (15/100)] = 162 pounds.

Weight Goal (20%) = 137.8/[1 − (20/100)] = 172 pounds.

The weight goal provides an estimate of what the person's weight would be if his/her fat-free weight component remained the same but the body fat changed to the desired goal. Sedentary adults who start an exercise program tend to increase muscle mass and lose fat weight. This results in a decrease in percent fat but sometimes without the projected weight loss. When a program uses only diet, both fat and fat-free weight are lost, often leaving percent fat relatively unchanged or even slightly increased, while total weight is reduced. It is important to monitor both body weight and percent fat during an adult weight-reduction program to be sure that the participant's body composition is being altered in the desired direction.

**Table 11.9** Standards for Evaluating Body Composition of Adults

| Body Composition Standard | Age Group In Years | | | |
| | Under 30 | 30–39 | 40–49 | Over 49 |
|---|---|---|---|---|
| **Men** | | | | |
| *High* | >28% | >29% | >30% | >31% |
| *Moderately high* | 22–28 | 23–29 | 24–30 | 25–31 |
| *Optimal range* | 11–21 | 12–22 | 13–23 | 14–24 |
| *Low* | 6–10 | 7–11 | 8–12 | 9–13 |
| *Very low* | ≤5% | ≤6% | ≤7% | ≤8% |
| **Women** | | | | |
| *High* | >32% | >33% | >34% | >35% |
| *Moderately high* | 26–32 | 27–33 | 28–34 | 29–35 |
| *Optimal range* | 15–25 | 16–26 | 17–27 | 18–28 |
| *Low* | 12–14 | 13–15 | 14–16 | 15–17 |
| *Very low* | ≤11% | ≤12% | ≤13% | ≤14% |

**Table 11.10** Standards for the Interpretation of Adults' Percent Fat Standards

| | |
|---|---|
| **High** | Percent fat at this level indicates the person is seriously overweight to a degree that this can have adverse health consequences. The person should be encouraged to lose weight through diet and exercise. Maintaining weight at this level for a long period of time places the person at risk of hypertension, heart disease, and diabetes. A long-term weight loss and exercise program should be initiated. |
| **Moderately High** | It is likely that the person is significantly overweight, but it could be high due in part to measurement inaccuracies. It would be wise to carefully monitor people in this category and encourage them not to gain additional weight. People in this category may want to have their body composition assessed by the underwater weighing method. |
| **Optimal Range** | It would be highly desirable to maintain body composition at this level. |
| **Low** | This is an acceptable body composition level, but there is no reason to seek a lower percent body fat level. Loss of additional body weight could have health consequences. |
| **Very Low** | Percent fat level at this range should only be reached by high-level endurance athletes who are in training. Being this thin may carry its own additional mortality. Individuals, especially females, this low are at risk of having an eating disorder such as anorexia nervosa. |

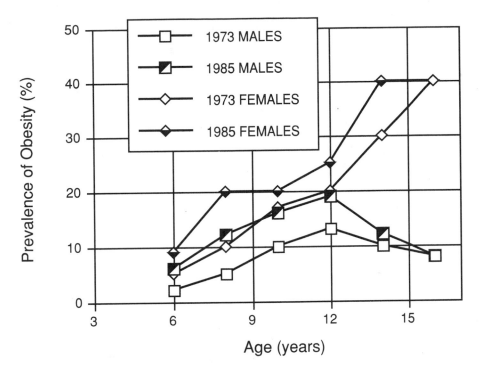

**Figure 11.14**
Prevalence of obesity based on 25% fat for males and 31% fat for females in 1973 (NHES 1973) and 1985 (NCYFS 1985). Graph developed from published data. (Lohman 1992.)

Defining weight goals from fat-free weight of children and youth is not appropriate. During these developing years, total body water and bone mineral content—components of fat-free weight—are not stable, introducing additional sources of inaccuracy.

Data provided in Figure 11.14 graphically shows that the body composition of American youth is changing in an unfavorable direction; children are fatter than they were 20 years ago. The changing activity pattern and nutrition of today's youth is likely responsible, and this is a concern of public health officials. As documented in Chapter 1, a reduction in the prevalence of overweight children is an objective of the *Healthy People 2000* program (U.S. Public Health Service 1990). Body composition tests are included in health-related youth fitness tests provided in Chapter 9.

Several investigators (Table 11.11) have used the two-component model to estimate body density of children from anthropometric variables. Children vary considerably in growth and developmental characteristics during their school years. In comparison to adults, children have a higher water and lower bone mineral content, and these values change during their developmental years. Figure 11.15 shows this age-dependent decrease in body water for boys and girls. Chemical maturity is not reached until late adolescence. Due to chemical immaturity, the two-component model over-estimates the percent body fat of children (Lohman 1992).

Many laboratories have the capacity to conduct underwater weighing studies, but very few have the capacity to measure body water and mineral content. Lohman (1992) developed skinfold equations based on the multicomponent

**Skinfold Assessments of Percent Fat of Children and Youth**

**Table 11.11** Means and Standard Deviations of Hydrostatically Determined Body Density and Concurrent Validity of Regression Equations for Youth

| Source | Sample Age | n | Body Density MEAN | SD | Regression Analysis R | SE |
|---|---|---|---|---|---|---|
| **Males** | | | | | | |
| *Cureton et al. (1975)* | 8–11 | 49 | 1.053 | .013 | .77 | .008 |
| *Durnin and Rahaman (1967)* | 12–15 | 48 | 1.063 | .012 | .76 | .008 |
| *Harsha et al. (1978)* | 6–16 | 79 | 1.046 | .018 | .84 | .010 |
| | 6–16 | 49 | 1.055 | .020 | .90 | .009 |
| *Parizkova (1961)* | 9–12 | 57 | * | * | .92 | .011 |
| **Females** | | | | | | |
| *Durnin and Rahaman (1967)* | 13–16 | 38 | 1.045 | .011 | .78 | .008 |
| *Harsha et al. (1978)* | 6–16 | 52 | 1.033 | .016 | .85 | .008 |
| | 6–16 | 39 | 1.041 | .019 | .90 | .008 |
| *Parizkova (1961)* | 9–12 | 56 | * | * | .81 | .012 |
| | 13–16 | 62 | * | * | .82 | .013 |

**Figure 11.15**
The percentage of body water content of fat-free weight of children declines with age. Not correcting for these differences in body water results in an overestimate of a child's true percent body fat. Graph made from published data. (Lohman 1992.)

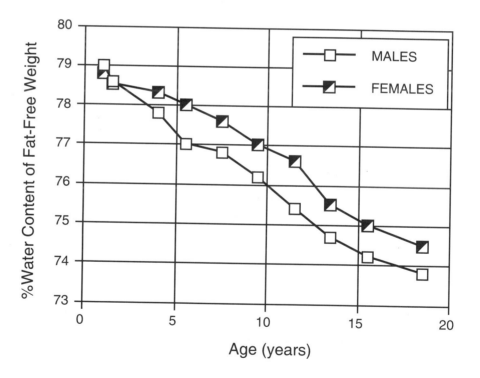

## Table 11.12 Skinfold Prediction Equations for Estimating Percent Fat in Children and Youth Considering Maturation Level, Ethnicity, and Gender

| Gender | Maturation Level | Racial Group | Equation |
|---|---|---|---|
| Σ *Triceps and Calf Skinfolds (SEE 3.8%fat)* | | | |
| Males | All | All | %fat = 0.735(ΣT&C) + 1.0 |
| Females | All | All | %fat = 0.610(ΣT&C) + 5.0 |
| Σ *Triceps and Subscapula Skinfolds (< 35 mm) (SEE 3.6% to 3.9%fat)* | | | |
| Females | All | Black | $\%fat = 1.33(\Sigma T\&S) - 0.013(\Sigma T\&S)^2 - 2.0$ |
| Females | All | White | $\%fat = 1.33(\Sigma T\&S) - 0.013(\Sigma T\&S)^2 - 3.0$ |
| Males | Prepubescent | Black | $\%fat = 1.21(\Sigma T\&S) - 0.008(\Sigma T\&S)^2 - 3.5$ |
| Males | Prepubescent | White | $\%fat = 1.21(\Sigma T\&S) - 0.008(\Sigma T\&S)^2 - 1.7$ |
| Males | Pubescent | Black | $\%fat = 1.21(\Sigma T\&S) - 0.008(\Sigma T\&S)^2 - 5.2$ |
| Males | Pubescent | White | $\%fat = 1.21(\Sigma T\&S) - 0.008(\Sigma T\&S)^2 - 3.4$ |
| Males | Postpubescent | Black | $\%fat = 1.21(\Sigma T\&S) - 0.008(\Sigma T\&S)^2 - 6.8$ |
| Males | Postpubescent | White | $\%fat = 1.21(\Sigma T\&S) - 0.008(\Sigma T\&S)^2 - 5.5$ |
| Σ *Triceps and Subscapula Skinfolds (> 35 mm)(SEE 3.6% to 3.9%fat)* | | | |
| Females | All | All | %fat = 0.546(ΣT&S) – 9.7 |
| Males | Prepubescent | Black | %fat = 0.783(ΣT&S) – 3.5 |
| Males | Prepubescent | White | %fat = 0.783(ΣT&S) – 1.7 |
| Males | Pubescent | Black | %fat = 0.783(ΣT&S) – 5.2 |
| Males | Pubescent | White | %fat = 0.783(ΣT&S) – 3.4 |
| Males | Postpubescent | Black | %fat = 0.783(ΣT&S) – 6.8 |
| Males | Postpubescent | White | %fat = 0.783(ΣT&S) – 5.5 |

model. Table 11.12 gives these equations. These equations use the sum of two different skinfold combinations: (1) sum of triceps and calf skinfolds and (2) sum of triceps and subscapula skinfolds. The gender specific triceps and calf skinfold equations can be used with children and youth of any age or ethnicity. The intercepts of the sum of triceps and subscapula skinfolds equations are adjusted to account for developmental and racial differences.

Tables 11.13 and 11.14 give the estimated percent fat values for the sum of triceps and calf skinfold for boys and girls. The table also includes standards for evaluating body composition of children. These standards are recommended by Lohman (1992) and are consistent with the adult standards previously presented.

## Bioelectrical Impedance Method

A somewhat new technique for measuring body composition is **bioelectrical impedance analysis (BIA).** It is based on the principle that the electrical resistance of the body to a mild electric current is related to total body water. Total body water and fat-free weight are highly related. The BIA method is simple and requires only the placement of four electrodes, two on the subject's ankle and two on the wrist. A current is transmitted into the subject, and the resistance in ohms is read directly into a microcomputer that calculates body composition.

**Table 11.13** Sum of Triceps and Calf Skinfolds, Estimated Percent Body Fat, and Standard for Evaluating Body Composition of Boys

| Σ Triceps & Calf | %Fat | Standard | Σ Triceps & Calf | %Fat | Standard |
|---|---|---|---|---|---|
| 4 | 3.9 | | 33 | 25.3 | **High** |
| 5 | 4.7 | **Very Low** | 34 | 26.0 | |
| | | | 35 | 26.7 | |
| 6 | 5.4 | **Low** | 36 | 27.5 | |
| 7 | 6.1 | | 37 | 28.2 | |
| 8 | 6.9 | | 38 | 28.9 | |
| 9 | 7.6 | | 39 | 29.7 | |
| 10 | 8.4 | **Low** | 40 | 30.4 | **High** |
| 11 | 9.1 | **Optimal** | 41 | 31.1 | **Very High** |
| 12 | 9.8 | | 42 | 31.9 | |
| 13 | 10.6 | | 43 | 32.6 | |
| 14 | 11.3 | | 44 | 33.3 | |
| 15 | 12.0 | | 45 | 34.1 | |
| 16 | 12.8 | | 46 | 34.8 | |
| 17 | 13.5 | | 47 | 35.5 | |
| 18 | 14.2 | | 48 | 36.3 | |
| 19 | 15.0 | | 49 | 37.0 | |
| 20 | 15.7 | | 50 | 37.8 | |
| 21 | 16.4 | | 51 | 38.5 | |
| 22 | 17.2 | | 52 | 39.2 | |
| 23 | 17.9 | | 53 | 40.0 | |
| 24 | 18.6 | | 54 | 40.7 | |
| 25 | 19.4 | **Optimal** | 55 | 41.4 | |
| | | | 56 | 42.2 | |
| 26 | 20.1 | **Moderately High** | 57 | 42.9 | |
| 27 | 20.8 | | 58 | 43.6 | |
| 28 | 21.6 | | 59 | 44.4 | |
| 29 | 22.3 | | 60 | 45.1 | |
| 30 | 23.1 | | | | |
| 31 | 23.8 | | | | |
| 32 | 24.5 | **Moderately High** | | | |

In the early stages of BIA technology, the accuracy of BIA was a major concern. One study showed that this method was no more accurate than the height and weight ratio body mass index (Jackson et al. 1988). Recent research (Lohman 1992) showed that with suitable equations, BIA estimates of percent body fat enjoy accuracy similar to skinfold estimates, except for the obese and very lean. Equations developed on the general population tend to underestimate percent body fat of the obese and overestimate the percent body fat of very lean subjects showing that more research is needed to develop generalized BIA equations.

**Table 11.14** Sum of Triceps and Calf Skinfolds, Estimated Percent Body Fat, and Standard for Evaluating Body Composition of Girls

| Σ Triceps & Calf | %Fat | Standard | Σ Triceps & Calf | %Fat | Standard |
|---|---|---|---|---|---|
| 4 | 7.4 | **Very Low** | 33 | 25.1 | **Moderately High** |
| 5 | 8.1 | | 34 | 25.7 | |
| 6 | 8.7 | | 35 | 26.4 | |
| 7 | 9.3 | | 36 | 27.0 | |
| 8 | 9.9 | | 37 | 27.6 | |
| 9 | 10.5 | | 38 | 28.2 | |
| 10 | 11.1 | | 39 | 28.8 | |
| 11 | 11.7 | **Very Low** | 40 | 29.4 | **Moderately High** |
| 12 | 12.3 | **Low** | 41 | 30.0 | **High** |
| 13 | 12.9 | | 42 | 30.6 | |
| 14 | 13.5 | | 43 | 31.2 | |
| 15 | 14.2 | | 44 | 31.8 | |
| 16 | 14.8 | **Low** | 45 | 32.5 | |
| | | | 46 | 33.1 | |
| 17 | 15.4 | **Optimal** | 47 | 33.7 | |
| 18 | 16.0 | | 48 | 34.3 | |
| 19 | 16.6 | | 49 | 34.9 | |
| 20 | 17.2 | | 50 | 35.5 | **High** |
| 21 | 17.8 | | | | |
| 22 | 18.4 | | 51 | 36.1 | **Very High** |
| 23 | 19.0 | | 52 | 36.7 | |
| 24 | 19.6 | | 53 | 37.3 | |
| 25 | 20.2 | | 54 | 37.9 | |
| 26 | 20.9 | | 55 | 38.5 | |
| 27 | 21.5 | | 56 | 39.2 | |
| 28 | 22.1 | | 57 | 39.8 | |
| 29 | 22.7 | | 58 | 40.4 | |
| 30 | 23.3 | | 59 | 41.0 | |
| 31 | 23.9 | | 60 | 41.6 | |
| 32 | 24.5 | **Optimal** | | | |

Table 11.15 provides an evaluation and comparison of the methods available to assess body composition. If accuracy is a major concern, the underwater weighing method with measured residual lung volume is the method of choice. The disadvantage of this method is that it is expensive and requires specialized equipment and trained testers. In addition, many do not enjoy the underwater weighing experience, and it is impossible to measure underwater weight accurately if the subject has a fear of water and cannot sit still fully submerged after an expiration. Using predicted residual lung volume rather than measuring it makes the underwater weighing method less accurate. The standard error increases from 1% to 3.5% body fat. With increased interest in assessing the body composition of children and elderly, more researchers will move to the multicomponent model.

**Comparison of Body Composition Methods**

**Table 11.15** Comparison of Methods Available to Evaluate Body Composition of Humans.

| Method | Strengths | Limitations | Accuracy—%Fat |
|---|---|---|---|
| Multicomponent | Most Accurate; Can be used for all age groups | Need expensive equipment; Very few labs have the capacity to measure body water and mineral content; Must measure residual lung volume | 1%fat, >3% if residual volume is not measured |
| Two component (Siri & Bro̊zek %fat equations) | Accurate with mature adults; Many labs have the capacity | Need expensive equipment; Cannot be used with children and elderly; Must measure residual lung volume | 1%fat, >3% if residual volume is not measured |
| **Skinfolds** Generalized equations | Inexpensive; Feasible for mass testing; Appropriate for most adults (ages 20–50) | Tester errors measuring skinfolds; Does not measure essential fat; Developed with two-component model | 3.5%–4.0%fat |
| Population-specific equations | Inexpensive; Feasible for mass testing | Tester errors measuring skinfolds; Does not measure essential fat; Developed with two-component model; Suitable for limited populations (e.g., young adult males) | 3.5%–4.0%fat for the limited population |
| Lohman's children's equations | Inexpensive; Feasible for mass testing; Based on multicomponent model | Tester errors measuring skinfolds; Does not measure essential fat | 3.6%–3.9%fat |
| Bioelectric impedance | Feasible for mass testing; Just need to attach four electrodes; Potential method of measuring body water | Validated on two-component model; Standard equations are not readily available; Lack accuracy with very lean and obese; Expensive equipment; Tester errors | 3.5%–4.5%fat |
| Body circumferences | Very inexpensive; Feasible for mass testing | Tester errors measuring circumferences; Does not measure essential fat; Developed on two-component model; Not very popular | 3.7%–4.5%fat |
| Body Mass Index (BMI) | Most feasible for mass testing (just need height and weight); Large normative databases available; Overweight standards are defined | Does not differentiate between fat and fat-free weight; Does not estimate %fat; Least accurate | ≥4.5%fat |

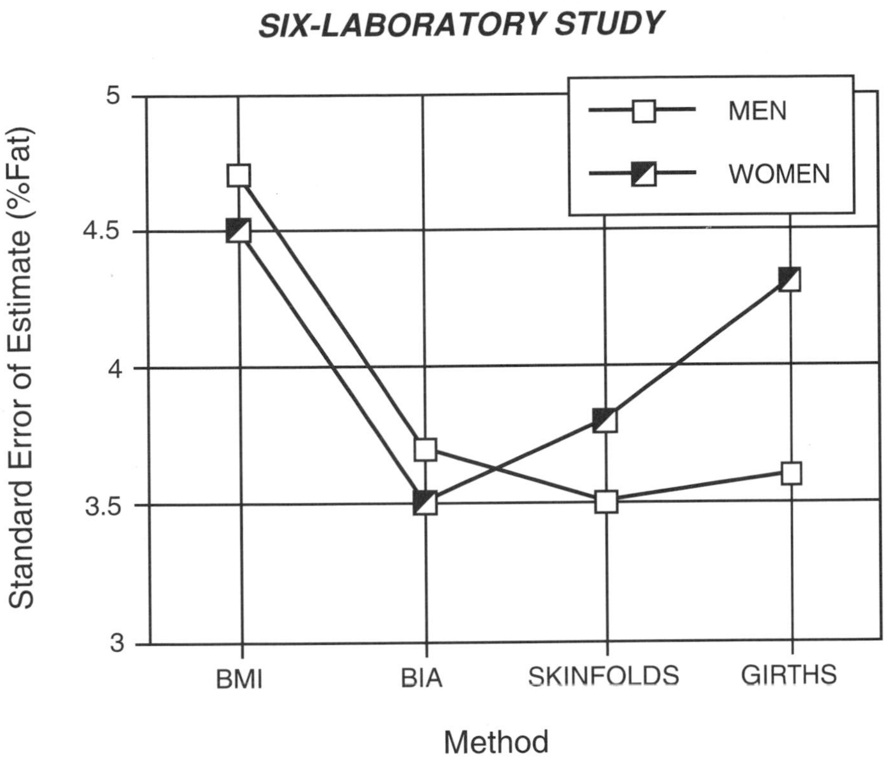

**SIX-LABORATORY STUDY**

**Figure 11.16**
The standard errors of estimate of hydrostatically determined percent body fat. Graph developed from data of the six-laboratories study. (Lohman 1992.)

In field setting, the most realistic options are skinfold, circumference, and BIA equations. Figure 11.16 shows a comparison of the accuracy of the BMI, skinfold, BIA, and body circumference methods of estimating hydrostatically measured percent body fat (Lohman 1992). Skinfold, BIA, and circumference estimates exhibited similar accuracy, with the exception that circumferences for women were less accurate. While the BMI method is the most practical method, it is the least accurate for evaluating the body composition of an individual. Body mass index is most suitable for population studies where the primary concern is to quantify the prevalence of overweight in a defined population.

A common problem associated with skinfold measurements is the measurement error among testers. With properly trained testers, percent body fat estimated from skinfolds can be reliably measured. Using three testers who varied in experience, but practiced together, the reliability was found to exceed 0.99 for the sum of seven and three skinfolds. The standard error of measurement was about 1.0 percent body fat (Jackson, Pollock & Gettman 1978). In a more comprehensive study (Jackson et al. 1978), both day-to-day and tester-to-tester measurement error of the skinfold, BIA, and hydrostatic estimates of percent body fat were examined. Table 11.16 lists these results. All reliability estimates were high, with standard errors of measurement about 1.0 percent body fat.

**Table 11.16** Reliability Estimates and Standard Errors of Measurement (%Fat) For Hydrostatically Determined Percent Body Fat, and Estimated Percent Body Fat from the Sum of Skinfolds, and Bioelectric Impedance (Jackson et al. 1988)

| Percent Fat | Males (n = 24) | | Females (n = 44) | |
| --- | --- | --- | --- | --- |
| | $R_{xx}$ | SEM | $R_{xx}$ | SEM |
| *Measured* | .97 | 1.1 | .97 | 1.2 |
| *Skinfold Estimated* | .98 | 1.0 | .99 | 0.9 |
| *BIA Estimated* | .96 | 1.4 | .97 | 1.5 |

The skinfold method is likely the most feasible option for general use and offers several advantages over the other field methods.

1. *Accuracy and reproducibility.* When testers are properly trained, it is reliable, and results are reproducible from day to day and tester to tester (see Table 11.16).

2. *Simplicity and cost.* The skinfold method is simple to perform, not embarrassing, easy to teach to others, and the equipment required is not expensive. While the BIA method may have similar accuracy, the equipment is much more expensive. The BMI method is most practical but less accurate.

3. *Fat deposits.* Recent work (Larsson et al. 1984) suggests that not only is total body fat related to health, but the location of the deposits is also important. Fat around the abdomen seems to be a greater risk factor to longevity than total body fat. Only anthropometric data can evaluate fat deposition.

4. *Education.* Individuals can gain a better understanding of the concept of excess body fat by actually measuring body fat. They may then use subjective assessments such as "pinch an inch" to gauge their progress.

5. *Measuring fat.* Gaining body fat results in the accumulation of subcutaneous fat, which is the fat that can be pinched. Thus, even if there is an error in estimating percent body fat, a reduction in the sum of skinfolds means a reduction in fat.

## Computer Calculations

This section provides equations for estimating percent fat from skinfolds for children and adults and computing a weight goal for a desired percent body fat level. The weight goal method is only suitable for adults. These equations were written to be compatible for use with database and spreadsheet microcomputer programs. They were used and checked for accuracy on a microcomputer database program. You will need to examine your program documentation to make the equations compatible with the program you have. Remember, the microcomputer mathematical operands are addition +; subtraction −; multiplication *; and division /.

The only values needed to estimate the percent fat of children are triceps and calf skinfolds. Separate equations are needed for boys and girls. The equations are

**Boys**

%FAT = (0.735*SUM) + 1.0

**Girls**

%FAT = (0.610*SUM) + 5.0

**CALCULATION EXAMPLE—BOYS**

|       | TRICEPS | CALF | SUM | %FAT |
|-------|---------|------|-----|------|
| JIMMY | 4       | 3    | 7   | 6.1  |
| TOMMY | 10      | 11   | 21  | 16.4 |
| TONY  | 15      | 11   | 26  | 20.1 |
| CHRIS | 20      | 14   | 34  | 26.0 |

**CALCULATION EXAMPLE—GIRLS**

|       | TRICEPS | CALF | SUM | %FAT |
|-------|---------|------|-----|------|
| MARY  | 4       | 3    | 7   | 9.3  |
| JUDY  | 10      | 11   | 21  | 17.8 |
| DEBRA | 15      | 11   | 26  | 20.9 |
| SUE   | 25      | 20   | 45  | 32.5 |

The generalized equations for adults use age in combination with the sum of seven skinfolds or the sum of three skinfolds. The sum of three for males includes chest, abdomen, and thigh skinfolds. The sum of three for women includes triceps, suprailium, and thigh skinfolds. The Siri equation was used to convert body density to percent fat. The equations are

**Men**

$BD(\Sigma7) = 1.11200000 - (.00043499*\Sigma7) + (.00000055*(\Sigma7*\Sigma7)) - (.00028826*AGE)$

$BD(\Sigma3) = 1.10938000 - (.0008267*\Sigma3) + (.00000016(*\Sigma3*\Sigma3)) - (.0002574*AGE).$

**Women**

$BD = 1.0970 - (.0004697*\Sigma7) + (.00000056*(\Sigma7*\Sigma7)) - (.00012828*AGE)$

$BD = 1.099421 - (.0009929*\Sigma3) + (.00000023*(\Sigma3*\Sigma3)) - (.0001392*AGE)$

$SIRI\ \%FAT = ((495/BD) - 450)$

## CALCULATION EXAMPLE—MEN

| SUBJECT | Σ7 | Σ3 | AGE | Σ7−BD | Σ3−BD | Σ7−%FAT | Σ3−FAT |
|---------|-----|-----|-----|---------|---------|---------|--------|
| JOHN | 85 | 42 | 25 | 1.07179 | 1.06851 | 11.8 | 13.3 |
| MIKE | 95 | 46 | 30 | 1.06699 | 1.06397 | 13.9 | 15.2 |
| TOM | 150 | 65 | 35 | 1.04904 | 1.04731 | 21.9 | 22.6 |
| PAUL | 191 | 78 | 42 | 1.03687 | 1.03506 | 27.4 | 28.2 |

## CALCULATION EXAMPLE—WOMEN

| SUBJECT | Σ7 | Σ3 | AGE | Σ7−BD | Σ3−BD | Σ7−%FAT | Σ3−FAT |
|---------|-----|------|-----|---------|---------|---------|--------|
| JANE | 85 | 42.0 | 25 | 1.05791 | 1.05464 | 17.9 | 19.4 |
| JUDY | 95 | 46.0 | 30 | 1.05358 | 1.05006 | 19.8 | 21.4 |
| KIM | 134 | 56.0 | 35 | 1.03963 | 1.03967 | 26.1 | 26.1 |
| DINA | 149 | 62.0 | 42 | 1.03406 | 1.03290 | 28.7 | 29.2 |

## Computing Weight Goal

The weight goal is a method of computing the person's weight for a desired percent fat level. This should only be used with adults. You must know the person's current percent body fat (%FAT) and body weight (WT). From this information, fat-free weight (FFWT) is computed and used to compute what the person's body weight would be for a desired percent body fat level (D−%FAT). The equations are

```
FFWT = WT − (WT* (%FAT/100))
GOAL = FFWT / (1 −(D−%FAT/100)).
```

## CALCULATION EXAMPLE—WEIGHT GOAL

| SUBJECT | WT | %FAT | D−%FAT | FFWT | GOAL |
|---------|-----|------|--------|---------|---------|
| JIM | 278 | 38.2 | 20 | 171.804 | 214.755 |
| JANE | 165 | 34.2 | 25 | 108.570 | 144.760 |
| BOB | 176 | 22.5 | 20 | 136.400 | 170.500 |
| MARY | 132 | 26.7 | 22 | 96.756 | 124.046 |

## Summary

Overweight is the excessive body weight for an individual's height while obesity is the excessive accumulation of body fat. Both have a negative influence on health. The limitation of body mass index (BMI) is that it does not differentiate between fat and fat-free weight. Body density is the ratio of body volume and dry land weight. The most valid method of measuring body density is by underwater weighing. Once density is known, standard equations are available to convert body density to percent body fat. These calculations are based on the assumption that the density of fat weight is 0.90 g/cc and lean weight is 1.10 g/cc. These density constants may vary somewhat among individuals, which introduces biological errors in calculating percent body fat, especially for children and the elderly. The multicomponent model that uses body water and mineral content corrects for these biological errors. The major source of measurement error of the underwater weighing method is the failure to measure residual lung volume. The most common field methods are skinfolds, bioelectrical impedance analysis (BIA), circumferences, and BMI. These methods are less accurate but more realistic for mass testing. Skinfolds are likely the most common field method used to estimate percent body fat, but with the development of more generalized equations, the BIA methods will become an attractive alternative. Body mass index is suitable for defining overweight in populations of individuals but lacks the accuracy to assess an individual's body composition.

**Formative Evaluation of Objectives**

*Objective 1*  Identify the methods used to measure body composition of youth and adults.

1. Outline the steps you would follow to measure percent body fat by the hydrostatic weighing method.
2. Outline the steps you would follow to measure percent body fat using the generalized skinfold equations.
3. Are the generalized skinfold equations suitable for children?
4. How do you estimate the percent body fat of children?

*Objective 2*  Identify the limitations of the two-component percent body fat model when applied to children and elderly.

1. What is the limitation of the two-component percent body fat model?
2. How does the multicomponent model adjust for the limitation?

*Objective 3*  Calculate percent body fat of youth and adults from skinfold equations.

1. A 42-year-old woman has a sum of seven skinfolds of 130 mm. What is her body density and percent body fat? What would these values be if she had a sum of three skinfolds of 64 mm?
2. A 38-year-old man had the following skinfold values: sum of seven of 142 mm and sum of three of 65 mm. What would be his estimated body density and percent body fat?
3. What is the percent body fat for a 15-year-old boy with a sum of calf and triceps skinfolds of 25?
4. Evaluate the body composition of a 12-year-old girl with a sum of calf and triceps skinfolds of 32.

*Objective 4*  Be able to evaluate body composition of youths and adults.

1. What is the percent fat level used to define level of obesity in children?
2. Why are adult body composition standards adjusted for age?
3. Is there a danger in having percent body fat too low?

*Objective 5*  Calculate weight goals for selected levels of desired percent body fat.

1. Assume a 165-pound woman's percent body fat is 35%. What would her weight be if she was 23%? How about 28%?

2. Assume a football player's body weight is 245 pounds and his measured percent body fat is 23%. If a coach would like the player's body composition to be between 10% and 15%, what would his weight range be?

*Objective 6*  Evaluate the accuracy of the various methods used to measure body composition.

1. What is the major source of measurement error for measuring percent body fat by the hydrostatic weighing method?

2. The standard error of prediction for estimating percent body fat from skinfolds ranges from about 3.5 to 4.0% body fat. What does this mean?

3. What is the limitation of using BMI to evaluate percent fat?

## Additional Learning Activities

1. Measure the skinfold thickness on several individuals. The secret to obtaining accurate percent body fat estimates from the generalized skinfold equations is to measure skinfold thickness correctly. Work with a partner and compare your results. Follow the instructions and pictures provided in this chapter.

2. Have your body composition determined by the underwater weighing method. This is the most valid method of measuring body composition. Be certain they measure your residual lung volume.

3. Many commercial fitness centers use electronic machines to estimate percent body fat of its members; a common method is the BIA method. Go to a center to have your body composition measured, and if you have had it done by the hydrostatic method, compare the results. Ask the person taking the measurements to explain to you how the machine works and how accurate the equations are.

4. If you have a microcomputer and the software, use a database program and develop a system for calculating percent body fat for the generalized equations. You will be surprised how easy and powerful database programs are. Examples are provided in the Computer Calculations section.

## Bibliography

Behnke, A. R. and J. H. Wilmore. 1974. *Evaluation and regulation of body build and composition.* Englewood Cliffs, NJ: Prentice-Hall.

Boileau, R. A., T. G. Lohman, and M. H. Slaughter. 1985. Exercise and body composition in children and youth. *Scandinavian Journal of Sport Sciences 7:*17–27.

Brŏzek, J. and A. Keys. 1951. The evaluation of leanness-fatness in man: Norms and intercorrelations. *British Journal of Nutrition 5:*194–206.

Brŏzek, J., F. Grande, and J. T. Anderson. 1963. Densitometric analysis of body composition: Revision of some quantitive assumptions. *Annals of New York Academy of Science 110:*113–140.

Cureton, K. J. 1984. A reaction to the manuscript by Jackson. *Medicine and Science in Sport and Exercise 16:*621–622.

Cureton, K. J., R. A. Boileau, and T. G. Lohman. 1975. A comparison of densitometric, Potassium-40, and skinfold estimates of body composition in prepubescent boys. *Human Biology 47:*321–336.

Durnin, J. V. G. A. and R. Passmore. 1967. *Energy, Work and Leisure.* London: Heinemann Educational Books, LTD.

Durnin, J. V. G. A. and J. Wormsley. 1974. Body fat assessed from total body density and its estimation from skinfold thickness: Measurements on 481 men and women aged from 16 to 72 years. *British Journal of Nutrition 32:*77–92.

Forsyth, H. L. and W. E. Sinning. 1973. The anthropometric estimation of body density and lean body weight of male athletes. *Medicine and Science in Sports 5:*174–180.

Golding, L. A., C. R. Meyers, and W. E. Sinning. 1989. *The Y's Way to Physical Fitness.* (3d ed.,) Chicago: National Board of YMCA.

Haisman, M. F. 1970. The assessment of body fat content in young men from measurements of body density and skinfold thickness. *Human Biology 42:*679–688.

Harsha, D. W., R. R. Fredrichs, and G. S. Berenson. 1978. Densitometry and anthropometry of black and white children. *Human Biology 50:*261–280.

Hodgdon, J. A. and M. B. Beckett. 1984a. *Prediction of percent body fat for U.S. Navy men from body circumferences and height.* Report No. 84–11, Naval Health Research Center, San Diego, CA.

Hodgdon, J. A. and M. B. Beckett. 1984b. *Prediction of percent body fat for U.S. Navy women from body circumferences and height.* Report No. 84–29, Naval Health Research Center, San Diego, CA.

Hodgdon, J. A. and M. B. Beckett. 1984c. *Technique for measuring body circumferences and skinfold thickness.* Report No. 84–39, Naval Health Research Center, San Diego, CA.

Jackson, A. S. 1984. Research progress in research design and analysis of data procedures for predicting body density. *Medicine and Science in Sports and Exercise 16:*616–620.

Jackson, A. S. and M. L. Pollock. 1978. Generalized equations for predicting body density of men. *British Journal of Nutrition 40:*497–504.

Jackson, A. S., M. L. Pollock, and L. R. Gettman. 1978. Intertester reliability of selected skinfold and circumference measurements and percent fat estimates. *Research Quarterly 49:*546–551.

Jackson, A. S., M. L. Pollock, and A. Ward. 1980. Generalized equations for predicting body density of women. *Medicine and Science in Sports and Exercise 12:*175–182.

Jackson, A. S., et al. 1988. Reliability and validity of bioelectrical impedance in determining body composition. *Journal of Applied Physiology 64:*529–534.

Katch, F. I. and W. D. McArdle. 1973. Prediction of body density from simple anthropometric measurements in college age women and men. *Human Biology 45:*445–454.

Katch, F. I. and E. D. Michael. 1968. Prediction of body density from skinfold and girth measurements of college females. *Journal of Applied Physiology 25:*92–94.

Katch, F. I. and E. D. Michael. 1969. Densitometric validation of six skinfold formulas to predict body density and percent fat of 17-year-old boys. *Research Quarterly 40:*712–716.

Larsson, B. et al. 1984. Abdominal adipose tissue distribution, obesity, and risk of cardiovascular disease and death: 13-year follow-up of participants in the study of men born in 1913. *British Medical Journal 288:*1401–1404.

Lew, E. A. and L. Garfinkel. 1979. Variations in mortality by weight among 750,000 men and women. *Journal of Chronic Diseases 32:*181–225.

Lohman, T. G. 1981. Skinfolds and body density and their relation to body fatness: A review. *Human Biology 53:*181–225.

Lohman, T. G. 1982. Body composition methodology in sport medicine. *Physician and Sports Medicine 10:*46–58.

Lohman, T. G. 1986. Application of body composition techniques and constants for children and youth. *Exercise and Sport Sciences Review 14:*325–357.

Lohman, T. G. 1992. *Advances in body composition assessment.* Champaign, IL: Human Kinetics Publishers.

Lohman, T. G. et al. 1984. Bone mineral measurements and their relation to body density relationship in children, youth and adults. *Human Biology 56:*667–679.

NCYFS. 1985. *Summary of findings from National Children and Youth Fitness Study.* Washington, DC: Department of Health and Human Services.

NHES. 1973. *Sample Design and Estimation Procedures for a National Health Examination Survey of Children* (National Center for Health Statistics Publication No. HRA 74–1005). Rockville, MD: Health Resources Administration.

Paffenbarger, R. J. et al. 1986. Physical activity, all cause mortality, and longevity of college alumni. *New England Journal of Medicine 314:*605–613.

Parizkova, J. 1961. Total body fat and skinfold thickness in children. *Metabolism 10:*794–807.

Pascale, L. et al. 1956. Correlations between thickness of skinfolds and body density in 88 soldiers. *Human Biology 28:*165–176.

Pollock, M. L. 1975. Prediction of body density in young and middle-aged women. *Journal of Applied Physiology 38:*745–749.

Pollock, M. L., T. Hickman, and Z. Kendrick. 1976. Prediction of body density in young and middle-aged men. *Journal of Applied Physiology 40:*300–304.

Ross, R. M. and A. S. Jackson. 1986. Development and validation of total work equations for estimating the energy cost of walking. *Journal of Cardiopulmonary Rehabilitation 6:*182–192.

Ross, R. M. and A. S. Jackson. 1990. *Exercise concepts, calculations, and computer applications.* Carmel, IN: Benchmark Press.

Sinning, W. E. 1978. Anthropometric estimation of body density, fat, and lean body weight in women gymnasts. *Medicine and Science in Sports 10:*234–249.

Siri, W. E. 1961. Body composition from fluid space and density. In *Techniques for Measuring Body Composition.* J. Brŏzek and A. Hanschel (Eds.) Washington, DC: National Academy of Science.

Slaughter, M. H. et al. 1988. Skinfold equations for estimating of body fatness in children and youth. *Human Biology 60:*709–723.

Sloan, A. W., J. J. Burt, and C. S. Blyth. 1962. Estimation of body fat in young women. *Journal of Applied Physiology 17:*967–970.

Tran, Z. and A. Weltman. 1989. Generalized equation for predicting body density of women from girth measurements. *Medicine and Science in Sports and Exercise 21:*101–104.

Tran, Z. V., and A. Weltman, and R. L. Seip. 1988. Predicting body composition of men from girth measurements. *Human Biology 60:*167–176.

U.S. Department of Health and Human Services. 1988. *The Surgeon General's Report on NUTRITION AND HEALTH.* p. 727. U.S. Department of Health and Human Services, Public Health Service. Washington, DC.

U.S. Public Health Service. 1990. *Healthy People 2000: National Health Promotion and Disease Prevention Objectives.* Washington, DC: U.S. Department of Health and Human Services.

Wilmore, J. H. 1969. A simplified method for determination of residual lung volumes. *Journal of Applied Physiology 27:*96–100.

Wilmore, J. H. and A. R. Behnke. 1969. An anthropometric estimation of body's density and lean body weight in young men. *Journal of Applied Physiology 27:*25–31.

Young, C. M. 1964. Prediction of specific gravity and body fatness in older women. *Journal of American Dietetic Association 45:*333–338.

Young, C. M., M. Martin, and W. R. Tensuan. 1962. Predicting specific gravity and body fatness in young women. *Journal of American Dietetic Association 40:*102–107.

# Evaluating Skill Achievement

## Key Words

accuracy tests
objective evaluation
rating scales
skill tests
subjective evaluation
wall volley tests

## Contents

## Objectives

The achievement of sport skills can be measured by three general means: skill tests, rating skills, and performance itself. Skill tests are an objective, often-used means of evaluating a variety of psychomotor objectives. These tests can be standardized or developed individually. Rating scales are instruments that standardize and define a performance that will be subjectively evaluated by a teacher. Finally, in some instances the performance itself can be used to evaluate achievement.

After reading Chapter 12, you should be able to:

1. Identify the four general types of sport skill tests.
2. Evaluate the four general types of sport skill tests using the criteria reliability, validity, and feasibility for mass testing.
3. Evaluate the weaknesses and strengths of rating scales.
4. Identify motor skills that are best evaluated by performance.
5. Outline methods that could be used to develop reliable, valid, and feasible measurement procedures for evaluating motor skill achievement.

# INTRODUCTION

A universal goal of physical education programs is to produce permanent, measurable changes in student psychomotor behavior, in skills ranging from touch football to modern dance, from volleyball to scuba diving. For the achievement of psychomotor objectives to be evaluated, the measurement procedures—tests, rating scales, or other instruments—must parallel the instructional objectives. Today the trend is away from standardized evaluation methods, whose objectives often vary from instructional ones (Klein 1971). Instead, it is the teacher—the person who has developed the instructional objectives—who must develop the procedures for evaluating them.

Sport skill tests are an objective method for evaluating motor skill achievement, and several of these tests are outlined in the chapter. From them, and the extensive bibliography of tests in the Appendix, you should be able to develop your own reliable, valid skill tests.

Rating scales are a subjective but systematic method for evaluating those skills that do not lend themselves to objective evaluation. The subjectivity of the method presents numerous problems, but there are procedures for constructing reliable, valid scales discussed in the text.

Finally, for certain skills (e.g., golf, bowling, archery) performance can provide an objective score for skill evaluation. The advantages and limitations of performance-derived evaluation are presented here as well.

# Sport Skill Tests

**Skill tests** require an environment similar to the game environment and standardized procedures for administration. The validity of skill tests is judged to some extent on the consistency between testing and performing environments. This does not mean you must recreate exactly the playing environment; it does mean that the movements and the activity must correspond to those of the actual sport. For example, you can use repeated volleying of a volleyball against a wall to measure achievement in the skill of volleyball passing; however, the student must be standing in the proper position.

The virtue of skill tests is a subject of ongoing debate. Many skill tests offer an objective, reliable, and valid method for evaluating motor skill objectives, while others do not. Do not use a skill test that does not meet your evaluation needs or the important criteria of reliability, validity, and feasibility for mass testing. Also, be sure to adopt tests that were developed on students of the same gender, age, and experience level as your students. You can also modify an existing test to meet your needs. Collins and Hodges (1978) describe many skill tests that might be adopted or modified for use in your testing program.

Although skill tests are most useful for the evaluation of learning, they can also be used for (1) placement, (2) diagnosis, (3) prediction, (4) comparative evaluation, and (5) motivation. The tests used to evaluate achievement can be placed into four groups: (1) accuracy tests, (2) wall volley tests, (3) total bodily movement tests, and (4) throws, kicks, or strokes for power or distance. A few tests have aspects of several groups and so are combination tests. Provided next are sample tests that illustrate each general group of skill tests.

# Accuracy Tests

**Accuracy tests** involve throwing, striking, or kicking an object toward a target for accuracy. Basketball free throws, badminton short serves, and volleyball serves are common accuracy tests.

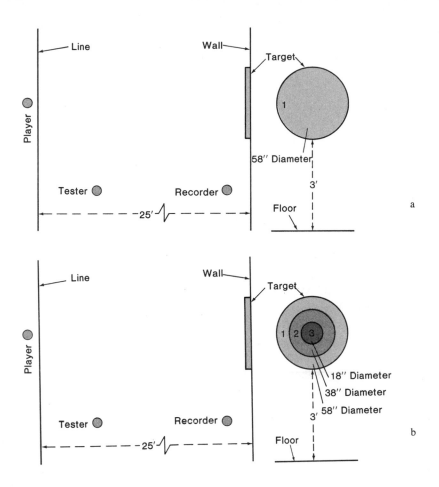

**Figure 12.1**
Two procedures for scoring an accuracy test. (Adapted from AAHPERD, *Basketball Skills Test Manual for Boys.* 1966. Reprinted by permission of the American Alliance for Health, Physical Education, Recreation and Dance, 1900 Association Drive, Reston, VA 22091.)

## Basketball Passing Test for Accuracy (AAHPER 1966a)

*Objective:* To measure the accuracy with which a player can make a two-hand-push pass at a target.

*Equipment:* Standard inflated basketballs; a target painted or drawn on a wall or mat, or on a piece of canvas hung on a smooth wall; chalk; and a measuring tape. The floor should be properly measured and marked as shown in Figure 12.1.

*Procedure:* The player stands behind a line 25 feet from and parallel to the target. Using a two-hand-push pass (chest pass), the player tries to hit the center of the target with the basketball. Passes must be made with both feet behind the passing line, and the two-hand-push pass must be used. After a practice pass, each student takes 10 passes.

*Scoring:* Award 3 points for hitting the center circle, 2 points for the next circle, and 1 point for the outer circle. Score hits on a line as though they

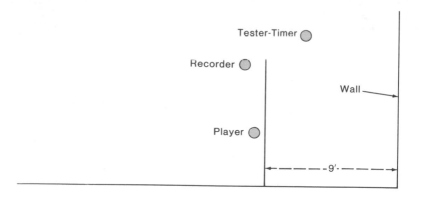

**Figure 12.2** AAHPERD Basketball Passing Test as an example of a wall volley test. (Reprinted by permission of the American Alliance for Health, Physical Education, Recreation and Dance, Reston, VA 22091.)

had struck the higher of the two adjacent circles (Figure 12.1b). Record points as they are made with the total points being the score. The maximum possible score is 30 points.

*Other considerations:* The basic disadvantage of accuracy tests is that the scoring system does not allow discrimination among skill levels. For example, it would be meaningless to use a single basketball pass as an index of passing skill because the score could range from only 0 to 3. This lack of variability reduces reliability. Two general procedures, however, can improve the reliability of accuracy tests. The first increases the variability of the target. A target with a range from 0 to 1 (Figure 12.1a) is less reliable than the recommended target, whose range is from 0 to 3 (part b). Given 10 passes, the range of scores on the first target would be from 0 to 10; on the second, from 0 to 30, a more precise measure. The second procedure increases the number of trials. Obviously 20 trials yield more reliable results than do 5 or 10. Ideally, then, 15 to 30 trials should be administered for most accuracy tests. Of course, too many trials can make a test unfeasible for mass testing.

## Wall Volley Tests

**Wall volley tests** require the subject to repeatedly stroke, pass, throw, or kick an object at a wall over a specified period of time with the number of successful trials the unit of measurement, or for a specified number of successful trials with time as the unit of measurement.

### Basketball Passing Test (AAHPER 1966a)

*Objective:* To measure the speed with which the subject can continue to pass and catch a ball.

*Equipment:* A level floor or ground; a smooth, solid wall; a stopwatch; and standard inflated basketballs.

*Procedure:* The player stands behind a line on the floor parallel to and 9 feet from the wall (see Figure 12.2). At the signal, "Go," the player passes the ball against the wall about head high, catches the rebound, and continues passing against the wall as rapidly as possible until ten passes have been completed. Any method of passing can be used, but the push pass is fastest.

A practice trial is allowed. All passes must be made from behind the line. The ball must be caught and passed, not batted. The ball can hit the wall at any height. If the ball is dropped, the subject must recover it and continue from behind the line until the ball has hit the wall ten times. Two complete trials are allowed.

*Scoring:* The test is timed from the instant the first pass hits the wall until the tenth pass hits the wall. (Although the player begins at the signal "Go," the watch is not started until the ball hits the wall.) Record the time in seconds and tenths of seconds. Record two complete trials, using the better score of the two.

*Other considerations:* In general, wall volley tests tend to be reliable, but because the testing and playing environments can differ considerably, validity poses a problem. Does repeatedly passing a ball against a wall truly measure a student's basketball passing skill? The original Dyer Tennis Wall Volley Test required the student to volley a tennis ball against a wall repeatedly for 30 seconds (Dyer 1935). The restraining line was only 5 feet from the wall, and students tended to tap rather than stroke the ball. In a revision of the test, the restraining line was moved back sufficiently to require the subject to use appropriate ground strokes (Hewitt 1965). Because the wall volley test environment differs from the game environment, it is especially important that students be allowed to practice the test. Then too, wall volleying can be a useful way to practice a skill, allowing the student both practice in the skill and greater familiarity with the testing environment.

Notice in the example basketball passing test the number of passes against the wall was set (10) and the score was the amount of time it took to complete the ten passes. An alternative procedure and scoring system for wall volley tests is to count the number of hits on the wall in a set length of time, usually 15 to 60 seconds. The Dyer Tennis Wall Volley Test just cited is an example. The advantage of the alternative procedure is that only one timer is needed and several students may take the test at the same time if sufficient wall space is available. The student's partner counts the number of hits and watches for correct form.

These tests require the subject to run a standardized test course using movements characteristic of the sport.

## Tests of Total Bodily Movement

### Basketball Control Dribble Test (AAHPERD 1984)

*Objective:* To measure skill in handling the ball that a player is moving.

*Equipment:* Standard inflated basketballs, a stopwatch, and six obstacles arranged as shown in Figure 12.3.

*Procedure:* The player stands on his or her nondominant hand side of Cone A with a ball in hand. At the signal "Go," the player begins dribbling with the nondominant hand to the nondominant hand side of Cone B and continues to dribble through the course using the preferred hand, changing hands

**Figure 12.3** AAHPERD
Basketball Control Dribble
Test as an example of a
total bodily movement test.
(Reprinted by permission of the
American Alliance for Health,
Physical Education, Recreation
and Dance, Reston, VA 22091.)

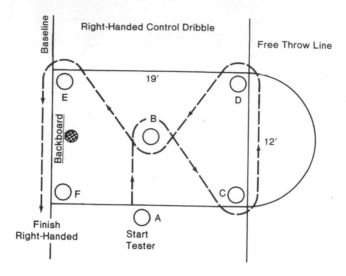

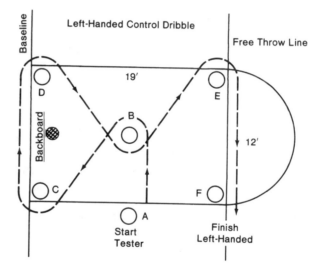

when desired until he or she crosses the finish line. The ball may be
dribbled with either hand, but legal dribbles must be used. Each player is
allowed three trials.

*Scoring:* The score in seconds and tenths of seconds is the time required to
dribble the entire course. The last two trials are timed and recorded; and the
sum of the two is the player's score on the test.

*Other considerations:* In general these tests are reliable. Their value, and thus
validity, is determined by the extent to which they relate to the objectives
being taught. Allow students to practice on the test course. They will learn
how to travel it more efficiently with each practice or trial. These types of
tests, like most skill tests, can also be used as skill practice.

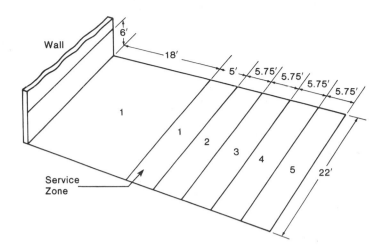

**Figure 12.4** Scoring zones for Cornish Handball Drive Test. (From C. Cornish, 1949. A study of measurement of ability in handball. *Research Quarterly 20:* 215–22. Reprinted by permission of the American Alliance for Health, Physical Education, Recreation and Dance, 1900 Association Drive, Reston, VA 22091.)

These tests, among the more common types of skill tests, measure the student's ability to throw, kick, or strike an object forcefully. Obvious examples are the football pass for distance, the football punt for distance, and the softball throw for distance. Two less obvious tests follow.

## Throws, Kicks, or Strokes for Power or Distance

### Badminton Drive for Distance

*Objective:* To drive a badminton shuttlecock for distance using an underhand stroke.

*Equipment:* A test station with two lines at right angles to each other, such as the sideline and center court line of a basketball court; and a 50-foot tape measure.

*Procedure:* Standing at the T formed by the two lines, the student drives an indoor shuttlecock as far as possible. The long service stroke is used. Ten trials are given each student. Trials in which the student obviously misses the shuttlecock are repeated.

*Scoring:* Each trial is measured to the last half foot. The score is the sum of the ten trials. To facilitate scoring, the measurement is taken at the point where the shuttlecock comes to rest, not where it first hits the floor.

### Cornish Handball Power Test (Cornish 1949)

*Objective:* To measure the power of the handball drive.

*Equipment:* The test course and scoring system are shown in Figure 12.4.

*Procedure:* Standing behind the service zone, the subject throws the ball against the front wall. Letting the ball hit the floor, the subject drives the ball into the wall as hard as possible, trying to make it rebound as far back as possible. The ball must strike the wall below the 6-foot line, and the subject must stroke the ball from behind the front service line. A retrial is allowed if the ball hits the front wall above the 6-foot line or if the subject hits the ball in front of the service line.

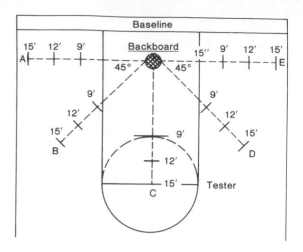

**Figure 12.5** Speed Spot Shooting Test. (Source: AAHPERD, 1984. *Basketball Skills Test Manual for Boys and Girls*, Reston, VA 22091.)

*Scoring:* The score is the value of the scoring zone in which each trial first touches the floor.

*Other considerations:* Normally such tests are reliable because the distance the object travels can be accurately measured. Attention must be paid, however, to each test's relevance to the instructional objectives. Certainly a modification of this test could be used in racquetball and tennis.

## Combination Tests

These tests are a combination of several of the four groupings just mentioned, usually speed and accuracy.

### Speed Spot Shooting (AAHPERD 1984)

*Objective:* To measure skill in rapidly shooting from specified positions.

*Equipment:* Standard inflated basketball, standard goal, stopwatch, marking tape.

*Procedure:* Grades 5 and 6 shoot from 9 feet; grades 7, 8, and 9 shoot from 12 feet; grades 10, 11, 12, and college shoot from 15 feet (Figure 12.5). Three 60-second trials are administered, with the first trial considered practice and the last two scored. During each trial a student must shoot at least once from each of the five spots (A–E) and may shoot a maximum of four lay-up shots, but not two in succession.

*Scoring:* Two points are awarded for each shot made, and one point is awarded for each unsuccessful shot that hits the rim. The final score is the total of the last two trial points.

### Passing (AAHPERD 1984)

*Objective:* To measure skill in passing and recovering the ball while moving.

*Equipment:* Standard inflated basketball, stopwatch, smooth wall surface, marking tape.

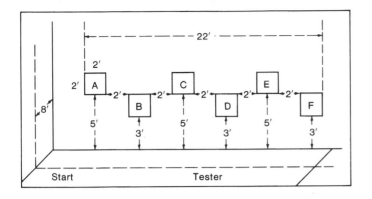

**Figure 12.6**
Basketball Passing Test.
(From Johnson, B. L. and J. K. Nelson. 1979. *Practical Measurements for Evaluation in Physical Education.* Minneapolis, MN: Burgess Publishing Co. and AAHPERD, *Basketball Skills Test Manual for Boys and Girls*, 1984.)

*Procedure:* Six squares are marked on the wall and a restraining line is marked on the floor 8 feet from the wall (Figure 12.6). Three 30-second trials are administered, with the first trial considered practice and the last two timed. The player, holding a ball, stands behind the restraining line and faces target A. On the command "Go," the player chest-passes at target A, recovers the rebound, and moves opposite target B. From behind the restraining line the player chest-passes at target B. This pattern continues until target F, where two chest-passes are executed. Then the player moves to the left, passes at target E, and continues to move left passing at each target in turn.

*Scoring:* Each pass that hits the desired target counts two points. Each pass hitting the wall but missing the target counts one point. The sum of the last two trial points is the final score.

## Rating Scales

**Rating scales** are useful for evaluating qualities that cannot be measured objectively, or at least not easily and efficiently. This section focuses on procedures for constructing and using rating scales; particularly to evaluate skill achievement.

### Subjective or Objective Evaluation?

Most of the measurement techniques discussed to this point have had good objectivity for the simple reason that most of the measurements conducted in physical education are objective rather than subjective. With **objective evaluation,** the test has a clearly defined scoring system, so the scorer does not affect the final score. Examples of objective tests are a 50-yard dash measured with a stopwatch, a standing long jump measured with a tape, a one-minute sit-up measured in number of executions, or a basketball free throw test. If a student makes seven free throws out of ten shots, two scorers would have little difficulty arriving at the same score. Remember, objectivity is the degree of agreement between two or more competent scorers. With subjective evaluation, a qualified person or persons judge(s) the quality of a performance and assign(s) a score, so the scorer can and does affect the final score. A subjective evaluation may be based on a defined scoring system, as in the scoring of gymnastics events in competition, or the evaluation may be just the impressions of each scorer. In the latter case, agreement between the scorers would probably not be high and objectivity would be low. Rating scales are designed to help objectify subjective evaluation by defining the scoring system, just as a tape measure defines the system of scoring the distance a person jumps.

Some people do not think highly of subjective evaluations, but it must be remembered that **subjective evaluations** are often used to determine the validity of objective tests. Judges' ratings are among the most widely-used criteria for validating skill tests for team sports. Although it is true that anything that exists can be measured, the system for measuring it may not be an objective test. Certainly, wherever feasible, objective evaluation should be used. But many important instructional objectives cannot be measured objectively. In fact, objective skill tests are not even available for gymnastics, folk dancing, fencing, and teamwork. For a number of the more complex team sports, it would be almost impossible to develop a test or test battery to validly measure total playing ability for two reasons:

1. The difficulty of identifying or measuring in a short period of time all the skill components that make up a given sport, and

2. The difficulty of objectively measuring the interaction among the skill components of a given sport, making the sum of the measurable components less than descriptive of the whole sport.

Subjective evaluation may also be more efficient than objective testing. Certain subjective scoring can be carried out while the students are practicing or competing, making it unnecessary to set aside special testing periods. Also, the number of trials required in certain tests for objective evaluation can make those tests unfeasible for mass testing. For example, assume that a teacher wants to evaluate student skills in serving and passing a volleyball for a class of sixty. The two recommended objective tests (AAHPER 1969) would require a total of 600 serves and 1200 passes to reliably evaluate these skills. Certainly a more efficient use of time would be to develop a rating scale and evaluate the students while they play the game.

## Problems with Subjective Evaluation

Subjective evaluation must be not only valid, reliable, and efficient, but also as objective as possible. We can satisfy these four criteria if the procedure is well planned.

The first stage in the planning process is the determination of which skills are going to be evaluated and how much each skill is going to affect the final score. Consider, for example, a teacher who, at the end of a volleyball unit, has not planned what to evaluate or how to weigh what has been evaluated. This teacher may have neglected not only to observe the same skills in each student, but also to weigh each equally in the final score. Serving skill may account for 35% of one student's final score and only 20% of another's.

The second stage in the planning process is the formulation of performance standards. Suppose that a teacher, having decided which skills to evaluate and their weight, begins to evaluate the students' serves without formulating performance standards. If the teacher expected well-placed, hard-to-return services and the first few students do not serve well, the teacher may unconsciously lower his or her standards, applying different criteria to the next students. These sliding standards would give two students of equal ability different scores.

The third stage in the planning process is a system for immediate recorded scoring. Even when a teacher knows what to evaluate, the weight of each evaluation, and the performance standards, unless the scores are recorded immediately, the evaluation will probably be neither reliable nor valid. Scores are too easily interchanged if the teacher tries to remember the score of each student and record it later.

In a sense, a rating scale reflects the careful planning procedure required to give reliability, validity, and objectivity to subjective evaluation. The scale lists the traits to be evaluated, reflects the teacher-determined importance of each trait, describes the performance standards, and provides a format for immediate recorded scoring.

The process of constructing a rating scale is threefold: (1) determining the purpose of the subjective evaluation, (2) identifying the basic components of the trait being evaluated, and (3) selecting the levels of ability for each component.

**Constructing a Rating Scale**

*Purpose.* The purpose of a rating scale determines the degree to which subjective evaluations must discriminate among ability groups. The more they must discriminate, the greater the number of classifications of ability. If, for example, posture is subjectively evaluated, only two classifications (acceptable-unacceptable) or three classifications (excellent-average-poor) may be needed. For grading purposes, three to five classifications are usually adequate; occasionally seven to ten are used in competition.

*Basic Components.* The trait being rated is almost always evaluated in parts or components, which must themselves be identified. The importance of each component and subcomponent must be defined so that points reflecting their relative value can be assigned. In Table 12.1, for example, three components are identified and three subcomponents are listed under each. These components and subcomponents reflect the instructional objectives of the activity.

*Levels of Ability.* The third step in the process is the decision of how many levels of ability should be assigned to each component. Two levels—pass-fail—are usually considered too crude an evaluation procedure. When three levels of ability are sufficient, a student can be rated above average, average, or below average on each subcomponent. A five-level scoring system is probably the most common: Each student is rated superior, above average, average, below average, or inferior on each subcomponent. Systems beyond five levels require that the teacher be knowledgeable enough about the characteristics being evaluated to identify small differences in ability or status. If a teacher creates more ability levels than he or she can identify, the reliability of the evaluations will be low. Remember that reliability and objectivity are improved when the rating scale lists exactly what is looked for in each subcomponent.

No rating scale, however well prepared, works unless it is used. You should have a copy of the scale for each subject and record the ratings on it immediately after the evaluation. There are also several ways to improve the effectiveness of a rating scale; increasing the number of qualified raters, retesting on several occasions, allowing sufficient time for both the test and the evaluation, preparing the students, and developing your own scale where possible.

**Using the Scale**

## Table 12.1 Sample Volleyball Rating Scale

Each of the three components of volleyball-playing ability has a point value of 15, and is scored on a 5-4-3-2-1 basis:

5 points—Exceptional ability, near perfect for the age and sex of the participant.

4 points—Above average ability, not perfect but quite skillful for the age and sex of the participant.

3 points—Average ability, typical for the age and sex of the participant.

2 points—Below average ability, characterized by more mistakes than is typical performance for the age and sex of the participant.

1 point—Inferior ability, far below typical performance for the age and sex of the participant.

For each subheading, circle the appropriate score.

**I. Serve**
   *A. Height above net*          5  4  3  2  1
   *B. Accuracy of placement*     5  4  3  2  1
   *C. Difficulty of return*      5  4  3  2  1

**II. Setting or Spiking—choose one**
   *A. Setting*
      1. Height above net         5  4  3  2  1
      2. Accuracy of placement    5  4  3  2  1
      3. Coordination with spiker 5  4  3  2  1
   *B. Spiking*
      1. Accuracy of placement    5  4  3  2  1
      2. Difficulty of return     5  4  3  2  1
      3. Coordination with setter 5  4  3  2  1

**III. General team play**
   *A. Hustle*                               5  4  3  2  1
   *B. Alertness—saves and play of difficult shots*  5  4  3  2  1
   *C. Teamwork*                             5  4  3  2  1

Total Score _____

***Number of Raters.*** The reliability and validity of subjective evaluations increase as the number of raters increases, as predicted by the Spearman-Brown prophecy formula and the validity prediction formula (Chapters 4 and 5), provided of course that the raters are qualified. One well-qualified rater is preferable to several poorly qualified raters. When there are several raters, objectivity improves if they decide before the rating what they are looking for and what standards to use. For example, assume there are four judges in a gymnastics meet—two college coaches and two high school coaches—and that each rates performers on a 10-point system. The college coaches may expect more of the performers than do the high school coaches. Thus, if the participants are junior high boys, the judges must decide whether a perfect score indicates perfect performance, or the best that can be expected of this age group.

***Number of Trials.*** Rating each student on several occasions within a short period—three days, for example—and using the average of the ratings as a score usually improves the score's reliability and validity. The justification and advantages of rating each person several times are the same as the reasons for using multiple trials on a physical performance test. By rating each person on several different days we minimize the chances of a student receiving a poor rating because of an off day, or a high score due to luck.

If you are able to rate a student on several different occasions, do not look at the student's previous ratings, which are likely to influence your evaluation. For example, if you know that a student was rated below average on the first performance, there is little chance that you will rate the student above average on a subsequent performance, even if the student deserves it. This preconceived idea of ability is a problem common to all forms of subjectivity evaluation.

***Testing Time.*** Allow enough time to rate an individual completely and to record the ratings immediately. It is better to rate only ten people each hour and to do a good job than to try to rate thirty people in an hour and to obtain invalid ratings.

***Student Preparation.*** As with objective tests, the students should know what is expected of them and what you will be looking for when you evaluate them. Let the students know that you plan to evaluate them in the near future so that they can prepare themselves if they want to. This makes the evaluation a type of formative evaluation and communicates to the students their weaknesses. Finally, students should be informed that they are being evaluated the day that ratings are made.

***Teacher-Prepared Scales.*** We believe that teachers should construct their own rating scales. The objectives of the course, the manner in which it is taught, the types of students, and their prior experiences are all variables that affect what is evaluated and how. Only a teacher-made rating scale can meet the evaluation needs of a specific situation. In preparing your own scales, you can look to others, like those shown in Tables 12.2 and 12.3, for help.

## The Performance

For many motor skills, performance is a reliable means of evaluating instructional objectives. Some authors refer to such measures as skill tests or rating scales, which in a sense they are. However, it is important to remember that in this context the performance environment is also the evaluation environment. The instructional objectives and the performance may thus be identical, and logical validity more readily assured. For example, a tumbling objective might be to execute a forward roll; when the student does so, the objective has been evaluated.

When performance is evaluated, it is usually in terms of achievement, but it could be in terms of developmental or biomechanical instructional objectives. Among the skills where performance can serve as a means of evaluation are the following:

*Archery.* Archery achievement is validly determined by measuring the student's accuracy in shooting a standardized target from a specified distance.

# Table 12.2 Badminton Rating Scale

The four areas of badminton-playing ability may all be rated during competition. However, the first two areas may be rated in a noncompetitive situation, if so desired, by asking the student to demonstrate the various serves and strokes.

Each subarea is scored on a 3-2-1 basis:

3 points—Above average ability, considerably more skillful than the performance typical of the student's age and sex.
2 points—Average ability, typical performance for age and sex.
1 point—Below average ability, far inferior to typical performance for age and sex.

For each subarea, circle the appropriate score.

## I. Serve
A. Position of shuttlecock upon contact—racket head strikes shuttlecock below waist level.                                    3  2  1
B. Position of racket at end of serve—if short serve, racket head does not rise above chest; if long serve, racket head stops between shoulders and top of head at end of serve.    3  2  1
C. Placement of serve—well-placed relative to type of serve and position of opponent.                                          3  2  1
D. Height of serve relative to type of serve—short serve is low over net; drive serve is low over net and deep; clear serve is high and deep.                                                     3  2  1

## II. Strokes—consider placement and quality of each stroke
A. Clear—high and deep.                                                                                                        3  2  1
B. Smash—hit from position above head and in front of body; path of bird is down.                                             3  2  1
C. Drive—sharp and low over net; hit from position about shoulder height; can be deep or midcourt, but not short.             3  2  1
D. Drop—hit from position waist- to shoulder-height; low over net; a hairpin-type shot.                                       3  2  1

## III. Strategy
A. Places shots all over court.                                                                                               3  2  1
B. Executes a variety of shots at the most opportune moments.                                                                 3  2  1
C. Takes advantage of opponent's weaknesses (for example, poor backhand, strength problem in back court, poor net play).     3  2  1
D. Uses own best shots.                                                                                                       3  2  1

## IV. Footwork and Position
A. Near center court position so flexible to play any type of shot.                                                           3  2  1
B. Has control of body at all times during play.                                                                             3  2  1
C. Body is in correct position when making each shot (usually determined by the feet).                                        3  2  1
D. Racket is shoulder-to-head-height and ready for use (wrist cocked) at all times; eyes are on the shuttlecock at all times. 3  2  1

Total Score _____

Suggested by Bill Landin, Indiana University.

**Table 12.3** Swimming Rating Scale for
Elementary Backstroke

The arm stroke, leg kick, complete stroke, and stroke efficiency are rated on a
three-point scale. Complete stroke and stroke efficiency are double-weighted so as to
be twice as influential as arm stroke and leg kick in the total rating.

Circle the appropriate score for each area.

**A. Arm Stroke**

    3 points—Arms do not break water or rise above top of head; elbows are kept at
          sides and fingers move up midline of body; stroke is powerful and
          smoothly coordinated.

    2 points—Arms do not break water or rise above top of head; elbows are usually
          kept at sides and fingers move up midline of body; stroke is reasonably
          powerful and reasonably well-coordinated.

    1 point —Arms break water and/or rise above top of head; elbows are not kept at
          sides and fingers do not move up midline of body; stroke is not
          powerful and/or poorly coordinated.

**B. Leg Kick**

    3 points—Legs drop at knees for whip kick; toes are outside of heels as feet
          spread; kick is powerful and smoothly coordinated.

    2 points—Legs drop at knees for whip kick but some flexation occurs at hips; toes
          are not outside of heels as feet spread, causing knees to spread; kick is
          reasonably powerful and reasonably well-coordinated.

    1 point —Legs do not drop at knees for whip kick, but are brought toward
          stomach by flexing at the hips; knees spread too wide; no power in
          kick; kick is poorly coordinated.

**C. Complete Stroke**

    6 points—Arms and legs are coordinated during stroke; arms are at sides, trunk
          and legs straight, and toes pointed during glide position.

    4 points—Minor deviations from the standard for 6 points occur.

    2 points—Arms and legs are not coordinated during stroke; glide position is poor
          with reference to arm-trunk-leg-toe position.

**D. Stroke Efficiency**

    6 points—Long distance is covered in glide; body is relaxed in water; swims in
          straight line; hips on surface.

    4 points—Average distance is covered in glide; body is relaxed in water; does not
          swim in straight line; hips slightly below surface.

    2 points—Little distance is covered in glide; body is not relaxed in water; does not
          swim in straight line; hips are well below surface (swimmer is sitting in
          water rather than lying on top of it).

**Total Score** _____

*Bowling.* The bowling average achieved under standardized conditions is an
objective measure of bowling skill. Subjectively evaluating bowling form
would certainly be possible.

*Golf.* If the school has access to a golf course, the student's score on several
rounds can serve as an objective index of golf skill. This criterion is well
accepted by touring professionals.

*Swimming.* The number of breaststrokes required to swim 25 yards is an objective measure of breaststroke ability. Stroke mechanics and/or form are commonly evaluated.

## Procedures for Evaluating Skill Achievement

We recognize that teachers are not researchers. The procedures below for the development of skill test batteries represent the application of scientific test construction principles to the public school teacher's situation. They also represent several years' work. Do not expect high-quality evaluation of psychomotor objectives to be instantly performed.

1. *Define what is to be measured.* This is one of the most important steps in the test construction process: If it is not carried out correctly, subsequent procedures will also be incorrect. Use your instructional objectives as the source of what is to be measured. These objectives describe the skills that should be achieved during an instructional phase, so they also define what needs to be measured.

2. *Select a measuring instrument.* Choose tests or rating scales that measure the achievement of the instructional objectives. In most instances the process of matching objectives and measuring instruments is based on logic. Remember that the skill learned during instruction must also be the skill used during the test. That is, individual differences in scores on a basketball dribble test must be due to individual differences in dribbling skill, not to unrelated factors.

    In selecting a measuring instrument, you can choose from among published skill tests, construct a rating scale, or use the performance itself. It may be necessary to alter an instrument to fit your instructional objectives. In constructing a skill test battery, skill tests and rating scales can be used together to evaluate the different motor skill components of an activity. For example, you can use a serving test to evaluate the achievement of volleyball serving skill and a rating scale to evaluate spiking skill. When it is impossible to evaluate all the skills you have taught, as it usually is, select those that are most important.

3. *Pretest the instrument.* Before you administer a test or rating scale to a class, try it out on a group of five to fifteen students. No matter how explicit test instructions appear, you will truly understand the test and its procedures only after you have administered it. Several important questions must be answered: Does the test seem to be valid? Does it measure the stated instructional objective? Does it seem to be reliable? Are the directions clear? What is the best way to standardize its administration? How long does it take to test one student? If the test is too long, you may have to set up several test stations and recruit and train additional testing personnel. At this point you should also develop standardized procedures for administering the test.

4. *Revise the test and testing procedures.* On the basis of your findings from the pretest, you may want to devise, delete, or add tests to the battery. If the changes are numerous, you should administer the revised test to another small group.

5. *Administer the instrument.* At the end of the instructional phase, administer the selected test to the class.

6. *Evaluate the administered test.* After you administer the battery, examine the reliability, validity, and feasibility of each test.

   a. *Reliability.* Because testing procedures and the variability of the group can affect reliability, it is important that you estimate each test's reliability for your testing procedures and students. If a test lacks reliability, it may be necessary to use additional trials, alter your testing procedures, or search for a better test.

   b. *Validity.* Once you have determined reliability, you must determine validity. In most instances, you can do so logically: If the test obviously measures an instructional objective, you can assume logical validity. For example, a test that requires a student to swim 25 yards in as few strokes as possible using the sidestroke is a valid test of sidestroke skill. If validity cannot be determined logically, you could compare the scores achieved by the best and poorest students in the class. If the achieved scores do not confirm your observations, the test is suspect. Or, you could compare the test scores with tournament standings. If the tests are valid, the two sets of scores should be related.

   c. *Feasibility.* Tests can be both reliable and valid, yet simply impractical for mass testing. If you cannot revise the testing procedures to make them applicable for mass testing, you must select or develop a new battery.

7. *Revise the final battery.* The final battery should consist of reliable, valid instruments that measure important instructional objectives. A battery normally consists of from three to five individual tests. Two criteria for compiling the final battery are (1) that the selected tests be reliable, valid, and feasible for mass testing, and (2) that the correlation among the final items be low. If the correlation between two tests in the final battery is high, one should be eliminated.

8. *Develop standards.* Once you have finalized the content of the battery, you must develop norm-referenced or criterion-referenced standards. T-score and percentile norms (see Chapters 3 and 6) are especially useful. T-score norms have the advantage of allowing you to sum the test items and calculate a total score for the entire battery. Criterion-referenced standards based on research finds or personal beliefs are useful because they are a minimum proficiency standard. Many published tests provide national norms; however, you should try to develop your own norms because testing procedures and climatic conditions vary.

The Research Council of the AAHPERD (formerly the AAHPER) published several sport skill tests in the late 1960s that were developed from the combined efforts of researchers, city directors of physical education, and public school teachers. Currently, test manuals are available for the archery, football, and volleyball tests. The manuals list administration procedures as well as percentile norms for boys and girls ages 10 to 18. They are available at nominal cost from the AAHPERD.

## Sample Sport Skill Tests

### AAHPER Sport Skill Test Series

The following criteria were used in developing the tests:

*Validity.* Each test should measure the student's ability to perform a skill basic to the sport.

*Reliability.* Accuracy tests should have reliability above .70; the other tests should have reliability above .80.

*Test environment.* Preference was given to tests that were also a method of practicing the skill.

*Scoring.* Preference was given to tests that could be scored objectively.

*Degree of difficulty.* Each test should differentiate among the various skill levels at each grade level.

*Variability.* The distribution of scores for each age level should be normal.

The report of a committee that evaluated the 1960s AAHPER series concluded that the procedures for the test items are vague (Morris 1977); that the items should be studied in typical physical education situations and the results reported; that a task analysis of the sport skills should be conducted if logical validity is to be used for the selection and retention of items; that some of the items fail to meet the criterion of reliability; and that, although the test items are supposed to measure skill achievement, some of them actually predict potential achievement. This last is of special concern, in that many of the tests include basic ability items (speed, jumping, agility) that predict, rather than indicate, skill ability. Another common criticism, although not presented by Morris, is that the various batteries each contain eight or nine items, which often take a good deal of time to administer or overlap in terms of skill tested.

The Measurement and Evaluation Council of the AAHPERD formed a task force in 1979 to revise and expand the AAHPER sport skill test series. The basketball and softball skills tests are revised and a tennis test added to the series. Presently, volleyball and soccer skills committees are at work.

The AAHPERD sport skills tests presently available are not without merit. With the exception of the basketball, softball, and tennis tests, a person should probably select two to four items from a test battery to administer to a class, keeping in mind the concerns of Morris (1977). A brief discussion of each battery follows, for your reference. Individuals planning to use these tests should obtain the test manuals from AAHPERD in order to have the complete administrative procedures, norms, and recommended drills.

**Archery.** The archery test requires the student to shoot two ends (12 arrows) at a 48-inch target from distances of 10 to 30 yards (AAHPER 1967a). Girls shoot from 10 and 20 yards; boys shoot from 10, 20, and 30 yards. The target has five zones, scored 9-7-5-3-1. Misses are scored 0.

**Basketball.** The basketball battery consists of four tests recommended for boys and girls, with minor changes for gender differences (AAHPERD 1984). The basketball battery is presently being revised and neither the 1984 or a new test manual is available.

*Speed Spot Shooting.* This test was presented earlier in the chapter (see page 348).

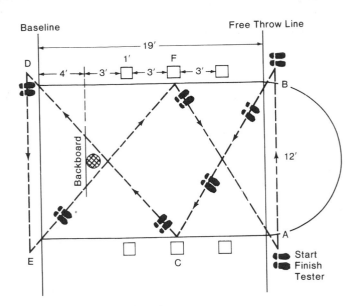

**Figure 12.7**
AAHPERD Basketball Defensive Movement Test. (Reprinted by permission of the American Alliance for Health, Physical Education, Recreation and Dance, Reston, VA 22091.)

*Passing.* This test was presented earlier in the chapter (see pages 348 and 349).

*Control Dribble.* This test was presented earlier in the chapter (see pages 345 and 346).

*Defensive Movement.* The purpose of this test is to measure basic defensive movement. A course of six cones is set up on the free throw lane of the court (see Figure 12.7). Three timed trials of side-stepping (slide-step) through the course are administered. The final score is the sum of the last two trial times.

In a factor analysis study of basketball skill tests, 21 items were administered to 70 male subjects (Hopkins 1977). Four factors were identified: (1) shooting, (2) passing, (3) jumping, and (4) moving with or without the ball. A similar study (Gaunt 1979), using 20 variables administered to 167 female subjects, also identified four factors: (1) lay up shooting, (2) passing, (3) explosive leg strength, and (4) dribbling. These findings influenced the selection of tests in this battery.

**Football.** The football battery (AAHPER 1966b) was developed for use with boys. It consists of the following ten tests.

*Forward Pass for Distance.* The test involves passing a football as far as possible. Distance is measured to the last foot, at right angles to the throwing line. A restraining line is 6 feet behind the throwing line to define the throwing zone. The best of three throws is scored.

*50-Yard Dash with Football.* The test involves sprinting 50 yards while carrying a football. The score is the elapsed time accurate to a tenth of a second for the better of two trials.

*Blocking.* The test course is an obstacle course consisting of three blocking bags. The boy must cross-body block each of the three bags to the ground.

The score is the elapsed time required to run the test course, accurate to a tenth of a second for the better of two trials.

*Football Pass for Accuracy.* The test involves passing a football at a circular target with diameters of 2, 4, and 6 feet. The target is placed so the bottom of the largest circle is 3 feet from the ground. Each boy tries ten passes from behind a 15-yard throwing line. Each pass is scored from 0 to 3 points.

*Football Punt for Distance.* The test involves punting a football as far as possible. The kicking zone, and administration and scoring of the test are the same as for the forward pass for distance.

*Ball-Changing Zigzag Run.* While running an obstacle test course, the student must change the ball from hand to hand. This is a timed test scored to a tenth of a second. The better of the two trials is the subject's score.

*Catching the Forward Pass.* The student starts on the scrimmage line 9 feet to the left of the center (a player), runs 30 feet straight down field, and turns at a right angle to the left. A passer standing 15 feet behind the center passes the ball to the student as he runs. The student is thrown ten passes. The same thing is done with the student 9 feet to the right of the center and turning to the right. One point is awarded for each pass caught. The score is the sum of the twenty passes caught.

*Pull-out.* On the command "Go," the student pulls out, runs around a goalpost that is 9 feet, 3 inches, from the starting position, and sprints straight downfield 30 feet. This is a timed test accurate to a tenth of a second. The better of the two trials is recorded as the subject's score.

*Kickoff.* The student is tested for the distance that he can place-kick a football off of a kicking tee. The player may take as long a run as desired to kick the ball. Three trials are given. The scoring is the same as for the forward pass for distance.

*Dodging run.* The student runs an obstacle test course while carrying a football. Two complete runs through the course are a trial and two trials are given. This timed test is scored to a tenth of a second. The better of the two trials is recorded as the subject's score.

**Softball.** The softball battery (AAHPERD 1991) consists of four tests recommended for boys and girls grades five through college.

*Batting.* The softball outfield is marked off into three power zones (for grades 5–8: 120 feet, 180 feet, and more than 180 feet from home plate) and into three placement areas (left, center, and right field) so there are nine scoring areas. Hit balls that come to rest in the farthest center field scoring area receive the most points. Less points are given for hits to right or left field and hits not reaching the farthest scoring area. The test consists of two practice trials and six test trials of hitting a ball off of a batting tee for distance and accuracy. The sum of the six test trials is the batter's score.

*Fielding Ground Balls.* A tester throws a ball on a smooth field and the student tries to field the ball cleanly. Two practice and six test trials are administered. Each test trial is scored based on how cleanly the ball is fielded and where the ball is fielded. The score is the sum of the points for the six test trials. The directions are specific as to dimensions and marking of the test area, ball velocity and placement, and assignment of points.

*Overhand Throwing.* The test involves throwing a softball for distance and accuracy. Players have 3 to 4 minutes of short-throw warm-up and then have two trials to throw the softball as far and as straight as possible down a throwing line. The trial scored is the ground distance the ball went before hitting the ground minus the number of feet the ball landed away from the throwing line. The better of the two trials is a player's score. This score is very reliable and more economical than the mean of two trial scores.

*Base Running.* This test involves running the first two bases for time. One reduced-speed practice trial and two test trials are administered. A trial score is the time it takes to run from home plate to first base to second base. The score is the better of the two trials for the same reason indicated for the overhand throwing test.

**Tennis.** The tennis battery (AAHPERD 1989) consists of two tests and an optional test recommended for boys and girls grades nine through college. The committee who developed this battery found that tennis is not taught at the junior high school level as much as previously believed. They found three test items that had acceptable reliability, validity, and administrative efficiency.

*Ground Stroke: Forehand and Backhand Drive.* The test measures the ability to hit ground strokes with both accuracy and power. The score for each trial is based on placement and power. The placement score is where the ball lands in a target area, with deep shots on the court receiving more points than shots near the net. The power for each shot landing in the target area is how deep on the court the second bounce lands. Placement scores are 0 to 4 and power scores are 1 to 3.

*Serving.* The test measures serving accuracy and power. As with the ground stroke test, the tennis court is marked with scoring areas and power zones. Students are permitted about 5 minutes of warm-up prior to being tested. Sixteen services are scored for placement and power. Accuracy of each serve is scored 0 to 2, and power for each serve landing in the tennis court is scored 1 to 2 depending on how deep the second bounce of the serve lands. The score for the test is the sum of the points for the sixteen trials.

*Volley Test (optional).* The test measures the ability to volley the ball accurately from a position near the net. The court is divided into seven areas which are scored 1 to 4 points. The tester hits ten balls to the forehand side and ten balls to the backhand side of the student. The student hits each ball over the net aiming at the target areas. The first four balls hit from each side are considered practice. The score on the test is the sum of the points for the twelve trials.

***Volleyball.*** The volleyball battery consists of four tests recommended for both boys and girls (AAHPER 1969).

*Volleying.* This is a wall volley test that involves volleying a ball above a 5-foot long line 11 feet above the floor. The score is the number of legal volleys during a 60-second period.

*Serving.* The court is divided into scoring zones that range from 1 to 4 points. Each student is awarded ten serves. For children younger than 12, the serving line should be located 20 feet from the net.

*Passing.* From the rear of the court the student must pass a volleyball above an 8-foot rope into a 6 × 4 foot target outlined on the floor. The ball is tossed to the student, who must pass the ball to either the right or left side of the court. A total of twenty passes, ten to each side, is allowed; 1 point is scored for each pass that goes over the rope and lands in the proper target.

*Set-up.* From the middle of the front court a student receives a pass from a thrower in the back court. The student must set up the volleyball by passing the ball over a rope (10 feet high for boys, 9 feet for girls) and into a 4 × 6 foot target outlined on the floor at the corner of the court next to the net. Each student is allowed twenty trials, ten set to the right and ten to the left. The sum of the twenty trials that go over the rope and land within the target is the student's score.

The final revision of the volleyball test is complete, and in late 1992 collection of normative data began. The revised test is for girls and boys in grades seven through college in beginning volleyball classes. The test consists of four items.

*Self-Volley.* The player starts by tossing the ball to himself/herself and tries to set it to himself/herself as many times as possible in one minute.

*Self-Pass.* This is the same as the self-volley except only forearm passes are counted.

*Wall Spike.* The player starts at least 6 feet from a smooth wall, tosses the ball to himself/herself, and hits the ball above his/her head so it hits the floor and rebounds off the wall. The player continues to hit the ball rebounding off the wall above the head so it hits the floor and rebounds. The score is the number of balls that hit the floor and then the wall in one minute.

*Serving.* The score is the number of serves out of twenty serves that land in the court. The points awarded are 1.0 for an underhand serve and 1.5 points for an overhand serve. All serves must be made from the regulation distance on a volleyball court.

## Other Sport Skill Tests

Following are numerous other sport skill tests as examples of the types of tests that have been used in the past. If these tests meet your needs, use them. However, we hope that many physical education teachers will use these tests as examples to construct their own sport skill tests.

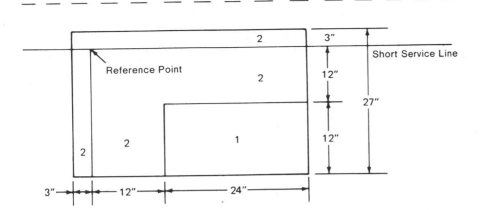

**Figure 12.8**
Scoring zones for the
Sebolt Short Service Test.
(Reprinted by permission of
Don Sebolt, Virginia Polytechnic
Institute, Blacksburg, VA.)

## *Badminton*

### Sebolt Short Service Test (Sebolt 1968)

*Objective:* To measure the achievement of the badminton short service.

*Validity and reliability:* Because the ability to serve the shuttlecock close to the
net and into the front middle corner of the opponent's service court is an
important badminton skill, logical validity is assumed. With college
students the correlation between performance on a ladder tournament and
the service test was .61. The intraclass reliability for the students was
estimated at .72 and .79.

*Equipment:* The test is administered on a standard court, with scoring zones as
shown in Figure 12.8. A string is stretched 16 inches directly above and
parallel to the net. A badminton racket and ample supply of new indoor
shuttlecocks are needed.

*Procedure:* Each student is given a 5-minute warm-up period on a practice
court before being tested. The test consists of twenty legal serves from the
right service court. The bird must be served between the net and the string
into the target area. Shuttlecocks served above the string are scored 0. If the
shuttlecock hits the string, another serve is allowed. Shuttlecocks that hit
the net are scored in the same manner as birds that clear the net.

*Scoring:* A scorer is needed for each test station. The student's score is the sum
of the twenty serves. The scoring zones are shown in Figure 12.8. A
shuttlecock that hits on the line is awarded the higher value.

*Other considerations:* An objective of the short serve is to serve the
shuttlecock near the net and have it land near or on the short service line.
The 3-inch band outside the service court, an important feature of the test,
encourages the student to serve for the line. In the game situation a
shuttlecock landing just outside the service court should be hit because the
player cannot be certain if the bird is in or short. If several test stations are
available, the test is feasible for mass use.

## Scott and Fox Long Service (Scott & French 1959)

*Objective:* To measure the accuracy of the badminton long service.

*Validity and reliability:* Because the ability to serve the shuttlecock deep into the opponent's backcourt is an important skill for singles, logical validity is assumed. A correlation of .54 was reported between the service scores and the subjective rating made by three judges during play. The internal-consistency reliability estimates with college women were .77 and .68.

*Equipment:* The test is administered on a standard court, with scoring zones marked as shown in Figure 12.9. A restraining rope at a height of 8 feet is placed parallel to and 14 feet from the net. The student needs a suitable racket and an ample supply of new indoor shuttlecocks.

*Procedure:* Before the test the student should be given sufficient opportunity for practice. Each student is allowed twenty trials that can be administered in groups of five to ten. The student tries to serve the shuttlecock in a legal manner over the rope into the highest scoring zone. Serves that hit the rope are taken over.

*Scoring:* A scorer is needed for each test station. The student's score is the sum of twenty serves. The scoring zones are shown in Figure 12.9. A 0 is awarded for serves that fail to land in the service court or that go under the restraining rope. Any shuttlecock that lands on a line dividing two scoring areas is awarded the higher value.

*Other considerations:* A weakness of the scoring system is that the student receives a 0 when a shuttlecock misses the back line by 1 or 2 inches. In the game situation a serve up to about 6 inches long may be good because the opponent may be forced to play the shot. Generally, for a long serve used in singles, the server wants to aim for the deep back line near the center T. We recommend scoring zones be used that encourage the student to aim for the back line. An alternate scoring zone is offered in Figure 12.9.

## *Golf*

### Green Golf Test (Green, East & Hensley 1987)

*Objective:* To measure the five basic skill components of golf: putting, chipping, pitching, using middle-distance irons, and driving.

*Validity and reliability:* A group of 146 subjects were administered each item of the test battery on each of two days near the end of a beginning-level golf class. Reliability coefficients were at least .70 except for the pitch shot for females and the short-putt for both males and females.

A group of 66 subjects completing a beginning-level golf class at the college level were used to validate the test. Multiple regression was used to estimate validity with the score on 36 holes of golf the criterion measure and the predictor variables the golf battery items. Validity was .72 for a two-item test battery of middle-distance shot and pitch shot, increasing to .77 for a four-item test battery of middle-distance shot, pitch shot, long-putt, and chip shot.

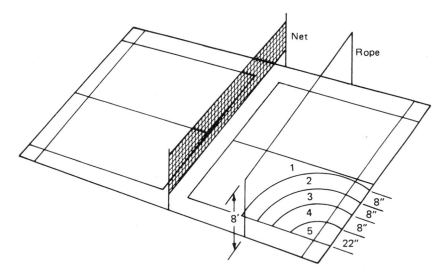

**Figure 12.9**
Scoring zones for the
Badminton Long Service
Test. (Adapted from Scott,
M. G. and E. French. 1959.
*Measurement and Evaluation in
Physical Education.* (p. 145).
Dubuque, IA: Wm. C. Brown.
Reprinted by permission of
M. Gladys Scott.)

Scott-Fox Scoring

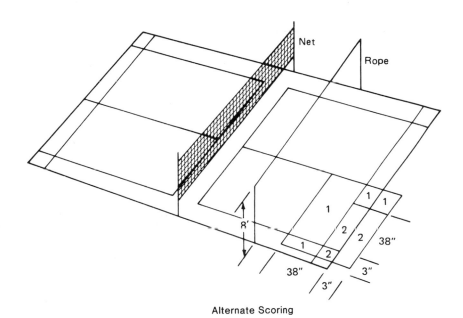

Alternate Scoring

*Items:*

*Middle-distance shot.* The test was four trials of hitting a ball at a target 140 yards away (males) or 110 yards away (females). The score was the sum of the perpendicular distance in yards each ball came to rest from the target.

*Pitch shot.* Six trials from 40 yards away from the flagstick were used. A seven through nine iron, pitching wedge, or sand wedge was used for the test. The score for the test was the sum of the distance in feet each of the six pitch shots were from the flagstick.

*Long-putt.* This test was putting from six proportionately spaced positions around the cup. All positions were 25 feet from the cup. The score was the sum of the distance in inches that each putt stopped from the cup.

*Chip shot.* Six trials from 35 feet away from the flagstick were used. The score for the test was the sum of the distance in feet each of the chip shots stopped from the flagstick.

### Gymnastics

#### Gymnastics Skills Test for College Women (Ellenbrand 1973)

The 16-item battery consists of the following events: balance beam (5 items), floor exercise (4 items), uneven parallel bars (5 items), and vaulting (2 items). The items were selected using the following criteria: contribution to the category in which they were placed, extent to which they were considered basic skills (as opposed to a variation of some skill), progression within the category, and similarity to a gymnastics performance.

*Objective:* To measure achievement of gymnastics skills.

*Validity and reliability:* Concurrent validity was estimated by correlating the scores of three judges of varied experience (an experienced gymnastics teacher, a college teacher with limited gymnastics teaching experience, a student majoring in physical education with a single basic course in gymnastics) with the ratings of two experienced gymnastics judges. The correlations were balance beam, .93; floor exercise, .97; uneven parallel bars, .99; vaulting, .88; and total test, .97. The intercorrelations among the four events ranged from .44 to .70, low enough to warrant the inclusion of all four. The reliability for each event and for the total test was investigated again using the three judges of varied experience. In addition the test was administered on a second day by one teacher. The intraclass reliability estimates were as follows:

| Event | Among Teachers | Between Days |
|---|---|---|
| Balance beam | .99 | .98 |
| Floor exercise | .97 | .99 |
| Uneven parallel bars | .99 | .94 |
| Vaulting | .97 | .99 |
| **Total tests** | .98 | .99 |

*Procedure:* The skills for each item were ordered from simple to difficult. The difficulty ratings were logically assigned. The student selects one skill under each item that demonstrates her achievement in that area. She should have an opportunity to practice. Deduct points for falls, but give students the opportunity to repeat stunts.

We present here the test items and difficulty ratings for the floor exercises only (see Table 12.4). For the floor exercise event, skills are performed on the length of mats provided. A return trip can be used if necessary. Connecting skills can be added if needed for preparation of a selected skill (e.g., a round-off to prepare for a back handspring). However, extra steps and runs should be avoided because they detract from the execution rating.

*Other considerations:* This test is designed to evaluate the instructional objectives of gymnastics for college women only; it should not be used for other students. However, the same logic could be applied to develop a test for any gymnastics or tumbling class.

## Racquetball

### Racquetball Battery (Poteat 1983)[1]

*Objective:* To measure basic racquetball playing ability of beginning players.

*Validity and reliability:* Twelve collegiate and professional racquetball instructors evaluated the skills test battery as to its logical validity and all agreed that the test battery items measured skills necessary for beginning racquetball players. Further, correlations between test items and expert ratings of the skill involved in the test item varied from .62 to .76.

Stability reliability coefficients for the items varied from .75 to .84. Internal consistency reliability coefficients varied from .85 to .91.

*Equipment:* A regulation racquetball court with official markings is necessary. Also, a racquetball racquet, stopwatch, measuring tape, and four racquetballs and marking tape are needed.

*Procedures:* The original battery consisted of forehand and backhand passing shot, service placement, forehand and backhand wall play, and wall volley tests. Because of high correlations between comparable passing and wall play items, the author suggests dropping the passing shot item but changing the wall play item so it has the same target area and scoring procedure as the passing shot and service placement items. The three suggested test items in their original form are presented here.

1. *Service placement.* The court markings for this test item are shown in Figure 12.10. The student stands in the center of the service area, bounces the ball, and hits it to the front wall so that it will rebound and hit in or pass through the 10 × 5 foot target area. The ball is served to the student's backhand. The student is allowed 10 attempts per trial and 2 trials. No points are awarded if the ball is an illegal serve or contacts the front wall higher than 5 feet above the floor. One point is awarded if

---

[1]Reprinted by permission of Charles Poteat.

# Table 12.4 Floor Exercise Items from Ellenbrand Gymnastics Test

## Test Item: Tumbling Skills (Rolls)

| Difficulty | | Skills | Difficulty | | Skills |
|---|---|---|---|---|---|
| .5 | a. | Forward roll to stand | 4.5 | i. | Back extension |
| .5 | b. | Backward roll to knees | 5.0 | j. | Dive forward roll (layout) |
| 1.0 | c. | Back roll to stand | 6.0 | k. | Back tuck somersault (aerial) |
| 2.0 | d. | Pike forward or back roll | 6.5 | l. | Back pike somersault |
| 2.0 | e. | Straddle roll (forward or back) | 6.5 | m. | Forward tuck somersault |
| 3.0 | f. | Dive forward roll (pike) | 7.0 | n. | Back layout somersault |
| 4.0 | g. | Handstand forward roll | 8.0 | o. | Somersault with a twist |
| 4.0 | h. | Back roll to headstand | | | |

## Test Item: Tumbling Skills (Springs)

| Difficulty | | Skills | Difficulty | | Skills |
|---|---|---|---|---|---|
| 1.0 | a. | Handstand snap-down | 5.0 | h. | Back handspring |
| 2.0 | b. | Round-off | 5.0 | i. | Front handspring on one hand |
| 2.5 | c. | Neck spring (kip) | | | or with a change of legs |
| 3.0 | d. | Head spring | 5.5 | j. | Series of front handsprings |
| 3.5 | e. | Front handspring to squat | 6.0 | k. | Series of back handsprings |
| 4.0 | f. | Front handspring arch to stand | 6.5 | l. | Back handspring to kip (cradle) |
| 4.5 | g. | Front handspring walk-out | 6.5 | m. | Back handspring with twist |

## Test Item: Acrobatic Skills

| Difficulty | | Skills | Difficulty | | Skills |
|---|---|---|---|---|---|
| 1.0 | a. | Mule kick (three-quarter handstand) | 4.0 | i. | Dive cartwheel |
| 1.0 | b. | Bridge (back arch position) | 4.0 | j. | Tinsica |
| 2.0 | c. | Handstand | 4.5 | k. | Dive walk-over |
| 2.0 | d. | Cartwheel | 5.0 | l. | Handstand with half turn or straddle-down to a sit |
| 2.5 | e. | Backbend from standing | | | |
| 3.0 | f. | Front limber | 5.0 | m. | One-handed walk-overs |
| 3.0 | g. | One-handed cartwheel | 6.0 | n. | Butterfly (side aerial) |
| 4.0 | h. | Walk-overs (forward and back) | 7.0 | o. | Aerial cartwheel or walk-over |

## Test Item: Dance Skills

| Difficulty | | Skills |
|---|---|---|
| 1.0 | a. | Half turn (one foot), run, leap |
| 2.0 | b. | Half turn, step, hitch kick forward, step, leap |
| 3.0 | c. | Half turn, slide, tour jeté, hitch kick |
| 4.0 | d. | Full turn (one foot), step, leap, step, leap |
| 5.0 | e. | Full turn, tour jeté, cabriole (beat kick forward) |
| 6.0 | f. | One and one-half turns, step, leap, step, leap with a change of legs |

*Scoring:* The score is the product of the skill difficulty and the execution rating. The following scale is used for the execution rating:

3 points: Correct performance; proper mechanics; execution in good form; balance, control, and amplitude in movements.

2 points: Average performance; errors evident in either mechanics or form; some lack of balance, control, or amplitude in movement.

1 point: Poor performance; errors in both mechanics and form; little balance, control, or amplitude in movements.

0 points: Improper or no performance; incorrect mechanics or complete lack of form; no display of balance, control, or amplitude in movements.

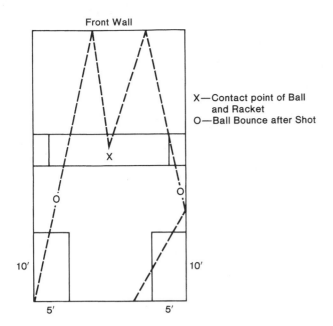

Front Wall

X—Contact point of Ball and Racket
O—Ball Bounce after Shot

10'        10'

5'        5'

**Figure 12.10**
Court markings for the service placement and examples of good serves. (Reprinted by permission of Charles Poteat, Lincoln Memorial University, Harrogate, TN.)

the ball bounces in the target area or passes through the target area. The ball may contact the side wall if the above criteria are met. Each successful serve is awarded one point. The maximum total is 20.

2. *Back wall play.* The court markings for this test item are shown in Figure 12.11. The student stands about 5 feet from the back wall and 20 feet from the side wall. He or she throws the ball to the back wall so that it bounces to the side wall, and then bounces on the floor. The player then returns the ball to the front wall so that the ball does not contact the side wall on the way to the front wall. The ball must contact the front wall at a height of five feet or less above the floor. The student is allowed 2 trials of 10 attempts per trial with the forehand stroke, and 2 trials of 10 attempts per trial with the backhand stroke. No points are awarded if the above criteria are not met. The score is recorded as the total number of successful attempts for both trials.

3. *Wall volley.* The student, holding two balls, begins the test from the service line 15 feet from the front wall. The student drops one of the balls and hits it to the front wall, then continues to rally the ball for 30 seconds. The ball may bounce any number of times on the return to the subject or the ball may be volleyed. The subject may not cross the service line to contact the ball, but may cross the line to retrieve a ball. Any stroke may be used to rally the ball. If the ball passes the player, he or she may put the second ball in play. Additional balls may be obtained from the test administrator. Two 30-second trials are given. One point is awarded for each legal hit to the front wall. The total score is the total number of successful attempts.

**Figure 12.11**
Court markings for the back wall play and examples of good attempts. (Reprinted by permission of Charles Poteat, Lincoln Memorial University, Harrogate, TN.)

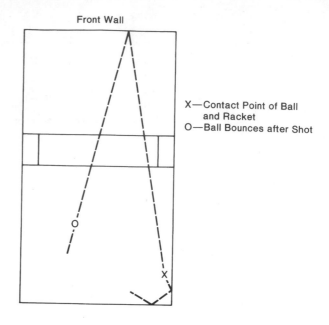

X—Contact Point of Ball and Racket
O—Ball Bounces after Shot

*Other considerations:* Poteat (1983) provides T-scores for scores on each test and percentile ranks for sum of the T-scores. He states that all items in his test battery have sufficient range to discriminate among students with varying ability. The test battery takes 15–18 minutes to administer to each student. If a single item is administered it probably should be a wall volley (Hensley, East & Stillwell 1979). Their wall volley test and most tests of this type allow the student to use either a forehand or backhand stroke. Karpman and Isaacs (1979) maintain there should be one of each.

Dowd (1990) hypothesized that beginning-level racquetball skill of college students is represented by serve, kill shot, and passing/defense shots. For males, Dowd found a volley component represented by the long wall volley and a drive serve component represented by the short-drive serve. However, for females, Dowd found a volley component represented by the long wall volley, a placement component represented by the forehand overhead ceiling shot, and a kill component represented by the forehand kill shot set up with a toss and hit.

## Soccer

### Soccer Battery (Yeagley 1972)

*Objective:* To measure basic soccer skills of beginning players.

*Validity and reliability:* The validity of each of the four test items was examined with two different criteria: (1) the ratings of four judges on the soccer juggling skill and (2) the composite standard score of the four tests. The concurrent validity coefficients were as follows:

|  | **Judges' Ratings** | **Composite Standard Score** |
|---|---|---|
| 1. Dribble | −.66 | −.80 |
| 2. Wall volley | .54 | .81 |
| 3. Juggling | .69 | .74 |
| 4. Heading | .38 | .61 |

A multiple correlation of .76 was reported between the criterion (the judges' ratings) and the dribble and juggling tests. The addition of the wall volley and heading tests increased the multiple correlation to only .78; thus, we recommend that dribble and juggling be used if a short form is wanted. With a sample of male physical education majors who were beginning soccer players, the following internal-consistency coefficients were reported: dribble, .91; wall volley, .90; juggling, .95; and heading, .64.

*Equipment:* The test was designed to be administered in a standard gym with the basketball floor markings used to outline the various test stations. Nine soccer balls inflated to 10 pounds and stopwatches accurate to a tenth of a second are needed. Two assistants are needed for each test.

*Procedures:* The four tests are as follows:

1. *Dribble.* The course for the dribble test is on half a basketball court, as shown in Figure 12.12. On the signal "Go," the student dribbles around the obstacles following the course. The test is scored by the time measured to the nearest second from the signal until the student dribbles the ball across the finish line between the four line markings and brings the ball to a halt using only the feet. It is legal to touch, knock down, or move any obstacle with the ball or the feet so long as the course outline is followed. Two trials are given, and the best time is used.

2. *Wall volley.* The test course for the wall volley consists of an unobstructed wall 8 × 24 feet, and a restraining line 15 feet from the wall (Figure 12.12). On the signal "Go," the student begins kicking the ball from behind the restraining line and continues kicking the rebounded ball to the kickboard area as many times as possible in 30 seconds. Any type of kick and any legal trapping method is permissible; however, to score a legal volley, the nonkicking foot must be behind the restraining line. Additional balls should be available in case the student loses control of the volleyed ball. The score is the number of legal volleys during the 30-second period. Two trials are given, and the best score is used.

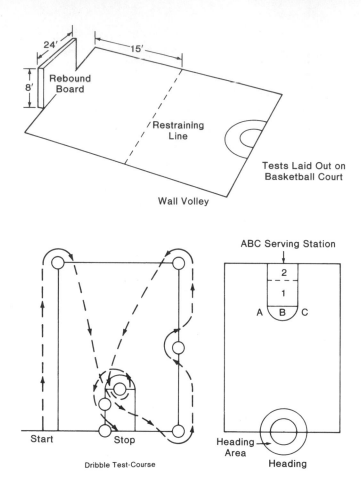

**Figure 12.12**
Test course for the Yeagley Soccer Battery Test. (Reprinted by permission of J. L. Yeagley, Indiana University, Bloomington, IN.)

24'

15'

8'

Rebound Board

Restraining Line

Tests Laid Out on Basketball Court

Wall Volley

ABC Serving Station

2

1

A   B   C

Start   Stop

Heading Area

Dribble Test-Course

Heading

3. *Juggling.* This test also uses half a basketball court as the testing area. The student starts at any point in the area, holding one soccer ball. On the signal "Go," the subject bounces the ball to the floor and then tries to juggle or tap the ball into the air with his or her other body parts as many times as possible in 30 seconds. All parts of the body excluding the arms and hands can be used to continue juggling the ball. (The primary parts used for juggling are the feet, thighs, and head; but the shoulders, chest, and other parts are also legal.) The ball is allowed to bounce on the floor any number of times between touches, although it does not have to bounce at all. It is to the student's advantage to keep the ball in the air for a series of rapidly controlled juggles. The student's score is the number of legal juggles completed in the 30-second period. Juggles outside the half court boundary are not counted. Each time the student controls the ball with the hands or arms 1 point is deducted. Two trials are given, and the best score is used.

4. *Heading.* The course for the heading test is also shown in Figure 12.12. The student stands at any point in the heading area, which is the far half of the center circle. The center line of the basketball court is the restraining line, behind which one foot must be placed when the ball is headed. The ball is thrown by the tester

from the three spots designed in the figure. The throw should be soft, ideally at the same arc on each trial, and no higher than 15 feet. A total of three tosses are administered from spots A and C, four tosses from B. The student being tested can refuse a poorly tossed ball. The student tries to head the tossed ball in the specified scoring zone. Ten trials are administered, and the total points of these trials constitute the subject's score. Balls landing on the line receive the higher value.

*Other considerations:* One advantage of this battery is that it can be administered in a gym. This not only controls for environmental conditions, but also allows the teacher to proceed with skill testing, even in bad weather. A test of total soccer skill ability is not available. Yeagley reported that the juggling test is used as an instructional technique for developing ball sensitivity "touch," very important in performing basic soccer skills. The juggling test was selected by the American Professional Soccer League for a national youth soccer skill test. Coaches and teachers in European countries have used ball juggling as the primary test item in national youth soccer skill contests for the past several years.

If four testing stations are available (two basketball courts), the test could be administered to a class of thirty students during a 50-minute class period.

The reliability of the heading test is somewhat low. For a total of twenty trials the estimated reliability is .78.

## Swimming

### Swimming Achievement for Intermediate Swimmers (Jackson & Pettinger 1969)

*Objective:* To measure achievement of swimmers defined at an intermediate level—that is, those who can swim one length of the pool with the front and back crawl, sidestroke, elementary backstroke, and breaststroke.

*Validity and reliability:* These swimming tests have been examined for logical and concurrent validity with college women, and for logical, concurrent, and construct validity with college men.

1. *Logical validity.* The objectives of the intermediate swimming course were defined in terms of stroke efficiency, mechanics, speed, and endurance. Tests were selected that logically measure these objectives.

2. *Concurrent validity.* The criterion for rating stroke efficiency and mechanics was the independent ratings of three judges over the five strokes. The criterion for speed and endurance was a 5-lap medley swim for time in which the swimmer was required to use each of the five strokes for one lap. The product-moment correlation between each of the tests and these criteria are listed in Table 12.5. Because most of the tests are intercorrelated, combinations of them could be used.
   a. Men. To measure speed and endurance, the multiple correlation between the criterion and a combination of a 2-length medley and a 15-minute swim was .94.
   b. Men. To measure stroke efficiency and mechanics, the multiple correlation between the criterion and a combination of a 15-minute swim and the breaststroke was .91.

**Table 12.5** Concurrent Validity Coefficients for Swimming Stroke Efficiency and Mechanics

| Test | Men | Women | Speed and Endurance for Men |
|------|-----|-------|-----------------------------|
| 1. 15-minute swim | .85 | .61 | .86 |
| 2. 2-length medley | .78 | .04 | .93 |
| 3. Front crawl | .61 | .63 | .53 |
| 4. Back crawl | .57 | .79 | .49 |
| 5. Sidestroke | .64 | .72 | .54 |
| 6. Elementary backstroke | .65 | .72 | .54 |
| 7. Breaststroke | .76 | .64 | .61 |

c. Women. To measure stroke efficiency and mechanics, the multiple correlation between the criterion and a combination of back crawl, 15-minute swim, 2-length medley, elementary backstroke, and breaststroke was .90.

3. *Construct validity.* The performances of three groups of varying ability were compared: intermediate male swimmers; certified water safety instructors; and the Indiana University varsity swimmers, who qualified for the 1968 Olympic swimming tryouts. For every test the means for the intermediates were the lowest and those for the varsity swimmers were the highest.

The reliability coefficients for each of the subtests were not calculated, but the concurrent validity coefficients indicated that the tests were reliable. In another study with college students the reliability estimates of two 25-yard trials of the breaststroke and elementary backstroke administered on two days (a total of four 25-yard trials) were high, .93.

*Equipment:* A timer (with stopwatch) is needed for the 2-length medley. For the other tests a scorer must count strokes or laps for each swimmer. Because this is a relatively simple procedure, other students can be used as scorers.

*Procedures:* The procedures for the seven tests in the battery are as follows:

1. *15-minute swim for distance.* On the starting signal each subject dives into the water and swims as many laps as possible in the 15-minute period. Counters should record the distance. This test can be administered either lengthwise or widthwise in the pool; the score is the number of lengths or widths swum during the 15 minutes. Some pools have distances marked on the side, or tape can be placed at 1-yard intervals on the pool deck. In this way the test can be scored to the last yard.

2. *2-lap timed medley.* Either a 10-pound diving brick or hockey puck is placed on the pool bottom at the halfway mark. Subjects start in the water. On "Go," they front crawl to the halfway line, surface dive, and retrieve the object to the surface. Using the sidestroke, they continue forward with the brick or puck to the far end, deposit it onto the pool deck, push off on their backs, and swim toward the starting end using the elementary backstroke. At the halfway mark, indicated by a line of pennants easily visible from the back position, they turn over and swim using the front crawl to the finish line. The score is the elapsed time measured to the last tenth of a second.

3. *The number of strokes to complete the length of the pool for each of five strokes.* For each of these tests the student starts in the water, pushes off, and swims 1 length. Because the efficiency of the push off is related to overall efficiency, it should be counted as the first stroke. The student should swim at a moderate pace—not a sprint, but not too slow. Strokes are counted until the swimmer touches the opposite end. Strokes and counting methods are as follows:

    a. Front crawl. Strokes are counted by noting the number of hand recoveries.

    b. Back crawl. Same as the front crawl.

    c. Sidestroke. Each power phase—that is, each complete arm-leg cycle—is counted as a stroke.

    d. Elementary backstroke. Same as the sidestroke.

    e. Breaststroke. Same as the sidestroke.

*Other considerations:* With the exception of the 2-length medley, these tests are feasible for mass testing. Using other students for scorers, it is possible to simultaneously test as many swimmers as the size of the pool allows. If the pool width is used, half the class can be tested while the remaining half serves as scorers.

The 15 minutes for the distance swim may be too long for younger students, and this should be altered accordingly. If widths are used for the stroke count tests, we recommend that the sum of four widths be used to ensure reliable measures.

***Red Cross Swimming Skills.*** The American Red Cross has identified basic swimming skills for various swimming classification groups. The skills are subjectively rated on a pass-fail basis. The ratings can be used for the formative evaluation of swimming achievement.

**A. Beginner skills**

1. Water adjustment skills

2. Hold breath—10 sec.

3. Rhythmic breathing—10 times

4. Prone float and recovery

5. Prone glide

6. Back glide and recovery

7. Survival float

**B. Advanced beginner skills**

1. Bobbing—deep water

2. Rhythmic breathing to side

3. Survival float—2 min.

4. Crawl stroke

5. Elementary backstroke

6. Survival stroke

7. Treading water—30–45 sec.

**Summary**

The achievement of psychomotor objectives is a universal goal of physical education programs. We can measure the achievement of psychomotor skills with three general procedures: skill tests, rating scales, and the performance itself.

Skill tests require the creation of an environment similar to the game environment and the standardization of procedures for administration. The validity of skill tests can be judged in part by the extent to which the testing environment duplicates the playing environment. There are four general types of skill tests:

1. Accuracy tests. Accuracy tests require the subject to throw, strike, or kick an object at a target for accuracy. Examples are the basketball free throw, the badminton short serve, and the volleyball serve.

2. Wall volley tests. Wall volley tests require the subject to repeatedly stroke, pass, throw, or kick an object at a wall. The score may be the number of successful volleys completed during a specified time period or the time required to execute a specified number of volleys.

3. Tests of total bodily movement. These tests require the subject to run a standardized test course using movements typical of the sport. Dribbling a basketball through an obstacle course is one example.

4. Throws, kicks, or strokes for power or distance. These tests require the subject to throw, kick, or strike an object (a football, a shuttlecock, etc.) for distance.

Rating scales are a device for evaluating skill achievement subjectively. They are used for evaluating qualities that cannot be efficiently measured by objective means. In a sense these scales add a measure of objectivity to subjective measurements and can yield reliable, valid measurements of skill achievement if they are properly constructed and used.

For some motor skills, the performance itself is a reliable, valid method of evaluating achievement. This type of evaluation tends to be content-valid because the performance environment is also the evaluation environment. Archery, bowling, golf, and swimming are skills that can be evaluated by performance.

The steps in the development of reliable, valid procedures for evaluating skill objectives are as follows:

1. Define what is to be measured.

2. Select a measuring instrument.

3. Pretest the instrument.

4. Revise the test and testing procedures.

5. Administer the instrument.

6. Evaluate the administered test.

7. Revise the final battery.

8. Develop norms.

*Objective 1*   Identify the four general types of sport skill tests.

1. Skill tests involve creating an environment similar to the game situation and standardizing testing procedures. Numerous skill tests have been published for a variety of sport skills. Skill tests can be categorized under one of four general groups. Summarize the characteristics of each group.

    a. Accuracy tests
    b. Wall volley tests
    c. Tests of total bodily movement
    d. Throws, kicks, or strokes for power or distance

*Objective 2*   Evaluate the four general types of sport skill tests using the criteria reliability, validity, and feasibility for mass testing.

1. In order for a test to be valid it must first be reliable. However, a test may be both reliable and valid but still not be feasible for mass use. In order to evaluate the achievement of motor skill objectives, the teacher must select skill tests that meet acceptable levels of reliability and validity and that can be administered in the public school. Each of the four general categories of skill tests has inherent weaknesses and strengths. Identify the basic weakness associated with each category and summarize the actions you could take to improve its effectiveness.

    a. Accuracy tests
    b. Wall volley tests
    c. Tests of total bodily movement
    d. Throws, kicks, or strokes for power or distance

*Objective 3*   Evaluate the weaknesses and strengths of rating scales.

1. In many evaluation situations it is neither feasible nor possible to measure motor skill achievement with an objective sport skill test. In these situations a rating scale is used. A rating scale is a subjective measurement procedure. Differentiate between the terms objective and subjective as applied to the evaluation of motor skill achievement.

2. List the weaknesses and strengths of rating scales.

3. Like all forms of measuring instruments, rating scales must be reliable. Certain procedures in the development and use of rating scales help guard against measurement error and ensure objectivity. Outline the procedures you should follow when constructing and using this type of measurement instrument.

*Objective 4*   Identify motor skills that are best evaluated by performance.

1. For many motor skills the actual performance may be used to evaluate skill achievement. List the basic advantage of using performance as a criterion for skill evaluation.

2. The text offers several illustrations in which skill achievement can be evaluated by performance. Identify an additional motor skill that could be evaluated in this way. Using your example, outline the specific procedures you would follow to evaluate achievement in the skill.

*Objective 5* Outline methods that could be used to develop reliable, valid, and feasible measurement procedures for evaluating motor skill achievement.

1. The text lists systematic procedures for evaluating skill achievement. Briefly outline these procedures.

## Additional Learning Activities

1. Many studies published in *Research Quarterly* have attempted to develop sport skill tests. References for several of these studies are in the Appendix. Select three or four articles and review them. Pay close attention to the methods used to establish the reliability and validity of the tests and the procedures used to develop the battery. Would you use the tests for your physical education class?

2. Often a published skill test does not fit the specific needs of a teacher, who must either revise the published tests or develop a new one. Select a sport skill and develop a test to evaluate it. You might alter an existing test, develop an alternate scoring system, or develop a new test. Administer the test to a group of students and calculate its reliability. Is your test feasible for mass use? Do the most highly skilled students achieve the best test scores?

3. A test can be valid for one group of students but not for another. Select a published sport skill test and determine the concurrent validity of the test with a group of students. In order to accomplish this you must select a criterion measure. (You may want to review Chapter 4 before you begin.)

4. Select a skill that cannot be evaluated with an objective skill test and construct a rating scale for it. With a classmate, independently rate the performance of a group of students and then calculate the correlation between your two ratings. How reliable were your ratings? Remember that reliability can be improved by properly training raters.

5. For some skills, performance provides an objective score for evaluating their achievement. Using a skill such as archery, bowling, or golf, estimate the stability reliability of the performance scores. Remember that for stability reliability you must have the performance scores of the same group of students for two different days.

## Bibliography

A more complete bibliography of sport skill tests, listed by sport, can be found in the Appendix.

AAHPER. 1966a. *Basketball skills test manual for boys.* Washington, DC.
———. 1966b. *Football skills test manual.* Washington, DC.
———. 1967a. *Archery skills test manual.* Washington, DC.
———. 1969. *Volleyball skills test manual.* Washington, DC.
AAHPERD. 1984. *Basketball skills test manual for boys and girls.* Reston, VA.
AAHPERD. 1989. *Tennis skills test manual for boys and girls.* Larry Hensley, (Ed.) Reston, VA.
AAHPERD. 1991. *Softball skills test manual for boys and girls.* Roberta Rikli, (Ed.) Reston, VA.
Collins, D. R. and P. B. Hodges. 1978. *A comprehensive guide to sports skills tests and measurements.* Springfield, IL: Thomas.
Cornish, C. 1949. A study of measurement of ability in handball. *Research Quarterly* 20:215–222.

Dowd, D. A. 1990. A factor analysis of selected beginning-level racquetball skill tests. Ed.D. dissertation, University of Georgia, Athens, GA.

Dyer, J. T. 1935. The backboard test of tennis ability. *Research Quarterly 6* (Supp.):63–74.

Ellenbrand, D. A. 1973. Gymnastics skills tests for college women. Master's thesis, Indiana University, Bloomington, IN.

Gaunt, S. 1979. Factor structure of basketball playing ability. P.E.D. dissertation, Indiana University, Bloomington, IN.

Green, K. N., W. B. East, and L. D. Hensley. 1987. A golf skill test battery for college males and females. *Research Quarterly for Exercise and Sport 58:*72–76.

Hensley, L., W. East, and J. Stillwell. 1979. A racquetball skills test. *Research Quarterly 50:*114–118.

Hopkins, D. R. 1977. Factor analysis of selected basketball skill tests. *Research Quarterly 48:*535–540.

Jackson, A. S. and J. Pettinger. 1969. The development and discriminant analysis of swimming profiles of college men. *Proceedings of 72d Annual Meeting, National College Physical Education Association for Men,* 104–110.

Karpman, M. and L. Isaacs. 1979. An improved racquetball skills test. *Research Quarterly 50:*526–527.

Klein, S. P. 1971. The uses and limitations of standardized tests in meeting the demands for accountability. *UCLA Evaluation Comment,* Vol. 2, No. 4 (January 1971), 1–7.

Morris, H. H. 1977. A critique of the AAHPER skill test series. Paper presented to the Measurement and Evaluation Council, AAHPER National Convention, Seattle, WA.

Poteat, C. 1983. A skill test battery to measure overall racquetball playing ability. Ed.D. dissertation, University of Georgia, Athens, GA.

Scott, M. G. and E. French. 1959. *Measurement and evaluation in physical education.* Dubuque, IA: Wm. C. Brown.

Sebolt, D. R. 1968. Badminton skill tests. Unpublished paper, Virginia Polytechnic Institute and State University.

Yeagley, J. 1972. Soccer skills test. Unpublished paper, Indiana University, Bloomington, IN.

# Cognitive and Affective Testing

# Evaluating Knowledge

## Key Words

## Contents

## Objectives

The process of evaluating knowledge is threefold: (1) constructing a knowledge test based on the cognitive objectives of the unit, (2) administering it, and (3) analyzing it. Before the actual construction, the type of test and the test items must be selected to be sure that the content is correct and the items themselves are well constructed. In addition, it is important to administer and score the test so that all people have the same opportunity to do well, and so that the scores themselves are valid. Finally, it is vital to analyze the test to determine the quality of each item and the test as a whole. This analysis indicates not only quality of the test, but also how it might be revised.

After reading Chapter 13, you should be able to:

1. Differentiate among various types of knowledge tests.
2. Define the levels of knowledge most applicable to physical education and adult fitness.
3. Outline the basic procedures used for constructing, administering, and scoring a knowledge test.
4. Evaluate knowledge test items.
5. Analyze knowledge tests in terms of test reliability and item analysis.

## INTRODUCTION

Knowledge is one of the objectives of most physical education programs. Teachers want their students to know the rules, etiquette, terminology, procedures, and strategy of various sports and physical activities. Students should understand the role of exercise on health and physical fitness and how to stay fit. Many health-related fitness programs have knowledge objectives. The extent to which these objectives are met can best and sometimes exclusively be determined with a knowledge test.

Knowledge is often retained longer than physical skill and fitness. Obviously people lose a degree of skill and fitness as they stop participating in sports, but they can continue to enjoy sports as spectators if they have acquired sufficient knowledge. Then, too, as health-related physical fitness programs become more popular, greater emphasis is being placed on the cognitive aspects of physical fitness and health (see Chapter 1). Knowledge, then, is a wanted objective of physical education programs and adult fitness programs and should be one of the first areas of attention in any measurement procedure.

Knowledge is also an objective in adult fitness programs and rehabilitation programs. The instructor or clinician wants the program participants to know why fitness is important, how to develop and maintain fitness, the importance of good diet, why stress management is important, the adverse effects of smoking, and why they received an injury and how not to become reinjured. To determine if program participants have this knowledge as they enter the program or are obtaining this knowledge as a result of handouts and verbal presentations during the program, a knowledge questionnaire (test) must be administered. This knowledge questionnaire is scored not to grade each participant, but to determine what information needs to be provided to program participants.

## Levels of Knowledge

There are different levels or degrees of knowledge. This is apparent whenever a group of people is tested: Their understanding of a given topic can range from superficial to thorough.

Bloom's **taxonomy** of educational objectives (1956) proposes six levels of behavior arranged in ascending order of complexity: knowledge, comprehension, application, analysis, synthesis, and evaluation. Each level corresponds to a level of knowledge. Bloom then divides the levels of behavior and provides illustrative questions for each subdivision. Table 13.1 lists Bloom's six levels and their subdivisions. Because the two highest levels are quite complex and usually exceed the educational objectives of a typical physical education activity course or adult fitness program, only the first four levels of knowledge in the taxonomy are presented, defined, and illustrated with a test question in Table 13.2. The educational objectives of most courses and programs do exceed Bloom's first level because teachers and exercise specialists want students and participants to acquire more than a superficial knowledge of the topics covered.

# Table 13.1 Bloom's Taxonomy of Educational Objectives

1.00 Knowledge
    1.10 Knowledge of specifics
    1.20 Knowledge of ways and means of dealing with specifics
    1.30 Knowledge of the universals and abstractions in a field

2.00 Comprehension
    2.10 Translation
    2.20 Interpretation
    2.30 Extrapolation

3.00 Application

4.00 Analysis
    4.10 Analysis of elements
    4.20 Analysis of relationships
    4.30 Analysis of organizational principles

5.00 Synthesis
    5.10 Production of a unique communication
    5.20 Production of a plan for operations
    5.30 Derivation of a set of abstract relations

6.00 Evaluation
    6.10 Judgments in terms of internal evidence
    6.20 Judgments in terms of external evidence

# Table 13.2 The First Four Levels of Bloom's Taxonomy

| Level | Definition | Sample Question for Golf Test |
|---|---|---|
| I. Knowledge | Recall of ideas, terms, facts, etc. | What is a slice? |
| II. Comprehension | The use of translation, interpretation, or extrapolation to understand certain ideas, terms, facts, etc. | What causes a slice? |
| III. Application | The use of general ideas, rules of procedure, or generalized methods in particular and concrete situations. | The following scores were recorded by four golfers on 9 holes. In what order should the golfers tee off on the 8th tee? |
| IV. Analysis | The separation of a phenomenon into its constituents so that its nature, composition, and organizational principles may be determined. | A golf ball is located on a hill above the cup, and the shot will be made downhill onto a very fast green. The ball is best played with what kind of grip and stroke, and off what part of the club face? |

For Application:

| Player | 1 | 2 | 3 | 4 | 5 | 6 | 7 | 8 | 9 | Total |
|---|---|---|---|---|---|---|---|---|---|---|
| A | 3 | 6 | 3 | 4 | 3 | 4 | 7 | 3 | 6 | 39 |
| B | 4 | 5 | 4 | 4 | 4 | 5 | 4 | 3 | 4 | 37 |
| C | 6 | 6 | 5 | 3 | 3 | 3 | 3 | 3 | 3 | 35 |
| D | 3 | 3 | 4 | 4 | 2 | 4 | 5 | 7 | 3 | 35 |

Although the majority of questions on many physical education knowledge tests require the students only to remember facts, some questions should draw on higher levels of knowledge. And certainly, as the class becomes more advanced, the number of knowledge questions should be smaller, and the number of questions from the higher levels of the taxonomy should be larger.

## Types of Knowledge Tests

**Knowledge tests** are either essay or objective tests and either mastery or discrimination tests. Each question on a knowledge test, whether stated as a question or not, is called an **item.** Teachers and exercise specialists must choose the type of test they want before they can begin to construct it.

### Essay versus Objective

An **essay test** is any test on which people answer each item with whatever information they choose and write their answers in sentences. The answer to an essay item may be short or long, depending on how much the person knows and how full an answer the item requires. **Objective tests**—true-false, multiple choice, matching, and the like—have potential answers provided with each test item. After reading an item, a person selects one of the provided answers. For example, T or F on a true-false item.

The question of which test to use—essay or objective—raises both philosophical and economic issues. Some educators believe that objective tests encourage students to memorize facts rather than integrate facts together into a total understanding. These people use essay tests on the theory that the students must have a total understanding to answer essay questions. Other educators maintain that essay tests allow students to write everything they know about the subject, while objective tests determine if they know only what has been asked. Students frequently complain after objective tests that the teacher did not ask any of the things they knew. We can think of the items on an objective test as a sample from an infinite number of items that could have been used.

Economically, objective tests are time-consuming to construct but quick to score, while essay tests are the reverse. It does not take long to construct three to five general essay-type items, but it takes considerable time to properly read and score each one. Whenever tests are to be used with many people, either in one testing session or over numerous sessions, objective tests are more economical than essays in terms of total time involvement. Once the objective test is developed, it is easy to use and score. This is probably the major reason why objective tests are used more than essay tests.

### Mastery versus Discrimination

A **mastery test**—a kind of formative evaluation with criterion-referenced standards—is used to determine whether the students or program participants have mastered the material. Items on the test pertain to information everyone is expected to know. Many of these items are easy, and often the entire class or group answers them correctly. However, the performance standards for mastery tests tend to be high. Bloom and his associates (1971; 1981) recommend that the criterion for passing a knowledge test be 80% to 90% correct answers. A mastery test is graded pass-fail or proficient-nonproficient. It is commonly used in physical education and adult fitness programs.

The purpose of a **discrimination test**—a form of summative evaluation with norm-referenced standards—is to differentiate among students in terms of knowledge. Each test item is written to discriminate among ability groups. Thus, discrimination tests include a larger number of difficult items than do mastery tests. They often do not elicit basic information because it does not discriminate sufficiently. As a result of using a discrimination-type test, a few excellent students will have high scores on the test while the rest of the students will have lower scores. Discrimination tests are seldom used outside of education.

Mastery tests tend to include items from the knowledge, comprehension, and application levels of Bloom's taxonomy (1956); discrimination tests tend to include items from the higher levels. Because discrimination tests are more difficult than mastery tests, their performance standards must be lower. The test mean and standard deviation need to be considered when developing the grading scale (see Chapters 3 and 6).

The decision about which test to use—mastery or discrimination—should depend on your educational purposes and how the test scores will be used. For a formative evaluation of student achievement, a mastery test should be used. For a summative evaluation of student achievement, a discrimination test should be used. Formative evaluation is graded on a pass-fail basis; summative evaluation allows the teacher to identify individual differences in achievement by assigning letter grades.

Some teachers have mistakenly used mastery tests to make summative evaluations. The reliability of letter grades based on scores of mastery tests is almost always low because most of the items are too easy to discriminate well. To achieve high reliability, test items must discriminate sufficiently so that the students' scores are spread out. Later in the chapter we will show that the larger the standard deviation, the higher the Kuder-Richardson reliability. Low reliability means, in turn, that the standard error of measurement (see Chapter 4) is similar in value to the standard deviation for the test.

An example should clarify these points. Assume a mastery test is administered in a first aid class and letter grades are assigned based on the test scores. Suppose that the grading standard for a 100-point test is A: 93–100, B: 87–92, C: 78–86, D: 70–77, and F: below 69. If the standard deviation is 8 and the reliability of the test is .44, the standard error of measurement for the test is 6. Thus, the probability is .68 that a student who scored 88 will score between 82 and 94 ($88 \pm 6$) if retested. Notice that 82 is a C and 94 is an A; the assigned grade is not reliable. If formative standards are used and a score of 80 or above is considered passing, the large standard error of measurement poses no problem because the student passes whether the score is 82 or 94. This is not to suggest that large standard errors are desirable or will not cause problems for other scores. For the person with a score close to the pass/fail cutoff score, the size of the standard error may be quite critical.

Similarly, assume that the instructional objectives for a physical education unit pertain to knowledge of the rules of a sport. The best policy in this situation is probably to use a mastery test for formative evaluation. If a student can correctly answer 80% of the items on the test, the teacher can assume that the student has enough knowledge to play the sport. The mastery test is designed essentially to measure knowledge of basic rules. Similar thinking would apply in an adult fitness program.

Of course, mere knowledge of the rules is not sufficient for playing a sport. The rules must be applied and several different rules may have to be considered to resolve a situation. To interpret rules the higher levels of the cognitive domain must be used. The teacher might use a discrimination test for summative evaluation of the students' ability to apply, analyze, and synthesize the rules in a game situation. Although students may know all the basic rules, they are likely to differ in their ability to understand, apply, and interpret them.

**Table 13.3** Sample Table of Specifications
for a Basketball Test

| | Type of Test Items | | |
|---|---|---|---|
| *Subject Topic* | *Knowledge* | *Comprehension* | *Application* |
| Rules | 15% | 5% | 0% |
| Player duties | 20% | 10% | 0% |
| Offensive plays | 10% | 10% | 10% |
| Defenses | 5% | 5% | 0% |
| Strategy | 0% | 0% | 10% |

**Construction**

Whenever possible, the teacher or exercise specialist should develop his or her own knowledge tests. A major advantage of instructor-made tests is that they tend to cover the material stressed in the unit in terminology the people understand. Thus, instructor-made tests tend to have logical validity (see Chapter 5). Another person's test not only may omit important material and include irrelevant material, but also may confuse people with the use of unfamiliar terminology.

**Procedure**

Typically, there are four general procedural steps to follow in constructing a good knowledge test:

Step 1. Construct a table of specifications.

Step 2. Decide the nature of the test.

Step 3. Construct the test items.

Step 4. Determine the test format and administrative details.

A table of specifications is an outline for the test construction. It lists the areas and levels of knowledge to be tested, as shown in Table 13.3. By adhering to a table of specifications, the test developer ensures that all the material on it is covered and that the correct weight is given to each area.

In deciding which type of test to give, consider the advantages and disadvantages of essay and objective tests, and then, if an objective test is chosen, of true-false, multiple-choice, or other types of items. There is no reason why a test must be composed of a single type of item, although all items of the same type should be grouped together. Tests that include both true-false and multiple-choice items, or some objective and some essay items, are not uncommon.

The third step is writing the test items. Begin this task well in advance of the testing session. It is important to allow enough time to develop items that are carefully conceptualized and constructed. In fact, after constructing the items, the constructor should read them, correct them, and then put them aside for at least a day before reading them again. A fresh look may pinpoint other errors and ambiguities.

Finally the test format is chosen. One important consideration is the directions, which should appear at the top of the test. The directions must clearly indicate how to take the test, what is the policy for guessing, whether a question may have more than one correct answer, etc. Another consideration is the presentation of the items. They

Part 4 Cognitive and Affective Testing

should be typed neatly with enough space to make them easy to read. When several items pertain to information supplied on the test (for example, a diagram), the information and the items should be on the same page. Examples of good test format are presented later in the chapter.

*True-False.* A **true-false item** consists of a short, factual statement. If the statement appears to be true, the person marks True or T; otherwise the person marks False, or F. This type of item is quite popular.

Advantages and Disadvantages: The advantages of true-false items are as follows:

1. The rapidity with which people can answer these items makes it possible to include many items on the test.
2. It is easier and quicker to construct true-false items than other types of objective items.
3. Test items can be scored quickly.
4. Factual information is easily tested.
5. Standardized answer sheets can be used.

The disadvantages are these:

1. Probably only the first level of Bloom's taxonomy (1956), knowledge, can be tested by a true-false test.
2. People have a 50% chance of guessing the correct answer.
3. It is easy for a person to cheat by glancing at another person's paper.
4. This type of item can encourage memorization rather than understanding of facts.
5. This type of item is often ambiguous, in that the test taker and the test maker may not interpret an item in the same way.
6. True-false items often test trivial information.
7. To ensure reliability, a true-false test requires more items than does a multiple-choice test.

Construction Procedures: Many people believe that true-false test items are easy to construct. Unfortunately this is not entirely the case. Although they are easier to construct than some other types of objective items, true-false items must be constructed with care, using the following rules:

1. Keep the statement short. If it is long, the test taker may have to read it several times, which means that fewer items can be asked.
2. Use only a single concept in any one statement. This way, if a person answers incorrectly, you can identify the concept he or she does not know.
3. Keep the vocabulary simple.
4. Do not reproduce statements exactly from the text unless your objective is for the student to identify the passage.
5. Whenever possible, state the items positively rather than negatively.

6. Avoid using words like "always," "never," "all," and "none." Absolute statements are almost always false, and many people know this.

7. Do not allow more than 60% of the items to have the same answer. People expect approximately half the items to be true, which influences their thinking as they take a test.

8. Avoid long strings of items with the same answers.

9. Avoid patterns in the answers like true, false, true, false, etc.

10. Do not give clues in one item to the answer of another. For example, don't let the statement in item 1 help answer item 14.

11. Avoid interdependent items. They put the person who misses the first item in double jeopardy.

Examples of Poor True-False Items: Ebel (1979) provides many examples of poor true-false items, but a sampling of poor items and the reasons why follow:

1. T(F) In soccer, the hands cannot touch the ball except when the ball is thrown in or when the player is the goalie.
   *Explanation.* The key word "legally" has been omitted. Also, two questions are being asked: (1) Can the hands be used to throw the ball in? (2) Can the goalie touch the ball with his or her hands?

2. T(F) Never go swimming just after you have eaten.
   *Explanation.* An absolute like "never" should not be used. A better item would be "It is not recommended that a person go swimming immediately after eating."

3. T(F) Physical fitness is important because a sound body and a sound mind usually go hand in hand, and, further, the physically fit person does not tire as easily as the unfit person and, thus, is usually more productive, but the fit person does not necessarily live longer than the less fit person.
   *Explanation.* The statement is too long and includes multiple concepts.

4. T(F) A timed run may be used to test cardiorespiratory endurance.
   *Explanation.* The statement is ambiguous because the distance of the timed run isn't stated.

*Multiple Choice.* A **multiple-choice item** is composed of a short complete or incomplete question or statement followed by three to five potential answers. The first part of the item, the question or statement, is called the "stem"; the answers are called "responses." After reading the stem, the person selects the correct response. Complete stems are preferred over incomplete stems. Multiple-choice items are the most popular type of item with professional test makers, and are commonly used by all people who construct knowledge tests.

Advantages and Disadvantages: Among the advantages of this type of item are the following:

1. Because people can answer each multiple-choice item quickly, many items can be included in the test.

2. Test items can be scored quickly.

3. All levels of knowledge in Bloom's taxonomy can be tested with multiple-choice items.

4. The chances of a person guessing correctly are slimmer than for true-false items, and decrease as the number of responses (plausible answers) increases.

5. Standardized answer sheets can be used.

Among the disadvantages of multiple-choice items are these:

1. Fewer items can be asked than with true-false items.

2. Considerable time is needed to think of enough plausible responses to each item.

3. There is a certain danger of cheating on multiple-choice items.

4. To some degree, multiple-choice items encourage memorization of facts without regard to their implications. This is more of a problem with items at the lower end of Bloom's taxonomy, and is generally less of a problem than it is with true-false items.

5. Students are unable to demonstrate the extent of their knowledge; they can respond only to the items as the instructor has constructed them. Of course this is a legitimate criticism of all objective test questions.

Constructive Procedures: Multiple-choice items are not easy to construct. The development of items with good stems and responses takes time, and it can be difficult to think of enough responses for an item. It is not uncommon to spend 15–30 minutes constructing a single item. However, if the following few rules are followed, you should end up with an acceptable test.

1. Keep both stems and responses short and explicit.

2. Make all responses approximately the same length. Beginning test constructors have a tendency to include more information in the correct responses than in the incorrect responses, a fact the test takers quickly pick up.

3. Use apparently acceptable answers for all responses. There is no excuse for writing obviously incorrect or sloppy responses.

4. If possible, use five responses for each item. This keeps the guess factors acceptably low (.20), and it is usually hard to think of more. It is desirable that all multiple-choice items on a test have the same number of responses.

5. If the stem is an incomplete sentence or question, make each response complete the stem.

6. Do not give away the correct answer with English usage. If the stem is singular, all responses should be singular. Words beginning with a vowel must be preceded by "an."

7. Do not give away the answer to one item in the content of another.

8. Do not allow the answer to one item depend on the answer to another. If people answer the first incorrectly, they will answer the second incorrectly as well.

9. Do not construct the stem in such a way that you solicit a person's opinion. For example, do not begin questions with "What should be done?" or "What would you do?"

10. If the items are numbered, use letters (a,b,c,d,e) to enumerate the responses. People tend to confuse response numbers with item numbers if the responses are numbered, particularly when standardized answer sheets are used.

11. Try to use each letter as the correct answer approximately the same number of times in the test. If the constructor is not careful, (c) may be the correct response more often than any other, which could help people guess the correct answer.

12. State the stem in positive rather than negative terms.

Examples of Poor Multiple-Choice Items: Again see Ebel (1979) for additional examples.

1. What should you do if the right front wheel of your car goes off the pavement as you are driving?

   a. Brake sharply.
   b. Cut the front wheels sharply to the left.
   c. Brake sharply and cut the wheels sharply to the left.
   d. Brake sharply and turn the wheels gradually to the left.
 *e. Brake gradually, maintaining control of the car by driving along the shoulder of the road if necessary. Then pull gently back onto the pavement when speed is reduced.
   *Explanation. (1) the stem asks for the student's opinion; (2) it is understood, but should be stated in the stem, that the right front wheel went off the right side of the pavement; (3) the longest response is the correct answer.*

2. A multiple-choice item is a

 *a. very popular and commonly used type of item.
   b. alternative to a true-false item.
   c. important type of knowledge test item.
   d. very easy type of item to construct.
   e. limited application type of item.
   *Explanation.* Responses b and c can be eliminated because the stem ends in "a" and they both begin with vowels. The best solution is to end the stem at "is" and to add "a" or "an" to each response.

3. What is the worst position in wrestling?

   a. on both knees
   b. flat-footed
   c. leaning forward
   d. weight all on one leg
 *e. none of the above
   *Explanation.* It is not clear from the question what is wanted and whether the wrestlers are standing or prone. In truth, the worst position is on the back because the wrestler is in danger of being pinned.

4. Pick the incorrect statement from the following:

   a. Only the serving team can score in volleyball.
 *b. In badminton, a person cannot score unless he or she has the serve.
   c. In tennis, a set has not been won if the score is 40–30.

d. In tennis, volleyball, and badminton, a net serve is served again.

e. In tennis and badminton, a player cannot reach over the net to contact the ball or shuttlecock.

*Explanation.* (1) When an incorrect response is to be identified, all responses should be stated positively so as not to confuse the students.

(2) In response e, it would be preferable to say "it is illegal for a player to reach. . . ."

***Matching.*** In a **matching-item** test, a number of short questions or statements are listed on the left side of the page and the answers are listed in order on the right. Matching items are a logical extension of multiple-choice items in that both provide the person with several answers from which to choose. Matching items are used less often than true-false or multiple-choice items, but they are very helpful in situations in which the same answers can be used with several test items. A sample matching test is shown in Table 13.4.

Advantages and Disadvantages: Among the advantages of matching items are the following:

1. You can save space by giving the same potential answers for several questions.

2. The odds of guessing the right answer are theoretically quite low because there are so many answers to choose from. In actuality, people will probably be able to detect that no more than five to eight answers apply to any given question.

3. These items are quicker to construct than multiple-choice questions.

The disadvantages of matching items are these:

1. Matching items usually test only factual information (the lowest level in Bloom's taxonomy).

2. Matching items are not particularly versatile, and a multiple-choice item often serves just as well.

3. Standardized answer sheets usually cannot be used with these items.

Construction Procedures: To develop a fair test, carefully plan the format and directions using the following rules:

1. State the items and potential answers clearly; neither should be more than two lines long.

2. Number the items and identify the potential answers with letters.

3. Allow a space at the left of each item for the correct answer.

4. Keep all items and answers on the same page.

5. Make all items similar in content. It is preferable to construct several sets of matching items rather than to mix content.

6. Arrange potential answers in logical groupings—all numerical answers together, all dates together, and so on. This saves people the time necessary to scan all the answers before responding.

**Table 13.4** A Sample Matching Test

---

## Volleyball

For each item on the left-hand side of the page, find an answer on the right-hand side. Place the letter of the correct answer in the space provided at the left side of each item. Each answer can be used only once.

*Items*

|  | | |
|---|---|---|
| _____ 1. The official height of the net in feet | a. | 6 |
| _____ 2. The number of players on an official team | b. | 8 |
| _____ 3. The number of points needed to win a game | c. | 12 |
| _____ 4. Loss of the serve | d. | 15 |
| _____ 5. Loss of a point | e. | 18 |
| _____ 6. Illegal play | f. | 21 |
| | g. | Net serve that goes over |
| | h. | More than 3 hits by receiving team |
| | i. | Reaching over the net to spike the ball |
| | j. | Stepping on a side boundary line |
| | k. | Serving team carries the ball |

---

## Golf

In items 7–10, determine which of the four clubs listed on the right is best suited for the shot described on the left. Each answer can be used more than once.

*Items*

|  | | |
|---|---|---|
| _____ 7. Tee shot on a 90-yard hole | l. | Three-wood |
| _____ 8. 100-yard approach to the green | m. | Two-iron |
| _____ 9. Fairway shot 140 yards from the green | n. | Five-iron |
| _____ 10. 200-yard shot from the rough | o. | Nine-iron |

---

7. Provide more answers than items to prevent people from deducing answers by elimination.

8. In the directions, tell the people whether an answer can be used more than once.

9. Have several potential answers for each item.

***Completion.*** In a **completion item,** one word or several words are omitted from a sentence, and the student is asked to supply the missing information. This type of item has limited usefulness and application, and is less satisfactory than a multiple-choice item. In fact, none of the better textbooks discuss this type of item in detail (Ahmann & Glock 1981; Barrow, McGee & Tritschler 1989; Ebel 1979; Gronlund 1982, 1985). Unless completion items are stated carefully, students may be uncertain what information the teacher wants. For example, consider the following item:

Three playing combinations in racquetball are _____, _____, and

_____.

Some people will answer singles, doubles, and cutthroat, while others, thinking about doubles play, will respond side-by-side, front-and-back, and rotation. Dizney (1971) suggests that acceptable answers to the item "$.02 and $.03 are _____?" must include "$.05," "5," "a nickel," "5 pennies," and "money." Obviously true-false or multiple-choice items could do the job with less ambiguity.

***Short Answer and Essay.*** **Short-answer** and **essay** items are appropriate when the teacher wants to determine the student's depth of knowledge and their capacity to assemble and organize facts. For each item students answer with whatever facts and in whatever manner they think appropriate.

Advantages and Disadvantages: The advantages of essay items are the following:

1. Students are free to answer essay items in the way that seems best to them.
2. These items allow students to demonstrate the depth of their knowledge.
3. These items encourage students to relate all the material to a total concept rather than just to learn the facts.
4. The items are easy and quick to construct.
5. All levels of Bloom's taxonomy can be tested with essay items.

Their disadvantages are these:

1. Essay items are time-consuming to grade.
2. The objectivity of test scores is often low.
3. The reliability of test scores is often low.
4. Essay items require some skill in self-expression; if this skill is not an instructional objective, the item lacks validity.
5. Penmanship and neatness affect grades, which again lowers the item's validity.
6. The halo effect; students expected to do well on the test tend to be scored higher than they may deserve.

Construction Procedures: Most teachers can construct reasonably good short-answer or essay items. However, if an item is hastily constructed, the students may not respond in the manner wanted. The biggest disadvantage of this type of item may be its grading. Teachers must key an item carefully to identify the characteristics wanted in the answer and to determine how partial credit points are assigned. Without an answer sheet, the reliability of scores is often low. For example, if a test item is worth 20 points and 5 specific facts should be mentioned in the answer, each fact is worth 4 points. If only 3 of the 5 facts are included, the student receives 12 points. Thus, if the teacher should grade the item again, the student is likely again to receive 12 points. Research that required an instructor to grade a set of essay tests twice has found the test-retest reliability is usually low. The objectivity of essay test grades has also been investigated by assigning two qualified teachers to grade a set of essays independently. The objectivity has seldom been high.

If the following rules for constructing short-answer and essay items are followed, the items should be satisfactory:

1. State the item as clearly and concisely as possible.

2. Note on the test the approximate time students should spend on each item.

3. Note on the test the point value for each item.

4. Carefully key the test before administration. This is the only way to identify ambiguous items.

**Sample Tests**

Ideally people should construct their own knowledge tests. Those constructed by others often do not have the terminology or material emphasis needed for every teacher and class. If, for example, two teachers do not use the same technique, the correct answer to a question about that technique will not be the same for both instructors. The content and emphasis of a knowledge test also are influenced considerably by the age, sex, and ability level of the students. Knowledge tests can quickly become outdated as ideas, techniques, and rules change.

There are several sources of knowledge tests. Some have been published in research journals, and most books and manuals about specific sports and skills include sample knowledge tests. McGee and Farrow (1987) published a book of test questions for fifteen different activities. Unpublished knowledge tests (theses, dissertations, tests constructed by teachers in your school system) are also available.

Several sample knowledge test items are included here.

### *Badminton*

Part I. True-False. If the answer is true, put a plus (+) to the left of the item number. If the answer is false, put a minus (−) to the left of the item number. Please respond to each item.

_____ 1. In singles play it is tactically poor to return your opponent's drop with another drop unless your opponent is completely out of position in the back court.

_____ 2. Proper position of the feet is more important in the execution of strokes made from a point near the rear boundary line than from a point near the net.

_____ 3. Players A-1 and A-2, a two-person team, are trailing in their game 5-3. They have just broken the serve of Team B, so A-1 will start the serve in the right service court for Team A.

Part II. Multiple-Choice. To the left of the item number put the letter of the answer that is most correct. Please respond to each item.

_____ 4. During the execution of a stroke the arm is straightened
   a. at no particular time
   b. just prior to contact between racket and bird
   c. at the moment of contact between racket and bird
   d. just after contact is made between racket and bird

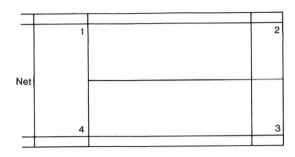

_____ 5. If your opponent is in the back left-hand corner of his or her court when you play the bird, what number in the diagram represents your best target?

    a. 1

    b. 2

    c. 3

    d. 4

Part III. Identification. Give the official names of the lines of the court that are numbered in the diagram, placing the name next to the number.

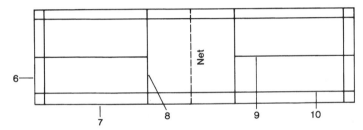

## Volleyball

Read the instructions that precede each section of the test before you answer any of the items in that section.

Part I. True-False. If the statement is true, blacken the a on the answer sheet. If the statement is false, blacken b on the answer sheet for that numbered statement.

1. To start the game, Team A serves. Team B's first server will be the player who started the game as the right forward.

2. If the spiker is left-handed, the "ideal" set-up will be on his or her right side.

3. The blocker's jump is begun just before the spiker's jump.

Part II. Matching. Read each numbered statement and choose the best answer from the five responses. Then, on the answer sheet, blacken the letter of the correct response for that numbered statement. Use the same five responses for items 4 through 7.

a. Point for Team A
b. Point for Team B
c. Loss of serve
d. Legal, play continues
e. Reserve or serve over

4. While Team B is serving, a player on Team A tries to play the ball, but it bounces off his or her shoulder and a teammate successfully spikes the ball over the net where it strikes the floor inbounds.

5. During the return of B's serve, a player on Team A spikes the ball, which lands inbounds on B's side of the net.

6. Team A serves. Team B sets the ball for its spiker, while Team A sets up a two-person block. During the spike-block play, Spiker B lands over the center line; however, one of A's blockers' hands goes over the net.

7. Team B serves. Team A sets the ball for the spiker, while Team B sets up a two-person block. Player A spikes the ball into Blocker B's hands and the ball bounds over Team A's end line.

### Wrestling Knowledge Test (Kraft 1971)
(This test has good directions, diagrams, and so on.)
Instructions to be read by the test examiner:

1. This test consists of 50 multiple-choice questions. Read each question carefully. Select the most appropriate answer and, using the pencil provided, mark your answer on the separate answer sheet. Do not mark on the test booklet. Scratch paper has been provided for use in any computations.

2. Mark a heavy black line in the box on the answer sheet. Be sure that the number on the answer sheet corresponds to the number in the test booklet. Do not make stray marks and carefully erase any answer you want to change. Questions with more than one answer will be marked incorrect. Do not fold, bend, or tear the answer sheet.

3. Mark only one answer for each question, but answer all questions. When you do not know an answer, make an intelligent guess. Your score will be the number of right responses.

4. Are there any questions?

5. You have approximately 45 minutes to complete the test.

1. If the final score of a match is Wrestler-A 5 and Wrestler-B 4, how many team points are earned by each wrestler?

   a. A 0, B 3
   b. A 3, B 0
   c. A 5, B 0
   d. B 5, A 0
   e. None of the above.

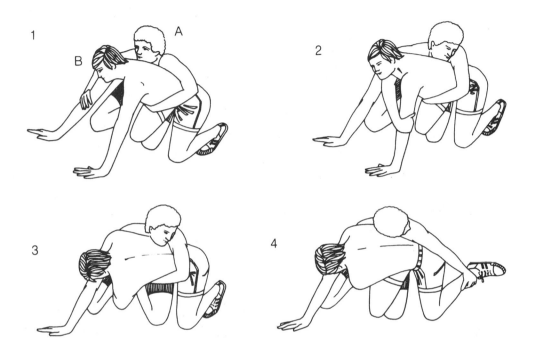

2. How many points are awarded Contestant A for successful execution of the maneuver illustrated?

   a. 0
   b. 1
   c. 1 or 2
   d. 2
   e. None of the above.

## Administration and Scoring

### Administration Procedures

A test setting should be quiet, well lighted, properly heated, odor-free, spacious, and comfortable. The failure to furnish a comfortable and distraction-free testing site places people at a disadvantage. Physical education teachers and exercise specialists often are not careful about the testing atmosphere and setting: The practice of instructing students to lie on the gym floor to take a test while other students participate in another part of the gym leaves much to be desired.

The teacher must also consider test security. During a test, students should all face the same direction. They should be sitting close enough to allow the teacher to see everyone, but far enough apart to preclude cheating and whispering. In a classroom, you may assign a student to every other seat or, better still, to every other seat of every other row. Encourage students to keep their eyes on their own papers and their papers covered. Sometimes alternate test forms, with the same items arranged on each form in a different order, are used. Also a procedure for collecting the papers is essential. If students stand around the teacher waiting to turn in their tests, they can exchange answers while they wait; and, students still taking the test can exchange answers while the teacher is busy collecting other students' tests.

If you plan to use the same test with several classes, you must ensure that students who have taken the test do not give the test items and answers to those yet to take it. If only two consecutive classes are to take the test, security poses no problem. However, if even as much as an hour elapses between the two administrations, the test's contents will probably be known to the second class. The best approach, then, is to use several forms of the test. Of course each form must test the same material. A common procedure with multiple-choice tests is to construct parallel items. For example, all forms of the test include an item dealing with the volleyball serve. With true-false tests, a common procedure is to reword some of the items on the second form so that the answer changes.

### Scoring Procedures

On an essay test, remove the person's name from the test paper to increase the validity and objectivity of scoring, and score each student's answer to a single item before going on to the next item. This procedure, and the use of a key, increases the likelihood that the same standards will be applied to all answers. Reliability suffers when an essay test is scored in a hurry. This is one reason why essay tests take so much time to score.

The scoring of true-false and multiple-choice items, although usually less time-consuming than essay questions, can be tedious if it is done by referring alternately to the answer key and each person's answers. Standardized answer sheets can speed up the scoring of true-false and multiple-choice tests. These answer sheets can be constructed by the teacher or exercise specialist or purchased commercially. A sample of a commercial, standardized answer sheet is shown in Figure 13.1. These standardized answer sheets have the advantage of being machine-scorable, thus eliminating the time needed to score the tests by hand. Machines to score tests vary from the large and expensive ones used by scoring services and universities to the small and inexpensive desktop model used by individual schools or programs. In addition, the use of standardized answer sheets makes it possible to reuse test booklets.

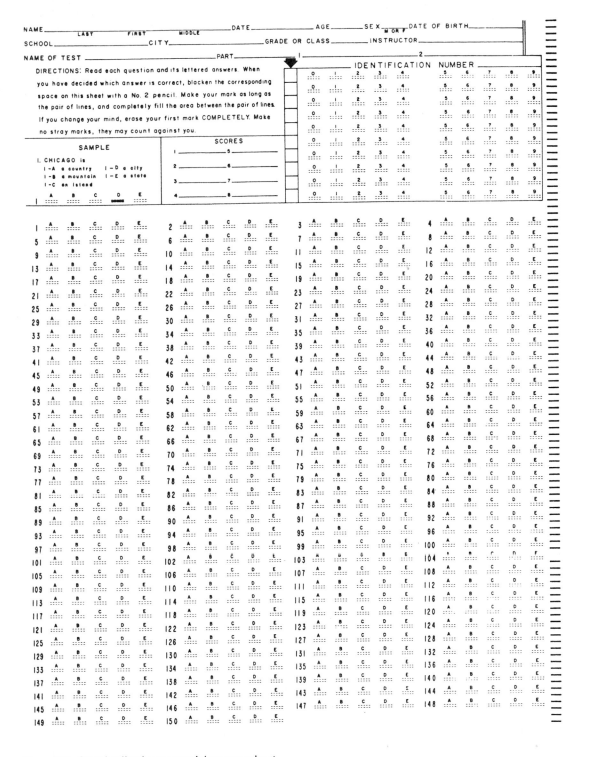

**Figure 13.1** Standardized commercial answer sheet.

A layover answer key—a standardized answer sheet on which the correct answers are cut or punched out—is used to score standardized tests by hand. To use a layover answer key, first scan the person's answer sheet to make sure there are no multiple responses to any of the test items. Then the layover answer key is placed on top of the answer sheet, and the number of visible pencil marks is the person's score. A 50-question true-false or multiple-choice test can be scored in 20 to 30 seconds using a layover answer sheet.

To score commercial answer sheets by machine, the person must use a pencil to mark the answer sheets. Many colleges and school districts offer free scoring services to their personnel. The answer key and answer sheets are fed into a machine that scores the tests and stamps a score on each answer sheet.

## Analysis and Revision

Most objective tests are used more than once. After the test has been administered and scored, it should be examined to determine the merits of the test and of each question, and to identify those items that should be revised or deleted before the test is used again. The failure to analyze a knowledge test after its first administration lowers the reliability and validity of the test scores.

After administering and scoring a test, the following characteristics should be examined:

1. Overall difficulty
2. Variability in test scores
3. Reliability
4. The difficulty of each item
5. The discrimination, or validity, of each item
6. Quality of each response in a multiple-choice item

## Analyzing the Test

***Difficulty and Variability.*** The overall difficulty of a test is determined by calculating the mean performance for the group tested. The higher the mean, the easier the test. The variability in test scores is determined by calculating the standard deviation. The larger the standard deviation, the more the test discriminates among ability groups.

***Reliability.*** The reliability of a knowledge test is usually estimated using either the Kuder-Richardson or coefficient alpha method. As indicated in Chapter 4, coefficient alpha is the same as an intraclass reliability coefficient. The test-retest method discussed in Chapter 4 is inappropriate because persons would be expected to do better the second day due to a carryover of knowledge and an exchange of information about the test.

The Kuder-Richardson Formulas 20 and 21 are typically used to estimate the reliability of a knowledge test. Nunnally (1978) states that with dichotomous items (items scored as either right or wrong) Formula 20's reliability coefficient is the same as coefficient alpha. (In Chapter 4 we illustrated coefficient alpha.) Formula 20 is time-consuming to use because the percentage of the class answering each item correctly must be determined. On the assumption that all test items are equally difficult, Formula 20 can be simplified to Formula 21. Although Formula 21 is commonly used,

# Table 13.5 Kuder-Richardson Formula Scores

|          |   |   |   |   |   | Item |   |   |   |    |   |
|----------|---|---|---|---|---|------|---|---|---|----|---|
| Person   | 1 | 2 | 3 | 4 | 5 | 6 | 7 | 8 | 9 | 10 | X |
| A        | 1 | 1 | 1 | 1 | 0 | 1 | 1 | 1 | 1 | 1  | 9 |
| B        | 1 | 0 | 0 | 0 | 0 | 1 | 1 | 0 | 1 | 1  | 5 |
| C        | 0 | 1 | 0 | 0 | 0 | 0 | 1 | 1 | 0 | 1  | 4 |
| D        | 1 | 1 | 0 | 0 | 0 | 1 | 0 | 1 | 1 | 1  | 6 |
| E        | 1 | 1 | 0 | 0 | 0 | 1 | 1 | 1 | 1 | 1  | 7 |

$\overline{X} = 6.2$
$s^2 = 2.96$

Ebel (1979) notes that it underestimates the reliability coefficient when test items vary in difficulty, which they usually do. Formula 21 should be considered an estimate of the minimum test reliability. The Kuder-Richardson Formula 21 is as follows:

$$r_{21} = \frac{k(s^2) - \overline{X}(k - \overline{X})}{(k - 1)(s^2)}$$

where k is the number of test questions, $s^2$ is the test's standard deviation squared, and $\overline{X}$ is the test mean.

*Problem 13.1:* Use the information in Table 13.5 to calculate the Kuder-Richardson Formula 21 reliability coefficient of the test.

*Solution:* Where **k** is 10, $s^2$ is 2.96, and $\overline{X}$ is 6.2, the reliability coefficient using Formula 21 is .23:

$$r = \frac{(10)(2.96) - (6.2)(10 - 6.2)}{(10 - 1)(2.96)} = \frac{2.96 - (6.2)(3.8)}{(9)(2.96)}$$

$$= \frac{29.6 - 23.56}{26.64} = \frac{6.04}{26.64} = .23$$

Formula 20 yields a correlation coefficient of .63, which as Ebel suggested is a higher value than the .23 yielded by Formula 21.

The Kuder-Richardson Formula 20 is as follows:

$$r_{20} = \left(\frac{k}{k - 1}\right)\left(\frac{(s_x)^2 - \Sigma pq}{(s_x)^2}\right)$$

where k is the number of test items, $(s_x)^2$ is the variance of the test scores $[\Sigma X^2/n - (\Sigma X)^2/n^2]$, p is the percentage answering an item correctly, q is $1 - p$, and $\Sigma pq$ is the sum of the pq products for all k items.

*Problem 13.2:* Determine the Kuder-Richardson Formula 21 reliability of the test presented in Table 13.5.

*Solution:* Using the figures in Table 13.5, we can calculate the following p, q, and pq for the ten items:

| Item | 1 | 2 | 3 | 4 | 5 | 6 | 7 | 8 | 9 | 10 |
|------|-----|-----|-----|-----|------|-----|-----|-----|-----|------|
| p | .8 | .8 | .2 | .2 | .0 | .8 | .8 | .8 | .8 | 1.0 |
| q | .2 | .2 | .8 | .8 | 1.0 | .2 | .2 | .2 | .2 | .0 |
| pq | .16 | .16 | .16 | .16 | .00 | .16 | .16 | .16 | .16 | .00 |

Where **k** is 10, $(s_x)^2$ is 2.96, and $\Sigma$**pq** is 1.28, **r** is .63:

$$r = \left(\frac{10}{10-1}\right)\left(\frac{2.96-1.28}{2.96}\right) = \left(\frac{10}{9}\right)\left(\frac{1.68}{2.96}\right) = \frac{16.8}{26.64} = .63$$

Remember that—all other factors being equal—the larger the standard deviation, the higher the reliability coefficient. If in Problem 13.1 the scores had been 9, 8, 7, 5, and 4; $\overline{X}$ was 6.6; and $s^2$ was 3.44, the reliability coefficient r using Formula 21 would have been .39. Thus, high reliability is harder to obtain with homogeneous groups than it is with heterogeneous ones.

As noted above, coefficient alpha is the same as Kuder-Richardson Formula 20 with dichotomous items. If the items have more than two possible answers (like answers A,B,C,D,E on a knowledge test or scores 1 to 5 on an attitude scale), Kuder-Richardson Formulas are not appropriate but coefficient alpha can be utilized. Coefficient alpha is commonly provided when computer analysis of a knowledge test is conducted.

## Item Analysis

The last two relevant characteristics of a test—the difficulty and validity of the items and the efficiency of responses—can be determined by an item analysis that is a procedure that is important but tedious to do by hand. This analysis should be conducted whenever a test is used the first time.

For the results of an item analysis to be reliable and valid, a large number of people (over 100) must have taken the test. There are several reasons why a large number is essential, one being that all ability levels are apt to be represented. Also, some estimates of correlation coefficients are used in the item analysis procedure, and coefficients based on small groups are often uncommonly high or low and thus untrustworthy.

The first step in an item analysis is to identify a top and bottom group from the total test scores. We will use the top and bottom 27% of the scores. Use only the tests of people in these ranges in the analysis. The next step is to make a chart on which to record the answer each person in the top and bottom groups chose for each item. Figure 13.2 shows a sample chart using the test papers of the top and bottom 16 students in a class of 60. You can see that 12 students in the top group and 5 students in the bottom group answered Item 1 correctly. By using only the top and bottom 27% of the test papers in the analysis, we minimize the work of constructing the chart and can also determine how well each item discriminates between the best and worst

| ITEM | CORRECT ANSWER | | RESPONSE a | b | c | d | e | OMIT |
|------|---------|--------|----|----|----|----|----|------|
| 1 | b | top | | 𝖳𝖧𝖫 𝖳𝖧𝖫 // | /// | / | | |
| | | bottom | // | 𝖳𝖧𝖫 | 𝖳𝖧𝖫 | // | // | |
| 2 | e | top | // | // | / | /// | 𝖳𝖧𝖫 /// | |
| | | bottom | // | /// | // | 𝖳𝖧𝖫 | //// | |
| 3 | c | top | | | 𝖳𝖧𝖫 𝖳𝖧𝖫 𝖳𝖧𝖫 / | | | |
| | | bottom | | /// | 𝖳𝖧𝖫 𝖳𝖧𝖫 /// | | | |
| 4 | a | top | 𝖳𝖧𝖫 | 𝖳𝖧𝖫 /// | /// | | | |
| | | bottom | 𝖳𝖧𝖫 𝖳𝖧𝖫 | // | //// | | | |

**Figure 13.2**
Chart showing answers selected by top and bottom groups in a class of students taking a given test.

students. With the information in the chart, it is possible to determine the difficulty and validity of each test item, and whether all responses functioned.

*Item Difficulty.*   Because each person answers each item correctly or incorrectly, we can calculate the percentage of people who chose the right answer. This percentage, called the **item difficulty** (D), is large when the test item is easy, and small when it is hard. We use the following formula to determine item difficulty:

$$D = \frac{\text{number right in top group} + \text{number right in bottom group}}{\text{number in top group} + \text{number in bottom group}}$$

*Problem 13.3:* Determine the difficulty of Item 1 in Figure 13.2.

*Solution:* Where the number right in the top group is 12, the number right in the bottom group is 5, and the number of students in each of the groups is 16, the item difficulty, D, is .53.

$$D = \frac{12 + 5}{16 + 16} = \frac{17}{32} = .53$$

*Discrimination Index.*   Item validity, or item discrimination, indicates how well a test item discriminates between those who performed well on the test and those who did poorly. If, as is wanted, an item is answered correctly by more of the better performers than the worse performers, it discriminates positively; if more of the worse performers answer the item correctly than do the better performers, the item is a poor one and discriminates negatively. The first time a test is used, it is not uncommon to find that a few items discriminate negatively. These items should be revised or rejected before the test is used again.

The **discrimination index** (r) is essentially a correlation coefficient between scores on one question and scores on the whole test. Thus its value ranges from +1 to −1; +1 corresponding to the best possible positive discrimination. The calculation of the correlation between scores on each question and on the total test is too time-consuming, but we can estimate it, using the top and bottom 27% of the class, with the following formula:

$$r = \frac{\text{number right in top group} - \text{number right in bottom group}}{\text{number in each group}}$$

*Problem 13.4:* Determine the discrimination index of Item 1 in Figure 13.2.

*Solution:* Where the number right in the top group is 12, the number right in the bottom group is 5, and the number of students in each group is 16, the discrimination, or validity, index r is .44:

$$r = \frac{12 - 5}{16} = \frac{7}{16} = .44$$

The discrimination index is quite easy to compute with a calculator; it can be tedious if done by hand.

It is apparent from the discrimination index formula that a positive value is obtained when more people in the top group than in the bottom group answer an item correctly; a zero value is obtained when the same number of people in both groups answer correctly.

We assume in determining item validity that the total test score is a valid measure of knowledge. Therefore, total test validity must be determined, usually by examining the logical validity, before the item analysis. Item validity has no meaning if the total test is not valid. Also, as noted earlier, all other factors being equal, the larger the standard deviation, the more reliable the test. The more a test discriminates, the larger the standard deviation tends to be.

It is worth noting as well that the difficulty of a test item affects the maximum attainable discrimination index. If, for example, the difficulty of an item is .50, a discrimination index of 1.0 is obtained if all people in the top group and none in the bottom group answer the item correctly. If, however, the difficulty of a test item is .60, the best possible discrimination (.80) is obtained when 100% of the top group and 20% of the bottom group respond to the item correctly. The maximum possible discrimination if item difficulty is .40 is also .80. As item difficulties go up or down from .50, the maximum possible discrimination index decreases. For this reason teachers who want to develop discrimination tests, rather than mastery tests, try to write as many test items whose difficulty is approximately .50 as possible—a difficult task.

**Response Quality.**   Ideally, at least some of the people whose test papers are analyzed should select each response of a multiple-choice item. The instructor can use the chart developed to do the item analysis to determine whether all responses were indeed selected. Figure 13.2 shows that all responses were selected in Item 1, but only responses b and c were selected for Item 3. Thus Item 3 might as well have been a true-false item.

*Item Analysis by a Computer.*    The **item analysis** just presented is time-consuming to do by hand. The computer (mainframe or micro) can be used to complete an item analysis. When standardized answer sheets are used the process is quite easy. As noted previously, many schools offer machine scoring. As each answer sheet is scored, the machine can record the student's name, test score, and response to each item. This information for the entire group is then submitted to the computer for item analysis. Computer analysis is more complete than the item analysis undertaken by hand because all the students' scores are used; the top group becomes the upper 50% of those tested. At many colleges, universities, and public school districts the item analysis service is free.

The *Statistics with Finesse* package (Bolding 1989) of microcomputer programs has the MULTIPLE CHOICE TEST option on the Test and Questionnaire Analysis disk that provides item difficulty, item discrimination, Kuder-Richardson reliability, and so on. To use this option the answers of each subject must be saved on disk. Using the File Management Disk, name each test question and then enter the answer of each subject to each test question. Answers must be numerically coded (example: A=1, B=2, C=3, D=4, E=5). The MULTIPLE CHOICE TEST program will ask for (1) "response variables" which are the names you assigned to the test questions, and (2) the correct answer to each test question.

A sample of the data from a microcomputer printout of an item analysis appears in Table 13.6. The test was administered to 52 people and was composed of 15 multiple-choice items. Notice much useful information accompanies the analysis. Having the raw score, percent of items correctly answered, and percentile rank for each person plus the mean, median, and standard deviation for the test provided can save the instructor a lot of calculations.

In the term analysis section of the printout, the correct answer for each item is starred (*). Because all calculations are done so quickly by the computer, frequencies and percentages are reported for each answer to each item. For item 6, of the 13 people in the upper quarter of the group in terms of total test score, 10 people selected answer C, 2 people selected answer D, and 1 person selected answer E. Similar information is reported for the 13 people in the lower quarter of the group in terms of total test score. Under the total count heading the number of people in the total group (n = 52) who selected each answer is reported. Thirty-four people selected answer C, the correct answer, which is 65% of the total group. A discrimination index is reported for each answer to each item based on the discrimination index formula used when calculating by hand and the frequencies under upper and lower quarter. For item 6, answer C, the discrimination index reported to one decimal place is .4 [(10 −5)/13]. The difficulty factor reported to one decimal place is based on the total count and total percent for the correct answer. For item 6, the difficulty factor is .7. Item 6 is a good item since all five answers functioned (see under total count heading) and the item discrimination and difficulty factor are acceptable. Notice that a negative item discrimination is desirable for the incorrect answers since it indicates that more of the lower quarter than upper quarter people selected the answer. Item 6 also fulfills this standard with the exception of answer B, which was not selected by any of the people in the upper and lower quarters. In looking over the item analysis, item 3 was very difficult (.4) with fabulous discrimination (.8), but it was basically a true-false item with answers B and C selected. Although item 5 was easy (difficulty = .9), it discriminated well (.4) and all answers functioned. Item 4 was not as good as item 5 due to low discrimination (.2). Item 8 was not good due to low difficulty factor (.4) and two answers with similar positive discrimination indexes. Item 10 is too hard. The reliability of the test is not provided, but it can be quickly calculated from the information on the computer printout using either the Kuder-Richardson 20 or 21 Formulas.

*Problem 13.5:* Determine the reliability of the knowledge test using the information in Table 13.6.

*Solution:* Where **K** is 15, **s** is 2.52 so $s^2 = 6.35$, and $\overline{X}$ is 9.9, the reliability coefficient using Kuder-Richardson Formula 21 is .50:

$$r = \frac{(15)\,(6.35) - (9.9)\,(15 - 9.9)}{(15 - 1)\,(6.35)} = \frac{95.25 - 50.49}{88.9} = \frac{44.76}{88.9} = .50$$

*Solution:* Using the figures in Table 13.6, we can calculate the following **p, q,** and **pq** for the 15 items, with **p** = Total % for the correct answer to an item and **q = (1 − p):**

| Item | 1 | 2 | 3 | 4 | 5 | 6 | 7 | 8 | 9 | 10 | 11 | 12 | 13 | 14 | 15 |
|------|-----|-----|-----|-----|-----|-----|-----|-----|-----|-----|-----|-----|-----|-----|-----|
| p | .81 | .56 | .42 | .87 | .87 | .65 | .88 | .37 | .71 | .13 | .50 | .75 | .77 | .71 | .87 |
| q | .19 | .44 | .58 | .13 | .13 | .35 | .12 | .63 | .29 | .87 | .50 | .25 | .23 | .29 | .13 |
| pq | .15 | .25 | .24 | .11 | .11 | .23 | .11 | .23 | .21 | .11 | .25 | .19 | .18 | .21 | .11 |

Where K is 15, $s^2$ is 6.35, and $\Sigma pq = 2.69$, the reliability coefficient using Kuder-Richardson Formula 20 is .62:

$$r = \left(\frac{15}{15 - 1}\right)\left(\frac{6.35 - 2.69}{6.35}\right) = \left(\frac{15}{14}\right)\left(\frac{3.66}{6.35}\right) = \frac{54.9}{88.9} = .62$$

## Revising the Test

After calculating the difficulty of and discrimination index for each item, the overall quality of the test and of each item must be determined so the test can be revised as necessary. A set of standards for evaluating discrimination type multiple-choice tests appears in Table 13.7.

Using these standards, we can evaluate the four items in Figure 13.2:

Item 1. D is .53; r is .44. All responses functioned; a good item.

Item 2. D is .38; r is .25. All responses functioned; an acceptable but difficult item.

Item 3. D is .91; r is .19. Only two responses functioned; essentially an easy true-false item. Revision might improve the responses. If left as is, it should be changed to a true-false item.

Item 4. D is .47; r is −.31. Three responses functioned. Revise or reject the item. Either the item itself or response b misled many of the top group. If this problem is corrected by revision, most students will probably answer correctly because ten of the bottom group did so this time. However, because it is unlikely that the item will ever discriminate and because two responses do not function, the item probably should be rejected.

**Table 13.6** Sample Item Analysis Printout

| Student ID | Student Name | Raw Score | % Right | Percentile Rank |
|---|---|---|---|---|
| 1234 | AC | 8 | 53 | 22 |
| 2562 | BZ | 9 | 60 | 42 |
| 2981 | CC | 13 | 87 | 87 |
| 3324 | DF | 12 | 80 | 75 |
| • | • | • | • | • |
| • | • | • | • | • |
| • | • | • | • | • |
| 2617 | GJ | 5 | 33 | 3 |

| | | | |
|---|---|---|---|
| No. of Respondents = 52 | Mean Score = 9.9 | High Score = 14 | |
| No. of Items = 15 | Median Score = 9.0 | Low Score = 2 | |
| | Stand. Dev. = 2.52 | | |

### Item Analysis

| Question | | Upper Quarter | Lower Quarter | Total Count | Total % | Discrim. Index | Diff. Factor |
|---|---|---|---|---|---|---|---|
| 1 | A | 0 | 0 | 1 | 2 | 0.0 | 0.8 |
| | B* | 13 | 8 | 42 | 81 | 0.4 | |
| | C | 0 | 0 | 1 | 2 | 0.0 | |
| | D | 0 | 3 | 4 | 8 | −0.2 | |
| | E | 0 | 2 | 4 | 8 | −0.2 | |
| 2 | A | 1 | 4 | 11 | 21 | −0.2 | 0.6 |
| | B* | 12 | 5 | 29 | 56 | 0.5 | |
| | C | 0 | 0 | 1 | 2 | 0.0 | |
| | D | 0 | 2 | 3 | 6 | −0.2 | |
| | E | 0 | 2 | 8 | 15 | −0.2 | |
| 3 | A | 0 | 0 | 0 | 0 | 0.0 | 0.4 |
| | B* | 11 | 1 | 22 | 42 | 0.8 | |
| | C | 2 | 12 | 29 | 56 | −0.8 | |
| | D | 0 | 0 | 0 | 0 | 0.0 | |
| | E | 0 | 0 | 1 | 2 | 0.0 | |
| 4 | A* | 13 | 10 | 45 | 87 | 0.2 | 0.9 |
| | B | 0 | 2 | 2 | 4 | −0.2 | |
| | C | 0 | 1 | 2 | 4 | −0.0 | |
| | D | 0 | 0 | 1 | 2 | 0.0 | |
| | E | 0 | 0 | 2 | 4 | 0.0 | |
| 5 | A | 0 | 1 | 1 | 2 | −0.0 | 0.9 |
| | B | 0 | 2 | 3 | 6 | −0.2 | |
| | C* | 13 | 8 | 45 | 87 | 0.4 | |
| | D | 0 | 1 | 2 | 4 | −0.0 | |
| | E | 0 | 1 | 1 | 2 | −0.0 | |
| 6 | A | 0 | 2 | 2 | 4 | −0.2 | 0.7 |
| | B | 0 | 0 | 3 | 6 | 0.0 | |
| | C* | 10 | 5 | 34 | 65 | 0.4 | |
| | D | 2 | 4 | 7 | 13 | −0.2 | |
| | E | 1 | 2 | 6 | 12 | −0.0 | |

* = correct answer

**Table 13.6** Sample Item Analysis Printout—*Continued*

## Item Analysis

| Question | | Upper Quarter | Lower Quarter | Total Count | Total % | Discrim. Index | Diff. Factor |
|---|---|---|---|---|---|---|---|
| 7 | A | 0 | 1 | 2 | 4 | −0.0 | 0.9 |
| | B | 0 | 0 | 0 | 0 | 0.0 | |
| | C* | 13 | 9 | 46 | 88 | 0.3 | |
| | D | 0 | 0 | 0 | 0 | 0.0 | |
| | E | 0 | 3 | 4 | 8 | −0.2 | |
| 8 | A* | 7 | 3 | 19 | 37 | 0.3 | 0.4 |
| | B | 0 | 2 | 6 | 12 | −0.2 | |
| | C | 4 | 8 | 20 | 38 | −0.3 | |
| | D | 2 | 0 | 7 | 13 | 0.2 | |
| | E | 0 | 0 | 0 | 0 | 0.0 | 0.7 |
| 9 | A | 0 | 0 | 0 | 0 | 0.0 | |
| | B* | 12 | 11 | 37 | 71 | 0.0 | |
| | C | 0 | 0 | 0 | 0 | 0.0 | |
| | D | 1 | 1 | 6 | 12 | 0.0 | |
| | E | 0 | 1 | 9 | 17 | −0.0 | |
| 10 | A* | 6 | 0 | 7 | 13 | 0.5 | 0.1 |
| | B | 6 | 10 | 36 | 69 | −0.3 | |
| | C | 1 | 0 | 3 | 6 | 0.0 | |
| | D | 0 | 3 | 4 | 8 | −0.2 | |
| | E | 0 | 0 | 2 | 4 | 0.0 | |
| 11 | A | 2 | 3 | 8 | 15 | −0.0 | 0.5 |
| | B* | 9 | 4 | 26 | 50 | 0.4 | |
| | C | 1 | 1 | 6 | 12 | 0.0 | |
| | D | 1 | 2 | 4 | 8 | −0.0 | |
| | E | 0 | 3 | 8 | 15 | −0.2 | |
| 12 | A | 0 | 8 | 11 | 21 | −0.6 | 0.8 |
| | B | 0 | 0 | 1 | 2 | 0.0 | |
| | C* | 13 | 5 | 39 | 75 | 0.6 | |
| | D | 0 | 0 | 0 | 0 | 0.0 | |
| | E | 0 | 0 | 1 | 2 | 0.0 | |
| 13 | A | 0 | 2 | 3 | 6 | −0.2 | 0.8 |
| | B | 0 | 3 | 6 | 12 | −0.2 | |
| | C | 0 | 1 | 1 | 2 | −0.0 | |
| | D | 0 | 1 | 2 | 4 | −0.0 | |
| | E* | 13 | 6 | 40 | 77 | 0.5 | |
| 14 | A | 0 | 0 | 0 | 0 | 0.0 | 0.7 |
| | B | 0 | 8 | 14 | 27 | −0.6 | |
| | C* | 13 | 5 | 37 | 71 | 0.6 | |
| | D | 0 | 0 | 0 | 0 | 0.0 | |
| | E | 0 | 0 | 1 | 2 | 0.0 | |
| 15 | A | 0 | 0 | 0 | 0 | 0.0 | 0.9 |
| | B* | 12 | 11 | 45 | 87 | 0.0 | |
| | C | 0 | 1 | 3 | 6 | −0.0 | |
| | D | 1 | 1 | 4 | 8 | 0.0 | |
| | E | 0 | 0 | 0 | 0 | 0.0 | |

Total in Upper Quarter = 13   Number of Respondents = 52
Total in Lower Quarter = 13   Number of Test Items = 15

* = correct answer

**Table 13.7** Standards for Evaluating a Discrimination Type Multiple-Choice Test

1. The total test
   a. The validity of the test is acceptable.
   b. The reliability of the test is acceptable.
   c. The mean performance of the class approximates that wanted by the teacher.
   d. At least 90% of the class finished the test (not applicable to speed tests).

2. Each test item
   a. Difficulty: No more than 5% of the test items have difficulty indexes above .90, and no more than 5% are below .10.
   b. Discrimination:
      (1) More than 25% of the test items have discrimination indexes above .40.
      (2) More than 25% of the test items have discrimination indexes between .21 and .39.
      (3) More than 15% of the test items have discrimination indexes between .0 and .20.
      (4) Less than 5% of the test items have zero or negative discrimination indexes.
   c. Responses: On each test item, each response was selected by at least 5% of the students whose test papers were used in the item analysis.

## Questionnaires

The construction of questionnaires follows procedures and strategies very similar to those for knowledge tests. Questionnaires are commonly utilized by teachers, exercise specialists, and researchers to quickly and economically collect information from a group. Often the group is widely dispersed so the questionnaire is sent and returned by mail. Information such as beliefs, practices, attitudes, knowledge, and so forth are commonly obtained by the use of a questionnaire. Student evaluation of instructor and course, participant evaluation of an exercise program, participant recall of exercise adherence or barriers to exercise, people's attitudes toward exercise, smoking, or drugs, and people's knowledge about the benefits of exercise and tension reduction are all examples of the use of a questionnaire. Several attitude questionnaires, rating scales, and inventories are presented in Chapter 14. Presented in Table 13.8 is a questionnaire that was sent to public school physical education teachers to determine their attitudes toward physical fitness testing.

Many things influence the success of obtaining information with a questionnaire. Of concern here is getting people to complete and return the questionnaire, particularly if it is mailed to them. A few things that influence the success of a questionnaire are cover letters, timing, appearance, form, length, and content. A letter from you and maybe some influential person on the front of the questionnaire will improve the return rate. Sending or giving the questionnaire to people when they have time to complete it will improve the returns. Sending a questionnaire to people two weeks before Christmas would be a mistake. A questionnaire should be typed, on good paper, with a neat and professional appearance to improve the return rate. The form of the questionnaire in regard to people understanding the directions and easily or quickly responding to the questions influences the return rate. If the questionnaire looks short people are more likely to return it than if it looks long. Using small type and both sides of the paper makes a questionnaire look short. If the content of the questionnaire is of interest to the people completing it and you are willing to share your results with them,

## Table 13.8 Example Questionnaire

**The AAHPERD Fitness Tests Opinionnaire**

The American Alliance for Health, Physical Education, Recreation and Dance (AAHPERD) presently distributes the Youth Fitness Test (used by the President's Council on Physical Fitness and Sport), which was introduced in 1957 and the Health Related Physical Fitness Test, which was introduced in 1980. AAHPERD must decide whether to continue to distribute the two tests, combine the two tests into one test, or discontinue one test. Numerous groups and committees have given AAHPERD their recommendations. However, public school physical education teachers have had very limited input on this important issue. This is your opportunity to make your views known. What AAHPERD does will influence what fitness tests are available to you in the future.

Endorsed by:  American Alliance for Health, Physical Education, Recreation and Dance
State Consultant for Physical Education, Georgia Department of Education

This opinionnaire should take less than 15 minutes to complete. Please complete each questionnaire and return it today in the stamped self-addressed envelope.

1. Are you aware of the Youth Fitness Test (due to college classes, reading, workshops, etc.)? (circle number)
   1. Yes
   2. No

2. Have you administered the Youth Fitness Test within the last three years? (circle number)
   1. Yes
   2. No

3. Does your school or school system require that you administer the Youth Fitness Test on a regular basis? (circle number)
   1. Yes
   2. No

4. If you were given the choice, would you administer the Youth Fitness Test on a regular basis? (circle number)
   1. Yes
   2. No

5. Are you aware of the Health-Related Physical Fitness Test (due to college classes, reading, workshops, etc.)? (circle number)
   1. Yes
   2. No

6. Have you administered the Health-Related Physical Fitness Test within the last three years? (circle number)
   1. Yes
   2. No

7. Does your school or school system require that you administer the Health-Related Physical Fitness Test on a regular basis? (circle number)
   1. Yes
   2. No

8. If you were given the choice, would you administer the Health-Related Physical Fitness Test on a regular basis? (circle number)
   1. Yes
   2. No

**Table 13.8** Example Questionnaire—*Continued*

9. What should AAHPERD do with the two fitness tests they presently distribute? (circle a number)
    1. Combine the two tests into one test of 9 items from which teachers could choose what items to administer.
    2. Discontinue the Health-Related Physical Fitness Test and continue the Youth Fitness Test.
    3. Discontinue the Youth Fitness Test and continue the Health-Related Physical Fitness Test.
    4. Continue to distribute both tests so teachers have a choice of tests.

Finally, we would like to ask a few questions to help us interpret the results and to give you a chance to make comments and suggestions.

1. Is your school located in a rural or urban area? (circle number)
    1. Rural
    2. Urban

2. What is the student population of your school? (circle number)
    1. 0–100
    2. 101–500
    3. 501–1,000
    4. 1,001–1,500
    5. Over 1,500

3. What is your school called? (circle number)
    1. Elementary School
    2. Middle School/Junior High School
    3. Senior High School
    4. Other (specify grade levels) _____

4. What is your age? (circle number)
    1. 20–29 years
    2. 30–39 years
    3. 40–49 years
    4. 50–59 years
    5. 60 years or older

5. What is your gender? (circle number)
    1. Female
    2. Male

6. What is the highest degree you hold? (circle number)
    1. Bachelors
    2. Masters
    3. Specialist
    4. Doctorate

7. Are you usually (presently or the majority of the time) a member of the Georgia Association for HPERD (GAHPERD) and/or the American Alliance for HPERD (AAHPERD)? (circle number)
    1. No, neither organization
    2. Yes, GAHPERD
    3. Yes, AAHPERD
    4. Yes, both organizations

the return rate may be fairly good. If the content of the questionnaire is threatening or too personal, this may hurt the return rate. For example, the question, "Please check the illegal drugs listed below that you regularly use" is threatening. Questions concerning a person's exact age or income are too personal and are better asked in intervals. For example, "Is your age a. 18–25, b. 26–40, c. 41–60, or d. 61–85?"

A more comprehensive discussion of questionnaire construction and use is not possible in the space provided in this book. The interested reader should consult any of a number of good texts on the subject such as Weisberg and Bowen (1977) and Sudman and Bradburn (1982) or research books with a chapter on the subject like Baumgartner and Strong (1994).

## Summary

Knowledge testing should be a component of most measurement programs. Before trying to construct a knowledge test, you must be aware of the types of knowledge tests and items, the advantages and disadvantages of each, and the construction process.

Certain techniques are necessary in administering a knowledge test, and their use can help you obtain reliable, valid scores. It is also important to be aware of the different techniques that can be used in grading a knowledge test after it is administered.

Finally, you should understand the importance of analyzing a knowledge test after it has been administered and should master the techniques used in item analysis. Improving the quality of knowledge tests through item analysis should be every teacher's goal.

## Formative Evaluation of Objectives

*Objective 1*   Differentiate among various types of knowledge tests.

1. Knowledge tests can be classified as either essay or objective tests. Differentiate between these two basic test types.

2. Knowledge tests can also be classified as either mastery or discrimination tests. Differentiate between these two categories in terms of the difficulty and the objectives of the tests.

*Objective 2*   Define the levels of knowledge most applicable to physical education and adult fitness.

1. The taxonomy for educational objectives lists six classes, or levels, of knowledge. Ranging from low to high, the levels are knowledge, comprehension, application, analysis, synthesis, and evaluation. Define the first four of these levels and write a test item for each.

*Objective 3*   Outline the basic procedures for constructing, administering, and scoring a knowledge test.

1. Listed below are basic steps that a teacher can follow in constructing a knowledge test. Summarize the major decisions made at each step.

   a. Construct a table of specifications.
   b. Decide what type of test to give.
   c. Construct the test items.
   d. Determine the test format and administrative details.

2. The teachers must consider the basic problems and procedures of test administration.

   a. What types of considerations should be given to the testing environment and test security?

   b. Is it advantageous to have alternate forms of the same test on hand?

3. Differentiate between the procedures used to score an essay test and those for an objective test.

4. Listed in the text are basic rules that professional test makers follow in constructing various types of test items. Briefly summarize these basic procedures, being sure to list the key points.

*Objective 4*  Evaluate knowledge test items.

1. In constructing a test, you can choose from several types of items. Each type has its advantages and disadvantages, as discussed in the text. Briefly summarize these advantages and disadvantages for each type of item listed below.

   a. true-false
   b. multiple-choice
   c. matching
   d. completion
   e. short answer and essay

2. What is wrong with the following multiple-choice item?

   a. The score of a student on a multiple-choice test is the number of correct answers minus some fraction of the number wrong. On a 50-item, 5-response test a student had 30 items correct and omitted 5. The student's score should be (1) 26; (2) 27; (3) 28; (4) 29; (5) 30.

3. What is wrong with the following two multiple-choice items that were together on an archery test?

   a. What is the term that designates a bow made of several pieces of wood and/or other materials? (1) Self-bow; (2) Laminated bow; (3) Multiple bow; (4) Chrysal bow.

   b. Which of the following is the smoothest shooting wood for a self-bow? (1) Birch; (2) Lemonwood; (3) Hickory; (4) Yew.

*Objective 5*  Analyze knowledge tests in terms of test reliability and item analysis.

1. Test reliability is useful for evaluating knowledge tests. Assume that a 50-item multiple-choice test was administered to 225 students. Calculate the test reliability from the following.

   a. A test mean of 37 and a standard deviation of 3.5.

2. It is difficult to write a reliable knowledge test on the first try. A test's quality will improve if an item analysis is conducted after the first administration and the test is revised accordingly. An item analysis consists of item difficulty and item discrimination.

   a. Define term difficulty and interpret the following item difficulties: (1) .68 and (2) .21.

   b. Define term discrimination and interpret the following discrimination indices: (1) .45, (2) .15, (3) .03, and (4) −.67.

3. Outline the basic procedures involved in an item analysis.

## Additional Learning Activities

1. Several of the books referenced in the text offer complete discussions of knowledge test construction and analysis. Read some of them to increase your familiarity with the subject.

2. Construct a knowledge test composed of some true-false and some multiple-choice items. Administer the test and do an item analysis.

3. As noted in the text, an item analysis can be obtained by using a standardized answer sheet and a test-scoring service on campus. Determine the type of standardized answer sheet to use and the procedures to follow in using your school's service.

## Bibliography

Ahmann, J. S. and M. D. Glock. 1981. *Evaluating student progress: Principles of tests and measurements.* 6th ed. Boston, MA: Allyn and Bacon.

Barrow, H. M., R. McGee and K. A. Tritschler. 1989. *Practical measurement in physical education and sport.* 4th ed. Philadelphia, PA: Lea & Febiger.

Baumgartner, T. A. and C. H. Strong. 1994. *Conducting and reading research in health and human performance.* Dubuque, Iowa: Brown and Benchmark.

Bloom, B. S. (Ed.). 1956. *Taxonomy of educational objectives: Cognitive domain.* New York: McKay.

Bloom, B. S. et al.1971. *Handbook on formative and summative evaluation of student learning.* New York: McGraw-Hill.

Bloom, B. S. et al. 1981. *Evaluation to improve learning.* New York: McGraw-Hill.

Bolding, James. 1989. *Statistics with finesse.* Fayetteville, AR.

Dizney, H. 1971. *Classroom evaluation for teachers.* Dubuque, IA: Wm. C. Brown.

Ebel, R. L. 1979. *Essentials of educational measurement.* 3d ed. Englewood Cliffs, NJ: Prentice-Hall.

Gronlund, N. E. 1985. *Measurement and evaluation teaching.* 5th ed. New York: Macmillan.

———. 1982. *Constructing achievement tests.* 3d ed. Englewood Cliffs, NJ: Prentice-Hall.

Kraft, G. C. 1971. "The construction and standardization of a wrestling knowledge test for college men." P.E.D. Dissertation, Indiana University, Bloomington, IN.

McGee, R. and A. Farrow. 1987. *Test questions for physical education activities.* Champaign, IL: Human Kinetics.

Nunnally, J. C. 1978. *Psychometric theory.* 2d ed. New York: McGraw-Hill.

Sudman, S. and N. Bradburn. 1982. *Asking questions: A practical guide to questionnaire design.* San Francisco: Jossey-Bass.

Weisberg, H. F. and B. D. Bowen. 1977. *An introduction to survey research and data analysis.* San Francisco: W. H. Freeman and Company.

# Measuring Psychological Dimensions of Physical Education, Exercise, and Sport Psychology*

## chapter 14

## Key Words

activity factor
affective domain
attitude
body cathexis scale
body image
evaluation factor
personality
potency factor
psychophysical
rating of perceived exertion (RPE)
semantic differential scales

## Contents

## Objectives

Measuring psychological dimensions is of interest to physical education teachers, exercise specialists, sport psychologists, and researchers. However, psychological dimensions are difficult to measure in a reliable and valid manner. As discussed in Chapter 1, regular vigorous exercise has a positive influence on cardiovascular health and longevity, but many who start exercise programs will quit. Affective behavior—interests, attitudes, appreciations, values, and emotional sets or biases—is not only difficult to measure, but also difficult to teach (Krathwohl et al. 1964). As Ebel (1972) has noted:

> Feelings . . . cannot be passed along from teacher to learner in the way information is transmitted. Nor can the learner acquire them by pursuing them directly as he might acquire understanding by study. Feelings are almost always the consequences of something—of success, of failure, of duty done or duty ignored, of danger encountered or danger escaped.

Provided in this chapter is an overview of the measurement problems and general instruments that are available.

After reading this chapter, you should be able to:

1. Evaluate the validity of physical education attitude scales.
2. Outline the procedures used to develop semantic differential scales.
3. Describe the nature of the Self-Motivation Inventory (SMI).
4. Describe the nature of body image scales.
5. Evaluate the validity and value of the psychophysical rating of perceived exertion scales (RPE).

*The help of Dr. Mary E. Rudisill of the University of Houston is appreciated in the revision of this chapter.

## The Evolving Discipline of Sport Psychology

The psychology of exercise and sport is a developing academic discipline, dependent on having reliable and valid instruments. Initially, general psychological scales (e.g., Spielberger's Trait and State Anxiety Scale) were used in sport psychology, but the more recent trend has been to develop sport- and exercise-specific scales. The sport-specific scales have their roots in the more general psychological scales. The publication of these specific scales reflects the evolution of sport psychology as a discipline independent of the general area of psychology.

Numerous sport- and exercise-specific scales have been published. The scales can be categorized into five general classifications: (1) sport attitudes and performance; (2) exercise and sport motivation; (3) anxiety, arousal, and performance; (4) attentional focus and styles; and (5) perceived exertion.

A major limitation of many scales is that their true validity has not been established, which can only be achieved through extensive research. Provided at the end of this chapter are the references of scales that have published reliability and validity data. The scales with an established research base are provided in more detail. Following is an overview of each general category.

### Sport Attitudes and Performance

Many of the early psychological scales were concerned with the measurement of attitudes. The methods of measuring attitudes and the validity of the physical education attitude scales are covered extensively in this chapter. An emerging type of attitude scale in sport psychology is concerned with the attitudes of athletes and dimensions of sport, such as cohesion in sport teams and leadership behavior.

### Exercise and Sport Motivation

This general category has received extensive attention. It is concerned with the intensity and direction of sport behavior. These scales are designed to measure the amount of effort an individual puts forth to accomplish a behavior, and whether the individual is avoiding or approaching a goal. Within the topic of exercise and sport motivation, there are several major areas of study: (1) intrinsic and extrinsic motivation; (2) goal-setting and goal-orientations; (3) achievement motivation; (4) causal attributions and dimensions; (5) self-esteem or perceived competence; and (6) group motivation. The self-motivation scale (SMI) is provided in this chapter.

### Anxiety, Arousal, and Performance

An important area in sport psychology is the influence of anxiety and arousal on performance. Researchers have sought to explain how anxiety and arousal can positively or negatively influence performance (trait—anxiety). Also, relationships between **personality** (anxiety levels—trait anxiety) and motor performance have been investigated.

### Attentional Focus and Styles

This area of sport psychology studies personality differences and attentional focus. During sport performance, attention is directed toward various aspects of the activity. Investigators have published scales to measure attentional focus (Albrecht & Feltz 1987; Van Schoyck & Grasha 1981).

### Perceived Exertion

The ratings of perceived exertion scales are used to rate exercise intensity or other subjective symptoms such as breathing difficulties or chest pain (Borg 1978). The RPE scales have a sound, extensive research base and are covered extensively in this chapter.

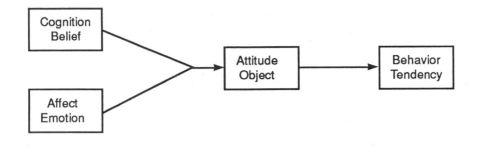

**Figure 14.1**
Attitudes are a function of beliefs and emotion. An attitude scale is used to measure a person's feelings toward the object. The true validity of the attitude scale is determined by the individual's behavior. Many have a positive attitude toward physical fitness but lead a sedentary life-style.
(Scale courtesy of R. J. Sonstroem.)

## Measuring Attitudes

Much of the physical education research in the **affective domain** has focused on attitudes (See Figure 14.1) and their measurement. "Attitudes concern feelings about particular social objects—physical objects, types of people, particular persons, social institutions, government policies" (Nunnally 1978). Attitudes are generally measured with scales that require a student to agree or disagree with a series of statements, worded both positively and negatively. Several types of scales are used to determine a respondent's degree of affect. The most common offer two alternatives (Disagree-Agree) or five alternatives (Strongly Disagree, Disagree, Undecided, Agree, Strongly Agree). A 7-step scale can be created by adding Very Strongly Disagree and Very Strongly Agree to the 5-step scale.

Nunnally (1978) recommends the use of a graphic scale demarcated with numbers, like that shown below, to clearly convey degrees of feeling. A graphic scale also allows greater flexibility in selecting the number of steps offered.

Completely disagree____ : ____ : ____ : ____ : ____ : ____ : ____ Completely agree
                            1     2     3     4     5     6     7

An attitude scale lists various statements that elicit one's feelings about the attitude object. The individual's attitude is determined by adding the scores of the statements. In scoring them, the positive statement scores are simply added as they appear; the point values for the negative statements, however, must be reversed by subtracting the score from the total number of levels plus 1. Using a 7-step scale like the one shown here, the marked score of a negative statement is subtracted from 8. For example, assume that a student marks a "2" next to the following statement: "If for any reason a few subjects must be dropped from the school program, physical education should be one of the subjects dropped." Notice that this is a negative statement in terms of an attitude toward physical education and that by scoring it with a low number the student is actually showing a positive attitude toward physical education. Using the 7-step scale, then, the marked negative score 2 becomes 6, correctly reflecting the student's positive attitude (i.e., $8 - 2 = 6$).

In contrast, assume that a student marks a 2 next to the following statement: "Participation in physical education activities establishes a more wholesome outlook on life." Because the statement is positive, a score of 2 on the 7-step scale indicates a negative attitude.

## Validity of Attitude Scales

An **attitude** scale is a self-report measure and suffers from the weaknesses typical of this type of instrument. Its principal limitation is that it reflects only what individuals know and are willing to relate about their attitudes. Students who like a teacher tend to respond more favorably than their true attitudes may warrant, and often favorable responses on a self-report scale are accompanied by contrary behavior. For example, students may express a favorable attitude toward physical activity and fitness yet be inactive and unfit.

Because it is unrealistic to establish an attitude scale's concurrent validity with actual behavior, most scales claim face validity. This involves defining the content area to be measured and devising attitude statements that logically relate to it. Usually an individual's attitude toward the content area is represented by the total score on the scale. Unfortunately this has created a serious problem of validity on physical education attitude scales. If you sum all the scores on the scale, it is essential that all statements measure the same general attitude.

Several physical education teachers and exercise specialists have published attitude scales. The targeted objects have included physical education (Adams 1963; Carr 1945; Edington 1968; Kappes 1954; Kneer 1971; Mercer 1971; O'Bryan & O'Bryan 1979; Penmon 1971; Seaman 1970; Wear 1951, 1955); athletic competition (Harris 1968; Lakie 1964; McCue 1953; McGee 1956; Scott 1953); creative dance (Allison 1976); and sportsmanship (Johnson 1969). These published scales report high reliability estimates ($\geq 0.85$), but their validity has not been established. In addition, the scales have not proved to be valuable to either the public school physical education teacher and exercise specialist or researcher. Many of these scales are fully published in other sources (Barrow & McGee 1971; Johnson & Nelson 1979; Neilson & Jensen 1972).

Kenyon (1968b) has demonstrated that attitude must be considered multidimensional. That is, there are several different types of attitudes toward an object and that the composite score must be split into several scores to validly measure each dimension. For example, assume that a scale measures two factors in a subject's attitude toward physical education: (1) the value of physical education for social development and (2) the value of physical education for health and fitness. By simply summing all the scores, two individuals with very different attitudes might receive the same total score. Yet, one may highly value physical education for social development; the other may consider it valueless for social development but important for health and fitness. Thus, the total score is not a valid representation of the true feelings of either person.

The ATPA scale for men consists of 59 items and the parallel scale for women consists of 54 items. Following is a description of the six dimensions. The complete instrument with instructions is provided in other sources (Baumgartner & Jackson 1982; Kenyon 1968c; Safrit 1981). The six dimensions measured by the ATPA are

Dimension 1. *Physical activity as a social experience.* Physical education teachers and exercise specialists maintain that physical activity meets certain social needs. Individuals who score high on this factor would value physical activities "whose primary purpose is to provide a medium for social intercourse, that is, to meet new people and to perpetuate existing relationships." The internal consistency reliability estimates for this scale are about 0.70.

Dimension 2. *Physical activity for health and fitness.* The importance of physical activity for maintaining health and fitness is generally recognized. Individuals who score high on this factor would value physical activity for its "contribution to the improvement of one's health and fitness." The internal consistency reliability estimates are about 0.79.

Dimension 3. *Physical activity as the pursuit of vertigo.* The pursuit of vertigo is the search for excitement: "those physical experiences providing, at some risk to the participant, an element of thrill through the medium of speed, acceleration, sudden change of direction, exposure to dangerous situations, with the participant usually remaining in control." The internal consistency reliability estimates ranges are about 0.88 for men and 0.87 for women.

Dimension 4. *Physical activity as an aesthetic experience.* Many people believe that forms of physical activity have a certain beauty or artistry. People who score high on this factor perceive the aestheticism of physical activity. The internal consistency reliability estimates were 0.82 and 0.87 for men and women, respectively.

Dimension 5. *Physical activity as a catharsis.* Many believe that physical activity can provide a release from the frustrations of daily living. The validity of this factor has not been fully established. A negative relationship was reported between catharsis scores and preference for "physical activity for recreation and relaxation." The internal consistency reliability estimates were 0.77 and 0.79 for men and women, respectively.

Dimension 6. *Physical activity as an ascetic experience.* Individuals who score high on this scale value the type of dedication involved in championship-level performance. Such activity demands long, strenuous, often painful training and competition, forcing a deferment of many of the gratifications of general physical activity. The internal consistency reliability estimates were 0.81 for men and ranged from 0.74 to 0.78 for women.

Kenyon's work is especially important. The publication of the ATPA scales marked a departure from using physical education as the attitude object. Rather, Kenyon's scales were designed to measure the reasons *why* individuals exercised. He recognized that exercise motives were multidimensional, that there were different reasons why people were physically active. The methods used to develop the six scales of the ATPA provide an excellent example of the use of construct validity.

## Semantic Differential Scales

A flexible device for measuring attitudes is the **semantic differential scale,** which asks the subject to respond to bipolar adjectives to measure attitude (Osgood et al. 1957; Snider & Osgood 1969). An example is shown in Table 14.1. The approach is flexible in that many different attitude objects can be measured without revising the scale. In Table 14.1, for example, the object "physical fitness" could be replaced with others such as "Intramural Football," "Physical Education Class," "Interschool Athletics," or some other concept.

**Table 14.1** Semantic Differential Scales Illustrated*

**Physical Fitness**

| | | | | | | | | |
|---|---|---|---|---|---|---|---|---|
| (E) pleasant | ___ : | ___ : | ___ : | ___ : | ___ : | ___ : | ___ : | unpleasant |
| (A) relaxed | ___ : | ___ : | ___ : | ___ : | ___ : | ___ : | ___ : | tense |
| (A) passive | ___ : | ___ : | ___ : | ___ : | ___ : | ___ : | ___ : | active |
| (E) unsuccessful | ___ : | ___ : | ___ : | ___ : | ___ : | ___ : | ___ : | successful |
| (P) delicate | ___ : | ___ : | ___ : | ___ : | ___ : | ___ : | ___ : | rugged |
| (A) fast | ___ : | ___ : | ___ : | ___ : | ___ : | ___ : | ___ : | slow |
| (E) good | ___ : | ___ : | ___ : | ___ : | ___ : | ___ : | ___ : | bad |
| (P) weak | ___ : | ___ : | ___ : | ___ : | ___ : | ___ : | ___ : | strong |
| (A) lazy | ___ : | ___ : | ___ : | ___ : | ___ : | ___ : | ___ : | busy |
| (P) heavy | ___ : | ___ : | ___ : | ___ : | ___ : | ___ : | ___ : | light |
| (E) unfair | ___ : | ___ : | ___ : | ___ : | ___ : | ___ : | ___ : | fair |

*Note: Any concept may be used: the concept "Physical Fitness" is illustrated.

When originally developed, the object being measured was stated in global, neutral terms such as "Intramural Football." A limitation of stating the attitude object in global terms is that the scale lacks the sensitivity to make strong behavior predictions. There is a major trend in sports psychology to move from the measurement of general to more specific traits (Ajzen & Fishbein 1980). This can be easily accomplished with semantic differential scales by including the intended behavior with the attitude statement. For example, the general attitude object "Intramural Football" could be replaced with the more specific phrase "My participation this year in the football intramural program."

The Children's Attitude Toward Physical Activity Inventory (CATPA-I) is a fine example of the use of semantic differential scales to measure attitude. The instrument was developed by Simon and Smoll (1974) and adapted by Schutz et al. (1985) to measure Kenyon's dimensions of physical activity. The general design of the CATPA-I is shown in Figures 14.2 and 14.3. The normative information of the scale is provided in other sources (Schutz et al. 1985).

## Semantic Dimensions

The process of developing semantic differential scales involves first defining the object to be evaluated and then selecting the bipolar adjective pairs. Numerous studies using various concepts have concluded that three major factors are measured by the semantic differential technique: evaluation, potency, and activity. Evaluation is the most common factor. It involves the degree of "goodness" the subject attributes to the object being measured. For most instances, **evaluation** is the only factor of interest. It is measured with the following types of bipolar adjectives.

| | | |
|---|---|---|
| good-bad | fresh-stale | fair-unfair |
| new-old | valuable-worthless | successful-unsuccessful |
| health-unhealthy | pleasant-unpleasant | honest-dishonest |
| beautiful-ugly | | |

Figure 14.2
CATPA-I inventory
subdomain descriptions.
(Schultz et al. 1985.)

Physical activity for social growth
Taking part in physical activities that give you a chance to meet new people.

Physical activity to continue social relations
Taking part in physical activities that give you a chance to be with your friends.

Physical activity for health and fitness
Taking part in physical activities to make your health better and to get your body in better condition.

Physical activity as a thrill but involving some risk
Taking part in physical activities that could be dangerous because you move very fast and must change direction quickly.

Physical activity as the beauty in movement
Taking part in physical activities that have beautiful and graceful movements.

Physical activity for the release of tension
Taking part in physical activities to reduce stress or to get away from problems you might have.

Physical activity as long and hard training
Taking part in physical activities that have long and hard practices. To spend time in practice you need to give up other things you like to do.

Figure 14.3
Scale format for the Children's Attitude Toward Physical Activity Inventory (CATPA-I), grades 7 through 11.

How Do You Feel about the Idea Below?

Physical Activity for Social Growth
Taking Part in Physical Activities that Give You
a Chance to Meet New People

Always Think about the Idea in the Box

If You Do Not Understand This Idea, Mark This Box ☐
and Go to the Next Page.

| 1. Good | | | | | Bad |
|---|---|---|---|---|---|
| 2. Of No Use | | | | | Useful |
| 3. Not Pleasant | | | | | Pleasant |
| 4. Nice | | | | | Awful |
| 5. Happy | | | | | Sad |

The second factor, **potency,** involves the strength of the concept being rated. Among the bipolar adjectives that measure potency are the following:

| | | |
|---|---|---|
| deep-shallow | light-dark | hard-soft |
| heavy-light | smooth-rough | thick-thin |
| strong-weak | dominant-submissive | rugged-delicate |
| full-empty | | |

The third factor, **activity,** is measured by adjective pairs that describe action, like the following:

| | | |
|---|---|---|
| excitable-calm | fast-slow | lazy-busy |
| stable-unstable | tense-relaxed | cheerful-sober |
| happy-sad | active-passive | dynamic-static |
| hot-cold | changeable-stable | |

## Construction of Semantic Differential Scales

The first step in constructing a semantic differential scale is the selection of concepts relevant to the general attitude being evaluated. The second step is the selection of appropriate adjective pairs. Two criteria determine the pairs: how well they represent the factor and their relevance to the concept in question.

Certain adjective pairs have proved valid for measuring the evaluation, potency, and activity factors. Because a minimum of three adjective pairs is suggested to measure a factor reliably, at least nine adjective pairs are needed to measure all three factors. Finally, the adjective pairs must be at the reading comprehension level of the students being evaluated and must relate logically to the concept in question.

The letters E, P, and A in Table 14.1 identify the factor measured by the adjective pair. These letters would not appear on the instrument itself. The various adjective pairs are randomly ordered to prevent those relating to a single factor from being clustered. It is also essential that both negative and positive adjectives appear in each column.

## Scoring and Interpretation

The respondent places a mark at that point between the two adjectives that best reflects his or her feeling about the concept. There are several ways to score semantic scales, but the one we find the easiest is to develop a key with the lowest point value assigned to the first space on the left side and the highest assigned to the last space on the right side. The scoring system would be

unsuccessful 1: 2: 3: 4: 5: 6: 7: successful

pleasant 1: 2: 3: 4: 5: 6: 7: unpleasant

Since the adjectives "successful" and "pleasant" are the positive ends of the scale, the pleasant-unpleasant scale scoring is reversed by subtracting "8" for the obtained score (i.e., $8 - 1 = 7$). The student's score on a factor is the sum for all bipolar adjectives that measure that factor. Thus, if all three factors are measured, each scale yields three scores. The reverse scoring and summing of scale scores can be easily completed by computer. A computer-generated scoring system for the semantic differential scales shown in Table 14.1 is shown in the Computer Calculations section found at the end of this chapter.

Part 4 Cognitive and Affective Testing

Because these data can be analyzed statistically, it is possible to develop norms from them. The semantic differential scale was designed to measure an individual's feelings about a given concept. Nunnally (1978) reports that the evaluation factor serves as a definition of attitude, so that responses to this factor's adjective pairs are excellent measures of verbalized attitudes. Often, just the evaluation factor is used. The potency and activity factors tend to be partly evaluative, but they also tend to reveal the respondent's interpretation of the concept's physical characteristics. Assume, for example, that two groups of students are administered a semantic differential scale for the concept "physical education class." One group is enrolled in a 12-week basic course in archery; the other, in a basic body-conditioning course that involves distance running and weight training. Although both groups might rate the physical education class "good" on the evaluation factor, their responses are likely to differ on the potency and activity factors. The archery students are apt to respond to the potency adjectives "delicate," and "weak." Students in the conditioning class are more likely to rate their class "strong" and "hard," and the activity adjectives "active," "fast," and "busy." Thus, all three factors would be useful to determine how the students feel about the concept.

## Motivation to Exercise—Adherence

As shown in Chapter 1, sedentary life-style and obesity are risk factors of many chronic diseases and mortality. These data are the basis for the development of adult and youth health-related fitness programs. So compelling are these data that in 1985, the Centers for Disease Control established objectives that call for 60% of 18- to 65-year-olds to be regular participants in vigorous exercise by 1990. Unfortunately, this objective is not being met. It is estimated that only 20% of Americans exercise regularly and intensely enough to meet current ACSM guidelines for developing fitness or for health promotion (Dishman 1988). In a typical adult exercise program 50% will drop out within 6 months to a year. Of major companies that provide employee fitness programs, only 20% to 40% of eligible employees will participate, but of these only 33% to 50% will exercise on a regular basis at a vigorous intensity—a small fraction of those eligible to participate.

The reasons individuals adhere to exercise programs are complex and not fully understood, but research suggests that adherence is due to one's exercise history, type of exercise program, and motives. Dishman and Dunn state:

> A review of existing data on the determinants of physical activity and exercise, in both supervised exercise programs and spontaneous activity in the population, indicates that advancing age and elapsed time after initial adoption of an activity routine are among the most consistent predictors of inactivity. (1988, p. 186)

Pollock (1988) has shown that the type of exercise is important. With adults, exercise that can be completed in one hour and at a moderate intensity enhances fitness and increases exercise adherence. It is commonly assumed that patterns of exercise and health habits for adulthood are established during early years. The behavioral determinants of physical activity and fitness are a complex and current exercise science research theme. See Dishman (1988) for an excellent and comprehensive text on this subject.

**Figure 14.4**
Sonstroem's 1975
psychological model for
physical activity.
(Source: Sonstroem, R. J. 1974.
Attitude testing examining
certain psychological correlates
of physical activity. *Research
Quarterly 45:* 93–103.)

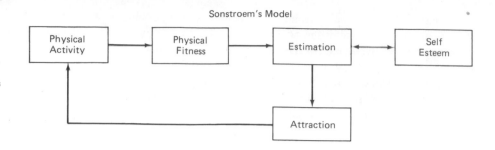

Sonstroem's Model

Provided in this section are the psychological instruments that are most often used to assess the motives of exercise. The primary reason adults start an exercise program is for weight control, and it has been estimated to be the major reason of nearly 60% of those who expressed an interest in joining a corporate health and fitness program (Baun & Bernacki 1988). The final psychological scale provided can be used to study one's attitude toward his or her body. The scale has been shown to be related to body composition.

## Physical Estimation and Attraction Scales (PEAS)

The Physical Estimation and Attraction Scales (PEAS) were developed by Sonstroem (1974) and incorporated into a model (see Figure 14.4) explaining psychological benefit of physical activity and motivation to participate in physical activity (Sonstroem 1978). The 33 Estimation items measure self-perceptions of (attitudes toward) one's own physical abilities. Estimation is conceived to be a component of general self-esteem. The 54 Attraction items assess interest in or attraction to vigorous physical activity. Of the 100 items, two pertain to the social aspects of physical activity, and 11 neutral items (not scored) are included to hide the nature of the scale. Examples of Estimation and Attraction items are presented below. The entire PEAS may be obtained from Baumgartner and Jackson (1982, 2nd edition), Safrit (1981, 2nd edition), or by writing to Dr. Sonstroem at the University of Rhode Island.

The Estimation items ask students to affirm or deny their own physical characteristics, fitness, athletic ability, or potential in motor performance. Examples of items include the following:

I am stronger than a good many of my friends.

It is difficult for me to catch a thrown ball.

I am in better physical condition than most boys my age.

Even with practice I doubt that I could learn to do a handstand well.

The Attraction items ask students to affirm or deny their personal interests or likes for certain forms of physical activity. Sample items are as follows:

Sports provide me with a welcome escape from present-day life.

I love to run.

Playing tennis appeals to me more than golfing does.

I enjoy the discipline of long and strenuous physical training.

Reliability and validity research had been conducted with boys in grades 8 through 12. Internal consistency reliability estimates of .87 and .89 and stability reliability estimates of .92 and .94 have been reported for the estimation and attraction scales, respectively (Sonstroem 1974, 1976).

Construct validity research has supported the two scales (Sonstroem 1974). Both estimation and attraction were found to be correlated with height, weight, and athletic experience and unrelated to intelligence quotient (Sonstroem 1974). Sonstroem (1976) found the scales to be relatively free of response distortion. Dishman (1980) identified a tendency for subjects to "fake bad" on the attraction scale under instructions to do so.

Repeated research has shown that self-perceptions of physical ability (Estimation scores) correlate well with actual physical fitness scores and with measures of self-esteem as Sonstroem's model hypothesizes (Dishman 1978; Fox, Corbin & Couldry 1985; Sonstroem 1978). Estimation scores have been significantly related to mental health scales of the Tennessee Self-Concept Scale (Sonstroem 1976). Physical fitness seems to bear no direct association with self-esteem, which suggests that what people think about their fitness and bodies is more related to positive mental adjustment than their actual fitness level. Estimation scores have been shown to increase following exercise experiences (Dishman & Gettman 1981; Kowal, Patton & Vogel 1978). Attraction scores have been found to be related to self-reports of participation in sport-type activities (Neale et al. 1969; Sonstroem 1978; Sonstroem & Kampper 1980). Sonstroem and Kampper (1980) administered the PEAS to grades 7 and 8 boys at the beginning of a school year. They found that Attraction, first, and Estimation, second predicted those boys who would subsequently try out for the touch football and soccer teams. Scores, however, failed to predict staying with a team for the entire season. Other research has shown that the Psychological Model for Physical Activity Participation is not successful at predicting adherence to an exercise program (Dishman & Gettman 1981; Morgan & Pollock 1978). Sonstroem (1988) has suggested that this failure of attitudes to predict exercise adherence may be caused by the types of general attitude statements found in the Attraction scale. Attitude items are for predicting behavior and should be statements that are very specific to the intended behavior and should measure attitudes toward actually performing this specific behavior. Attitude specificity is discussed in the introduction to this chapter.

In general, the PEAS may be employed for most of the testing purposes outlined at the beginning of the chapter. In terms of individual diagnosis and remediation, it would seem useful in identifying students with low self-perceptions of ability and with low attitudes toward physical activity. Its greatest utility, however, appears to be in the area of research in the psychological benefits of exercise. Sonstroem and Morgan (1989) have proposed a model that explains how exercise program experiences influence self-esteem by means of such variables as physical self-efficacies and physical competence. They suggest that physical competence can be assessed by the Estimation scale.

The research that led to the development of the PEAS was conducted with adolescent males only. While similar model relationships have been found in college males, results tend to be somewhat different with college females (Fox, Corbin & Couldry 1985; Safrit, Wood & Dishman 1985). Little data are available on females in general. Estimation and Attraction means have generally been lower in college females as opposed to males. Recently, Safrit, Wood, and Dishman (1985) tested large numbers of college males and females, and they found

Attraction items for women to be different from those for men. A common 12-item Estimation scale is recommended for both sexes.

## Self-Motivation Inventory (SMI)

Dishman and Ickes (1981) developed a Self-Motivation Inventory (SMI) designed to measure potential exercise compliance. The 40-item scale consists of 20 positively keyed and 20 negatively keyed statements. The subject is instructed to read each item and select an alternative that best describes how characteristic the statement is when applied to the subject. The alternatives are

A) Extremely uncharacteristic of me. (Point value = 1)[1]

B) Somewhat uncharacteristic of me. (Point value = 2)

C) Neither characteristic nor uncharacteristic of me. (Point value = 3)

D) Somewhat characteristic of me. (Point value = 4)

E) Extremely characteristic of me. (Point value = 5)

This is a Likert-type scale scored with a value of "1" for alternative A to "5" for alternative E. The subject's score is the sum of all items after the negative statements have been corrected (i.e., point value −6). The scale, item polarity, and scoring method are provided in Table 14.2. A microcomputer program for scoring the SMI is shown at the end of this chapter in the Computer Calculations section.

Using a sample of over 400 undergraduate men and women, the internal consistency reliability was estimated to be 0.91. Stability reliability has been found to be high, exceeding 0.86 (Dishman & Ickes 1981). The SMI was found to be the best psychological instrument for discriminating among those who would and would not adhere to exercise in athletic and adult fitness environments. A major finding in the adult fitness setting was that the decision to adhere or to drop out of a prescribed exercise program appears to be largely dependent on body composition and the behavioral disposition of self-motivation (Dishman, Ickes & Morgan 1980). This suggests that both biological and psychological variables need to be considered when studying the complex problem of exercise adherence.

## Body Image

**Body image** is both the attitude one has toward the body and the way in which one's own body is perceived. Psychologists have discovered that an individual's feelings about his or her body reflect anxieties and values.

Body image can be measured with projective tests and self-report inventories. Projective tests require a psychologist for scoring and interpretation, which makes them inappropriate for use by physical education teachers and exercise specialists. The most common self-report inventory used is the **Body Cathexis Scale** (Secord & Jourard 1953), which focuses on those aspects of body image related to an individual's satisfaction or dissatisfaction with different parts of the body and their functions. The scale assumes the following:

1. Feelings about the body are related to feelings about the self.

2. Negative feelings about the body are related to anxiety about pain, disease, or bodily injury.

3. Negative feelings about the body are associated with insecurity.

---

[1] Note, the point value is here for clarity. It would not be on the scale when administering the SMI.

# Table 14.2 Self-Motivation and Adherence to Exercise Inventory

| Key[1] | SMI Statement |
|:---:|---|
| − | 1. I'm not very good at committing myself to do things. |
| − | 2. Whenever I get bored with projects I start, I drop them to do something else. |
| + | 3. I can persevere at stressful tasks, even when they are physically tiring or painful. |
| − | 4. If something gets to be too much of an effort to do, I'm likely to just forget it. |
| + | 5. I'm really concerned about developing and maintaining self-discipline. |
| + | 6. I'm good at keeping promises, especially the ones I make to myself. |
| − | 7. I don't work any harder than I have to. |
| − | 8. I seldom work to my full capacity. |
| − | 9. I'm just not the goal-setting type. |
| + | 10. When I take on a difficult job, I make a point of sticking with it until it's completed. |
| + | 11. I'm willing to work for things I want as long as it's not a big hassle for me. |
| + | 12. I have a lot of self-motivation. |
| + | 13. I'm good at making decisions and standing by them. |
| − | 14. I generally take the path of least resistance. |
| − | 15. I get discouraged easily. |
| + | 16. If I tell somebody I'll do something, you can depend on it being done. |
| − | 17. I don't like to overextend myself. |
| − | 18. I'm basically lazy. |
| + | 19. I have a very hard-driving, aggressive personality. |
| + | 20. I work harder than most of my friends. |
| + | 21. I can persist in spite of pain or discomfort. |
| + | 22. I like to set goals and work toward them. |
| + | 23. Sometimes I push myself harder than I should. |
| − | 24. I tend to be overly apathetic. |
| + | 25. I seldom, if ever, let myself down. |
| − | 26. I'm not very reliable. |
| + | 27. I like to take on jobs that challenge me. |
| − | 28. I change my mind about things quite easily. |
| + | 29. I have a lot of will power. |
| − | 30. I'm not likely to put myself out if I don't have to. |
| − | 31. Things just don't matter much to me. |
| − | 32. I avoid stressful situations. |
| + | 33. I often work to the point of exhaustion. |
| − | 34. I don't impose much structure on my activities. |
| − | 35. I never force myself to do things I don't feel like doing. |
| − | 36. It takes a lot to get me going. |
| + | 37. Whenever I reach a goal, I set a higher one. |
| + | 38. I can persist in spite of failure. |
| + | 39. I have a strong desire to achieve. |
| − | 40. I don't have much self-discipline. |

1. Scoring: the point values for each response are: (1) extremely uncharacteristic of me; (2) somewhat uncharacteristic of me; (3) neither characteristic nor uncharacteristic of me; (4) somewhat characteristic of me; (5) extremely characteristic of me. Items negatively keyed are scored 6 − X, where X is the assigned value (1 to 5). SMI score is the sum of the 40 items.

The Secord and Jourard Body Cathexis Scale consists of forty-six words describing body parts (hair, hands, ankles) or functions (keenness of senses, digestion, sex drive). The respondent considers each body part or function and rates his or her feelings using the following scale:

1. Wish strongly a change could somehow be made.
2. Don't like, but can put up with.
3. Have no particular feelings one way or the other.
4. Am satisfied.
5. Consider myself fortunate.

The subject's score is the sum of the responses to each item. A high score represents a positive body image. Secord and Jourard (1953) estimated the internal consistency reliability of the scale at .88 and .92 for men and women, respectively.

Langston (1979) administered the scale to three different groups of college women and factor analyzed each set of responses. She found a general factor related to perceived size and body weight, and several additional factors related to other body parts and functions. She also found that the body image factor related to perceived size and weight was significantly correlated (–0.47) with the percentage body fat measured with skinfolds (Jackson, Pollock & Ward 1980). This showed that women who had the highest levels of body fat were the most dissatisfied. Langston used ten items to measure body weight and size factors.

| | | |
|---|---|---|
| 1. Figure | 5. Hips | 8. Shape of legs |
| 2. Waist | 6. Weight | 9. Upper arms |
| 3. Size of abdomen | 7. Appetite | 10. Body build |
| 4. Thighs | | |

All forty-six items of the Secord-Jourard scale appear in the original source (1953). If you use the entire instrument, you will need the help of a psychologist for valid interpretation of the results. We recommend, instead, that a body image inventory be restricted to those items related to the size and weight factors.

## Psychophysical Ratings

Individuals are able to perceive and rate strain during physical exercise. The **rating of perceived exertion (RPE)** is a valid and simple method for determining exercise intensity. The RPE scale was developed by the Swedish psychologist Gunnar Borg (1962, 1978, 1982) and is used extensively for exercise testing and exercise prescription. It is Borg's opinion (1982) that perceived exertion is the single best indicator of the degree of physical strain because the overall perception rating integrates many sources of information elicited from the peripheral working muscles and joints, central cardiovascular and respiratory functions, and central nervous system. "All these signals, perceptions and experiences are integrated into a configuration of a 'Gestalt' perceived exertion" (Borg 1982).

Borg has published two RPE scales. The first is a category scale with values ranging from 6 to 20, which assumes a linear relation between exercise heart rate and RPE rating (Borg 1962). The second scale was developed to be consistent with the nonlinearity of psychophysical ratings (Borg 1978, 1982).

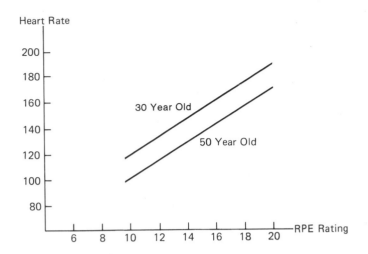

**Figure 14.5**
Graph shows the change in the heart rate and RPE ratings with the decrease in maximal heart rate associated with aging. RPE ratings ≥ 18 are typically an indication that maximal heart rate has been reached. (Graphics by MacASJ.)

6
7  Very, very light
8
9  Very light
10
11  Fairly light
12
13  Somewhat hard
14
15  Hard
16
17  Very hard
18
19  Very, very hard
20

**Figure 14.6**
The 15-grade category scale for rating perceived exertion (RPE scale). (Source: Dr. G. Borg, Dept. of Psychology, University of Stockholm, Stockholm, Sweden.)

## Borg's Category RPE Scale

The Borg category RPE scale increases linearly with exercise heart rate. The scale has been shown to correlate between 0.80 and 0.90 with heart rate, $\dot{V}O_2$, and lactic acid accumulation (Borg 1982). The scale values range from 6 to 20. This was proposed to denote heart rates ranging from 60 to 200 b·min$^{-1}$. For example, a rating of 15 was meant to correspond with a heart rate of 150 b·min$^{-1}$. Borg did not intend that the heart rate-RPE rating be taken literally because many factors can affect exercise heart rate. Age, exercise mode, environment (e.g., heat, humidity), anxiety, and drugs (e.g., beta blocker drugs that are used to control high blood pressure) all can affect exercise heart rate. The influence of aging on RPE is illustrated in Figure 14.5.

The RPE scale (Figure 14.6) is very popular and very easy to use. Research by Pollock, Jackson, and Foster (1986) shows that the scale provides an excellent estimate of exercise intensity and can be used to prescribe exercise and regulate exercise testing. RPE values of 12 and 13 represent exercise intensities at about 60% of heart rate

**Figure 14.7**
Borg's category scale with
ratio properties (RPE).
(Source: Dr. G. Borg, Dept. of
Psychology, University of
Stockholm, Stockholm,
Sweden.)

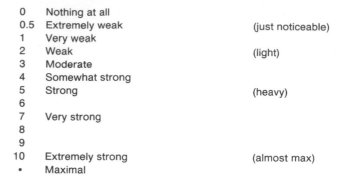

| 0 | Nothing at all | |
|---|---|---|
| 0.5 | Extremely weak | (just noticeable) |
| 1 | Very weak | |
| 2 | Weak | (light) |
| 3 | Moderate | |
| 4 | Somewhat strong | |
| 5 | Strong | (heavy) |
| 6 | | |
| 7 | Very strong | |
| 8 | | |
| 9 | | |
| 10 | Extremely strong | (almost max) |
| • | Maximal | |

reserve[2] and $\dot{V}O_2$ Max. Ratings of 16 and 17 correspond to about 90% of heart rate reserve and 85% of $\dot{V}O_2$ Max. These ranges have been valid for both leg and arm exercise and subjects on beta blocker drugs that lowered $\dot{V}O_2$ Max and maximal heart rate (Pollock, Jackson & Foster 1986). The instructions used for the RPE scale during exercise testing are[3]

> You are now going to take part in a graded exercise test. You will be walking or running on the treadmill while we are measuring various physiological functions. We also want you to try to estimate how hard you feel the work is; that is, we want you to rate the degree of perceived exertion you feel. By perceived exertion we mean the total amount of exertion and physical fatigue. Don't concern yourself with any one factor such as leg pain, shortness of breath, or work grade, but try to concentrate on your total, inner feeling of exertion. Try to estimate as honestly and objectively as possible. Don't underestimate the degree of exertion you feel, but don't overestimate it either. Just try to estimate as accurately as possible.

## Borg's Category Scale with Ratio Properties

It has been shown that psychophysical ratings are not linear (Borg 1978). This has led to the development of a category scale with ratio properties (see Figure 14.7). The new scale is not only suitable for rating exercise intensity, but other subjective symptoms such as breathing difficulties, aches, and pains (Borg 1982). The scale has also been found to be useful for judging the difficulty of work tasks, such as carrying 50-pound bags or shoveling coal (Jackson & Osburn 1983).

The feature of the ratio RPE scale is that numbers anchor verbal expressions that are simple and understandable for use by most people. The expressions are placed in the correct position on the ratio scale where they belong according to their quantitative meaning. A simple range of 0 to 10 is used to anchor the verbal expressions. It is permissible to use fractional ratings (e.g., 2.5 or 3.8) and values above 10. The ratio RPE scale has been shown to correlate highly with both blood lactate and muscle lactate level, which are the biochemical markers of cardiorespiratory and muscle fatigue (Borg 1982).

---

[2]Percent Heart Rate Reserve = [X(Max HR – Rest HR)] + Rest HR, where X is the desired percentage and HR is heart rate (Pollock, Wilmore & Fox 1984).

[3]Instructions developed by William Morgan Ed.D., University of Wisconsin, Madison, WI. Published with permission.

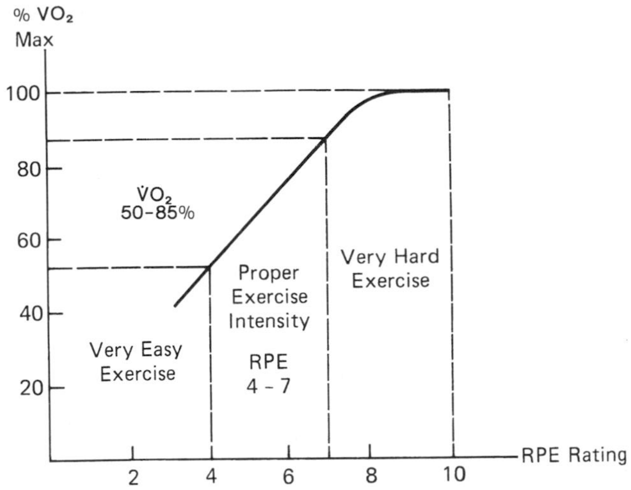

**Figure 14.8**
Relation between ratio RPE
scale and exercise intensity
(% VO₂ Max).

The ratio properties of the new RPE scale result in a nonlinear scale. This is shown in Figure 14.8. Ratings of between 4 and 7 are consistent with an exercise intensity window between 50% and 85% of $\dot{V}O_2$ Max. The instructions[4] for the ratio RPE scale are

> We would like you to estimate the exertion you feel by using this scale.
> The scale starts with 0 **"Nothing at all"** and goes on to 10, **"Extremely strong"**—that is **"Almost max"** you should say 10. For most people this corresponds to the hardest physical exercise they have ever done, as for example the exertion you feel when you run as fast as you can for several minutes till you are completely exhausted, or when you are lifting or carrying something which is so heavy that you nearly can't make it.—Maybe it is possible to imagine exertion or pain that is even stronger, and that is why the maximum value is somewhat over 10. If you feel the exertion or pain to be stronger than **"Extremely strong"** (almost max) you can use a number that is over 10, for example 11, 13 or an even higher number.
> If the exertion is **"Very weak"** you should answer with the number 1. If it is only **"Moderate"** you say 3 and so on. Feel free to use any number you wish on the scale, as well as half values as for example 1.5 or decimals as 0.8, 1.7 or 2.3. It is important that you give the answer that you yourself feel to be right and not that which you think you ought to give. Answer as honestly as possible and try neither to overestimate nor underestimate the degree of exertion that you feel.

**Psychophysical** ratings are used for many different purposes. Some of the more common uses include the following:

## Uses of Psychophysical Ratings

1. *Exercise testing.* The RPE scale is used to judge exercise intensity when administering a graded exercise test on a treadmill or cycle ergometer. The objective of an exercise test is to slowly and systematically increase the exercise intensity from submaximal levels to maximal. Often, percent of maximal heart rate is used to quantify exercise intensity. But, in most

---

[4]Personal communication with Dr. Gunnar Borg, Department of Psychology, University of Stockholm, Stockholm, Sweden, November 1985.

**Figure 14.9**
Recommended training zone for exercise prescription. (Adapted from Pollock, Wilmore and Fox 1984.)

| | | |
|---|---|---|
| Oxygen Uptake | 50% ⟶ | 85% |
| Heart Rate Reserve | 60% ⟶ | 90% |
| RPE (6–20) | 12 ⟶ | 16 |
| RPE (1–10) | 4 ⟶ | 7 |

instances, maximal heart rate is not known and must be estimated from age (Max HR = 220 − age). However, there tend to be errors in this estimate (± 10 to 15 b·min$^{-1}$). The RPE ratings are used to determine when a subject is reaching his or her maximal tolerance (≥17 on the 6–20 RPE scale and ≥7 on the 1–10 RPE scale).

2. *Exercise prescription.* Percentage of $\dot{V}O_2$ Max is the most valid method of prescribing exercise, but this is typically not known. Therefore, percentage of maximal heart rate reserve is recommended. A difficulty with this method is that maximal heart rate must be known. It has been found that RPE ratings (see Figure 14.9) are an excellent method of selecting the proper intensity for exercise and can be used to supplement heart rate estimates (Pollock, Jackson & Foster 1986).

3. *Quantification of energy expenditure.* Many adult fitness programs seek to quantify energy expended through exercise, which is often expressed in kilocalories. This can be done very accurately with aerobic exercise modes such as walking, jogging, or cycling because external work can be quantified (see Chapter 10). There are other popular aerobic exercise modes such as aerobic dancing or playing tennis where external work cannot be quantified. Individuals vary in the intensity to which they exercise. The computer logging system at the Tenneco Health and Fitness center and the CSI logging computer program (see Chapter 2) both use psychophysical ratings to estimate exercise intensity when external work cannot be measured. To illustrate, more calories would be expended when playing tennis at an RPE rating of 7, Very strong, as compared to a rating of 3, Moderate.

## Uses of Psychological Scales

Psychological scales are readily available and easy to administer and score. This enhances their use, but also presents a potential danger. Psychological instruments, especially personality inventories, can be threatening and potentially harmful when administered and interpreted by the untrained or naive. The legitimacy of using psychological instruments can be clarified by asking two simple questions.

1. Do you have a need and right to secure such data?

2. Are you capable of validity interpreting and using the test results in a way that will help the person being tested?

It is difficult to conceive any valid purpose for the use of psychological scales such as personality inventories and behavior rating scales by public school physical education teachers and exercise specialists, but other psychological inventories have legitimate educational and research purposes. Some specific examples follow.

1. *Achievement of class objectives.* A common objective of physical education programs is the development of a positive feeling toward class activities and physical activity in general. Semantic differential scales would be especially useful to evaluate this.

2. *Administrative planning, curriculum development, and evaluation of teaching methods.* Again, semantic differential scales could provide data that could be used to evaluate the effectiveness of instruction units and methods of instruction. Children may improve their physical fitness, but they could develop negative feelings toward physical activity in general. Psychological scales could be used for these purposes.

3. *Individual diagnosis and remediation.* The identification of children with a low self-concept or body image could be very important. Altering a child's attitude in a positive direction could enhance his or her mental health.

4. *Research.* A current problem in physical education and exercise science is a lack of understanding of the psychological motives of sports participation and exercise adherence.

Although medical research has clearly established that lack of exercise and obesity are major cardiovascular disease risk factors (see Chapter 1), we still do not know why some people are physically active and others are not. This will be a major area of research in the 1990s. The PEAS and SMI scales will be used to study these issues.

Provided next is a bibliographical listing of sport psychology studies that have published scales providing some information on the reliability and validity of scales.

## Sport Psychology Scales

### Exercise and Sport Motivation

Carmack, M. A. and R. Martens. 1979. Measuring commitment to running: A survey of runner's attitudes and mental states. *Journal of Sport Psychology* 1:25–42.

Corbin, C. B., A. B. Nielson, L. L. Eorsdorf, and D. R. Lauraie. 1987. Commitment to physical activity. *International Journal of Sport Psychology* 18:215–22.

Gill, D. L. and T. E. Decter. 1988. Development of the sport orientation questionnaire. *Research Quarterly for Exercise and Sport 59.* 191–202.

Griffin, N. S. and M. E. Crawford. 1989. Measurement of movement confidence with a stunt movement confidence inventory. *Journal of Sport and Exercise Psychology 11:*26–40.

Griffin, N. S., J. F. Keogh, and R. Maybee. 1984. Performer perceptions of movement confidence. *Journal of Sport Psychology 6:*395–407.

McCready, M. 1984. Locus of control and adherence to exercise program. Unpublished Master's thesis, University of British Columbia, Vancouver.

Pemberton, C. L., L. M. Petlichkoff, and M. E. Ewing. 1986. Psychometric properties of the achievement orientation questionnaire. Paper presented at the NASPSPA Conference, Scottsdale, AZ.

Rudisill, M. E., M. T. Mahar, and K. S. Meaney. 1989. The development of a motor skill perceived competence scale for children. Paper presented at the American Alliance for Health, Physical Education, Recreation and Dance, Boston, MA.

Rychman, R. M., M. S. Robbins, B. Thorton, and P. Cantrell. 1982. Development and validation of a physical self-efficacy scale. *Journal of Personality and Social Psychology* 42:891–900.

Schutz, R. W. and F. L. Smoll. 1977. Equivalence of two inventories for assessing attitudes toward physical activity. *Psychological Reports 40:*1031–34.

Vealey, R. S. 1988. Sports confidence and competitive orientation: An addendum on scoring procedures and gender differences, *Journal of Sport and Exercise Psychology 10:*471–78.

Vealey, R. S. 1986. Conceptualization of sport-confidence and competitive orientation: Preliminary investigation and instrument development. *Journal of Sport Psychology 8:*221–46.

## Anxiety, Arousal, and Performance

Hart, E. A., M. R. Leary, and W. J. Rejeski. 1989. The measurement of social physique anxiety. *Journal of Sport & Exercise Psychology 11:*94–104.

Martens, R. 1977. *Sport competition anxiety test.* Champaign, IL: Human Kinetics.

Martens, R., D. Burton, R. S. Vealey, L. A. Bump, and D. Smich. 1982, May. Competitive State Anxiety Inventory-2. Symposium presented at the NASPSPA conference, College Park, MD.

## Attentional Focus and Styles

Albrecht, R. R. and D. L. Feltz. 1987. Generality and specificity of attention related to competitive anxiety and sport performance. *Journal of Sport Psychology 9:*231–48.

Van Schoyck, R. S. and A. F. Grasha. 1981. Attentional style variation and athletic ability: The advantage of a sport-specific test. *Journal of Sport Psychology 3:*149–65.

## Sport Attitudes and Performance

Chelladurai, P. and S. D. Saleh. 1980. Dimension of leadership behavior in sports: Development of a leadership scale. *Journal of Sport Psychology 2:*34–35.

Smith, F. S. 1976. The index of organizational reactions (IOR). *JSAS Catalog of Selected Documents in Psychology 6:*MS No. 1265.

Widmeyer, W. N., L. R. Brawley, and A. Carron. 1985. *The measurement of cohesion in sport teams: The group environment questionnaire.* London, Ontario: Sports Dynamics.

## Perceived Exertion and Performance

Borg, G. A. V. 1973. Perceived exertion: A note on history and methods. *Medicine and Science in Sports 5:*190–93.

Rejeski, W. J. 1985. Perceived exertion: An active or passive process? *Journal of Sport Psychology 7:*371–78.

# Computer Calculations

This section illustrates computer-generated methods of scoring semantic differential scales and the SMI scale developed by Dishman and Ickes (1981). These equations are written to be compatible for use with database, spreadsheet, and statistical programs (e.g., Statview 4.01) that have this capacity. They were used and checked for accuracy on a microcomputer database program. You will need to examine your program documentation to make the equations compatible with the program you have. The microcomputer mathematical operands are addition +; subtraction −; multiplication *; and division /.

## Scoring Semantic Differential Scales

Illustrated is the method used to score the Semantic Differential Scales shown in Table 14.1. These are illustrated by assigning three students constant values (1, 4, and 7) for the 11 adjectives pairs that are named E-1, A-1, P-1, etc. The computer-generated scoring system reverses the scoring to assign the high score to the positive end of the scale which are

> EVAL—pleasant, successful, good, and fair;
>
> ACT—tense, active, fast, and busy;
>
> POT—rugged, strong, and heavy.

The final step involves summing the scales to produce Evaluative (EVAL), Activity (ACT), and potency (POT) scale scores.

The database program used is given below. Note, some programs require that the variables used in an equation be surrounded by « ».

```
EVAL = (8 - «E-1») + «E-2» + (8- «E-3») + «E-4»
ACT = «A-1» + «A-2» + (8- «A-3») + «A-4»
POT = «P-1» + «P-2» + (8- «P-3»)
```

|      | E-1 | A-1 | A-2 | E-2 | P-1 | A-3 | E-3 | P-2 | A-4 | P-3 | E-4 | EVAL | ACT | POT |
|------|-----|-----|-----|-----|-----|-----|-----|-----|-----|-----|-----|------|-----|-----|
| Jane | 1   | 1   | 1   | 1   | 1   | 1   | 1   | 1   | 1   | 1   | 1   | 16   | 10  | 9   |
| John | 4   | 4   | 4   | 4   | 4   | 4   | 4   | 4   | 4   | 4   | 4   | 16   | 16  | 12  |
| Jim  | 7   | 7   | 7   | 7   | 7   | 7   | 7   | 7   | 7   | 7   | 7   | 16   | 22  | 15  |

## Scoring the Self-Motivation Inventory (SMI)

Illustrated is the method used to score the SMI shown in Table 14.2. The program involves reversing the negatively worded items by subtracting a value of 6, and then summing all 40 items. The items are identified by I-1, I-2, I-3, . . . , I-40. Shown are examples of three subjects where one was assigned all "1s", the second all "3s", and the last all "5s." Because of the number of items in the scale, it was programed to compute a score for all negatively (NEG) and positively (POS) worded statements. The subject's SMI Score was the sum of NEG and POS.

```
NEG = (6-«I-1»)+(6-«I-2»)+(6-«I-4»)+(6-«I-7»)+(6-«I-8»)+(6-«I-9»)+
(6-«I-14»)+(6-«I-15»)+(6-«I-17»)+(6-«I-18»)+(6-«I-24»)+(6-«I-26»)+
(6-«I-28»)+(6-«I-30»)+(6-«I-31»)+(6-«I-32»)+(6-«I-34»)+(6-«I-35»)+
(6-«I-36»)+(6-«I-40»)
POS = «I-3»+«I-5»+«I-6»+«I-10»+«I-11»+«I-12»+«I-13»+«I-16»+«I-19»+
«I-20»+«I-21»+«I-22»+«I-23»+«I-25»+«I-27»+«I-29»+«I-33»+«I-37»+
«I-38»+«I-39»
SMI SCORE = «POS» + «NEG»
```

|      | I-1 | I-2 | I-3 | I-4 | I-5 | ... | I-39 | I-40 | NEG | POS | SMI | SCORE |
|------|-----|-----|-----|-----|-----|-----|------|------|-----|-----|-----|-------|
| JOE  | 1   | 1   | 1   | 1   | 1   | ... | 1    | 1    | 100 | 20  | 120 |       |
| MARY | 3   | 3   | 3   | 3   | 3   | ... | 3    | 3    | 60  | 60  | 120 |       |
| JANE | 5   | 5   | 5   | 5   | 5   | ... | 5    | 5    | 20  | 100 | 120 |       |

## Summary

The psychology of exercise and sport is developing as an academic discipline. This is mirrored by the development of psychological testing instruments. The scales can be categorized into five general categories: (1) sport attitudes and performance; (2) exercise and sport motivation; (3) anxiety, arousal, and performance; (4) attentional focus and style; and (5) perceived exertion. A major limitation of many of these scales is that their true validity has not been established.

Most of the published physical education attitude scales were developed on the assumption that a single factor was being measured. Scales that gauge attitudes toward physical education report high reliability, but their construct validity—what factors are measured—is yet to be determined. The Kenyon and Sonstroem scales are multi-dimensional instruments that have established construct validity. Semantic differential scales that use bipolar adjectives to measure feelings about concepts are a flexible technique for measuring attitude.

Many adults who start exercise programs will quit. It has been shown that adherence to exercise is related to self-motivation as measured by the SMI. Body image scales measure attitude about the body. Research has shown one general factor (related to body size and weight) that itself relates to the subjects' percent body fat.

The psychophysical RPE scales have been shown to be useful for determining exercise intensity. Borg has developed two scales, either of which can be used for (1) exercise testing; (2) exercise prescription; and (3) quantifying the energy expended through exercise.

## Formative Evaluation of Objectives

*Objective 1*   Evaluate the validity of physical education attitude scales.

1. Attitude scales are self-report instruments designed to measure attitudes by the way one responds to statements. In terms of validity, what is the basic weakness of this type of measurement?

2. Kenyon's attitude scale offers a valid method of measuring attitudes toward physical activity. The scale measures six different types, or dimensions, of attitudes. Identify and briefly describe each.

3. The Physical Estimation and Attraction Scales were developed to explain motivation toward physical activity. Identify and briefly describe each scale.

*Objective 2*   Outline the procedures used to develop semantic differential scales.

1. Semantic differential scales provide a flexible method for evaluating attitudes. Research indicates that three basic factors are measured with these scales: evaluation, potency, and activity. Define these concepts and list three adjective pairs that measure each of them.

2. Outline the process you would follow to develop semantic differential scales.

3. Outline the procedure for scoring semantic differential scales that would calculate a score for each of the three factors.

4. What are the concepts being measured by the Children's Attitude Toward Physical Activity Inventory? What semantic dimensions are being used with the CATPA-I?

*Objective 3*   Describe the nature of the Self-Motivation Inventory (SMI).

1. What does the SMI predict?

2. How might one use the SMI?

*Objective 4*  Describe the nature of body image scales.

1. What is the definition of body image?
2. How is body image measured?
3. Is body image related to one's physical characteristics?

*Objective 5*  Evaluate the validity and value of the psychophysical rating of perceived exertion scales.

1. What are the similarities and differences between the two Borg RPE scales?
2. How can the RPE scales be used?
3. In order to improve aerobic fitness, one should exercise at what level on the RPE scales?

**Additional Learning Activities**

1. Several studies have sought to determine the correlation between attitude and physical fitness. Review the articles published in the *Research Quarterly* to determine whether a positive attitude is associated with a high level of physical fitness. How was attitude measured? How was physical fitness measured?

2. Select either the CATPA-I or the PEAS and administer it to a group of students. Can you develop a microcomputer or SPSS program to score the scale?

3. Select a concept (e.g., physical fitness, athletics, aerobic dance) of particular interest to you and develop semantic differential scales to measure attitude toward the concept. Administer the scales to various groups and determine whether the groups' means differ. You might use male and female physical education majors as your groups. You may want to consult a basic statistics text to determine whether the means between the groups are significantly different.

4. Administer the CATPA-I to a group of children. Be sure to read the proper instructions (Schutz et al. 1985) and administer either the scale for 3rd graders or the scale for older children.

5. What are the reasons adults do not continue exercise programs? Conduct a review of the exercise science literature to answer this question. A good place to start is to conduct a computer search for research published by R. K. Dishman.

6. Learn how to use either of the Borg RPE scales. This can be accomplished several ways. If you take a maximal exercise test, relate the submaximal ratings with percent of heart rate reserve, or $\dot{V}O_2$ Max. A second method is to exercise at an exercise intensity that will produce an aerobic training effect and rate this intensity by either the 6 to 20 or 1 to 10 scale.

# Bibliography

Adams, R. S. 1963. Two scales for measuring attitude toward physical education. *Research Quarterly 34:*91–94.

Ajzen, I. and M. Fishbein. 1980. *Understanding attitudes and predicting social behavior.* Englewood Cliffs, NJ: Prentice-Hall.

Albrecht, R. R. and D. L. Feltz. 1987. Generality and specificity of attention related to competitive anxiety and sport performance. *Journal of Sport Psychology 9:*231–48.

Allison, P. R. 1976. An instrument to measure creative dance attitude of grade five children. Ph.D. Dissertation, University of Alabama, Tuscaloosa, AL.

Barrow, H. M. and R. McGee. 1971. *A practical approach to measurement in physical education.* 2d ed. Philadelphia, PA: Lea & Febiger.

Baumgarter, T. A. and A. S. Jackson. 1982. Measurement for evaluation in physical education. 2d ed. Dubuque, IA: Wm. C. Brown.

Baun, W. B. and E. J. Bernacki. 1988. Who are corporate exercisers and what motivates them? in *Exercise adherence: Its impact on public health.* Champaign, IL: Human Kinetics Books.

Borg, G. 1962. *Physical performance and perceived exertion.* Lund, Sweden: Gleerup.

Borg, G. 1977. *Physical work and effort.* Wenner-Gren Center, Stockholm, Sweden: Pergamon Press (Oxford).

Borg, G. 1978. Subjective effort in relation to physical performance and working capacity. In *Psychology: From research to practice.* New York: Plenum Publishing.

Borg, G. 1982. Psychophysical bases of perceived exertion. *Medicine and Science in Sports and Exercise 14:*371–81.

Carr, M. G. 1945. The relationship between success in physical education and selected attitudes expressed in high school freshmen girls. *Research Quarterly 16:*176–91.

Dishman, R. K. 1978. Aerobic power, estimation of physical ability, and attraction to physical activity. *Research Quarterly 49:*285–92.

Dishman, R. K. 1980. The influence of response distortion in assessing self-perceptions of physical ability and attitude toward physical activity. *Research Quarterly for Exercise and Sport 51:*286–98.

Dishman, R. K. 1984. Chapter 29: Motivation and exercise adherence. In J. Silva and R. Weinberg (Eds.). *Psychology foundation of sport.* Champaign, IL: Human Kinetics.

Dishman, R. K. 1988. *Exercise adherence: Its impact on public health.* Champaign, IL: Human Kinetics Books.

Dishman, R. K. and A. L. Dunn. 1988. Exercise adherence in children and youth: Implications for adulthood. In *Exercise adherence: Its impact on public health.* Champaign, IL: Human Kinetics Books.

Dishman, R. K. and L. R. Gettman. 1981. Psychological vigor and self-perceptions of increased strength. *Medicine and Science in Sports and Exercise 15:*118.

Dishman, R. K. and W. Ickes. 1981. Self-motivation and adherence to therapeutic exercise. *Journal of Behavioral Medicine 4:*421–36.

Dishman, R. K., W. Ickes, and W. P. Morgan. 1980. Self-motivation and adherence to habitual physical activity. *Journal of Applied Social Psychology 10:*115–32.

Ebel, R. L. 1972. What are schools for? *Phi Delta Kappan 54:*3–7.

Edington, C. W. 1968. Development of an attitude scale to measure attitudes of high school freshmen boys toward physical education. *Research Quarterly 39:*505–12.

Fox, K. R., C. R. Corbin, and W. H. Couldry. 1985. Female physical estimation and attraction to physical activity. *Journal of Sport Psychology 7:*125–36.

Franzi, S. L. and S. A. Shields. 1984. The body esteem scale: Multidimensional structure and sex differences in a college population. *Journal of Personality Assessment 48:*173–78.

Harris, B. 1968. Attitudes of students toward women's athletic competition. *Research Quarterly 39:*278–84.

Part 4  Cognitive and Affective Testing

Jackson, A. S. and H. Osborn. 1983. Validity of isometric strength tests for predicting performance in underground coal mining tasks. Houston, TX: Employment Services, Shell Oil Company.

Jackson, A. S., M. L. Pollock, and A. Ward. 1980. Generalized equations for predicting body density of women. *Medicine and Science in Sports 12:*175–82.

Johnson, B. L. and J. K. Nelson. 1979. *Practical measurements for evaluation in physical education.* Minneapolis, MN: Burgess.

Johnson, M. L. 1969. Construction of sportsmanship attitude scales. *Research Quarterly 40:*312–16.

Kappes, E. E. 1954. Inventory to determine attitudes of college women toward physical education and student services of the physical education department. *Research Quarterly 25:*429–38.

Kenyon, G. S. 1968a. A conceptual model for characterizing physical activity. *Research Quarterly 39:*96–105.

Kenyon, G. S. 1968b. Six scales for assessing attitude toward physical activity. *Research Quarterly 39:*566–74.

Kenyon, G. S. 1968c. Values held for physical activity by selected urban secondary school students in Canada, Australia, England, and the United States. Washington, DC: U.S. Office of Education.

Kneer, M. E. 1971. Kneer attitude inventory and diagnostic statements. In *A practical approach to measurement in physical education.* Philadelphia, PA: Lea & Febiger.

Kowal, D. M., J. F. Patton, and J. A. Vogel. 1978. Psychological states and aerobic fitness of male and female recruits before and after basic training. *Aviation, Space, and Environmental Medicine 49:*603–6.

Krathwohl, D. R. 1964. *Taxonomy of education objectives handbook II. The affective domain.* New York: McKay.

Lakic, W. L. 1964. Expressed attitudes of various groups of athletes toward athletic competition. *Research Quarterly 35:*497–503.

Langston, K. F. 1979. The relationship between body image and body composition of college females. Ed.D. Dissertation, University of Houston, Houston, TX.

McCue, B. F. 1953. Constructing an instrument for evaluating attitudes toward intensive competition in team games. *Research Quarterly 24:*205–10.

McGee, R. 1956. Comparison of attitudes toward intensive competition for high school girls. *Research Quarterly 27:*60–73.

Mercer, E. L. 1971. Mercer attitude scale. In *A practical approach to measurement in physical education.* Philadelphia, PA: Lea & Febiger.

Messer, D. and S. Harter. 1986. *Manual for the adult self-perception profile.* Denver, CO: University of Denver.

Neale, D. C. 1969. Physical fitness, self-esteem and attitudes toward physical activity. *Research Quarterly 40:*743–49.

Neilson, N. P. and C. R. Jensen. 1972. *Measurement and statistics in physical education.* Belmont, CA: Wadsworth.

Nunnally, J. C. 1978. *Psychometric theory.* New York: McGraw-Hill.

O'Bryan, M. H. and K. G. O'Bryan. 1979. Attitudes of males toward selected aspects of physical education. *Research Quarterly 40:*343–82.

Osgood, C. 1957. *The measurement of meaning.* Urbana, IL: University of Illinois Press.

Penmon, M. M. 1971. Penmon physical education attitude inventory for inner-city junior high school girls. In *A practical approach to measurement in physical education.* Philadelphia, PA: Lea & Febiger.

Pollock, M. L., A. S. Jackson, and C. Foster. 1986. The use of the perception scale for exercise prescription. In *The perception of exertion in physical work.* Wenner-Gren Center, Stockholm, Sweden: 161–76.

Pollock, M. L., J. H. Wilmore, and S. M. Fox III. 1984. *Exercise in health and disease.* Philadelphia, PA: W. B. Saunders.

Riddle, P. K. 1980. Attitudes, beliefs, behavioral intentions, and bchaviors of men and women toward regular jogging. In *Research Quarterly for Exercise and Sport 51:*663–74.

Safrit, M. J. 1981. *Evaluation in physical education.* Englewood Cliffs, NJ: Prentice-Hall.

Safrit, M. M., T. M. Wood, and R. K. Dishman. 1985. The factorial validity of the physical estimation and attraction scales for adults. *Journal of Sport Psychology 7:*166–90.

Schutz, R. W., F. L. Smoll, F. A. Carre, and R. E. Mosher. 1985. Inventories and norms for children's attitudes toward physical activity. *Research Quarterly for Exercise and Sport 56:*256–65.

Scott, P. M. 1953. Attitudes toward athletic competition in elementary school. *Research Quarterly 24:*353–61.

Seaman, J. A. 1970. Attitudes of physically handicapped children toward physical education. *Research Quarterly 41:*439–45.

Secord, P. F. and S. M. Jourard. 1953. The appraisal of body cathexis: Body cathexis and the self. *Journal of Consulting Psychology 17:*343–47.

Simon, J. A. and F. L. Smoll. 1974. An instrument for assessing children's attitudes toward physical education. *Research Quarterly 45:*407–15.

Snider, J. G. and C. E. Osgood. 1969. *Semantic differential technique: A sourcebook.* Chicago, IL: Aldine.

Sonstroem, R. J. 1974. Attitude testing examining certain psychological correlates of physical activity. *Research Quarterly 45:*39, 103.

Sonstroem, R. J. 1976. The validity of self-perceptions regarding physical and athletic ability. *Medicine and Science in Sports 8:*126–32.

Sonstroem, R. J. 1978. Physical estimation and attraction scales: Rationale and research. *Medicine and Science in Sports 10:*97–102.

Sonstroem, R. J. 1988. *Psychological models in exercise adherence: Its impact on public health.* Champaign, IL: Human Kinetics Books.

Sonstroem, R. J. and K. P. Kampper. 1980. Prediction of athletic participation in middle school males. *Research Quarterly for Exercise and Sport 51:*685–94.

Sonstroem, R. J. and W. P. Morgan. 1989. Exercise and self-esteem: Rationale and model. *Medicine and Science in Sports and Exercise 21:*329–37.

Van Schoyck, R. S. and A. F. Grasha. 1981. Attentional style variations and athletic ability: The advantage of a sport-specific test. *Journal of Sport Psychology 3:*149–65.

Wear, C. L. 1951. The evaluation of attitude toward physical activity as an activity course. *Research Quarterly 22:*114–26.

Wear, C. L. 1955. Construction of equivalent forms of an attitude scale. *Research Quarterly 26:*113–19.

# Appendix

Most of the sources listed are available to public school teachers.

**Additional References for Selected Sport Skill Tests**

**Tests and Measurements Books**

Barrow, H. M., R. McGee, and K. A. Tritschler. 1989. *Practical measurement in physical education and sport.* 4th ed. Philadelphia, PA: Lea and Febiger.

Hastad, D. N. and A. C. Lacy. 1989. *Measurement and evaluation in contemporary physical education.* Scottsdale, AZ: Gorsuch Scarisbrick.

Johnson, B. L. and J. K. Nelson. 1986. *Practical measurement for evaluation and physical education.* 4th ed. Minneapolis, MN: Burgess.

Miller, D. K. 1994. *Measurement by the physical educator: Why and how.* 2d ed. Dubuque, IA: Brown and Benchmark.

Strand, B. N. and R. Wilson. 1993. *Assessing sport skills.* Champaign, IL: Human Kinetics.

**Archery**

Shifflett, B. and B. Schuman. 1982. A criterion-referenced test for archery. *Research Quarterly 53:330–35.*

Zabick, R. M. and A. S. Jackson. 1969. Reliability of archery achievement. *Research Quarterly 40:254–55.*

**Badminton**

French, E. and E. Stalter. 1949. Study of skill tests in badminton for college women. *Research Quarterly 20:257–72.*

Lockhart, A. and F. A. McPherson. 1949. The development of a test of badminton playing ability. *Research Quarterly 20:402–5.*

Miller, F. A. 1951. A badminton wall volley test. *Research Quarterly 22:208–13.*

Thorpe, J. and C. West. 1969. A test of game sense in badminton. *Perceptual and Motor Skills 27:159–69.*

**Basketball**

Miller, W. K. 1954. Achievement levels in basketball skills for women physical education majors. *Research Quarterly 25:450–55.*

Stroup, F. 1955. Game results as a criterion for validating basketball skill tests. *Research Quarterly 26:353–57.*

**Bowling**

Martin, J. and J. Keogh. 1964. Bowling norms for college students in elective physical education classes. *Research Quarterly 25:325–27.*

Olson, J. K. and M. R. Liba. 1967. A device for evaluating spot bowling ability. *Research Quarterly 38:193–210.*

**Field Hockey**

Chapman, N. 1982. Chapman ball control test-field hockey. *Research Quarterly 53:*239–42.

Schmithals, M. and E. French. 1940. Achievement tests in field hockey for college women. *Research Quarterly 9:*84–92.

**Golf**

Brown, H. S. 1969. A test battery for evaluating golf skills. *Texas Association for Health, Physical Education and Recreation Journal* May, 4–5, 28–29.

Shick, J. and N. Berg. 1983. Indoor golf skill test for junior high school boys. *Research Quarterly 54:*75–78.

West, C. and J. Thorpe. 1968. Construction and validation of an eight-iron approach test. *Research Quarterly 49:*1115–20.

**Gymnastics**

Johnson, B. L. 1973. A screening test for pole vaulting and selected gymnastic events. *Journal of Health, Physical Education and Recreation 44:*71–72.

**Softball**

Broer, M. R. 1958. Reliability of certain skill tests for junior high school girls. *Research Quarterly 29:*139–43.

Central Association for Physical Education of College Women. 1959. Fielding test. In *Measurement and Evaluation in Physical Education.* M. G. Scott and E. French. Dubuque, IA: Wm. C. Brown.

Davis, R. 1959. The development of an objective softball batting test for college women. In *Measurement and Evaluation in Physical Education.* M. G. Scott and E. French. Dubuque, IA: Wm. C. Brown.

Fox, M. G. and O. G. Young. 1954. A test of softball batting ability. *Research Quarterly 25:*26–27.

Scott, M. G. and E. French. 1959. Softball repeated throws test. In *Measurement and Evaluation in Physical Education.* M. G. Scott and E. French. Dubuque, IA: Wm. C. Brown.

Shick, J. 1970. Battery of defensive softball skills tests for college women. *Research Quarterly 41:*82–87.

**Swimming**

Bennett, L. M. 1942. A test of diving for use in beginning classes. *Research Quarterly 13:*109–15.

Fox, M. G. 1957. Swimming power test. *Research Quarterly 28:*233–37.

Rosentswieg, J. 1968. A revision of the power swimming test. *Research Quarterly 39:*818–19.

**Tennis**

Avery, C., P. Richardson, and A. Jackson. 1979. A practical tennis serve test: Measurement of skill under simulated game conditions. *Research Quarterly 50:*554–64.

Broer, M. R. and D. M. Miller. 1950. Achievement tests for beginning and intermediate tennis. *Research Quarterly 21:*303–13.

DiGennaro, J. 1969. Construction of forehand drive, backhand drive, and service tennis tests. *Research Quarterly 40:*496–501.

Hewitt, J. E. 1965. Revision of the Dyer backboard tennis test. *Research Quarterly 36:*153–57.

Hewitt, J. E. 1966. Hewitt's tennis achievement test. *Research Quarterly 37:*231–37.

———. 1968. Classification tests in tennis. *Research Quarterly* 39: 552–55.

Johnson, J. 1957. Tennis serve of advanced women players. *Research Quarterly 28:*123–31.

Kemp, J. and M. F. Vincent. 1968. Kemp-Vincent rally test of tennis skill. *Research Quarterly 39:*1000–1004.

Purcell, K. 1981. A tennis forehand-backhand drive skill test which measures ball control and stroke firmness. *Research Quarterly 52:*238–45.

Scott, M. G. and E. French. 1959. Scott-French revision of the Dyer wallboard test. In *Measurement and Evaluation in Physical Education.* M. G. Scott and E. French. Dubuque, IA: Wm. C. Brown.

Shephard, G. J. 1972. The tennis drive skills test. In *Tennis-Badminton-Squash Guide—1972–74.* Washington, DC: AAHPER Publications.

## Volleyball

Broer, M. A. 1958. Reliability of certain skill tests for junior high school girls. *Research Quarterly 29:*139–45.

Clifton, M. 1962. Single hit volley test for women's volleyball. *Research Quarterly 33:*208–11.

Cunningham, P. and J. Garrison. 1968. High wall volley test for women. *Research Quarterly 39:*486–90.

Kronquist, R. A. and W. B. Brumbach. 1968. A modification of the Brady volleyball skill test for high school boys. *Research Quarterly 39:*116–20.

Liba, M. R. and M. R. Stauff. 1963. A test for the volleyball pass. *Research Quarterly 34:*56–63.

Mohr, D. R. and M. J. Haverstick. 1955. Repeated volleys tests for women's volleyball. *Research Quarterly 26:*179–84.

# Glossary

## A

**AAHPERD HRFT** One of the first health-related fitness tests sponsored by AAHPERD 249

**AAHPERD YFT** A youth fitness test developed by a group of physical educators who met and selected tests on the basis of logic 247

**Absolute Endurance Test** An endurance test that uses a weight load constant for all subjects tested 208

**Accuracy Test** A test in which the student projects an object at a target for a score 342

**ACSM** The American College of Sports Medicine, which is a leading exercise science professional organization 249

**Activity Factor** A semantic differential factor that involves motion; measured by adjective pairs such as fast-slow and excitable-calm 424

**Aerobic Fitness** Physical working capacity or $VO_2$ Max 272

**Affective Domain** A system used to categorize affective behavior to help teachers formulate affective objectives 419

**Agility** The ability to change the direction of the body or body parts rapidly 226, 246

**Analysis of Variance** A statistical technique for dividing total test variance into parts 100

**Anorexia Nervosa** Excessive diet and exercise resulting in extreme weight loss 325

**Apple II** One of the first microcomputers that was especially popular in American public schools. The computer is no longer manufactured by Apple Computer Company 31

**Attitude** A feeling about a particular object, such as a physical object, a certain type of person, or a social institution 420

## B

**Backup** Making copies of important information 35

**Balance** The ability to maintain body position 235

**Basic Physical Ability** A trait, more general than a psychomotor skill, that provides the foundation for the successful execution of many different psychomotor skills; also called *psychomotor ability* 196

**Bell-Shaped Curve** See *normal curve* 63

**Binary** A numbering system based on two values, 0 and 1 33

**Binary Digits** Used to quantify the capacity of a microcomputer 32

**Bioelectrical Impedance Method (BIA)** A technique for measuring body composition based on the principle that the electrical resistance of the body to a mild electric current is related to total body water. 329

**Bit** One binary value 33

**Body Cathexis Scale** A self-report scale used to measure body image 428

**Body Composition** The classification of the body into fat weight and lean body weight 251, 306

**Body Density** A value used to calculate percentage body fat; calculated with the underwater weighing method, it is determined by the following formula (307):

$$\text{Body density} = \frac{\text{weight}}{\text{volume}}$$

**Body Image** The attitude one has toward the body and the manner in which one's own body is perceived 428

**Body Mass Index (BMI)** The ratio of weight and height and defined as BMI = Weight/Height$^2$, where weight is in kilograms and height is in meters 310

## C

**Cardiorespiratory Function** The ability to continue work; depends on efficient respiratory (lungs) and cardiovascular (heart and blood vessels) systems 248

**Cardiovascular Disease**   The leading cause of death of Americans. The most common are heart disease and strokes 11, 296

**Central Tendency**   The tendency of scores to be concentrated at certain points; measures of central tendency that include the mode, median, and mean 65

**Chrysler-AAU**   A youth physical fitness test that includes both motor fitness and health-related fitness test items. The test is administered at Indiana University (IU) 253

**Circulatory-Respiratory Endurance**   A component of motor fitness characterized by moderate contractions of large muscle groups over long periods of time 246

**Circumferences**   Anthropometric measurements used to measure the distance around the body. Some common circumference measurements include waist, abdomen, and wrist 312

**Classification Index**   A mathematical formula used to combine age, height, and weight to predict excellence in the ability to perform a wide variety of motor tasks 194

**Coefficient of Determination**   The amount of variability in one measure explained by the other measure 93

**Completion Item**   A knowledge test item that asks students to complete or fill in the blanks in the item 394

**Computer Hardware**   Refers to the electronic and mechanical equipment used to process data. This would include microcomputers, printers, storage discs, screens, or other auxiliary equipment such as scanners and modems 31

**Computer Software**   Refers to the programs or applications that allow one to use a computer 31

**Concurrent Validity**   The degree to which scores on a test correlate with scores on an accepted standard 142

**Construct Validity**   The degree to which a test measures some part of a whole skill or an abstract trait 144

**Continuous Scores**   Scores with the potential for an infinite number of values 58

**Coronary Heart Disease**   A major form of cardiovascular disease that affects coronary arteries, the arteries that deliver oxygen and nutrients to the heart muscle (myocardium). A build up of plaque restricts the blood flow through the coronary arteries 11

**Correlation**   A mathematical technique for determining the relationship between two sets of scores 91

**Correlation Coefficient**   A value between –1.0 and 1.0 that indicates the degree of relationship between two sets of measures 92

**Criterion-Referenced Standard**   A standard that explicitly defines the task to be achieved 18

**Criterion Score**   An individual's recorded score; the score used to represent a person's ability 125, 147

**Criterion Variable**   See *dependent variable* 95

**Cross-Validation**   If the prediction formula and standard error seem acceptable, the prediction formula should be proven on a second group of individuals similar to the first 97

**Curvilinear Relationship**   A relationship between two measures that is best described by a curved line 93

**Cycle Ergometer**   A machine that regulates the work performed while cycling; workload can be accurately altered by increasing or decreasing the resistance on the ergometer 281

# D

**Data**   A set of scores 39

**Database**   A structured collection of information that is arranged consistently and logically 38

**Decision Validity**   An indication of the validity of a criterion-referenced test using logic 148

**Dependent Variable**   The Y variable of a regression equation and is often called the criterion variable 95

**Desktop Publishing**   The computer application that allows for the easy combination of text and graphics to produce quality publications 38

**Desired Weight**   A body weight determined for a specified percent body fat 325

**Digital**   The form in which a microcomputer expresses its commands 32

**Discrete Scores**   Scores with the potential for a limited number of specific values 58

**Discrimination Index**   A value indicating how well a knowledge test item differentiates between the high- and low-scoring students 406

**Discrimination Test**   A test designed to identify different ability groups based on test scores  386

**Distance Run Tests**   Running tests used to evaluate cardiorespiratory function; normally of 1 mile or longer in distance, or 9 minutes or more in duration  255

**Domain-Referenced Validity**   An indication of the validity of a criterion-referenced test expressed as a numeric value  148

**Dynamic Balance**   The ability to maintain equilibrium while moving from one point to another  236

**Dynamometer**   An instrument used to measure strength by recording force exerted  207

# E

**Essay Test**   A test that asks students to respond to questions in writing  386

**Evaluation**   A decision-making process that involves (1) the collection of suitable data (measurement); (2) a judgment of the value of these data against a standard; and (3) a decision based on these data and standards  15

**Evaluation Factor**   A semantic differential factor that involves a degree of "goodness"; measured by adjective pairs such as good-bad and beautiful-ugly  422

**Exercise Epidemiology**   The study of diseases associated with physical inactivity  253

# F

**False Negative Stress Test**   The stress test fails to identify coronary heart disease in patients who have heart disease  20

**False Positive Stress Test**   The stress test results indicate coronary artery disease in patients who do not have heart disease  21

**Fat Weight**   In measuring a person's body, the weight in pounds that is body fat  307

**Fat-Free Weight**   See *lean body weight*  307

**Final Grade**   The grade assigned at the end of a unit or grading period  165

**Flexibility**   The range of motion about a joint  232, 247

**Floppy Disk**   Transfers information through a disk drive; stores 800K worth of information  33

**Formative Evaluation**   The process of judging achievement at the formative stages of instruction to determine the degree of mastery and to pinpoint that part of the task yet to be mastered; often used as a form of student feedback  17

**Frequency Polygon**   A graph of a frequency distribution with scores along the horizontal axis and frequencies along the vertical axis  63

# G

**General Motor Ability**   The theory that individuals who are highly skilled on one motor task will be highly skilled on other motor tasks  195

**Generalized Equations**   Equations that can be validly used with heterogeneous samples  319

# H

**Hard Disk**   Stores 20 megabytes, equal to about 25, double-sized 800K disks  33

**Hardware**   The electronic and mechanical equipment used to process data  31

**Health-Related Physical Fitness**   A scientific body of knowledge that links the positive effects of regular, vigorous exercise with the prevention of degenerative disease  247

**Heart Rate**   The number of times per minute that the heart beats or ejects blood. Heart rate increases with exercise or increased workload  273

**Hydrostatic Weighing**   The underwater weighing method used to determine body volume, which is then used with dry land body weight to calculate body density  306

# I

**Independent Variable**   The X variable of a regression equation and often called the predictor variable  95

**Individual with Disability**   An individual requiring special program or testing considerations due to limited ability to perform certain activities  186

**Instructional Objectives**   Objectives that make clear to both students and teacher what is to be accomplished, including: (1) the task to be learned; (2) the conditions under which the task will be performed; and (3) the criterion-referenced standard that will be used to evaluate the achievement  xiii

**Internal-Consistency Reliability Coefficient**   The degree to which an individual's scores are unchanged within a day  117

**Interval Scores**  Scores that have a common unit of measure between consecutive scores but not a true zero point 58

**Intraclass Correlation Coefficient**  A correlation coefficient that estimates test reliability; derived with analysis of variance 118

**Isokinetic Strength**  Strength that is measured by recording the force exerted through the entire range of motion. 208

**Isometric Strength**  Strength that is measured by recording the force exerted against an immovable object 206

**Isotonic Strength**  Strength that involves moving an object through a defined range of motion; often measured with a 1-RM test, which is the maximum weight that can be lifted during one repetition 207

**Item**  A question or statement on a knowledge test; one of the tests in a battery of tests 386

**Item Analysis**  An item-by-item analysis of a knowledge test to identify valid questions 407

**Item Difficulty**  The difficulty of a knowledge test item; the percentage of a group that correctly answers an item 405

# K

**K**  1,000 bits of information 32

**Kappa Coefficient**  An indication of the reliability of a criterion-referenced test; one of two commonly used 134

**Kiloponds (kp)**  The unit of measurement used to quantify resistance on a bicycle ergometer; kp represents the unit of resistance in kilograms 273

**Kinesthesis**  The ability to perceive the body's position in space and the relationship of its parts 237

**Knowledge Test**  A paper-and-pencil test that measures knowledge 386

**kpm**  The unit of measurement used to quantify the intensity of exercise on a bicycle ergometer. This is a product of the resistance in kp and the rpm. $\dot{V}O_2(ml\cdot min^{-1})$ can be determined from kpm 273

# L

**Lean Body Weight**  The weight of the body with the fat tissue removed; also called *fat-free weight* 306

**Leptokurtic Curve**  More sharply peaked than a normal curve 63

**Line of Best Fit**  See *regression line* 96

**Linear Relationship**  A relationship between two measures that is best described by a straight line 93

**Logical Validity**  A validity technique based on the subjectively established fact that the test measures the wanted attribute 141

# M

**Mainframe Computer**  A computer with enormous capacity allowing for storage of huge amounts of information and the ability to conduct complex data analyses 30

**Mass Testability**  The degree to which a large number of students can be tested in a short period of time 181

**Mastery Test**  A test that determines how well students have mastered the material 386

**Matching Item**  A knowledge test item that asks students to match columns of questions and answers 393

**Maximal Oxygen Uptake ($\dot{V}O_2$ Max)**  The amount of oxygen one utilizes during exhausting work; the criterion for validating field tests of cardiorespiratory function 274

**Maximal Stress Test**  A diagnostic medical test that systematically increases exercise to determine physical working capacity and changes in exercise blood pressure and the exercise EKG. This is an initial screening test for cardiovascular disease 277

**Mean**  A measure of central tendency, or average; obtained by dividing the sum of the scores by the number of scores 69

**Measurement**  The collection of information on which a decision is based 15

**Median**  A measure of central tendency, or average; the score below which 50% of a group scored 65

**Megabyte**  1000 K 32

**MET**  A unit used to quantify oxygen consumption. A MET equals a $\dot{V}O_2$ of 3.5 ml·kg$^{-1}$min$^{-1}$ and is the oxygen uptake at rest 273

**Microcomputer**  A general term referring to a complete, tiny computing system. A microcomputer, often termed a personal computer (PC), can easily sit on your desk. It is similar to a mainframe computer, but smaller, and functions essentially in the same manner 31

**Microprocessor**  The major electronic chip of a microcomputer. These electronic components regulate the speed or power of the microcomputer  33

**Minicomputer**  Smaller than a mainframe, but functions in essentially the same manner  30

**Mode**  A measure of central tendency, or average; the most frequent score for a group of people  65

**Motor Educability**  The ability to learn motor skills easily and well  195

**Motor Fitness**  A category of the psychomotor domain that is defined by the component's strength, power, and endurance  246

**Motor Skill**  The level of proficiency achieved on a specific motor task; also called *psychomotor skill*  196

**MS-DOS**  Represents Microsoft Desk Operating System and is the program used to operate MS-DOS machines. Some of the leading MS-DOS microcomputers include Compaq, IBM, and Dell  31

**Multicomponent Model**  The method used to measure percent body fat from the underwater weighing method. The model assumes that the density of fat is $0.9$ g·cc$^{-1}$ but also uses total body water and bone density to adjust density estimate of the fat-free weight component  310

**Multiple-Choice Item**  A knowledge test item that asks students to select an answer from three or more provided answers  390

**Multiple Correlation**  The correlation between a criterion and two or more predictors that have been mathematically combined to maximize the correlation between the criterion and predictors  98

**Multiple Prediction**  The prediction of the value of one measure based on the performance of two or more other measures; also called *multiple regression*  98

**Multi-Stage Exercise Test**  A method used to estimate $VO_2$ Max from two or more submaximal workloads and heart rates  284

**Muscular Endurance**  The ability to persist in physical activity or to resist muscular fatigue  221, 246

**Muscular Power**  Traditionally, the maximum force released in the shortest possible time; more appropriately, the rate at which work can be performed by involved muscle groups  218, 246

**Muscular Strength**  The maximum force a muscle group can exert during a brief period of time  206, 246

# N

**Natural Breaks**  A grading technique that assigns grades by breaks in the distribution of scores  160

**Negatively Skewed Curve**  Long, low tail on the left, indicating few students received low scores  63

**Nominal Scores**  Scores that cannot be ordered from best to worst  59

**Normal Curve**  A symmetrical curve centered around a point that is the mean score; also called *bell-shaped curve*  63, 84

**Norm-Referenced Standard**  A standard that judges a performance in relation to the performance of other members of a well-defined group  18

**Norms**  Performance standards based on the scores of a group of people  18

# O

**Obesity**  The excessive accumulation of fat weight  306

**Objective**  A test where two or more people score the same test and assign similar scores  15

**Objective Evaluation**  A test in which the student's performance yields a score without a value judgment by the scorer (see *subjective measure*); also a test that asks students to respond to questions by selecting one of two or more provided answers  349

**Objective Tests**  True–false, multiple choice, matching, and the like  386

**Objectivity**  The degree to which multiple scorers agree on the magnitude of scores  114

**Ordinal Scores**  Scores that can be ordered from best to worst but that do not have a common unit of measure  59

**Overweight**  That weight that exceeds the "normal" weight based on gender, height, and frame size  306

**Oxygen Uptake**  The amount of oxygen one uses for a given level of exercise  273

# P

**Percent Body Fat**  That proportion of total weight that is fat weight  306

**Percentile**  A score that has a specified percentage of scores below it fixed  75

**Percentile Rank**   A score value that indicates the percentage of scores below a given score  73

**Personality**   The general psychological construct that explains an individual's motives; can be measured by many different psychological instruments  418

**Physical Best**   The health-related fitness test sponsored by AAHPERD. In January 1994, the test was discontinued when AAHPERD decided to endorse the Prudential FITNESSGRAM® health-related fitness test  171

**Platykurtic Curve**   Less sharply peaked curve  63

**Positively Skewed Curve**   The tail of the curve is on the right  63

**Posttest Procedures**   The analysis and recording of test scores  185

**Potency Factor**   A semantic differential factor that involves the strength of the concept; measured by adjective pairs such as strong-weak and smooth-rough  424

**Power**   The rate at which work is performed; calculated with the following formula (219):

$$\text{Power} = \frac{\text{work}}{\text{time}}$$

**Power Output**   The rate of work used to define exercise intensity. The power output for a cycle ergometer is increased by placing more resistance on the flywheel and increasing the cycle peddling rate. The power output for treadmill exercise is increased by increasing treadmill speed and increasing the grade  273

**Prediction**   The estimating of the value of one measure based on the value of one or more other measures; see also *multiple regression*  95

**Predictive Validity**   The degree to which one measure can predict performance on a second measure  143

**Predictor Variable**   See *independent variable*  95

**President's Challenge**   A test battery with slight modifications of the AAHPERD YFT and consisting of five tests  254

**Pretest Planning**   The procedures that must be followed before a test is administered; includes knowing the test, developing test procedures and directions, and preparing the students and the testing facility  183

**Prevalence**   Refers to the disease rate within a defined group of people (cohort). It is the percentage of individuals within the group affected  6

**Program Evaluation**   Determination of the extent to which a program achieves the standards and objectives set forth for it  169

**Proportion of Agreement Coefficient**   An indication of the reliability of a criterion referenced test; one of two commonly used  134

**Prudential FITNESSGRAM®:**   The leading American health-related fitness test. The test was developed at the Cooper Institute for Aerobics Research, Dallas, TX  250

**Psychomotor Ability**   See *basic physical ability*  196

**Psychomotor Skill**   See *motor skill*  196

**Psychophysical**   A term used to describe scientific methods used to integrate psychological and physical parameters. An example of a psychophysical test is Borg's RPE scale  433

# R

**RAM**   Stands for random-access memory. This type of memory allows for information to be "written in" or "read out" of the computer's memory very rapidly. Information in RAM is stored on a temporary basis and disappears when the computer is turned off  32

**Range**   A measure of the variability or heterogeneity in a set of scores; the difference between the largest and smallest scores  70

**Rank Order**   Straightforward, norm-referenced method of grading  161

**Rank Order Correlation Coefficient**   *Rho* or *Spearman's rho;* calculated when the scores for the two sets of scores are ranks  92

**Rank-Order Grading**   A grading technique that assigns grades after ordering the scores  161

**Rating of Perceived Exertion Scale (RPE)**   A scale developed by Dr. G. Borg of Stockholm, Sweden that is used to rate the intensity of exercise  280, 430

**Rating Scale**   A set of standards or a checklist for measuring performance subjectively  349

**Ratio Scores**   Scores that have a common unit of measure between consecutive scores and a true zero point  58

**Regression Line**   Often termed the "line of best fit" and is the line that is defined by predicting the dependent variable from the independent variable  89

**Reliability**   The degree of consistency with which a test measures what it measures  114

**Residual Lung Volume**   The amount of air remaining in the lungs after a full expiration. This measurement is used when estimating body density by the underwater weighing method 308

**ROM**   The read-only memory. It is a semiconductor memory device where information required to operate the computer system is permanently stored 32

# S

**Semantic Differential Scales**   A method of measuring attitude by having someone react toward an object or concept by responding to bipolar adjective pairs 421

**Short-Answer Item**   A knowledge test item that requires the student to write a short answer to the item 395

**Simple Frequency Distribution**   An ordered listing of a set of scores, complete with the frequency of each score 61

**Simple Prediction (Regression)**   The prediction of the value of one measure, the dependent variable, using another measure, the independent variable 95

**Single-Stage Exercise Test**   A method used to estimate $VO_2$ Max from one submaximal workload and heart rate 285

**Skewed Curve**   A curve that is not symmetrical; see *normal curve* 63

**Skill Test**   A test that measures physical skill, not fitness 342

**Skinfold Calipers**   An instrument used to measure the thickness of subcutaneous fat tissue 312

**Skinfold Fat**   The subcutaneous fat tissue that lies just below the skin 265

**Software**   The programs that allow one to use a computer 31

**Speed**   The ability to move rapidly 225, 247

**Spreadsheet**   A computer program that allows the user to work with numbers in rows and columns and use equations to complete various calculations 38

**Stability Reliability Coefficient**   The degree to which an individual's scores are unchanged from day to day 116

**Standard Deviation**   A measure of the variability, or spread, of a set of scores around the mean 70

**Standard Error of Measurement**   The amount of error expected in a measured score 131

**Standard Error of Prediction**   A value indicating the amount of error to expect in a predicted score 96

**Standard Error of the Mean**   A value indicating the amount of variation to expect in the mean if subjects were tested again 99

**Standard Score**   A test score calculated using the test mean and standard deviation; usually expressed as a *z* or *T* 77

**Static Balance**   The ability to maintain total body equilibrium while standing in one spot 236

**Step Tests**   Tests used to evaluate cardiorespiratory function by having the subject repeatedly step up and down from a bench at a prescribed cadence 284

**Subjective**   A test lacking a standardized scoring system, which introduces a source of measurement error 15

**Subjective Evaluation**   A test in which the scorer must make a value judgment before assigning the performer a score 350

**Submaximal Exercise Test**   A test used to evaluate cardiorespiratory function by measuring one's ability to perform work at submaximal workloads and then predicting $VO_2$ Max from submaximal heart rate 281

**Summative Evaluation**   The process of judging achievement at the end of instruction 17

# T

**T-Scores**   Used to combine different tests together; usually rounded off to the nearest whole number and rarely negative 78

**t-Test**   An inferential statistical test used to determine if two means are equal in value 100

**Taxonomy**   A classification for parts of a system; the educational taxonomies for the cognitive, affective, and psychomotor domains are used to formulate educational objectives 384

**Teacher's Standards**   A grading technique that compares students' scores to a standard developed by the teacher 161

**Tensiometer**   An instrument used to measure strength by recording the tension applied to a steel cable 207

**Test-Retest Method** The procedure used to correlate the scores of a test administered on each of two days; used to establish stability reliability 116

**Texas Youth Fitness Test** A motor fitness test, split into physical fitness components and motor ability components 247

**True–False Item** A knowledge test item that asks students to answer either *True* or *False* 389

**Two-Component Model** The method used to measure percent body fat from the underwater weighing method. The model assumes that the density of fat is 0.9 $g \cdot cc^{-1}$ and the fat-free weight is 1.0 $g \cdot cc^{-1}$ 309

# U

**Underwater Weighing** Determining a person's body weight in water; one method used to determine body density. See also *hydrostatic weighing* 306

**Useful Score** A test score that can be used immediately or inserted into a formula with little effort 182

# V

**Validity** The degree to which a test measures what it is supposed to measure 114, 140

**Variability** The degree of heterogeneity in a set of scores; measures include the range and the standard deviation 70

**Variance** The square of the standard deviation 72

**VO₂ Max** See *maximal oxygen uptake* 272

# W

**Wall Volley Tests** Skill tests that require the student to repeatedly volley a ball against a wall 344

**Word Processing** A common microcomputer application that allows for easy typing, editing, "cutting," "pasting," and revising of all entered text 36

**Work** The ability to apply force over distance; calculated with the following formula: (218)

$$Work = (force)(distance)$$

# Z

**z-Score** A standard score with mean 0 and standard deviation 1 77

# Name Index

George, J. D., 287
Gettman, L. R., 333, 429
Gill, D. L., 437
Girardi, G., 184
Gire, E., 195
Glaser, R., 18, 19
Glass, G., 58
Glencross, D. J., 218, 219
Glock, M. D., 394
Golding, L. A., 213, 215, 224, 235, 282, 284, 299, 321
Goodrick, G. K., 38
Grande, F., 309
Grasha, A. F., 420, 438
Gray, R. K., 218
Green, K. N., 364
Griffin, N. S., 437
Griggs, T., 204
Gronlund, N. E., 157, 394
Gross, E., 194, 195

## H

Hagberg, J. M., 277
Haisman, M. F., 318
Harris, B., 422
Harris, C. W., 195
Harris, M., 206, 233
Harris, S. S., 10
Hart, E. A., 438
Hart, J. W., 13, 203
Heath, R. W., 75
Henry, F. M., 147, 196
Hensley, L. D., 364, 370
Hermiston, R. T., 204
Herrin, G. D., 13, 203, 204
Hetherington, R., 147
Hewitt, J. E., 345
Hickman, T., 318
Hintermeister, R., 286
Hirschland, R. P., 233, 247
Hodgdon, J. A., 312
Hodges, P. B., 342
Hodgson, J. L., 22, 275, 277
Hogan, J. C., 4, 200, 201, 202, 208
Holloszy, J. O., 277
Hopkins, D. R., 359
Hopkins, K., 58
Horvat, M. A., 186
Hosmer, D., 278
Howley, E. T., 275
Huck, S. W., 100
Huettig, C., 186

## I

Ickes, W., 430, 438
Isaacs, L., 370
Ismail, A., 206

## J

Jackson, A. S., 4, 7, 11, 13, 20, 38, 43, 48, 125, 144, 145, 148, 189, 200, 203,
204, 206, 212, 215, 219, 225, 226, 237, 248, 251$n$, 255, 273, 274, 275, 278, 279, 280, 282, 282$n$, 285, 288, 289, 298, 299, 306, 310, 311, 315, 318, 319, 320, 333, 334, 335, 373, 422, 428, 432, 434, 436
Jackson, A. W., 141
Jensen, C. R., 422
Johnson, B. L., 422
Johnson, G. B., 195
Johnson, M. L., 422
Johnson, R., 147
Johnson, R. E., 190
Jourard, S. M., 430, 432

## K

Kachigan, S. K., 96
Kalakian, L. H., 186
Kampper, K. P., 429
Kappes, E. E., 422
Karpman, M., 370
Katch, F. I., 318
Katz, S., 10
Kendall, F. P., 223
Kendrick, Z., 318
Kenyon, G. A., 144
Kenyon, G. S., 422
Keogh, J. F., 437
Kerlinger, F. N., 98
Keys, A., 318
Keyserling, W. M., 13, 203, 204
King, H. A., 31
Klein, S. P., 342
Kline, G. M., 286
Kneer, M. E., 422
Kovar, M. G., 5
Kowal, D. M., 429
Kraft, G. C., 398
Krathwohl, D. R., 419
Kraus, H., 233, 247
Kusumi, F., 278

## L

Lakie, W. L., 422
Landon, T. E., 202
Langston, K. F., 432
LaPorte, W. D., 169
Larson, L. A., 195, 206
Larsson, B., 334
Laughery, K. R., 203
Lauraie, D. R., 437
Lavay, B., 190
Lavay, B. W., 186
Leary, M. R., 438
Leighton, J., 232
Lemon, P. W. R., 204
Leon, A. S., 10, 13
Lev, J., 94
Lew, E. A., 24, 325
Lewis, C., 197
Liba, M. R., 206
Lindquist, E. F., 58, 75

Lohman, T. G., 23, 251, 306$n$, 309, 310, 312, 319, 324, 325, 329, 330, 333
Looney, M. A., 20
Looney, M. L., 150

## M

Mach, R. S., 204
MacLeod, D., 206
Mahar, M., 282, 285, 437
Manning, J., 204
Margaria, R., 220, 221
Marriott, B. M., 204
Martens, R., 437, 438
Martin, M., 318
Mathews, D. K., 220, 221
Maybee, R., 437
McArdle, W. D., 318
McCloy, C. H., 194, 195, 206, 218, 219, 229, 233
McCready, M., 437
McCue, B. F., 422
McGee, R., 170, 394, 396, 422
McKee, M. E., 121
Meaney, K. S., 437
Meeter, D., 147
Mercer, E. L., 422
Metheny, E., 195
Meyers, C. R., 213, 215, 224, 235, 282, 284, 299, 321
Meyers, D. C., 206
Michael, E. D., 318
Mitchell, J. H., 274
Morgan, W. P., 429, 430
Morris, H. H., 358
Morrow, J. R., Jr., 10, 48
Mosher, R. E., 424

## N

Nagel, F. J., 274
Naughton, J. P., 274
Neale, D. C., 429
Neilson, N. P., 422
Nelson, J. K., 422
Nie, N. H., 98
Nielson, A. B., 437
Nitko, A. J., 19
Noakes, T. D., 274
Nunnally, J. C., 128, 144, 402, 421, 427
Nutting, S. M., 202

## O

O'Bryan, K. G., 422
O'Bryan, M. H., 422
O'Connell, E., 204
Osburn, H. G., 203, 432
Osgood, C. E., 423
Owen, C. A., 17

## P

Paffenbarger, R. J., 325

# Subject Index

Body density
  computing, 308
  converting to percent body fat, 309
  measuring, 307–8
Body image, 430, 432
Body mass index, 300, 310–11
Body plethysmograph, 308
Body weight, correlation with arm power, 219
Borg's category RPE scale, 433–34
Borg's category scale with ratio properties, 434–35
Bowling, evaluating achievement in, 355
Brozek method, 309–10
Bruce protocol, 278, 279, 282, 283, 299
BYU jog test, 287–88, 289, 292, 300

## C

Calculated conversion tables, 79
Calculators, 59
California Physical Performance Test, 189
Caloric expenditure, 272
Calorimetry, indirect, 277–78
Cardiorespiratory endurance, measuring, 225
Cardiovascular disease, role of aerobic physical activity in preventing, 9–10
Central tendency, measures of, 65–73
Children and youth, skinfold assessments of percent fat of, 327–29, 335
Children's Attitude Toward Physical Activity Inventory (CATPA-I), 424
Chrysler Fund-AAU physical fitness program, 48–50, 245, 253, 266–67
  award program in, 254
  in testing individuals with disabilities, 190
  test items on, 253–54
Circulatory-respiratory endurance, as component of motor fitness, 246
Circumference, body, 312
Civil Rights Act Title VII, 4
Classification index, 194–95
Coefficient alpha, 128–29
Coefficient kappa, 134–36
Coefficient of determination, 93
Combination tests, 348–49
Completion item test, 394–95
Computer
  in applying two-way ANOVA to data, 127–28
  item analysis by, 407–8
  percentiles and percentile ranks on, 76–77
  in score analysis, 59
  types of, 30
Computer calculations, 438
  in body composition, 334–36
  in VO₂ Max measurements, 297–301
Computer literacy, 34–35
Computer virus, 35*n*
Concurrent validity, 139, 142–43
Confidentiality, of testing, 180
Construct validity, 139, 144–46, 202
Content validity, 202
Continuous scores, 58

Cooper Medical Clinic, 18–19, 22
Cornish handball power test, 347–48
Coronary heart disease, 11
  and occupational physical activity, 6–7
Correlation, 89, 94
Correlation coefficients, 92–93
  accuracy of, 93–94
  interpreting, 93
  intraclass, 117–30
  multiple, 98
  Pearson-product-moment, 142, 143
  prediction-regression analysis of, 94–99
  simple, 95–97
Correlation technique, 91–94
Criterion-referenced standards, 18, 155–56, 266–67
  examples in developing health-related, 22–24
  limitations of, 20–21
  nature of, 19
Criterion-referenced tests
  reliability of, 133–36
  validity for, 148–50
Criterion-related validity, 202
Criterion score, 113, 125, 139, 147
  selecting valid, 147–48
Critical region, 102
Critical value, 102
Cross-validation, 97
Curls, 214
Curl-up test, 224
  in youth testing, 251–52
Curvilinear relationship, 93
Cut score, 204
Cycle ergometers, 271
  power output of, 273
  submaximal protocols for, 281–82

## D

Database programs, 38–39, 40
Data collection for program evaluation, 169–70
Death, leading causes of, 11
Decision validity, 139, 148
Degrees of freedom, 102
Descriptive values
  measures of central tendency, 65–73
  measures of variability, 70–73
Desktop publishing, 38
Digital form, 32
Disabled individuals. *See* Individuals with disabilities
Discrete scores, 58
Discrimination index, 405–6
Discrimination test, 386–87
Distance run test, 255–60
  methods, 256–60
  validity of, 255
Domain, 148
Domain-referenced validity, 139, 148
Dyer Tennis Wall Volley Test, 345
Dynamic balance, 235, 236–37

Dynamic flexibility, 233
Dynamometers, 207

## E

Elderly, 5
E-mail network, 40
Employment testing, 4
Endlink, 40*n*
Endnote, 40*n*
Endurance. *See also* Muscular endurance
  absolute, 208
  common test items for, 260–65
  muscular, 221–25, 245
Endurance run, 253
Essay test, 386, 395–96
  scoring, 400
Estimation, 133
Ethnic composition, 6
Evaluation, 14–15
  factor in semantic dimensions, 424
  formative, 17–18, 155, 170–71
  functions of, 16–17
  objective, 349–50
  standards for, 18–23, 155–56
  subjective, 154, 350–51
  summative, 17–18, 155, 171–72, 387
  systematic model for, 15–16
Exercise, motivation to, 426–32
Exercise stress test
  accuracy of, 21
  estimating VO₂ Max without, 288
Expert ratings, 142

## F

Factor analysis, 145–46
Factor loadings, 145
False positive tests, 21
Fat-free weight, 307
Fat weight, 307
Fax, 39
50-yard dash, 226
Final grades, 165–69
Fine psychomotor abilities, 237
Fitness, 245
  common test items for, 255–65
Fitness evaluation, distinguishing between stress test and, 295–97
Fit Youth Today (FYT), 249
Flexed-arm hang test, 221, 253, 261
Flexibility, 13, 232–35
  common test items for, 260–65
  as component of motor fitness, 247
  dynamic, 233
  measurement of, in youth, 252
Floppy disk, 33
Football, sports skills tests for, 359–60
Formative evaluation, 17–18, 155
  in program evaluation, 170–71
F-ratio, 106
Frequency polygon, 63
F-test, 124